THE DIARY OF
ROBERT SHARP
OF SOUTH CAVE

Life in a Yorkshire Village
1812–1837

I have none. R. Moxon Bills [...]

1827
Friday
19th Jany

Our old Friend at the Saw & Mill lately sent some Flour by
his Man to Old Rachel Levett, which was not of a superior
quality; so the next time that the man went, Hannah
said to him, Now your master blames you for this black
flour, he says he told you only to put a handful or two
of the black wheat into it. What a liar he must be
exclaims the man with an Oath, for he told me himself
to make it all of that Black Wheat, but you know him,
you know him, says the Man. Now honest Tom says he
must have his man instructed better, he is a decent man
and all that, but then he had not ourse to say that this flour
might have been made, after some ordinary bad stuff had
been ground; Tom thinks there is as much evil in
speaking truth when against him, as in telling a wilful lie.

Saturday
20th Jany

What a difference in the manners of those called farmers, to
what there formerly was. When a Company of these Gentry
meet now in public, there is generally one of the party, with
a little more brass in his countenance than his neighbours
who is placed at the head of the table and dignified with
the name of Chairman, and there the Company sit spreing
their bottoms, with Port & Sherry in cut glass Decanters
before them, when the impudent fellow at the head of
the table (who ought to be put under it) gets up and says
Gentlemen I beg to give a toast or sentiment, or something of the kind: then Gentlemen I give wheat not below
than 70s pr Qr, this is drunk with as much applause
as the Company is capable of bestowing. Formerly
farmers used to meet at Market and 3 or 4 of them drank
grog all out of a plated tankard (I do not admire very
much this slavering method but so it was), the first who
drank said neighbour I wish all your healths and may
God send a good harvest, (or something similar to this)
they knew then that a good harvest was a blessing
which they ought to be thankful for, and they would
have pronounced that Man a daring blasphemer,
who wished for bad harvests. They never knew
the miseries of over-production; thankful were they
to the giver of all good, not for abundant Crops.

RECORDS OF SOCIAL AND ECONOMIC HISTORY
NEW SERIES 26

THE DIARY OF ROBERT SHARP

OF SOUTH CAVE

Life in a Yorkshire Village 1812–1837

EDITED BY

JANICE E. CROWTHER

AND

PETER A. CROWTHER

Published for THE BRITISH ACADEMY
by OXFORD UNIVERSITY PRESS

Oxford University Press, Great Clarendon Street, Oxford OX2 6DP

Oxford New York
Athens Auckland Bangkok Bogota Bombay
Buenos Aires Calcutta Cape Town Dar es Salaam
Delhi Florence Hong Kong Istanbul Karachi
Kuala Lumpur Madras Madrid Melbourne
Mexico City Nairobi Paris Singapore
Taipei Tokyo Toronto Warsaw

and associated companies in
Berlin Ibadan

Published in the United States by
Oxford University Press Inc., New York

© *The British Academy, 1997*

First published 1997
Reprinted 1998

British Library Cataloguing in Publication Data
Data available

ISBN 0–19–726173–6

Typeset by the editors
Printed in Great Britain
on acid-free paper by
The Cromwell Press Limited
Trowbridge ,Wilts

FOREWORD

With this 26th volume in the new series of *Records of Social and Economic History* the series reaches the nineteenth century for the first time, and thus makes a start on marking out suitable territory in the modern period — and in due course in the contemporary as well — for this type of record publication. Robert Sharp was the local schoolmaster in an East Riding market village, who kept a detailed diary from 1826 to 1837, which he sent in instalments to his son who was in London, and before that sent the same son a steady flow of letters with family and local news, between 1812 and 1825. These letters and diary have been known to local historians for some time, but are now for the first time transcribed in their entirety and made available to the wider audience of social historians which they deserve to reach. They have a twofold significance. They form a detailed record and commentary on village life and affairs by an acute and sympathetic observer who was a villager himself and of a different social level from the well-known country parson diarists, an observer whose literacy and level of education made him into an active participant in many village concerns as a measuring surveyor, tax assessor and collector, clerk to the local friendly society, and scribe for his less literate neighbours (Sharp says little about the school or his work as schoolmaster in the diary, perhaps because he did not regard his job as newsworthy). Secondly, they record something of the political opinions and general views of a largely self-educated, intelligent, and well-read man, who was well informed about events in the world outside his village, read *The Times* and Cobbett's *Weekly Political Register* regularly, and had a good knowledge of English literature. These documents, ably and informatively edited by Janice and Peter Crowther, are at once a source for social history and an enjoyable read.

July 1997

F. M. L. Thompson
Chairman, Records of Social and
Economic History Committee

CONTENTS

LIST OF ILLUSTRATIONS

Frontispiece: Facsimile of a page from the Diary

MAPS

PLATES

Between page xxxii *and page* xxxiii

PREFACE

Robert Sharp's diary has been well known to historians of South Cave and its neighbourhood for many years. It has, however, never before been transcribed in its entirety, and the present volume owes much to the support of the Archivist of the East Riding of Yorkshire Council, Mr Keith Holt, who provided us with facilities for making a copy of the work on disc.

The diary has travelled from South Cave to London and back again. Initially it was sent in instalments to Robert Sharp's son, William, who was apparently responsible for having it bound, and at some time in the later nineteenth century it was sent back to South Cave, into the care of the Dennis family. It was first mentioned in print in 1909, when William Richardson included extracts from the diary as an appendix to his book, *The Parish Registers of South Cave*. Richardson referred to the diary as belonging at that time to Mr William Sharp Dennis. Mr Dennis died in 1956, and the manuscript became the property of his daughter, Miss Florence Dennis, who was herself a school-mistress in South Cave. When David Neave, with a Workers' Educational Association class, wrote *South Cave: a Market Village Community in the 18th and 19th Centuries* (1974), the diary provided much useful information about life in the village. Before her death in 1972, Miss Florence Dennis deposited the manuscript for safe keeping in the East Riding Record Office, now the East Riding of Yorkshire Council Archives Service, where it still remains.

We are particularly grateful to Mr Keith Holt, Mrs Carol Boddington, and their staff, who have provided us with helpful support and assistance at all times. We would also like to thank Miss Pamela Martin, Mrs Jennifer Stanley, and the staff of the Beverley Local Studies Library (East Riding of Yorkshire Council), and Miss Jill Crowther, and her staff at the Hull Local Studies Library (Kingston upon Hull City Council), for their friendly and knowledgeable assistance. We have made much use of the facilities of the Brynmor Jones Library, University of Hull, where we have had the advantage of the expert assistance of, among others, Mr John Hooton and Mr John Morris. The staff of the Publications Office of the British Academy have given us their valuable guidance in the formatting of the text and the production of camera-ready copy. We are much indebted to our cartographer, Mrs Wendy Munday, and our photographer, Mr Alan Marshall. Both brought not only expertise, but also enthusiasm to the project. We would also like to thank Mr Roland Wheeler-Osman for photographing Jane Sharp's sampler. The sampler belongs to one of the great-great grandsons of Robert Sharp, Mr Neville Brown, and his wife Margaret. He has provided us with background knowledge, even to the extent of searching his boyhood memory for the location of sections of South Cave Beck, now culverted, and of walking along its course during a cold, grey November day. We are likewise indebted to many people in South Cave and its vicinity, who have attended the University of Hull and Workers' Educational Association local history classes over the last few years. The most notable is

Mrs Mollie Cutts, who, in addition to organizing the classes, provided students with traditional Cave cheese-cakes. Other people who have provided us with information and assistance are Mr Michael Bott, Keeper of Archives and Manuscripts, University of Reading; Mr Peter Donovan, Senior Library Assistant, City of Westminster Archives Centre; Ms Judith Hodge, Principal Librarian, Huddersfield Library; Dr Peter Matthias; Mr Bryan Sitch, formerly of Hull Museums; staff of Skipton Public Library; Professor F. M. L. Thompson; Mr David Tucker; Professor J. D. A. Widdowson, Centre for English Cultural Tradition and Language, University of Sheffield; Professor Donald Woodward; and Mr William Young, St Martin-in-the-Fields Archives.

Finally we would like to thank, most particularly, Dr Joan Thirsk, without whose encouragement and support the diary would never have been published.

The work of preparing the manuscript for publication was divided between the two editors thus: both transcribed and checked the manuscript; Janice Crowther compiled the biographical appendix, gathered the information necessary for the maps, and was responsible for the illustrations and the family tree; Peter Crowther wrote the introduction, was responsible for the greater part of the footnotes, compiled the glossary, the bibliographical appendix and the index, and prepared the diary in camera-ready form for publication.

Robert Sharp was an admirer of the work of Oliver Goldsmith. This extract from the *Deserted Village* seems in many ways to fit both the character of the diarist and his position in South Cave, though we trust that with the publication of his diary, Robert Sharp's name will not be 'forgot'.

Beside yon straggling fence that skirts the way,
With blossom'd furze unprofitably gay—
There, in his noisy mansion, skill'd to rule,
The village master taught his little school.
A man severe he was, and stern to view;
I knew him well, and every truant knew:
Well had the boding tremblers learn'd to trace
The day's disasters in his morning face;
Full well they laugh'd with counterfeited glee
At all his jokes, for many a joke had he;
Full well the busy whisper, circling round,
Convey'd the dismal tidings when he frown'd—
Yet he was kind, or if severe in aught,
The love he bore to learning was in fault.
The village all declar'd how much he knew;
'Twas certain he could write, and cipher too,
Lands he could measure, terms and tides presage—
And even the story ran that he could gauge.
In arguing too, the parson own'd his skill,
For even though vanquish'd he could argue still;
While words of learned length and thundering sound
Amaz'd the gaping rustics all around—
And still they gaz'd, and still the wonder grew
That one small head could carry all he knew.
But pass'd is all his fame: the very spot,
Where many a time he triumph'd is forgot.

EDITORIAL METHOD

Omissions

In order to publish the letters and diary in a single volume of manageable proportions, certain passages from the original manuscript have been omitted from this edition. The excisions amount to approximately 20,200 words out of a total of 275,800 words in the original, which corresponds to a reduction of about seven per cent. In thus abbreviating the diary, the editors have attempted to retain everything that is of social and economic importance, whilst at the same time preserving its human interest and faithfulness in reflecting the general tenor of the day-to-day life of the village and its diarist. With this general aim in mind, we have excluded obviously trivial and unimportant entries as well as passages devoted exclusively to literary, philosophical, or pedagogical digressions. In particular the following types of entry have been excised:

a. Robert Sharp's own literary productions, for example, two copies of his letters to newspapers composed as examples of literary style which appear in the Letters section, and his serialized moral tales in the section for 1829.

b. Extended commentary on literary and biblical texts.

c. Digressions on grammar and letters of the alphabet.

d. Remarks on the history of Barmston (but not his personal recollections of it).

e. Extended references to, and commentary on, relatively trifling topics taken from old magazines and almanacs.

f. Trivial entries such as 'Nothing particular this day' or 'Went to collect sess at Ellerker but met with little success'.

g. Entries devoted exclusively to the weather unless it was significant, for example, in its bearing on crop growth or the harvest.

In order to compensate for any loss of significant information, by the omission of the titles of books or periodicals consulted by the diarist in material in category 'b' above, all titles of works mentioned in the letters and diary have been listed in Appendix 3, even if the only reference to them is in an excised passage.

All passages deleted from the diary have been indicated by the marks of omission—three points. Three points at the beginning of a daily entry immediately after the date indicates that the first part of that entry has been omitted; three points at the end of an entry, if followed by an entry for a date later than the next day's date, indicates that one or more entries have been omitted by the editors and not that Sharp has not written entries for those days.

Punctuation and Capitalization

As far as possible punctuation and capitalization follow that of the original manuscript. Very occasionally punctuation has been supplied by the editors, when it has seemed necessary to make the sense of a passage more readily understood. All such editorial insertions are indicated by square brackets. When a full stop has been inserted to mark the end of a sentence, the initial letter of the first word of the next sentence has been capitalized. Similarly, when the diarist has uncharacteristically begun a new sentence without a capital letter, one has been supplied by the editors. Such case changes are few and unimportant and have not been indicated in the text. Slips of the quill, for example the mistaken repetition of an article, have been silently corrected to avoid an appearance of undue pedantry. The only other departure from a strictly faithful rendering of the original manuscript is with regard to the use of superscript letters. Sharp used these in some of his abbreviations of personal forenames, for example T$^{hos.}$ and W$^{m.}$, but for technical reasons, it was not possible to reproduce superscript characters at the transcription stage, and it seems preferable to retain the normal characters as transcribed rather than attempt to replace them retrospectively with the original superscript characters. Letters crossed through in the manuscript, indicating corrections, are shown as crossed through in the text. Later insertions, written between lines in the manuscript, have been enclosed within arrow marks, thus > <. Words of doubtful transcription are followed by a question mark in square brackets.

Archaic and Dialect Words

The distinction between some archaic words, that is words no longer in general use, and dialect words is sometimes blurred. Appendix 1 lists all the words in the diary that are known to be in present-day use in the East Riding dialect as well as words that are rarely or no longer used but which are listed in printed glossaries of the East Riding dialect such as F. Ross, *et al. A Glossary of Words Used in Holderness in the East-Riding of Yorkshire* (1877). Some of the words listed in the appendix may well be common to other Yorkshire or North of England dialects. With some notable exceptions (for example, 'throng' meaning 'busy'), Sharp, himself, rarely used dialect words, except consciously for special effect, when he always underlined the word or words in dialect. He did, however, frequently report the speech of others verbatim, and in some cases quite extensive passages of speech are quoted in dialect. In most instances, the general meaning should be deducible by non-dialect speakers, and individual words will be found in the appendix of dialect words. Where the editors have judged that a whole phrase or sentence might not be easily comprehensible, a translation in standard English has been inserted in square brackets. The meanings of archaic or unfamiliar words, not considered to be dialect, have been explained in footnotes.

Weights and Measures

Weights and measures have been transcribed as written. The imperial system was in use during the period covered by the letters and diary. The most commonly used values, with their usual abbreviations and metric equivalents, are listed below. Less common measurements which feature in the diary are explained in the footnotes.

Money

4 farthings	=	1d. (penny)	
12d. (pence)	=	1s. (shilling)	1s. = 5p.
20s. (shillings)	=	£1 (pound)	
21s. (shillings)	=	1 guinea	

Weight

16 oz. (ounces)	=	1 lb. (pound)	1 lb. = 0.45 kilograms
14 lb. (pounds)	=	1 stone	1 stone = 6.35 kilograms
2 stones	=	1 qr. (quarter)	1 qr. =12.70 kilograms
4 qr. (quarters)	=	1 cwt. (hundredweight)	1 cwt. = 50.80 kilograms
20 cwt.	=	1 ton	1 ton = 1.02 tonnes

Volume

2 pints	=	1 quart	1 quart = 1.14 litres
4 quarts	=	1 gallon	1 gallon = 4.55 litres
2 gallons	=	1 peck	1 peck = 9.09 litres
4 pecks	=	1 bushel	1 bushel = 36.40 litres
8 bushels	=	1 qr. (quarter)	1 quarter = 2.91 hectolitres

Distance

12 in. (inches)	=	1 ft. (foot)	1 ft. = 0.305 metres
3 ft. (feet)	=	1 yd. (yard)	1 yd. = 0.91 metres
22 yds. (yards)	=	1 chain	1 chain = 20.12 metres
10 chains	=	1 furlong	1 furlong = 201.17 metres
8 furlongs	=	1 mile (1760 yds.)	1 mile = 1.61 metres

Area

30 ¼ square yds. = 1 perch (P.)[*]			=25.29 sq. metres
40 perches	= 1 rood (R.)[*]	=1210 square yds.	=1011.56 sq. metres
4 roods	= 1 acre (A.)[*]	=4840 square yds.	= 0.405 hectares

[*] Abbreviation as used by Sharp but not a standard one.

Special Calendar Days

Many of the regularly occurring events in South Cave's calendar year, such as Cave Fair, the Club feast, and the autumn sittings were referred to by the diarist and his neighbours not by the date of the month but by the name of one of the quarter days or saint's feast day. The quarter days are:

Lady Day	25 March	Old Lady Day	5 April
Midsummer Day	24 June	Old Midsummer Day	6 July
Michaelmas Day	29 September	Old Michaelmas Day	11 October
Christmas Day	25 December	Old Christmas Day	6 January

Saints' feast days mentioned by Sharp:

Candlemas Day	2 February	Old Candlemas Day	14 February
St. Swithin's Day	15 July		
Martinmas	11 November	Old Martinmas	23 November

Feast days connected with Easter were (and are) moveable:

Lent is the period of 40 days before Easter. The first day of Lent is Ash Wednesday, which is preceded by Shrove (Pancake) Tuesday. Whit Sunday or Pentecost occurs on the seventh Sunday after Easter. The next Sunday after Whit-Sunday is Trinity Sunday, which is followed by Trinity Monday, when Cave Fair began.

Appendices and Maps

The text of the diary is followed by three appendices, namely a glossary of dialect, a bibliographical list of books, poems, and periodicals mentioned in the diary, and a biographical list of the more prominent persons who feature in it. The names of the persons who appear in this list are italicized in the index. For ease of reference, and to show the descent of the diary insofar as this can be traced, a family tree of the members of the Sharp family has also been included.

The five maps show: (1) the geographical location of South Cave with respect to other Yorkshire towns, villages, and major topographical features, (2) the parish of South Cave and its neighbourhood, illustrating the major roads, toll bars, farms, and topographical features recorded by the diarist, and (3–5) the village of South Cave, depicting the major buildings and residences of the most important people mentioned in the diary.

ABBREVIATED REFERENCES

All the works listed below have been used as sources of information for footnotes. Periodicals, and collective works generally known by their titles, together with archival sources are listed under the abbreviated forms by which they are identified in the footnotes. The method used to refer to other works listed below under author(s) is as follows: (1) if an author appears only once in the list as a single author, the work is cited by the author's surname, e.g. Balchin; (2) if a work is by two authors, both names are cited, e.g. Rayner and Crook; (3) if a work is by more than three authors but listed under the first named, it is treated as a single author work; (4) if two or more works by a single author are listed, the date of publication is added in parentheses after the author's surname, e.g. MacDonagh (1988), MacDonagh (1989); (5) if two or more authors share an identical surname, they are distinguished by their initials, e.g. Jackson, C., Jackson, E.

Where parliamentary Acts have been used as sources of information, they have been cited by regnal year and chapter in the text of the footnote. The Acts themselves may be consulted in the *Statutes at Large*.

Throughout the footnotes, the diarist has been cited by his initials, RS.

Manuscript Collections, Periodicals, and Collective Works (Abbreviations)

ALLR	*All England Law Reports Reprint* ... 1824–34 .London, 1966.
AR	*Annual Register*.
CPR	*Cobbett's Political Register* (*Cobbett's Annual Register*, *Cobbett's Weekly Register* etc.)
DNB	*Dictionary of National Biography*.
EB	*Encyclopaedia Britannica*. 11th ed. 1910–11.
EP	*English Poetry: the English Poetry Full-text Database*. CD-ROM edition. Chadwyck-Healey Ltd. 1992–
ER	*English Reports*, vol.161 (Ecclesiastical, Admiralty, Probate and Divorce).
ERYARS	East Riding of Yorkshire Archives and Record Service
HA	*Hull Advertiser*.
HP	*Hull Packet*.
NQ	*Notes and Queries*.
ODQ	*Oxford Dictionary of Quotations*. 3rd ed. Oxford: OUP, 1979.
OED	*Oxford English Dictionary*
PP	*Parliamentary Papers*.
TM	*The Times*.
VCHYER	*Victoria County History: a History of the County of York: East Riding*; edited by K. J. Allison. Oxford: OUP, 1969–89. – Vols. 1–6.

Books, Theses, and Periodical Articles

Addison, R. *A Topographical History of Leavening at the Close of the Eighteenth Century* (1831).

Ahier, P. *Legends and Traditions of Huddersfield*. Huddersfield: Advertiser Press, 1940–5. – 2 vols.

Allen, J. *The Stranger's Guide to Ferriby ... and South Cave ...* Hull: sold by J. Rayner, 1841.

Allison, K. J. *'Hull Gent Seeks Country Residence', 1750–1850*. Beverley: EYLHS, 1981.

Baines, E. *History, Directory & Gazetteer of the County of York ...* Vol. 2: *East And North Ridings*. Leeds, 1823.

Baker, F. *Methodism and the Love-feast*. London: Epworth Press, 1957.

Balchin, A. T., 'The Justice of the Peace and County Government in the East Riding of Yorkshire, 1782–1836'. Ph.D. thesis, Hull University, 1990.

Barnard, M. *A History of Australia*. 2nd ed. London: Angus and Robertson, 1963.

Beach, V. W. *Charles X of France: his Life and Times*. Boulder, Col.: Pruett, 1971.

Bell, J. *A Copious and Practical Treatise on the Game Laws ...* London: W. Crofts, 1839.

Brenan, G. *A History of the House of Percy ...* London: Freemantle and Co., 1902. – 2 vols.

Bulmer, T. *History, Topography and Directory of East Yorkshire ...* Preston: T. Bulmer and Co., 1892.

Butterworth, S. 'The Old *London Magazine* and Some of its Contributors', *Bookman*, vol. 63, Oct. 1922.

Campbell, J. L. *Lives of the Chancellors*. Vol. 8: *Lives of Lord Lyndhurst and Lord Brougham ...* London: John Murray, 1869.

Carnall, G. 'The *Monthly Magazine*', *Review of English Studies*, n. s., vol. 5, 1954.

Carr, R. *Spain, 1808–1939*. 2nd ed. Oxford: Clarendon Press, 1982.

Clarke, S. R. *The New Yorkshire Gazetteer or Topographical Dictionary*. London: Henry Teesdale and Co., 1828.

Crowther, J. E. *Beverley in Mid-Victorian Times*. Cherry Burton: Hutton Press, 1990.

Crowther, J. E. 'New Light on Beverley: Street Lighting in the Nineteenth Century', *East Yorkshire Local History Society Bulletin*, no. 32, autumn 1985.

Crowther, J. E. 'Parliamentary Enclosure in Eastern Yorkshire, 1725–1860'. PhD thesis, Hull University, 1983.

Cunnington, C. W. and P. *Handbook of English Costume in the Nineteenth Century*. 3rd ed. London: Faber and Faber, 1970.

Curtis, S. J. *History of Education in Great Britain*. 5th ed. London: University Tutorial Press, 1963.

Dale, R. W. *History of English Congregationalism*, London: Hodder and Stoughton, 1907.

Dawson, W. H. *History of Independency in Skipton from 1770 to 1890*. London: James Clarke and Co., [1891].

Dod, C. R. *Electoral Facts from 1832 to 1853* ... edited by H. J. Hanham. Brighton: Harvester Press, 1972. Includes facsimile reprint of 2nd ed. of 1853.

Dodd, G. 'London Shops and Bazaars' in: *London*; edited by C. Knight (1841–43), vol. 5.

Dowell, S. *A History of Taxation and Taxes in England* ... 3rd ed., with a new introduction by A. R. Ilersic. London: Cass, 1965. – 4 vols.

Drabble, M., ed. *The Oxford Companion to English Literature*. 5th ed. Oxford: OUP, 1985.

Evans, E. J. *The Contentious Tithe: the Tithe Problem and English Agriculture, 1750–1850*. London: Routledge & Kegan Paul, 1976.

Fairfax-Blakeborough, J. *Yorkshire, East Riding*. London: Robert Hale Ltd., 1951.

Foster, J., comp., *Pedigrees of the County Families of Yorkshire*, London: W. W. Head, 1874. – 3 vols.

Fussell, G. E. *The Farmer's Tools: the History of British Farm Implements, Tools and Machinery AD 1500–1900*. Reprint ed. London: Bloomsbury Books, 1985. – Originally published 1952.

Gosden, P. H. J. H. *Self-help: Voluntary Associations in the 19th Century*. London: Batsford, 1973.

Greenwood, J. *Greenwood's Picture of Hull*. Hull, J. Greenwood, 1835.

Greig, G. R. *The Life of Arthur, First Duke of Wellington*. London: Longman, 1862.

Gutch, Mrs., ed. *Examples of Printed Folk-lore Concerning the East Riding of Yorkshire*. London: D. Nutt for the Folk-lore Society, 1912.

Hackwood, F. W. *Inns, Ales and Drinking Customs of Old England*, London: Bracken Books, 1985.

Hall, J. G. *A History of South Cave* ... Hull: Edwin Ombler, 1892.

Hall, I. and E. *A New Picture of Georgian Hull*, York: William Sessions Ltd., 1979.

Harris, A. 'Bones for the Land: the Early Days of an East Yorkshire Industry', *East Yorkshire Local History Society Bulletin*, no. 31, 1985.

Hartley, W. C. E. *Banking in Yorkshire*. Clapham: Dalesman Books, 1975.

Henriques, U. R. Q. 'Bastardy and the New Poor Law', *Past and Present*, no. 37, 1967.

Hobsbawm, E. J. and Rudé, G. *Captain Swing*. London: Lawrence and Wishart, 1969.

Hone, W. *The Every-day Book; or, Everlasting Calendar* ... London: Hunt and Clarke, 1826–7. – 2 vols.

Imrie, M. *The Manor Houses of Burton Agnes and their Owners*. Cherry Burton: Hutton Press, 1993.

Jackman, W. T. *The Development of Transportation in Modern England.* 2nd ed. London: Cass, 1962.

Jackson, C. E. *British Names of Birds.* London: Witherby, 1968.

Jackson, G. *Hull in the Eighteenth Century.* London: OUP for the University of Hull, 1972.

Kinzner, B. L. *The Ballot Question in Nineteenth-century English Politics.* New York: Garland, 1982.

Knight, C. B. *A History of the City of York.* 2nd ed. York: Herald Printing Works, 1944.

Kussmaul, A. *Servants in Husbandry in Early Modern England.* Cambridge: CUP, 1981.

Lawson, J. *A Town Grammar School through Six Centuries: a History of Hull Grammar School* ... London: OUP for the University of Hull, 1963.

Leatham, I. *A General View of the Agriculture of the East Riding of Yorkshire.* London: printed by W. Bulmer, 1794.

Legard, G. 'Farming of the East Riding of Yorkshire: Prize Report', *Journal of the Royal Agricultural Society,* vol. 9, pt. 1, 1848.

Leys, M. D. R. *Between Two Empires: a History of French Politicians and People between 1814 and 1848.* London: Longmans, Green and Co., 1955.

MacDonagh, O. *The Hereditary Bondsman, Daniel O'Connell, 1775–1829,* London: Weidenfeld, 1988.

MacDonagh, O. *The Emancipist, Daniel O'Connell, 1830–47,* London: Weidenfeld, 1989.

Macmahon, K. A. *Roads and Turnpike Trusts in Eastern Yorkshire.* York: EYLHS, 1964.

Macturk, G. G. *A History of the Hull Railways,* Hull: Hull Packet Office, 1879.

Malcomson, R. W. *Popular Recreations in English Society, 1700–1850.* Cambridge: CUP, 1973.

Markham, J. *The Beverley Arms: the Story of a Hotel.* Beverley: Highgate Publications, 1986.

Markham, J. *Colourful Characters.* Beverley: Highgate Publications, 1992.

Markham, J. *Nineteenth-century Parliamentary Elections in East Yorkshire.* Beverley: EYLHS, 1982.

Mattingly, H. and Sydenham, E. A. *The Roman Imperial Coinage.* Vol. 1: *Augustus to Vitellius,* London: Spink, 1923 (reprinted 1948).

Mingay, G. E., ed. *The Agrarian History of England and Wales.* Vol. 6: *1750–1850.* Cambridge: CUP, 1989.

Morison, S. *The English Newspaper: Some Account of the Physical Development of Journals Printed in London between 1622 and the Present Day.* Cambridge: at the University Press, 1932.

Mudford, W. *The Life of Richard Cumberland, Esq.* ... , London: Sherwood, Neely and Jones, 1812.

Neave, D. *East Riding Friendly Societies.* Beverley: EYLHS, 1988.

Neave, D. and Turnbull, D. *Landscaped Parks and Gardens of East Yorkshire*. York: Georgian Society for East Yorkshire, 1992.

Neave, D. *Londesborough: History of an East Yorkshire Estate Village*. Londesborough Silver Jubilee Committee, 1977.

Neave, D. *South Cave: a Market Village Community in the Eighteenth and Nineteenth Centuries*. 2nd ed. Howden: Pye Books, 1984.

Nicholson, J. *Folk Lore of East Yorkshire*. London: Simkin, Marshall, Hamilton, Kent, & Co., 1890.

Oliver, G. *The History and Antiquities of the Town and Minster of Beverley* ... Beverley: printed by M. Turner, 1829.

Park, G. R. *Parliamentary Representation of Yorkshire* ... Hull: the author, 1886.

Patton, J. G. *A Country Independent Chapel (Swanland, E. Yorks., Congregational Church)*. London: A. Brown and Sons, 1943.

Pevsner, N. *London. – Vol.1: The Cities of London and Westminster*. 3rd ed., revised by B. Cherry. Penguin Books, 1973. – (The Buildings of England).

Pevsner, N. *Yorkshire: York and the East Riding*. 2nd ed., [edited] by D. Neave [*et al.*]. Penguin Books, 1995 – (The Buildings of England).

Pigot and Co. *National and Commercial Directory ... of the Merchants, Bankers, Professional Gentlemen, Manufacturers and Traders ... in the Counties of Chester, Cumberland, Durham, Lancaster, Northumberland, Westmoreland and York* ... London: Pigot and Co., 1834.

Pine, L. G. *The New Extinct Peerage, 1884–1971* ... London: Heraldry Today, 1972.

Pressnell, L. S.. *Country Banking in the Industrial Revolution*. Oxford: Clarendon Press, 1956.

Purvey, P. F. *Coins of England and the United Kingdom*. 20th ed. London: Seaby, 1984. – (Standard Catalogue of British Coins, vol. 1).

Quayle, E. *The Ruin of Sir Walter Scott*. London: Hart-Davis, 1968.

Rayner, J. L. and Crook, G. T. *The Complete Newgate Calendar*. London: Navarre Society Ltd., 1926. – 5 vols.

Richardson, W. 'Notes on the Early History of Misssions to the South Sea Islands with Special Reference to the Rev. Charles Barff ...' South Cave, 1895. – Bound volume of Ms. account and cuttings from newspapers and periodicals including an article by the author on Barff and his family taken from the *Hull and District Congregational Magazine*, July and Aug. 1898. The bound volume is kept at the Hull Local Studies Library, Albion St., Hull.

Richardson, W. *Some East Yorkshire Worthies*. Hull: A. Brown and Sons Ltd., 1914.

Robinson, H. *The British Post Office: a History*, Princeton, N.J.: Princeton U. P., 1948.

Rose, L. *The Massacre of the Innocents: Infanticide in Britain, 1800–1939*. London: Routledge & Kegan Paul, 1986.

Ross, F. *Celebrities of the Yorkshire Wolds*. London: Trübner and Co., 1878.

Ross, F., *et al. A Glossary of Words used in Holderness* ... London: Trübner and Co. for the English Dialect Society, 1877.

Sambrook, J. *William Cobbett*, London: Routledge & Kegan Paul, 1973.

Sheahan, J. J. *General and Concise History and Description of the Town and Port of Kingston-upon-Hull*. London: Simpkin, Marshall and Co., 1864.

Sheahan, J. J. and Whellan, T. *History and Topography of the City of York, the Ainsty Wapentake, and the East Riding*. Beverley, 1855. – 2 vols.

Sibree, J. *Fifty Years' Recollections of Hull* ... Hull: Brown and Sons, 1884.

Smith, E. A. *Whig Principles and Party Politics: Earl Fitzwilliam and the Whig Party, 1748–1833*. Manchester: Manchester U. P., 1975.

Smith, F. B. *The People's Health, 1830–1910*. London: Croom Helm, 1979.

Soloway, R. A. *Prelates and People: Ecclesiastical Social Thought in England, 1783–1852*. London : Routledge & Kegan Paul, 1969.

Stevenson, J. *Popular Disturbances in England, 1700–1832*. 2nd ed. London: Longman, 1992.

Strickland, H. E. *A General View of the Agriculture of the East Riding of Yorkshire* ... York: Wilson, 1812.

Sumner, W. L. *The Organ: Its Evolution, Principles of Construction and Use*. 3rd ed. London: Macdonald, 1962.

Sutherland, J. *The Life of Walter Scott: a Critical Biography*. Oxford: Blackwell, 1995.

Thirsk, I. J. *The Rural Economy of England: Collected Essays*. London: Hambledon Press, 1984.

Thompson, F. M. L. *Chartered Surveyors: the Growth of a Profession*. London: Routledge & Kegan Paul, 1968.

Timbs, J. *Curiosities of London, Exhibiting the Most Rare and Remarkable Objects of Interest in the Metropolis*. New ed. London: J. S. Virtue and Co., 1867.

Tomlinson, W. W. *The North Eastern Railway: Its Rise and Development*. Newcastle-upon-Tyne: Reid, 1914.

Trout, A. E. 'An Old Yorkshire Congregation: South Cave Congregational Church', *Transactions of the Congregational Historical Society*, Sept. 1931.

Tucker, D. N. 'Norwood House' – an unpublished typescript article deposited in Beverley Local Studies Library.

Walpole, *Sir* Spencer. *A History of England*. London: Longmans, Green and Co., 1911–14. – 6 vols.

Ward, J. T. *East Yorkshire Landed Estates in the Nineteenth Century*. York: EYLHS, 1967.

Watson, G., ed. *The New Cambridge Bibliography of English Literature*. Vol. 3: *1800–1900*. Cambridge: University Press, 1969.

White, W. *History, Gazetteer, and Directory of the East and North Ridings of Yorkshire*. Sheffield: William White, 1840.

White, W. *History, Gazetteer, and Directory of the West-Riding of Yorkshire with the City and Port of Hull*. Sheffield: William White, 1838. – 2 vols.

Whitehead, J. *Sunk Island: the Land that Rose from the Humber*. Beverley: Highgate Publications, 1991.

Wolff, M., *et al.*, comps. *The Waterloo Directory of Victorian Periodicals, 1824–1900*. Phase 1. Waterloo (Ont.): Wilfred Laurier U. P. for the University of Waterloo, 1976.

Woodcock, Henry. *Piety among the Peasantry: being Sketches of Primitive Methodism on the Yorkshire Wolds*. London: J. Toulson, 1889.

Woodforde, J. *The Strange Story of False Teeth*. London: Routledge & Kegan Paul, 1968.

Woodward, D., ed. *The Farming and Memorandum Books of Henry Best of Elmswell 1642*. London: OUP for the British Academy. 1984. – (Records of Social and Economic History, n. s. 8).

Wright, J., comp. *The English Dialect Dictionary*. London: Frowde, 1898–1905. – 6 vols.

INTRODUCTION

Overview

The author of the letters and diary, Robert Sharp (1773–1843), was the schoolmaster of South Cave, an East Riding market village, from 1804 until his death in 1843. The letters, which cover the period from 1812 to 1825, were sent to his son who worked initially for a Hull bookseller and later for the London publishing firm, Longman's. The diary proper begins in 1826 and, like the letters, was sent to his son in instalments. These instalments were later bound together with the letters into a single volume. Apart from a gap for the year 1828, the diary continues almost uninterruptedly until 1837, ending just two weeks before the accession of Queen Victoria to the throne. It thus covers that highly significant period of nineteenth-century British history between the Napoleonic Wars and the Victorian era which included the passing of the Reform Act of 1832.

The chief importance of Robert Sharp's writings is not as a record of the history of rural education—indeed, he rarely mentioned his work as a school teacher—but as an exceptionally intimate portrayal of village life in the early years of the nineteenth-century. Many of the published diaries of the period have been written by local clergymen, who were usually of a higher social status than most of their parishioners so that their viewpoint was necessarily more distant and detached than that of Robert Sharp, who himself came from humble origins. As one of the most educated men in the village, he was involved in almost every aspect of village life where his skills of literacy and numeracy were required. He was thus in a unique position to record the affairs of the village and its inhabitants. Of particular interest is the detailed picture that emerges of the day-to-day administration of local affairs by the parish officers, as observed by one who was himself a parish officer (deputy constable and tax assessor) and assistant in various capacities to the other officers. In the earlier years of the diary, this long-established system of almost autonomous local administration, based on the unpaid service of prominent parishioners, supervised by the Justices of the Peace, but largely independent of central government, was almost indistinguishable from what it had been in the previous century and earlier. However, in the later years of the diary it is possible to detect how it was beginning to change, through increasing government intervention and effective legislation, especially the passing of the Poor Law Amendment Act in 1834 and the Highways Act in 1835. Another feature of village life at that time, which is well illustrated in the diary, is its pronounced cyclical nature based on a regular calendar of traditional events and customs, marking the passage of the year. These range from the procession of the plough boys at the New Year, through Easter with its visitation dinner and the wearing of new clothes, followed on Trinity Monday by Cave Fair with its potters and cheesecakes, the Club feast after Old Midsummer, hare feasts on 5 November, the sittings at Martinmas, and finally to Christmas with the traditional yule clog and frumenty.

Although the main strength of this diary is in its portrayal of village life at a significant period of British history, yet it is also important because the diarist took such a lively interest in what was happening outside the village both nationally and internationally. He not only expressed his own opinions on the wider questions of the day but reported on the reactions of others. The diary, likewise, illustrates to what extent a small market village was affected by national trends and events, for example, emigration, Catholic Emancipation, parliamentary reform, the abolition of slavery, agricultural unrest, the new Poor Law, the Corn Laws, the Beer Act, the coming of the railways, and the social effects of industrialization. Very little of national importance, especially in the main period of the diary from 1826 to 1837 (except of course 1828), has escaped the attention of the diarist.

The Letters and the Diary

The letters and diary are bound together in a single volume which is kept at the East Riding of Yorkshire Archives and Records Service in Beverley (DDX/216/4). The volume was deposited there by the late Miss Florence Dennis of South Cave, a descendant of the diarist through his daughter Eliza. The volume is made up of 377 sheets of paper. The letters comprise the first 41 sheets, which range in size from 6¼ in. × 7½ in. (16 cm. × 19 cm.) to 13½ in. × 8½ in. (34·5 cm. × 21·5 cm.). The diary proper is written on 336 sheets, most of which measure 13½ in. × 8½ in. (34·5 cm. × 21·5 cm.). The sheets which deviate from this size are contained in four sections of 4, 10, 23, and 16 sheets respectively, each measuring 12½ in. × 7½ in. (31·5 cm. × 19 cm.) and a fifth section (spanning the period 18 January to 24 October, 1831) of 19 sheets, which measure 15¼ in. × 9½ in. (38·5 cm. × 24 cm.). The sheets in this particular section, being longer than all the other sheets in the volume, have curled over at the bottom, damaging the paper so that in some cases the writing at the foot of the page is either very difficult to read or illegible. Elsewhere, as befitted a man who lived largely by the pen, cut his own quills, and made his own ink, the writing is uniformly neat and legible. The letters themselves (17,500 words) make up less than seven per cent of the bound volume (275,800 words) and because of the very long gaps between letters, especially the earlier ones, when for some years no letters exist, the collection is obviously very incomplete. The letters begin in 1812 with a short letter to the young William from his sister, Jane, and then from 1813, with two exceptions, another letter from Jane and a joint letter from his mother and father, all the letters are from Robert. The last letter before the diary starts is dated '25th Decr. 1825'. The letters were obviously saved as a collection by Robert's son, William, to whom they were addressed, as many of them have been annotated by him with descriptive comments such as, 'My Sister Jane July 16. 1812' and 'My Father

Feb 10 1820'. This may suggest that William, himself, was responsible for binding together the letters and diary and this view is repeated by the South Cave historian, William Richardson, in his book, 'The Parish Registers of South Cave', published in 1909, which has an appendix containing a selection of extracts from Robert Sharp's diary. Unfortunately, it has not been possible to trace the history of the diary from the date of the last entry (5 June 1837) when Robert asked 'a nephew of Mr. Beaumont' to take the last instalment in 'a parcel to Wm.' and decided that he would 'not begin another Sheet,' until it is mentioned (in the work cited above) as being back in South Cave in the possession of the diarist's great grandson, William Sharp Dennis.

The diary was sent to William in instalments by his father as a record of what concerned his family and what was happening in his home village. There is no indication whether or not Robert was keeping a diary for his own use before 1826 during the period covered by the letters. The first entry for the diary in the bound volume starts rather abruptly on 19 May 1826 without any explanatory preamble which would, perhaps, suggest that he had begun the diary before that date. It is of course impossible now to know whether William had not received, had lost, or had simply not begun to collect any earlier entries. Very few gaps in the diary over the next eleven years are unexplained apart from the missing year—1828. The only possible clue provided by the diarist for this major gap in the sequence is in the entry for 2 January 1829, when he wrote 'Went to West Ella this morning ... my mother looks remarkably well, I had not been there since July last having been so poorly, but I hope my illness is entirely gone, as at present I feel very well.' The diary instalments were usually sent to William in his 'box', one of two chests which plied regularly back and forth between South Cave and London either by coach or by sea. The Sharp parents sent William food from South Cave, fruit, fowl, eggs, pies, and game, and in return William sent them a variety of goods obtainable from the capital, including books, journals, items of clothing both new and second-hand, confectionery, tobacco, and medicaments. One significant gap in the diary is for the period 2 October to 17 December 1835. This instalment was despatched to Hull on 18 December in a basket 'containing a Goose dressed a Standing Pork Pie some few fine apples—a little Spice loaf and a Sovereign and a half together with my Journal up to this time and a letter for a few popular Books such as Cock Robin, little Red Riding Hood &c. &c.' The basket and its contents were loaded aboard a steam packet bound for London, but alas, shortly after departure, a fire broke out on board destroying the cargo and forcing the boat to run ashore at Grimsby. Fortunately, such accidents were few, and the diary has been largely preserved in its entirety for the span of years that it covers.

A notable feature of the diary is the increasing brevity of the daily entries in the later years of its coverage. It is easy to speculate why this should be so: Robert himself had been writing it day after day for several years and may well have been experiencing a diminution in his own enthusiasm for the task. William, too, as he got older would no doubt have become increasingly preoccupied with his growing family responsibilities and professional duties in London, and perhaps correspondingly less concerned with events in far off South Cave. If this were so, it would be only natural if he were to be less responsive to the news contained in his father's journal, and that Robert himself, sensing his son's diminished interest, would lack the stimulus previously given him to write at greater length. Whatever the reason, the diary entries became markedly more abbreviated after 1829: in sheer volume the greatest word count for a single year is for 1827 (41,000 words), followed by 1829 (30,000 words) and the part-year 1826 (29,000 words); thereafter 1830 to 1833 each have 20–24,000 words, whilst the remaining four years are all less than 20,000 words each. Fortunately, there is no strong correlation between the length of a daily entry and the degree of interest that it provides the reader.

Robert Sharp and his Family

Robert Sharp was born on 22 September 1773 in the village of Barmston, about six miles south of Bridlington on the Yorkshire coast. He was the eldest of four children born to John Sharp, a shepherd, and his wife, Elizabeth Harrison. The other children were Thomas (born 1775 and later to become the Independent minister at Skipton),[1] Mary (born 1778), and Milcah (born 1783). Mary, who later lived in Hull and provided a home for Robert's young son William, when he obtained his first job in that town, subsequently left him a substantial legacy at her death in Liverpool in 1832. Milcah married a James Ramsdale and lived in the village of West Ella (see map 2), where she was later joined by her mother and father after their retirement. She eventually died of cancer, after having first undergone an apparently successful mastectomy. Robert had a very happy childhood in Barmston and was often later in life to look back upon it with great nostalgia. He was educated by his maternal uncle, the Barmston village schoolmaster, Robert Harrison, to whom he later paid fond tribute as his chief mentor.

Robert left Barmston in 1786 when he was 13. From later remarks made in his diary, it appears that he went to Bridlington, where he apparently stayed until taking up his appointment as schoolmaster of South Cave in 1804. Robert himself made very few references to this period of his life in his writings and very little can be gleaned from other sources. It is possible that he was apprenticed as a shoemaker, since he was certainly earning his living by that trade in 1803 shortly before taking up his post at South Cave in the following year. The evidence for this is contained in the baptismal register of the Zion Independent Chapel at Bridlington[2] where the words 'Shoe Maker' are appended to the entry for 'Jane Daughter of Robert and Ann Sharp Born 28th

---

[1] Dawson 55–84.

[2] ERYARS Mf 2 [3020].

April and Baptised August 19th 1803. Willm. Vint Bridlington'.[3] Further confirmation of Robert's occupation before he became a schoolmaster is provided by a reference to him in a later reminiscence by a former pupil, who recalled that his teacher's nickname at the school was 'Cobbler Dick'.[4] The diarist himself never once referred to his former occupation in his diary. Almost the only references to the years spent in Bridlington are when he recalled visits made to Barmston at Martinmas, and a reminiscence of his acquaintanceship with two old Quaker ladies living in the town. Writing in 1829 (15 November), he recalled that 'they had a good many Books, and I was allowed and invited to ransack amongst them as much as I liked, where I could get amongst Books it was always a treat to me.' He added that this acquaintanceship was '40 year since' so that his recollection would go back to about 1789 when he would be 16 years old. His love for books and reading remained with him throughout his lifetime, and it seems likely that most of his learning was acquired as a result of self-education; certainly there is no evidence to suggest that he received any formal education after the age of 13 when he left his uncle's village school at Barmston.

In 1795, at the age of 21, Robert married Ann Read, who was about three years younger than her husband. They were married in Bridlington at the Priory Church. In all they had six children, the first four of whom were baptized at the Zion Independent Chapel in Bridlington. Their children were: John (May 1796; died February 1797), William (June 1798), Mary (May 1801; died in infancy), Jane (April 1803; died 1815 aged nearly 12), Elizabeth (April 1805), and John (March 1806; died 1816 aged nearly 10). Thus two children died as infants, two as grown children, and only two survived to adulthood: William and Eliza.

Initially the letters were sent to William in Hull where he stayed with his aunt Mary, Robert's sister. William was aged 14 when he received the first letter in the collection and was working for John Craggs, a North Cave man, who operated as a bookseller, binder, stationer, and paper manufacturer in Silver Street in Hull. From November 1821, William was living in London and working for the prestigious firm of London publishers, Longman's. He was to work there until his death in 1870 and occupy the office of 'head at the counter', a position in which he was eventually succeeded by his elder son, also William. (Together their careers at Longman's spanned 75 years, from 1821 to 1896).[5] William's own marriage to one Hannah Hicks took place on 12 April 1828. Apart from William, born 1831, he had a daughter, Mary Barker, born in 1829 and a great favourite of her paternal grandparents, as well as another son,

---

[3] The occupations of all the fathers of the baptized children listed on that page of the register have been supplied, but most of the other entries do not include the name of the officiating minister, so that there is no doubt that the description of 'shoe maker' refers to RS and not to Vint.

[4] Record by the South Cave historian, William Richardson, in his ms. 'Memoranda and Copies of Documents' kept at Hull Local Studies Library, of an interview with John Dunn on 3 Aug. 1899. 'Mr. Dunn will be 86 in October ... he went to the Cross School. M^r. Sharp (Cobbler Dick) being then the schoolmaster ...'

[5] *Ex inf.* M. Bott, Keeper of Archives and Mss. (including the Longman archives) at Reading University.

born *c.* 1833 and named Robert Harrison after his great great uncle who had taught Robert in Barmston.

Eliza lived at home with her parents until her marriage in 1829 to a South Cave saddler, John Conder. She does not seem to have been nearly so favoured in her father's affections as was William. Maybe it was a case of absence makes the heart grow fonder. At all events Robert does not even record her wedding in his diary. Perhaps, too, he had higher expectations than a saddler for son-in-law. Eliza went on to have a large family and her eldest daughter, Ann, successfully established herself in her grandfather, Robert's affections, as is obvious from a reading of the diary.

In 1804, at the age of 30 Robert became the village schoolmaster of South Cave and remained there until his death in 1843. He and his wife and their young family took up residence in the schoolmaster's house, which formed part of the Market Cross hall, in the upper storey of which was located the village school (often known for that reason as the Cross School). Although he enjoyed teaching, and wrote that some of his 'best days have been spent in [that] employ' (23 March 1832), there is very little of this aspect of his life in the diary. Like many countrymen at that period, Robert had more than one occupation. Just as his fellow villagers contrived to be simultaneously shopkeepers and farmers or publicans-cum-blacksmiths-cum-farmers, so Robert himself was not simply a schoolmaster. As one of the few éducated men in the village, he fell in for almost any odd job requiring a knowledge of reading and an ability to write. This involved writing letters for his neighbours, filling in forms, writing out and witnessing wills, helping with the parish accounts and books, drawing up land tax bills, writing lists of voters, jurors, militiamen, helping with censuses, surveys and all the other business that affected the parish and its inhabitants. As well as these occasional or seasonal employments, he was regularly employed as a private tutor and acted as the village's tax collector, being selected every year as one of the two tax assessors. Much of his spare time was spent in attempting to collect (often from unwilling payers) the various forms of 'sess'—the local taxes or assessments for the upkeep of church, poor and highways. In addition as the local sub-distributor of stamps, he acted as a government agent, selling the official excise stamps required for various legal documents and transactions, and delivering the surcharges which were part and parcel of the national governmental system of taxation. Robert was an experienced accountant and book-keeper and his services in this field were much in demand. For several years he acted as a deputy village constable, as well as assisting the officers of the parish in carrying out their duties in more informal ways. Throughout the year, usually on Saturdays, but also in the evenings after school during the warmer months, Robert was regularly out in the fields and closes with his measuring rods and chain, employed by the local farmers to measure land and crops, usually as a preliminary to their sale. For this work he was paid a standard fee. Another regular source of income was supplied by his role as clerk to the village friendly society, known as the Club. For this he received a regular stipend of 30s. paid annually in November; in addition he received a pint of beer at every meeting and 1d. for every member whom he notified when there was to be a funeral of a Club member. In addition, for a period of about five years, from 1828 to 1833, the Sharps ran a village shop selling food and general stores. Although this gave them both considerable satisfaction, it did not in the end prove profitable and they gave it up.

The character and personality of Robert comes over very strongly in the letters and the diary. He was pre-eminently an intellectual—an avid reader of books and newspapers (see Appendix 3 for a list of titles mentioned in the letters and diary) and a keen student of current affairs on which he commented extensively. He was also very interested in his fellow-men and wrote shrewdly and affectionately but with wry humour on the characters, foibles, and behaviour of his neighbours in South Cave. Although he was himself a serious and abstemious man with strongly held moral and religious views, yet at the same time he was remarkably tolerant and sympathetic in his attitude to those whose lifestyle was less regular than his own. He was an affectionate and loving father and grandfather, and seems to have been very happily married, making numerous affectionate references to his wife, Ann. Robert Sharp led a busy but regular and largely uneventful life. He has described his daily routine for a typical week in the diary entry for 6 June 1827: it reveals the steady, unhurried lifestyle of a man at ease with himself and content with his lot where 'one day is so much like another that there is but little variation' in a 'life with as little deviation as possible'. Unlike some of his more intemperate fellow villagers, who were likely to spend their nights drinking and brawling at the Bear or the Fox and Coney, Robert liked nothing better than an evening by his own fireside reading a book, or a congenial meeting with his fellow-cronies at the house of his friend, the village cobbler, Old Willy Atkinson, where they would all sit around the fire smoking their pipes and discussing everything from the latest corn prices to the coming of the railways and the outcome of the next election.

In his political outlook, Robert Sharp was a keen (though not uncritical) follower of Cobbett and a Whig sympathizer, being strongly critical of the big farmers and landowners and sympathetic to the under-dog in the persons of the persecuted Roman Catholics (whom he opposed on doctrinal grounds), the black slaves, or the poor. His liberal views often put him in the position of being at variance with his neighbours: 'I do not know how it is but I am generally in the Opposition and frequently in the Minority, here they are all mad against any relief to the Catholics; whether it be a natural Sympathy that causes me to wish well to the oppressed or a spirit of Contradiction in Argument that urges me to oppose the domineering Spirit at present abroad I cannot say, perhaps it is a little of both.' (28 Feb. 1829). As so many of his neighbours were farmers, it is not surprising that he was so often on the opposite side in his views on economic matters. Echoing Cobbett, Robert believed that the Corn Laws were wholly detrimental in their effect on keeping up prices, and thus causing hardship to the poorer classes, and thought that the farmers would do better to campaign for lower rents rather than petitioning to keep up the price of corn artificially. On the other hand, the farmers were less likely to share his sympathy with the poor since the burden of the poor rate fell most heavily upon their shoulders. It is notable how frequently the diarist paraphrased Cobbett's views on economic matters, for example, in his condemnation of paper currency and those who supported that system—'the Rag-rooks'—or in his advocacy of the plan to reduce poverty by allowing the poor to rent a small plot of land with which to become self-sufficient. He even used Cobbett's own terms of opprobrium, describing farmers, for example, as 'great Bull-frogs' (28 Sept. 1829). However, Cobbett's influence seems to have waned after 1832 (when he became MP for Oldham) as there are only a few scattered references to him in the diary after that year. Although Robert Sharp may have been ideologically opposed to his farming neighbours, it does not seem to have affected his personal relationships with them, as many of his close personal friends, for example, Giles Bridgeman and the Marshalls, were farmers. Farming dominated South Cave and like his neighbours Robert took a keen interest in agricultural matters, whether it was the price of wheat, the state of the harvest, or the operation of the Corn Laws.

In matters of religion, the diarist, although a devout Christian, was a bitter critic of the Anglican Church and its clergy. At the time when the diary was written, the state of the Church of England was at a low ebb, and visibly in need of reform: parson magistrates out of touch with their parishioners, tithe-hungry vicars, often absent, and their churches run by impoverished curates, anti-reformist bishops, many of them like the Bishop of Durham scandalously rich, and the extensive practice of plurality—all of these shortcomings helped to explain both the widespread unpopularity of the church and its clergy at that time as well as the increasing appeal and popularity of the nonconformist sects. Robert Sharp rarely lost an opportunity in his diary to rail against the established church and its clergy. At times his antipathy towards them was almost more than he could bear: 'there is no conception how tired and disgusted I am of all that belongs to the Church, I cannot much longer put up with it.' Unfortunately for him, he had little choice in the matter, as he was required to attend the church services as part of his job—being responsible for taking a roll-call of his pupils before the Sunday services, and required to sit with them in order to supervise their behaviour. Although he was brought up by his parents in Barmston as a member of the Church of England, his sympathies seem to have been wholly with the dissenters. Indeed, his own children were baptized in the Zion Independent Chapel at Bridlington, and his wife, Ann, and his daughter, Eliza, were frequently mentioned as having attended Chapel. It is possible that Robert may have been influenced by his brother, Thomas, who had left the Church of England to become an Independent minister.

Associated, perhaps, with Robert's dislike of the established church was his abhorrence of the National School system. The National Society for Promoting the Education of the Poor in the Principles of the Established Church had been formed in 1811, and in 1817 on the appointment of the new vicar, Edward Barnard, some 13 years after Robert Sharp's appointment as its resident schoolmaster, the Cross School was newly designated as a National

School. Details of the meeting at which the resolution was passed are given below. It is sufficient to note here that the new regime laid down strict regulations for the day-to-day management of the school and provided for its supervision and regular inspection by a committee of seven persons including the vicar and churchwardens. Teaching had to 'be in strict conformity with that adopted in the District School at Beverley, and the same books ... made use of.' The sudden imposition of this system, and the degree of control and opportunity for interference by the ecclesiastical authorities that were implicit in it, must have been anathema to Robert Sharp. From various cryptic remarks made by him in the diary and from the later report of a contemporary writer,[6] it seems that he struggled against the system and eventually succeeded in getting rid of it. Edward Barnard seems to have more or less accepted defeat by 1827, when the diarist wrote: 'But I have been pestered with, (what, aye I wonder what!) three Parsons this afternoon pretending to look over and examine the School, they know not how much I detest their officiousness. Old Kit told my wife on Sunday last that Edwd. Barnard would not pay his Subscription any longer to the School, so I told their Reverences if that was the case I should certainly give it up, but the Curate assured me it was not the case' (1 May 1827). By 10 December 1829, he could write: 'I have had a travelling Schoolmaster from Beverley to examine what he calls the national School, but I told him I had nothing to do with those who had sent him, he sent a letter last week, which I never opened so he took it with him and paid the Postage. He wished me to write to Mr. Gilby, but I told him I had nothing to write about, I could only say in the words of Scripture "Answer him not a word." ' In 1833, when a sermon was preached on behalf of funds for the National Society, he was able to look back on the struggle with complacency: 'This day the Parson had what he called a Sermon for the benefit of the — Institution [i.e. the National Society] after which a Collection was made. I had a single farthing in my Pocket and I kept it there. I will not encourage them to ruin others as they wished to do to me. No No. no encouragement' (20 Jan. 1833).

When the diary finished in 1837, Robert Sharp was nearly 64 years old. He continued teaching at the school but by 1840, numbers had declined and standards must have deteriorated since the then vicar, Edwin Hotham, proposed that a new school be established as the Cross School had become 'the wreck of what it once was'. However, it appears that Robert Sharp remained as its schoolmaster until his death, at the age of 69, on 5 May 1843. For some 39 years he had played an active part in the affairs of the village and educated several generations of its inhabitants. He was buried in the village churchyard. In 1985,[7] the inscription on the gravestone was recorded as 'Sacred/ to the memory of/ ROBERT SHARP/ who departed this life/ 5th May 1843 aged 69 years'. Sadly the gravestone has since been lost or destroyed in a building development, and but for the foresight and family affection of that member of

---

[6] 'The school was conducted for a short time on the National plan' (Allen78).

[7] *South Cave and Broomfleet Monumental Inscriptions* (1985) 15.

the Sharp family (probably William) who bound up and preserved the pages of the diary, all memory of this observant, witty, and sympathetic chronicler of South Cave would have been lost irrevocably. It is pleasing to think that Robert Sharp himself would have been glad to know that his diary would eventually be appreciated by a wider audience: 'I am glad that he (Wm) likes the Journal, as praise to a writer is animating, and Censure is the next agreeable sensation; the worst situation an Author can be placed in is not to be noticed at all' (24 January 1827).

The Village Background

Topography and Population

The village of South Cave[8] lies at the foot of the south-western corner of the Yorkshire Wolds, about 11 miles west of Hull, a little to the north of the modern A63 road near its junction with the A1034. It is linear in shape and is divided into two distinct parts, separated since the eighteenth century by the grounds of the Barnard family's Gothic house, Cave Castle, which is now (1995) a hotel and restaurant. It is likely that the West End, where the parish church stands, is the more ancient settlement, and that the eastern end of the village containing the market place may represent a later extension based on the growth of trade and the development of the village's market from the early Middle Ages. Much of the eastern part of the parish covering Great wold and Little wold lies on chalk land higher than 120 metres above sea-level and reaches 160 metres on the top of Great wold. The escarpment dips abruptly to about 60 metres. The village itself stands on a broad belt of Jurassic sand, clay, and limestone. Further west the outwash sands and clays of that part of the parish situated in the vale are everywhere below 15 metres above sea level.[9] During the period of the diary, the parish was more extensive than at the present day, and extending southwards to the Humber which formed its southern boundary for some three miles,[10] it contained 7,480 acres,[11] and included the townships of Broomfleet and Faxfleet.

South Cave's beck which runs through the village from east to west has now been put into a culvert. Mill Beck, which also features in the diary, is situated to the west of the village and runs approximately from north-west to south-east.

The population of South Cave increased only slowly in the nineteenth century and census figures show that it did not exceed 1,000 until 1931. During the years covered by the diary, it remained relatively stable at about 800 to 900.

---

[8] See Maps 1–5.
[9] *VCHYER* iv. 37–9.
[10] Clarke 55.
[11] Allen 72.

In 1831 Robert Sharp acted as the official census enumerator, and reported the results of his survey in the entry for 7 June in that year: 'I have finished taking the Population and here is the result. 173 inhabited houses, 181 Families. 1 house building. 9 houses unoccupied. 109 families engaged in Agriculture. 49 in trade and 23 other classes. — There are 407 Males & 426 females Total 833'. In 1821 the population had been higher at 885, possessing 168 inhabited houses and 9 empty houses; the reduction in population between 1821 and 1831, he explained as being due to the absence of the lord of the manor, Mr. Barnard, and his servants, and to the number of villagers who had emigrated to America. As shown in the return, by far the bulk of the population was engaged in agriculture.

The Social and Economic Life of the Village

The Community. Although most of the village community was engaged in agriculture (and all were ultimately dependent on it), as the above census return makes clear, yet because South Cave was an important market village and thus larger than many of the other villages in the neighbourhood, so it had a correspondingly greater proportion of shopkeepers, traders, craftsmen, and professional men in its population. Many people of course, particularly at that time, before society had become more specialized, followed more than one occupation simultaneously and defy precise classification. Nevertheless, it is worth glancing at Baines's directory for 1823 to get some idea of the occupational profile of South Cave just before the diary proper began.[12] It lists seven 'persons of superior quality', three teachers, two attorneys, five innkeepers, three blacksmiths, six shoemakers, two tailors, three wheelwrights, five butchers, two bricklayers, four shopkeepers, 14 miscellaneous traders, and 17 farmers. Labourers and servants are not listed. Nonetheless the list does give some idea of the variety of occupations which were followed at that time in South Cave. In his capacity as teacher and parish officer, Robert Sharp must have known everyone in the village, yet only a small proportion of the community featured regularly in his writings as close acquaintances and friends. Most of those who were included in that group seemed to have belonged to the professional classes such as Dr and Mrs Sonley, or to have been craftsmen such as Old Willy Atkinson the shoemaker, or shopkeepers such as John Holborn the glazier, or—and this is by far the largest group—were farmers, among whom he seems to have had his closest friends, such as Robert and Thomas Marshall, and Giles Bridgman. People lower down the social scale, such as horse-dealers and labourers, were as often as not mentioned only in relation to their misdemeanours. A list of those people featuring most regularly in the diary is contained in Appendix II.

---

[12] Baines ii. 186-7.

PLATE I

South Cave Town Hall

PLATE II

South Cave Market Place showing the Town Hall and the 'Fox and Coney'

PLATE III

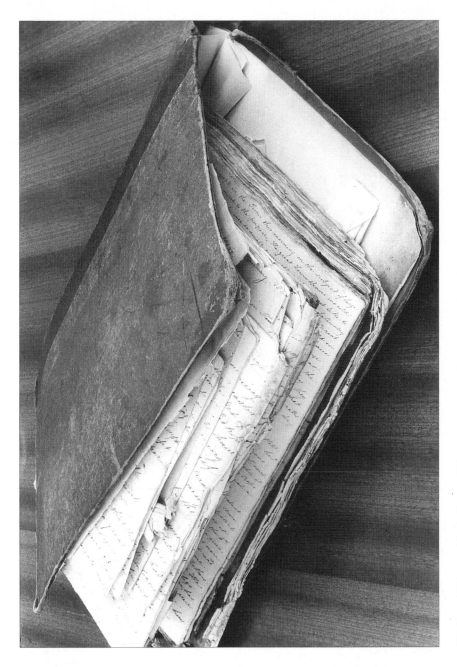

The Bound Volume of the Letters and Diary

PLATE IV

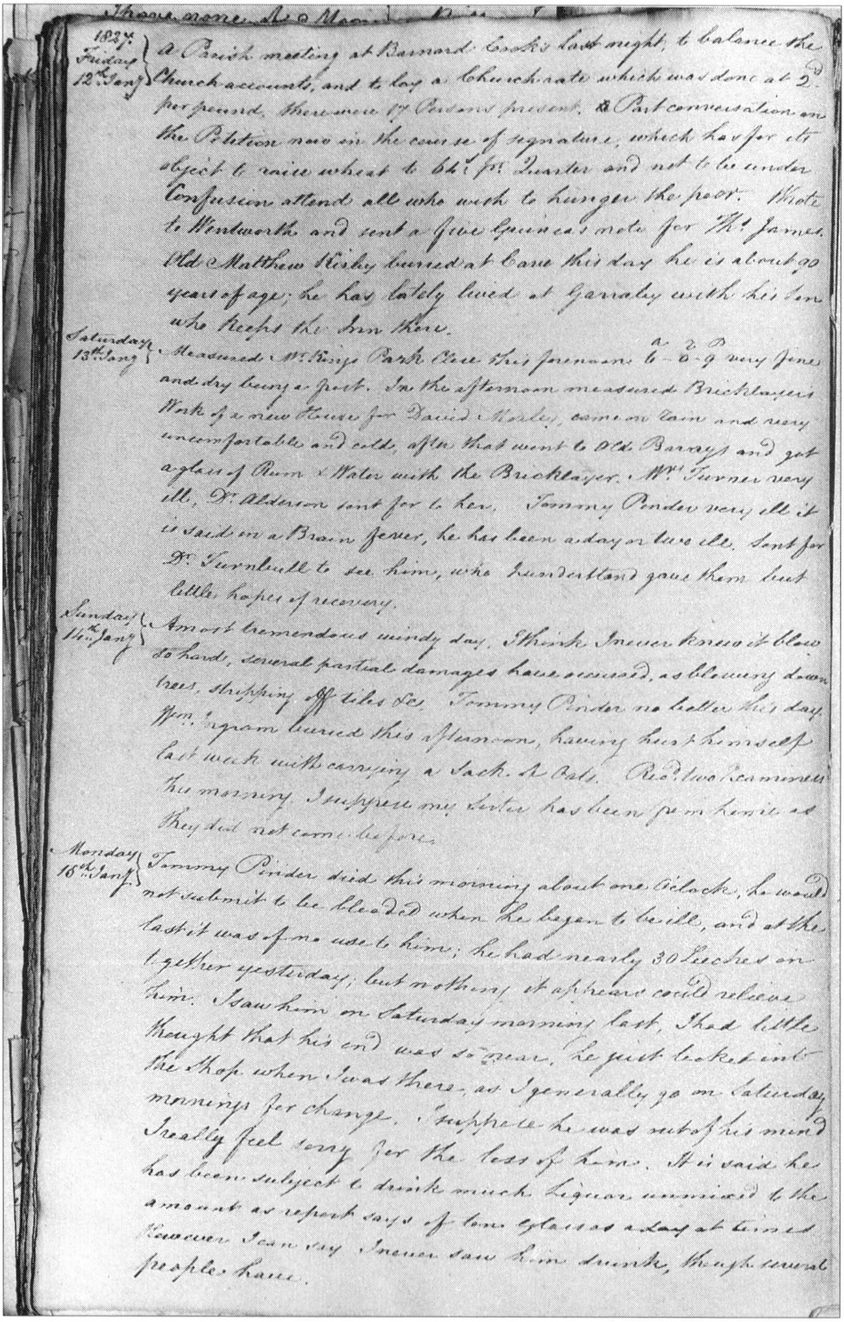

1827 Friday 12th Jany } A Parish meeting at Barnard Cook's last night, to balance the Church accounts, and to lay a Church rate which was done at 2d per pound, there were 17 Persons present, & Part conversation on the Petition now in the course of signature, which has for its object to raise wheat to 64s. pr. Quarter and not to be under Confusion attend all who wish to hunger the poor. Wrote to Wentworth and sent a five Guineas note for Ths. James. Old Matthew Kirby buried at Cave this day he is about 90 years of age; he has lately lived at Garraby with his Son who keeps the Inn there.

Saturday 13th Jany } Measured Mr. Kings Park Close this forenoon 6–0–9 very fine and dry being a frost. In the afternoon measured Bricklayers Work of a new House for David Morley, came on rain and very uncomfortable and cold, after that went to Old Barrays and got a glass of Rum & Water with the Bricklayer. Mrs. Turner very ill, Dr. Alderson sent for to her. Tommy Pinder very ill it is said in a Brain fever, he has been a day or two ill. Sent for Dr. Turnbull to see him, who I understand gave them but little hopes of recovery.

Sunday 14th Jany } A most tremendous windy day, I think I never knew it blow so hard, several partial damages have occured, as blowing down trees, stripping off tiles &c. Tommy Pinder no better this day. Wm. Ingram buried this afternoon, having hurt himself last week with carrying a Sack of Oats. Recd. two Examiners this morning. I suppose my Sister has been from home as they did not come before.

Monday 15th Jany } Tommy Pinder died this morning about one O'clock, he would not submit to be bleeded when he began to be ill, and at the last it was of no use to him; he had nearly 30 Leeches on together yesterday, but nothing it appears could relieve him. I saw him on Saturday morning last, I had little thought that his end was so near, he just looked into the Shop when I was there, as I generally go on Saturday mornings for change. I suppose he was out of his mind. I really feel sorry for the loss of him. It is said he has been subject to drink much Liquor unmixed to the amount as report says of ten glasses a day at times however I can say I never saw him drunk, though several people have.

A Page from the Diary

PLATE V

Cave Castle, c. 1812

J. Bigland, The Beauties of England *(1812)*

PLATE VI

Saturday Market Place, Beverley, c. 1830

T. Allen, A New and Complete History of the County of York (1826-31)

PLATE VII

All Saints' Church, South Cave

PLATE VIII

Jane Sharp's Sampler

South Cave's Public Houses. Much of the social life of the village centred around its six public houses: the Bay Horse, the Bear, the Fox and Coney, the Three Tuns, the Windmill, and the Blacksmith's Arms. As well as drinking places, they provided venues for meetings, dinners, dances, games, and singing, and served as convenient resorts in which to conduct deals and commercial transactions. Of the six main houses during the years of the diary, five—the Bear, the Blacksmith's Arms, the Fox and Coney, the Three Tuns, and the Windmill were all in the Market Place—and only the Bay Horse was at the West End. (See Maps IV–V). The Blacksmith's Arms was licensed and fitted out as a new public house from an existing private house in the Market Place in 1825. Only two of these public houses have survived to the present day (1996): the Bear and the Fox and Coney. Since Robert Sharp frequently referred to a public house not by its name but by the name of its landlord or landlady, their names are listed here: Bay Horse: 1827– James Levitt; The Bear: –1832 Richard Newlove, 1832–5 Edward Fewson, 1836– J. Turner; Blacksmith's Arms: 1825–31 Matthew Pickering, 1831–3 Barnard Cook, 1833– Sarah Cook; Fox and Coney: –May 1829 Barnard Cook, May–Aug. 1829 Sarah Cook, Aug. 1829–1835 David Morley, 1835– William Hudson; Three Tuns: –1831 John Tindale, 1831– John Fenwick; The Windmill: William Cousens. In addition to the public houses, licensed and controlled by the Justices of the Peace at the annual Brewster Sessions held in Beverley, there were, according to Robert Sharp, three beer shops established in South Cave after the Beerhouse Act of 1830. These were the Gate (landlord Robert Donkin) and the Carpenter's Arms (landlord Charles Smith), both established at the West End in 1833, and the Half Moon (landlord John Waudby) opened in Church Street in 1834.

South Cave Friendly Society. Robert Sharp held the position of clerk to the South Cave Friendly Society or 'Club' as he always termed it. Although there is literary evidence that some friendly societies existed in England before the end of the seventeenth century,[13] and others, such as the Norman Society (1703), had been founded by Huguenot refugees in London in the first decade of the eighteenth century,[14] they were at that time still neither common nor widespread throughout the country. Founded in 1770, the South Cave society was one of the earliest friendly societies to become established in the East Riding. It was preceded in the region only by those of Hull and Howden, and pre-dated, by almost a quarter of a century, the legislation incorporated in George Rose's Act of 1793, which led to the more extensive development of such bodies both regionally and nationally.[15] The Club had been founded for the purpose of providing relief for its members when they were incapacitated by sickness or old age, and to ensure that they would be given a decent funeral on their death. It met in one of South Cave's public houses, selected on a rota

[13] In Daniel Defoe's *Essays on Projects* published in 1697 (Gosden 4).

[14] Ibid. 6–7.

[15] Neave (1988) 9.

system, on the first Thursday of each month, when every member paid one shilling into the communal fund or 'box', and was allowed to spend at the Club's expense up to threepence a meeting on drinks. Detailed regulations existed to ensure good behaviour and members who contravened those rules were fined, the money being paid into the box. Some of the capital was occasionally used to grant mortgages to members. If a member became incapacitated and thus unfit for work on account of sickness or old age, he was entitled to draw seven shillings a week from the box for a period of one year and thereafter three shillings and sixpence. Other benefits included the member's funeral expenses and a fixed sum to be paid to his dependants on his death. From about 1830, some members who were intending to emigrate, and who did not wish to lose their benefits, were allowed to 'exclude' themselves from the Club and exchange their benefit rights for a lump sum from the box, the amount to depend on how much they had already paid in.[16] Such applications must have been too numerous, however, for within less than two years Robert noted: 'Last night was the Club night, Mattw. Pickering wanted to have some money out and be excluded, but he could not accomplish his purpose, indeed I think there will be no more money paid to Members for excluding themselves' (2 September 1831). The annual Club Feast, which was an important event in the social life of the village, was held on the first Thursday after Old Midsummer's day (6 July). Robert Sharp described the celebrations of one such occasion in his entry for 12 July 1827: 'Club feast day, it was at Newlove's where they had a Booth fixed in the yard, and the Members all dined together, at two tables set the whole length there were about 120 members, a very good plain dinner, and good order kept, Mattw. Smith towards night got very drunk and some Boys got some Soot, Tallow & Reds, and daubed his face all over, making him look wilder than an American Savage.'

For his services as clerk to the Club, Robert received 30 shillings per annum, paid each November, together with one pint of free ale at each meeting plus one penny for every member whom he notified when there was to be a funeral of one of the members. Throughout the period of the diary, membership of the Club ranged from 100 to 130 or more members.

The Barnards. From the mid-eighteenth century and throughout the period of the diary and beyond, the major landowners and principal family in the parish were the Barnards. South Cave was originally divided into two main manors, South Cave East Hall and South Cave West Hall. In 1748, the manor of South Cave East Hall was purchased by Leuyns Boldero, a Pontefract lawyer. In 1769 Boldero assumed the arms and surname of Barnard on the death of his uncle, Dr Henry Barnard of Beverley. In 1785, two years after his father's death, Henry Boldero Barnard succeeded in acquiring the West Hall manor, and in addition purchased the Rectory and advowson of South Cave and the manor

---

[16] e.g. James Milner received £12 (4 Feb. 1830).

of Broomfleet,[17] thus securing the family's dominant position in South Cave for at least the next century. Henry was the prime mover in the enclosure of the parish in 1785–7, which gave him the opportunity to lay out the park and rebuild the East Hall Manor House in Gothic style with battlemented walls as the family seat.[18] It was thereafter known as Cave Castle, a name which it retains to the present day. H. B. Barnard's son, Henry Gee Barnard, succeeded to the estate in 1815, holding it until his death in 1858, so that he was Lord of the Manor throughout the diary period. He was less interested in the estate than his father had been, and as the diarist made clear was often an absentee landlord: 'This is Mr. Barnard's Rent day, he is as great a stranger here, as any Irish Absentee Landlord is on his own Estate in Ireland, not one Shilling of the Rents which arise from his Estate is spent by him here' (6 March 1834). There are numerous references to Barnard's rent days in the diary: it appears that they were held twice a year on the first Thursday in March and on the first Thursday in August. His tithe rent day was on the first Thursday in January. Much of his business was conducted by his steward, initially Christopher (Kit) Corner, but from 1827, Richard Marshall.

Manorial courts were held twice a year, in spring and October, at the Bay Horse public house. The proceeding of one of these meetings was described by the diarist:'[Mr Barnard's steward] will enter on duty and Cry "Oyes! Oyes! All mander of Persons who have business at the Court Leet, Court Baron and customary Court of H.G. Barnard Esq. come into Court and do suit and Service or you shall be amerced" meased was the old Bailiff's word, then the Steward of the Court Mr. Spofforth dismisses the Court with God save the King & the Lord of this Manor, to which the Old Bailiff always added "and the Steward of this Court" ' (17 May 1827). During the period of the diary, the court still appointed two of the village's officers, the constable and the pinder, but by that time other regular offices such as that of flesh greaves had fallen into disuse.

Markets and Fairs. South Cave's status as a market village dates back to the early Middle Ages, possibly as early as the twelfth century. By the late eighteenth century it had become an important trading centre for corn, partly as a result of improvements in arable farming in the area, and partly on account of its proximity to the Humber. In Baines's 1823 directory, it was reported that 'a great quantity of corn is sold, and sent by the Humber and its branches to Leeds, Wakefield and the other populous towns of the West Riding, in vessels, which bring back coals, lime, flags, free stone, and various other articles.'[19] The market continued to operate successfully during the period of the diary but declined rapidly from about 1840 when the new railways began to eliminate South Cave's advantage in having easy access to water transport. The market was held every Monday in the Market Place and in the Market Cross hall in the

[17] Neave (1984) 2.

[18] Neave and Turnbull (1992) 26–7.

[19] Baines ii. 186.

rooms immediately below the school in which Robert taught. The building had been built in 1796 expressly to provide accommodation both for the market and the school.

Cave Fair was an important event in the village year. It was held annually on Trinity Monday and Tuesday, the first day being devoted to trade and the sale of animals and the second day to a pleasure fair, when races and games were organized. Traditionally the fair was associated with the making and eating of cheesecakes, produced according to traditional local recipes, and it was eagerly anticipated by the South Cave villagers who prepared for the event by spring-cleaning and 'colouring' their homes in readiness for the traditional visits made at fairtime by friends and relatives from outlying villages and towns. Robert Sharp never failed to make some reference to the fair in the 11 years covered by the diary. He described the first day of the fair, in 1827: 'Cave fair commenced this morning, with Cattle lowing, Dogs barking, Asses braying, Boys whistling, trumpets blowing & every other characteristic for a Country fair; — It was very dusty all the day, Cattle sold best in the morning, they were rather dull after, Robt. Marshall sold 6 Beasts for two shillings a piece less than he had bid the last week, — I expect Wm. would eat Cave fair Cheesecakes this day in London. No Company this day but John Read' (11 June 1827), and the second day, in 1829: 'This is the great day of all the days in the year with us for display. I dare say not many good Clothes would be left at home, there were shews as usual. Mary Martin and the Red Barn, and the murdering of Daft Jamie all by the way of amusement!!' (16 June 1829). Sometimes the festivities extended beyond the first two days of the week to the Wednesday or Thursday: 'Horse Racing, Ass Racing, Foot racing, Blobbing for Oranges in a Tub full of Water, Running Wheel-Barrows blinded and other Rustic amusements, concluding with getting drunk by those who could afford it and those who could not pay were thankful to others that would afford them the gratification' (17 June 1829). The fair was always attended by potters and attracted many other traders, mostly cattle and horse dealers. The 1841 census, taken on the Sunday before Cave Fair, revealed some 300 visitors staying at South Cave and about 800 in the surrounding villages.[20] In addition to the fair on Trinity Monday, a cattle fair, known locally as 'back end fair', was inaugurated on the second Monday (24 October) after Old Michaelmas (11 October) in 1831. It continued to be held on 24 October annually for the remaining years of the diary period but was subsequently fixed on the second Monday after Old Michaelmas.[21]

South Cave's annual hiring fair or statute sittings was held in November on the two Thursdays immediately before Old Martinmas (23 November). Statute hirings were held at all the market towns and principal villages in the East Riding on certain days, known as hiring days, which varied according to the custom of the locality, but were generally within the period of the three or four weeks preceding Old Martinmas. Elsewhere in the country, sittings were

[20] Neave (1984) 22.
[21] *VCHYER* iv. 52.

held at other periods, usually Michaelmas in the southern and eastern counties, but in Lincolnshire mainly around May Day.[22] In the 16th and 17th centuries, statute sittings were held under the supervision of a Constable or Justice of the Peace in order to regulate the contracts made between masters and servants and to determine the rate of the wages to be paid, but by the beginning of the 19th century, they had become essentially a form of free labour exchange at which young men and women themselves negotiated wage agreements with the farmers in the neighbourhood, and were hired by them as farm servants for the coming year.[23] It was customary for servants to 'live in' at the farm where they worked. At the end of the year's engagement, the servants received their wages for the year and for a short time were able to enjoy an unaccustomed period of leisure. The annual hiring fair was thus a festive occasion in the year—a time when the young servants, often from isolated farms, were able to mix with their family and friends and enjoy a holiday with money in their pockets. It is not surprising that a certain amount of rowdy behaviour occurred at some sittings. In South Cave, the first of the two Thursdays of sittings days, known as the Burton sittings, coincided with the annual meeting of the Constables of Hunsley Beacon at South Cave, who celebrated the occasion by holding a dinner at one of the village's inns.

Transport and Communications. Although a landing place was situated at Crabley sluice on the Humber near Broomfleet,[24] the steam packets plying between Hull and Selby did not call there but only at Blacktoft, too far to the westward to be convenient for passenger traffic from South Cave. In consequence most persons wishing to travel from South Cave were dependent, at least initially, on the roads. The old Roman road which led northwards from Brough to York via Newbald, a major trading route from Lincolnshire to the North, passed through South Cave's Market Place. This road was turnpiked in 1771 with toll bars erected at Brough, and at Kettlethorpe north of South Cave. The other major road in the parish, also turnpiked (in 1774), was the old 'post road' from Hull, which ran in an east-west direction from Kirk Ella past Raywell and Riplingham, across Weedley and along the northern parish boundary, where it was known as Swinescaife Road, towards North Cave and Wallingfen. This road was furnished with toll bars at Riplingham and Wallingfen (see map). Another road, not turnpiked, ran uphill westwards from the Market Place, where it was known as Porter Hole (or Poulterer's Hole), towards Beverley via the village of Walkington. It was this route (a journey of about nine and a half miles) which Robert Sharp normally took, when travelling to Beverley on parish business, often on horseback, occasionally on foot, and once memorably in a gig driven by his fellow tax assessor, Thomas Robinson of Mount Airy (30 March 1831). The condition of the roads, even the turnpikes,

---

[22] Kussmaul 50–51, 151–63.

[23] Ibid. 60–61.

[24] *VCHYER* iv. 39.

was often very bad especially in wet or snowy weather. In his diary entry for 21 June 1826, Robert complained that he soon found himself 'in the Chalk road enveloped with dust, and here I cannot but observe how careful the makers of Roads have been to exclude the Pedestrians from the smallest comfort as no footpaths are thrown up for their accommodation, they must plod on in Summer amidst dust and in Winter nearly stick fast in puddle.' The worst roads in the parish, however, seem to have been those leading to Broomfleet in the low-lying area towards the Humber. They were described as 'horse belly deep' (10 January 1834), and only a man of Broomfleet could find anything good to say about them: 'There has been a letter from a young man who went from Broomfleet last year to America, which only gives a very poor account of his prospects, he says the Roads there are worse than at Broomfleet; if they are they need not be called Roads at all, at all' (10 August 1831).

South Cave's inhabitants were linked to the outside world by a variety of coaches and carriers' carts, all offering regular services. In 1826 the 'Rodney' coach was recorded as leaving the Fox and Coney in South Cave's Market Place for Hull at eight o'clock in the morning and returning at four o'clock in the afternoon. In the same year, Blanchard and Cousens operated a carrier service from South Cave to Hull on Tuesdays and Fridays, leaving the village at four o'clock in the morning and returning at nine in the evening.[25] William Cousens was the landlord of the Windmill and a close neighbour of Robert Sharp. The service was later operated by William and his son, Richmond Cousens. Another carrier service was provided by Frank Smithson of Howden, who called in at South Cave on his way to Hull at half past 12 on Monday afternoon and returned at three p.m. the following day on his way back. By the year 1834, two additional carriers were operating from the village, John Fenwick and Robert Donkin. By 1833 a post coach to South Cave was operating from Edward Miles's livery stables in Carr Lane, Hull, from which it departed every afternoon, except Sundays, at five p.m.[26] In that same year a rival coach service was set up by R. J. Chaffer. It ran between North Cave and Hull, calling at the Fox and Coney, South Cave, at a quarter to eight every morning except Sundays, and arriving in Hull, at the Black Horse, Carr Lane, at half past nine and leaving from there at half past four in the afternoon for the return journey.[27] By 1840, there were no less than four different coaches passing through South Cave each day, with four carriers operating regular services to Hull and one carrier operating a Saturday service to Beverley.[28]

The village post office was run by Barnard Cook, landlord of the Fox and Coney, and later of the Blacksmith's Arms. In 1826 letters were scheduled to arrive at 3 p.m. and were sent off at 4 p.m.[29] By 1834 the hours had changed so

[25] Baines ii. 187.

[26] Greenwood 192.

[27] *HA* 8 May 1835.

[28] Neave (1984) 27.

[29] Baines ii. 186.

that post arrived at 6.30 a.m. and was despatched at noon.[30] Normally the cost
of the postage on letters was paid by the recipient. Franked newspapers were
sent free of charge provided that they contained no written messages. Robert
Sharp frequently complained that newspapers sent to him either failed to arrive
or were sent to the wrong destination and arrived late. Nevertheless the post
seems to have been generally efficient and quick: a letter or newspaper sent
from London would normally be expected to arrive in South Cave the following
day and vice versa.

Administration of Village Affairs

Much of the life of the parish centred around the good ordering of local affairs,
which were administered by parish officers elected by the parish vestry. Parish
meetings, often in one of the village inns, were held periodically throughout the
year to deal with such matters as the election of officers and setting a poor rate
or considering the churchwardens' or highway accounts. The system had
scarcely altered in its essentials since the Poor Law Act of 1601, which made
the overseers of the poor responsible for the local administration of the Poor
Law. It was based on the principle of 'service', since the officers were not paid,
and was underpinned by the authority of the magistrates. In South Cave, the
parish officers (two for each office) were selected at a meeting of the parish,
held at or before Easter-time (except in the case of the highways surveyors who
were chosen in early October), to serve for the ensuing year. They were the
churchwardens, the assessors, the highways surveyors, and the overseers of the
poor. These officers were chosen in rotation from a restricted group of the more
important members of the local community, mostly farmers. In the case of
churchwardens, one was elected annually at a parish or vestry meeting by the
parishioners and one was appointed by the vicar. The other officers were also
appointed annually—their names coming up in rotation on a list. The
appointment of officers had to be ratified by the local magistrates, who usually,
but not always, 'rubber-stamped' the pair of names presented to them. In
practice, officers were not always chosen in strict rotation because if, for
example, an individual was especially well qualified for an office and willing to
fill it, then he might serve for a longer period than the appointed year. Robert
Sharp had served as one of the pair of assessors from 1809, and continued to do
so throughout the period of the diary. However, all appointments (other than
churchwardens) had to be authorized, and the appointees sworn in, by the local
magistrates at Beverley.
       In South Cave, where a manorial court still functioned, the office of
constable remained a court prerogative. However, like the officers chosen at the
parish meetings, the office of constable (or constables since there was usually a
deputy or second constable) was unpaid and held for one year. The court also
appointed the village pinder. Apart from this latter office, which was usually

[30] Pigot & Co. 691.

held by a person of lesser standing in the village, all the parish offices during the period of the diary were held by a limited number of prominent parishioners. The same names crop up again and again as the holders of office and not always the same office, since a person could be a churchwarden one year, a constable the next, and an overseer of the poor the following year. In the period 1825 to 1837, Robert Sharp, mentioned only 26 names as holders of the five main parish and manorial offices, each of which was normally held by two persons. Obviously this restriction in the number of persons holding office could be advantageous to the interests of good government, in that the office holders would become very experienced in their work, and would be able to draw on the experience of their colleagues in such a close-knit group. (Indeed they might have it forced upon them)! However the main reason why so few people were involved was probably because the holder of an office, especially an overseer of the poor, had to be a person of some means. An officer frequently had to lay out money for expenses, in the course of his duties, that might not be re-imbursed for some time from the parish rates: 'This Evening with the Overseers collecting Poor Sess Ths Wride one of the Overseers had laid out about £20 and very fearful he was he should not get it again, however this night I managed to pay him so that he would sleep comfortably' (13 October 1831). Parish officers were responsible for the accounts books associated with their offices, although the actual accounting work in almost all cases seems to have been done by Robert Sharp. The highways accounts book and poor books had to be taken to the magistrates at Beverley for examination and approval.

Unlike the other parish officers, the Parish Clerk was a paid official of the church and held his office for as long as he gave satisfaction to the vicar. who had appointed him. During the period of the diary, John Reynolds served as the parish clerk in South Cave.

At the period when the diary was written, especially during the earlier years, the intervention of the central government in local affairs was comparatively unintrusive. Its will was expressed through the Justices of the Peace whose influence over local affairs was pervasive and extended well beyond the punishment of misdemeanours. Magistrates were drawn from the local gentry and land-owning classes and included members of the local clergy—the parson magistrates—who were themselves often the younger sons of gentry families. They exercised a supervisory function over the work of the parish officers and were responsible in their judicial capacities for the administration of the law. At Beverley, annual brewster sessions were held at which the magistrates were enabled to exercise control over the behaviour in public houses throughout the region by the issue or withdrawal of licences. Magistrates also met regularly in petty sessions, for which the presence of at least two magistrates was required, and dealt there with cases brought before them by the parish officers. However, even a single magistrate had the power to deal with minor breaches of the peace and to arbitrate in disputes, of which there are many examples in the diary. In the East Riding, at the beginning of the diary period, there were some 40 magistrates. The nearest court of petty sessions to South Cave was at Riplingham where it was held in a room in the Blacksmith's Arms.[31] Robert Sharp frequently recorded cases which were referred to the magistrates there from South Cave by the parish officers, for example, in his entry for 22 February 1830: 'The Overseer has been at Riplingham today with Thos. Shaw's wife's daughter, who said she was married some time ago, but the last week it transpired that she was not married. She has been this day to swear to her Settlement, when an order of removal was granted to remove her to Ellerker.'

The School

At the enclosure of South Cave in 1785–7, the parish was allotted approximately nine acres in lieu of common rights. In 1797 this land was let out at a nominal rent to Jonathan Scott for a period of 30 years in return for a payment of £300. This sum together with money raised from a public subscription was applied to the erection in 1796 of the two-storey Market Cross hall in South Cave's market place. It was a dual-purpose building, in which the ground floor was used as a market hall and the first floor set aside for use as a school. A school house was provided for the schoolmaster, in consideration of which he was expected to teach two poor boys free. It was to this school that Robert Sharp, his wife, Ann, and their young family, came in 1804. In the advertisement for the job, which appeared in the *Hull Advertiser* on 14 January 1804, it was stipulated that both a master and mistress were required, which suggests that girls as well as boys attended the school. The outgoing schoolmaster was a Mr. Witty.

As mentioned above, the school was completely reorganized in 1817 with the arrival of the new vicar, the Revd Edward Barnard, who successfully moved that the school should be run according to the system of the National Society, apparently against the wishes of its schoolmaster. In the East Riding of Yorkshire Archives and Records Service at Beverley, a copy of a contemporary pamphlet[32] records the public meeting at which the vicar's resolution was adopted, and details the regulations by which the school was to be henceforth governed. Part of this document is here reproduced:

Printed Regulations for the Management of the National School, South Cave (dated 1817)

At a General Meeting of the Inhabitants of the Township of South Cave, held in the Vestry, on Thursday, the Seventh day of August 1817 It was moved and unanimously Resolved,
1. That the Parish School, raised upon the Mortgage of certain Church Lands, shall be opened to all Inhabitants of the Township, (who are subscribers of not less than Four Shillings per annum for each Child) for the purpose of educating

---

[31] Balchin 201, 210.

[32] ERYARS DDMT 464

their children in the principles of the Established Church, in Reading, Writing, and Arithmetic, free of all expense. No Children to be admitted into the School under seven years of age.

2. That the school shall be conducted on the system of Dr. Bell; that it shall be placed in Union with the East Riding District Society for National Education; that the mode of Instruction shall be in strict conformity with that adopted in the District School at Beverley, and the same books shall be made use of.

3. That the expenses thereof shall be defrayed by voluntary Subscriptions, to be paid quarterly on the first day of October, January, April and July respectively, and that the first quarter's Subscription, due in October, be paid in advance.

4. That the direction and regulation of the school, and the disposal of the Funds, be given to a committee of seven persons, to be chosen from the subscribers.

5. That Two Visitors, one Male and the other Female, be chosen from the Subscribers whose office shall be to overlook the School, once a month at least, and report any abuses to the Committee.

6. That Mr. Robert Sharp, be the School-Master, with a yearly salary of Fifty Guineas, and liberty to take into the School, Children from other places, provided that he does not depart in any instance, from the Rules laid down by the Committee.

7. That Parents who refuse to pay their Subscriptions, when they become due, or to make their children comply with the Rules laid down by the Committee shall be deprived of all benefit of the School.

By virtue of the power committed to us by the Fourth Resolution above written, We the undersigned, constituting the Committee for the management and regulation of the National School of South Cave, and of the Funds thereto belonging, do institute the twelve following Rules and Regulations, and do order, that, after printed copies of them are distributed, they be duly enforced and the fines appointed therein, strictly levied.

Witness our hands this fifth day of October 1817.}   Edward W. Barnard, Vicar

          Barnard Cook }
          Wilkinson Ayre}   Churchwardens
          Teavil Leeson.
          Francis Day
          Robert Leeson
          George McTurk.

1. The Year shall commence on the first of October and there shall be a month's holidays at the end of it, from the first of September to the first of October, inclusive.

2. No Children shall be admitted for less than one quarter of a Year.

3. The sum of Four Pounds shall be allowed to the Master, to provide a Fire for the School-Room.

4. The Committee shall meet in the School-Room, at the expiration of every quarter, for the purpose of inspecting the progress of the Children, rewarding the best scholars, hearing complaints, receiving donations, &c. &c.

5. There shall be a Public General Examination, at the expiration of the year; at which all the Township shall be requested to attend; notice of the appointed day shall be published a week before, and every scholar who is absent, shall be expelled from the school, unless he produces to the Committee, a proper Certificate of Sickness, or some sufficient cause of absence.

6. A Box to be called the Reward Box, shall be hung up at the entrance of the School-Room, for the purpose of receiving the Fines and Charitable Donations, which shall be distributed among the best children, at the quarterly Meeting of the Committee.

7. A Sum not exceeding three Guineas, shall be set apart yearly, as a fund, in aid of the Reward Box.

8. The School shall be opened every day, (Saturday and Sunday excepted) and Prayers begin at Nine o'Clock in the Morning, and at Four in the Afternoon.

9. All the Children shall assemble in the Church, on Sundays, morning and evening, a quarter of an hour before the service begins; to have their names called over, and shall sit together in some convenient place, under the eye of their Master: but if a Parent be present, he may take his children into his own pew, if he chooses, after they have answered to their names. And if any Parents dissent from the Church, and wish to take their children to their respective places of worship, they may do so, upon giving satisfactory testimony to the Committee, when required, that the children are really thus employed, and not suffered to neglect and mis-use the Lord's Day.

10. Every child, who is absent without leave from the Master, shall forfeit one Halfpenny for every half day's absence from School, and one Penny for every half day's absence from Church. These fines to be put into the Reward Box. See Rule 6th.

11. A Reward Ticket shall be given to the head of every Class, every day; six of which shall entitle him to a Reward out of the Box or Fund, at the quarterly Meeting of the Committee.

12. Every Monitor shall receive a Reward of one Penny per week, from the Fund, and the Usher, if one be necessary, two Pence per week.

On the back of the last page of this pamphlet, which is blank in the original printed version, a report is written in manuscript of a second meeting on the same topic which was held the following year. It confirms the resolutions and regulations approved at the first meeting, with some minor amendments, and adds an additional resolution: *'That an 8th Resolution be added to those already printed as follows. Resolved, that it being principally the object of the Parish to afford the means of education to the Poor, their children shall be received at a less Subscription than the children of the richer class. The rate shall be as follows— The poor shall send one child for 6[s.] 0*
two children for 10[s.] 0
three or more for 4s each
The richer class shall send one child for 16/-
two for £1·4
three or more for 10/- each

If there be any dispute as to which class a person belongs, it shall be decided at a special meeting of not less than five of the committee'.

It is impossible to know for how long and to what extent these detailed regulations were actually enforced, but certainly by 1826 it would seem that regulations 4 and 5 governing quarterly inspections and annual public examinations had been discarded as the diarist would almost certainly have mentioned such events, if only to complain about them. The annual September holiday (regulation I) seems likewise to have been dropped as Robert specifically referred to an interruption at school on 29 September 1826:'Watson Arton came this forenoon at School time with the Ellerker Highway Book to Balance. I do not like to be broken in upon when I am engaged, and I wonder how people can be so unthinking as to suppose I can spare time to attend to them.' School breaks seem to have occurred during the Christmas holiday, at Easter, at Cave Fair, and more informally around August at harvest time, when the children are often mentioned as being in the fields helping with the harvest. It appears most likely that, having won the struggle over the question of its status as a National School, Robert was left alone to manage it according to his own best judgement, and without too much outside interference.

The number of pupils in the school declined from a peak around 1819, when there were 80 pupils and 1823, when there were 50, to 1835, when there were only 30 pupils and the master's salary had fallen to only seven pounds.[33] Perhaps increasing competition was partly to blame as White's 1840 directory records three additional schools in South Cave for that year, one run by Thomas Holberry (also recorded in 1834), and two dame schools, run by Ann Ellerton and Sarah Sykes, respectively.

Church and Chapel

The parish church of All Saints is situated at West End and according to an inscription inside the nave was rebuilt in 1601. Much, however, of the medieval church remains, but successive restorations have obscured its architectural history.[34] According to the diary, services were held twice each Sunday, in the morning and in the afternoon. Robert Sharp regularly attended both services, in the company of his pupils for whom a special gallery had been built in 1818/19.[35] A succession of vicars held the living during the period of the letters and diary. They were: Daniel Garnons, 1783-1817; Edward William Barnard, 1817–28; Stephen Creyke, 1828-34; and Edwin Hotham, 1834–44. Of these, only Garnons, who was of more humble origins than his successors, was resident in South Cave during his incumbency. The vicar's residence, which was a small cottage built in 1787, was said to have been unfit for habitation and

[33] *VCHYER* iv. 58.

[34] Pevsner (1995) 700.

[35] *VCHYER* iv. 56.

was probably an inducement towards absenteeism for those who could afford it. After Garnons, all the other incumbents were appointed by the Barnards and were in some way related to that family; Edward W. Barnard, for example, was Henry Gee Barnard's younger brother. From 1826 until 1834, the church was served by a full-time curate, John Rodmell, the son of a Hull postmaster. The living was reckoned to be a comfortable one: between 1818 and 1828 the vicar's income ranged from £275 to £325, whilst in 1824 his outgoings only amounted to a little over £60, which included the curate's salary of £40.[36]

South Cave was somewhat unusual for an East Riding village in having a strong Independent or Congregational following, whose origins dated back to the seventeenth century. By 1730 a chapel had been built in West End, and it remained in use until a replacement was erected on the same site in 1873. Ann Sharp and her daughter Eliza attended services at this chapel and it was here that the diarist's brother, Thomas Sharp, the Congregational minister at Skipton in the West Riding, preached a sermon on 23 July 1826: 'At Church this morning heard a Sermon of about the same length as last Sunday viz. about a quarter of an hour. My Brother preached in the Evening at the Chapel[,] it is many years since he preached here before, his text was the 5th. Chapter John 28th. & 29th. verses, he exerted himself a good deal and preached about an hour[.] We went to Mr. Turk's after the Service and staid a short time.' During the period spanned by the letters and diary, the ministers of the Congregational Chapel at South Cave were William Tapp, 1791 to his death in 1819; Revd Whitridge, occasional preacher but non-resident 1819–20; George Nettleship 1821 until his resignation in 1823; Seth Kelso, 1824–28; William Stott 1829 until his death in 1839.[37] Robert Sharp had apparently quarrelled with Nettleship during his ministry, according to the remarks made in a letter of 1825, and did not have a very high opinion of him: 'The little Dandy parson yclep'd Nettleship was preaching and begging here one night[.] Robt. Marshall asked me if I intended to hear him[.] I told him I should shew myself very weak if I did, but said he[,] forget and forgive, yes so I will forget when my memory fails, but at present I perfectly recollect the dirty tricks of the little fellow.'

Wesleyan Methodism became established in South Cave as early as 1782, when the house of George Turner was certified as a meeting place for Methodists. Richard Milner (1744–1829) was an early stalwart of Methodism in the village and was much admired by Robert Sharp 'Richd. has been a member of the Methodist Society considerably more than half a Century. He remembers his Mother taking their part from the very first, but his Father was very much against them. Richd. is a very worthy old Man' (5 September 1827) and again on Richard's death 'He has done much for the cause of Methodism, and has not left a better man behind him, he was respected by all, even those who had no sense of Religion could not help esteeming him' (17 August 1829). A Wesleyan

---

[36] Neave (1984) 45.
[37] Trout 9–15.

chapel was erected in Church Street in 1816 but its congregations were never very large in the early nineteenth century.

Primitive Methodists first made an appearance in South Cave in 1819, when William Clowes began his preaching tours in the area. Robert Sharp recorded open-air meetings around South Cave: 'There has been a Camp meeting of the Ranters this day at Cockle-pit row, on the Brough road, which I understand has not been very strongly attended; indeed the day has been rather against it, for it has been rather cold and blustering' (24 September 1826), and again at nearby Newbald (2 August 1835). On 12 December 1836, he reported: 'at night the Ranters had a Missionary meeting at the west end Chapel (which they borrowed) there was I understand a large Congregation and a tolerable Collection. We neither of us were there.' In the following year, the Primitive Methodists built their own chapel in South Cave, in Church Street.

National Affairs

Although much of the diary is concerned with parochial matters, it contains many references to the wider world of national and international affairs. The outside world is reflected in the diary in two ways: firstly in the diarist's reports and comments on national and international events, and secondly in his descriptions of how developments of national importance manifested themselves at the local level of the parish. As an educated and intelligent man, Robert Sharp took a keen interest in current affairs, on which he kept himself informed by his daily reading of newspapers, in particular the *Times* and the local *Rockingham*, and *Hull Packet*, and periodicals such as the weekly *Examiner* and *Cobbett's Political Register*. From such sources as these, he was able to report and comment on a wide variety of national events and issues. Many of the reports, especially those relating to foreign affairs, were relatively brief and factual, such as the report on the death of the Russian tsar, Aleksandr I (25 February 1825),[38] the war in Portugal (14 May 1827), the arson attack on York Minster (6 February 1829), the Treaty of Adrianople (26 October 1829), the abdication of King Charles X of France (5 August 1830), the siege of Antwerp (10 December 1832), the battle of Cape St. Vincent (17 July 1833), and the burning of the Houses of Parliament (20 October 1834).

On other issues, he commented in greater detail and with more frequency. Major political issues and events rarely went unremarked. Elections and the fortunes of the various Whig and Tory ministries received extensive commentary. For example on the resignation of Lord Liverpool's old Tory ministers, when Canning had been called to form a new government, he wrote: 'Saw in the Rockingham that seven of the Ministers have sent in their resignations. — Amongst the rest the Lord Chancellor, I never expected that he would have parted with his office but with his life. I think from what has

---

[38] Dates in parentheses correspond to the date of the diary entry and not to the date of the event.

transpired there will be no cause of grief to the Country on his Account. I am rather surprised that Mr. Peel is amongst the number, as he appears to be well respected in general, and has made himself useful' (15 April 1827). And on Canning's new ministry, his neighbour, Mr Tinsdill was reported to be: 'very full of the new ministry, saying there certainly can not be one more disagreeable to the Country than the last one. I suppose the great object with most is to gratify their own ambition, and look close to their own interest, there may perhaps be some solitary exemptions, but such men are looked upon like a white Crow in a rookery' (20 April 1827). Later in the same year, the diarist reported: 'All the ministerial places appear to be now filled up: it appears Mr. Herries has been appointed Chancellor of the Exchequer after it having been offered to two others, with what ability Mr. Herries may fill the situation, time will tell; it is a great thing in any ministry to be unanimous' (8 September 1827). Later, in 1830, he wrote about the unsuccessful attempts of Wellington's cabinet to make economies: 'Ministers have said they will make retrenchment to some amount, but it does not seem that they will take off any of the taxes, so of what use will their proposals be, if the same amount of taxes are to be paid? what will they do with the Surplus? Mr. Hume I think does what he can, and Colonel Davies who appears to be made of stern stuff, says they may dismiss a number of the forces and be all the better for it. But for my part I can see no benefit in Economy if the People still have the same to pay' (25 February 1830).

The question of parliamentary reform was already beginning to excite interest, early in 1831, when in his entry for 2 March of that year, the diarist wrote: 'we are all anxious at our meeting house to hear the Report of the Ministers plan of reform, — but I believe our old friend the Freeman, had rather hear tell of Parliament being dissolved than any plan of reform carried into execution.' The preoccupation and excitement over the issue of reform that was being felt throughout much of the country was echoed by Robert Sharp in his writing: there are more than a score of references to it in the diary to the end of 1832, of which the following are examples: 'The Reform meets with Opposition from several of the Speakers who wish things to remain as they are, but I think they will be thrown into the back Ground—It seems to make little impression here, indeed here are very few who know any thing of the Matter— Mr. Shackleton who is perhaps as well informed or rather better than many amongst us, is delighted with the proposals of Lord John Russel. — Hedon appears to be the only Borough in our neighbourhood which is to be disenfranchised, and by Accounts which I have heard it merits its doom' (10 March 1831), 'Recd. the Paper this morning containing an Account of the Division in the House of Commons on the second reading of the Reform Bill the numbers were very near being 302 for it and 301 against it; how zealous the Gentry are who think and say that all is right, but will this be right with them?' (25 March 1831), 'I have read the opening speech of the Campaign on reform, the Ministers I think to their credit are resolved to persevere and Sir Robt. Peel will persevere too, but it is in contradiction; Now what will the <u>born</u> Legislators do with this same reform measure, they will for their own sakes I think pass it; I do not know they can do any better' (29 June 1831), 'So the reform Bill has passed the second reading by an overwhelming Majority, one would think that the Antis might be convinced, that they are engaged in a hopeless work, the Country is against them, this is certain, now for the incurables, if they see their own interests, and they appear to know it, they will fall in and swim gently with the stream. I think they will' (10 July 1831), 'Recd. the Morning Chronicle of Saturday last giving an Account that the Reform Bill was lost in the House of Lords, by a majority of 41. What the result will be we must wait to discover; I suppose our old friend the Freeman of Bristol & Beverley and formerly a Voter for Westminster will be pleased at the Result' (10 October 1831), 'The reform Bill I see has got through the House of Commons favoured by a great Majority, now for its ordeal in the Lords; It is my own Opinion that it will not pass the born Legislators, but I may be mistaken: so may others who are sure that it will be passed by their Lordships' (29 March 1832), 'Heard this Evening at Mr. Atkinson's that the Ministry of Lord Grey is again in Power; it is seldom that I mind any thing of the ins or the outs but I think at the present the recall of Lord Grey is a healing measure: all the Antis may see that if there be no reform, there will be confusion worse confused' (17 May 1832), and 'No Paper this morning—yesterday the Overseers recd. the Reform Act, with instructions to give Notice to those qualified to Vote to send in their claims, and one Shilling with each claim; these Shillings are to go in aid of the Poor rates; the Notices are to be put on the Church Doors on the 25th. July' (22 July 1832).

Other topics dealt with in similar depth by Robert Sharp include the Corn Laws, especially in the earlier years of the diary, when he seems to have been very much under the influence of Cobbett in his opinions and preoccupations, and Catholic Emancipation. These questions, perhaps to a greater extent than governmental politics and, certainly, foreign affairs, had more local importance, with the result that the diary entries in which they appeared were based as much on the diarist's personal observations as on what he had read in newspapers. To take one example, the question of Catholic Emancipation seems to have been regarded as a major issue in the minds of many of Robert Sharp's neighbours. It provoked controversy, leading to personal quarrels between friends and, especially in Beverley, a staunchly protestant borough, it was the focus for public meetings and debate. There are no less than 15 entries relating to this topic in the diary for the year 1829, when the Catholic Emancipation Act was finally passed. Among those dealing with the question locally are: 'Politics with us are little attended to, the people have some Idea that Roman Catholics are strange formidable Creatures that would count nothing of running red hot pokers into the Bodies of the Holy protestants. I have asked some of them if they wish for a better neighbour than Billy Dodd of Ellerker, as he is one of the frightful bugbears, this sometimes rather nonplusses them but they get over it by saying it is for want of power in his party. He is a very quiet fellow and will take a glass with any Heretic and be as merry as any of them, caring no more for them than they do for the Pope' (5 January 1829), 'There has been a meeting of the East Riding Clergy at Beverley to petition against any further concession to the Catholics, the Revd. Jn. Gilby L.L.B. Rector of Barmston with a thousand a year for scarce ever preaching was Chairman' (25 January 1829), 'A Lady (Mrs. Wrottesley Mother to the young Lady who keeps the School at Brantingham) asked me yesterday how the people at Cave were affected to the Catholics, I told her they were nearly without exception stanch protestants, which she was very glad to hear. I did not think it worth while to Volunteer my own Opinions, but suggested that persons of any religious persuasion ought not to be debarred from Civil rights, when she immediately said but what will become of the Church and its ministers' (1 March 1829), 'The Anti-catholic meeting at Hull on Monday last has gone off in the manner I expected, the requisitionists had all their own way, not one word from the Opposition against the Petition, it was in fact a meeting, where there would not have been any chance for Argument; I am informed that it was at one time the intention of the Vicar of the High Church to have offered some Arguments in favour of Conciliation, but this was abandoned before the meeting took place' (5 March 1829), 'There was an Anti-catholic meeting at Beverley on Thursday last, at the New Sessions house, but as there were some Gentlemen of liberal Opinions, the Protestants as they proudly call themselves adjourned to the Market Place that they might not be disturbed by the Opposition. The liberal Gentlemen were Mr. Bethell of Rise, the Revd. J. Coltman[,] Mr. Beverley[,] young Mr. Beverley[,] Mr. Schonswar & Mr. Popple' (8 March 1829), 'The feeling of the Country is certainly against concession to the Catholics. I dislike their Doctrine and mummery as much as any one, but at the same time I would not debar them from having the same privilege as their fellow subjects, for I do not consider that the Religious Opinions of any ought to be held up as marking them out to execration by the Vulgar' (9 March 1829), 'Old Willy in hopes of an Election as he has no doubt this Parliament will be dissolved if the House of Lords do their duty and turn out the Catholic relief Bill, even if this should not be the case he is fully persuaded the King will not sign it. How little such persons know of the history of their Country, neither King nor Queen has refused to sign any Bill past by both houses for more than a hundred years, and surely the King is better advised than to refuse signing what he has recommended' (19 March 1829), 'This Catholic business makes friends quarrel. Mr. Levitt of Ellerker and Geo. Hodgson have split and called one another after having been thick as thieves for seven years past. Geo. called Levitt's friend George Coulson the Mayor of Hull, a great Leather nose, and Levitt got to hear of it, but George would not deny that he had called him, and repeated that he was nought else but a great Leather nose, and did not know what Catholic emancipation meant, neither did he know what the principles of Protestantism were for which he is such a stickler' (30 March 1829), and finally 'The Old Cobler at Walkington has got a notice in his plantation that no Papists nor Popish Priests will be suffered to enter there: it happens that he is always opposed to the Parson, and in this case he the Minister was of the liberal Party, which with Tithe eaters has not been very common. I think this Plantation cannot be more than 4 or 5 yards square!!' (2 May 1829).

Large-scale emigration was a national phenomenon of the nineteenth century, particularly in the earlier decades, and was neither confined to the years spanned by the diary nor to the South Cave region. It is interesting to note, however, that almost all emigration activity in that area, according to the diary and in the period covered by it, occurred in the years 1829 to 1831. Enthusiasm for emigration seems to have been well under way by the autumn of 1829: 'America and Swan River Mania is very prevalent here at present. James Milner and most if not all of his family are attacked with it, but I think if he has a mind to Americanise he cannot raise the needful to get him there. Robt. Nicholson they say talks of Swan River, he married one of Matthew Pickering's daughters, and his wife will not hearken to his folly. There is a Joiner who served his time with G. Petfield and married his Sister who talks of emigrating, as the sure way to independence' (26 November 1829). Most of the specific cases of emigration mentioned by the diarist, apart from those convicts transported to Australia, relate to emigrants to North America. In all, over 30 references to emigration appear in the diary. Many of the references relate to local people auctioning their property prior to their embarkation abroad, but there are also references to emigrants writing home to report on how they were faring in their adopted country, and in some cases to their returning home again. Most of the emigrants by their own report seem to have found conditions to their liking and to have done well: 'There has been a letter from James Milner in America (this morning.) He is at a place called Kingston in one of the Canadas, he and all his family have fallen in for work at good Wages (of course) he does not intend to proceed to Michigan this Summer. Some of his Companions have gone on there' (15 August 1830) and again 'A Letter from Ths. Milner in America they are at Kingston in Canada, the Account it said is very satisfactory, but highly Coloured, James by his business they say clears 4 or 5 Acres of Land in a week so that if he goes on in this way for a year (half year) he will have a snug farm of his own' (14 January 1831). Many of the men of the parish seem to have gone alone, in some cases sending for their families after having established themselves in America. Robert Sharp also referred to cases where the parish had itself paid the passage money of emigrants or of the families of emigrants who would have been left at home by their menfolk, presumably calculating that it would save expense in the long run by not having them as a burden on the parish. One such case involved a lump-sum expenditure of £16: 'A Parish meeting last night to consider of a proposition made by a Man who has a Wife and 3 Children belonging the Parish who wishes to go to America, he proposed taking 16 pounds which was at length agreed to, the Passage money will be £8–10–0 and he has his Victuals to find for the Voyage[;] he is going to Quebec[,] the time of the Voyage is estimated at 6 weeks so that the Poor fellow will not have much left to establish himself in a foreign Land' (16 April 1829). Some emigrants, as has been noted previously, raised money towards the expense of their fares abroad by arranging to take a cash payment from the 'Club' in lieu of benefits due to them by reason of the subscriptions which they had already paid.

The later years of the diary coincide with a period of increasing government intervention in local affairs, and it is interesting to see how a small rural community at that time was affected by the legislation of central government. In many cases the effect of legislation was minimal. The passing of the Factory Act of 1833 might have been of interest to the diarist, but its provisions found little application in South Cave. Similarly the issue of slavery may have been the occasion of petitions circulating in the village, but probably few villagers were seriously interested in, or affected by, the 1833 Abolition of Slavery Act which followed. On the other hand some Acts had more direct application: the Beerhouses Act of 1830 resulted in the establishment of three new beerhouses in the village. Perhaps one of the most important Acts in its effect on the administration of village affairs was the Poor Law Amendment Act. Robert Sharp made more than 20 references to this Act which, taken together, provide a good illustration of how its provisions were applied in South Cave and district, and the progress made there in the establishment of the revised system. Legislation for the new Poor Law passed through Parliament in the summer of 1834—'It seems the Poor Law, (miscalled amendment Bill) has passed the house of Commons, if this Bill be a boon to the Poor, it is the queerest piece of good that I ever heard of; it will increase the Poor Rates, instead of diminishing them' (2 July 1834). Details of the Act's provisions reached South Cave in the month following its passage into law—'The Poor act has arrived together with questions to be answered, I suppose it is much like other Acts, nearly past all human comprehension, however I have not yet read it' (17 September 1834). The new legislation embodied in the Act was to change radically the traditional system of poor relief, centred on the parish and administered by parish officers, by placing it in the hands of boards of guardians of newly formed poor law unions, who were themselves regulated by the Poor Law Commissioners. It is very evident from the attitude of the diarist that the changes were resented as an intrusion on the local community's independence, and offended against its pride in holding responsibility for its own affairs: 'Yesterday we had a Poor Law Commissioner or otherwise a Lacquey belonging to them he is going to establish a Union of Parishes and have a Workhouse at So. Cave, he proposed sending Letters to the different Parishes to meet to consult or rather to hear instructions, for I do not suppose that if they were opposed to the project they would be attended to. Talk of Irish Oppression indeed when every Parish in England is prevented from conducting their own affairs!!' (8 June 1836). Subsequent entries in the diary describe the stages in the establishment of the new organization in the region: 'The assistant Poor Law Commissioner has sent notices to twenty Townships or Parishes or more for the Overseers to meet him on Monday next the 27th. June at the School Room, to consult with him, on the Union of Parishes. I think Dis-union would be as proper a name' (20 June 1836); 'A meeting in the School this Evening of several Overseers to meet the Assistant Poor Law Commr. when it was settled that a Union of several Parishes is to take place and most probably a Workhouse will be provided here for the Union, there did not appear to be the least Opposition; for all were complying and quiescent' (27 June 1836); 'A Packet this day from the Poor Law Commissioners, commanding the Rate payers of this Parish to elect a Guardian, to the Beverley Union, which consists of 36 Parishes or Townships, the day of Election is fixed by them (the Comms.) for the 15th. Novr.' (2 November 1836); 'Another packet of Explanations and Instructions from the Poor Law Commrs. which only makes confusion worse confused; however dark it is we shall grope our way out in some manner' (3 November 1836); 'I was at the West end this afternoon placing a Notice on the Church door, according to the orders of the Lords in the ascendant viz. the Poor Law Comms.' (5 November 1836); 'Thos. Leaper has been nominated to be Guardian for this Parish which is to join the Beverley Union, so that we shall soon have the Machinery in progress' (8 November 1836); and finally—'The first meeting of the Guardians elected for the Beverley Union is this day held at Beverley, when they meet to obey the commands of their Superiors the high & mighty the Commissioners of the Poor Law: I like none of the set' (16 November 1836). No doubt such a sentiment was echoed in countless small rural parishes throughout the country by other parish officers who had been long accustomed to manage their own affairs without outside interference.

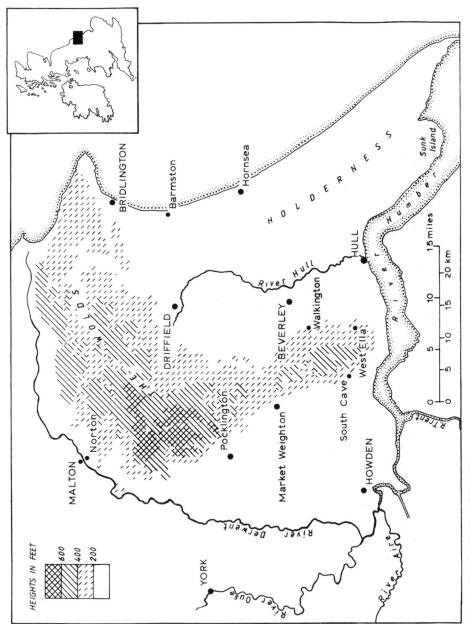

Map 1. The East Riding of Yorkshire

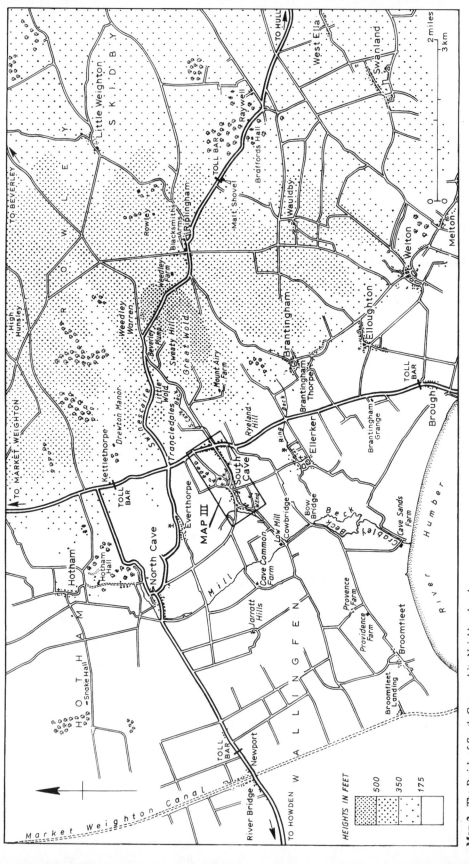

Map 2. The Parish of South Cave and its Neighbourhood

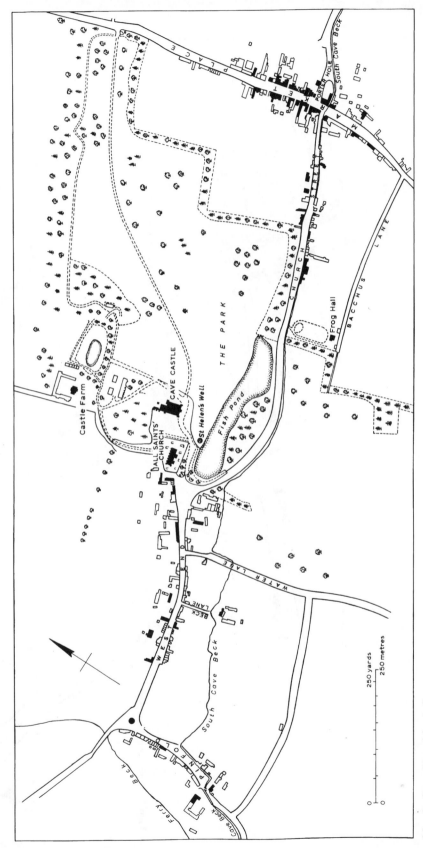

Map 3. Street Plan of South Cave

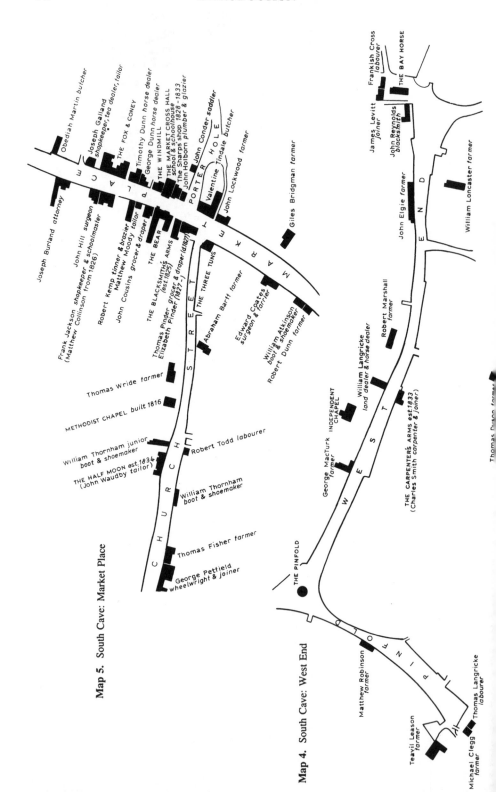

Map 5. South Cave: Market Place

Map 4. South Cave: West End

1812 July 16th [sister, Jane, to brother, William]
[On front of sheet]:

Dear Brother Wm
My Sister Jane July 16. 1812

[On reverse]:

South Cave 16th July 1812

Dear Brother Wm

I wonder you could not read my Letter[.] I only missed a Line and I think this will be better, and I hope it will please you, we are all well and I hope you are the same so if you cannot read this you may do as you li[ke] with it, only do not send it back so no more

from your loving Sister
Jane Sharp

1813 Feb. 1st

South Cave, 1st Febr. 1813

Dear Wm

You say you do not know what to write about. I expected you would have told us whether you had received your Guinea or not: as to the Hat buying I think you had better let it alone until I come to Hull for I am afraid you will give too much for it. I cannot at present say when I shall come. I have had a bad face for a Month past, it proceeded from a pimple; the wind got into it and swelled my face very much, I undertook the Cure of it myself and healed it, not in a very handsome manner; it looked like a large Carbuncle, so then I applied to Dr. Sonley who had to apply Caustic to it to eat it down. I am still patched up: so I may as well stay at Home as come to Hull to be laughed at. You say you have got a young Man into the Shop from Nottingham, I hope it will be an Advantage to you, if he be steady & serious. if you find he likes loose Company have no Connection with him, any further than what good manners require ...

Send 2 Skains[1] of Embroidering Silk like the Pattern & 4 Quire[2] of wove Letter Paper to sell at 1 Shilling & 4 Quire of Do. — to sell at 1/6, send them all with the Reviews if you have got them

I remain your loving Father
Robt. Sharp

[Letter continued by his mother, Ann Sharp]:

---

[1] Variant of 'skein', a linear measurement of thread or yarn wound upon a reel. A skein of cotton is approximately 120 yards (*OED*).

[2] One quire equals 24 sheets (*OED*).

Dear William

you Say that you dont know What to right about but if i had Such a father and Mother as you have i never Should be at a loss[.] you never told me ow you liked your puddings nore nothing i sent you[.] wen you send your box you must send that bottl[e] back that i sent your A[u]nt with and send me Word if her ye[a]st ans[w]er and mind you send your Stokings to wash[.] you only sent them W[h]ite on[e]s[.] you had too pare of them new on[e]s Dorty [i.e. dirty.] i Sent you a pare of new on[e]s by them Books of Mr crags so you have a pare for every Week[.] if you send them to wash you must send them by the parsel[.] you have not sent a 1 pocket Hankerchif this Munth so you must have too verry Dorty on[e]s[.] i should like you to send your things that you may be clean[.] i have sent you som[e] apples[.] you must eat one after Denner[.] your father says i better send you nothing but if you have bellyake you must not eat them[.] i hope you Do not forget to return go[o]d thanks for your Helth agane[.] i am verry thankful for it[.] your father as been verry pourly sins [i.e. since] he was at Hull but is much better but walking oversets im[.] He wanted to cam [i.e. come] on sathuday but i told im not for is feet is so bad with walking[.] he wil com wen the Wedder is better[.] you must mind to get right silk embroidering Silk at towers[3] you got [w]rong last time[.] it is trepence a cane[4]

> I remain your loving
> > Mother
> > Ann Sharp

[Below in the handwriting of RS]:

You need not take the Gin which is sent except your Belly be bad[,] it will be no worse for keeping, here is 6d. to pay for the Silk—1/6d to buy Quarter of a Stone of Biscuits[,] if you like you may keep one or two for yourself

[In margin]: My Father & Mother Feb 1. 1813

1813 Feb. 14th. [sister, Jane, to brother, William]
[On front of sheet]:

> Robert Sharp
> My Sister Jane Feb 14 1813

[On reverse]:

> South Cave 14th February 1813

Dear Brother William

I have got a Shilling given by Mrs Sonley which I have sent you. I hope you will come to Cave again: it wants just 17 weeks to Cave Fair[5] which

---

[3] William Frank Towers, haberdasher, clothier and glover of no.1, Whitefriargate, Hull (Baines ii. 310).

[4] A measurement of length from Fr. 'canne' or It. 'canna'. On the Continent it varied from 7' 3 ½" (Naples) to 6' 5²/₃" (Provence) but in England was probably somewhat in excess of 2 yards, or about 2 metres in present-day terms (*OED*).

[5] Held annually in Trinity week. (See Introduction).

will so[o]n be here, it is nine weeks to Easter and 8 week after[.] I hope you are very well[.] My Father will be at Hull on Tuesday but I dare not trust so much Money with him[.] John says what a letter that will be Jane[.] I remane

your loving Sister

Jane Sharp

1813 June 24th

So. Cave, 24th. June 1813

Dear Wm

We recd. your Letter on Tuesday and were sorry to hear that you were sick, but hope you are now better. You would find some Eggs and if they do you as much good as Eggs & Bacon did Wm. Gardam when he was sick you will need nothing else. Wm. Gardam was once very ill, and several of his neighbours went to see him; amongst the Rest was Wm. Tindle, he asked Billy how he was, he replied, "varry bad my lad varry bad": Noh Noh! I can soon cure thee; nay nay you cant[,] I can eat nought — nought at all my lad my lad O I's varry bad, I think thou can eat a bit of Bacon[,] I'll gang yam and send thee sum, so he went home and told his wife poor Billy was varry bad, but he had undertaken to cure him so he order'd her to Fry about a Pound of good Fat Bacon & half a Dozen Eggs, which was done as soon as possible, and he carry'd his medicine to his patient, and gave him proper directions how to take it, and to eat it all up at once and he would be bound for it that it would keep off sickness: So Billy set to in good earnest, and soon finished it and he said it had done him more good than all Sippyty Sauces he had gotten, & he presently recovered. When Billy is ill if he sees parson he tells him he shall come to Church on Sunday but parson tells him he will never go till he be carried, yes yes I will however, for I find I's ganging: you may Recollect that Billy once went to ask for Mr. Barnard before he had got up so he left strict word that he wanted something varry particular with him, which he could not tell to onny yan of Sarvants, but when he gat up he was to be told to go to him in Beverley Plump Close: Mr. Barnard got up & was told Billy wanted something very particular with him and where he was to be found so he rode out to wait upon Billy, when he got there he said well Wm. what is it you want with me; whya Sor I'se varry glad yeve cum'd for I want to ax you if you think I mun put my lad Prentis tiv a Breechesmaker; this was too much for Mr. Barnard's gravity[,] he was forced to turn his Horse about & laugh, but Billy stood with his Stick in one hand & the other upon his back, & looked for an answer which he soon got, you Fool what business had you to send for me two miles[,] put your lad to what you like, so no more of Billy at this time.

I think the Coachman charged you very high; your Mother has not got your Apron washed[,] she says you have two with you. Send the little Basket which came with the Cheesecakes[,] give your Aunt the Letter for your Grandmother, to send the first Opportunity.

I remn. your loving Father

Robt. Sharp

[In margin]: My Father June 24/1813

1815 Nov. 16th
Dear Wm

     I shall most likely write you a long letter at this time, — you said neither you nor your Aunt, knew the meaning of the Letter I wrote to Barmston[6] so that it follows of consequence you could not be pleased with it — I can only say it was very different with me when I accidentally fell in with the Account of it, and the names of the Inhabitants, and the very Houses that they lived in and the Land occupied by them, about 80 years ago, but now they are all changed and I think not above one of their descendts. live in Barmston, and I do not know indeed whether or no he be of the Family I mean — it may be with him as with our Family name: as there was then a Willm Sharp but I dare say not one of our Ancestors, thus one generation passeth away and a new one rises in their places.

     You wish to know what Bronze is, and what Country produces it; it is the produce of no particular place, but it is a Compound Metal, consisting of one part of tin, Ten of Copper and a little Zinc. The famous Horses of Chio which Bonaparte brought from Venice to adorn his Triumphal Arch are made of Bronze — they are supposed to be upwards of 2000 years old — the Statue of King William in the Market Place at Hull, I suppose is Bronze. Medals are often made of Bronze — Bronze is also the name of a Colour used in painting, which is applied with Varnish. I suppose your Ornaments will be of this kind. I have sent you some extracts from a Poem called Waterloo, by G. Walker[7] perhaps you have it the price is 3s. It is in the Old English Ballad Style ...

I have none of Moxon Bills,[8] I never liked them but if others are partial to them, let them enjoy their opinions. I hope all will be paid to the holder of their notes. — you said you sent 1/6d but you only sent 1s. This has been the sittings day, very throng and wages low[.] We are well at present.

South Cave 16th Nov. 1815
[On reverse]: My Father Nov 16/1815

---

[6] This letter has not survived, although an earlier letter, written on 1 Feb. 1813, also contained passages (omitted from this edition) on the history of Sharp's birthplace, the village of Barmston.

[7] George Walker (1772–1847), London bookseller, publisher and novelist. The ten verses of the poem quoted by RS in this letter have been omitted.

[8] The Hull Commercial Bank established in 1791 (or 1792) by Richard Moxon and Edmund Bramston in new premises in Whitefriargate, Hull, had passed into the hands of Richard, George and John Moxon in 1795 on the death of Bramston. They continued to manage it until its liquidation in November 1815 (Jackson, G. 212).

1817 Feb. 24th
South Cave, 24th. Feb.y 1817.
Dear Wm.

I have sent you the remainder of your money together with two Crown Pieces of your mother's[;] nobody will take them here and if they should be stopped altogether after the time the new Coin is issued there will be a loss in them, you must make inquiries and if you find that they will not go you had better change them, get 4 new Crown pieces for the four Crowns sent herewith.

Those which I have wrapped separately I would advise you to keep at all events they are as under

Half Crown.	James 2nd
Shilling -----------------------	Wm 3rd
Do. -----------------------	Queen Anne
Sixpence---------------------------	Do.
Shilling --------------------	George 1st.
Shilling & Sixpence	George 2nd
Do. --------Do. ------------	George 3rd

and 2 four pence pieces

If you are satisfied that they will pass Current after this time you need not get them changed, but if they will not[,] get them exchanged for new ones, they are all heavier than the respective new Coins — I expect, but I have not seen a new Crown piece — 15s.6d. of the last coinage is of the weight of 16s.6d. of the new or present Coin[9]

there are 2 plain Sixpences which you must try to get 2 new ones for & be particular in sending them back if you cannot, as they are not my own—
  £ s. d   £ s   s d
there is 2–11–0 and 1–5, you had which is £3–16–0 without the 9–8 you have to save
        s
here is 6– for the Books & send the other we have ordered—the two Crown pieces of your Mothers is a present from her to you

[On reverse of sheet]: My Father Feb 24. 1817...

[9] The transfer of the Mint from its old quarters in the Tower of London to a new site in Tower Hill marked the full-scale introduction of a 'token' silver coinage in which the coins had an intrinsic value lower than their face value. From 1816 the Mint began to issue a complete re-coinage. The 'old' crowns may have been the 18th cent. crowns of George II issued from 1732 to 1750. Although other silver coins were issued from 1816 or 1817, the new crown coin was not issued until 1818, so William should have been able to pass his old crowns as 'Current' (Purvey 223, 230, and 235–6).

1820 Feb. 10th
So. Cave, 10th. Feb.y 1820.
Dear Wm.

I have to complain, that you neither sent the Ink ingredients, the Indian rubber nor <u>Jne Corner's Book</u>, and as for the Copy Slip I shall receive it along with the Beauties of Lancashire,[10] Can you tell when that will be? do endeavour to send what we desire. You must send a Skein of marking Silk same as the pattern. — I am glad you sent me the Bks to look over. I have read Cobbett's address, and in reading it I almost forgot that it was the writing of the furious demagogue. I was led to think this man must be writing for the good of the public, but the Cloven foot sometimes was seen, and then it appeared he was only zealous for party views, or else he was resolved to be moral out of contradiction, for Religion the fellow has none at all ...

You wish for the particulars of the Proclamation here on Monday last, I shall gratify you as follows. On Sunday I received intelligence that the most high and mighty Prince George of Wales, would be proclaimed King[11] the following day at the Market Cross, by Mr. Peter Oxtoby of Market Weighton a Sheriff's officer vulgarly called a Bum Bailiff;[12] I myself I! with Mr. Robt. Marshall my Colleague made it as public as we could on the Sunday. We informed Mr. Barnard who promised to attend the ceremony, but he was prevented. We likewise waited on most of the other respectables in Cave to give them notice of the important event. Accordingly we ordered the singers to begin singing at half past eleven on Monday morning, and a Band of Music to attend at twelve O'clock at the Cross Steps. Some short time before twelve the Company began to assemble at Mr. Cook's,[13] (the Herald Mr. Peter having arrived) from whence the procession began moving a few minutes after; in something like the following order

Musicians,
The Herald, and a Bum Bailiff!
Constables
Lawyers, and Doctor
A military officer

---

[10] John Britton and Edward Wedlake Brayley, *The Beauties of England and Wales; or; Delineations, Topographical, Historical and Descriptive of Each County* ... London: Vernor, Hood and Sharpe, 1801–15. – 18 vols. of which vol. 9 by John Britton, published 1807 and 808 pages in length, was devoted to Lancashire, Leicestershire, and Lincolnshire. In addition, a reprint of the section on Lancashire, pages 5–312 of vol. 9, from a parallel 18-vol. edition of the same work, published by George Cowie and Co., was re-issued as a separate volume, entitled 'A Topographical and Historical Description of the County of Lancaster' [c.1815]. The reference is probably to this separate publication.

[11] i.e. King George IV, eldest son of George III; he had been Prince Regent since 1811 on account of his father's insanity.

[12] Used contemptuously of the meanest kind of bailiff, said to be derived from one who sneaks close to a debtor's back or catches him in the rear (*OED*).

[13] The Fox and Coney: Barnard Cook remained landlord of this, South Cave's principal public house, until May 1829.

A Publican, and Churchwarden
Guardian of the Poor
Farmers
The people on all sides
Bobby Todd, with a Cask of Ale in a Wheelbarrow

The procession having arrived opposite the Cross, the Herald desired all present to be uncovered while he read the proclamation, which he did with a great degree of boldness[,] he being in the habit of haranguing the multitude at times, in his quality of an Auctioneer; The Ceremony over three Huzzas were given for the new King, and the populace most loyally began to pay their respects to the Ale Barrel with the head knocked in, just before the Cross; O what a charming scene it was to see Pots, tins and Mugs in contact, dipping into the delightful beverage, and from thence to their mouths, where it ran down the narrow passage of their throats like Soap suds down a Sink-hole.

Nearly five pounds were subscribed and loyalty was kept up at all the Public houses until a late hour; The day passed over in harmony, and we feel as well satisfied with his Majesty as ever people were with a King; excepting some discontented spirits, who were resolved, after having freely sacrificed to Sir John Barleycorn, to have a King of their own making; and whether by Accident or choice it so happened that Mr. Wm. Cressey, attained to that honour, and was chaired and proclaimed with three times three, but sometimes when at the summit of Ambition, we are the nearest to misfortune, and so it happened to King Cress, for the multitude, who are never pleased long together, tumbled his Majesty into the Beck, and repeated their cheering. You must understand I was not a witness to this, as it came to pass sometime after midnight. So much for the proclamation.

You see how much paper I have wasted in the above long letter. I thought to have said something on the folly of troubling ourselves so much about Politics; but I will say nothing about it at present, for we may meet with unhappiness plentifully, without making ourselves uneasy respecting the Government. I had forgot to say any thing of the ~~Book~~ Man in the Moon,[14] There seems to be some humour in it but I do not think I understand it, — but it does not come up to the House that Jack built.[15] I cannot give you an Ansr. before next Wk respecting the London Mag.[16]

[14] William Hone, *The Man in the Moon*, with 15 woodcuts [by George Cruikshank]. London: William Hone, 1820. — Satirical verses on George IV and others. There were at least 27 editions or impressions of this work up to 1825. William Hone (1780–1842) was a London author and bookseller who began publishing political satires against the government from 1817 onwards, many of them illustrated by Cruikshank.

[15] William Hone, *The Political House that Jack Built* ... London: William Hone, 1819. Some 49 separate editions or impressions of this satirical work were published by the author between 1819 and 1820; they were illustrated by 13 woodcuts executed by Cruikshank.

[16] Originally known as Baldwin's *London Magazine* to distinguish it from its short-lived rival known as Gold's *London Magazine*, this famous literary journal was founded in 1820 and continued under successive proprietors until 1829. Its first and most successful editor was a Scotsman, John Scott, who

We want the Supplement for the Monthly Mag.[17] published in August last and the Supplement for the present Vol. ending Jany. 1820.

[In pencil underneath] We must keep Cobbett a week longer
[In margin]: My Father Feb 10 1820 ...

1821 Dec. 25th
South Cave, 25th Decr. 1821
(Christmas Day)
Dear Wm.

In the first place I will give you an account of the Letters and papers we have received from you lately. On Monday the 17th inst a Newspaper marked of the trials you had heard at the Court of King's Bench, in my Opinion (and who is qualified to form a better judgment on the point?) the line with which it was marked was superior to the celebrated Painter's line of Beauty. On Tuesday the 18th. we recd. from Hull the letter and parcel containing Cobbett's works. I have lent them to Mr. Day, who enquired of me if I had lately seen any of the Works in question; he is so fond of his Sermons that he says he will buy them. In his Cottage Economy[18] he says he knows of no law human or divine to restrain a poor Man working in his Garden on a Sunday, if the necessity of his family require it, for my own part I do not think that any such case of necessity can ever exist, then he justifies his Argument by a piece of very bad reasoning — namely because some particular persons are obliged to do some kind of work on the Sunday therefore it follows that there is no law to prevent a poor man working in his Garden on a Sunday, this is downright Sophistry and unworthy of Cobbett, for he knows very well that if every so many persons commit a crime it still remains no less a crime for that. On Friday the 21st. we recd. the letter and Farthings,[19] when I first saw them I was surprised as I mistook them

died as a result of a duel occasioned by a quarrel with Lockhart of the rival *Blackwood's Magazine.* Among the *London Magazine*'s contributors were Charles Lamb, William Hazlitt, John Clare, De Quincey and Carlyle (Butterworth 12–17; Watson iii. 1844).

[17] The *Monthly Magazine* ran from 1796 to 1843. It was founded by Sir Richard Phillips, who published it for 28 years until 1824, when it was bought by Messrs. Cox and Baylis. Dubbed by Southey, 'the Dissenters' Obituary', it published a wide range of articles, on literature, science and politics. Its readership was made up of Unitarians and other nonconformist groups as well as freethinkers and radicals of various religious persuasions. Among its contributors it included Malthus, Godwin, Hazlitt and Southey. Within a year of the change of ownership, the last editor under the Phillips regime, John Thelwall, was dismissed, and thereafter editorial policy reflected the changed character of the magazine which was 'put on a par with other periodicals' and political topics excluded (Carnall 158–64; Watson iii. 1841).

[18] William Cobbett, *Cottage Economy: Containing Information Relating to the Brewing of Beer, Making of Bread, Keeping of Cows, Pigs, Bees, Ewes, Goats, Poultry and Rabbits, and Relative to other Matters Deemed Useful in the Conducting of the Affairs of a Labourer's Family.* London, 1822. This work was originally issued in 7 monthly parts (1821–2), one of which provided the source of RS's reference.

[19] The last issue of copper farthings, which featured the head of George III, had been in 1806. The Mint resumed the issue of farthings in 1821, with pennies and halfpennies following in 1825. The new

for Sovereigns but I was quickly undeceived. The Brittania is a beautiful figure; the head I can say very little for, — on Sunday we recd. the letter and Newspaper, and much satisfaction they caused us, we are particularly glad to hear that you have recovered so wonderfully, for which both you and us ought to be thankful. I am glad to find that Mr. Day was so kind as to make an offer of lending you money but I am still more glad that you had no occasion to borrow, however the Gentleman's kindness is no less, and I hope you will evince the same Gratitude, as though you had not had a Farthing. I am sorry that the Partridges did not arrive safe; with respect to the Box which contained the Apples, Gingerbread and Stockings, we sent it to Hull on the 7th inst. and desired your Aunt to send it you by the first conveyance which I expect was done as we have not heard any thing from her since. I hope before you receive this you will have received it. You say you think the parcel would come cheaper in the Barton Coach,[20] I do not think it would make much difference, and then the conveniency of the Rodney[21] is so much greater, that when we have any small parcel we shall always send it by this Conveyance. Eliza could read your letter nearly as well as myself[;] she had got it read over before I got up, and much Joy it diffused in our small Family, it is with infinite pleasure we hear from you, — I really do think the Situation[22] you are in will be found by you to be a pleasant one, as you will see so much of the busy scenes around you, and it will certainly give you a great insight into your business by attending every day so many different Shops, and I think it will be more conducive to health a great deal than being constantly confined in a Shop. In short it is such a situation as I should wish for you, for it is a place of trust and Confidence by having money delivered to you every day and only accounting once a week; I know you are qualified to keep all your accounts correctly, which you will of course take a pride in doing. — You say in one of your letters that the Chapels are fast approaching the Church in Gowns[,] Bands and other appendages of Popery, which John Knox the Scottish reformer would have called the cast off Rags of the Whore of Babylon. I am afraid that the Simplicity in the worship of Dissenters, is in a great measure changed for shew and splendid decoration. I am much pleased with your description of Westminster Abbey, and hope I shall have the pleasure of being conducted by you to see this temple of the mighty dead, should all be well with us the next harvest. Last Sunday night after your Mother and Eliza were gone to Bed I took a solitary walk into this venerable

farthings depicted a portrait bust of George IV, with draped neck and head wreathed in laurels (Purvey 232 and 242).

[20] From Barton, on the south bank of the Humber, the Royal Mail departed daily at 9 a.m. for London, the journey taking approximately 22 hours. The returning Royal Mail was due back at Barton at 6 p.m., when the Express Post Coach left for London, each day (except Sunday). Both coaches connected with the Waterloo Steam Hoy which left Hull at 7 a.m. and 4 p.m. to cross the Humber to Barton (Baines ii. 349, 353).

[21] The Rodney Post Coach from Hull passed through South Cave at 8 a.m. daily on its way to Sheffield and London, via Booth Ferry, where a ferry crossed the River Ouse (Baines ii. 187, 349).

[22] William Sharp had joined the staff of the London publishing firm, Longman's, only in the previous month. (See Introduction).

pile where I staid till near midnight. I entered at the great Western door and what a sight struck my eyes! The lofty Aisles I viewed with astonishment and wonder, the great Iron gates of the Choir were opened and I trode the marble floor until I reached the east end of the church or rather chancel, where I admired the beautiful Altar of White marble, but this was not the place for me, I passed almost with unconcern the monument of Lady Eliz. Nightingale[23] and made the best of my way to the southern extremity of the Cross Aisle which you know is the place called "Poets' Corner". the monument you lately saw. I noticed one you did not mention, which is to Dr. Watts,[24] I then walked to the north end of the Cross Aisle where is the monument to ~~the Earl~~ Lord Mansfield[25] sitting in his robes with a piece of parchment in his left hand and as he did not know where to put his right hand, he laid it on his knee. I can say nothing adequate in praise of Henry the 7th Chapel only it is supposed to be the finest piece of Architecture of the kind in the World. all this which I have been describing was more endeared to me by knowing that you had viewed many of the same monuments but a few days before. — You say a Yorkshireman is easily known in London, I do not wonder at it, — I once heard some person (whether Londoner or not I have forgot) on the hearing of your Maternal Grandfather say that such a person whom he had heard preaching was a poor Creet-shure (Creature) to which your Grandfather replied he was indeed a poor preacher, so that you see Creature is here pronounced to be mistaken for preacher; however if any improvement can be made in your pronunciation you will act wisely to adopt it. I heard the Archbishop of York pronounce the word mercy with an a, as marcy which is certainly broad Yorkshire, but you know there are many persons' examples I would follow before those of Archbishops. — It will be towards the latter end of January before your Mother will be able to get your Shirts ready to send in the next Box.

The weather here is very wet and I suppose it is the same with you; On Sunday last I was in the Vestry of the Church, with the Parson, and a Man of Broomfleet by name John Baitson, when either to confound us by his knowledge or astonish us by his ignorance when talking about the weather he said it is very "contracted weather", and confounded and astonished I certainly was, for I could not even guess what kind of weather he meant; I scarcely ever heard an expression but I could make something of the meaning, but this was perfectly

---

[23] The monument of J. G. Nightingale (d. 1752) and his wife (d. 1734) is situated in the north transept (west wall of the east aisle) of Westminster Abbey. It was made in 1761 by Louis-François Roubiliac and shows Mr Nightingale standing against an arch and seeking to protect his wife from the figure of Death in the form of a gruesome skeleton pointing a lance at her (Pevsner (1973) i. 448–9).

[24] This monument is located in the north transept (in a bay on the south wall of the south aisle) of the Abbey. It commemorates Dr Isaac Watts (1674–1748), the hymn writer. He is shown with pen in hand, listening to an angel. The monument was made in 1774 by Thomas Banks (Pevsner (1973) i. 460).

[25] This monument is located in the north transept (east side of the west aisle) of the Abbey. It commemorates William Murray, 1st Earl of Mansfield (1705–93), Lord Chief Justice, and shows him, dressed in robes and wearing a wig, seated on a tall circular pedestal with Wisdom and Justice standing to the left and right. At the rear Death as a naked youth leans on an extinguished torch. The monument was erected by John Flaxman in 1801 at a cost of £2,500. (Pevsner (1973) i. 450–1).

unintelligible. This Box which we now send, will go in the inside of the last, and the last will go in the inside of the next we send, so that they will fit one into another like the Sentences in the Agricultural Report, which Cobbett compares to a nest of Pill Boxes.[26]

Mr. Day has lent me the Beauties of Cobbett in three twopenny numbers,[27] the first part contains the life of Paine, the second is called the "Torch of Truth" and part third "Politics for the People" they are extracts from his Works, ["]Published by H. Stemman, 68 Princes Street, Leicester Square" with Medallion Portraits of Thomas Paine and William Cobbett. — They shew the changeableness of the Man. — Were you here we should be asking you twenty Questions before you could answer one, but I will ask you a few now, and you can answer them at your leisure.

1. What time do you rise in the morning?
2. What do you get to your Breakfast?
3. What time do you begin work?
4. Where do you dine?
5. What do you chiefly get to dinner?
6. Do you get tea in the afternoon?
7. Where do you get your Supper?
8. Have you a room to yourself?
9. What time do you leave work at night?
10. What does your Dinner cost you?
11. How much is your Weekly Expences?

I sent you a newspaper on Saturday last which I expect you would receive on Monday morning, it had a few lines written on the bottom of the 2nd. and 3rd. pages. You need but send me the title of the Act relative to sending newspapers by the Post, as I can refer to the Act if I know the title.[28] I would advise you to eat Greens to your Dinner or Carrots sometimes, as I find them both of a laxative Quality; and could you get good Porter; to drink a very little at a time; but it is in general such a Diabolical mixture of Coculus Indicus[29] and other pernicious ingredients that it is scarcely prudent to let it come within ones lips. — you must persevere in taking a few pills occasionally just before you go to bed at nights, as you find yourself costive. — I went last week to see a collection

---

[26] Cobbett's critique of the *Report of the Select Committee on Distress in Agriculture* took up much of his *Weekly Register* between Sept. and Nov. 1821. The passage alluded to here (CPR 40 xvi (3 Nov.) 1821, 1043) refers to that section of the *Report* concerning rents, prices, and changes in the currency.

[27] William Cobbett, *The Beauties of Cobbett*. London: H. Stemman, [1820?]. – 3 pts. – Extracts designed to discredit the author.

[28] The principal Act of 1764 (4 Geo. III c. 24) had been further modified by the Act of 1802 (42 Geo. III c. 63), entitled: 'An Act to Authorise the Sending and Receiving of Letters and Packets, Votes, Proceedings of Parliament and Printed Newspapers by the Post ...'

[29] *Cocculus indicus*, the dried berries of *Anamirta cocculus*, found in Malabar and Ceylon. 'The berry is a violent poison and has been used to stupefy fish, and in England to increase the intoxicating power of beer and porter.' (*OED*).

of Wild Beasts which stopped here on their way to Hull, amongst the rest was a very large fierce looking Lion, with a shaggy mane the first of that description I ever saw; his roar was most dreadful[.] A man's life would not have been worth a moment's purchase if he had met him in the desert. — There is a beautiful little Poem which I have seen in some Collections many years ago called "Hassan or the Camel driver", which I had rather see again than all the works of Lord Byron which I have yet seen, if you should happen to meet with it, preserve it for me, after reading it yourself, — one line is "What if the Lion in his rage I meet"! another Couplet I recollect is,

> "The Lily peace outshines the silver Store,
> And life is dearer than the golden Ore".[30]

You must procure some Ink rather more different from the colour of your paper than the last you wrote with. I was at Barnard Cook's on Monday night where I shewed your new Farthings [to] Mr. Brown of Brough the same young man who was at our house at Cave fair[.] Said if I would let him have one, he would treat me with a Glass of any thing I chose, to which at length I consented, so you see I have one Farthing less than I had; I now recollect the following lines which if I had thought upon at the time might have kept me one 960th. part of a pound richer than I am

> "Weigh every small expence and nothing waste
> Farthings long sav'd amount to pounds at last".

You will instantly discover that this is a maxim of thrift, with a great deal of meaning in it, but as you know Poor Richard's maxims of Industry and Frugality[31] I need not enter into a comment to darken the words of the text. — James Marshall was here on Monday[,] he is very glad to hear you are better and so indeed is Robt. and all the Marshalls and all our other Friends who know that you have been ill.

Now for the Contents of this present Box[:] here is one Goose Pie with a few Slices of Old Ham in it. And another Pork and Beef. Here are likewise some Sausages & Black puddings of your Mothers own making, with Mince tarts made on purpose for Christmas[.] We hope you will receive all in good order and Condition, which you may either enjoy in a Solitary or social manner as you think the most conducive to your own interest. Only I think you must get your kind Landlady to boil your Sausages, and invite her to Sup with you, and if either or both of the young men Clerks in your department are kind to you, you may let them taste of a Yorkshire pie. — Here is likewise what I must not forget namely five Gold Guineas, which if you want do not spare them, and if you do not want put them in your purse, and the Chink of them I think will sound as

---

[30] The quotations are from 'Eclogue the Second, Hassan; or, The Camel Driver' by William Collins (1721–59) (*EP*).

[31] *Poor Richard's Almanack* was written and published annually by Benjamin Franklin (1706–90). Each issue contained a number of popular sayings and proverbs expressed in Franklin's own words. They were collected together and published in the issue for 1758 and subsequently reprinted under a variety of titles such as *Father Abraham's Speech, The Way to Wealth, Poor Richard's Maxims* etc. RS quoted from the work on 3 occasions in his letters and diary (25/12/21, 25/4/27 and 15/5/29).

sweetly in your ears, as the sound of Bow Bells in the ears of Cockneys. We have had Robt. Marshall to dine and drink tea with us to day and at this present is set by the fire side while I am writing. I have strict charge to remember him to you, which here I do. Now you see I have written you a pretty long letter, made up of the first thoughts that came into my mind — well I expect you will receive this Box on Thursday evening so be sure to write on Friday, which will come in due course on Sunday morning, I hope you will be able before you write to give a good account of the last Box, Your Mother & Eliza's kindest love to you along with my own
So Remain

> your loving Father
> R Sharp

[In margin]: My father Dec 25. 1821

1822 Apr. 24th
So. Cave, 24th. Apl. 1822
> Wednesday night
Dear Wm

We recd. the Exn. [Examiner][32] this morning with an Account of the terrible disaster which happened to the last Basket of Eggs[.] We have now sent another and hope better fortune will attend it. You have not said in your note this morning how you are, and that is the chief thing we want to hear about, pray for the future never omit mentioning your health, we naturally fear the worst when we hear nothing.

We recd. the Letter on Friday with one inclosed for John Turk, which he was glad to receive but I have not seen him since, but have had related to me the following dialogue between him and Robt. Marshall[:]

John. — This Wm. Sharp is a wonderful lad, he really is Robt. without joking why you see he can write a Sheet of Paper and never be at a loss for ought to say.

Robt. Why I should wish to write to him but then I am like you I dont know what to write about, what I can but tell him old house stands where it did, and I have been at Ruffham field and Hogmanpit as nearly past getting to, the Wallingfen roads are so bad.

John, That's just like me, I could not tell him a bit more, for when I begin to write and think I have a little in my head, then I may be want to write a word that I don't know how to spell, and so sitting musling (musing) to know how to spell I may be write it wrong and forget all I was thinking about.

Robt. As for spelling you know John he would put up with that because he would find out what we meant, if there was any meaning in it.

---

[32] *The Examiner* was, in its earlier years, a strongly radical weekly newspaper. It was published in London from 3 Jan. 1808 to 26 Feb. 1881. The first proprietors were John Hunt and J. H. Leigh Hunt (1808–25); they were succeeded by Robert Fellowes (1828–30?) and Albany Fonblanque (1830?–65) (Watson iii. 1809).

Jno.   There must be a difference Robt. in families[,] I'll never believe but there is, why you see his Father would begin to write and there he would go on without stopping at all until he had done; what can one say about it, it must be a gift Robt. don't you think it is.

Robt.   Yes it is a gift that's for certain

Jno.   You know and so do I that I have not that gift, but I could like to write to Wm. for all that but you see Ive neither Pen Ink nor paper

Robt.   But you have advantage of me you know you have a letter book

Jn. –   It weant dea [won't do], it weant dea mun to write to him out of a Book what he wad no/know it at yanse [he would know it at once], no I mun he sum thing om mesan when I deah begin [no I must have something of my own when I do begin].

R Sharp

PS. you will perceive from the foregoing that I have fallen into the Error which I wished to correct in you, — but I now tell you that we are well & do not neglect to always let us know how you are when you write. I have just seen Jno. Turk he says he could like to write but does not know what to say, he says he should have been a whole day in writing a letter as long as the one you have sent him, but he knows you always were quick at writing.

[In margins]: My Father April 24. 1822
        Wm Sharp [written reversed]

1825, Jan. 31st
South Cave, 31st. January. 1825
Dear Wm.

The Box arrived safe from you on Friday night the 21st. January last, and happy were we to hear from you, it being so long since we had any thing from you before. The Hymn Book gives particular satisfaction, so do the Pocket Books, the Ladies dresses will serve for patterns in fact they are very acceptable, the Mint Lozenges are of curious construction and very good. I need scarcely say that I am gratified with the Articles particularly for me[;] they are novelties, as I have seen none since I was with you. With respect to the Portrait[33] which you esteem the very image of me, I think & hope it is not a likeness, it is remarkably grim. I must acknowledge that when I was in London, I was a shade or two darker than common, what with being at Sea and the hot weather after. I was surprised at my own countenance, indeed if I be exposed to the Sun but for a day it has a remarkable effect in tanning me. — I have read over carefully Johnson's Typography,[34] the first Volume is particularly interesting and

[33] Unfortunately not traced.

[34] John Johnson, *Typographia; or, The Printer's Instructor* ... London: Longman and Co., 1824. – 2 vols.

perhaps the second may be equally so, to printers whom it more immediately concerns. The excursion to Windsor[35] I told you I would keep it for the Library if you say what was the price of it, I expected you would have let me know and I could have sent the pay in the Box again. I have likewise returned the Steam Packet companion[36] which was very amusing in the Voyage home. You say yours is but a gloomy life but I know you cannot be very gloomy with a Book before you, a student's life must be for the most part Solitary, then in the days you are at the very fountain head of literature, and you can improve yourself in many things, indeed I think there is a great deal of pleasure in reading merely for amusement, at least I know I should have more satisfaction in employing my time in that manner than in frequenting the most fashionable places of dissipation and immorality. You say you should like to see my Journal of the short time I was in London, but it unfortunately happens that I have mislaid the few remarks I made on the great City for which I am very sorry that I cannot gratify you, but I will endeavour to tell you what struck me the most and I know you will be surprised when I tell you that the <u>Door of Death</u>[37] you shewed me which came out of the Newgate into the old Bailey was one of the most prominent, I did not like Sterne take a single Captive,[38] and see how he spent but one day, the sight of which overpowered him; but I immured myself in the Dungeon loaded with Chains and what is still more with Crimes, the melancholy days and tedious nights passed in dreary horrors, at length the day of trial comes, I am found guilty and sentenced to undergo the dreadful punishment of the law, I took a last farewell of all friends, and the dismal passage was traversed the first and the last time. I could not bear up against the accumulated horrors around me, I may say that I passed through the comfortless realms of despair; — No! I find I cannot even bear to see a public execution, my fortitude would be so shaken to see the guilty wretches that I could not endure the scene — no more of this.

The first public building which struck me with surprise was Somerset house (for I had not then seen Saint Pauls) I was lost in amazement at the sight of such a Building[;] it has something so majestic on entering the Square that I cannot pretend to describe. The Statue of George facing nearly the principal

[35] John Evans, *An Excursion to Windsor in July 1810, through Battersea ... and Hampton Court ... Also a Sail down the River Medway, July 1811, from Maidstone ... to the River Nore, upon the Opening of the Oyster Beds.* London: Sherwood, Neely and Jones, 1817.

[36] Thomas Nicholls, *The Steam Boat Companion; or, Margate, Isle of Thanet, Isle of Sheppey, Southend, Gravesend and River Thames Guide ... with Descriptions of every ... place ... on each Side of our River, from the Custom House to Margate ...* London, 1823. Although the title does not exactly correspond with RS's reference, it seems most probable that this is the work to which he was referring since it would be both up to date and relevant to the course of his trip down river, on the return journey to Hull.

[37] Also known as the 'debtor's door'. Newgate was the famous London prison built on the site of earlier buildings by George Dance (jun.) in 1768–78 and subsequently demolished to make way for the Central Criminal Court, Old Bailey (1900–07) (Timbs 697–9).

[38] The reference is to 'The Captive. Paris' in Laurence Sterne's *A Sentimental Journey through France and Italy* first published in 1768.

entrance is almost as Black as London smoke can make it, the front towards the Thames is admirable; — As for Temple Bar it has nothing more to recommend it than the North Bar at Beverley[,][39] it is I think a disgrace to the City. You know what I felt on seeing St. Pauls for you were with me, the exterior is amazing and commanding, but to behold the inside work especially the Convex Surfaces of the Dome is astonishing. One cannot help wondering how such a stupendous design should have ever entered into the mind of man. You know how fearful I was in looking down from the Whispering Gallery on the pavement below; it even now is very powerful on my feelings, the view from the top was grand and magnificent, the five Bridges all in perspective before you, and the tiny passengers and Coaches in Cheapside seemed like a sight in fairy land. Then look what way you would nothing but buildings to meet your eye until you fairly glanced over the whole some twenty miles into Surrey. It is a charming place is this noble Cathedral, I have it now in my mind's eye, and as much afraid as I was I do not know but I should be again tempted to ascend the flights of steps once more if I had an opportunity. Guildhall seemed to me like being at home I was so well acquainted with the redoubted Hero's before, but not one word did their Gogships reply when I gave the Compliments of their old friend Willy to them, so adieu great Gog and thou Magog[40] continue in thy place that the Cockneys may have something to talk of and boast about, for in former times, these were but the common statures of most men born within the sound of Bow Bells, O London look now on thy puny progeny and weep over thy degenerate Sons.

The exchange struck me with a good deal of surprise I knew it by the description but did not expect to see such an assemblage of Statues and in so fine a state as I found them, I need not say anything of the Tower that grand storehouse of death, where you at one view see Arms for 150,000 men in the finest possible condition, I saw these and the Horse armoury and other curiosities but I had to pay for them, a sight without cost always pleases me the best, or we will say a trifling cost; but I believe imposition is the order of the day, for Towers and Temples cannot be entered except you first satisfy the Cerberus who attends, I shall say nothing of Westminster Abbey, only the person who goes round with you I will not say shews it but hurries you on as fast as possible, that he may dismiss you and walk (to him) the same dull round, and chink again the Silver, from some other inquisitive visitor, I could have wished to have been turned loose in the midst of the illustrious dead who are there deposited, but no such thing, for the guide is like Time and Tide he waits

[39] Beverley's North Bar is the only survivor of the 3 brick-built bars, or town gates, which originally belonged to the town. It dates from 1409. Newbegin Bar was demolished in 1790, and Keldgate Bar in 1808 (*VCHYER* vi. 178–80).

[40] These 2 gigantic effigies, each 14 feet high, in London's Guildhall were carved in 1708 by Richard Saunders to replace 2 earlier figures destroyed in the Great Fire. According to legend, Gog and Magog were the survivors of a race of giants descended from 33 wicked daughters of Diocletian and their demon lovers. They were brought back to London (then called Troy-novant) by their captor, Brute, and forced to serve as porters at the gate of the Royal Palace (*EB* xii. 190).

for no man, well let him mind his drudgery I had more real delight in a cursory visit than he had in receiving his impositions not fees.

The first Sunday we were in London which I think was the 5th. Sept. you know we saw nearly all the Churches from the Tower to the Temple which is the whole extent of the City, the little miniature Church of St. Stephens Wallbrook[41] is fitted up in a handsome manner and appears grand as a drawing room. The temple Church appeared the most ancient of any we saw, except perhaps St. Bartholomews. I admire St. Bride's for its lofty and I think beautiful Spire or Steeple altho' Sir Richard Phillips says it is but a deformed Mass, but here I beg leave to differ in opinion with him. Should the Committee appointed to prevent the building of the Houses in Fleet Street which were burnt down, succeed in their endeavours it will be a grand view through the opening,[42] and here by the bye the Fire was very near you and would cause some alarm, the sight must have been awfully sublime, I should admire a fire the most of any thing provided I could see it without any persons suffering either bodily or in their property.

On the Sunday in the afternoon we went you know in a Stage from the Bank, how far I cannot say, but after we alighted we walked in Hyde Park, where we saw nothing very particular until near the end of Picadilly I think where the Brazen image of a fellow called Achilles stands,[43] he appears like a Giant having been aroused from his Sleep in a dream, and immediately getting up had forgot to dress himself, but luckily he found an old Fish-Kettle which in his hurry he took up instead of his Shield, to guard him from the Assaults of his Foes. The Barber's Bason of Seville of which Don Quixote made a Helmet was nothing to the Fish-Kettle shield of the redoubted A-kill-ease.

I have said nothing of the Bridges — Waterloo is a fine level Bridge and convenient for heavy loads passing over it, but it is not so grand as Blackfriars, but in my opinion Westminster is the grandest Bridge over the River.

So much for buildings of Brick, Stone and Mortar. I think the place where Moxon lodged when I was there is not far from Shoreditch Church, but I did not know it then; I was sorry to hear of the sudden death of his Landlady so soon after we were there. I have had two letters from London the last week in answer to two which I wrote respecting a Man who is here at present in the Workhouse, he had been confined in an Asylum at Bethnal Green and was sent there by the Parish of Saint Saviours in the Borough, but as he was only a

---

[41] One of the City of London churches built after the Great Fire to the design of Sir Christopher Wren. St. Stephen Walbrook was built in 1672–9, the domed design foreshadowing that of St. Paul's (Pevsner (1973) i. 177–80).

[42] On 14 Nov. 1824 several houses on the south side of Fleet Street were destroyed by a fire. The space created by the fire was used subsequently to lay down 'an architectural avenue to St. Bride's Church' (Timbs 156).

[43] The 36 feet high iron statue of Achilles was erected in Hyde Park in 1822 in honour of the Duke of Wellington. It was made by Sir Richard Westmacott from the metal of captured French cannon (Pevsner (1973) i. 590–1).

casual Pauper, the application to them is of no use; the man is a native of Scotland and says he is a Lieutenant in the Navy on half pay on the Superannuated list, but as he appears to be deranged, he does not know who draws his pay, he says he will set off to London, and the Lord Mayor will soon right him. — Do you recollect the Literary Gazette[44] which was to be sold as waste paper, I should like to have some of them if you can conveniently purchase them. — I see the Index for the Examiner is published so that you may send it the next time you send a Box, and there is a Portrait of Lord Byron belonging the last year's paper which you may send with it if you have it. — We have sent you no Sausages &c this season for we could not fall in for a Pig at Cave, we bought one at Ellerker but did not get the inside, they have been remarkably scarce and dear, and we have not had a single Hare this Season or else we should have sent you one.

All our friends are well, Robt. Marshall was glad to hear from you, and with us will be happy to see you in the spring if you can make it convenient, perhaps it will be about Cave fair, which this year will be the latter end of May; give my best respects to all the friends you think proper, with whom I made a short acquaintance, when in London, not forgetting little Parsons, and the Philosophical Mackenzie ...

Your mother has made you three white Pocket handkerchiefs, but she thinks they ought to be a little finer, but at present there is none to be had here, she will look out for some against a future opportunity, you can say how you like these and then it will be known what will suit. Your Linen is all very beautifully got up, it fortunately happened to be very fine bleaching weather so that they are in excellent condition. I hope they will answer safe.

Cobbett keeps up his Spirits. I expected he would have declaimed against the Decision of the Judge who said it was not lawful to publish Police reports, but I have been strangely out in my conjectures, for he appears to be delighted with the Shackles imposed on the "vile London press".[45] For my part I think it proper to publish the reports, and I hope the Police Offices will be soon open Courts, I do not like secret proceedings in the cause of Justice. — The history of the reformation is what Cobbett at present seems to have set his mind upon, it is a subject that will give him full scope of talking against the powers that be, for it is his invariable practice to praise no man, save and except those who have bought his Apple Grafts, and adopted his method of growing Swedish Turnips or straw platt: yet it appears that he is at present enamoured with the Catholic association.[46] Some of his remarks when not upon the subject

---

[44] Published from 25 Jan. 1817 to 26 Apr. 1862, when it was incorporated in the *Parthenon*. William Jerdon was its principal editor for more than 30 years (1817–50) (Watson iii. 1821).

[45] Cobbett considered that it was 'wise and just' to prevent newspapers from reporting details of court cases before the accused had been found guilty or innocent. He had recently written 2 articles on the subject, occasioned by a current court case involving the privacy of a person accused of indecency, in *CPR* 52 x (4 Dec.) 1824, 595–614 and 53 iv (22 Jan.) 1825, 190–237.

[46] Daniel O'Connell had revived an older Catholic Association in 1823 with the principal aim of promoting the candidature of MPs pledged to support Catholic emancipation. In *CPR* 52 xi (11 Dec.)

of Politics are very good, for instance what he says of Household manufactures, I can recollect the time very well when it would have been thought a Crime for any woman not to spin a Web of Linen at least in the year, but these times are over, no wheels are seen and idleness and gossiping have usurped their places[;] the change is not for the better, — I can say in praise of your mother that she is the constant manufacturer of our Stockings, indeed I do not think she could be idle, activity with her is natural[,] perhaps if more were to follow her example it would be the better for the community at large for the greatest population is made up of individuals, and an idle population will be sure to proceed from bad to worse; I do not like the "Cotton Lords" proceedings with the poor Slaves under their care nay I am wrong under their power.[47]

Rail roads are all the talk at present,[48] we often canvass the scheme over at old Willy's but not a soul of us can tell how they are to be laid down, nor what kind of Carriages are to run upon them, whether they are to go by art Magic, or which is nearly the same by steam, or whether the animals called Horses are to have the honour of dragging along the cumbrous loads and stupid travellers that are to be sported upon them, for the sole use and benefit of the Speculators on this occasion. Some are (of us I mean) sure that the road will come through Cave from Selby to Hull, others are afraid that some little hills will be impediments,[49] but of this I can assure you we are completely in the dark about this same Iron road, not the least ray from a Gas light[50] has ever shone upon our minds, to make us comprehend this levelling of hills and raising the vallies, if you happen to light of about three pennyworth of information on the subject you may let me have it, as I think it will be fully as much as we shall be able to read over, for you know we shall have to explain and comment as we go on, so that if we had a great book we should not be able to go through it in a reasonable time. — I had forgot to say when mentioning Cobbett's history of the reformation that I once when a Boy read a Book called England's reformation, it is in Verse and is I believe a satire on the

1824, 680–92 a reprint of the Catholic Association's *Address to the People of Ireland* is prefaced by a short article on the Association by William Cobbett.

[47] Possibly a reference to an extract from a speech at a meeting of cotton spinners printed, under the title 'Cotton Lords', in *CPR* 53 iv (22 Jan.) 1825, 239–44.

[48] The mid-1820s was a peak period of speculation and interest in railways. It has been estimated that in 1824 and 1825 no less than 60 railways were projected by various companies that had been formed for that purpose, including a Leeds and Hull Railway Company, which intended to build a line as a section in the proposed rail link from Hull to Liverpool (Jackman 532–3; Tomlinson 97–9).

[49] South Cave was eventually connected to Hull by rail but not via Selby and not until 60 years later, in 1885, when the Hull and Barnsley Railway was opened. It was the last major new railway company to be promoted in the 19th c. and was relatively short-lived with the last through train running in 1961, and the line itself finally closing in 1964. The first line to link Hull with the West Riding was the Hull-Selby Railway, opened in 1840, which took a more southerly route avoiding South Cave and its 'little hills' (VCHYER i. 392 and 395–6).

[50] The streets of Beverley, a town visited frequently by RS, had only the previous month been lit by gas for the first time (Crowther (1985) 15).

reformation, I think the Author's name is Ward,[51] but from that time to this I have not seen the Work, yet I have some faint recollection of it; it mentions several of the Abbeys being despoiled by the Duke of Somerset to build his Palace in the Strand adjoining the Thames, where Somerset house now stands. I had a short conversation on Saturday night last with an 84 degrees man,[52] alias a Manchester traveller; I asked him if the report was true that had been so often published, of the extreme heat of the factories, he did not at all deny it but said the work could not be carried on without such heat, but as to the healthiness of the persons employed, men, Women and Children, he was lavish in the praise of. I told him I understood a Man grew old at about 40 and was not worth much after who had been brought up in these places of confinement, this word was treason to the feelings of our traveller, he could scarce have been more alarmed had he been set upon a Barrel of Gunpowder with a spark nearly in contact, he said so far from being confined there was no persons who enjoyed themselves more in parading about the streets and enjoying themselves. I said the West India planters gave just the same reason for Slavery as was given for the stifling heat in the Cotton-factories namely that Sugar could not be supplied without the labour of Slaves, he did not appear to just envy the state of the Slaves but believed their sufferings had been greatly exaggerated; In conclusion I told him the plea he urged was very weak and one under which all kinds of injustice had been committed, namely the Tyrants' plea of necessity; thus ended our conversation not much to the edification of either party.

I now conclude with my best wishes for your welfare, accept your Mother and Eliza's love and give her Comps. to Mrs Warwick[53] & Mrs Powell we are all well at present & hope you are the same[.] I do not know whether I have said so before or not in this long letter, and I cannot at present get time to read it all over, So I rem.

                        Your loving Father
                        R Sharp
[On reverse of sheet]: Wm. Sharp
            London-town
[Below, reversed]: My Father Jany 31.1825

1825 July 11th
So. Cave, 11th July 1825.

---

[51] Thomas Ward (1652–1708) was a convert to Roman Catholicism and served for a spell in the Pope's Guard but lived in England from 1685 to 1688 where he produced several, then, controversial works. Later he settled in France and subsequently died there. His historical work, *England's Reformation from the Time of King Henry VIIIth to the End of Oate's Plot*. 4 Cantos, was first published in Hamburg in 1710 with numerous subsequent editions as follows: London, 1715 (2 vols.), 1716, 1747, and 1804; Dublin, 1814 (2 vols.) and Manchester, 1815 (*DNB*).

[52] Apparently a reference to *CPR* 51 viii (21 Aug.) 1824 in which Cobbett wrote of the 'wretched creatures ... locked up in ... hellish factories for fourteen hours a day in a heat of eighty four degrees'.

[53] Mrs Warwick was William's landlady at that time and for the next 2 years.

Dear Wm.

The Boxes arrived safe on the Tuesday after you sent them off; the Old Catalogues &c are all new to me and I like to see them; the Mint Drops are excellent. — I think we shall give up the Monthly Magazine as it has for the last few months been the Vehicle of Thelwall's Lectures[54] on nothing that can be understood then he crams in his L.L.T. Poetry and all his notes and notices are more than I can find any delight in. I think I shall order the Imperial[55] instead of it as it is but 1 shilling a No. I never saw above one or two Nos. but I did not dislike them. — I have sent you three Sovereigns for the Novels you sent which cost you £2–12s–6d so that there is 7s/6d for yourself, and likewise 4d. for the Reading easys. I like the Novels very well they are good and neat, as respects the execution — You wish to know all the tittle-tattle of So. Cave but if you know a little it will be perhaps as much as I know myself. The little Dandy parson yclep'd Nettleship[56] was preaching and begging here one night[.] Robt. Marshall asked me if I intended to hear him[.] I told him I should shew myself very weak if I did, but said he[,] forget and forgive, yes so I will forget when my memory fails, but at present I perfectly recollect the dirty tricks of the little fellow. — Old Sam Ayre I daresay is in his old melancholy mood as I suppose for I never enquire after him but I never see him out, and if it please heaven to spare my eye-sight, I never desire to see him again. — The Marshalls are all very far gone in the Cornu-mania[.] Miss[57] takes a deal of pains in cultivating their acquaintance and they seem a good deal elevated by her con, con what, why consideration — Robt. is better but at present he does not seem much inclined for Miss but she exerts herself all she can, therefore she will catch him if he does not mind. Old Rachel Levitt continues the same as when you were here, she calls her Son James, and tells him he cannot find his way back to London, she says she might as well have sent him to Broomfleet for improvement as to London, he has laid a Floor, she says she can almost put her feet through the joints in the boards, then she turned to him and says a little snaffling devil, there is nothing she says can get their little shambling Jim from home. Old Willy received the Blacking some time since which you ordered for him, it all came in 6d. pots just what he wanted! If you were to send Old Willy a description of St. Paul's I believe he would be much pleased, they sold for twopence when he was in London, perhaps the price now may be Sixpence, you must direct it for him and inclose it when the Box comes again, he has not yet

---

[54] Reformer, writer and political activist, John Thelwall (1764–1834), was noted for his Jacobin sympathies. Arrested for sedition in 1794 and under sentence of death, he was fortunate in being acquitted. After his trial he left London but continued to advocate the radical cause in his writings and lectures in the provinces. Later he became the last editor of the *Monthly Magazine*, in its active liberal phase under Sir Richard Phillips, but lost his post under the new owners in Nov. 1825 (*DNB*)

[55] *The Imperial Magazine* published 1819 to 1834.

[56] George Nettleship (1794–1881) became minister to the Independent Chapel, South Cave, in Sept. 1821 but resigned, apparently after 'differences', in June 1823 (Trout 10–11).

[57] i.e. Miss 'Kitty' [Mary] Corner, daughter of Kit Corner, a shopkeeper in South Cave and steward to Henry Gee Barnard. (See Appendix 2).

got any drawers made for his nails, the Kidney beans you sent are coming up[;] we gave a few of them to the Old Cardinal alias Mr. Holborn who set them in his Garden so that we may see them every day. We got our yearly Stock of Coals in the last week, and a hard job it was, it is such an awkward place to get to and so far to carry. Club[58] feast was on Thursday last, and your Mother's School feast[59] on the same day quite a grand display, the Scholars went round town with the Club Music before them, they looked very neat and in many persons Opinions it was a fairer sight than the Club itself, I should think we had as much stir in proportion to the place, as what was witnessed by you at the laying the foundation of London Bridge.

Val. Tindle hav[e] a Dog that can crack nuts very cleverly and eat the Kernels, I saw him exhibit one night in Tommy Pinder's Shop, he went through the work very adroitly. — Tom remains very lank sided yet, Young Tib is as frisky as any of her tribe[,] she is often threatened for trespassing in the Garden but she seems to take very little notice, for the first opportunity she is capering again as before. Tom jumped·upon the table one night and broke our best Tureen and very quick he was in getting himself out, when he came in again he seemed to have forgotten all about it — Mr Tinsdill has ordered Robt. Marshall to Scarborough[.] I think he will go, for he conceits himself being far from well, & what with Physic Bleeding[,] Blistering & cupping,[60] it is enough to make a stronger minded man than he is fancy himself not right. We have another new Doctor come to the Town[,] his name is Smith he comes from Hull and I think served his time with Sherwin. I think here is a poor prospect for him, he is at Val. Tindle's where Mr. Leeson lodged, but you know opposition is the order of the day[.] I think I have almost put Frank Jackson down[:] five of his Scholars have come to me since you were here, I know he cannot live by his Academy and I have no desire he should. Robt. Marshall and Mr. Turk were at Howden on Saturday last, Georgy rode a Galloway of Mr. Shackleton's, they were about three hours in riding there and as many back again, Robt. says to him come put on, put on, On! I am at full speed, I can go no faster, I don't know what Mr. Shackleton bought such a Beast as thee for, I would sooner walk to Provence every day than get upon thee — then they jogged on again when old Georgy broke out, now what is thou doing now setting up thy back and Shitting on the road Shit, Shit, Shit all the way, had it been once in my time I would have turned thee adrift and thou might have gone to where thou would for any thing

---

[58] i.e. the South Cave Friendly Society. (See Introduction).

[59] In the original advertisement for the vacant teaching post at the Market Cross School at South Cave in the *Hull Advertiser* on 14 Jan. 1804, it was specified that 'a Master and Mistress' were required. Ann Sharp thus held the position of mistress at the school in her own right and was not simply officiating at this occasion by virtue of being RS's wife.

[60] Bleeding was regarded as a sovereign remedy at that time. There were 3 methods in use: venesection, in which blood was drawn from a vein, usually in the arm; the application of leeches; and cupping. In this latter method a glass vessel was heated and applied to the patient's skin. As the air inside the vessel cooled, it tended to form a vacuum and exert a drawing effect on the skin which was scarified before the application of the glass to enable the blood to flow (Smith, F. B. 111).

I care about thee, Mr. Shackleton need not be afraid of me borrowing thee again thou hast given me satisfaction this time; Robt. asked him if it hotched or was uneasy, Aye I don't know that I shall get home with a whole Skin, — He had two Sticks at sitting [i.e. setting] off[:] a small switch to flag on his horse, and a strong one to walk with when he arrived at Howden, but the switch was soon worn then he had to lay on with the other, he stopped to pull a stick from a Willow tree but was deceived for the beast would not stop then when he wanted it. now I think I have said plenty on this subject.

I think there has been some alteration in a late Act in the last Sessions, respecting sending Newspapers by the Post, I think that according to an extract I saw, it will not be necessary to have a member's name on the address. You can inform yourself of this and let me know, for I do not know the title of the Act.[61] — All your Linen &c is now sent back in excellent order and likewise a small Loaf &c which we hope will come safe to hand, the Box would have been sent sooner, had it not been on Account of the death of your Grandfather,[62] who died as you have been informed on the 23d. June, in a good old age, he was a remarkably quiet and peaceable man; I cannot tell you much of his Ancestors, his Father was a Shepherd and lived at Reighton, your Grandfather had two Brothers, and some Sisters, he had one died young a favourite one, her name was Jane, the name is still dear to me as your Sister Jane was called after her, I can say no more on this head.

John Ramsdale was here one Saturday[,] he had taken the liberty of falling sick for a week, and to spend his time he came a day here, he says he does not like Hull, he likes to be amongst Horses better than in a Counting house[.] I asked him if he read much, but he said he read but little and as for writing he hated it, a pretty Article this for a Cheesemonger, but such there must be, he is a good looking lad.

I have got a pair of black breeches made out of the Trowsers you sent last, very good ones, and a Waistcoat made of one of the Coats, so that I am quite set up in this line. — The newspapers have come very regular ever since you were here excepting when you had forgot Friday one week, the paper did not arrive until Monday. — I hope you enjoy your health well, we are all well at present, I have lately suffered in Tooth Ach and pain in my mouth, but it is much better now & I hope it will continue so for the future. Who and what are the two new Sheriffs Crowther and Kelly?[63] is it Kelly the Bookseller the N.[?]

---

[61] RS was apparently referring to 6 Geo. IV, c. 68, entitled 'An Act to Regulate the Conveyance of Printed Votes and Proceedings in Parliament, and Printed Newspapers ...' 22 June 1825. It permitted franking by other 'authorised franking person[s]' as well as by MPs, but did not thereby create a precedent as the Acts of 1764 and 1802 had not restricted the privilege solely to MPs. The system of franking newspapers was widely abused and finally abolished in 1834 (Robinson 245).

[62] This was Robert's father, John Sharp. See Appendix 2 for biographical details.

[63] Elections for London sheriffs were held annually around midsummer by the common council of the Livery Companies, when the 2 candidates with the highest poll of Liverymen's votes were elected for the ensuing 12 months. In 1825 Mr. Kelly and Alderman Crowder were elected. See n.19 (1832) on the disputed legacy of Alderman Crowder (*TM* 1 July 1825, 3 c and 2 July 1825, 4 c).

man. Your Shirts all appear right as to number. All the Ginger is gone that you sent[;] it was very good. I have not heard whether T. Harper has come back or not[.] I saw his mother on Saturday and she had not then heard of him, it is a bad Speculation he has had in going to London upon expences without a situation, there are some people who think if they were at London they have nothing to do but as they like, it is best to let them try, as nothing but experience will teach some persons.

    I see the Rebellion of the Beasts[64] is published[,] there was a notice of it in the Examiner a short time ago[,] they hardly know what to make of it; have you seen it? Now I have given you a fair specimen of what you may call tittle tattle which will at least amuse you for there is not much instruction in it. I will now conclude with my best wishes for your welfare, and remain

    Your loving Father   R Sharp

[On back of sheet, reversed]: Tomorrow is Beverley Sessions, you may remember the last when we walked there and back, There are two men of North Cave to be tried for stealing Wool from Newbald. Mr. C's gamekeeper Boast is[,] or very nearly[,] implicated in the transaction as he was to have been the receiver but the two thieves one of the name of Constable & the other Moore were discovered putting it over the wall into Boast's yard, so Boast said they were stealing the Wool from him. Moore was convicted and Recd Sentence of Death some about two years since for Stealing Corn from Richd. Wilson at Ferriby, he was imprisoned one year but seems to be no Better.

[In centre]: Mr. W Sharp
           London
[In margin]: My Father July 11. 1825

[On additional sheet]: An after thought.
You said you wished I would give you my Opinion on Cobbett's rise and fall of prices,[65] I think what he says is convincing at least to me, the Pencil marks tell but little to say this a lie and the other truth is easily said but to set aside his chain of reasoning is another affair, we all know that Agricultural produce is at present at an exorbitant height compared with other countries and for what I see to the contrary the cause may be as Cobbett has stated it, but I cannot at present enter into it ...

---

[64] John Sprat, *pseud.* [i.e. James Henry Leigh Hunt], *The Rebellion of the Beasts; or, The Ass is Dead; Long Live the Ass!!!* By a late Fellow of St. John's College, Cambridge. With dedicatory epistle by John Pimlico. London: J. H. L. Hunt, 1825. Also a 2nd ed., 1825. James Leigh Hunt was the editor of the Radical anti-government newspaper, *The Examiner.*

[65] Prices were a current preoccupation of Cobbett; see, for example, *CPR* 54 xi (11 June) 1825 and 54 xii (18 June) 1825.

1825, Sept. 29th
Dear Wm.

The large Box arrived safe on the Tuesday after you had sent it all safe and in good order, the Lozenges and Tobacco are both very acceptable[.] I shall wish your health in smoking a pipe of it, but there was not the smallest token for Eliza, judge of the disappointment after loosing all the Gordian knots with which the Box was fastened when nothing appeared, I saw her brighten with pleasure when she got hold of the Blue paper containing the Ginger, to be sure it is excellent Ginger, but then it would not be very ornamental, affixed in any part of a Lady's dress, — The Rebellion of the Beasts you sent is a curious concern[,] I hardly know the drift of it. the Book of Morals daubed with Elephant's dung is a happy hit, at many explanations which priests are in the habit of making to keep up their superiority over the commonalty. I cannot as I said before make out the meaning of much of the Book, but I will read it again, — We have been dinned I know not how long with the notes of preparation for the musical festival at York,[66] all the Country has been in an uproar about it, and happy were they who could hear the foreign squallers, in a language they could not understand, but happier the squeakers when they saw the number of gulls before them so willing to part with their money, for what I question not one in a hundred knew anything about. I suppose it has been a fine time for the citizens of Old Ebor, but it is over now and Doncaster Races succeeds, the knowing ones are all talk about Memnon, Alderman, and forty more famous horses for the Saint Leger (a horse racing saint! I wonder where he lived, most likely in some stable for there his followers pay their respects to him and his ministers are no other than Jockeys and Stable Boys) I know not who has won for I never enquire after the sports of the noble vulgar [*written in margin*: I wrote this last week] ...

Old Willy Newlove asked me one day if I had ever seen a Book of Arabian nights. I told him I had; he said a Gentleman once lent him one to amuse him when he had his leg broken, he said it was the queerest Book he ever saw in his life, and he does not believe it was all true for all it belonged to a Gentleman. Such a heap of tales and never a one of them neither beginning nor end; I suppose he meant that the beginning of a Chapter did not commence with a tale. I never read the Arabian nights, for want of an opportunity, as they never fell in my way ...

Robt. Marshall has taken Richd. Kirby's farm at the Common, as Mr. Barnard wanted to raise his rent 50 pounds a year. Rd. turned stupid and would not take again so he has thrown himself out like an old fool as he is, now he repents not taking again when it is too late, as the Farm is not yet too high

---

[66] The second of a series of music festivals, held each Sept. in York, between the years 1823 and 1835 inclusively. The main concerts were held in the Minster with additional evening concerts and fashionable balls in York's Assembly Rooms. Attendance at the Minster performances totalled 20,873 with total receipts for the festival amounting to £20,876. The profit on this occasion was £1,900, this sum being equally divided among 4 hospitals: York County Hospital and the 3 general infirmaries of Leeds, Hull and Sheffield. See also n.25 (1835) (Knight 626–7).

rented; he seems to have no regard for his Family. If I were a Landlord I would raise my Farms according to the times, and not let the ignorant Rustics pocket all the profits of high prices, well may they wish for high prices when they are at low rents, there is not one amongst them all, but what would complain every rent day and oftener too, to his Landlord if prices were low. I would let no farms on long leases for these are only beneficial to the tenants, and cannot be to the Landlord; in what are called good times, the tenant pays his rent and makes a fortune out of his lease, but should the times be low he cannot fulfil his contract, then what is there for the Landlord? he may send his tenant to prison or give him a present to give up his lease and quit, it is best for a landlord to be guided by the prices of produce, at low prices he cannot get a high rent, and certainly his folly would be great to let his farms at low rents in dear times.

Mr. Bridgman's housekeeper about a fortnight ago mixed some arsenic with treacle & water, on a plate to kill flies, and set it on a table in the kitchen, when a Boy of Jas. Hunter's — about seven years old tasted some of it, which made him sick, and in spite of all that could be done to save him he died in about two or three hours from the time he took it, a Coroner's inquest was held the next day when a Verdict of accidental death was recorded.

Matthew Pickering has got licence for a public house[67] and is now fitting it up for that purpose, to the dissatisfaction of the other publicans, which he seems to think little about, the house is the one where Richd. Milner lived ... I was at West Ella on Saturday last, your Grandmother is very well: I heard Mr. Chalmers had seen you a short time ago, I am always glad to hear of any person having seen you that I know. Major Sykes[68] I am informed met with a misfortune after leaving London, having had a hole cut in his trunk and all his clothes stolen out of it. — I came home by Swanland and Ferriby, they have not yet begun to inclose the Fields, but they are partly staked out, and the work will commence it is expected before the winter[69] — N. Shaw has built a new house in Swanland field between there and West Ella.

A great deal has been said and written on contagion and noncontagion, Dr. Maclean[70] appears to be in his natural element when in a Pest house, the same as a Salamander in the fire. I have seen very little satisfactory in support of his ideas; for it is admitted by the noncontagionists that though the plague or whatever disorder that has been for ages a terror to the earth is not spread by actual contact or in wearing the apparel of the individuals who are afflicted; still the Air or Atmosphere may be in such a state that the disorder will be

[67] This was the Blacksmith's Arms of which Matthew Pickering was the landlord from 1825 until 1831 when he emigrated to America. He was succeeded as landlord by Barnard Cook. The Blacksmith's Arms was renamed the Prince Albert, the latest reference to it being in 1858.

[68] Major Richard Sykes of West Ella. (See Appendix 2).

[69] See n.24 (1826).

[70] Dr Charles Maclean (fl.1788–1824) was educated as a physician. He entered the service of the East India Company and travelled as a surgeon on voyages to Jamaica and India, where he settled for a time and made a study of fevers. In 1796 he published a dissertation on the source of epidemic diseases, in which he set out his theory that such diseases were not contagious (DNB).

rapidly spread, if not from one person to another, yet numbers will be afflicted with the same disease, How do the anti-contagionists reconcile this with their Doctrine? Upon the whole I think several disorders are contagious such as the Plague, Small Pox, and others, but my thinking so does not make them so, but how is the fact to be known whether they are or are not so?

James Levitt has been at the York musical meeting[,] he saw John Pinder there, the little fellow with a broad brim'd hat, he was at a public house with him, when the little tailor ordered a bottle of Porter with quite a London air, "bring me a bottle of Porter, and let it be mild, and let me have a Pipe and be quick" then he pulled a little Gold watch out of his waistcoat pocket to see how long the waiter would be, and at the same time to display his little watch to the Gazers who wondered to see so much trick by a little quack. — Young Teavil Leeson has been here some time[,] he is a Dandy from Dowgate[71] with a Coat neither strait nor wide[,] a sort of a Moxon Coat, which would do for an excursion to France, for it seems to have Wallet looking pockets which would be useful to stow Brandy bottles in.

I have seen Jno. Pinder since writing the above[,] he is dressed in a dark coloured Coat & Waistcoat & white Pantaloons[,] he has rather a broad brimmed hat but is very decent and becoming, he says he never met with you in London, he is for returning again he says, he has lately been working in Lombard Street[.] I think he said No. 33.

The Turks were all very glad to hear of you and desire their best respects to you, they have had 5 Servants this year not all at a time mind you, but fairly one after another, the old cry is still kept up, Servants are but little worth, and how should they be any otherways in the manner they are brought up!! There is hardly a brawl amongst them all that their mother will suffer to be contradicted, when they can scarcely walk, the dear creatures must have their own way, and when they grow up they do not forget all their masterships at home, and they are not going to submit to others, why should they! whom they have been told are no better than themselves.

Mr. Tinsdill has sent a lot of Lancets to sharpen at Millikins & Co.[72] in the Strand[,] you can send them the first opportunity, he was glad to hear you were well, he still reads Cobbett, and is a great admirer of him. I like him pretty well at times, but he is continually bawling against Bank Bills, a deal of it I hardly understand: his Gardening is amusing as well as when he gets begun to call the Broad Sheet Fellows, poor Thwaites[73] he thrums him over to some purpose, the Ass of the Morning Herald, the linen Draper fellow &c.

I have sent as under

---

[71] Dowgate, one of the 26 wards of London.

[72] Millikin and Wright, surgeons' instrument makers at 301 The Strand (Kent's *London Directory for 1826* per City of Westminster Archives Centre).

[73] Thwaites, editor of the *Morning Herald* at this period, was the subject of a fierce attack ('And now, Thwaites, late Linendraper, thou despicable Creature ...') by Cobbett for his vacillating editorial policy on the subject of the state of the national economy (*CPR* 55 x (3 Sept.) 1825, 606).

	s	d
Norwich Union .—	12	1
Lottery ——————10		6
Tinsdill Bk————2		6
£1. 5.		1

I am obliged to you for the Crusaders[,][74] I expected to read of Wars and Battles between the Lion Richard and the Saladin but instead of that the greatest business seems to have been for these two to show their respect for one another in the most friendly manner, and thus it ended and the grim figures each returned home, and not one Battle is recorded between the Christian and Infidels in the whole of the Vols.

We have sent you some fine Ribstone pippins and pears of our own growth, Old Willy gave us a few pears for you some time ago for which I thanked him kindly in your name; no box yet made for his nails all in the same disorder as usual. We are all well for which we ought to be thankful and we hope you continue the same; your Cloaths are all returned in the best manner with the Silk Handkerchief you mentioned, all inclosed in the great military Box, if the old one can be returned it will be useful.

I remn. your loving Father

R Sharp

Eliza has fallen in for some Virgin honey in the Comb which she has sent you & hopes you will like it. We shall provide some honey for you by the next time the Box comes, of a superior quality.

[In margin]: My Father. Sep 29/1825

[Listed in pencil at foot of sheet]:

4 Night Shirts
8 Shirts
36 Collars
32 Cravats
2 Pairs Drawers
4 Silk Handkerchiefs
5 Night Caps
9 Pairs Stockings

---

[74] Louisa Sidney Stanhope, *The Crusaders: an Historical Romance of the Twelfth Century*. London, 1820. – 5 vols. Although there are other works of the same title in this period, this is the only one to be published in more than one volume.

1825, Dec. 25th
So. Cave, 25th. Decr. 1825.
Dear Wm.

As we are preparing a Box with Christmas cheer for you, I shall employ myself with writing as far as I am able what may be at least amusing to you. Robt. Marshall was here last night when we had Furmity as usual, we smoked a little of the <u>fine</u> tobacco you sent and wondered how you were spending the night, but I took upon myself to say that I knew very nearly how you were engaged it being about eight O'clock I concluded that you had not then left the Shop, which was assented to as most likely. Robt. has been ill with the Quinseys in his throat, he has got better of that complaint but is still under Mr. Tinsdill's care for some imaginary complaint[;] he has had Leeches, Blisters, Pills, drenches[,] Boluses, and other articles[75] which issue from Apothecaries in pretty large quantities, he can eat well & sleep well so I think there is not much danger attending him[.] I advise him to give up all sorts of nauseous drugs, and rely on the Cookery of Sister Becky; I dined with him today out of roast Goose & Giblet Pie and for a sick man he did very well, if he had been well we should have made dreadful havoc[;] he desires his kindest respects to you. —

We have had rumours innumerable true and false respecting the Banks,[76] some people are yet fool hardy and prefer ragged paper to sterling gold, not so with me for I had some Bills by me (Robt. having paid me the money he had) I went to Beverley with them on Saturday the 17th. Decr. I had 6 five Guinea notes & 6; 5 pound notes of the East Riding Bank[77] which I presented for Cash, they rattled over some of the Old Lady's paper which I declined[,] they assured me it was good as Gold, I told them I was as well satisfied with their Bills as the Bank of England's, but says I Gold if you please for the Bills which I present, when one of the Clerks turned to Duesbery[78] one of the partners and said what must we do? give him gold, give him gold he said, so he counted out to me 61 beautiful new Sovereigns which had never been in circulation & 5s. in Silver, which settled my account with them. I then went to the other Bank with Notes of theirs amounting to £26–5s here again I was offered paper in exchange but I stood staunch for Gold and obtained it; the chinking of Sovereigns has to me a great deal more pleasing sound than the

---

[75] A drench was a medicinal drink or potion, a bolus was a large pill (*OED*).

[76] The national financial crisis of Dec. 1825 resulted in the closure of many country banks and prompted the government to ban the circulation of currency notes valued at less than £5 (Walpole ii. 190–200).

[77] The East Riding Bank (Bower, Duesbery, Hall and Thompson) in Lairgate was one of 2 banks in Beverley at that time. It was established in 1790 by Sir Christopher Sykes and partners although it was only subsequently given the name 'East Riding Bank' by which it was known for most of the 19th c. There were branches in Hull and Malton (*VCHYER* vi. 118).

[78] Thomas Duesbery was a prominent Beverley citizen who had served as an Alderman since 1800 and continued to do so until 1835. He had also been twice Mayor of Beverley in 1800/01 and 1810/11 (*VCHYER* vi. 203, 205).

rustling of Old Rags converted into paper with a promise upon it; I will make one and all of the <u>Rag-rooks</u> a promise that if I have a single pound to lay by I will not have it in any of their promises, but in the portly picture of his sacred Majesty in Sterling gold; I should have been in a fine Situation had they shut up their Rag Shops, and a fool I should have called myself if that had been the case, and what satisfaction would that have been to me? I know I was very uneasy for a few days before I got the chinking gold[.] Let those put their confidence in Banks who gain by them[,] for my part I despise their <u>accommodation</u>, how do you think they accommodate me? why by making me pay for mutton as much more nearly than it is worth, and for flour a shilling a stone more than it would be were it not for such accommodation; I hate Banks as much as Joseph Galland hates monkeys[,] he says "Curse the monkeys nasty deavils", and I say same by the banks.

I have returned the Edinburgh review[79] which you sent, I am much pleased with the Character of Milton he has often met with injustice, but here is a great deal in his favour[.] Cobbett's came safe to hand last week, I expected a little more from him than he has said on the paper system but as his last register is the 10th. he will I doubt not pay all off in his own coin he has much grounds for exultation at the present, and he is not so modest as to deny the credit which is due to him for his endeavours to blow up the thing, I expect a rattling tirade from him on the subject of issuing the small notes though I shall not be at all surprised if he praise the measure and if we are to have Bills I think we had better have the Old Lady's than any of her illegitimates; — I took ten one pound notes last Thursday which were the first I have seen, and sent them to Hull for Stamps the day after; They were dated 1821.[80]

The newspaper arrived this morning[.] I think you frequently send a Thursday paper, should it have been here yesterday? I like to have it on Sundays best, I am often out on Saturdays. It contained the Semicolon from which I infer that you are well,[81] I expect you receive the paper regular every Thursday morning; I am writing now your Mother & Eliza being at the Methodist meeting, all still about me except that it blows hard, but upon the whole it has been a very fine Christmas day, yesterday was as fine as summer. — Old Willy

[79] Founded by Francis Jeffrey (1773–1850), Henry Brougham (1778–1868) and Francis Horner (1778–1817) and initially edited by Sydney Smith (1771–1845), the *Edinburgh Review* was a combative and reformist Whig literary and political quarterly. First published in Oct. 1802, it continued until Oct. 1929. Sydney Smith was replaced as editor by Francis Jeffrey after the first issue (Watson iii. 1853–5).

[80] The accidental discovery of a large quantity of old £1 notes in the vaults of the Bank of England and their subsequent issue for country circulation had been an important factor in restoring confidence at the time of the financial panic of Dec. 1825 (Walpole ii. 193).

[81] Franked newspapers were sent free on condition that they contained no written messages. The Sharps, like many other people, contrived to circumvent this regulation by using a system of coded marks to convey pre-arranged messages. In the diary entry for 15/4/27, RS noted that newspapers were frequently examined at the General Post Office, where it was found that 8 in 100 contained messages that should have been sent by letter. Elsewhere (17/3/36) he wrote that he was not in favour of a total repeal of the tax on newspapers since he feared that such a measure would be accompanied by the imposition of postal charges on their delivery; he would prefer a reduction in the tax and 'the Paper sent free as usual'.

is very well and drives on in the Leather, nails & Blacking concern every thing disarranged as before. I generally spend an hour or two there a few nights weekly; our sittings of late have been taken up almost entirely with the money concerns of the Country, to the exclusion of Old Willy's favourite topic an Election but it will come in its turn. I saw that stupid thing called the Doncaster Gazette[82] on Saturday with the first intelligence of the death of the magnanimous Alexander,[83] I have very little doubt but he has been murdered, he happened to die as Roger Pinder said by his old horse when he shot it on purpose, well I think I shall not put on mourning for <u>Alleck</u>.

There is one pleasure in writing to you which every parent does not enjoy, and that is I have never to find fault with you nor caution you against any vicious habit so that when you read over my scrawl I hope it is with pleasure unalloyed by pain — your duty you know so well that no caution is necessary, and your letters to me are received with the greatest satisfaction, you are a source of comfort to us all, I do not know that one day passes without something being said about you. — Old Willy Stather Ambrose's great uncle is dead and has left him (excuse these nasty blots I have done it with turning over the paper.) a hundred pounds the same as his other Brothers & Sisters but nothing to his mother[.] Thos. Fisher, Ambrose's uncle is the Executor he gets the largest share; John Arton of Ellerker is lately dead. How he has left his affairs I hardly know, but it is said Watty & his mother are joint executors, and will get most of what there is, which I expect is not so much as he ought to have died worth, having had what the farmers say [is] the advantage of all the good times. Things go on with us much as usual no worse, we have bought a pig of friend Abraham the price I do not know as we never have any agreement, for he will haggle hard at making a bargain but give him his own way he will be rather below than above the common price[.]

Monday 26th Decr. 1825

Your Mother & Eliza very busy making Black puddings, Sausages &c. so that we hope you will get all in excellent order. I see Mr. Craggs has advertised for another assistant, so that the last has not been long with him, he also wants 2 or 3 apprentices in the various branches of his business.

All the mint Lozenges are gone[;] they were excellent. I have likewise used the last the Galls[84] which you sent[,] they were greatly superior to any I

---

[82] *Doncaster, Nottingham and Lincoln Gazette* (179–? – Dec. 1881). Continued as: *Doncaster Gazette*. Jan. 1882 onwards.

[83] Tsar Aleksandr I of Russia, principal architect of the Holy Alliance, died of a fever, and possibly excessive bleeding by his doctors, on 1 Dec. (18 Nov. O.S.) 1825 at Taganrog in southern Russia (*EB* i. 561).

[84] Iron-gall inks were prepared by mixing extracts of gall-nuts, bark, etc. with green vitriol. From the 16th c., recipes for the preparation of ink were given in domestic encyclopaedias. RS has numerous references elsewhere in the diary to making ink, e.g., on 17/11/26 'Made some Ink this morning, the hot weather has been against Ink, causing it to mould so much, it will be better now; besides in hot weather it evaporated and dried up very much'; also on 7/3/27 'Made some Ink of the last Galls I have left'.

ever bought here, you may send another pound when the Box comes for which I
have sent 2/6. I have sent as follows

	s	d
Mr. Tinsdill's Lancets	3	6
2 Abstracts	2	–
For Galls	2	6
	s8	0

I remn. your
　　　　　loving Father
　　　　　　　　R Sharp
[On reverse of sheet]:　　My Father
　　　　　　　　　　　Decr 25.1825

THE DIARY

Friday 19th May

Went this afternoon to measure some Land for Thos. Marshall[.] When I got there he had Flour to dress for themselves[1] to make Cheesecakes for the Fair, he says their custom is scarcely worth noticing for two reasons, the first is they never pay for what he supplies them with, and the next is they find as much fault as any other Customer; but there are two good things attending them[.] One is they take a good weight of stuff off his hands and the other it is gain livering or else he will be d—d he would not have their Custom at any rate. Wanted him to settle with me but so throng he could not get time and to convince me of it, we sat down in the Close on a Bank and talked for about two hours, but settling with friend Tom is a serious concern.

Saturday 20th May

Went down to West end this morning after paying the poor, then conversed with Old Willy awhile, Market this day in the afternoon, Robt. Marshall came up[,] I was standing at the Cross Steps, when old Kit said to Robert come wilt thou come in and taste Cheesecakes, instantly Miss Kitty squall'd out Mr. Marshall do come in and taste Cheesecakes. His answer was he had got tea and was not at present disposed, then do come on Monday morning to breakfast with us—I was there all the time but no notice taken of me or any invitation given so I said I will not stop here any longer so off I went, and this is a Lady's behaviour who aspired to more gentility than her neighbours. I did not want any thing she had even if I had nothing of my own, which no thanks to her I had, as good as hers.

Sunday 21st. May

Nothing particular this day, we have no Company for the fair so that we can enjoy ourselves in a comfortable way. Robt. Marshall & Mr. Bellard called in the Evening and smoked a pipe or two and then departed in peace.

Monday 22nd May

Cave fair day very dusty and disagreeable, Cattle sold low but there were purchasers at the prices, it seems to be the want of Rain that keeps Stock so low. Old Kit and Miss invited me in to taste their Cheesecakes, and as an inducement they said they had no company, but I recollected Saturday so did not go in, did they think I was not Company good enough for any they could command? Let them think so if they will, so do not I think.

Tuesday 23rd. May

Very dry and dusty this day, a good deal of Company in the town as usual, a great many people to tea this afternoon, Mary Ramsdale came this day from West Ella, she is the only relation we have had; this has been a very quiet fair, no fighting nor gaming going on.

---

[1] i.e. for Thomas Marshall's own immediate family.

Wednesday 24th May

At Beverley this day swearing to the Assessed tax Bills,[2] rode with Watson Arton in his Gig a very comfortable Journey. Dined at Mr. Smelt's where there were a Methodist preacher I believe, and two young Ladies from Hull, another preacher came in after dinner, and a good deal of small talk ensued[.] The last mentioned parson said Job was a heathen, I let him get to the end of his harangue, and then I asked him if he really thought Job was a heathen, "a perfect Man and upright and one that feared God and eschewed evil", Now Sir says I is this the Character of a heathen, well says he there were but two Classes of people in those days Jews and heathens, and we know Job was not a Jew therefore he was a heathen, I think Sir says I you come to your conclusion rather hastily, let me just ask you another question are you sure there were any Jews in the time that Job lived; I could not get an answer but a kind of evasion, saying had Job lived now I should have called him a Christian; I concluded by observing, that I thought he seemed a great deal more like a Christian than a heathen, and left him by observing I never heard Job called a heathen before.

Thursday 25th. May

A Balloon went up this day from Beverley,[3] it came in sight here about One O'clock it seemed not larger than a Blown bladder, I thought the first sight I had of it, that it was directly over Val. Tindle's house, I went down to the west end after it, but before I got over Mr. Bridgeman's Close I lost sight of it, I have not yet heard for certain where it alighted, Snaith is mentioned as the place, from what I have since heard I think it was considerably to the South of us in its passage over.

Friday 26th May

Mary Ramsdale went away this morning and Eliza with her, to see her Grandmother; went this forenoon to see Crows shot in the Rookery with an Air Gun[;] got eight given to me which I brought home, a Pie or two in a Season is as much as I wish for.

---

[2] RS was re-appointed annually as one of South Cave's two tax assessors throughout the period of the diary. His duties included the return of information on the assessed taxes paid by the village's inhabitants. At that time, people were subject to a very wide range of taxes on articles of consumption and manufactured goods as well as on such items as horses, carriages, and dogs. Drawing up a tax bill was no easy task as there was an elaborate scale of charges and exemptions on certain articles (Dowell iii. 155–62).

[3] This balloon was inflated by coal gas from the newly established gasworks at Beverley. An account of the flight is given in Oliver (p. 264)—'In the succeeding year, these [gas] works were appropriated to the purpose of inflating a balloon for an aeronautic expedition; and on the 25th May, 1826, Mr Brown made a splendid ascent from Mr Thompson's yard ... The balloon took a south westerly direction, and Mr Brown descended with some degree of violence on the moors between Crowle and Thorne, and received some injury in the spine. Being conveyed to the latter town he was bled, which gave him immediate relief, and he was able to proceed in a post chaise to Sheffield to fulfil another engagement of a similar nature.'

Saturday 27th May

Went this afternoon to measure some paring[4] in Weedley Warren it came on Rain. I took Shelter under a hedge for about an hour, when it became nearly fair, but such a mist that there was no seeing more than a few Yards before them so I came away again without measuring the land, which is put off to a future Opportunity, when I got below Mount Airy it was quite clear, so much difference is there between Hills and Plains.

Sunday 28th May

At Church this forenoon, no service in the afternoon, I staid at home from noon, one of my toes was rather sore & painful so staid at home to give it ease.

Monday 29th May

A very cold day, began School again this morning after Cave fair, no business doing in the Corn line, buyers are slack in bidding prices, but I don't think myself that the prices will be much lower, altho' the Farmers are very fearful.

Tuesday 30th May

Called at Old Willy's after Schooltime, he is very anxious for an Opposition for Bristol at the insuing Election, old as he is he would gladly take a Journey to that place in case of such an event. I told him I had seen in a London paper no less than five Candidates spoken of for that City which elevated him uncommonly. After this went to Brantingham and from thence to Ellerker, to collect Poor & Church sess[5] for Ellerker, Gave Mr. Todd eight pounds in part of the poor Rate, got home between nine and ten, Eliza had been out at a party at Mr. Rd. Marshall's I should have said according to Miss Kitty's phraseology Mrs. Richard. Miss Kitty was entertaining the Company with several Old Stories from the Newspapers which by some of the gapers were all swallowed as gospel.

Wednesday 31st May

Went to Weedley Warren to Measure some paring, a beautiful night, the Hills looked quite charming indeed all nature seemed to enjoy itself; it is troublesome walking up and down the Hills, spent about 3 hours, arrived at home between eight and nine, — quantity measured 18a–1r–32p.

Thursday 1st. June

After School time went to the West end and measured a small Close, which Ths. Levitt either has bought or thinks of buying, then went to Old

---

[4] The practice of paring and burning was common on the Yorkshire Wolds when old grasslands were converted to arable. A thin layer of the surface was pared off, dried and heaped up. The piles were then burned and the resultant ashes were spread upon the ground and ploughed in to enrich the soil (Strickland 201–3).

[5] The poor assessments were rates or taxes levied on property owners according to the value of their property and applied to the support of the poor of the parish. The church rate was the oldest form of local taxation in England. The sums raised were used for the upkeep of the fabric of the church and its services, and for the payment of its officials, such as the parish clerk and the sexton. RS acted as the collector of poor and church sess for both South Cave and Ellerker.

Rachel's[6] and got a pint of Ale. She is just in the same way as usual, she calls her son James as much as ever, and says he dare not go back to London, she says he has committed some crime and now lounges about here to be a burthen to her. This was the Club night which I attended, got pretty soon through the business, and at home before ten O'clock

Friday 2nd. June

A Parish meeting at the Church respecting the poor the chief consideration of which was, to make the Paupers live on the least possible allowance, I have to communicate the result on Monday morning when the poor are paid which is not a very agreeable task. One Woman on Monday last threw a Stone at me at the Cross Steps because a Shilling a week had been stopped in her pay. The Assessors wanted me to get an order for her and commit her to the house of Correction but I declined having any thing to do in that way.

Saturday 3rd June

Went down to the West end this morning, and in the afternoon I went to measure some land at Ellerker, I staid and drank tea at Mrs. Arton's, when Watty enlarged on the breed of his Bull, and how many Cows they had had the last Week, called in at Old Willy's, a person had been canvassing for Votes for Beverley for a Candidate of the name of Stewart.[7] It is a high time with those called or miscalled Freemen.[8]

Sunday 4th. June

Went to the Chapel this Forenoon there being no service of the Church until the afternoon, attended Church in the afternoon, a Stranger from Beverley preached, left Church and came home. I never go out on a Sunday after I come home but pull off my best Coat and put on another that I may not so soon Spoil it, I had forgot to say on Friday we received a parcel from William which as usual always gives me much pleasure, he wants to know how the Silk gowns look, I can say very elegant, Eliza had hers made at Hull very neat and plain[;] I do not like them very gaudy, her Mother had hers made at Cave and has it on today but not for the first time. They are both highly prized.

Monday 5th June

Wrote to Wm. this day by Wm. Purdon who with his wife are going to London: wrote Copy of the Land tax Bill[9] for Mr. Robinson, who is Agent for Mr. Duncombe for the Yorkshire election — very little done at the market this day, the farmers as usual calling the Ministers for making an inroad into the

---

[6] At that time the Bay Horse was South Cave's only licensed house in the West End; the other 4 public houses were all in the Market Place. Rachel Levitt was the landlady until her death in 1827, when she was succeeded by her son, James Levitt.

[7] John Stewart, a wealthy Tory outsider candidate, who was duly elected on 9 June (Markham (1982) 46).

[8] In the early 19th c., Beverley had one of the largest electorates in the country: about 1,300 freemen (including non-residents) had the right to vote out of a population of 5,401 in 1801 (Markham (1982) 10).

[9] The Land Tax was a fixed tax on land and property. Over 90 people paid the tax in South Cave at this time. The bill was being used, in this case, as a record of who held the franchise.

Corn laws[10] which they look upon as their <u>vested</u> rights, filled up the returns of expences of the Poor for the last year to send to the House of Commons.[11]

Tuesday 6th June

It is distressing to think of the sufferings of the Manufacturers, there is no doubt but in general when their wages are good they are very improvident, Can nothing be done to free them from the thraldom in which they are bound by this abominable Cotton? There is now no domestic manufacture of Linen carried on as there was since I recollect, formerly every Woman, at least all housekeepers span their own Linen[,] there was then a Weaver in almost every Village, and a high day it was when a good web was brought home, — but now if you find a weaver in the Country he must buy his Yarn spun by machinery, as there are no spinners left in the Country; the good Women say they can buy Cloth much cheaper than they can spin, but they forget that one of the former home spun Shirts would wear three of these machine Articles, Idleness has had a great share in putting a stop to spinning in Farm houses & Cottages.

Wednesday 7th June

At west end this evening, Robt. Marshall out with John Stather who is canvassing the Freeholders for Mr. Bethell;[12] I hope he will be successful, altho' I rather fear it; after that went to Old Willy's. He is going off to Beverley in the morning the day of Election being fixed for Friday, he has not yet promised his Vote. I hear there is a great stir at Hull made by an Irishman of the Name of O'Neil[13] who is a candidate, I hope they will send the fellow back instead of into the house of Commons. What is known of him! Why nothing, it is said Mr. Sykes has been waited upon to offer himself, but he ought not to be waited on, they ought to elect him without either expence or ceremony.

Thursday 8th. June

Nothing talked about but the Election, the enquiry amongst the Freeholders for the County is not who is the most suitable man but who will pay them best for their Journey to York, I wish they may not get Sixpence, but let them stay at home, and others Vote who stand more on principle than profit.

---

[10] In May, when there were riots as a result of a combination of a depression in the manufacturing districts and the highest prices for wheat since 1819, the government had allowed about 300,000 quarters of bonded foreign wheat to be released onto the home market. Further quantities of grain were authorized to be imported in case of need, and subsequently about 500,000 quarters were actually brought into the country and sold duty free (Walpole ii. 208–9).

[11] Alarmed by the rise in parochial expenditure on the poor, the government now required regular returns to be made by the overseers, on whose behalf RS was acting.

[12] Richard Bethell (1772–1864) was a member of a local landowning family, active in politics, whose seat was at Rise in Holderness. He held the office of High Sheriff in 1822 and was for many years chairman of the Riding Quarter Sessions. Although declining the poll at York in 1826, he served as a liberal Tory in the Reform Parliament of 1830–1 and represented the East Riding as one of its MPs from 1832 to 1841 (Ward 39).

[13] Augustus John O'Neill was a government supporter and advocate of free trade and a modification of the Corn Laws but an opponent of Catholic Emancipation. He was returned as Member for Hull together with Daniel Sykes in the 1826 election but did not stand for re-election at the general election of 1830 (*VCHYER* i. 206).

Friday 9th June

Election at Beverley and Hull this day, there are two new Members returned for Beverley, I believe both Tories, poor Wharton[14] the old member who has served them for 38 years has been compelled to retire after having spent an immense fortune amongst the worthless <u>Freemen</u>. Heard this night by the Carrier that the Irishman at Hull carries it with an high hand, he has all the Ragamuffins on his side[.] Mr Sykes stood second and the Courtly Villiers[15] last on the poll, may he remain there is my wish.

Saturday 10th. June

An idle day with me this, in the forenoon wrote a letter for Wm. Cousens to Manchester inclosing his half year's Rent, most of the afternoon at Tommy Pinder's he being getting in a Hogshead[16] of Sugar, no certain account of the Election at Hull.

Sunday 11th. June

Heard this morning that the Election at Hull had closed[,] the Irishman and Mr. Sykes being the successful Candidates. I am sorry that Mr. Sykes is not first in the poll, he ought to have been so, if the <u>jolterheads</u> had the least spark of Gratitude left in them, but it seems they had not; he is not only a useful member for the Town of Hull but valuable to the whole Country. Saw Old Willy today after his Journey to the Election at Beverley, he is in hopes of being called to Bristol but as far as I see his presence may be dispensed with.

Monday 12th. June

A very hot Day yesterday, the whole talk at the market was respecting the Corn laws, the Farmers say it will be the <u>ruination</u> of England if Prices are not kept up, then a little bit of Pity for their dear generous Landlords who have racked them up so high, that they seem proud of their Situation; for my own part I do not think it will benefit the manufacturers, or distress the Agriculturists in any great degree, to admit Foreign Corn with what is called a protecting duty, but that is the place where the rub lies to know what will protect one Class and not injure another. I think 12s. – pr. Quarter duty on Wheat quite high enough but others think differently.

Tuesday 13th. June

Almost overset with heat this day, Old Willy wants sadly to be off to Bristol but to his grief he sees nothing in the Paper of any Opposition going on there, I believe he has promised one Vote for the County of York for Mr. Bethell. A few mornings ago I am informed the following was put up on

---

[14] John Wharton, a Whig with radical views from a minor county family of Skelton Castle (Yorks., N.R.) served as MP for Beverley from 1790 to 1796 and from 1802 to 1826 (*VCHYER* vi. 127 and 129–30).

[15] Charles Pelham Villiers (1802–98), later to become MP for Wolverhampton and a leading advocate of free trade, was the nephew of the Earl Clarendon and brother of the Hedon parliamentary candidate, Thomas Hyde Villiers (DNB).

[16] A cask of capacity varying according to commodity and locality, but in the case of sugar at this period probably amounting to between 14 and 18 cwt (*OED*).

Kemp's Shop Window, he being rather in the same way as I am myself, not liking to get up very soon in the morning

> Friends and neighbours do not weep,
>
> He is not dead but fast asleep,
>
> He's neither broke nor run away,
>
> He'll open out sometime to day.

Whether the above be a genuine Cave production or not I can not say, but I think I could make him something as good in the same line if he would put it up, and here it is

> Friends and neighbours you may weep
>
> While I enjoy myself in Sleep,
>
> And if I break or run away,
>
> Not one of you my Debts will pay!!

So much for Robt. Kemp commonly called the Lantern maker.

Wednesday 14 June

Heard from Wm. He had seen Wm. Purdon & Wife and had furnished them with a picture of London, which I expect would not be of much use to the Man of Broomfleet. — heard by the Carrier that the Popularity of the Irishman has much diminished at Hull since Friday last, there was preparations making on Tuesday for burning him in Effigy, Scarcely an Orange Ribbon[17] last week could be suffered, now it is Sykes and Orange for ever, I am very glad that the fools have been so finely taken in.

Thursday 15th. June

... At Barnard Cook's this Evening posting up the Accounts in the Highway Book,[18] young Barnard as drunk and wise as ever, the more liquor he has in him, he appears to think the more wisdom, he has a strange Sottish look, and nearly all shrunk away.

Friday 16th June

Recd. a small parcel this morning by Wm. Purdon which gave me great pleasure. Went to the West end this Evening got a Glass of Whiskey with Mr. Shackleton, I am not very fond of it.

Saturday 17th. June

Went this morning to measure a Close for Robt. Marshall at the Common, after that went round his Closes with him to look at his Stock, this is the first day I have seen any Wheat shot, in all probability this will be a forward Wheat harvest. Rain is very much wanted[,] the Summer pastures all look of a Russet

---

[17] Political party colours, as used in the East Riding, varied to some extent according to locality. Orange normally denoted the Whig and Radical interest. In most parts of the East Riding, blue was adopted by the Tory candidates and their supporters; however in Hedon (and later in the century, probably from the mid-1830s, in Beverley) their chosen colour was crimson. Pink was occasionally used by candidates in Beverley who wished to emphasize their independent and moderate stance (Markham (1982) 24).

[18] Under the Highway Act of 1555, every parish was responsible for the state of its own roads. In South Cave, 2 highways surveyors were appointed annually in October and a rate was levied for the upkeep of the highways in the coming year. Throughout the period of the diary, RS balanced the highway accounts on behalf of the surveyors of South Cave and sometimes of Ellerker, too, and often collected the highway 'sess' on their behalf.

Colour; dined with Robt. Marshall, and in the afternoon drank tea at T. Pinder's.

Sunday 18th. June

Recd. 2 papers from Wm. this morning. I am glad to see that Waithman and Wood have been successful at London. Cobbett I see has lost his Election at Preston (in the Hull advertiser) I should have liked to have seen him in Parliament. Mr. Bethell has declined contesting Yorkshire, but [it] is thought that his friends will yet bring him forward. Papers have been stuck up this morning to that effect. Mr. Robinson the Agent for the Tory candidates Duncombe and Wilson[19] has likewise been posting up Papers in their behalf, it will be a complete farce to return 2 Whigs & two Tories, as their Votes will neutralize each other and Yorkshire the largest County in England, will appear as though it had not a single Vote in the House of Commons.

Robt. Marshall came up in the Evening and smoked a pipe of London tobacco.

Monday 19th. June

Sent a newspaper[,] the Globe & traveller[,][20] to my Brother at Skipton, only very poorly this day, but better towards night. Farmers this day at market talking about sowing turnips, many of them enquiring the price of Bones for manure,[21] but all agreeing they need not sow until rain comes, still they are preparing and some of them sowing every day!!

Tuesday 20th. June

I think there is not a more uncomfortable thing (at least to me) to see a person lolling about in a Chair, spending his time with nothing, never looking at a Book, for my part sooner than be debarred from reading, I would suffer the odious punishment of the tread Mill. Great anxiety about the County Election tomorrow, two Steam Packets are engaged for Milton & Marshall[22] from Hull to York, one of which went this day, and took in Voters from Blacktoft.

Wednesday 21st. June

After School time went to Weedley to measure some land paring 15a–3r–18p and Swarth[23] 13a–2r–21p. there was a Quantity of Whins in the Close with which I always feel pleased, they shew something of the state of Land when the

---

[19] The Tory candidates for the Yorkshire election, named by RS, were Richard Fountayne Wilson and William Duncombe; the other candidates were John Marshall, Richard Bethell and Lord Milton. However, Richard Bethell, a supporter of Catholic Emancipation, subsequently withdrew from the contest before polling took place. Since Yorkshire returned 4 members, from 1826, the remaining 4 candidates were automatically elected (Markham (1982) 43).

[20] See n.108 (1827).

[21] Sir Tatton Sykes of Sledmere claimed to have been 'one of the first persons' on the Yorkshire Wolds to have used bones as field manure, *c*. 1810. By the 1820s the practice was spreading rapidly throughout East Yorkshire (Harris 8–11).

[22] Viscount Milton and John Marshall were returned as MPs for Yorkshire together with Richard Wilson and William Duncombe. Milton had previously been a successful candidate in the elections of 1807, 1812, 1818, and 1820 when Yorkshire was represented by only 2 members. John Marshall was a prominent Leeds merchant, a Whig and a Unitarian (Markham (1982) 8 and 43).

[23] A synonym for 'sward', meaning the grassy surface or sod of pasture or grassland (*OED*).

commons were open and the poor were indulged, nay had the right to procure them for firing. I seemed while among the fine yellow King Cups to be in some superior Climate, but on coming back again I soon found myself in the Chalk road enveloped with dust, and here I cannot but observe how careful the makers of Roads have been to exclude the Pedestrians from the smallest comfort as no footpaths are thrown up for their accommodation, they must plod on in Summer amidst dust and in Winter nearly stick fast in puddle. — Bought a Set of China 1 Doz. Cups, 1 Doz. Saucers[,] Teapot, a milk Jug[,] 2 Basons and 2 Plates, double gilt edged all for 12 Shillings; but as we neither want them nor have any place to put them in for display, we have packed them in a Basket and put them in the Garrett Closet, if this be not encouraging manufacturers I know not what is!!

Thursday 22nd. June

Very dry yet, at West end this Evening. Robt. Marshall gone to Mr. <u>Wad's</u> Clipping, I suppose condoling with one another on the low price of Wool, about 9d. or 10d. pr. lb. Last year it was about 16d. but the prices not suiting some of the wise ones, they have their last year's Stock in hand, this is the beauty of Speculation, selling for little more than half price and being out of their money all the time. The last time I was at Ferriby I saw what may be called the first fruits of an Inclosure,[24] viz. a Board put up with notice that any person trespassing on the land would be prosecuted. No walking in the field now without danger of the tread mill, nothing now but dust to gratify the weary traveller.

Friday 23rd. June

This sort of Journalizing suits very well for any who cannot continue a narrative; as the writer is tied [to] no subject he may be concise as he pleases one day on a subject, then he may spin out another amazingly for his amusement another day; I had often wondered why Diaries were written, but it seems the persons wanted to appear as something and did not know how to proceed: <u>of course I disclaim all this.</u>

Saturday 24th. June

Went to Broomfleet this morning to measure some land belonging Mr. Briggs which Wm. Purdon farms. Pasture 6a–1r–20p. Meadow 11a–2r–33p. on the Humber side, the river is encroaching greatly on the land, some years ago the last mentioned Close contained more than 14 Acres. Dined with Wm. Purdon, then walked back, a very sultry day, called at Robt. Marshall's and drank tea, after which he came up and got a pipe with me. One of my toes very much blistered with my walk, and another blister in the bottom of the same foot, very painful, the roads are all like unslacked lime. Mr. Bethell did not come forward on the day of Election at York, to the great disappointment of many who intended to sell themselves, to the highest bidder for their <u>independent</u> Votes.

[24] North Ferriby, with Swanland, Kirk Ella, West Ella and Willerby, was enclosed under an Act of 1824, although the award was not signed until 1837 (Crowther (1983) 91).

Sunday 25th June

Not out this morning my foot being very sore, and there is no Service at Church this forenoon, so I was the Housekeeper. Eliza is out at Hotham[,] she went yesterday. We had some new Potatoes this day to dinner for the first time this season, We had Green Pease the last Sunday, for all the weather is so dry and scorching Pease appear very plentiful. I believe wheat in general looks well but spring Corn viz. Barley and Oats are very short on the Ground, the farmers complain that there will be very little either Hay or Straw except Rain come very shortly; Our young Cat stole a piece of Veal this morning and made her escape with it into the Old Cardinal's Garden, she has not been suffered to come into the house all day, she has the Character of being a great thief which she seems to think little about.

Monday 26th June

All the talk this day at Market of the scarcity of Water, in some places Cattle are to drive for Miles to Water, it really is uncommonly dry, and the Sky for many days has not shewn a single Cloud, nothing but a wide expanse of Blue, clear as an Italian Sky. Sent to the Stamp office at Hull by the Carrier £107–5–0. People drink this weather to cool themselves, which I believe has rather the contrary effect, as it serves to inflame, rather than cool.

Tuesday 27th. June

A man going about with advertisements this morning for a new Guide & Directory for Hull, the price to be 5s/6d published by William White & Co.[25] but I do not know who they are. I shall not subscribe for it. A Thunder storm came on this Evening about 6 O'clock and the Rain poured down for about half an hour, which will be a great relief for the Country. Recd. a Rect. for the Money I sent yesterday to the Stamp Office.

Wednesday 28th. June

A very sultry hot day, a few Drops of Rain at times, a heavy shower at the Common about eleven O'clock, a fine time now for Sowing turnips. At west end in the evening, our friends sorry to hear that the market at London on Monday last was 2s. pr. quarter lower for wheat; it cannot rise before harvest except a very wet unfavourable season takes place; Settled with Ths. Fisher for the Constable Accounts[26] for the last three months.

Thursday 29th. June

Isaac Wilson in his paper of the 16th. inst. said that the Poll was settled at Preston and Cobbett thrown out, but it appears the contest is still continued, but without any probability of his being returned. I think the accounts of the contest was all very garbled, it is said that Cobbett is a great blackguard, but it appears he has fallen into company with greater blackguards than himself, then there is

[25] *The Directory, Guide and Annals of Kingston-Upon-Hull and the Parish of Sculcoates ... together with Neighbouring Towns and Villages in Lincolnshire and Yorkshire.* Leeds: William White and Co., 1826.

[26] By an Act of 1662 (14 & 15 Chas. II c. 12), the village constable was empowered to levy a local rate to meet the expenses arising from his duties, which included collecting the county rate and apprehending malefactors.

no want of money to Crush him, — Hunt conducts himself with great self possession in Somersetshire, but he will not be able to sit in Sir Thomas' Leather breeches, indeed it seems hopeless to continue the contest any longer, but he is not the man to be daunted with trifles.

Friday 30th. June

I got up sooner this morning by an hour than I expected, so set to work and entered a Rate in the poor book, which wanted doing, after that put in all the disbursements up to Monday last. I never like to be much in arrears with the Accounts, as they are best to manage when not run a great length; — Re[ceive]d. a parcel from Wm. this night by the Carrier, containing two of Cobbett's & a Court Calendar, I am glad to hear he is well, I expected that Cobbett's conduct at Preston had been blackened to the utmost, I should have liked to have seen him in Parliament, but that is over ...

Sunday 2nd. July

At Church this morning Mr. Boyce of Beverley[27] preached a decent Sermon, on the meetness of the Saints for heaven, he is a very indifferent reader. I have observed this Election that the Candidates who have the least number of Votes, are generally the most confident of succeeding, but I think Mr. Turk's advice to his Son Willy, when he asked him how he must ride his Galloway once at the Race at Cave fair, is the better plan to proceed upon[,] he said get first and keep first and then you will be sure to win. — I think Mr. Brougham has very little chance of being returned for Westmoreland. Cobbett I see is out of Preston as I expected, he did not it appears give them a parting Speech, it is rumoured that the Election at Beverley will be petitioned against.

Monday 3rd. July

Thos. Fisher got struck with a horse this forenoon, on the upper part of his Cheek, near his eye. I went in to see him[,] he was in bed and looked very ill, but I understand from Mr. Tinsdill he is not in immediate danger. This is the beginning of the Dog days I have been told, when misfortunes are always prominent, for this I cannot vouch, but this warm weather has certainly an effect in making Animals very restless, being so much pestered with Flies and Insects.

Tuesday 4th. July

Mr. Ed. Barnard the Vicar called this day, with his new Curate, he is Son to the Postmaster at Hull. Mr. Barnard the Esquire met Matthew Smith today, and said well Cooper here is very hot weather, O yes Sir very, I have just been begging a drink of one of your tenants, well how much did you get, I don't know Sir exactly they brought it in a Tin perhaps most of a Quart[,] well and did you drink it all? O yes Sir! this dry weather nearly chokes me, well I suppose you like Liquor, O no Sir no Liquor, a Sup of Ale for me; well what you will[,] call at Mr. Cousen's and get a pint or two more, I don't know Sir, but I think I shall, ah well I thought you would, — I return you thanks Sir for the very great honour you have done me, well what is that Matthew? Oh just in

---

[27] i.e. Revd Henry Boyce of Beverley.

employing me to work for you once <u>more again</u> just once <u>more again</u>, I look upon it as an honour to work for you Sir, bless you Sir I work for most of the Gentlemen round and now once <u>more again</u> for you.

Wednesday 5th. July

London must be the headquarters of Iniquity as well as law[,] not a paper but some depredation is announced, all sorts of Schemes the rogues have in practice, to live in Idleness, scarcely any company exempt from their depredations. I see by the Times of Saturday last that Hunt retired from the Contest very cleverly by making Dickinson a present of one of his best bottles of blacking which he told him he might split with Sir Thomas; Dickinson almost redeemed all his former behaviour by his manner of receiving it, but Sir Thomas stood "Fool confess'd". — This is Beverley Fair day[,][28] many people have gone to it from this place, some I dare say that have no more business there than I have, and that is none at all. I see a Review of Moxon's Book[29] in the Imperial Mag. for July, it is very fair I think.

Thursday 6th. July

Went to see Thos. Fisher, he is confined to his Bed, and does not know whether he will lose the sight of one eye or not, at present he cannot open it, he seems very weak, and the weather being so hot is much against him. This is the Club night, paid for Wm. Richardson's[30] funeral 12 pounds, he died in York Castle. This was the man on whose account Mr. Hume presented a petition in the House of Commons. The Child that was confined with him is liberated and I believe is now at Everthorpe, Richardson was father in law to the Boy. the man is now safely out of the way of all contempt of the Court of Chancery, and free from John Doe and Richard Roe.

Friday 7th July

Bought 2 Doz. Lead pencils of a German Jew who came about this day, he likewise gave me a receipt to make Ink powder which perhaps at some time I may try, he had some with him in Bottles, which he mixed with water, and then it was fit for immediate use, but I do not know whether it can be relied on or not; Spent most of this Evening at Mr. Atkinson's when the Old Gentleman said the County of Sussex joined Essex, I told him it was South of the Thames, on the Sea Coast adjoining Kent, but I could not persuade him that it was so, and as he has been a traveller he thinks he knows better than his neighbours,

---

[28] At this time Beverley had 4 fairs a year: on the Thursday before old Valentine's day (i.e. 25 Feb.), Holy Thursday, 5 July, and 5 Nov. They were known respectively as Candlemas, Holy Thursday or May Day, Midsummer, and Ringing Day Fairs. All were for horses and cattle but the last 2 also included pleasure fairs (Oliver 286; *VCHYER* vi. 222–3).

[29] Edward Moxon, *The Prospect and other Poems*. London, 1826. See also n.42 (1831).

[30] William Richardson had fallen foul of the law in a dispute over a life interest of £700 that had led to the filing of a bill in Chancery which, because of his ignorance of the proceedings, he had failed to answer and was as a result committed to York Castle for contempt. On his death, he left an orphan child in the prison which was subsequently taken care of by some 'professional gentlemen in this place [i.e. Hull]', according to the editor of the *Hull Packet* (*HP* 6 June 1826).

but I think I know the local situation of most Counties, as well as many people and certainly better than some, this is a proof of it.

Saturday 8th. July

A rather gloomy morning, rain anxiously looked for, it had been a fine rain yesterday at Hull for about two hours, it came as near to us as Riplingham, but we had only a few drops; Robt. Marshall turned his Cattle into 16 acres of meadow yesterday, as the pastures are so bad and the meadow scarcely worth mowing, Hay is selling at very high prices and it is very likely that Fodder will be found very scarce in the Winter as there will be very little straw.

Sunday 9th. July

The new Curate[31] preached this morning at the Church, and read prayers in the afternoon, he appeared rather timid, I think his voice not very good, but only hearing him once, I can hardly form an opinion, he appears a good natured young man, and if he conduct himself in a becoming way, he may meet with encouragement. — I was very poorly on Friday evening whether it proceeded from the hot weather or no I cannot say, but after a night's rest I was better in the morning, we are obliged to have all Doors and Windows open to catch a little Air when we can.

Monday 10th. July

A Great falling off in the Revenue this Quarter, the greatest deficiency appears in the Stamps. I can only say on my own account that, I never had a better Quarter, it averaged £100. This at 2 pr. Cent is something. It keeps very dry yet here, at Cottingham last night there was a heavy rain; it is indeed a critical time especially for Turnips, should the weather continue dry there will be no Turnips of any account here, nothing done in the Corn line this day, all the enquiry is for old beans, they are nearly the price of Wheat, which cannot hold long, Wheat must of necessity maintain the highest price. Old John Pawson called upon me to lectrify (rectify) his accounts[.] I told him I would lectrify all next week, Oh very well then I will try to put off till then.

Tuesday 11th. July

A Water Jury[32] Supper this Evening at Wm. Cousens'[,] there were ten supped[.] As Thos. Fisher who is the Constable is so ill I had to act for him, all very comfortable. I came home a little after ten O'clock, — Mr. Atkinson at Hull this day, no rain yet, but I believe there are places worse off than we are for Water; as the Beck still continues to run with a small stream and the Wells in general hold out yet. Geo. Hodgson of Ellerker says he does not care what sort of Laws the Parliament makes if they only do not make an Act to compel him to work!

---

[31] John Rodmell, curate at South Cave from 1826 until 1834 (See Appendix 2).

[32] Commissioners of Sewers had been established for marshland areas as early as the 16th c. The Commissioners, who were appointed from local landowners, were assisted by juries of 24 men for each division. It was the juries' task to inspect drains and banks and report on any deficiencies. In South Cave, RS wrote out lists of pains (penalties) and carried out other clerkly duties for the juries.

Wednesday 12th. July

Went down to the West end this night and took a walk in the Moors with Robt. Marshall, he had been ploughing up part of his Swede Turnips he had sown, and sowing afresh with white Turnips.

Thursday 13th. July

This is the Club feast day, it rained uncommonly fast in the forenoon[.] Wm. Cousens had a Booth fixed in the Yard for the Members to dine under, the Rain quickly found a passage through, it became fair weather before noon, and we had a comfortable dinner it came on to rain very fast about four O'clock but as the Dinner was over it was not of so much consequence, it has indeed been a fine Rain, which was very much wanted. Robt. Marshall's house was broken into last night and a Flitch of Bacon, two pair of Shoes 2 good Shirts, a new Hat and other things stolen out, the Robbers had taken the Bacon out of the Chamber where his men sleep. The house was entered by the Parlour Window, it having been left unfastened. Went to Timothy Dunn's this Evening to witness the Signatures of himself and wife, for some Property sold by her at Bridlington Quay.

Friday 14th. July

Robt. Marshall says the thieves who broke into his house have used him very badly, he will be obliged to have another pair of new Shoes & a Hat, he says he will buy a Gun and have it charged and if he sees any persons at an unreasonable time about his premises he will fire at them. — Received a Box from William this Evening quite glad to hear that he is well. Robt. Marshall was here when the Box came and is happy to hear that he is still remembered by him, Wm. I am to mind and not forget to give his best respects to Wm. when I write, and mind to tell him of the disaster he has undergone. The mint drops are excellent.

Saturday 15th. July

This is Saint Swithin's Day which has not passed over without Rain, but what influence the weeping Saint can have on the weather I am at a loss to determine. Bought two small Hams this Day one of which is intended to be sent to Wm. Called to enquire after Thos. Fisher, he is much better, but it is feared his eye will be lost, he cannot move the lid without help, it is indeed a serious accident. — Cobbett seems in excellent Spirits after his defeat at Preston, as to the Times and him, they are a good deal like Thos. Marshall and Richard Kirby, they always quarrel between themselves when there is none other to vent their rage upon. I do not exactly know what harm the South American loan[33] can do to the people of this Country collectively, without doubt individuals will suffer, if I had bought a Bond of £100 pounds which should turn out to be of

---

[33] This was the Colombian Loan, one of a number of foreign loans (see *CPR* of 12 Aug. 1826 for details) at this period which were funded by bondholders. Owing to the unstable political conditions prevailing among the South American republics at this time and partly as a result of its unsound financial policy, the Colombian government, despite strenuous efforts, found itself unable to pay out any of the dividends on the loan which were due to the bondholders (*AR* 1826, Hist. 402–6).

little value it is certainly a loss to me, but to the Nation at large it is a matter of no moment.

Sunday 16th. July

A Dull gloomy morning it had been a little rain in the night time[.] I took my Umbrella with me, but before noon it cleared up and became very fine. I heard the shortest Sermon I think I have heard preached[,] it was rather under a quarter of an hour, I saw a piece in the times headed "Poor old Cobbett" where it seems to be insinuated that he has not spent all the money which he has given an account of, I suppose he will be in a short time falling foul of the "Bloody old Times".

Monday 17th. July

Barnard Cook began harvest this day by cutting some Wheat at Ryeland hills. There has been more Wheat offered for Sale this day than for any one Market day these three months past. It is rather a falling article and when that is the case there are always most sellers, there is still great fears of Turnips not growing, the flies are so destructive to the plants which make their appearance. Very warm and dry again but not so much so, as it was a little time since ...

Wednesday 19th July

... It has been rather a dull day but no rain. Ringing this night at the Church, it being the King's Coronation day.[34]

Thursday 20th July

A Drizzly day this but very little rain fallen. Heard this day that Mr. Miles (who married a Sister of Old George Grayson) is dead by a fall from his horse which kicked him when down. I was well acquainted with him a very steady serious man, he was a Farmer at Bessingby near Burlington,[35] a particular acquaintance of Daniel Porters — But as <u>Will</u> says

No medicine in the world can do thee good,

In thee there is not half an hour of life.[36]

Friday 21st. July

A rainy night last night, a fine clear morning this, wrote letters to Mr. Croft and both Mr. Barnard's for Barnard Cook to let them know he was authorized by the General Post Office to charge 2 Guineas a year for their private letter Bags.

Saturday 22d. July

At Ellerker this afternoon getting ripe Berries & Tea at Mrs. Arton's. I think I eat more than agreed with me, when I got home at night my Brother had arrived at Cave, he is very well, he had been at Hull & West Ella, all the week. My mother has been very poorly in her leg but is now better again. My Brother

---

[34] i.e. the anniversary of King George IV's coronation. He had succeeded to the throne in 1820 and was ceremonially crowned in 1821.

[35] An old form of the name of Bridlington.

[36] Quotation from *Hamlet, Prince of Denmark*, act 5, scene 2.

had been at the ordination of the Chapel Minister at Swanland[37] on Wednesday last.

Sunday 23d. July

At Church this morning heard a Sermon of about the same length as last Sunday viz. about a quarter of an hour. My Brother preached in the Evening at the Chapel[,][38] it is many years since he preached here before, his text was the 5th. Chapter John 28th. & 29th. verses, he exerted himself a good deal and preached about an hour[.] We went to Mr. Turk's after the Service and staid a short time. I was not very well this Evening, not disposed for any Supper.

Monday 24th. July

Felt very well this morning having had a good night's rest, I am afraid the distress of the Country is not yet at its height, the Farmers cannot bear the thought of this country ever importing corn from abroad, and here the Simpletons think it will be so much against their interest, then they begin to sympathize with the Government, and cry out how are the Taxes to be paid if Agriculture be depressed? They take the merit of the Land paying all the Taxes[.] I only wish the "Life and Fortune Gentry had all to pay" they deserve to suffer, for they were the greatest zealots for a furious and destructive war when they found they could double their Rents, I do not know one of them who has paid Sixpence more in taxes than he was compelled to pay.

Tuesday 25th. July

My Brother went away this morning after Breakfast for West Ella, a very fine morning. Harvest pretty generally begun I believe, Wheat appears a fine Crop, I hope favourable weather will be afforded for gathering it in good order. It appears very dull when a Friend goes away after staying with one a short time, there is the pleasure of meeting, but the pain of parting, yet it is so ordered in this world that in most cases the dearest relations must for the most part live in a state of separation. Mr. Tinsdill has had plans drawn to build a new house, he having bought the house of Parson Brown's at the top end of the Market place next to G. Holborn's, but I think he will not build this Summer. I understand the estimates of the Builders are much higher than the Architect would undertake the building for. James Levitt & James Milner made the estimates,—Entered a Church Rate in the Book this evening not having gone out from home at all.

Wednesday 26th. July

The Times recd. this morning gives an account of the Printing trade being in a very depressed state at present, I hope it will quickly revive. I think Cobbett has committed himself dreadfully in recommending the People about Manchester not to meet unarmed, this advice must tell against him for where

[37] The new minister was John Hayden from Homerton College. His induction service as pastor of Swanland Independent Chapel took place on 19 July 1826 and was attended by numerous local Yorkshire Congregational ministers. He stayed at Swanland for 8 years before moving to High Wycombe, where he remained as the local minister for 34 years (Patton 38–9).

[38] The Independent (Congregational) Chapel, which had been built in the West End by 1730 and remained in use until it was replaced in 1873 (Neave (1984) 48).

multitudes meet and have the means of offence or resistance in their power, the consequences may be fatal. I think therefore the advice given is not good. I wish there was no occasion for meeting about starvation, but that everything would go on prosperously, there is no method of relieving the starving population but by Government advancing money to find them some kind of employment, voluntary Contributions are not calculated to remedy the want of employment, indeed relief without employment cannot answer. — Recd. this morning a small parcel from Wm. I think Cobbett's greatest antipathy at present is against the Morning herald, though Anna Brodie, & Dr. Black[39] come in for their share of his abuse. He still recommends the hoarding of Gold, it is indeed much better than having beggarly notes of no value but the promise, which hundreds lately have found to be but of small value. — Wrote a letter this Evening for Thos. Thompson South Wold Ellerker to a relation at Turnham Green respecting some money in the Funds. At west end this Evening smoked a pipe with Robt. Marshall, then went to Mr. Shackleton's and staid about an hour, getting him to sign a Paper for the Composition of his Taxes.

Thursday 27th. July

The weather is very dry again. Mr. King's are leading Wheat today, I think they are too soon with it, as they only began to cut it on Monday last, it often happens that Corn is got in worse condition in fine Weather, than when it is more precarious, as it is often too much hurried in a fine Season. Barnard Cook is likewise leading Wheat this day. Billy Kirby says Oh what a Sermon your Brother preached, there was no botheration nor belch about it, it was as easy to understand as A.B.C. now here is a point in this, for Billy cannot read, and how easy A.B.C. may be to him I cannot say!!

I see the account is contradicted that Walter Scott has been appointed the King's printer, the Newspapers contradict one day what they have confidently asserted the day before, it appears as the Poet says that truth lays deep, even in a Well, and is not easily drawn out.

As this is the last day I can journalize or Diarify on this Sheet I must draw to a conclusion. — Work is very little in demand and at low prices, Some of the greasy butcher's want to raise the price of Mutton, even if Sheep were as cheap as they were in old Will's time, when he says

"A Score of good ewes may be worth two pounds."[40]

I hope the price of Provisions will be kept low, otherwise we may expect to hear of dreadful doings, may the Lord in his mercy keep the Population of this Country from being dependent on the Lords of the Soil or their Vassals — called Farmers for their tender mercies would be cruel. The great overgrown Farmers are an abomination in the earth, if it depended on them we should be racked up in the prices more than their Landlords rack them in their rents, but

[39] Anna Brodie was the wife of Alexander Brodie, D.D., and the daughter of the proprietor, John Walter I. Although Cobbett sometimes attacked her specifically, he also seems to have used her name eponymously when referring to *The Times* in a more general way. John Black was editor of the London *Morning Chronicle*, 1819–43.

[40] Quotation from *Second Part of King Henry IV*, act 3, scene 2.

by the wise laws of Providence there are always some and they a great number that must of necessity bring their Articles to Market in a regular way.

Friday 28th July

Sent by the Carrier this morning Wm.'s Box for London, I hope it will arrive safe, and the Contents gratify him. I thought I heard Footsteps on the Stairs this morning about Sunrise. I got up and looked about but all was safe and quiet, I suppose I had been awaked rather suddenly by some noise in Cousen's Yard as it is the morning he goes to Hull.

Saturday 29th. July

Every one busy with Harvest, met with Thos. Marshall this morning so busy that he could not spend a single minute about paying any money, but I kept him talking about 2 hours sometimes astride of his old Horse and sometimes down. Mr. Barnard came past as we were talking, and said Well Thomas what you ride with a halter, Why yes Sir, I don't like bridles much for a halter is useful to hang a horse to a Gate or ought of that Sort. Tom has a man left him because he was called pretty well now and then by his master, but honest Tom says he cannot call the Numbhead half enough with the words in the English language[,] there are not letters sufficient to make words suitable for them, he thinks he has called them all he could think of and much more than he can think about, he would give aught for some fresh words to throw at them. Eliza and her Mother out at Hotham this day so I am housekeeper.

Sunday 30th. July

Wm. Loncaster took a Bee hive last night and put the Comb in a Sieve to drop into a Bowl below, which he placed carefully in the Parlour, the Window of which was set open this morning, about Noon the Bees found the sweet treasure, and made a claim of it Thousands strong, this almost nonplus'd Old Lonc. but he muffled up his hands in old Stockings and put some sconce before his face and boldly removed the Sieve, Bees, and honey into the Yard; but the little Insects did not yet wish to leave the precious sweet, persuading being out of the question. Old Lonc muffled up ordered some straw to be put on the Sieve and set on fire, and this caused them to depart, but here an accident happened; for the fire taking deeper hold than was expected burnt the Sieve, sides and bottom, let in the Comb & Bees into the Bowl below but not to be beat the old Gentleman ordered a ladle to be brought and scooped out the Bees, honey and all and threw all together on the ground, and ordered the Boys who were looking at the operation to tread the Enemies under their Feet, so here he conquered his Foes and lost his spoil!! Heard another quarter of an hour's Sermon at Church this morning, it is quick work. A Very hot day this the Ground seems to be as dry as it was before the rain.

Monday 31st July

A Very hot day Rain much wanted for Turnips in many places they have entirely missed growing. Farmers very throng with the Wheat harvest it has become ripe very suddenly. About nine O'clock at night it lightened very much with a few Claps of Thunder, only a few drops of rain; this hot weather makes me quite languid.

Tuesday 1st. August

Called up this morning by Mr. Levitt of Ellerker to serve an order on two Men who had taken his Corn to cut, and refused to begin of it. I went down to Cave Sands to serve the order on them summoning them to appear at Brantingham[41] this forenoon at half past ten O'clock met the Parties at Brantingham when they would have sworn on one side there was an agreement and on the other none, however they agreed for a shilling an acre more than the first bargain. Got home about noon and sent for a Pint of Ale to Dinner, which is a very unusual thing with us, I should think all the time we have been at Housekeeping we have not had half a Dozen Pints of Ale at Dinner when we have had none but our own Family. Went to see Thos. Fisher, he is much better but he has totally lost one eye, — after that went to Mr. Tinsdill's and staid about an hour, he is quite delighted with Cobbett's writings lately.

Wednesday 2nd. August

A Fine Rain sometime towards this morning, it rained very fast, but our Water tub did not get filled. Colder a great deal today, a high blustering wind with rain at intervals ...

Thursday 3rd. August

James Levitt has begun business at Hull, in partnership with a young man of the name of Kidd, son of Kidd of Dairy Coates near Hull, they carry on their business at 47 Dock Street. Young Barnard Cook lately had a fit, much likely brought on by drinking and intemperance, he is better now. — This is Mr. Barnard's rent day. I have no doubt but his ears will be assailed by complaints, on the dry weather having such an injurious effect on the Crops both of grass, and spring corn; as for Wheat they cannot complain for the Crop is in general very good, and I hope it will be got, in a good state. I hope he (Mr B) will not give them any thing again, for the Farmers beat all others with complaints, there is never a day in the year but they complain either of one thing or another.

Friday 4th. Augt.

Went with the old Cardinal to his Close, he never knew such a dry Season, which I almost wonder at, as he is famed for something out of the common way. He can recollect of Lambs being bought at Pocklington Fair (as tomorrow) for twenty pence a piece good ones and small Lambs for 15 or 16 pence each. — It is expected that this year the price will not be more than half of what it was the last. Served an order on a Woman of the name of Savage for breaking a neighbour's window. She is to appear at Riplingham[42] on Monday next.

---

[41] Brantingham was not the location of a regular court of petty sessions, for which the presence of at least 2 magistrates was required. However, Edward Barnard, South Cave's vicar had joined the bench in 1820, and lived at Thorpe Brantingham Hall. It would therefore be convenient to refer minor local disputes and other matters that could be dealt with by one magistrate to him (Balchin 88).

[42] The division of Hunsley Beacon had 3 courts of petty session located, respectively, at Beverley, Riplingham, and Sculcoates. The court at Riplingham was held in a room in the Blacksmith's Arms (Balchin 201 and 210; *PP* 36 (1845) 335–6).

Saturday 5th. Augt.

At West Ella this day seeing my Mother she looks pretty well, but has part pain in her Legs they are a good deal swelled but much better than they have been. I came back by Swanland Ferriby &c most of the Wheat is safely got in, and other Corn is in hand, as fast as can be got forward with. Major Sykes is at West Ella now, he had seen Wm. a short time ago, he said he was very well & very throng, both which I was glad to hear[;] these are all the particulars I have heard. I did not speak him.

Sunday 6th. Augt.

The weather still very dry. I never saw the Pasture land so much burnt up as it is at present. The ground is in comparison as bare as a public road. It is wonderful how the Cattle live, yet they do live and look well, it is surprising what little meat they can do with, especially when they have plenty of water.

Monday 7th. August

Got up this morning between 3 & 4 O'clock to serve an Order on Wm. Wilkinson & Timothy Dunn who had taken some Turnips to Hoe for Rd. Clark of Riplingham, but they agreed to go back to their Work, so I had nothing to do but carry in the Summons, and the other Summons which was got for the Woman breaking the Window, which was compromised without attending before the Magistrates, they had my Expences to pay. I see by the Paper this day there has been a great deal of Rain in London especially in Bridge Street in the neighbourhood of Bride Lane.

Tuesday 8th. August

John Holborn mended our Sky light it having had several squares broken, it wanted mending most part of the last year, but never got done before this day. Went to Drewton this Evening with some tax papers for Geo. Metcalfe, got back about seven O'clock. The leaves of some particular trees are all shrivelled up with the heat and falling off the same as in Autumn.

Wednesday 9th. August

Saw by the Paper this morning that Wm. had sent a parcel which he expected that we should receive last night, but it did not arrive, he does not say whether he has received his Box or not, — Old Nanny Thornton will water her Cows nowhere but close against Abraham Barff's, which friend Abraham does not approve of, he drives them off sometimes and threatens to put old nanny into the Beck, but it has no effect upon her. One day after bickering as usual, Abraham in his own yard says to her "Come here thou Old yellow faced rubbish and I will slap thy face for thee". Nanny immediately accepted the invitation and skipped across the Beck and said now strike, if I be nearer enough to thee, with that Old Nanny Barff armed with a sweeping brush interfered to keep her son Abe from being guilty of such a breach of the peace as was likely to ensue. Nanny Thornton says a fine Son thou has, that thou art forced to stand before him with the brush to keep him quiet. Hold thy noise says Mrs Barff and look at thy own Son Bobby, thou should have called him Jack, for he is as fond as Jack Thornton ever was, Say thou nought about Jack Thornton says old Nanny for he is dead, and cannot answer for himself. Why says Mrs. Barff Bobby can speak for him and answer as well as he could if he were here. A Fine Shower this afternoon about 3 O'clock.

Thursday 10th. Augt.

Some West Country Manufacturers with Music here this day begging, there have been three Sets within a short time, — Richd. Marshall's Ass threw him a few days ago and broke one of his Ribs, it likewise threw him again yesterday, he is in no danger. Recd. a letter from Charles Staniforth Esqr. informing me that he was appointed Distributor of Stamps for the East Riding, and enquired to know if I wished to continue Sub-distributor at So. Cave, wrote him back, I should be glad to continue if it meet his approbation. Mr. Tinsdill, Mr. Bridgman & myself signed our names as witnesses to Mr. Robinson's will, which appears to be a long one it being written on twelve Sheets of Paper.

Friday 11th. Augt.

Robt. Marshall's Galloway has fallen with him and broke its knees, he said he would never ride it more, and he sold it the same day to Wm. Newlove who is going to take it to Horncastle fair the next week along with other Horses. Mr. Barnard set out on a Journey on Monday, but on the Road his Gig shafts broke and backwards over he and his Groom came, but without receiving any injury. So that what [with] Gigs, Horses, and Asses we have had several falls. Mr. Staniforth was here today[,] he seems to be a very pleasant man. I was afraid the Stamp Office was to have been at Beverley which would have been very inconvenient to me as there is no conveyance from thence regularly, but he says he shall have an office in Sculcoates from whence I shall be supplied. There will be a separate distributor for Hull. Recd. a parcel from Wm. this night we expected it on Tuesday last, glad to hear he is well.

Saturday 12th. Augt.

I do not think Turnips will be so bad a Crop as was reported. I have seen several Closes the Crops of which will not be much to complain of, provided it come rain in any reasonable time; Potatoes have fine flourishing tops as I ever saw, but in comparison nothing at the Roots. Some of our fine Butchers were at Hull the other Day, and one of them Geo. Cottam by name who married one of Gledhill's daughters after getting his load at Hull, rode over a flint heap and came down, when he begun crying and ran back to Ferriby to tell the People he was killed dead!! He cried all the way home, and his wife said to him my "Pratty creature thou's kill'd", but he is still able to smoke in the town street, notwithstanding his own and his wife's evidence that he was killed! David Dennis who married Robt. Todd's "lahtle lass" had bought her a new Gown piece at Hull, he being drunk amongst the rest lost his new Gown, his companions having got it from him and torn it all in pieces so that our "lahtle lass" got no new Gown.

Sunday 13th. Augt.

The Curate has given notice that he shall examine in the Catechism all who have not been confirmed above 9 years of age, to begin next Sunday in the afternoon, and explain its meaning to them, I suppose he thinks it will be easier than reading two Sermons a day, though not many people would wish for easier work than reading at the most about 20 minutes at a time, but some people wish to do very little for their money. I know that one industrious Schoolmaster does more good to Society than several parsons in general do. — Therè is a notice I see in Longman's monthly Catalogue of a Book called the "Antiquarian Trio"[43] containing amongst other things a Description of Rudstone Church & Obelisk. I have seen what is here called the Obelisk, which is a single rude Stone standing about 30 Feet high above the Ground, but I have never seen any plausible conjecture for what purpose it was intended for, it has no inscription on it.

Monday 14th. Augt. [There are two entries for this date.]

I see by the Times this morning that a young man of the name of Dunn[44] from Hull has been robbing his employers Sewell & Co. Compton Street having got acquainted with an abandoned Woman of the name of Smith, whom he first knew in a house of ill fame near Covent Garden which he entered about two O'clock in the morning, it would have been much for his happiness that he had been in bed at the time — May this be a warning to all young men entrusted with their master's property not to live in the habits of dissipation nor spend more than their income. A Dutchman let his income be what it will, always contrives to save something out of it, which makes him in a great measure independent.

Monday 14th. Aug.

Sent a paper to my Brother this day, as I suppose he has got home before this time. Recd. a Paper from London this morning called the "London Mercury"[45] but by whom sent I cannot say —It is the first number published on Saturday last.

Tuesday 15th. Aug.

Mr. Atkinson gave us some Pears to send Wm it unfortunately happens that he is not in time when we have a Box to send, therefore we shall be under the necessity of making free with them ourselves. I have sent this day by Cousens to see if he can get 3/s- for the Box allowed to him; the last time it was sent to London it was paid for at both places, which must be an imposition. Mr. Barnard is pulling down Old John Dunlin's house and going to build 4 or 5 Cottages in its place, but how unlike the Cottages of old I need not say, formerly every Cottage had at least two Rooms on the Ground Floor, a house and Parlour which last was almost universally the lodging Room, the Chamber was the whole length of the two low rooms and in winter generally stored with Apples,

[43] Cole, John. *The Antiquarian Trio, consisting of Views and Descriptions of 1. Duke of Buckingham's House. 2. Rudston Church and Obelisk. 3. Effigy in the Old Town-hall* ... Scarborough: John Cole, 1826.

[44] Henry Dunn was the son of a Hull watchmaker. He had been employed by Messrs. Sewel and C. Cross, linen drapers in Compton Street, London, for about a year before he was discovered to have been systematically robbing the firm. He was found guilty and given a sentence of death later commuted to transportation for 14 years. (See the diary entries for 25/8/26, 25/9/26, and 16/12/26. See also *TM* 11 Aug. 1826, 3 e).

[45] This short-lived newspaper had only been published for the first time on the previous Saturday (12 Aug.). It survived until 23 Dec. 1826, when it was incorporated into the *Weekly Times*.

for an Orchard was the general appendage to a Cottage in those times; then there was what was called a backer end under the same Roof which was excellently adapted, for putting any kind of lumber and used occasionally to thrash the little Corn which was either grown, or gleaned by the industrious Cottager's wife. Cottagers in general kept Cows in those happy times, and to be beholden to the Parish was looked upon as a scandal.

Wednesday 16th. Aug.

Recd. the Receipt back from Hull of the Carriage of Wm's Box to London, the Wharfinger says it was entered as paid, if this be the case, and it appears that it is, the charge must have been made wilfully in London. However I shall send the Receipt and see if the money cannot be recovered. Recd. the same No. of the London Mercury as on Monday last, I likewise received last night by the Carrier from Hull a parcel of prospectuses of the same paper, which I shall not interfere with as Agent, because if I got any orders I should most likely be left to pay for them. John Hall brought a parcel this day from William[.] He says he saw him on last Sunday morning, and [he] is very well[;] the parcel contained the 11 Copies of the History of England,[46] Hall looks very well[,] he is going to stop until the latter end of September.

Thursday 17th. Aug.

The Times called Cobbett a "comical miscreant", and the "Vagabond" in an Article on the "Poor Man's Friend",[47] it appears there is another poor Man's friend published by H. Stemman Leicester Square or in one of the Streets of that neighbourhood, the object of the Article is to recommend the latter, and condemn Cobbett's work, but the Vagabond will not mind much what is said by Anna Brodie, but he will most likely make some remark upon it in his own way and his way is not the most polite, this it must be allowed he does not practice much.

Friday 18th. Augt.

There is a paragraph in the Times this morning on the subject of large Farms, which is much to the purpose. The great Leviathans would swallow up all, if it be ever so small a mouthful they do not like to see another enjoy it. I should wish to see it general in the Country, for every married Labourer to have sufficient land at the same rent the Farmers pay to keep him a Cow the year round[;] this would in a great measure make him independent, for he would then have an opportunity of feeding a Pig or two for his winter's use aye and Summer too, for Bacon is very good at any time of the year. I cannot tell what objection the Landlords can have to receive the same rent from Cottagers as from the great Jolterheads; they really do want taking down at least one year in three, for they get so powerful in their own views when in prosperity, that they think the Poor of almost a different species, the Poor rates will never be high

---

[46] See n.14 (1833) for a reference to a work of this title.

[47] *The Poor Man's Friend; or, Companion for the Working Classes, Giving Them Useful Information and Advice: being the System of Moral and Political Philosophy Laid down and Exemplified by William Cobbett.* London: H. Stemman, 1826.

enough until the great Monopolizers be forced to give up their Farms, but that will not be yet. Eliza went to West Ella this night after School time.

Saturday 19th. Augt.

Uncommonly dry weather yet & hot almost past bearing, lent Jno. Hall two Newspapers today, he says they will be quite a treat to him, he was at Hull yesterday. I have been giving notice to the Publicans that Brewster Sessions[48] will be held at Beverley on the 6th. Sept. next. The weather is excellent for harvest[,] the Corn as dry as possible it can be, but great complaints of the scantiness of the Spring Crops[.] All the wheat in this neighbourhood is got in, and in general a good Crop, for which I am very thankful.

Sunday 20th. Augt.

John Coupland died this morning after a short illness of about 24 Hours, he has worked for Sam Ayre for nearly 30 years. Ann Giles was buried this afternoon she is about 21 years old, Sister to Jackey Giles, he has not been heard of these last four or five years, there has not been a funeral here since the 6th of April last. The Parson after Church time asked the Children some questions which he calls catechising, but which questions were about as suitable to their capacities, as though he had read to them a dissertation in Greek. The learning of some people makes them as ridiculous as the ignorance of others. Eliza came home this morning from Hull and West Ella[.] She says her Grandmother is pretty well, but her legs appear much inflamed. John Hall it is said here, has given up his place to come to see his Friends, if his place was of no more value than they are he will not lose much by giving up, but if it was worth keeping, he has made but a poor Speculation to visit the Old Scarecrows.

Monday 21st. Aug.

A Thunder Shower about 12 O'clock last night, when it rained very fast for a short time, it has cooled the Air and made it much pleasanter than it was. I have lately read a report of the Corn Laws made in 1814 before the House of Commons, one witness says that the Farmers could live if Wheat was 72s. pr. Quarter providing the Property tax was taken off. Another says that they cannot get on with Wheat under 80s. pr. Qr., it came out in evidence that most of the Witnesses were land Valuers, appointed by the Land Leviathans to value their estates, and they knew that to please their employers it was their interest to get the land to as high a rate as they could. Cast up Thos. Pashley's Malt Book for the last Season he has made about 400 Quarters.

Tuesday 22nd. Aug

John Hall is gone out this morning in a Gig with Miss Kitty and two of his relatives, a pretty load they are, I think he does not look much of a Whip, and is glad to follow his vocation here rather than in the Streets of the crowded City, where he and his freight, would most likely soon come in contact with the dirty kennel — I don't know where they have gone they went out at the North end of the Town. I think to Market Weighton.

---

[48] See n.95 (1827).

Wednesday 23rd Aug

A Fine moderate rain today, there will be many people I expect go out on purpose to get a wetting. My Father after a dry time when it came a rainy Day would be sure to be out in it if possible and get wet through, he was as fond of a rainy day after a drought as a Duck is of water. Wm. complains of the Bugs disturbing him so much that he cannot sleep quietly at nights, I wish they would all set off to explore the North Pole, or South Pole either. In the "Fortunes of Nigel"[49] it is said in Scotland, they eat Raw Oatmeal Cakes baked upon a Peat fire. Page 275. Vol. 1.

Thursday 24th. Augt.

It is said that the manufacture of Carpets was only introduced into England about the year 1750,[50] in ancient times the Floors of Rooms were strewed with Rushes; A foreigner visited this Country about the time of the Reformation, and gives an account of the Dirty state of even the best sort of People at that time, to which the covering of their floors a good deal contributed. The farmers are most terribly afraid that foreign Corn will be permitted to come into this Country: I suppose they think nothing of the starvation of a few hundred thousand people in comparison to keeping up the Prices of Corn, or in other words the Rents of their Landlords. I do believe the Boobies would rather pay high rents to sell Corn high, than be content with the same profit at a lower rent.

Friday 25th. Aug.

My Sister was here yesterday from Hull she came from West Ella in the afternoon and went away after Tea; I gave her the receipt to send to Wm. for the Box which was paid for twice over[.] I hope he will get it righted, I had rather spend twice the value of it as be imposed on. — My Sister says the young man called Dunn lately apprehended in London for robbing his employers is the Son of a Watchmaker in Hull, I think who lives in Blackfriar Gate.

Saturday 26th. Augt.

Measured about 4 Acres of Turnips (hoeing) in the Moors for Robt. Marshall with whom I staid and dined, in the afternoon measured a Close for Watson Arton, top Close in the Warren 14a–0r–23p drank tea with Watty & Mudda, got home about eight O'clock[,] went in to Mr. Robinson's where I got a bottle of Ginger beer.

Sunday 27th. Augt.

Recd. the Examiner for last Sunday this morning, it having missed coming before this time, — At Church the Parson catechising the Children; according to his plan if indeed he has one, it would be as well to teach the Catechism out

[49] Sir Walter Scott, *The Fortunes of Nigel* ... Edinburgh: A. Constable and Co., 1822. – 3 vols. (8⁰). – 2nd ed., Edinburgh and London, 1822. – 3 vols. (12⁰). Also published in his: *Novels and Romances* ... Edinburgh: A. Constable and Co., 1824. – 7 vols.

[50] The person generally credited with the introduction of a carpet factory into England is a Frenchman, Père Norbert, who became a naturalized Englishman and changed his name to Peter Parisot. In 1750 he operated a small carpet-weaving workshop in Paddington, but transferred the business in the following year to Fulham, where he established a training school and factory to manufacture pile carpets (*EB* v. 395).

of a Dictionary, as he wants all the words explaining, he however has some merit or sincerity, for he acknowledges he does not know how to make the Children understand what he means, and how should he!!!

Monday 28th. Augt.

Higher prices asked this day at the Market for Corn; if I had the power that is at present vested in the Ministers the 500.000 Quarters of Foreign Wheat should soon see day light in this Country, it appears that Oats are as much wanted as Wheat, but let the Wheat come in and it will have an effect on all other kinds of grain. Watty Arton brought me a hundred Quills today, the first new quills I have had this Season.

Tuesday 29th. Augt.

What various appearances in our times Charity puts on, sometimes the Ladies take into their heads to work, and then sell their nick nacks and give the proceeds to the poor, to keep them in idleness, would there not be more sense in employing the poor than giving them what keeps them in the state they are? Then there is that begging Set called the Bible Society,[51] which contrive to cheat the poor Booksellers out of their profit, by just being so accommodating as selling the Books and enjoying the benefit themselves; I am almost sick of hearing tell of Charitable institutions; then if you say any thing against these popular follies, you are either disloyal or an infidel, however I will take care and give nothing to the wily beggars.

Wednesday 30th. Aug.

Sent a Pound note to pay for the Club at Burlington[52] which is like money thrown away, as the Person who pays for me sent me word last year he would pay no more. I expected he would not, but the silly fool has been paying for a full year, I have however given him notice not to pay for me any longer. The Harvest appears to be all over for this year. Old Willy says that Tailors are the most ancient trade, but I told him Gardeners had the precedence, at least <u>Will says</u> (in Hamlet) "there is no ancient Gentlemen but Gardeners, Ditchers and Grave makers; they hold up Adam's profession". Went to the Mill this night to see my old friend Tom, but he had just set off for a load of Corn about half after seven O'clock, the first load today, he likes a fresh job when it is time to leave work, so I did not stay to see him, which I dare say he will think very fortunate.

---

[51] The British and Foreign Bible Society was founded in London in 1804 with its stated aim being 'to encourage a wider circulation of the Holy Scriptures, without note or comment'. Its influence spread rapidly throughout Great Britain by means of its auxiliaries, i.e. local societies, affiliated but self-controlled with subsidiary branches and associations. In the first 12 years of its existence, the Society had received no less than £420,000 from its auxiliaries (*EB* iii. 906).

[52] Excluding an all-female friendly society, there were at least 2 other friendly societies in existence at Bridlington by 1804, when RS came to South Cave; they were the Amicable Society (founded 1796) and the Union Society (also known as the British Marine Society, and founded 1795) (Neave (1988) 45).

Thursday 31st Augt.

Mrs. Sonley has gone to Hull to have her Breast cut for a Cancer,[53] I think it will be dangerous at her age. I asked old Willy what sort of needles he thought Adam used in making his Fig leaf suit; he said he took a stick about a yard long and peeled off the outside bark, and then stripped down the inner rind within about an inch of the end, then his needle was thread and he began work. I think this hypothesis of the Old Gentleman is very plausible, but what is there that we do not know at Cave?!! John Davis and some others were fetching Water from Mill Beck, not a drop of Water runs down to the West end, and very little in the Market Place. Took a walk this Evening up Porter hole with Old Willy as far as the New Bridge, famed for making Articles of Clay, especially by the dirty boys.

Friday 1st. Septr.

This is the first Day of Death amongst Partridges &c. there seem to be a great many this Season, but few I know will fall to my Share, it will be rather dangerous walking in the Fields today for fear of random Shots; Mr. Barnard has gone from home[,] he set out on Monday last, so that his Game is left to the keeper, but others will not scruple who can come in for a Shot. I think the following is a[s] great a bouncer as pen and Ink need be employed upon. A French Priest & a Dutch Captain were matched to eat Oysters, the Priest eat 138 Dozen and then gave in, the Dutchman did not relax until he had eaten 186 Dozen — with which he drank 8 Bottles of White Wine: and by way of Des[s]ert eat a whole Fowl after and drank two more bottles of wine. A Parish meeting this Evening at the Church. Anthony Burton wants to sell his house to the Parish for a weekly annuity, but whether the bargain will be made or not I cannot say.

Saturday 2nd. Septr.

Wrote a letter for Matthew Pickering this morning to the Barley Mow Brewery, Limehouse, London advising them of the return of some empty Porter Casks. Went to Brantingham with four Orchard Robbers who had been stealing Apples and Filberts from Mr. Barnard's Orchard on Sunday last, near St. Helen's Well, they were fined One Shilling each and paid the expences, Mr. Barnard told them he had by a late law[54] the power of sending them to the tread Mill from one to three months, but he added he did not like this harsh law, he is not like the Parson Magistrates in Devonshire, who glory in committing Children to the tread Mill. In the afternoon went to Ellerker and measured top

---

[53] The operation of mastectomy had been performed at least as early as the 18th c. Henry Fearon's *A Treatise on Cancer* (1784) proclaimed 'a new and successful method of operating, particularly in cancers of the breast'. The operation, performed without antiseptics, and while the patient was fully conscious, is described by the diarist and novelist, Fanny Burney, who underwent a successful operation in 1811, and who survived for another 29 years. Mrs Sonley, who was the widow of Dr Sonley, had the operation at the age of 74 but died almost exactly a year later, having been 'ill for a long time'.

[54] i.e. An Act to Amend the Law in Respect to the Offence of Stealing from Gardens and Hothouses, 7 Geo. IV 1826 c. 69, passed on 31 May 1826. This act empowered a single Justice of the Peace to commit an offender, convicted of stealing fruits or vegetables, to imprisonment with hard labour for up to 6 calendar months.

Cave Gates Close belonging to Ths. Allison who occupies the farm where Heslewood formerly lived, the quantity 6a–0r–12p Measured another Close at the bottom of Ellerker Wold 5a–1r–24p. Drank tea with Ths. Allison and got home before eight O'clock.

Sunday 3rd. Septr.

At Church twice today as usual; the Parson at his work amongst the Children, armed with a huge Octavo which he called Archbishop Secker's Lectures on the Church Catechism[55] which he fired off to the confusion of the understanding of the Children, it all appears to be uphill work. If he be not tired, I know I am with hearing him; I believe the man means it for good, but he appears to be at a loss to adapt what he has to say to the capacities of the Children. I think I shall note no more of these proceedings.

Monday 4th. Septr.

Got a new great Coat made, Eliza bought the Cloth some time since of the same travelling merchant as I & Wm. met with at Js. Pearson's at Everthorpe when he was here; it is broad Cloth for which she gave only 10s. pr. yard, it appears a good piece of Stuff. The Jolterheads are all in amazement at the Ports being open for the importation of Corn, some of them call the Ministers in no measured language for their folly. One cries they are going to knock down the prices, that Farmers cannot live, others say there is no corn to come in and that prices will get higher than ever, but I do not see how they need to dread this, when they are endeavouring all they can to keep up the prices, certainly if the Order in Council favour them in this they need not abuse the Authors of it. One Man who has 200 Quarters of old Beans says he will gladly take 5s. pr. Qr. less for them than he had bid the last week, his name is Goundrill a Corn dealer.

Tuesday 5th. Septr.

I do not know what reason the Ministers can have for not suffering Barley & Wheat to come in as well as other grain. I think there will be no duty to pay for what is permitted to come in at present, this looks like an opening to demolish the Corn laws. I hope it will be followed up with Spirit, this appears to be as wise conduct as the Ministers have for some time shewn.

Wednesday 6th. Sepr.

At Beverley this day at Brewster Sessions as Constable, it began to rain about Noon, and continued all the afternoon and night. I had not my great Coat with me, I got wet through I never saw the Water run down the roads in greater quantity. In the morning all burnt up and not a drop of water to be seen, but at night the Ponds by the road side half filled[.] I hope the rain will have a beneficial effect. Bought half a Dozen Silver tea Spoons for which I gave two pounds.

---

[55] This was the standard Anglican catechism by Thomas Secker, Archbishop of Canterbury: *Lectures on the Catechism of the Church of England*. Various editions from 1769 onwards, e.g. 14th ed., London: Rivington, 1821.

Thursday 7th. Septr.

The employment of the lower Classes is to satisfy their hunger, and of the upper to find out the purpose of creating hunger. Wm. Cade's Shop was broken open last night and about two Stone of Beef Stolen. On Friday night last the West end Carrier's Cart was robbed of 3 Dozen of Porter in Bottles. It has been a drizzling rain most of this day, the weather appears quite changed, a Stormy east wind has now taken place, the Club night, two fresh members admitted, got home about half past nine O'clock.

Friday 8th. Sepr.

A Fine rainy morning; it is pleasant to see the Water run down the Street after so long dry weather. Cleared up about noon, and a fine sun shining afternoon, nature looks quite revived. John Hall is gone to Scarborough this week to see some Old Companion, or acquaintance, who they say has begun business there, I rather wonder Miss Kitty has not accompanied him, as She has taken a deal of pains to lead him about while here. South Cave has paid its proportion (being £4–0–2) of an Assessment on the Division of Hunsley Beacon for damage sustained by some Inhabitants of Sculcoates, in having their windows broken at the time of the Hull Election.[56] The Irishman[57] ought to pay all expences for had it not been through him and his silly supporters there would not have been the outrages committed which there were. Besides what business had he and his procession in Sculcoates? He had nothing to do there, indeed I do not know what business he had at Hull. Went to West end this night, the Grass closes look as if they had just been dyed a new Green. It is surprising how a great a change there has been in the pastures in so short a time.

Saturday 9th. Sepr.

Went down to the Mill this morning to see after my old friend the long Miller, but he had set out with his Wife and Daughter on a Journey to the Wolds so that I came back no better than I went. In the afternoon went with Robt. Marshall to Weedley to choose a Ram, while there we two drew a bucket of Water out of the Well[58] which is 113 yards deep, it takes ten minutes to draw up a bucket and is hard work for two men. People talk of the tread mill but I apprehend that a man forced to draw water here would find a far greater punishment, than the frightful tread mill. In looking into the well the water may be just discerned, like a small bright place, the depth of water is about 4 or 5 yards. Drank tea at Weedley, and arrived at home soon after eight O'clock where we smoked a pipe of London Tobacco which is almost done.

---

[56] Extra-ordinary rates were levied on individual wapentakes to raise compensation for occasional riot or arson damage occurring in the wapentake or division. Sculcoates, where windows had been damaged during the 1826 Hull election campaign, was in the Hunsley division in which South Cave also was located (Balchin 297).

[57] i.e. Augustus John O'Neill. See n.13 (1826).

[58] The well at Weedley Farm, approximately 2 miles east of South Cave, is marked on the O.S. 6 in. map of 1855 but the present (1995) owners of the farm, the Sergeant family, have no knowledge of it.

Sunday 10th. Sep

Some of my Friends are mourning this day, but not for their Sins, but because Oats and Beans have fallen in price, and they are afraid they will not have it in their power to realise so much by a good deal as they expected, but as they have a good deal of Fool hardiness, and not much in want of money they cannot think of selling now, indeed it is rather cause of wonder they ever sell, for when the prices are rising they are afraid of selling too low; and in a falling market they hang back, because so little money is raised; but then at times they are forced to sell.

Monday 11th. Sepr

No business done in the Market except for Seed Wheat, the Dogs of Farmers all strive to bite one another with seed Corn, asking higher prices than if Factors were buying it. I think Teavil Leeson is a match for the fellow who wrote the account of the Oyster eaters; he says he has a friend who has <u>180.000</u> Quarters of Oats on hand, this cannot be beaten in a common way.

Tuesday 12th. Sepr.

Spent a little time with the Old Cardinal this Evening, he as usual was telling amazing tales, particularly concerning a Dog which he once had called "Wigs", if he said Wigs I am going to fetch Galloway up, off went Wigs opening all the Doors in the House, went into the Stable, took out the Halter and run with it to the Close, where he arrived long before his Master, who would find him, with the Halter laid down close beside the Horse; Once he threw a piece of old rag upon a Bundle of Sticks which an Old Woman had on her head, which Wigs observed, after passing her some time he ordered Wigs to fetch the Old rag, who immediately set off, jumped on the Old Woman's back, threw her down and brought the rag in triumph to his Master. &c &c &c

Wednesday 13th. Sepr.

Recd. a parcel from Wm. last night. I was at the time reading Boswell's life of Johnson, but it was immediately laid down, for the entertainment I anticipated, from hearing how Cobbett stood affected after his defeat at Preston, he seems to bear it admirably for he says it was a triumph. I see he wants the Expences making up which has been incurred, so that there is yet an Opportunity for any of his Disciples or admirers to come forward with their Cash. No Newspaper this morning. I suppose it has got into a wrong Bag: therefore must wait until another day. I am glad to hear that Wm. has got the Money returned for the Carriage of the Box.

Thursday 14th. Sepr.

Recd. two Papers this morning, and was like the Ass between the bundles of Hay, not knowing which to begin to read first, however I even thought it was as well to begin in order so I read the oldest first. Ths. Marshall says that fellow was very wise who called the lower Class the Swinish multitude for he swears they are as fond as his old Sow, Oh, he says there is no comprehending the Stupidity, and what vexes Tom worse the asking high wages by the labourers, in these times when <u>he says</u> the Farmers are hard set to live; it is a grievous thing to him to have the Poor rates to pay, for they are so unthankful a set who are relieved, that he can hardly conceive there should be so much ingratitude. But I wonder what they are beholden to him for, as he gives them nothing but what he is obliged to do; Though to do our long friend Justice, I do not think a poor person can go to a better house, for there is always something to eat for any who go about the house; I believe he would fill the Bellies of the hungry but at the same time would not wish to have any credit for so doing.

Friday 15th. Sepr.

Very dry again a fine Sun all the day, rain appears to be almost as much wanted as before it lately came. Frank Jackson and all his family are fairly off to Hull; he took in his friend the old Cardinal for some money borrowed, for which he only recd. twenty pence pr. pound. This was as bad as though a rag shop had shut up, at least to the Cardinal. I think he had a five pound York note when the Bank[59] shut up, and so long since as December nothing has been paid, nor any dividend declared, but I have lately seen in the Papers that it is expected a dividend of 5s. in the pound will be paid in October next. — It happened very fortunately for myself that I had no rags by which I lost any thing & none of my own will I keep.

Saturday 16th. Septr.

Measured the following Crop of Richard Kirby, to whom Robt. Marshall succeeds, Ings Close 19a–1r–2p, from thence went to a Close of Beans near Provence house, and measured about 20 Lands for Labourers who had pulled the Beans, then from there down Jarratt Hills lane to a Close of Oats Stubble facing Wm. Laverack's house at the Common which measured 9a–2r–18p then measured another Close Wheat Stubble not far from the Mill 5a–2r–36p. Called at the Mill and measured about 6 Acres of Turnip Hoeing in Ths. Marshall's new field Close, it is about 15 Acres and has the finest looking Crop of Turnips I ever saw grow, it is low land and the dry Season has been particularly in its favour; from thence we went (that is Robt. Marshall & myself) to his house where we arrived about 2 O'clock, Awd Beck had got a Duck roasted for Dinner which I enjoyed very well after so much walking, after Dinner got a Pipe of Tobacco and a Glass of Rum & Water, then returned home, pretty well tired.

Sunday 17th. Sepr.

The Curate shewing some High Church pranks, a Child was brought from Broomfleet to be baptised & Christened this day, which he refused to Christen; because the proposed Sponsors had not received the Sacrament: he would not baptise the Child neither; The Father offered to become Godfather & the Mother to be Godmother, but this was likewise refused by the Clerical Gentleman, so the Child was taken back as it came, — I can scarcely keep myself within bounds to hear of such doings especially here. If I was in the Parents' place, I would not trouble the Parson any more on that head. Can this

---

[59] Wentworth, Chaloner, Rishworth and Co. had branches in Bradford, York, and Wakefield. The bank was the first, and one of the largest, of the provincial banks in Yorkshire to collapse in the general financial crisis of the winter of 1825/26. The York bank, managed by Robert Chaloner, eventually paid its creditors 15s. 2d. in the pound but that sum was not reached until 1834 (Hartley 33–4, 40–3).

be law? I wish these Gentlemen in the Church were compelled to do their duty without asking any questions, for a sorry duty it is to make the Godfathers and Godmothers promise and do for others, what they cannot for themselves. John Hall called this Evening he is going to Manchester in the morning to look out for a Situation there; if he does not succeed he will stay about a fortnight & then go to London.

Monday 18th. Sepr.

I had forgot to mention or note that I got settled with my old friend the long Miller on Friday night last, he paid all up without either cursing or swearing, which is rather remarkable, but he did let off in the swearing line a little, against the idle Clowns who receive the Money which he works and sweats to obtain. He has not been at Market since the rent day about 6 weeks ago when he contrived to get so drunk as to want help to get home.

Tuesday 19th. Sepr.

A Very Stormy night last night and rained very hard, I got up about four O'clock to set Washing tubs, it rained down so much, it still continues raining, and I am in the hope we shall have sufficient now, as it is the equinoctial time, when we are generally visited with a storm. This is the great race day at Doncaster under the Patron <u>St. Leger,</u> when the stakes of his name are to be run for, it has a sort of odd sound a Horse racing Saint. I do not know the Legend of this holy man, perhaps Hone in his every day book[60] can say something about him. Horse racing intelligence is what I never read in the newspapers, but to some kind of readers I understand it is the most interesting.

Wednesday 20th. Sepr.

A Cold Stormy easterly wind but not much rain, Old Willy was looking in the Plan of London last night for St. Martin's Church which is the one he was married at, but he could not find it <u>drawn out</u> which he rather wondered at; it is without doubt a fine building; when I was in London[61] it contained within its Vaults the Bodies of the King and Queen of the Sandwich Islands.[62] I see by the Times this morning there is likely to be some stir with the supporters of the Bible Society, it is no more than I have looked for; I expect there is good pickings from the Simpletons who give away their money, but for what purpose the receivers do not tell them. — Wrote to the revd. Mr. Barnard this day,

---

[60] William Hone, *The Everyday Book; or, A Guide to the Year Relating the Popular Amusements, Sports, Ceremonies, Manners, Customs and Events Incident to the 365 Days in Past and Present Times.* London: William Hone, 1825.

[61] In the summer of 1824.

[62] In 1824, King Kamehameha II, King of the Hawaian (Sandwich) Islands, and his wife visited England, where they both contracted measles and died as a result of it. Their bodies were kept for some weeks in the vault of St. Martin's church before being removed on 7 Sept. of that year to the frigate, 'Blonde', which conveyed them and their suite to Honolulu, arriving there on 19 May the following year (*TM* 15 July 1824, 2 c; 9 Sept. 1824, 2 b; 18 Sept. 1824, 2 c; 20 Mar. 1826, 3 f).

telling him it will be right to give notice to the occupiers of the School land[63] to quit the same at Lady day next.

Thursday 21st Sepr.

Last night it was enquired amongst several persons "what news", when one said Watt's horse had lost last at Doncaster races, ("What's Watt" — or his horse either to me) but it was added his jockey had won, for he had bet against the horse he rode; well then here is a fine Specimen of the honesty and morality of Horse racing; I exclaimed this wants putting down as much as Knacks[64] at Cave fair; Yes but it is Gentlemen's employment, well then the sooner stopped the better and let them employ themselves to more purpose, I think an account of horse racing is not worth polluting the Columns of a newspaper with. — Well but how was Driffield fair for Sheep yesterday? Why bad as can be. Lambs not half price they were the last year. Well but recollect they were extremely dear last year, and take the two years together you will have more than an average price, yes but the low price should not come last!! I wonder how the Market was at London on Monday says another? — Oh much the same, Aye it is either much the same or lower; Corn would have sold well if the fond fellows who rule us had kept the foreign Corn out of the Country — yes but then it was feared some part of the Country would suffer. — Aye but it is certain that Landholders must suffer now. — I thought to myself I should be glad if their time was come.

Septr. 22 Friday

A Fine morning — Dr. Johnson advises one of his friends if he keeps a Journal not to note the weather, but he never gave such a charge to me, and if he had I do not know that I should have obeyed it.— This is my Birth day of which I have acquainted no one, so that it will pass over without any observation as formerly. It is Forty years since I left home, and some of my early Companions I have seldom seen since that time; some I have accidentally seen and been surprised at People looking old, whom I had in my mind, as rosy Girls and Boys, I suppose the same feelings would animate them at the sight of me. Some of them I have never seen since, and I think there is not one who now lives at Barmston the place of my birth, and I do not know whether there are any householders now who were then there, all, all, is changed: yet notwithstanding I still like to retain a grateful remembrance of the place of my Birth[.] How often have I thought when returning from a Visit to my Parents, that could I live at Barmston, I should envy no one the choice of any other place. I have been at Cave more than 22 years, and here indeed I think I am likely to continue. May I be thankful to God for all his mercies. In general I have been blessed with good health, may I be grateful for it.

---

[63] A total of just over 9 acres had been variously allotted to the churchwardens and other parish officers at the enclosure of Wallingfen (1777–81) and South Cave (1785–7). In 1797 these allotments were let to Jonathan Scott for a period of 30 years at a nominal rent in return for a payment of £300 which was used to defray the cost of building and maintaining the Cross school and market building. The reference 'to quit the same' would apparently refer to the termination of the 30-year lease (Allen 78).

[64] 'Knack', a deceitful or dishonest trick, a dodge (*OED*).

Saturday 23rd. Sepr

Went to Ellerker this forenoon to measure some harvesting for Charles Rudd at the Sands, about 20 Acres, pretty near the Humber side, it was a pleasant day, and the Vessels passing looked very picturesque, having their sails full set, and not far from the shore. Dined at Charles Rudds and got a glass of Rum and Water after. When going away met with Mr. Thos. Leason, who would have me go on to his house, where I went and got tea, the first time this Season in Candle light. Got well home about 9 O'clock.

Sunday 24th. Sepr.

Young Teavil Leeson has left his place at London for what cause I cannot say, but it is long before his time was out — There has been a Camp meeting of the Ranters[65] this day at Cockle-pit row, on the Brough road, which I understand has not been very strongly attended; indeed the day has been rather against it, for it has been rather cold and blustering. Heard yesterday from my mother who I am glad to find is very well. Mr. Turk has gone to Bradford to see his son Wm. the Physician to stay about 3 weeks.

Monday 25th. Sepr.

I saw by the Paper that the young Man, Dunn from Hull has been tried & found guilty; I can feel for the Situation of his Parents, who most likely had placed strong hopes upon his being a Comfort and Credit to them; but all their hopes by his misconduct are blasted, and all that is left for them is to reflect, with a melancholy satisfaction that his life has not been forfeited to his Crimes. — Weighton fair this day, heavy complaints by the sellers who had Lambs and lean Sheep to sell. I understand the Stock was large, and some persons had nothing bid for their lots. Fat Sheep sold pretty well, high enough however for the Consumer. Butter in the Market this day 21d. pr. lb., famous prices these for the farmers wives, but we must lay the butter very thin. Mr. Craggs' Rag Warehouse was broken into on Friday night last and about a Ton of Rags stolen therefrom. He was searching a house in this town on Sunday night about 12 O'clock, but found nothing, the house is where Old Peggy Medd used to live. Mr. Craggs has put out hand bills offering a reward of 10 Guineas for the apprehension of the thieves.

Tuesday 26th. Sep

Mushrooms are uncommonly plentiful this Season, they have been scarce for a number of years. I can recollect my Mother making Catsup and selling at five Shillings half an Anker,[66] she likewise bottled small mushrooms and sold them at so much a bottle; — I accidentally met last night with an Old

---

[65] The Primitive Methodists, or Ranters, were a revivalist and evangelical off-shoot of the main Wesleyan Methodist movement. The sect spread rapidly from its beginnings in Staffordshire and arrived in the East Riding in 1819, when William Clowes came to Hull. It flourished in the region, particularly in the 1820s and 1830s, so that by mid-century, the East Riding had become one of its main strongholds in the country (Woodcock 32 and *passim*).

[66] An anker was a measure of wine and spirits, used in Holland, North Germany, Denmark, Sweden and Russia. It varied in different countries, but as used in Rotterdam, which was the measurement adopted also in England, it amounted to 10 old wine gallons or 8½ imperial gallons (*OED*).

Schoolfellow whom I had not seen for more than 40 years. I had not the least recollection of him but by name, I knew he was a bigger lad than I was at that time; he is now a Farmer at Gembling not far from Lissett; we talked over what had occurred in former times, and parted I dare say without the least regret; but I, with a certain something undefined at the remembrance of former days.

Wednesday 27th. Sepr

Heard from Wm. this morning who says Hall had been in London 2 or 3 days, so that his Manchester expedition has been very short, indeed I could not see the least probability of his succeeding there; The Old Cardinal said he Hall was likewise going to Liverpool, which I credited very little, but the old Monk is so credulous that he will believe almost any thing.

Thursday 28th. Sep

A Fine rain most of this Forenoon, the weather very warm. This is Howden Shew time, where good horses sell very well, but there are several of inferior kinds which will not be good to get into their owners Pockets.

Friday 29th. Sep

Watson Arton came this forenoon at School time with the Ellerker Highway Book to Balance. I do not like to be broken in upon when I am engaged, and I wonder how people can be so unthinking as to suppose I can spare time to attend to them. Watty had been at Howden Shew with three Horses two years old each which he sold for something more than a hundred pounds in the whole; Richd. Marshall sold one the same age for 31 pounds it cannot be said that the price of Horses is low, for what can pay better than these prices on an average. Sent to Hull this day by Cousens to the Stamp Office £40–1–6 the amount of the last quarter, which is but small compared with the Quarter before. Two men have been taken for stealing Mr. Craggs' Rags, one a very bad Character of the name of Wilson of North Cave the other I understand is a man from Gilberdike, I do not know his name, it is said the Rags or part of them were found at York. Bought of T. Pinder a piece of Stuff for a pair of Breeches at 5/6 pr. yd. which comes to 9s–7d and eight Pearl buttons for the knees 8d. — It is seldom that I get my Cloaths made to fit me and I do not think I am very difficult, the last pair of Breeches I had made, came down to the Calf of my leg, something like a Dandy coachman they would not do for me so I was obliged to have them cut shorter.

Saturday 30th. Sepr.

I have not a very high opinion of Fidlers in general, what a miserable employment fiddling must be, and yet how anxious many people are to be called good fidlers; Horsehair and Catgut rubbed together makes what is called delightful music, so it may to those who relish it; I am sure I do not admire the fidlers jigs, indeed a person makes himself look ridiculous by nodding his head and keeping his elbows in motion as though he had got St. Vitus's dance. It is now said that Wilson is not one of the Rag merchants, but that they are two travelling Potters, who are committed to the House of Correction at Beverley. — The Revd. Mr. Barnard called this day, to desire me to give notice for a meeting on the 9th. October next, respecting the School land, — He has set himself on having an Organ in the Church with a part of the Rent of the land, and the other part to be given to the School — I cannot help smiling at the thought of a <u>Box Organ</u>,[67] but it will be rather a grave matter to give a hundred pounds for the play thing. Caught a fine young Pigeon between our house & Cousen's.

Sunday 1st. Octr.

Miss Kitty says Hall has gone to Brighton where he has got a situation, he could have had a place in London but there was as great a number of young Men as in the last place he had so he declined: It is not long since Miss said that the last Situation he had in London was the most comfortable a person could have; I thought it was no great thing and it appears it has proved so. I think Dr. Johnson proved the firmness of his mind the morning after he had been attacked with a paralytic stroke when he was deprived of his voice, he wrote to several of his friends, telling them of the circumstance. Had he been a person who could not have written I have no doubt but it would have been taken for granted that his understanding was impaired, as he would not have had the means to make himself intelligible.

Monday 2nd. Octr.

Got a Mett of Wheat this day of Henry Arton, never asked what it was to be, it is in part payment, so that [it] is scarce worth while enquiring about the price. I have been reading Boswell's Life of Johnson which is very entertaining. I never saw Johnson's Journey to the Hebrides or western Islands, I suppose it is an amusing Book. Corn still keeps up its price particularly Oats, although there are such large supplies; what the price would have been if the ports had not been opened for importation, can hardly be known. I see by an Account of what is called an Agricultural meeting at Andover, that the Farmers there are tired of giving their support for the increase of Rents, they complain that the Corn laws have done them no good; these Farmers appear to show a spark of Wisdom above their Fellows in general.

Tuesday 3rd. Octr.

Engaged in balancing the Highway Books, they go in tomorrow so that all must be fairly stated this day. Green Corn is growing amazingly amongst the Stubbles, some say it is part of the Seed which has laid in the Ground until this time, but whether it be so, or corn that has been shaken it will be very acceptable to the Farmers who are scarce of Fodder; the weather is much in their favour it being particularly fine, without any Frosts at nights; some Grass closes are beautiful to see, they are so finely clothed in cheerful green.

Wednesday 4th. Octr.

Heard from Wm. this morning that the Military Chest is coming again, which caused his mother so much pleasure, that she seemed delighted to give

---

[67] A 'box' organ is so called because the pipes are enclosed within a swell box, faced on one or more sides with a set of balanced shutters. When these are closed, the tone is almost completely muffled, but when opened, usually by means of a pedal, the sound bursts forth with a 'swelling' effect, producing a rich and powerful volume of reed-tone. The swell organ was invented or at least introduced into England by Messrs. Abraham Jordan in 1712 at St. Magnus the Martyr, London Bridge (Sumner 169, 191–3).

me the information when I got up. I am also glad myself at all opportunities to hear from him. I see by the Papers that Hunt[68] has been at a public meeting in London where a requisition to the Lord Mayor was agreed on, to call a meeting respecting the Corn laws. Abolish them I say.

Thursday 5th. Octr.

Thos. Marshall came in last night and stayed until 11 O'clock when once he gets set, he is in no hurry of rising, for he has so many tales to tell of impositions which have been attempted upon him that he is very amusing. He has been annoyed this summer by a set of great <u>Stoving</u> Lads washing in the Mill Beck on Sundays, on one Side he has a Summer eaten Close, and on the other Side meadow, the great <u>hoving</u> beggars always choose the Meadow Side, he saw them one Sunday <u>maybe</u> 12 or 13 or more of them, 4 of them at the time naked in the Beck, which he took care to clear of them by Cobbling them pretty well with Clods; and then begun to <u>reason</u> and expostulate with them, telling them they did him a great deal of hurt by treading his Meadow and making it so bad to mow, wishing they would exercise on the other Side of the Bank, when <u>yan great gloring Raggal</u>, said you may Summer eat this side, <u>Curse-be-to-thee</u> said Tom am I to summer eat my Meadow a purpose to please such a <u>feal</u> as thee. He complains of being hampered by the Labourers as usual, and swears they are longer now in picking their teeth after getting their meat, than they formerly used to be in eating, then they are cocking up their heads and looking at the Sun, indeed they will mind ought or nought rather than their work, and the interest of their masters. He had a drain to dress which he offered to a Labourer for seven Shillings, nay mayster says he I <u>sud</u> have ten, but however nine, dean't tell me about <u>sud</u> have, what I <u>sud</u> have five and twenty Shillings a piece for Lambs and now am forced to take 20 shillings, but I tell thee 7s. is <u>my</u> price for this Drain, and I'll keep it on purpose for a standing job when any body wants work, he has told one fellow of it, who he does not doubt will ask him 14s.!! so that he is likely to keep it undone, there is about 3 days work in it; the first fellow has been doing nought for 3 days the time he might have done it, but Tom says he has given him over high wages ever since Martinmas last, while he can afford to keep holiday now; besides he has kept him an Ass all the time which he rode to work on. Now says Tom what do you think of a fellow like this? then he concludes with a hearty swearing at the fond Devils.

Robt. Marshall & the Revd. Jn. King are appointed Surveyors of the Highways for the ensuing year. Club night a very throng meeting but got done in good time and at home before ten O'clock. The air a good deal cooler this day, it having been a frost the last night. Days shorten fast the Sun not shining on the bottom of the School Window after 4 O'clock at night.

---

[68] Henry Hunt (1773–1835), commonly called 'Orator Hunt', was a staunch radical and associate of William Cobbett. He had presided over the great protest meeting in St. Peter's Field, Manchester, in Aug. 1819, which developed into a riot that was brutally suppressed by the authorities and became known as the 'Peterloo Massacre'. He was arrested and tried for conspiracy for which he was sentenced to 2½ years in prison. He was subsequently elected as MP for Preston in Aug. 1830 but lost his seat in 1833 (*DNB*).

6th. Octr. Friday

The Times this morning seems to think that the Corn question will meet with the same treatment as Catholic emancipation. I have not the least doubt but every exertion will be made by the Landholders to keep up the rents of their Dirty Acres, but I have some small hope that they will be defeated in their attempts, not to cram dear Corn down the throats of the People but to keep it out of their mouths altogether. I devoutly wish that every poor Man by his exertion and industry, may be able to maintain himself and family without the degradation of applying either to Charity, or unfeeling Overseers; as to the worthless I can have very little pity for them. Am at West Ella this day seeing my Mother who is very well for her Age, her leg is much better since it has been poulticed.

Saturday 7th. Octr.

Recd. Wm's Box last night all safe, with a great treat for me in the reading way, The mint Drops and Pills were received with great gratitude, from the good thinking lad. I am glad to find that he employs himself so well in Reading, he will have both amusement and interest in the History of our Country, I know that Historians are very subject to give us their own views, instead of Facts. Hume is very partial to Royalty, and at every opportunity is ready to sneer at Religion, for which I do not admire him. Wm. has the advantage of me in having access to what writer he pleases and I am glad to find that he makes so good use of his time. At Ellerker this afternoon at Mr. Leason's settling with him for the Church sess which I have been collecting for him. Mr. L. says he cannot sit to read an Hour in an Evening without falling asleep; this shows that there is no relish for the work. I should be unhappy to be debarred from reading.

Sunday 8th. Octr

Wm. says he hopes I continue my Journal. I have done so from the time I sent him the last Sheets, I hope the present scrawl will at least afford him some entertainment. I am very sorry to hear of the unfortunate young man's destiny which he mentions. I cannot tell how his mother feels, but I know I should not survive were he in the same situation; It is in the nature of Guilt to harden, a prison is a dangerous place, even if a culprit be dismissed he generally is worse when set at large than before his committal. I read in the Edinburgh Review the Remarks there made on the Hamiltonian System[69] of acquiring languages. I think it merits being attended to from the Specimens of the Italian with the English literal translation it does not appear to be difficult to understand. Robt. Marshall here this evening, smoked a pipe or two of Tobacco; he was glad to hear that Wm. keeps well.

---

[69] James Hamilton (1769–1829) first taught the Hamiltonian linguistic system in Philadelphia in 1816, printing explanatory texts for the use of his pupils. It was successfully adopted in the American universities as well as in Boston and Canada. In 1823, Hamilton came to London and taught in several major British cities. His system was defended in 1826 by Sydney Smith in the *Edinburgh Review* and in the *Westminster Review* (*DNB*).

9th. Octr. Monday

Cobbett is quite entertaining in his Rural Rides, he indeed excels in rural descriptions; he sees as well as all may who do not shut their eyes, the poverty and degradation of what were once called the lower Classes, then the Peasantry, and at a late meeting some Sir John whose name it is not worth while to remember, except with execrations, called them the poor Devils, so here they must be at the lowest Ebb of scandal and what is all this for? Even because the poor are nearly in a state of starvation, it is amazing that things should be in the state they are, some wallowing in all kinds of extravagance and Luxury, while others are depressed almost below humanity. Wrote a notice to Wm. Green at Brantingham to quit the House and Land which he holds of the Churchwardens of So. Cave for which he pays £20 pr. Ann. 30s. a month is expended in Bread, a pound for a Sermon on Easter Tuesday, and 1 pound yearly for a Dinner at Cave fair and another at Christmas in the Workhouse, where there are only two Paupers at present Sarah Thornton & Wm. Marshall. Potatoe tops look very black from the effect of the Frost on Thursday night last.

Tuesday 10th. Octr.

Wrote an Agreement for Wilkn. Ayre to let a Cottage at Ellerker to a labourer there for eight pounds a year with 2 small gardens, wrote a notice for a tenant of Wilkn Ayre's to quit at Lady day next. Paid W. Cousens 2s/6d for Wm's Box from London, very low charged this time, sent the Parcel to my Sister this day by the Carrier, a fine moist forenoon; in the afternoon rather brighter. A man of the name of Foster of Faxfleet was robbed on Friday night last between the Ings Bridge & Sands lane end by two men, one of them of the name of Turner who used to live in the House beside the Pinfold So. Cave, I once helped to take him for stealing some Ducks, he turned evidence and impeached his Companion who was imprisoned a year, & the King's evidence was cleared. Thos. Fisher is gone to Justice this day, having been sent for by one of the Magistrates Mr. Saltmarsh; as Turner is in custody I do not know of what use So. Cave Constable can be for, but time will tell. The man's father who was robbed was here this morning before I got up, he says his Son has sworn to Turner as one of the Men who robbed him; notwithstanding this a farmer of Broomfleet said yesterday he did not believe the man had been robbed but he had been drunk and lost his money and Watch 10 Pounds he says he has lost, while others say he had no such Sum of money. Spoke for a Hare this evening to send to William which I hope will be ready.

Wednesday 11th. Octr.

This is Hull fair day,[70] I never was there at the time and without something particular occur it is not very probable that I shall attend for the future. I have numerous applications for work in the jobbing line, better employers than payers a great deal. One wishes I would just write a notice to his

---

[70] Hull's regular autumn fair (established by a grant in 1598) replaced the earlier St. Augustine's Fair, which was first held in 1293. By 1823, the date fixed for the beginning of Hull Fair was 11 Oct., but in practice it became customary to start on the Saturday nearest to that date and continue for the next 7 days (*VCHYER* i. 411–2; Baines ii. 252).

tenant to quit; another wishes I would just make an Agreement or Memorandum, for letting some Property, then another if I would just draw a plan of some Land just in a rough way then another sends a handful of Old Black Pens to mend, enough to defile me by touching them; then again if I would just write a few lines for him, then others with their tax Papers to fill up just by way of amusement for me, then others asking advice just to hear what I say when they are resolved on following their own Opinions. I think these are amongst the miseries of life: there being no profit attending them, otherwise they would not be so tiresome. Mr. Bridgman and Old Willy have set off this day for Malton fair,[71] where they generally go once a year at this time, several of Mr. B's relations living in that part, he has likewise a good deal of Property in that neighbourhood. It is very likely that he will get all that belongs Old Willy, so he treats him with an annual excursion at no expence. This is the way of the world everyone anxious for more even if they possess more than is sufficient for them.

"Will you lend me ten Shillings"
"Says the Bells of Saint Helen's"

Why may not South Cave Fair be as good a subject as jingling Bells here it is, short metre

> A Hare! A Hare!
> Says Sammy Ayre.
> Let us catch it,
> Says Willy Padgett.
> Let me have it,
> Says Kester Levitt.
> She's a sweet one,
> Says Sammy Leighton.
> She's an odd one,
> Says Joseph Purdon.
> Oh! for a Dog,
> Says Tommy Hogg.
> Click her by leg,
> Says Johnny Clegg.
> Kill her with Fork,
> Says Georgy Turk.
> Step into Gap,
> Says Mr. Tapp
> I see her run

---

[71] In 1823, 5 fairs were held annually at Malton: Monday and Saturday before Palm Sunday; Saturday before Whitsuntide; Saturday before 15 July; on 11 and 12 Oct.; and on Saturday before Martinmas Day. The first was famous for horses, and the others for cattle (Baines ii. 478).

Says Bobby Dunn.
Come to <u>Winder</u>,
Says Johnny Pinder
It's diverting,
Says Ralph Martin,
I'll have a look,
Says Barnard Cook.
Where is she now?
Says Willy Dow,
I really dont know,
Says Sammy Shaw
She's run away,
Says Old John Day!!! and there's an end ont.

Thursday 12th. Octr.

A very fine morning quite warm, I see by the Times this morning there is a project for two prices, Paper & Cash, viz Paper one fourth of Gold, it appears to be a wild scheme, however I cannot understand it. Cobbett has often said that the time would come when this would take place, then the value of Sovereigns will shew itself. Sent my quarters Subscription 10s/6d to the Schoolmaster's Association.[72] I have now paid up three years. I hope at some time it may [be] a benefit to me. Mr. Ringrose is very ill at Leeds or at least was on Monday. I have not heard of him since, he has four Doctors to attend him, he has been obliged to have his water drawn from him, he has had a wound on one of his Legs for some years which has Closed up, and has a bad effect on his whole frame. Mr. Levitt of Ellerker where Land has been advertised for sale some time, told me yesterday he would sell it in Lots, but I think he wants more for it than it is worth; But if he be obliged to Sell he must take such prices as it will bring. It is generally supposed to be deeply mortgaged, and when this is the case a Man is not the master of his own property. The Land is not in such high condition as formerly, it has been so often cropped that it wants a good deal of management to bring it round.

Friday 13th. Octr.

I got a slight cold yesterday and was very restless all the night but am better again this morning. I had a good deal of fever, but towards morning I rather began to sweat, which is the only thing that brings me round again. A

---

[72] The Hull, East Riding and North Lincolnshire Schoolmasters' Association was the first attempt at professional educational organization in the region and was founded in 1823. RS having 'paid up three years' must have been one of the founder members. Although more a friendly society than a professional organization, it was recorded in 1825 as resolving to petition Parliament against the land tax and poor rate assessment on school buildings. The association held annual meetings each Whit Tuesday and members who failed to attend were fined 2s. 6d. The subscription, paid quarterly, was 2 guineas per annum, and in 1827, when the membership stood at 41, the association's funds amounted to over £375. By 1836 its funds had risen to £926 19s. 8d., yet at the same time its membership had fallen to only 30. Membership must have continued to fall as it seems to have gone rather rapidly into decline after that date and appears to have ceased to exist by about 1838 (Lawson 193–4; *HA* 26 Dec. 1823, 19 May 1826, 25 May 1827, 12 June 1835).

Stormy rainy morning; at west end last night, Robt. Marshall had gone to Mr. Wads at Drewton, Frank Wood has taken Mr. Clarke's farm at Riplingham, for his Son, it belongs Mr. Duesbury at Beverley, and contains about 250 Acres. Clarke gave notice to quit, he being a good deal annoyed in his yard by Mr. Thompson, who exercises nearly as much right in it, as Clarke himself.

Saturday 14th. Oct.

At Beverley this day meeting Mr. Walker the Surveyor of taxes, now that the amount is small, the trouble is proportionally large, there is abundance more of work now than when the Property tax[73] was paid; I suppose the reason is, Money is scarce and all methods must be used to enforce the payment to the utmost. I rode Robt. Marshall's Horse which carried me very well. I dined with Mr. Walker at the Beverley Arms, none but us two in the Room, we had Wine after Dinner which he thought was not very good, but as I seldom drink wine I refrain from giving an opinion of it. I found I could drink it. — There is a new Landlord at the Cross Keys, where I called as I came from Dinner about four O'clock where there was a large Company drinking Poonch (as Dr. Johnson used to call it) for the profit of the new Landlord, and the loss of themselves. I found it would not do for me to make a Fool of myself by staying amongst them, so I set off without any Company, and got home about half past six. Robt. Marshall came up this night when we played two or three Games at Draughts;[74] we never play for any thing, so that it is more amusement. The Times did not arrive this day.

Sunday 15th. Oct

Two Papers this morning, the one that missed yesterday came today. A Fire made in the Room this day the first time for this Season; about Hull fair, people generally begin to wear Clothing a little thicker, and to have fires which is an indication that Winter is coming on; but the weather yet is remarkably fine, and I hope will continue so some time longer, — I see there is a great deficiency in the Quarter's Revenue, — were an individual to go in the manner that Government does, he would soon be in a state of insolvency, indeed it appears all that is aimed at now, is to pay the interest if possible, taking no thought of keeping down the principal, but a change certainly must take place, — We none of us were at Hull fair.

—I hope the Bookselling trade is reviving, as I see many new works advertised. Absolute John has a Catalogue of 50 new Publications, may the business continue in prosperity. The Sun shone upon the bottom of the Middle Window of the School this day no longer than about 3 O'clock. The dreary winter makes its approach, in the Country; while the same Season is looked for with joy and anxiety in the great City; Dissipation there is the order of the Day or rather night, for I suppose there are many who see very little of Daylight; — There

---

[73] Probably a reference to the removal in 1825 of the house tax from households assessed under £10 per year and of the window tax from dwellings with less than 8 windows (Dowell iii. 174 and 184).

[74] Draughts was a popular game in England at the beginning of the 19th c. following the publication of Sturge's *Guide to the Game of Draughts* which was first published in 1800 and went into several editions (*EB* viii. 547).

was a Hare killed in the Street nearly opposite Mr. Robinson's this day in the Market time, poor puss had got lost, — Attended the Sale of Anthony Burton's house this Evening at Barnard Cook's. Ned Coates was the purchaser, but how he will raise money to pay for it is another consideration, it is very unlikely he can do it himself, but he may have been employed by some person, the purchase money was £46. Mrs. Tinsdill at our house talking while after 9 O'clock.

Tuesday 17th Octr.

Made some Ink this morning, the hot weather has been against Ink, causing it to mould so much, it will be better now; besides in hot weather it evaporated and dried up very much. I have read most of Moore's life of Sheridan,[75] I see Mr. Canning first came into notice in 1794 ... Old Willy and Mr. Bridgman arrived safe at home yesterday but I did not see them until this Evening. I generally go two or three times a week, and get a pipe there. Old Willy finds no Tobacco, so any who have a mind may treat themselves at their own expence.

Wednesday 18th. Octr.

No Times again this morning this is twice in less than a week, which the Paper has missed, if they have been regularly put in, there must be neglect or carelessness some where. I should like to have it remedied. There is a Sale at North Cave this day, and tomorrow. Mr. Constable's who was formerly in partnership with Mr. Boyes[76] at Hull, I suppose he is sold up under an execution or writ of some kind, he has got as far as he can. Walker's affairs were greatly involved, and his Son in Law it appears was not calculated to put them in a better state ... Heard that Mr. Ringrose is getting better.

Thursday 19th. Octr.

... Recd. two papers this morning. Wm. says Craggs had applied to him offering him a part of his business, which he has properly declined, he knows the Man — and his wife — and their manners. I remember the agreement that was made with him before and the manner in which it was fulfilled, he Wm. was to have an increasing Salary for 3 years, but that cringing fellow Wells wormed himself in, the Salary instead of an increase, fell off more than the last quarters revenue, even to nothing. These things cannot easily escape my memory. A Water Jury Supper at Matthew Pickering's this evening when I purpose attending, these Jury men are properly called Expenitors, or Expenditors,

My mind's independent and free,
I court not the World for applause;
With my Friends I would ever agree,
And I fear not the worst of my foes.
   RS.

---

[75] Thomas Moore, *Memoirs of the Life of the Rt. Hon. R. B. Sheridan.* London: Longman, 1825 (4°). Two subsequent 2-vol. 8° editions were published in 1825, and a 4th ed., also in 2 vols., in 1826.

[76] Boyes and Constable, ironmongers at 48 Market Place, Hull (Baines ii. 267).

Oct. 20 Friday

Packed up Wm's Box last night just before 10. O'clock having waited until that time in expectation of a Hare to send him. I am sorry to be disappointed as I was promised a week ago to have one against the time; and for fear of forgetting[,] Eliza went on Wednesday night to see about it, but all our care did not ensure success, for which I am very sorry. Robinson of Mount Airy and Mr. Shackleton of Province have each of them lately got threshing Machines,[77] they are nearly as prejudicial to the poor threshers as the Power Looms are to the hand weavers. The Drill for sowing Corn[78] is the best invention for not abridging labour, as it requires rather more hands than sowing without it; and there is an advantage in the sparing or saving of Seed Corn, another advantage is that the growing Corn is a great deal better to hoe than when sown in the common way. I was at the Water Jury Supper last night but came away before ten O'clock. Recd. half a letter from my Sister at Hull, from my Brother who is well, he wants to know if I shall expect the Times back again which I send him, I shall desire him to take care of them as they will be as safe with him as myself.

Saturday 21st Octr.

At the West end this forenoon, all my friends throng in the fields so that I soon came back again. In the afternoon at Ellerker helping (I should have said <u>assisting</u>, as help is nearly obsolete in the polite world) Mr. Levitt to value his land which will be offered for Sale at the George Inn at Hull on Tuesday next, there is about 119 Acres, which we valued at from £30 to £90 pr. Acre, the whole something more than £7000, if the prices bid come any thing near this it will be sold though I think not by Auction as there will be a Duty of Sevenpence a pound to pay; so that it is most likely it will be disposed of by private contract after the Sale. Drank Tea at Mr. Levitt's, and got back about seven O'clock; staid at Old Willy's about an hour, when I got home, Robt. Marshall was waiting for me[,] he staid till after nine O'clock. The Times missed again this day, this is three times in one week, I have some jealousy of Old Barnard keeping the paper a day longer than he ought to do; but perhaps I am wrong, however I have threatened him I shall write to London to know where the stoppage is.

Sunday 22nd. Oct

The Paper which should have been here yesterday arrived today, so that there were two this morning. A Very heavy rain about noon, but cleared up

---

[77] Experiments had been made with mechanical threshing machines in Scotland in the early years of the 18th c. but there are no recorded references to the use of a threshing machine in the East Riding until 1794, when Isaac Leatham reported that he knew of only one in the county. In 1812, Strickland wrote that threshing machines in the East Riding were becoming 'very general on the considerable farms throughout the district', and by the late 1820s, they were in general use all over the country and had to a large extent superseded the flail and the traditional practice of winter hand-threshing. Farm labourers' fears that their use would deprive them of winter work contributed to the outbreak of agricultural unrest in 1830. Steam-powered threshing machines were not introduced until the 1840s (Fussell 161; Leatham 30; Strickland 88).

[78] See n.48 (1827).

finely in the afternoon. I see by the Rockingham[79] that the last voyage of the Steam Packets from Hull this Season will be on the 11th Novr. next.

Monday 23rd. Octr.

The three men who stole the Rags from Mr. Craggs were tried at the Sessions at Beverley last week and were found guilty, and sentenced to be transported for seven years each. One of them appears to have been a hardened offender, when sentence was past upon him, he said the next time he went a thieving should be with a Rogue and not a fool. Old Lundy the Carrier of No. Cave is blamed as being connected with the robbers, it is said they were at his house until the time of night that the robbery was committed. Not a single sample of Corn shewn in the Market this day, as the prices are dull none of the full farmers are disposed to sell; I hope the time will come when they will be obliged to put up with moderate prices.

Tuesday 24th. Oct

A Customer of Old Willy's in the Leather and nail line, telling us he had heard Cobbett's register read lately, where he says in about a year or perhaps rather more from this time wheat will be at 3s/6d or 4s pr. Bushell; I told him I had heard that Cobbett was a false prophet. Aye but what sort of prophets are the great ones who rule us? Oh Billy holds them up says he[,] he is a <u>buttoner</u> he fits all tight on, let them try to get up the prices of Corn again and persuade me (says he) it is my benefit to pay sixpence for threepennyworth of bread, they deserve to be choked who believe this doctrine. — A very fine clear day, it is a glorious Wheat seed time, a great part of the Wheat in this neighbourhood is sown, and a good deal of it appearing above ground, it being so warm that it very soon vegetates. I rely upon Providence, being above all intermedling Statesmen. Got a glass of some kind of made wine at Timothy Dunn's this Evening.

Wednesday 25th. Octr.

A rainy morning but turned out fine after. Fine days at this time of the year make one regret the long days that are past, we do not expect fine weather at this time much longer. The days now by chance are bright, as old age sometimes seems to be not much impaired, but it is a kind of false brilliancy. In spring when the days are the same length as now, we look with delight for the Summer, the harbinger of which is a fine Sunny day. A meeting at Church this Evening afterwards adjourned to Old Rachel's, where arguments silly enough were advanced to shew that a Labourer with a Family might be in a better situation, if he would, than applying to the Parish for relief, certainly there can be no pleasure to the poor fellows in exposing their wants.

Thursday 26th. Oct

Richd. Marshall bought Mr. Levitt's Wold Close at the Sale on Tuesday last for £26 pr. Acre, it is less than I expected it would be sold for. Teavil

---

[79] Originally entitled the *Rockingham and Hull Weekly Advertiser*, it was first published on 2 Jan. 1808 and continued until 1844, having been re-named the *Hull Rockingham and Yorkshire and Lincolnshire Gazette* in 1828. It was a Whig organ, said to have been founded by members of the Sykes family and John Cowham Parker, and was published weekly on Saturdays (*VCHYER* i. 429).

Leeson bought Trancledale's Close, on the Drewton road side, for £60 pr. Acre, and Mr. Briggs of Hull the Common Close at the same price, these lots were all that were sold — Mr. Baron of Drewton sent us a Hare this day, had it just come a week sooner, it would I trust now have been in London: it certainly was not soon enough but still it is not too late, that is for ourselves, but I had rather it had been otherwise.

Friday 27th. Oct

Young Teavil Leeson was fined at Beverley last Saturday ten pounds for shooting without a licence and not being qualified, it was at Newbald or Sancton where he was sporting. He might as well have been employed in dusting some musty parchments. Court day[80] where I have always dined since I came to Cave, and receive as a present half a Guinea, it is a sinecure but a very small one truly, yet it is something. Sixteen at Dinner, all good company so long as I stayed amongst them, which was till near Seven O'clock.

Saturday 28th. Octr.

... A cold day gloomy and a high wind. Robt. Marshall and Richard Kirby staid at the Court last night after the rest of the Company, and got to falling out. Robt. struck at Kirby and gave him a black eye, for he aggravated him so much that he could not guide himself. He is afraid Kirby will get an order for him, which if it be the case he must make up, as an Assault has been committed. Robt. has been wishing ever since that he had never gone.

Sunday 29th. Octr.

Methodists both this day and for some time past been making a great hurry, in converting persons, especially a many Lads and lasses, the Curate at Church both this and the last Sunday preaching against any change of heart or regeneration, all the new birth that is required he says is communicated by baptism. I never heard this unscriptural doctrine preached before, I have given the parson to understand that I neither approve nor believe his doctrine. Even the Parish Clerk told him that he (the Clerk) never heard such preaching before so manifestly contrary to all preaching he had ever been acquainted with.

Monday 30th. Octr.

Wm. Loncaster was sworn in Constable on the Court day, much to his satisfaction. Old Ths. Robinson was once leading Beans out of one of the Strays up Porter hole, with his Son Tom fixed upon the load, Old Tom however contrived to throw the Waggon over as soon as he got out of the Close, with his Son Tom in the midst of it; On which he cried out O my Bayn! my Bayn! he's killed! he's killed! if thou be dead my Bayn shout out!! Tom was safe and answered his Father, who then thought he was not killed, this is a specimen of Wisdom formerly at So. Cave; it contains a great deal of feeling that is certain.

Tuesday 31st. Octr.

A Fire in the School this day for the first time this Season. Yesterday afternoon I was not very well, but I went to the Market as I had taxes to collect, but came home before Seven O'clock, and got a Bason of Gruel made, and took

---

[80] The manorial court met twice a year in the spring and autumn. (See Introduction).

it without any liquor in it. I then went to Bed about Seven and found myself quite better this morning; I believe it to be very hurtful for people to take liquors when they are ill, because if there be any disposition to fever, this will encourage it, and inflame the frame.

Wednesday 1st Nov

Heard from Wm. that he had got the Box safe, & that he was very well; Old Willy has got a Box with Partitions for his Nails to stand in the Window, which is a very great improvement of the plan he was on before, he happened to fall in for it second hand at a moderate price. Bought 3 hundred quills of Jn. Stather of Everthorpe ...

Thursday 2nd. Nov.

In a trial in the King's Bench the Lord Chief Justice said that Banker's call the Bank or office their "<u>Shop</u>" and they are the only persons that do so now. So this nation of Shopkeepers have vanished within a very few years; has the Country in general been ashamed of Bonaparte's affixing their calling upon them as a stigma? if this be the case it shows a great want of firmness — saw Richd. Kirby last night his eye looked black, but said nothing of his affray last week, — Club night, Matthew Smith nearly beat to raise his money, he had it up within sixpence, and none of his friends would advance it for him, at last Robt. Dunn lent him 6d. which set him completely at ease; he is so drunken and worthless that [it] is in vain offering to assist him. Got home by nine O'clock.

Friday 3rd. Nov.

The newspaper missed again this morning, so that this is a Blank day for me — An old Sailor and his wife begging. I told him I would give him 3d. and in sending out for change he launched out into the history of his life, he was born at the Cape of Good hope, was in the Bay of St. Helena when Bonaparte was buried, I asked him if he had ever seen him, O many a time master, he once gave me five Shillings when ashore at St. Helena, this I did not credit[.] I never (said he) prayed for Bonny's death, he was a good friend to England, (so say the Farmers now) now says I here is a penny more for you because you did not pray for the death of the Captive. He seemed struck, and said they ought to have taken Bonny into the English Service, then left me with many marine thanks.

Saturday 4th. Nov

Taxes paid in this day at Beverley, but I did not attend as Robt Marshall had to go I sent the money with him £145–6–3, it came on very wet and stormy in the afternoon so that I was better at home. The Paper which missed yesterday came this morning, it having the South Shields Post mark on it, so that it had gone a long way north of us.

Sunday 5th. Nov

My wife very ill since Friday, attacked with a violent purging and sickness. I went to desire Mr. Tinsdill to see her last night, he gave her a mixture which relieved her considerably in a short time; and a large blister[81] put on her body

---

[81] Blisters were usually mustard plasters, applied to the skin to raise blisters.

at night which was very painful; she was much better today, and I hope will continue recovering. Very cold today.

Monday 6th. Novr.

My wife in a mending way having got up this morning before eight O'clock and eaten some breakfast. Hall has sent Miss Kitty word that when he left Cave which was on Monday he went to Manchester and stayed two days, from thence to Liverpool and stayed two days, from thence to Bristol, yes to Bristol from Liverpool and staid two days more, — now from what Wm. said, Hall was in London either on Friday or Saturday after he left Cave, so that travelling & stoppages must be settled by himself and Miss. Hall appears to draw a long Bow, for it is a great shot from Liverpool to Bristol, & thence to London.

Tuesday 7th. Novr.

A very hard frost this morning, quite a contrast to the weather we had in the Summer. Hare feasts at the Public houses last night to keep up the 5th. Novr.[82] I was not at any of them. I had some invitation, but as I could not attend to them all, I did not attend to any of them; — Old Rachel Levitt says a woman from No. Cave called at their house last week, she was going to Justice to get an order for her husband abusing her, — Old Rachel asked her if she was good natured to him, she said he did not deserve to be good natured with. Now I'll tell you how to do and I'll warrant he will not abuse you any more, go home this night and make him a good Cup of tea and say nothing of what has happened & you may depend on it he will have no thought of behaving ill to you again. This was good advice from a woman who is rather <u>silly betimes</u>.

Wednesday 8th. Nov

... at the Hare feast at Barnard Cook's on Monday night, Mrs. Cook and Robt. Dunn were fighting, the Landlady has given her adversary a black eye, and swelled lip; I suppose there was a good deal of drunkenness going on in the Town, but I saw nothing of it.

Thursday 9th. Novr

Heard this morning of the dreadful accident of the Grimsby Steam packet blowing up,[83] Several lives are lost, and many persons wounded, but at present it is all hearsay, and the accounts are so contradictory that there is no reliance

---

[82] RS recorded hare feasts being held in the public houses at South Cave in the years 1826, 1827, 1829, 1834 and 1836. The custom was recorded for Leavening in the northern Yorkshire Wolds at the end of the 18th c., but no other references to hare feasts in association with 5 Nov. have been traced, although it may be relevant that there was said to be a widespread belief in early 19th c. Yorkshire and Lincolnshire that everyone had the right to shoot game with impunity on that day (Addison 12; *NQ* 7th ser. 6 (1888) 404–5).

[83] Early on the morning of 7 Nov. 1826, the Grimsby steam packet, 'Graham', burst its boiler while secured to an anchored Scottish steamer, the 'United Kingdom', which had been forced by bad weather to take shelter in the Humber. At the time of the explosion, the deck of the 'Graham' was crowded with passengers, who had disembarked from the larger vessel in order to continue their interrupted journey by landing at Hull and proceeding from there by coach. Six people were killed and several more seriously injured. The 'Graham' herself remained afloat and was towed into Hull (*HP* 14 Nov. 1826, 2–3).

to be placed on them. This is the Sittings day[84] here[,] a Constable meeting at Barnard Cook's where Mr. Smelt the chief Constable presided. Miss Smelt and a niece dined at our house, we had a roast Goose for Dinner, having got a Goose of Henry Arton in part payment; — My wife a great deal better, she attends the School every day having never been a day absent.

Friday 10th. Novr.

Barnard Cook has given notice to Mr. Smelt that he will not buy Burton Sittings[85] to be held at Cave any more, as some of the Publicans will contribute nothing towards the expence which is three guineas. I think it is likely they will be held at Cottingham, another year if not held here as usual.

Saturday 11th. Nov

At west end this morning but did not fall in for Company to hold on with, Robt. Marshall at Howden, & Richd. out amongst his Stock. Since James's death the different branches of the family can hardly agree; Mrs. Bellard the Sister from Hessle has been here a month without ever speaking to the Miller.

Sunday 12th. Nov

I have been at Houses sometimes very well furnished as far as Chairs & tables go, but not a Book to be seen, and no information to be had of any, I think books an absolutely necessary appendage, to those however who have any pretensions to knowledge; And a piece of the best furniture for a poor Man is to hang up in his House a Pig for his use ...

Monday 13th. Nov

A Dull November day. The Market for Corn much as it has been for some time past. Oats would have been a famine price had none been imported, and even with this help, they are very dear; We shall soon know whether the new parliament will be kept in awe by the tribe who call themselves the landed interest; or whether other classes of Society, are to be legislated for, and not kept under the tyranny of a Corn Monopoly; certainly some independent member or other will stand up for the rights of the poor who suffer.

Tuesday 14th. Nov

A Stranger at the Market yesterday holding forth, that a person who had £500 a year in the funds was much better off than another person who had the same income from land; as the fund holder was not burthened with the poor rates and taxes on his income; but such men as these are both ignorant and selfish, for if the poor rates were not paid as they are: the Landlords would immediately turn round on their tenants and want in Rent what is now paid to the poor, this I know to be their patriotism.

Wednesday 15th Novr.

Recd. a parcel this morning by Miss Corner from Wm: she does not know what it is to be as she has not yet seen Cousens to pay him. I suppose the

---

[84] Sittings at South Cave were held on the first 2 Thursdays before Old Martinmas (23 Nov.). (See Introduction).

[85] The earlier of South Cave's 2 hiring days was known as Burton Sittings.

creature intends to charge half the expence of the Box, this I shall not think to be right — Hall's letter to Wm. appears to have a fault that cannot be excused notwithstanding his <u>respected friend</u>, the fault is it cannot be read. I shall exert myself to look out for a Ham against Christmas for the London Market. I hope we shall procure a Hare by that time, indeed one thing with another I have no doubt we shall fit up a very interesting collection.

Thursday 16th. Nov

This is Cave Sittings Day very fine and Sunshining. A Town's Meeting last night at Tindale's where there was the most quarrelling I ever knew at a meeting of this kind but not at all on the Town's affairs[.] Wm. Cousens & Matt. Pickering begun the fray Pickering having two Guineas a year less licence to pay than Cousens on account of his house not being rated so high, they called each other every thing but <u>respected friends</u> — Then Ths. Levitt and old Loncaster began, so fierce that one would have thought that it would have soon been over but it was kept up with spirit a long time. Ths. Levitt told Loncaster he was the town's fool, and the town was not very wise or else they would not have appointed a real fool Constable. There were several people drunk, but I enjoyed nay saw it quite composed as I take care never to drink so much as to lose the little sense I possess. I came away about half past ten. Several staid until four or five O'clock the next morning.

Friday 17th. Nov

I have read all the Rural Rides of Cobbett he is very excellent at description, he has just opened on the Greek Patriots. I expect he will give them no quarter, but cut them up in his own way. One of our Poets, (Pope) says "self love and social are the same" but self interest appears to be a very different thing from the good of the public; there is one thing I admire in Cobbett, and that is his unsparing censure of the profession of Players, he seems to think (with myself) not much more of Music meetings, I do not know how the sound of the Box Organ may affect me, but the Vagabond players shall never fatten of any thing from me.

Saturday 18th. Nov

The Newspaper missed again this morning, the almost only morning that I particularly wished to see it, to see the commencements of the opening of the new Parliament. I wish I was beside the numbskull, that puts it in a wrong bag if that be the case; or perhaps it may be some political Postmaster, that may be spelling at it until another Post Day. I began last night to read the life of Dr. Clarke,[86] it was indeed a Book I much wished to see, and in this I have been gratified. A very fine day.

Sunday 19th. Novr.

The Plantations on the top of Mount Airy are now a rich Russet Colour, in a little time longer the trees will be stripped of all their Beauty: I had two

[86] William Otter, Bp. of Chichester, *The Life and Remains of Edward Daniel Clarke, Professor of Mineralogy in the University of Cambridge.* London: Cowie and Co., 1825. – 2 vols. (8°). Originally published in 1824 as a single-volume 4° edition.

Newspapers this morning. I cannot tell where the one that ought to have come yesterday has been as there is no Post mark on it as mis-sent. I read Dr. Clarke's description of the Island of St. Kilda last night, it is a singular place of curiosity, but it appears that the Poor Inhabitants who live in the midst of herds and Flocks, are not allowed so much as to taste the Flesh of them: the cravings of nature being satisfied with the Wild Birds with which the Island abounds.I think where the Countries are most fertile the poor live the worst.
Monday 20th. Novr

I agree with Cobbett respecting the Newspapers, for not one of them ever mentions him except they can catch something at him to hold him up to ridicule, but he contrives generally to pay them off, and makes them grin one against another like a set of Farmer's wives in the Market when butter settles, it is amusing to see these Doxies in a falling market, how they cry out and shew their teeth some of which are not the most handsome.
Tuesday 21st. Novr.

I am very fond of Dr. Clarke[.] I have finished the first Volume there is so much maternal feeling in his letters, that makes him quite amiable, wherever he was he was thinking of something that would be agreeable to his mother. — We have in the School a fine plant in a Flower Pot, very full of large yellow flowers which looks very pleasant at this time of the year, its name I do not know. Sun left the middle Window Bottom in the School this day about two O'clock. — Miss Kitty having carefully weighed the Box from Hall and the parcel from Wm. found the Box to weigh 5lb. and the parcel 7lbs so that she wanted 7/12 of the Carriage it was all only 1£–7s but she was partly shamed out of it by telling her we never charged a Farthing when a parcel came for any person in our Box. I do not like to be beholden to her, and still more I dislike to be imposed upon by her. I shall beg Wm. not to send any more under her care.
Wednesday 22nd. Nov.

Went to Old Willy's after School time last night, and heard most of what was and what was <u>not</u> going on in the neighbourhood. Came home about Seven O'clock and sat down in Company with Dr. Clarke until about ten. I ascended with him this Evening the highest Egyptian pyramid and took a view of the Sandy plain below: &c &c. I then went to fasten the Doors but unfortunately I laid down the Key upon the side board and attempted to lock the door with the second Vol of the Dr. but I soon found out what was the matter, and soon got all rights again, — a very dull day this[,] no Sun appearing.
Thursday 23rd. Novr.

Some of the wise Farmers saying that no duty less than 15s. pr. Qr. on wheat will be effectual to perpetuate the Monopoly with which the Country is cursed, only think of 15s. pr. Qr. on land yielding 4 Qr. pr. Acre which is 3 Pounds; about as much more as the rent, it is no wonder that the <u>Jolterheads</u> had rather have high prices as low Rents, for it is evident that the price between 50s. and 70s. is more than the rent, so let wheat be at 70s. the farmers can afford to pay 2 Pounds an Acre for their land better than cultivate it at 50s. without any rent; this is plain as two and two are four, but is the Country to be taxed about 12 Million yearly purposely to let the Farmers and Landlords starve a great part of the Community. I yet hope to see foreign Corn admitted at very low Duties, for whatever is laid on as duty is to support the Tribe of <u>Frogbellies</u> in their insolence. — Peter Wood of Beverley died yesterday he has been ill a long time, nearly two years.

Friday 24th. Nov

Paid by this Township a double County rate[87] about £42–0–0 there has been as much more paid since Lady day last; great alterations are making in York Castle[88] at the expence of the County, this double County rate in the East Riding amounts to £6074–7–8 but no matter, Palaces like jails must be supported. I have seen it observed that Parsonage houses and jails are the best looking Country buildings now a days

These County rates! These County rates,

They make the Farmer's Crazy,

The unpaid, unprais'd Magistrates,

Make those who pay uneasy.

Old Richard Milner walked to Hull yesterday and back, he is 81 years old.

Saturday 25th. Nov

A very Stormy night last night, came on Snow, two poor fellows at Ellerker were fined five pounds each on Monday last by the Magistrates at Riplingham for shooting Hares at Cave Sands on the 5th. or rather the 6th. Novr. last.

Sunday 26th. Nov

A very fine frosty morning put on my new great Coat for the first time, before noon it came on a heavy fall of Snow and continued most of the day; went to dine with Robt. Marshall he had a roast Goose, all very comfortable: got my Coat pretty well snowed upon.

Monday 27th. Nov

A Holiday this day being Martinmas Monday a good deal of rabble in the town, few of the Men who have been working hard all the year, can guide themselves properly when they have a little leisure time: My writing I think is nearly like the King's Speech it is often concerning — nothing.

---

[87] The county rate was levied by quota on individual parishes. It was the business of the High Constable of the hundred (in the case of South Cave, this was Hunsley) to require each petty constable to collect the rate from the householders of his parish. The money was applied to the judicial and administrative expenses of the riding, and also to road-building, the upkeep of bridges and the support of poor prisoners amongst other things. By the early 19th c., the rate had substantially increased and was very unpopular.

[88] In 1825, following the recommendations of a committee of Yorkshire magistrates set up to investigate and report on the requirements of the county gaol, it was decided to enlarge the area of the Castle and erect additional prison buildings. The works were commenced in 1826 and not completed until June 1835. The project involved compulsory purchase of a large house in Castlegate together with its grounds, as well as Clifford's Tower and the mound on which it stood. A massive 35-foot high wall was erected and extensive new prison buildings and a new residence for the Governor were also built at a total cost of £17,875, paid for by the 3 ridings (Knight 610–11).

28th. Novr. Tuesday

The Frost changed into Rain, at night I put on my great Coat it rained so fast, but my Shoes took in water at the Bottom so I was not much better for my great Coat. Heard this Evening that Old Sam Ayre died this afternoon, whether or not he was ill before, I never enquired, I was satisfied that he was gone. God forbid that I should say that I am sorry to hear of his death, the Old Sinner lifted up his Arm against me as much as he could, but was prevented doing me harm; so why should I be sorry to have my enemy under my feet.

Wednesday 29th. Nov

It is said Old Sam had some kind of a Fit the day before he died; However Old <u>Blashkite</u> is gone, the town will hear no more his folly from himself, he has spent all his time and had good opportunities of acquiring Property, and has not added any thing to what he originally had; indeed he went crazed to see his neighbours prosper in the world; I hope there is not such a disposition as his, left amongst us, then what was it to any of those he hated whether he went mad or not? This was one of his maxims, he said he could bear malice for 20 years then take a fresh lease: but his lease and his malice are ended. I think I have said more about him than he deserved.

Recd. a parcel from Wm. containing Cobbett's & the Drs. lancets. Wm. says he gives up all Scotchmen as bad. But he was gratified with Sir W. Scott; it is rather too sweeping to condemn a whole Country for a few Individuals. I am very happy that Wm. keeps well. I have not formed a decided Character of Cranmer, from what I know it is favourable at present. I am fully satisfied that Henry 8th. was a great tyrant.

Thursday 30th. Nov

Cobbett is very severe on Mr. Hume respecting his management of the Greek Subscription,[89] I think he says no more than is just. It is lamentable to find persons in public situations, thinking more of their own private interests than the good of the Community for whom they are employed; I myself wish Mr. Hume had not acted as he has done, that his enemies might not have had the advantage which he has given them, of lessening him in the estimation of the World. Cobbett hates his enemies, and despises his friends, he abominates the Times, which thinks like himself as much as the Courier, who is so opposite to him.

Friday 1st. Decr.

There is one of the best satirical pieces in the last Examiner (alias Tom Tit) on the King's speech which I almost ever read on any subject, it is a real cutter. — Recd. £2–10–0 being one moiety of a fine paid by a poor man of Ellerker for killing hares, one half of the fine is given to the Poor of the parish

---

[89] Joseph Hume, a leading member of the Greek Committee, had been accused by Cobbett, in his *Political Register* of 4 Nov. 1826 and subsequent issues, of malpractice in his handling of the funds raised to support a loan to be made to the cause of Greek Independence. Under his management the original price of the bonds had fallen from £59 to only £13, although Hume personally had contrived to be part-compensated for his own financial loss in the affair.

where the crime was committed; but I believe it is generally applied by the Overseers in aid of the Poor-rate. Can this be right?

Saturday 2nd. Dec

The Curate has actually refused to bury a Child, because it was baptized at the Chapel. He would not read the Burial Service over it, so that it was put into the Grave without the help of this sprig of Prelacy, I believe a Case like this has been tried, and the Clergymen have been compelled to bury all that have been baptised. I shall make further enquiry where the case is to be found. There is in London a Society for protecting the rights of Protestant dissenters;[90] I must have some information from it on the subject, if I can find how to address them. This same Journeyman Priest buried Sam Ayre the day after the poor innocent Child was refused Christian burial as it is called; Sam was baptised at the same Chapel, but then Sam had received the Sacrament, he had been Churchwarden, and was a Church goer, but then the case of refusal of Michl. Clegg's Child was it having been baptised by Dissenters. I should think this piece of Priestcraft does not know that Archbishop Tillottson[91] was baptised by Dissenters, which did not hinder him from rising in the Church.

Sunday 3rd. Dec

Got my leg bitten by a Dog on Friday night last. I went to Mr. Tinsdill to get it dressed, he says it will be no worse, I hope it will not; but I particularly dislike to be wounded by a Dog. Went to North Cave yesterday to see if I could fall in for a Ham for Wm. but without success, it is a time of year when such Hams are particularly scarce.

Monday 4th. Dec

An Association meeting for the prosecution of Felons[92] at Barnard Cook's this night, when Mr. Craggs attended with his account of Expences for apprehending the Men who stole his Rags: the expences were 37 pounds, I think it will break up the Society, Craggs drank 8 Glasses of Brandy and water, he was very drunk he then treated the Company with a Bowl of spiced wine which he called scalded wine; Abraham Barff rather controlled him; but the little Gentleman said it was well that Abraham was so old, or there was nothing

---

[90] This was the Society for Defending the Civil Rights of the Dissenters. (John W. Wickes, *Per lege si vis. A Letter Addressed to the ... Bishop of Peterborough in Answer to an Appeal made to the 'Society for Defending the Civil Rights of the Dissenters' relative to ... Church Burial by the Established Clergy* ... Stamford, [1808].).

[91] Archbishop John Tillotson (1630–94) was the son of a Puritan clothier in Sowerby, West Yorkshire. He had a successful career in the Church and rose to become the Archbishop of Canterbury from 1691 to 1694 (*DNB*).

[92] This was the New Association for the Prosecution of Felons, which held its meetings in South Cave. It was one of many such anti-criminal, self-help societies which flourished in the early part of the century, before the establishment of regular provincial municipal and later rural police forces, brought in by the Municipal Corporations Act of 1837 and the succeeding Acts of 1839, 1840, and 1856. According to a surviving handbill of 1825 (East Riding of Yorkshire Archives Office. DDMT 501), the South Cave Society had in that year 19 members, 3 from South Cave, and the rest drawn from other villages in the neighbourhood.

would have prevented Craggs from throwing Abraham out of the Window; poor Abe it was a chamber window too.

Tuesday 5th. Dec

A very cold Day can scarcely keep warm, turned a Blackguard fellow out of the Passage today who was behaving ill, he threatened what he would do, I threatened nothing but walked him out; he was not very formidable; A Person who has been brought up amongst Stock (Beasts & Sheep) not a fundholder, told me that the weekly price of Sheep at Turnips ought to be the price of a pound of Mutton, but this Season the price for Turnips is at least 3 times as much and the Price of Beasts feeding weekly the price of a Stone of Beef. He says a Sheep will lay on a pound of meat in a Week, and an Ox a Stone of meat.

Wednesday 6th. Dec

Busy preparing the Militia list,[93] this Martinmas time is not suitable for this business, there are so many men not Settled in their places. I believe there are a good many not yet hired. Ambrose the London Joiner is here at present. Eliza has seen him, he has come to settle his <u>Ancles</u> (Uncles) affairs, but all he has to settle is to receive what was left him, it is now a year since the Old man's death, and the time when the Legacies are paid. He told Eliza he had not seen <u>Walliam</u> lately as he had been in the <u>Cantry</u>. Country — I explain as I go on, because I do not know that every one into whose hands this may fall, understands the <u>refined</u> Language: which seems to have been thrown away as worthless by some and picked up by others as a prize.

Thursday 7th. Dec

Called at Mrs. Fisher's to leave a notice paper saw Mr. Ambrose, he said he had not seen <u>Walliam</u> lately, I asked him where he now lived he said in <u>Wallington</u> Street or Place or some Willington or another near the <u>Alliphent</u> and <u>Kestal</u> in the Borough, he wants exceedingly to be in Town again, to which I have no objection. — Club night tonight got done before ten.

Friday 8th. Decr

Mr. Burland the Attorney who lives at Everthorpe undertook to conduct Mr. Craggs, as far on his way home as he had to go, on Monday night, but both Craggs and his Galloway rolled so in the road that the Attorney brought them back to the Fox; when Barnard Cook sent a man with Cragg's who after a good deal of trouble got him home; the Man was rewarded by having the Door shut in his face, and not a penny given him. I make no remarks.

---

[93] Under the Militia Act of 1757 (30 Geo. II c. 25), each parish had to provide a list of all the able-bodied men in the parish between the ages of 18 and 45 from which the names of those liable for service were chosen by ballot. During the period of the diary, when there was no real threat to the nation's security, there was only one muster of the East Riding's militia regiment and that was in 1831. Most of those who actually served in the militia were paid substitutes and many parishes organized a system of insurance whereby those eligible for balloting could pay a fixed sum into a fund, before the ballot took place, so that those who were eventually chosen for service (or balloted) could draw from it the money required to pay for a substitute. RS described this system in operation at the muster of 1831 in his entry for 12 Apr. that year.

Saturday 9th. Dec

Went to Brantingham this forenoon to swear to the delivery of some notices for taxes; very fine morning, called at Mr. Atkinson's where there was a Sheffield tradesman who supplies the Old Gentleman with Articles in the hardware line; I ordered 200 Needles, and a penknife and a half, that is a new blade to be put in an old haft.

Monday 11th. Decr.

Last night I had to go down to the Workhouse with a poor young woman to get her lodgings, she had neither Shoes nor Stockings, and was almost starved to death, she is one of the Victims of the accursed Cotton trade; there is scarcely a day but some of the Poor creatures who have been brought up in these abominable Mills, are begging their bread; Happy would it have been for England if never a pound of the infernal <u>Fuzz</u> had ever found its way into this Country. Had it not been for Cotton we should not have been taxed as we are; when the Country went mad, Cotton was to do every thing; and indeed it has done every thing but make us prosperous and happy.

Tuesday 12th. Decr.

The Markets are rather lower, which has made the Farmers to grin horribly again, it is surprising what a pleasure they must take in uttering their Complaints in a Market Room where they drink and smoke until they can hardly distinguish one another; Sometimes their hardship is they have sold the wrong kind of Corn first, at others they solace themselves by bestowing on those who wish any alteration in the Corn laws, the Epithets of Fools, and <u>ruinators</u> of the Country. This is their Chorus, "keep up Corn and the Country will prosper", aye, aye, that is the doctrine of those who feel for none but themselves.

Wednesday 13th. Decr.

Recd. a parcel from Wm. last night, containing new Cravats. Cobbett is most fierce on Mr. Hume, but what good will he do? For my part I am sorry to see the mighty fallen so low. Mr. Waithman,[94] I think will expose the Bubble companies, Mr. Chairman Brogden[95] must writh[e] under the lash which the Alderman applies to him. Wm. charges us not to forget the Ham and indeed we do not, I have tried almost all over but cannot succeed for one; however I hope the Box will be fitted up to his satisfaction. — Old Willy had bought half a Pig yesterday, and was getting it salted in the Evening, he sent for some Ale to treat his friends with, as some of them told him the Bacon would stink if there was no lewance when it was salted. — Abraham is going to kill us a Pig I think on Thursday or Friday, that we may be in time for the Metropolitan Christmas market.

---

[94] Robert Waithman (1764–1833), a radical and reforming politician, was Lord Mayor of London in 1823 and Member of Parliament for London from 1818 to 1820 and 1826 to 1833 (*DNB*).

[95] James Brogden, MP for Launceston, had been accused by Waithman in Parliament of being involved in the financial improprieties of the notorious 'bubble' companies.

Thursday 14th. Decr.

At west end last night Richd. Marshall had a pain in his mouth which was perhaps increased, by hearing the Market on Monday at London was considerably lower; these low prices will be the end of many gasping farmers, the accounts in a manner stop their Breath; — Went to Loncaster's with the Militia list which goes to Beverley this day. Got a pipe and a Glass of Gin and water with the Constable, staid with him till about eight O'clock last night, and then came home, a very fine Moonlight night. My Wife spoke to the Gamekeeper to get us a Hare against Monday night next, which he has promised to do without fail; We have likewise spoken for a Goose to be ready against the same time; Necessity compels us at times to forgo what we wish to have, which is the case at present with respect to not procuring a ham, this is to be sure not pleasant, but it must be endured. Old Loncaster was at Beverley this day with the Militia list, he told me it was talked for certain that War was claimed by England, but against whom he could not say. However I had a shrewd guess that it was in favour of our dear old Ally sweet Portugal.

Friday 15th. Dec

Got our Pig this day it weighs somewhere about 18 Stone, but what the price is I cannot say, but expect it will be about 7s. pr. Stone, we never bargain with Abraham for the price, he will not do to be haggled with, but let him have his own way, and he will not impose upon his Customers. It is a beautiful Pig, indeed there can be none to beat Abm. for cleanliness and good keeping. I never interfere with Salting, so I forgo all claim to the excellent qualities of the Bacon when cured, but then I run no hazard of it not being good.

Saturday 16th. Dec.

Very wet Stormy Day and so dark we can scarcely see any thing in our Kitchen. Throng getting a Box fitted up to be ready by Monday to send off to the great City. All busy making Minced tarts and a Pork pie for William. Saw in the Paper this day that sentence of Death had been passed on the young man named Dunn from Hull, which is respited or mitigated to 14 years transportation. So then we are really going to defend Portugal against the tricks of Spain;[96] all that I fear is it may involve us in War with either one power or another; I think very little of the Portuguese; but it is the fashion at present to praise them.

Sunday 17th. Dec

The newspaper missed again this morning, so that I had no news this Day. A Gloomy dark day. a sermon at Church on the necessity of Fasting, had it been for contriving to feed the hungry who are obliged to fast, the attempt would

---

[96] Portugal at that time was in a state of great internal tension. A counter-revolution of the absolutist forces, led by the marquess of Chaves, had broken out in opposition to the newly formed but legitimate constitutional government under Saldanha. The rebels were receiving secret support from Spain and civil war seemed imminent. In these circumstances, Canning despatched a force of 5,000 British troops under Sir William Clinton to restore order and disband the counter-revolutionary force under Chaves. The move was successful and Spain remained at peace with Britain (*AR* 1826 Hist. 322–44).

have been praise worthy, but parsons I think try all they can to make themselves contemptible.

Monday 18th. Decr

The newspaper which ought to have come yesterday arrived this morning, having like the last been at South Shields, certainly the Postmasters either can not see, or else are incapable of reading, or it could not happen that such mistakes could be so frequently made.

Monday night 8 O'clock

    Exit

        RS

[in pencil]:

Best respects to Mrs. Warwick,

Mrs. Powell, Fred & Co. and

to Mr Jones & Moxon

A Pot of Currant Jelly for the Roast Hare.

Tuesday 19th. Decr.

Sent off Wm's Box last night with the Carrier with directions to go by the Barton Coach, and to be delivered immediately on arriving. I hope the Contents will please him. Wrote a letter to Wentworth near Rotherham, respecting Thos. James who lives there and has a Wife and six Children, he has been ill, and come upon the Parish for relief; He was Apprentice with Joshua Cade when I first came to Cave. A very fine day.

Wednesday 20th. Decr.

Old Willy asked a Man who came in if he ever saw a Stick with one end; Aye Scores you old Fool says the man; I should like to see a stick with only one end, only one end says the man, you fool they were like other Sticks two ends to be sure, but it's no use talking to you. — Our Old friend is famous for this kind of low wit, but he frequently overmatches himself.

Thursday 21st. Dec

At west end last night, the markets still keep lowering for Corn, which has the same effect upon the Farmers, as a hoar frost upon a Grass field, it makes them look very black.

They cry certainly this War will do some good to the Country; poor Creatures, what situation must we be in when War is hailed as a blessing? the last war is recollected with very grateful feelings; I myself wish sincerely for peace. This is called the shortest day, but as the Sun has shone nearly the whole of it, it appears not so short as some we have had, when Night appears to usurp the day.

Friday 22nd. Decr

Mr. Blyth from Beverley visiting the School this day. I do not want any of them to visit and inspect me, if they would contrive to make the Salary better it would be something to thank them for. Blyth is now the Curate of St. Mary's at Beverley. he has given up the National School at Beverley, and talks of taking six boarders if he can meet with them at 40 Guineas a year, which must be very good pay; he desired his respects to William which I told him I should remember.

Saturday 23rd. Decr

Mr. Barnard's has a large party this week, they were shooting a good deal in the Park and Grounds adjoining this day. I did not think it would have been safe or prudent to have come near them. I understand they killed 28 Pheasants; I dare say the poor birds are pretty good to hit; they have been many of them brought up tame so that they are not very shy. — This is the market day as Christmas day is on Monday, but there was very little attendance.

Sunday 24th. Decr

Recd. the Paper this morning with a hint on the Cover that if not delivered regularly complaint will be made, to those who are likely to remedy it: I likewise judge from it that Wm. has received his Box, so that the notice may answer two purposes: I have examined the Covers but can find no official intelligence of the arrival of the good things.[97] I see by the paper that there is a young man a bookseller in a dreadful situation being under sentence of death for setting his house on fire, it is a dreadful crime, and a dreadful suffering is attached to it. May we all be guarded from evil ways is my prayer.

Monday 25th. Decr

Christmas Day ushered in by the Waits[98] about one or two O'clock in the morning, what they call singing a Christmas Carrol, but in reality disturbing the good easy people who have a mind to enjoy sleep at the proper season; then these same disturbers have the impudence to beg of the Inhabitants to reward them, for undertaking to keep them awake; I promised them I would not give any thing and I stood to my promise. Then about five or six O'clock in the morning all the impudent lads and lasses in the Town running about for Christmas Boxes. I know a Box on the ears would have been the best reward. At Church in the forenoon, in the afternoon I staid at home, getting ready the Balance of my Stamp account, which is to be sent tomorrow £83–4–0. I do not think so much of the sacredness of Christmas day as many people do, for what command is there to set it above the Sabbath? Robt. Marshall and Mr. Bellard came in the Evening and smoked a pipe.

Tuesday 26th. Decr

Measured a small Close of Turnips for Wilkinson Ayre at Ring Beck 4a–1r–30p, came home by the way of Ellerker. I said before I should not like to be too near the Shooters who are at Mr. Barnard's, and it appears I did not judge of them rashly, for Tommy Pinder felt and heard shot whistling about him in his own Garth today, the Sportsmen I suppose being in the Flatts. — Recd. a receipt for the money sent to the Stamp Office. — Wandering about as this is a

---

[97] See n.81 (Letters).

[98] Waits were originally a body of musicians maintained by a city or town at public charge. By the 18th c., the name had come to be applied to parties of people who sang at the front doors of dwellings at Christmas time—in other words, carol singers.

holiday, cannot see to read at the Kitchen fire side, and no fire in the Room for fear of dirtying it.

Wednesday 27th. Decr.

Heard from Wm. that the Box had arrived safe and <u>very good</u>. I hope he would enjoy it. A Fine mild Christmas rather frosty this morning, I am just going out to see if I can catch Folly as it flies. Now I am back Mrs. Bowser formerly Ann Turk has presented her husband with a young Bowser, but the Old Women say it should not have been a Christmas Box. — but come it is that's truth. John Reynolds the Parish Clerk once by way of amusement went to a play, and so highly amused was he with the performance that he fell asleep; yes he really fell fast asleep. I don't know I ever heard a finer hit at the Vagrants than this. Wilkinson Ayre asks £300 a year for Old Sam's farm about 120 Acres. I have known many of these 300 a year Gentlemen, very soon come down, and what other can they expect if they live at twice the amount. Wrote or filled up a letter for Barnd. Cook to Mr. Cary 86 St. James's Street London, containing an account of the Gentlemen's houses in the neighbourhood.

Thursday 28th. Dec

Went to West Ella this morning very fine & clean walking it having been a hard frost the last night, called at Ferriby where I wanted some rent for the Workhouse, sent for the Overseer to the Public house but he did not attend, so I went to see for him and received the Money due; then went to Swanland to Mr. N. Shaw's to receive some rent due from them, Mr. Shaw is very poorly being troubled with Rheumatism; he asked me to stay dinner with him, there was a piece of Cold Beef on the table, but as I am not very partial to cold meat I excused myself, and went on to West Ella, where I arrived just in time to get a Bason of Broth &c at my Sisters; I then went to see my mother whom I found very well, in health but troubled very much with lameness. I then about three O'clock thought I would go to Hull, where I arrived between five and six. Staid all night at my Sisters. She seems very well, I think her Nephew John and her have agreed almost as long as they can; I asked John if he ever read, he said yes he had been reading a <u>Sary</u> book[99] that night, or else he did not think he had read a book for two years before. So much for this hopeful Nephew.

Friday 29th. Dec

Left Hull this morning about Eleven O'clock; Margaret Craggs died last night a little before twelve. I was in the shop last night and this morning too, they have a Shopman from London who was with Hurst and Robinson I think his name is Hallowell, he seems an easy kind of person, in fact not much like one who has been in London for seven years. — Dined with my Mother and drank tea with her about 3 O'clock when I set off for home where I arrived about half past five, very bad walking the frost having broken up, and I did not feel very well, however I got safe home. Bought some Ink glasses at the Shop opposite Craggs's.

---

[99] i.e. a story book.

Saturday 30th. Decr

The Fox hounds met this morning at Cave Castle[,] they have not been here since Wm. and I went upon Mount Airy to see them, at least I think not. I went this morning into the Park to see them, it was a beautiful morning the Sun shining clear, and many horsemen in Scarlet, with all the Shale Rag in the town and neighbourhood to gaze into the bargain; the Dogs went down by the Stables, and came out into the road beside the lodge, after frightening the poor Pheasants amazingly, they flew about in great numbers; the Sportsmen and Dogs then came down the Street and went up Porter hole to Mount Airy, in nearly the same direction as when we were there before, but I did not go on the Hills this time after them; I suppose they found a Fox, but he contrived to get away, for which I cannot blame him. After this another silly Fox jumped out of a Whin Bush before the hounds and was worried almost immediately.

Sunday 31st Dec

The funeral Procession of Margaret Craggs came through here this forenoon, on its way to North Cave; I see it is strongly reported that the difference between Spain & Portugal is made up. I hope it is, for I do not like to hear of the sound of War. This year ends with a beautiful day, and here is an end of another Sheet of Foolscap.

Monday 1st. January

Heaps of Boys running about for new year's Gifts, we had the first up stairs into both the School Rooms, I suppose to ensure luck for the year; then I dare say we were very careful to fetch something in before any thing was carried out, so that we stand a fair chance of being fortunate. A good deal of talk at Market amongst the farmers on what they call the low prices of Corn; and on the mistaken notions of the manufacturers in wishing for foreign importation[,] it is amusing to hear these people try with all the little sense they have to prove that dear corn is a blessing to the Country; and as their Auditors are of the same opinion with themselves they come to the conclusion that the country will be ruined if Corn becomes cheap.

Tuesday 2nd. Jany

Begun School again this morning, having had a holiday the last week. Many of the Boys with faces as simple as Ths. Leaman when he boiled his Clock. — Thos. had a wooden Clock commonly called a Cuckoo Clock, which had got so dirty and dusty that it wanted cleaning, as clocks sometimes do; so Tommy got on the Pot with clean water, and thought he could soon boil off all the extraneous matter, which was soon the case, but when he wanted his wheels in their proper places, he was at a fault; for neither wheels nor pinions were willing to occupy their old places, having swelled to such a degree that they fully defied the ingenuity of Tommy to put them together again, beside by boiling & drying, some of them split, and Tommy was thus bereft of his fine Cuckoo Clock.

Wednesday 3rd. Jany.

A very hard frost last night, and a little snow, it still freezes this day very keenly; heard from Wm. that he had spent a very pleasant Christmas day, I am glad that the articles which were sent him, pleased him & his friends. I see by the Paper that Counsellor Bric has lost his life in a Duel;[1] It is surprising that these men of honour should set all laws human and divine at defiance. Only hang up the Principals and seconds engaged in this species of Murder, and if that will not stop them, what will?

Thursday 4th. January

Recd. a letter from my Brother, by the way of Hull, respecting the Burial of Dissenters in Parish Church yards. He has given me notice of a Pamphlet

---

[1] John Bric, a Dublin barrister, had served as clerk to Daniel O'Connell from 1815, and was closely connected with the Catholic Association. He was killed in a duel, which was fought with William Hayes, a solicitor, on the outskirts of Dublin on 26 Dec. 1826. The duel was occasioned by an insulting remark made by Bric concerning an unsuccessful election candidate (Callahan), in the presence of Hayes, who was related to Callahan as well as being his political agent (Mac Donagh (1988) 304; *TM* 29 Dec. 1826, 4b).

published in London, on the subject in the year 1809,[2] which I shall endeavour to procure. — At west end last night, after that went with Robt. Marshall to Barnard Cooks, on the subject of the Highways. A very severe frost again this morning. I think I scarcely ever knew it keener all our School windows are so frozen that it is impossible to see through them, and yesterday they did not get entirely melted. — When I was at Hull the last week Oranges and Apples on the same stall were selling at the same prices viz. a penny each; it seems rather particular that Apples which are a home production, should be sold as dear as Oranges which are all foreign produce. Is it the scarcity of Apples this Season which makes them so dear? And what does the scarcity arise from? Is it for want of planting trees? Or ignorance in selecting the best kinds?

Friday 5th. Jany

A very great fall of Snow the last night, but more moderate this morning. Club night last night at Wm. Cousens's, also a supper for the Plough Lads[3] which made very throng work. No Newspaper this morning, perhaps it may be on account of the Snow; altho' the Post came in here at the regular time. Wilkn. Ayre has had three horses died this week, in some kind of distemper ...

Sunday 7th. Jany

A Fine mild morning. Yesterday I had two newspapers both packed up together, so it appears that the one which did not come on Friday had not been sent off. The Curate at Church explaining to the Children what Election meant, but I defy any one to guess what it was. This is his explanation, All persons are the Elect who have been baptised, with a reservation to those baptised by authorised Clergymen!!!

Monday 8th. Jany

A Petition in the Market this day for signatures to keep up the price of Corn, or in other words praying for no alteration in the Corn laws. One Overgrown farmer I heard tell off asserting that Wheat could not be afforded for less than 70s. per quarter; I hope it will be long before this price be realised. I did not sign the Petition. Heard in the Market that the Duke of York died on Friday night last.[4] Many Eulogies on him, and lamentations for him, some saying he has not left so good an one behind him, but it beats me to know wherein his goodness lay.

---

[2] John W. Wickes, *Accipe si vis. A Letter Addressed to the ... Lord Bishop of Peterborough, in Answer to the Opinion of Sir William Scott ... as to the Legality or Illegality of Refusing Church Burial to Dissenters.* Stamford: printed and sold by J. Drakard, [1809]. Pp. 44. (8°).

[3] Traditionally the farming year began with the start of spring ploughing on Plough Monday, the first Monday after Epiphany. In many villages in the East Riding, this event was customarily celebrated in a festival performed by the local plough lads, who blackened their faces, dressed themselves in fancy costumes, and dragged a wooden plough around the neighbourhood. Entertainment was provided by music and mummery. The money, which they collected, would usually be spent on a feast and drinks at a local public house (Gutch 87–9).

[4] Prince Frederick Augustus, duke of York and Albany and second son of George III. He died on 5 Jan. 1827 at the age of 63. Whilst serving in the army in 1789, he fought a famous duel with Captain Charles Lennox in which, although neither party was hurt, the duke was lucky to escape with his life (*DNB* and *TM* 8 Jan. 1827, 4 a).

Tuesday 9th. Jany.

Several if not all the tenants of Mr. Peters at Hotham have incurred his high displeasure, for presuming to Petition that Mr. Stillingfleet may be permitted to succeed his Father in the living at Hotham; they even presumed so far upon their own free Agency as to get a petition without acquainting their most high and mighty Landlord, who in a rage like other imbeciles has given them notice to provide for themselves; when he cannot legally give them notice to quit before Michaelmas next to leave the Lady day following.

Wednesday 10th. Jany.

Saw in the Paper this morning the official account of the Death of the Duke of York; the Paper in mourning. Norrison Marshall not well I went to see him last night, he had fallen down in the Chamber floor, in the morning; when Mr. Tinsdill was sent for; he the Dr. says will soon be better; he calls his complaint the Mumps, he had a swelled face, down into his throat, but it has now settled; I staid about two hours up Stairs with him. At west end this evening, reckoned up Robt. Marshall's following Crop which he has to pay for on the 14th. Feby. Young Bowser is dead. Hung up our Bacon this night ...

Friday 12th. Jany

A Parish meeting at Barnard Cook's last night to balance the Church accounts, and to lay a Church rate which was done at 2d per pound, there were 17 Persons present. Part conversation on the Petition now in the course of signature, which has for its object to raise wheat to 64s. pr. Quarter and not to be under. Confusion attend all who wish to hunger the poor. Wrote to Wentworth and sent a five Guineas note for Ths. James. Old Matthew Kirby buried at Cave this day he is about 90 years of age; he has lately lived at Garraby with his Son who keeps the Inn there.

Saturday 13th. Jany

Measured Mr. King's Park Close this forenoon 6a–0r–9p very fine and dry being a frost. In the afternoon measured Bricklayer's Work of a new House for David Morley, came on rain and very uncomfortable and cold, after that went to Old Barny's and got a glass of Rum & Water with the Bricklayer. Mrs. Turner very ill, Dr. Alderson sent for to her. Tommy Pinder very ill it is said in a Brain fever, he has been a day or two ill. Sent for Dr. Turnbull to see him, who I understand gave them but little hopes of recovery.

Sunday 14th. Jany

A most tremendous windy day. I think I never knew it blow so hard, several partial damages have occurred, as blowing down trees, stripping off tiles &c. Tommy Pinder no better this day. Wm. Ingram buried this afternoon, having hurt himself last week with carrying a Sack of Oats. Recd. two Examiners this morning, I suppose my Sister has been from home as they did not come before.

Monday 15th. Jany

Tommy Pinder died this morning about one O'clock, he would not submit to be bleeded when he began to be ill, and at the last it was of no use to him; he had nearly 30 Leeches on together yesterday; but nothing it appears could relieve him. I saw him on Saturday morning last, I had little thought that his end was so near, he just looked into the Shop when I was there, as I generally go on Saturday mornings for change. I suppose he was out of his mind I really feel sorry for the loss of him. It is said he has been subject to drink much Liquor unmixed to the amount as report says of ten Glasses a day at times. However I can say I never saw him drunk, though several people have.

Tuesday 16th. Jany

The Curate & Churchwardens begging for the relief of the distressed Manufacturers in obedience to the King's letter to the two great Archbishops;[5] I really think this Cotton business is worse than nothing as other classes at present have had the wretched weavers just to keep alive. Mr. Barnard has given twenty pounds to begin with, I gave one Shilling and I suppose many who can better afford it will give less. Mrs. Turner (Mr. Robinson's Aunt) died this forenoon, she was literally worn to a thread, some few years ago she was very jolly & stout, but for some time past she has been very much reduced.

Wednesday 17th. Jany

Recd. by the Carrier last night from Wm. the judgment of Sir John Nichols, on the burial of Persons baptized by Dissenters[6] I am glad to find that the survivors of such persons are not to beg as a favour to have their friends interred in the Parish Church yard; it is their undoubted right, if a case of this kind occurs here again I will by some means endeavour to bring the Orthodox Gentleman, (if not to reason) at least to fulfil his duty, by pleading the law on the subject, of which he must indeed be very ignorant. Wm. wishes the Journal to be continued; which indeed I carry on every day if not in a regular method, at least pretty fully. At Mr. Bridgeman's last night with a few neighbours paying him for their Cows bulling. I generally have an invitation to pay at that time, so that I am seldom forgot as he takes the will for the deed. I was at poor Tommy's funeral this afternoon he was buried at Brantingham. I think there were more than 200 people attended. It came on snow before I arrived at home.

Thursday 18th. Jany

A Fine morning. Recd. the Examiner this morning which is soon as can be expected. The times very copious on the approaching funeral of the Duke of York. All the honours paid to a nauseous Carcase will not in the least procure any favour from a righteous judge. In general the failings of the deceased are raked up with particular diligence; in the case of Tommy Pinder every one now knows that he has shortened his life by excessive drinking. But in the case of

---

[5] 'To the Archbishops of Canterbury and York for a Collection in aid of the Subscriptions entered into for the Relief of the Manufacturing Classes in the United Kingdom'—this letter was first issued on 16 Dec. 1826 and a copy of its text printed in *The Times* for 29 Dec. 1826, p. 3, col. 6.

[6] The Revd. John Wight Wickes, Rector of Wardly cum Belton, had refused to bury the infant child of two of his parishioners, John and Mary Swingler, who were Calvinistic Independents and had had the child baptized according to the rites of that sect. In an action brought to determine the legality of the Revd. Wickes's refusal, held at Arches Court, on 9 Nov. 1809, the judge, Sir John Nicholl, ruled that a minister of the Established Church could not refuse to bury the baptised child of a dissenter (*ER* clxi. 1320).

Royalty how carefully are all the faults kept in the back ground, and nothing brought forward but what would pass for a picture of perfection. Those who believe the Scriptures are not ignorant that the great and the noble are in no more estimation in the sight of God, than the most distressed Lazarus that ever lived.

Friday 19th. Jany

Our old Friend at the Low Mill lately sent down some Flour by his Man to Old Rachel Levitt's which was not of a superior quality; so the next time that the man went Hannah said to him, Now your master blames you for this black flour, he says he told you only to put a handful or two of the black wheat into it. What a liar he must be exclaims the man with an Oath, for he told me himself to make it all of the Black Wheat, but you know him, you know him, says the Man. Now honest Tom says he must have his man instructed better, he is a decent man and all that, but then he had not sense to say that this flour might have been made after some ordinary bad stuff had been ground. Tom thinks there is as much evil in speaking truth when against him, as in telling a wilful lie.

Saturday 20th. Jany.

What a difference in the manners of those called farmers, to what there formerly was. When a Company of these Gentry meet now in public, there is generally one of the party, with a little more brass in his countenance than his neighbours who is placed at the head of the table and dignified with the name of Chairman, and there the Company sit apeing their betters, with Port & Sherry in cut glass Decanters before them; when the impudent fellow at the head of the table (who ought to be put under it) gets up and says Gentlemen I beg to give a toast or sentiment, or something of the kind: then Gentlemen I give Wheat not lower than 70s. pr. Qr. this is drunk with as much applause as the Company is capable of bestowing. Formerly farmers used to meet at Market and 3 or 4 of them drink good Ale out of a plated tankard (I do not admire very much this slavering method but so it was), the first who drank said neighbours I wish all your healths and may God send a good harvest, (or something similar to this,) they knew then that a good harvest was a blessing which they ought to be thankful for; and they would have pronounced that Man a daring blasphemer, who wished for bad harvests. They never knew the miseries of over-production; thankful were they to the giver of all good, for abundant Crops.

Sunday 21st. Jan

Our old friend Mr. Atkinson very ill, he was taken ill in Bed on Friday morning about four O'clock; I think it was most likely a fit of some kind; when I saw him on Friday I thought he would not recover, but he is rather better today, he has been very drowsy, he was bled on the Arm, first, then had Leeches on his temples, next blooded in the temples with the Lancet; then cupped between his Shoulders, which I think has been of great Service to him; he has been up every day, but some of his friends have staid at nights with him. I think he is likely to recover now, as he has eaten pretty well today.

Monday 22nd. Jan

A very Cold frosty morning. By the Paper I see there has been a great deal of crowding about St. James's, to see the laying in state of the Royal Duke. John Bull's delight is in crowds, but what benefit is it to any of the Bull family even if the dead Corpse of the Commander in Chief could be seen? Some people are pleased with one sight and some another; but nothing comes amiss to Mr. Bull. John Turk has been here, he is out of a Situation, he could like to begin business for himself, but he does not know how to raise the means. He says he has had a very good year the last year but he has broken his employers!!! He often fell in with Longman's traveller I asked him how they became acquainted. Oh nothing easier he says, when he heard he was Longman's traveller he asked him if he knew a respectable young man in their house of the name of Sharp, which he did very well, then an acquaintance commenced immediately.

Tuesday 23d. Jany

Very cold again this morning, a good deal of snow last night. Mrs. Turner buried this forenoon, with all the Pomp and Pride of Circumstance, she has been kept a week, and is now interred in the Vault in the Church yard. I think it is needless to describe the Procession, there was a Hearse and two mourning Coaches, with the usual supply of hired mourners, that is they who had scarfs and gloves to ensure their attendance. Mr. Atkinson I think is no better altho' it is the opinion of some of his friends that he is. He says he has no pain, he is very drowsy and looks exceedingly ill. I should wish for him to get better.

Wednesday 24th. Jan

When I arrived home from Mr. Atkinson's last night, the Box had arrived from Wm. which was as soon as I had expected it. All was safe. I read his letter in the first place, which he calls rigmarole, but I believe it is the best kind of letter writing when anything is put down that comes into the mind of the writer; these formal letters are no better than so many sleepy Essays on different subjects. I am glad that the Christmas fare pleased so well, it was our desire that it should and this is all the satisfaction we require. The Gowns are very much liked, the tobacco I have not yet seen. But all is right, & his letter pleases me very well. I am glad that he (Wm) likes the Journal, as praise to a writer is animating, and Censure is the next agreeable sensation; the worst situation an Author can be placed in is not to be noticed at all. A very great fall of Snow last night. Quartered 24 Soldiers chiefly recruits on their way to Hull.

Thursday 25th. Jan

Sometimes articles of small value are highly prized, as was the case with a pair of old Shoes which Wm. sent in his Box, his Mother just wanted a pair of the kind as the others she had from him were just about worn, and now she feels so comfortable about her feet the like was never. Mr. Atkinson a great deal better today, he slept at Mr. Bridgeman's last night so that none of his friends were wanted to attend him; he feels very weak, but his appetite he says is as good as ever. Some person has lent him Bell's life in London,[7] a very <u>fit</u> companion for a sick man. Very hard frost last night and this day.

Friday 26th. Jan.

Last night I sat down to read Cobbett, and very cold it was, but I was left by myself at the fire-side; I never like a very great fire, I would rather have a little one and sit very close to it, which I always do when I have an opportunity. — Cobbett does belabour Mr. Canning and his furies, It was certainly not a point of wisdom in the Secretary to make use of such an expression; as unleesing the furies[.] It seems to go as far as any of the revolutionary Jacobins. He (Cobbett) still augurs evil from the Paper System, how far he is right time will determine. Robt. Marshall came last night to have a pipe of the London tobacco which we pronounced very good; we had likewise a Glass of Rum & Water to drink Wm's health, which we did with much fervency. May the blessing of God Almighty be upon him.

Saturday 27th. Jany

It is said that Mr. Barnard of Brantingham has let his house for two or three years to Lord Muncaster,[8] who has an Estate at Warter; Geo. Holborn is Gamekeeper to his Lordship, but I have heard he is about tired of his Situation, as there are so many Poachers; and he perhaps may have sense to think that it is not worth his while to venture his life in defence of such Worthless Animals as Hares and Partridges. Robt. Marshall went to Brantingham this afternoon to ask for the promise of the Farm which Mr. Barnard had in his hands (for his brother Jeremiah) but it was promised so that he has not the first chance. A Fine moderate day but a hard frost.

Sunday 28th. Jany

Mr. Edwd. Barnard it is said is going abroad but into what Country I do not know. I suppose he wants to live in a cheaper way. The weather rather softer this forenoon; towards night it began to thaw rapidly, it is surprising how the snow wastes away, when the air is clear of Frost; there were ten Men cutting snow in the Swinescaife road yesterday — it is almost entirely drifted up, there has not been so much snow of late as at present. Rosy Hunter died this morning after an illness from October last.

Monday 29th. Jan

All the farmers on the tip toe of expectation that Corn will rise in price, Mr. Levitt of Ellerker says the Parliament will be the greatest fools in existence if they do not lay a duty of 30s. pr. quarter on Wheat imported; I told him I was

---

[7] *Bell's Life in London and Sporting Chronicle* was a Sunday newspaper founded by Robert Bell on 3 Mar. 1822. It was subsequently bought by William Clement, who in 1827 acquired at auction the rival newspaper, Pierce Egan's *Life in London*, which had been intended for the same readership. W. R. Macdonald was appointed editor of the amalgamated newspaper which continued until 29 May 1886, when it was incorporated in *Sporting Life* (Morison 242–6; Watson iii. 1809–10).

[8] This was Sir Lowther Augustus John Pennington, 7th Bt. and 3rd Baron Muncaster, born 13 Dec. 1802, died aged 35, 30 Apr. 1838. He married (15 Dec. 1828) Frances Catherine, youngest daughter of Sir John Ramsden, Bt., by whom he had 7 children (4 sons and 3 daughters). The Muncaster seat was at Muncaster Castle, Ravenglass, Cumberland (Pine 203).

led to believe that they would not lay on half so much, well then he says they may bid farewell to the prosperity of England, all the ordinary land will be thrown out of Cultivation, well I replied so much the better if it will not pay for the expence laid out upon it. Let it return to grazing, then the poor may eat mutton, and so do with less wheat. Oh but England cannot be supplied with Corn from abroad; the supply will be stopped and famine will ensue. No fear of this for every Country is glad to exchange its produce for others which it needs. — I wonder it has never come into the heads of none of the Wiseacres to cultivate Tea in England, as for this Article we are entirely at the Mercy of foreigners, and yet no tea drinkers is ever at a loss for a supply provided money be at hand, even this trade is monopolized, and yet the supplies are abundant. The West India Merchants again are monopolizers of Sugar. But the greatest wretches of all are these who want to make a monopoly of Corn.

Tuesday 30th. Jany

It is reported that Wm. Fisher (who married one of Mr. Robinson's daughters of Mount Airy) has taken Mr. Barnard's farm at Brantingham. Sent five pounds in a letter to Malton for some Paupers belonging this place. I have begun to read Mill's history of Chivalry,[9] the author seems to be delighted with his subject, and I have no doubt but he treats it in a proper manner; — This is a glorious day fine and Sunny for the time of the year it is a great contrast to the weather last week at this time.

Wednesday 31st. Jan.

No Newspaper from Wm. this morning; Mr. Barnard had a Paper missed last week, he wrote the same day to Mr. Freeling concerning it, whether he got an answer or not I cannot say. He also wrote at the same time to the Postmaster at Market Weighton. The paper he takes is the Morning Herald.[10] To say the truth it is not pleasing to be disappointed, if one did not expect them regular, there would be no disappointment.

Thursday 1st. Feby. 1827

A Parish meeting last night, and as subscriptions are the order of the day it was resolved that a subscription should be attempted to find the poor of the Parish some Coals. I am to draw up the resolutions, to be shewn to the Lord of the Manor in the first place on Saturday next. It is not meant that the money subscribed should go in aid of the Poor Rate, but in addition to any relief which the poor now receive; Who would have thought such disinterested persons were to be found amongst us !! The newspaper that ought to have come yesterday has not arrived this morning, and it is the one of all the week, in which we hear from Wm. Our School smoked so much today that I was obliged to take the fire out, a very stormy day it is.

[9] Charles Mills, *The History of Chivalry; or, Knighthood and its Times*. London, 1825. – 2 vols. Also another ed. 1826.

[10] The *Morning Herald* was one of the principal London daily morning newspapers. It was published from 1 Nov. 1780 to 31 Dec. 1869 and was founded by the then editor of the *Morning Post*, Henry (later Sir Henry) Bate Dudley (1745–1824), one-time Curate of Hendon and nicknamed the 'Fighting Parson', who retained the ownership until his death (*DNB*)

Friday 2nd. Feb.

Club night last night Matt. Smith who is one of the honourable members was very drunk, some persons heated a pipe and put [it] in his old Jacket pocket which soon raised a smoke, as if Matty had a steam engine in his Pocket; but the pipe was not to be confined, and it was so hot that Matty could not hold it so it burnt itself out at his pocket bottom. The Club Box removed from Cousens's to Newlove's last night, as they have it a year each alternately. This is a cold day a Shower of Snow in the forenoon with a Stormy north wind.

Saturday 3rd. Feb.

Recd. a parcel from Wm. last night, he tells us he has left Mrs. Warwick's for which we feel concerned, as we fancied he was at home there, his mother is much troubled about it, However let him be where he will I rely on him conducting himself in a proper manner with credit to himself. I thought when I was in London that Jones was of a light trifling disposition but I depend on Wm. not being led against his better judgment. Cobbett on the Corn laws is almost above himself it is the best exposition I ever saw, of the frantic cry of the Agriculturalists that they bear exclusive burdens; just as if they were the sole consumers of all the fruits of the land. — Measured a Close of Turnips for Mr. King and another for Henry Arton. Then divided the Garth where John Dunlin lived into five parts for so many Cottages which Mr. Barnard has built on the place.

Sunday 4th. Feb

Heard by Ben. Tapp from my Brother yesterday, he had been at Skipton the Sunday before, he is very well and has a good congregation. I am glad to hear that he is comfortable. Ben has been travelling for Bowden's[11] he has been out seven weeks, he complains of trade very much in the west. Money he says is very bad to get. Rob. Marshall and Old Loncaster both came up this night and got a pipe with me. I cannot say that I am very fond of Company on a Sunday night.

Monday 5th. Feb.

When I wanted to cast up the dimensions of Mr. King's Close behold the figures had got rubbed out so that I shall have to measure the Close over again, which is not a very pleasant job. 24 Recruits came here about noon which I billetted at the public houses in the Market place, they all seem to be ragged and are Irish chiefly. I have read over the History of Chivalry, it really is true to the title page as nothing but Chivalry can be found in it. I cannot say that it is very amusing or instructive, altho' one sees a little more of its folly than is to be found in Walter Scott.

Tuesday 6th. Feb

I have got a Cold which makes me ill, I slept very badly last night, and did not get up till nearly nine this morning. I eat my breakfast pretty well, but I feel starved all the day. I hope I shall soon be better. A fine day not much frost. Mr.

---

[11] Two Hull merchants of this name are listed in Baines's 1823 directory: James Bowden of 18 High Street, and William Bowden of West Parade, Hull (Baines ii. 336).

Lane preaching at Everthorpe last night, he is going to preach here this evening. I suppose he is begging for his Chapel which he has built at Hull;[12] it is just opposite the new Church, so near that they can hear each other sing. It is said to be a large building.

Wednesday 7th. Feb

I am better this morning having applied to my old medicine last night, a Bason of Gruel. Recd. the Paper this morning without a word of writing, is this the effect of Wm.'s new lodgings?; if it be I care not how soon he quits them. Now it is very little trouble writing a few words, and it is what we have been so long accustomed to that we do not feel right without hearing at least once a week. Last Wednesday the paper never came at all, so that it is a fortnight now since we have heard by this conveyance. — Ths. Marshall came last night, when he was presented with a taste of the Tobacco which Wm. sent. Aye now says Tom "this is bacca", and then it looks so well too to think of an old friend, for I really always did take him for a friend; all are the friends of Tom where he can get any thing.

Thursday 8th. Feb

Richd. Marshall fell down from the Granary yesterday the Steps giving way, he fell backwards upon the Steps, but not much worse, some Skin on one of his legs was broken and he felt rather stiff. Mr. Barnard sent Old Willy a pheasant yesterday, the old Gentleman has got pretty well again, but I think his memory fails. I think the Lord Chancellor has decided very properly, in not suffering the accomplished Wellesley to have the education of his Children,[13] in his letter he had given some very fine specimens of his capability for the undertaking; however he is not impudent enough to intimidate the Court. Made 26 Copy Books very good paper, as I was nearly out ...

Saturday 10th. Feb.

Ths. Pinder's Widow has administered to his Effects, he died without a Will; she had £25–4–0 to pay, the personal property just under £800. I suppose the Goods are valued very low, but only think what a hardship for the Government to demand the above Sum. The Overseers going about begging for the Poor of this Parish. Mr. Barnard gave them twenty pounds for which he is greatly to be recommended, the Overseers gave each of them 2 Pounds, and several others 1 pound each; it is to be hoped it will be applied to the real use of those for whom it is collected. The Curate would not give a single penny,

[12] The first stone of the Tabernacle in Sykes Street, Hull, had been laid on 21 June 1826 and the chapel was opened on 7 Jan. 1827, when the Revd Lane was its first minister and part proprietor. Numerous nonconformist chapels and meeting houses were being founded in Hull at this time and Lane himself went on to found the Mariners' Church at Prince's Dock-side in Feb. 1828, and later the Bethesda (House of Mercy) Chapel in Osborne Street on 3 July 1842. He occupied the pulpit of this last building until his death, aged 89, in Oct. 1862 (Sibree 65-66; Sheahan 406, 422 and 436).

[13] William P. T. Long Wellesley had attempted to regain the legal custody and education of his 3 children who had been left in the care of his dead wife's sisters at her own request before she died. He was deemed to be an unfit person to have charge of them, and the Lord Chancellor, John Scott, 1st Earl of Eldon, turned down his petition on 1 Feb. 1827. Four years later, in 1831, he abducted his infant daughter and was ordered to be imprisoned for contempt of court (*ALLR* 189–213).

neither would he read over the Notice in the Church last Sunday, to let the parishioners know the intention of the meeting that was held for the purpose above named. The Parson was uncommonly anxious to beg under the authority of the King's letter. I have not heard how much they got, nor whether he gave any thing himself or not. Recd. a letter from Wm. this morning containing a punctual Direction to his lodgings. I hope he will find himself comfortable. His Clothes are got up in a superior stile and bleached so fine & white that they are inimitable. Very cold day.

Sunday 11th. Feb.

I do not know how the Minister will proceed with respect to the Corn laws, indeed those who are more in the Secret of State affairs can but at present form a guess. This is certain it will require much wisdom to satisfy all the different orders of Society, for one be favoured another suffers: the general opinion seems to be that a reduction of taxation would be the most calculated to give satisfaction, but how far this can be carried into effect under existing circumstances, admits of much doubt. I should like to see Caxton's "Historye of Reynart the Fox, folio Price £210",[14] better than any Petition which will be presented to Parliament this Session. There is another curious Book in the Catalogue, called "Speculum Humanae Salvationis"[15] folio £200 with wood Cuts, besides several other scarce old Printed Books. I like to read Catalogues: Jonathan Scott said he got all the learning he had from Road Posts; so I get part of mine from perusing Catalogues.

Monday 12th. Feb

After all the noise that Cobbett has made respecting his Petition, I see it has fallen to the Ground, for want of properly recognizances,[16] so Mr. Sykes's fifteen pounds will be useless for this purpose.

Thos. Marshall said to his Brother Jerry, if I was thee as thou wantest a Farm I would go and bid five shillings an acre more for Old Loncaster's farm than he gives for it. Nay says Jerry I would be without a farm for ever sooner than I would do such a dirty action, had I taken Mr. Barnard's farm at Brantingham, I should not have had any trouble with an offgoing tenant. Whya nea maybe nut says Tom, but then thou does not consider that is over dear by half, and so thou wouldst lose thy money, rather than have any now neice? But I tell thee I would have this old devil's farm if I could get it, and send him off packing. Tom does not like Old Lonc. because he does not grind with him, all this is a secret, for Loncaster knows nothing of Tom's proposal.

---

[14] Reynard the Fox. *This is the Table of the Historye of Reynart the Foxe* (tr. W. Caxton). fol. Westminster: W. Caxton, 1481.

[15] *Speculum Humanae Salvationis.* Augsburg: Gunther Zainer, [1471?]. 269 leaves. Numerous commentaries on and translations of this Latin devotional work were subsequently published.

[16] Cobbett announced the failure of his election petition, on account of a technical breach of the regulations governing its presentation, in a written address 'to the electors of Preston', printed in *CPR* 61 viii (17 Feb.) 1827, 449–67.

Tuesday 13th. Feb

Packed up and sent off Wm.'s Box last night, to go by the Carrier to Hull this morning, with instructions to enquire the name of the Vessel, and to what Wharf she goes to in London. It is 23 years this day since I came to Cave, there are but two farmers living on the same Farms as when I came viz. Giles Bridgman & Barnard Cook, some of them have been changed four or five times over. — then as now it was very cold weather.

Wednesday 14th. Feb

Enquired of Carrier last night for the name of the Vessel in which Wm's Box is going, which is the Brothers Capn. Chs. Wood, for Beal's Wharf London, wrote to Wm. to let him know. Recd. the paper this morning as usual with an account that he is well, glad to hear it. Mr. Barnard of Brantingham has let his house to Lord Muncaster, he is to go to it on the 20th. of this month. Wm. Fisher has taken his farm at I dare say a great rent, but so it is, the farmers are continually complaining, and if there be a farm to let, the Landlord can have almost what rent he likes for it, and they are in the right to make as much as they can for their property, and let the tenants try their skill to make the rent secure.

Thursday 15th. Feb

Robt, Marshall paying for his following Crop last night the Sum of about £117. When I was set reading by myself last night a little after nine O'clock I heard a great noise which sounded almost like a heap of Shop window shutters falling down very quickly: I went to the door to see the cause, several people at their doors with Candles in their hands, all amazed, Some persons said it was a Ball of Fire which had burst in the Street, I saw nothing of the kind, but the noise started me very much. Some of the Ladies said there was a strong smell of Sulphur but, I snuffed up nothing but the cold north wind.

Friday 16th. Feb

A very great fall of Snow and a hard frost last night. I see by the paper this morning that the Corn question in Parliament is put off till the 26th. inst. this almost confirms the report that the Ministers have no plan ready, for all the talk that was made that their resolutions were fixed long ago, however it completely paralizes speculation, and monopolists are hindered from putting their schemes into execution.

Saturday 17th. Feb

A very winter like morning, snowing fast, but the wind is southerly, so I hope it will be a change. Very little news of importance in the Papers. I see Mr. Hume[17] is still strenuous for Economy, particularly in the Navy estimates. There has been a good deal of expence incurred by the Government, in building Mills to supply the forces with unadulterated flour. The wretches who have mixed up their deliterious ingredients with the Flour deserve condign

---

[17] Joseph Hume (1777–1855) was an energetic and effective MP and leader of the radical party. He supported the cause of political reform and Catholic emancipation as well as the repeal of the combination laws and other liberal measures, and devoted himself to the question of public expenditure by advocating a policy of 'retrenchment' (*DNB*).

punishment. The noise which was heard in the Street on Thursday night is said to have been occasioned by some Boys firing Gun powder, scattered on the Ground. — When I first came to Cave the Millers had bells hung round the necks of their Cadging horses,[18] but Ths. Marshall has the merit (if any) of discontinuing the practice, he used to take the Bell off when he arrived at T. Pinder's Corner, in the time when the property tax was paid, for fear I should hear him and ask him for money, and as he generally contrives to keep his money in his Pocket as long as possible; he thought these tinkling bells gave notice of his appearance or approach. The Custom now is entirely dropped.

Sunday 18th. Feb

An uncommon cold windy, frosty, snowy day, it blows the Snow so that it drifts very much. A Farmer prophesying the last night that Mutton would be 9d. pr. lb. before Ladyday, it is not long to that time, then we shall see. To hear the Farmers talk you would think there is nothing but famine staring us in the face, No Stacks scarcely to thrash, and all the Corn been sold as it has come to hand, and yet these Gentry have the affrontery to petition parliament, to keep foreigners from sending us a supply. At a Dinner party of a few of them in a neighbouring village a day or two ago, I enquired if they had not had a grand dinner (it was at Wilkn. Ayres) Oh no nothing extravagant, a very neat little dinner, a piece of Roast Beef, a Turkey and Chine &c. &c. Oh thinks I, this is a plain dinner is it, I should think it a very good dinner to have any one of the articles. I suppose they know nothing of a roasted Turkey stuffed with Sparrows, and if they did they would set themselves against it because Cobbett has recommended it, not that they know any thing about him but a sort of dread when his name is mentioned, as he is sometimes held out as a Scarecrow in the Newspapers which fall into their hands; but to do them justice it is not often that they read.

Monday 19th. Feb.

I see that Cobbett's Register has been voted out of the Catholic Association on the Motion of O'Connell, but I expect he will hear of this in Cobbett's peculiar manner.[19] These Catholic Chiefs are much like Cobbett, they deal in domineering, but Cobbett is not to be put down so easily as his register, is voted out. Rotsey who used to drive the Coach through here died suddenly on Saturday last near Booth ferry, he had been there, and was running to get on board the Steam packet, afraid of missing it, when he dropt down dead; So uncertain is our tenure of this life.

Tuesday 20th. Feb.

Very Cold frost again today. Bought a watch key my old one being worn so much that I could not use it any longer. A Travelling Bookseller was lately

---

[18] In general terms 'cadgers' were itinerant dealers or carriers, but in Yorkshire, at least, they were more specifically the agents of local millers, delivering flour and soliciting orders on their behalf. The term was used in this sense by RS and was so used also by Henry Best of Elmswell in the 17th c. in his farming and memorandum books (*OED*; Ross (1877); Woodward 289).

[19] For Cobbett's reaction, see *CPR* 61 viii (17 Feb.) 1827, 467–8; 61 ix (24 Feb.) 1827, 562–70; and 61 x (3 Mar.) 1827, 598–606.

about with <u>excellent</u> Works for Sale; I think the highest priced Book was the Young Man's Companion,[20] indeed he appeared to recommend it as superior to most other Books, I was at Robt. Marshall's when he was there, he offered <u>Awd Beck</u> a Cooking Book for 1s. which he affirmed contained all things necessary to be know by any Cook whatsoever; the large Books he said were good for nothing but muddling their heads, and then they would be either under or over doing the Joints, under their Care; but with all his Rhetoric he could not so much as sell one.

Wednesday 21st. Feb

Recd a letter from London this morning from a person of the name of Abbotts, Skinner Street Snow hill, who is a Wine & Spirit merchant, for which I paid the Postage 11d. He wants an Agent to quit his puffed Wines and Spirits, but he shall not have one in me. I think he might have paid the Postage of his letter. I wish I had not opened it. I see by the Hull packet that the Brothers has sailed for London, and as the wind keeps fair, I am in hopes that Wm. will soon receive his Box. — Hay is selling at one Shilling a Stone which is a very exorbitant price, it is the Scarcity of Fodder that makes it so dear. Even 6d. pr. Stone is a great price; I have heard my Grandfather say that once in a scarce time he gave 6d. pr. Stone, and fetched it two miles on his back. I never knew a time like the present, Turnips in general are all rotten, so that they are nearly done.

Thursday 22d. Feb

Put another Wafer[21] in the Letter I received yesterday, and re-directed it and sent it back to No. 10 Skinner Street Snow Hill, so that Mr. Abbott will have the postage to pay back again, which will be of as much service to him as it was to me. Old Barny Cook thrashing wheat with a machine, it looks as if he wanted money, as his rent day is next Monday; if this was not the case he had not much occasion to thrash his Corn so suddenly, as he has no great stock left. I see Lord Liverpool has been taken very ill, some of the Farmers were so elevated as to say that providence has interfered so far as to put a stop to any alteration in the Corn laws. This is not my opinion.

Friday 23d. Feb

A Parish meeting last night, when I and Robt. Marshall were again nominated Assessors for the ensuing year. There was likewise a consultation how the money which has been given, is to be laid out, and the proper persons to receive it, there was a good deal of talking on the subject, some thinking one entitled to it, and some another. I think there will be much dissatisfaction in the distribution of it. The Sum is about 40 pounds. — No Newspaper this morning.

---

[20] J. A. Stewart, *The Young Man's Companion; or, Youth's Instructor* ... 2nd ed. Oxford: Bartlett and Newman, 1814. Pp. 861. Other works exist under this title, e.g. by William Mather, but apart from one published in Manchester in 1805, all date back to the 18th c. and Stewart's work seems to be the nearest in time to the diary entry.

[21] A small disk of flour mixed with gum and non-poisonous colouring matter, or of gelatine or the like similarly coloured, which when moistened was used for sealing letters, attaching papers, or receiving the impression of a seal (*OED*).

I generally receive the Examiner on Fridays but it has not come this day. Very hard frost continues yet.

Saturday 24th. Feb

Danl. Sykes when at home frequently calls at a Cottage in the Wood, between Raywell & Wauldby, to hold talk with Old Jno. Clark the Occupier. When he came from London after the first meeting of Parliament he had been at; he called to ask Old Jno. how he was. Jn. after thanking him for so kindly calling to see him, said "Now Sor you wad make sum on em hear ye at Lunnon" how John I dont understand you "Dear e me Sor what youve a <u>fine Seat</u> now e Parliment" Oh John you have been wrong informed, <u>I sat down upon a Bink end</u>, any ways where there was room; just like a lad going to a fresh school, I durst not say a word until I saw their ways: "wounds says Jno. that's mighty queer. I thought sike a Gentleman as you wad ha known how to talk till em". Well I think I shall tell them a little now I have seen some of their ways. "Aye now I e'en thought you wad, you may depend on't they'll tak notish of what ye say, But then they dean't kno' ye se weel as I dea, or else they ought to be sham'd ov theirselves".

Sunday 25th. Feb.

Recd. 2 Papers from Wm. yesterday morning, the Examiner not come to hand at all this week. Attended to give bread away at Church this afternoon,[22] One of the Churchwardens being from home. It thaws this day but keeps very cold. I see Taylor the Orator, Philosopher and Fool[23] has been obliged to find Bail for his good behaviour, on account of some of the nonsense he has been trying to promulgate. Now I wonder whether men of this description think they could make the World happier by voting out all religious obligations? James Levitt and his Partner have dissolved Partnership at Hull after a very short connection. Old Rachel very ill having been taken with a fit two or three days ago, her Complaint is an enlargement of the heart. F. Ruston, Js. Milner & 2 or 3 more have given up going to Chapel, <u>for what? aye for what</u>? not because the Preacher[24] does not preach well, but because he is <u>dirty</u>, (what is that to them) Last Sunday they had no singing, but this day they have done pretty well, Eliza was there this afternoon, and assisted powerfully. Thos. Marshall says she is worth a hundred pounds for it. Tom could like to let the discontented see that he can do without them.

Monday 26th. Feb.

Cast up the measurement of a Close for Ths. Marshal 13a–1r–3p which I measured on Saturday last; Tommy told me it was of very little use measuring it as he knew what it was, which was 15a–1r–0p at the least, but it would satisfy

---

[22] See n.2 (1836).

[23] Robert Taylor (1784–1844) had studied for the church at St. John's College, Cambridge and become a curate but later adopted anti-Christian views which he promulgated at public lectures in London. He was twice imprisoned for blasphemy in the course of a turbulent career (*DNB* and *TM* 20 Feb. 1827, 4 c and 22 Feb. 1827, 4 a).

[24] Revd Seth Kelso. See n.113 (1827).

them who bought the Turnips just to run it over: I told him as soon as it was done that there would not be 14 Acres of it. Whya, says Tom I always yam'd there was more than that of it, what look at it; my eye tells me there is more than you've made of it, that Old Kitt always told me there was 15 Acres. Curse him yan can believe nought he says; besides it makes one look so fond to tell the Man that bought the Turnips there were 15 acres, and now it turns out 13 and a Rood, and then what is worse than all, it comes to so much less money. D—n, it you must be wrong. No. No my old friend I said to him.

Tuesday 27th. Feb.

The Examiner for last week arrived yesterday. A very blowy morning. All the Snow nearly gone. I hear that the Corn question is put off till Thursday next, but it is no great matter, as it appears nothing will be done for the benefit of the Country in general. The Agriculturalists affirm that there is not sufficient Corn, to serve until the next harvest, still they are anxious to retard a foreign supply, although they acknowledge it will be wanted. This is Pancake Tuesday but we have had none to dinner, not having time to fry them, although we bought a new frying pan a short time ago.

Wednesday 28th. Feb

Heard from Wm. this morning that he had received his Box safe which we are glad to hear. He says he had sent a parcel which he expected would have been here last night but it has not yet come. — Old Barny says he will be most of his rent out of pocket this year. Last year he sold his Turnips for £75 this year the same quantity for £21. his wheat has been short in the Crop more than a Quarter an acre, and his Oats altho' he has 5 quarters an acre (which is a great crop this year) he says he ought to have had 9 or 10. He had 3 quarters of Beans on 4 Acres, a decent crop would have had 4 quarters an acre. His Hay like all others has been a very short crop. Now do these complainers take into consideration the advanced price of several of the Articles. A Rainy afternoon which prevented me from going out to measure a Close of Turnips after School time.

Thursday 1st. March

This is Mr. Barnard's rent day. I do not expect the tenants will make any complaints to their Landlord this day; but could they be heard after they have dined at Barnard Cook's (who provides a dinner on the occasion) when the Bottles are before them containing what they expect to be Wine, Instead of elevating them, and enlarging their hearts for the feelings of their fellow Creatures, there will be such a dismal noise of Complaints, that a bystander would think some woful Calamity had happened; but no such thing; it is only their tender hearts afraid that the Landlords should be obliged to <u>lower their rents</u>, was ever any thing so feeling? Yes, this touches them still nearer, afraid that produce <u>will be</u> <u>lower</u>, this is it that they continually dwell upon, whether eating or drinking or whatsoever they do, they do all to keep up prices.

Friday 2nd. March

Walter Scott in a public Company at Edinburgh, has acknowledged that he is the Author of the Scotch Novels I do not think that there is much surprise in the confession.[25] It is without doubt a task that he has performed which will be never again done by any one individual. I see there has been a meeting in London to subscribe for the erection of a Monument to the Duke of York, one would think people are careless about their money, they are not taxed enough by the Government, but must tax themselves; though when the list is examined, it appears there are Churchmen & Soldiers who have been long living on the Vitals of the Country; I do not see the use of a monument at all, to the late illustrious Commander.

Saturday 3rd. March

Expected the Parcel from Wm. last night but it did not come, Carrier brought the Organ last night, and it was taken down to the Church this morning, it is to be set up the next week; then we shall have a machine to praise God with; most of the Church work is done by machinery, all prayers are read (sometimes very ill) by a man in a white robe, and there is another not far from him who every now and then, begins either to mock or correct the man in white; the machines used for this purpose are called common prayer Books, alias Mass Books. Now here is every thing regular as can be done; and all by machinery; any Boy of tolerable Capacity, of ten or twelve years of Age, might conduct all the business in a workman like manner, but is this worshipping the ever living God? the Poet says

How decent and how wise
How charming to behold,
Beyond the Pomp that charms the eyes,
And rites adorn'd with Gold.[26]

Our Saviour charged his disciples not to use vain repetitions, But who that hears the Service of the Church, and reflects on it, but must think that the Compilers of it, have set Christ's words at defiance. Advanced £100 to Mr. Robinson to be secured on Mortgage of Robt. Kemp's house, new built where old Mrs. Young used to live. This is a very important transaction in my life and as such I note it down. The interest is to be 5 pr. Cent. which will be a pretty thing at the year's end. Measured part of a Close for Thos. Robinson of Ellerker 11a–2r–31p.

Sunday 4th. March

Recd. from Wm. the Morning Herald of Friday, which pleased me to find him so attentive, to what he knows gives me satisfaction; I am now beforehand with the knowing ones I think for my own part Mr. Canning proposes the duty

---

[25] Scott chose to keep secret his authorship of *Waverley* (published 1814) and the series of Waverley novels which followed that work. It was not until 1827 that he finally acknowledged publicly that he was their author. Contemporary observers found it difficult to believe that Scott could have found sufficient time to produce so many anonymous works while simultaneously living such an obviously full and busy public life (Sutherland 172).

[26] This is a slight misquotation from the poem by Isaac Watts (1674–1748), 'The Beauty of the Church; or, Gospel, Worship and Order'. The second line should read 'How glorious to behold' (*EP*)

too high; viz the standard at 60s. and 20s. duty,[27] now Wheat must be very low abroad to be brought in here and pay the duty, freight, Warehouse rent and the Merchants' profit. I think the expences inclusive of the duty cannot on an average be less than 10s. pr. qr. especially if any profit be allowed to the importer and who would wish to trade without? then this brings foreign wheat of the same quality as ours to just half the price. It almost looks like prohibition, like the old law until the price arrives at 80s. in this Country. Sir Thomas Lethbridge[28] appears to be pretty well satisfied with what is proposed; which will no doubt operate as a Stimulus, to some popular member to try to lower the duty but most likely it will not be done.

Monday 5th. March

No Newspaper this morning so that I have sent my Brother the Morning Herald which came yesterday. A hard frost last night but fine Sun shining today altho' cold. I am now fully convinced that the duties on Corn proposed by Mr. Canning are too high, as all the Farmers are delighted with it, I do not know but some of them would be drunk this day on the strength of it, they say it appears to be very fair and what the Country can afford and likewise they themselves can live if wheat can be kept at, or above 60s. pr. Qr. indeed if Flour never exceed 2s/6d pr. Stone, there will not be much complaint, provided employment can be had.

Tuesday 6th. March

Mr. Barnard has gone to London, he generally goes in the Spring after his rent day, he will perhaps stay three months or more. Mrs. Pinder had a chest of Tea and another of Coffee on board the Jubilee one of the London smacks which ran on shore near Yarmouth in the late storm. She has now got to Hull and the Chests are arrived safe, with an expence of about 5 Pounds upon them, which will take away the profit. I think it seems rather hard that goods on board should be subject to the expences. But this appears to be the custom.

Wednesday 7th. March

The Parcel from Wm. arrived last night, with an account that he had received the Chest safe and all excellent in the inside. I recd. two papers this morning packed up together, so that if news be like wine which improves in the keeping, I am very well off this day[.] It is all new to me. It is plain as a mathematical demonstration that the Duty on Corn is too high, for all the farmers are as eloquent in the praises of Mr. Canning as their capacities will allow, Oh, what a man he is to hit upon such a scheme, it appears he wishes the farmers to live, aye, aye, they are the support of the nation. Now it is only a very little while since these same men were wishing that the Govt would be as fatal to their Saviour (Mr. C) as the Fit had been to Lord Liverpool, now there is nothing but praises upon him, because he has touched a string of which they

---

[27] The Corn Bill of 1827 had been prepared by the previous government under Lord Liverpool. It failed to become law when Canning's coalition government was unable to defeat the Duke of Wellington's amendment to raise the threshold price from 60s. to 66s. (See n.72 (1827).

[28] Sir Thomas Buckler Lethbridge (1778–1849) assumed a prominent role as leader of the ultra-Tories after the formation of Canning's coalition ministry in Apr. 1827 (Walpole ii. 360-3).

like to hear the Sound, he has cried high prices this is their dear delight. I hope
the Landlords will not forget them, and as this is their hobby, let them have
high rents. It would be cruel to part high prices from high rents.

Made some Ink of the last Galls I have left; a moderate day, There is a fine
Cover on one of the Registers which I must preserve, it has been a Wrapper to a
No. of Hogarth's works, there are such droll figures on it as I can scarcely make
out, but it is very fine. In this Case I am almost like an ignorant Congregation
whom a Minister treats to a display of hard words, and by chance a scrap of
Latin, none of which they understand: but they get an idea that the Parson is a
very fine man; for he has words they do not understand, then he can talk an
outlandish language. So these figures with monkey heads, must be something
above the common vulgar.

Friday 8th. March

A very Stormy night and continues the same this day. No Paper this
morning. Wrote a notice to the Savings Bank at Beverley for the Club; to pay
the Money belonging them; to the Treasurer of the said Club, who is Jno.
Murgatroyd. Read the last Nos. of Cobbett to the 24th. Feb. he has no
compassion for Lord Liverpool; The Elegy on Bric is as ludicrous as can be well
conceived.[29] He still persuades his readers to keep Gold when they get it. I have
not followed this advice for last week the money I advanced was in Sovereigns;
which we have had by us more than a year, so that if the value of them advance,
there is the loss of interest to be deducted. I cast a lingering look at them when I
parted with their Golden faces. I mean it for the best.

Friday 9th. March

Cobbett tells a very plausible tale of being deceived by the man who was to
have been his Surety. He is of course prevented of prosecuting his Petition. I
should have liked to have seen him in Parliament, not that I know he would
have done any great good, but he would have annoyed some of the sensitive
Gentlemen very much. He would have minded very little been coughed at. By
the way this shews the Manners of the members of the honourable house. There
are many of them just calculated for Aye, and, No, and in addition to set up a
sort of Horse cough. — What ministerial men the farmers are now, they see
their own interests clear as mud; they have some misgivings that the Corn
duties will not pass. But still at this time they fancy Mr. Canning omnipotent.
— I am certain the duties are too high. Recd. a letter from Mr. Dryden of the
Stamp office that Mr. Willock is appointed distributor of the East Riding,
likewise a letter from Mr. Willock, for the names of my Sureties who are Robt.
Marshall and Saml. Shaw, two as respected persons as can be; I do not know
who Mr. Willock is. Two papers this day, one seemed as if [it] had been stopped
which should have come yesterday.

---

[29] 'The Lives, Loves, Deaths, and Burials of Lawyer Bric and the Fair Shoy-hoy' (*CPR* 61 ix (24 Feb.)
1827, 566–8).

Saturday 10th. March

The weather has been of late very boisterous, very cold for young lambs, for which the season has commenced; but as Sterne's Maria says, "God tempers the wind to the shorn lamb",[30] so the weather may be likewise tempered to the feelings of the tender young lambs. It is a very scarce time for fodder. Many times have I reproached myself for not giving some thing to a poor prisoner in the Fleet, who stood at a Window with a Box in his hand: his pale emaciated figure shewed that he was a sufferer; if I ever live to see such another object in the same place, I certainly shall drop some small pittance into the Box, and not stand self accused for negligence or hard heartedness. I do not much admire the law for incarcerating Persons for debt and what is called contempt of Court. Jeremiah Marshall going to Hull this day to enter on the Livery Stables, occupied by Ths. Reynolds. Reynolds has taken the Public house at North Cave where Mr. Walker lived. Long debates on the Catholic question which is lost by a very small majority, in a full house.

Sunday 11th. March

No Paper again this morning. A Sermon at Church this afternoon where the Parson was endeavouring to prove that the Penitent Thief on the Cross was not a <u>Thief</u>, he had a good many Conjectures, on it but nothing satisfactory; I do not know but we shall make this same thief a saint if we only had a name for him, for Saint Thief or Saint No-thief would sound rather odd. And why may not he be a saint as well as St. Cross, or St. Sepulchre? I think his Claims are better. The Organ now stands brazening in the Front of the Gallery like a tall Bully, or rather like a genteel Sentry Box, we have not been favoured today with its pealing, or rather bealing. Indeed they say there are two unmanageable Pipes in it, for play they will whether wanted or not, they will not conclude with the others, but blow out by themselves after the rest have done ...

Tuesday 13th. March

A Fine morning but cold. It appears that some of the Farming monopolists wish for the Duty to be paid on Corn at the time it is imported; but if this be the case it may as well be prohibited until it reach 70s. pr. Qr. for who would offer to import at 55s: the price here, and bring in foreign wheat at that time and pay 30s. pr. quarter duty, would not this be saying as much as you shall not import at all at low prices. Let the English warehouses be the Depot of Corn for all nations, and if the merchant cannot find a market here let him be at liberty to take it to any other Country where he can make a profit. Shipping wants employment, but none will they have if this mad scheme be put in execution. It cannot be, it must not.

Wednesday 14th. March

Recd. two Desk Penknives from Sheffield which I ordered some time since, of a tradesman who supplies Mr. Atkinson with Nails &c. I sent one of the handles to get a new blade put in, the other is a new one. I likewise ordered 200 needles for Mrs. School which have likewise come at the same time. The

---

[30] French proverb cited in this form in Laurence Sterne's *A Sentimental Journey.*

needles were 20d. pr. hundred which I understand are too dear, so that I must mind better and know the value another time before I order any more. Mr. Croft having written to the Post Office at York to complain of his papers being repeatedly stopped; even three times the last week. Barnard Cook had a letter this morning from the Post master at York with Mr. Croft's letter inclosed, where he charges Barnard with opening his Papers and letting his Customers read and soil them. I have written a letter for him in answer to York, totally denying the Charge, he says he never once either opened or suffered his papers to be opened in his house; He is suspicious that it is old Anthony Burton who carries the letters, that lends the Papers to his friends; indeed I have often known him lend Newspapers to the Old Cardinal and others; There was not one London Paper arrived last Sunday. I am in hopes the complaint may do good to the public.

Robt. Marshall has had 25 Lambs 5 of which are dead.

Thursday 15th. March

At Brantingham last night at Saml. Ringrose's he paid all I wanted of him, he has got very well again; Old Tommy Brigham who occupies his own farm seems to be fairly overset; for the little meat he had he wasted it before winter came on, then he had nothing for his Cattle. He has been offering to let his farm to Mr. Ringrose, he asked him 250 Pounds a year rent for it. O, thou old nasty beast Sammy says thou's broken thyself twice and now thou wants to break me but I'll take care of thee, I think 100 pounds would be over much for thy 60 Acres of bad poor land a deal of it. Why says Tommy there is no harm done Mr. Ringrose if you don't wish to have it. Hold your noise about harm says Sammy, what was there no harm in your stopping twice, and is there no harm in wanting to break me, harm! harm!! I think there has been harm enough faith. Then there is no harm in having Cattle and hungering them, and is there no harm in selling them for less than their worth? O — thou nasty old beast hold thy noise. — Poor Tommy can neither sell nor mortgage, or else his farm would soon go after his Stock, but he seems very happy and says it is all providence.

Friday 16th. March

Richd. Marshall had three Sheep worried a day or two ago which they killed and sold for about 24s: including the Skins, two more were badly bitten but are likely to live, the Dog belonged to a man who sells Fish. Coming up from the West end last night, I saw lights in the Church, the lovers of Sounds I suppose playing the Organ, but I had thoughts of Auld Kirk-Alloway in a bleeze, and should the same Old musician be here as was there, who, "screwed the pipes an gart them skirl"[31] I thought it would be as well to be out of the way, for fear Tam O'Shanter's fate should be mine. I certainly had the advantage of a running stream beside me, then it was not witching time of night; as it was only between seven and eight; I got home without any disaster.

---

[31] The quotation is from Robert Burns's poem, 'Tam O'Shanter: a Tale', and refers to the drunken Tam O'Shanter's sight of Kirk Alloway in a blaze of light and the Devil ('the Old musician'), in the shape of a black beast, playing the bagpipes and making them scream before the assembled company of dancing warlocks and witches.

— Old Rachel Levitt died last night, the last time I saw her was on Sunday last. she has been worse than common about a fortnight back. — Mr. Canning just seems to be in no place as his friends have advanced the price, and duty on Barley and Oats, after he said no alteration would be allowed, but it seems he has not power to carry his own measures.[32]

Saturday 17th. March

Newspaper missed coming again this morning. A very stormy day. I was at West end this forenoon, when <u>Awd Beck</u> had got a Lamb in the house at fire side, to which she had a little pastoral discourse. Now says she wilt thou neither drink nor suck, thou knowst I brought thee in when thou wast almost starved to death, wast not thou standing with all thy four legs together fit to drop down, and did not I stand watching to see if any of the Ewes would own thee? and did they not all go away and leave thee? and thou couldst not help thyself, and then I took thee and brought thee in here to fire side. And hast not Obed Martin who gathers Lambs' Skins just said that thou wilt soon be fit for him? but he shant have thee if only thou wilt suck thy milk and live. All this was said and more, but the poor lamb made no reply.

Sunday 18th. March

"Now see! what numbers to the Church repair,
    More for the Music than the Doctrine there"[33]

The above is a bitter Satire against these preachers, who have thinned their Congregations so much by their preaching, that they are glad of any means, no matter what only the Churches be filled. We have had the great "<u>Fum</u>" sounding today, making a great blishering noise, but I dare say no more, for fear the said great wooden inclosed Fum, should persecute me for a libel if this ever see the light. Some judges of harmony say it is very sweet music. Old Rachel Levitt was buried this afternoon. Aged 71 years. Both the Papers this day.

Monday 19th. March

Robt. Marshall had a Sheep blown into the Mill Beck, and drowned on Saturday last, the wind was so strong. Richard Marshall has an Old Mare dead, there are many horses die with Sand in the inside of them, supposed to be from drinking water that was muddy, and eating the Grass so near in dry weather. It is surprising how the Land owners keep the Ministers in awe. I should not be at all surprised but the Lords will be for higher duties on Corn than even the Commons have in their Wisdom (or Folly, which?) thought proper to propose.

---

[32] In the passage of the 1827 Corn Bill through Parliament, Canning had agreed to raise the medium price of barley from 30s. per quarter, as had been proposed originally, to 32s., and the duty from 10s. (medium price) to 12s. Oats were likewise raised from 21s. per quarter to 25s., and the duty at that medium price was raised from 7s. to 8s. In the event the Corn Bill was defeated. (See n.72 (1827)) (*AR* 1827 Hist. 79).

[33] Apparently a creative misquotation from Alexander Pope's *An Essay on Criticism Written in the Year 1709* (1711): 'Not mend their minds; as some to Church repair, / Not for the doctrine, but the music there ...'—(*EP*)

Tuesday 20th. March

There has been a report some time of building a new Church at Welton,[34] there was a meeting yesterday, when several of the Farmers not tenants to Mr. Raikes opposed the Scheme, but they were not succes[s]ful. The expence is estimated at £1400 which Mr. Raikes will advance at 5 per cent, with an engagement that the whole shall be paid off in 20 years. Mr. Harland a farmer at Melton says if this be carried into execution, and he continues on his farm so long, it will cost him £400, he appears to be most decidedly against it; as well he may if this be the truth.

The landed Gentlemen with Sir Thomas Lethbridge at their head like an old Pedlar, lead Mr. Canning about like a Jack Ass, he sometimes seems rather restive, and gives a Kick or two, but no Pedlar feels any alarm when his Ass kicks a little; for he knows it is like nothing at all.

Wednesday 21st. March

Recd. a parcel from Wm. this morning, am glad to hear that he is well. Our old friend Willy Atkinson is learned in various ways, indeed he seems an universal Genius. In Chronology he is unmatched, his text Book is the Newgate Calendar;[35] he knows the time when De la Motte[36] the french spy was executed, when Dr. Dodd[37] was hanged for forgery, and he can tell the date when sixteen string Jack[38] was in his glory, besides numbers more of whom he has an account. In Geography he is well skilled from Cave to London and from thence to Bristol; he is particularly acquainted with the situation, manners, & customs of Long Acre and Saint Martin's lane, Paternoster Row and little Britain he is not quite so certain in; and if there be one point in which he fails, it is in believing that Canterbury is a Seaport town; Now from his description I think he has been at Rochester, which he mistakes for Canterbury; I suppose no Ecclesiastic would make this mistake. He knows something of the Association of Ideas, for he never hears Parliament mentioned, but Beverley Election rushes into his mind, with all its eating, drinking, bribing and blue Ribbons flying about.

Thursday 22d. March

Three Soldiers with a Deserter from the 5th. Regt. of Foot going to Hull, they had taken the deserter at Nottingham. I always feel sorry for the poor

---

[34] No completely new church was ever built at Welton, but the existing church, St. Helen's, may have been repaired or slightly rebuilt at this time as a result of Mr. Raikes's proposal. The major rebuilding and restoration of the church, however, was carried out by G. G. Scott in 1862–3 (Pevsner (1995) 739–40).

[35] A. Knapp and W. Baldwin, *The Newgate Calendar, Comprising Interesting Memoirs of the Most Notorious Characters who have been Convicted of Outrages on the Laws of England ... with Anecdotes and Last Exclamations of Sufferers.* London, 1824–6. - 4 vols. (8°).

[36] Francis Henry De La Motte, executed at Tyburn 27 July 1781 for high treason (Rayner and Crook iv. 153).

[37] William Dodd was hanged at Tyburn on 27 June, 1777 (Rayner and Crook iv. 114).

[38] John Rann, commonly called 'Sixteen String Jack' on account of his habit of wearing breeches with 8 strings at each knee, was convicted of highway robbery and hanged at Tyburn on 30 Nov. 1774 (Rayner and Crook iv. 99).

fellows who have been enlisted and then desert. — Robt. Marshall has got a foal the first this Season in the town. — I had forgot when on the subject of Old Willy's Geography, that he believes Italy to be in Asia; but he does not pride himself at all on the situation of foreign Countries. Cobbett thinks that Mr. Canning would not have pressed on the Corn Bill in the manner it is, if he had not been threatened; I think the members for Cities &c who are not so far gone in the land Mania, ought to have tried more than they have for a different result. The farmers see their own interest or think they see it, in the present measures; but after all it may only be the interest of their Landlords.

Friday 23d. March

A meeting last night to let the lanes,[39] by Auction for the first time, they let for £20–14–6. Last year they were let for £13–5–0, Beverley road lane up Porter-hole last year was let for 4 Pounds to Timothy Dunn, this year Rd. Kirby has taken it at 8 Guineas. I think it is the best plan to let them to the highest bidder, then everyone has a chance of taking. Complaints have sometimes been made by some of being excluded; they are let on a safe plan as the money is paid for them at the time of letting. In the debates in the Times on Tuesday last, there is a resolution relating to Barley paying 2s/6d pr. Qr. under 33s. and when at or above that price for every quarter 6d. duty. Likewise when Oats are under 24s. a duty of 2s. pr. Qr. and at or above that price the duty to be 6d. pr. qr. Are these statements true? If they are where is the duties that were proposed? It is impossible to know for a Week together the meaning of our Corn legislators. Measured Thos. Fisher's Tofts 6a–3r–12p.

Saturday 24th. March

At Church this forenoon Copying Registers[40] for the last year; The Parson would not let the Books come out of the Church, as I always had them before, so I shut myself up in the Vestry not very warm; and I am not quite so fond of the Situation as old Harry Bentley was; he would not he said wish for a pleasanter dwelling than it is, so cheering to look out of the Windows on the Graves and Grave-Stones; this was Harry's Opinion of a pleasant view. — In the afternoon taking an account of my Stock of Stamps. In the Evening at the West end settling with Loncaster who is the Constable.

Sunday 25th. March

A Windy Day and Cold, but the Sun Shining makes it appear pleasant. The Crows in full activity building and repairing, scolding, fighting, and watching each other, altho' all of one Community there are often bickerings, at

---

[39] The roads that were laid down as a result of parliamentary enclosure were usually between 40 and 60 feet wide. Only the centre was used as a carriageway, so that the wide grass verges were available for grazing tethered animals. Every year, in many townships, including South Cave, the lanes were let for grazing to the highest bidder and the money so raised was used by the surveyors of the highways for the repair of the roads (Crowther (1983) 540).

[40] The Convocation of Canterbury ordered in 1597 and 1603 that an annual transcript of the parish registers should be sent to the bishop for preservation in the diocesan registry, the so-called 'bishop's transcript'. With the passing of Rose's Act in 1812, Parliament laid down measures for the safer custody of parish registers, for greater uniformity in their maintenance, and for more accurate bishops' transcripts (*EB* xxiii.. 40).

this Season amongst them, but there is no doubt they would all join against a common Enemy. Gooseberry trees are nearly in full leaf, grass grows very little, but it may be discerned that the land is rather greener. Even Nettles under hedges and Wall sides, remind one by their fresh life that Spring is approaching.

Monday 26th. March

Cobbett has rubbed down Sir Francis pretty roughly,[41] it appears that when self interest is contrasted with Patriotism the latter in general gives way. What will the Electors of Westminster say to Sir F's conduct, in speaking so much in favour of the landlords? will they think they have been properly heard by the mouth of their representative? I should think not.

Tuesday 27th. Mar

It was said not long ago that Barley would be from 3 to 4 pounds a quarter at Seed time, but that time is now at hand, and the sellers have the consolation to find that in general those who wanted to sow, have silently laid in their Stock of Seed; I suppose Barley is not dearer now than it was in December, notwithstanding the astounding cries of a bad crop. It has happened in this instance that the wise ones have overshot their mark; In fact there seems to be at present as much Corn as there can be found money to pay for it. Sent by Cousens £98–18–0 the amount of Stamps, last Qr.

Wednesday 28th. March

Recd. a returned letter this morning from London which I wrote some time since to Malton on Parish business; Recd. the rect. from the Stamp office for money sent yesterday, with half a Sovereign returned for being too light; I did not much like it when I took it. Wrote to the Norwich Union to insure Kemp's house. Very cold and rainy today. Balanced up the Constable's Accounts for the last 5 months. Plenty of news this day having 2 papers from Wm., he says he is well & that there is nothing new nor disagreeable, from which I infer that all is agreeable. I am glad to hear it.

Thursday 29th. March

At west end last night very rainy and Stormy, it was uncommonly dark when I came back, I slipped off the road into a Spring besides Thornam's, but without any injury except getting wet on one of my feet, and the Stocking dirtied on the other leg. This morning it snows again. Winter lingers 'ere it gives up its reign to Spring ...

Friday 30th. March

When Mr. Garnons was the Vicar here (in days gone by)[42] Old Harry Bentley was his Clerk; at the Churchwardens Easter Dinner and Visitation the Clerk was permitted to dine at the same table with his master, but when the Wine began to take effect and elevate the heart of the honest old Clerk, he

[41] Cobbett had published a lengthy attack on a speech made by Sir Francis Burdett on 9 Mar. 1827 (*CPR* 61 xii (17 Mar.) 1827, 705–34).

[42] Daniel Garnons was Vicar of S. Cave from 1783 until 1817 when he was succeeded by Edward William Barnard (Hall, J. G. 43).

would desire an explanation of some Theological point from his Master; but he was generally pretty soon overpowered by the Juice of the Grape and incapable of answering satisfactorily; so that Harry used to prick up his ears and assert that he knew more of Religion than his Master did. This was not to be endured by some of the Vicar's hearers who gave up their spiritual Concerns to the Parson, and looked upon themselves as insulted by the Clerk's arrogance; and a Resolution was carried that the Assistant to the Parson, should not for the future be suffered to dine with the (great) Churchwardens & Vicar. So after that time Harry dined alone and took his Chirping pint,[43] reflecting & meditating and feeling thankful that he had not to answer to any earthly tribunal for his Religion.

Saturday 31st. March

More alterations proposed in the Corn laws, they will be such a farrago, of Winchester & Imperial[44] that I question whether the proposers understand their own meaning; one thing is certain that the influence of the landed interest is predominant, they must be protected, let who will suffer; this appears to be very partial legislating; oppressing one part of the Community for the benefit of another; Every alteration which has been made is for both higher price and higher duty—Miss Stephenson of Ferriby Mill was married on Thursday last to Hall a Tobacconist of Hull. — At Brantingham this afternoon measuring Wm. Brigham's Turnip land 13a–1r–24p this has been a very bad season for me in measuring, as the Turnips in several places have missed and in others have been sold by the lump. I was asked by Mr Brigham to stop tea, but his Housekeeper whispered him that they had no butter without churning, which it appears she did not want to do this afternoon, so I excused myself and came home without.

Sunday 1st. April

A very fine soft spring day; I think parliament have been spending their time to very little purpose; the landed gentry appear not yet to be satisfied with their monopoly, it is reported I see that they intend to move that no Corn be warehoused without paying the duty, if this turn out to be the case it would have saved much time to have prohibited the bringing Corn in altogether; It is evident they feel for none but themselves. All their cry is for profit, profit.

Monday 2nd. April

Mutton 8d. pr. lb. how the Sellers of Fat Sheep now lick their lips and fill their mouths with mutton while fat runs out of the sides of their mouths, famous times for them, their eyes now stand out with fatness; but how are the poor and distressed to procure a bit of flesh meat at this price? their looks answer that they feel the gnawings of hunger, it is a distressing thing when an able man is

---

[43] Cheering or producing merriment; by 19th c. used only as part of a traditional phrase such as 'chirping cup' or, as here, 'chirping pint' (*OED*).

[44] Grain was measured by capacity, the 2 commonest measures being the bushel and the quarter, which varied somewhat according to local custom. The 2 standard measures in general use were the Imperial and Winchester bushels and quarters, which were themselves not exactly equivalent, the Winchester quarter being 97% of the Imperial quarter (Mingay vi. 91, 978, 1124–6).

willing to work that he cannot earn so much as will supply the cravings of his family; Luxury and want now rule with wide sway.

Tuesday 3rd. April

Balancing up the Poor Accounts for the last year; there is to be a meeting this Evening to examine them, and to nominate Overseers for the ensuing year; The expences this year have been less by more than Seventy pounds, than they were the last year, from this it appears that distress has not so much power amongst us, as in some places; It is to be observed that there is no superfluity allowed to any who receive relief, they are compelled to put up with the smallest pittance.

Wednesday 4th. April

A Parish meeting last night to balance to the Poor accounts at Wm. Cousens' the old Overseers nominated again. At Beverley this day getting sworn in Assessor with Robt. Marshall; there were races at Beverley[45] this day called Hunter's Stakes; and as some of my friends were anxious to go to see them, I out of mere good nature accompanied them, but I tired and came into Beverley again before the last race, which they assured me was the best, there having 12 or 13 horses run. I took a survey more of the Company than the racing, and what a motley group they were: There was the Lord Macdonald, and Mr. Hodgson who keeps hounds for the amusement of those who have nothing else to do but accompany them, — There was Dog Bob, an old fellow clothed in red (and mounted upon one [of] the horses of some of the honorables) with a great whip in his hand cracking along the course to clear it. There was another blackguard called Teapot Jack also clothed in Scarlet who seemed a fit companion to Capt. Ramsden & Co.—there were some who I fancy esteemed themselves Ladies, likewise solacing themselves, then there were Booths for supplying Liquor, and accommodating Pickpockets, and some poor fellows going about selling Lolly pop, nuts & oranges. Amongst the rest not fruit sellers was Walmsley of Hull who could see both ends of the Course at once, and several &c &c. I got home about eight O'clock. Rode Wm. Cousens' Galloway.

Thursday 5th. Apl

Club night long debates about advancing £120 on mortgage to Geo. Lester of Broomfleet, the Old Cardinal opposed it all he could but he was fairly put down and £60 in part of the money was taken out, the remainder to be paid on Saturday, when the treasurer will receive it from the Savings Bank. I was pleased to see the Old Broad brim put down, they were going to put the proposal to the Vote but he said it was of no use as there was only himself against it. He was the very first man who gave his consent about a month ago for it.

Friday 6th. April

Bought a Silk handkerchief and half a hundred needles of a travelling merchant from Hull of the name of Dawson who lives in Finkle Street, he says

---

[45] Horse racing on Beverley Westwood was first established in 1690 and continues to the present day (1995) on the same site (*VCHYER* vi. 206).

he has been a merchant but the times have been so much against him, that he is obliged to do any thing honestly for his support, he is rather a respectable looking man, and very clean in his appearance. What he says may be true. What a miserable dividend there will be to the Creditors of Hurst & Robinson[46] it appears to be worse than Frank Jackson's who paid 20 pence per pound. He had £40 of the Old Cardinals who received as many times 20d. for his money in pounds.

Saturday 7th. Apl.

Measured a Close of Turnip land at Ellerker for Mr. Todd 10a–2r–23p. Served a Summons on Wm. Loncaster, the <u>Constable</u> for an Assault on Prince a Saddler of River Bridge, this is the second time that the Constable has committed Assault since he came into Office, the last time he had 7s–6d to pay to make it up with the Man he had struck at, but this time he says he will take it to the Sessions rather than pay any thing. He is particularly unfortunate as a Peace officer, when he gets embroiled. — Mr. Oldfield was buried this afternoon at Elloughton, he died at Brough.

Sunday 8th. Apl.

This is Palm Sunday there are plenty of full grown Palms:[47] the weather has been uncommonly fine for the last week past. Wheat grows amazingly, and Grass fields look very green, fruit trees as far as I have seen are very full of blossom Buds, the seed time for spring Corn is very fine, so that if it please providence to send moderate weather there is every probability of plenty blessing the land. Most of the farmers now have their Corn drilled in Rows, instead of sowing by what is called the broad-cast method. Drilling is I think superior.[48]

Monday 9th April

Abraham Barff once on a Market day bet a Wager of Five Guineas with Hotham Miller that he would shew him a hundred pounds that night before twelve O'clock; so Abraham set off to fetch his money and the Miller ran out to be out of the way, when he Abm came back, which was not long first he enquired for the Miller but was told that he was gone, so Abe went from one public house to another to seek him and at last found him, and said now here is the money, the Miller got his hands before his face and told him he could not or did not see it, why its here Abraham says look at [it], I won't, I won't, was the reply, but presently twelve O'clock struck without the Man of Meal seeing the

---

[46] This London financial house, collapsed in Jan. 1826. It had been acting as the London agent for Sir Walter Scott's publishers, Ballantyne and Constable. Since the financial affairs of all the parties were closely intertwined, the fall of the London company brought financial ruin to both Scott and his publishers. Hurst, Robinson and Co. were left with liabilities of £300,000 and eventually paid out 15d. to the pound (Quayle 189–228).

[47] i.e. willow branches and catkins used to represent palms for the celebration of Palm Sunday.

[48] A successful seed-drilling device had been designed by Jethro Tull in 1701, but general adoption of the new system was slow. In 1794, it was recorded that 'the drill is very little used' in the East Riding (Leatham 30), but by 1812 'drill husbandry had made some advances in the best cultivated parts of the East Riding' (Strickland 124) and by 1848, drilling had 'become universal' (Legard 109).

Money; so it was given against Abraham that he had lost his wager, but the Company proposed that he should be off the bett if he would treat them with a Bowl or two of Punch, but to this he would not accede, so they treated themselves out of his money, and poor Abraham lost the whole, comforting himself that he had been robbed of it.

Tuesday 10th. April

Yesterday Mr. Willock the new Stamp Distributor was here along with Mr. Dryden to get the Stock transferred into his name, which was soon done, every thing being ready to their hands, with which they were much pleased, they had not found so great regularity in any of the Stamp Offices they had visited. I always like to keep every thing properly and do not like to put off to another day what I can do on this, but where the maxim of putting off is followed, confusion is generally the result.

Wednesday 11th. April

Measured Mr. Levitt's Trancledales last night the part next the Drewton road 12a–1r–32p, and the top part 6a–1r–33p. Teavil Leeson has bought the whole the low part at £60 pr. acre, and the top part I think under 40 pounds pr. acre, there is a part of it about 1a–3r–21p Copyhold the rest is Freehold. Heard this morning from Wm. that he is well, and has nothing more to say, this is quite satisfactory as far as it goes. The weather not so fine yesterday and today as it was last week. Ran a thorn into my leg last night very near the place where I was bitten by a Dog, which I think I often feel yet, it was on the foreside of the leg on the bone: Sometimes I think it is only my timidity and there is nothing in it; but this I know I do not like to be lacerated by a Dog: I know the Dog which bit me was not mad, but it sometimes happens that Dogs which are not mad have caused much trouble, and been dangerous to their victims.

Thursday 12th. April

At west end last night, I seldom miss on Wednesday nights except something extra happen. There was a large Sheep fair last Saturday at Caistor in Lincolnshire, where Hogs (that is Sheep of one year old) were in great abundance and contrary to expectation were in good condition. The best prices did not exceed 26s. each. Some of our friends who kept their lambs last year, made themselves sure of 30s. apiece for them this Spring, and now they are fearful that they are not worth more than a Guinea. This year some of them talk of making their lambs fat, so that this will help to supply the market, indeed it appears that Stock of all kinds is as plentiful as money.

Friday 13th. Apl

Eliza and her Mother gone to West Ella and Hull today, I was at Church in the morning being Good Friday, the Clerk let me know there would be Service in the afternoon, but I told him I could not attend as I had engaged to measure Mr. Levitt's Wold Close, which I did containing about 19a–2r–0p the close which Richard Marshall has bought, they expect to settle for it about this time.

Saturday 14th. Apl

Went to Ellerker this morning to measure all the Garths and Old Inclosure about the town, but did not finish, I measured about 32 different parcels and gave up about six O'clock not having got any dinner or refreshment of any kind but a pipe of Tobacco, it rained all the way home, Miss Kitty and her father would have me to Tea with them, and as my fire was out, I accepted the invitation, Old Kit assuring me that I was as welcome as themselves. They say that Hall has got to London again into Regent Street, mind at the <u>West end</u>.

Sunday 15th. Apl

Easter Sunday I am still Housekeeper alone, excepting two Cats. I broiled some Bacon and boiled 3 Eggs to my dinner. A very pleasant growing day, every thing looking remarkably well, No newspaper this day, I saw yesterday that they frequently examine the Newspapers at the General Post office and on an Average there are eight in a hundred, where intelligence is sent by them instead of letters. Saw in the Rockingham that seven of the Ministers have sent in their resignations.[49] — Amongst the rest the Lord Chancellor, I never expected that he would have parted with his office but with his life. I think from what has transpired there will be no cause of grief to the Country on his Account. I am rather surprised that Mr. Peel is amongst the number, as he appears to be well respected in general, and has made himself useful. Eliza & her Mother arrived about 7 O'clock this Evening.

Monday 16th. Apl

A large Show of Horses this day, and a throng market for Cave the owners of Horses treating their Customers with Punch and Wine, some of them will stand a Chance of being most of their expences out of Pocket, as they say there are some of the horses very worthless; but the owners have always something to say in praise of their own, however I made none of them any poorer for I did not get a single glass with them; they in general know their customers therefore I was not asked to partake.

Tuesday 17th. Apl.

This is Easter Tuesday I was at Church in the morning and staid till the Churchwardens were chosen,[50] who are Barnd. Cook and Mr. Atkinson, there was 30 Dozen of Penny rolls given away.[51] I did not attend the Churchwardens dinner as I had a close to measure at the Common, so I went down in the

[49] In Feb. 1827, Lord Liverpool suffered a paralytic stroke bringing his long-running ministry to an end. After Canning had been asked by the King to form a new ministry in Apr., Lord Liverpool's old Tory ministers, Wellington, Peel, Eldon, Bathurst, Melville, Westmorland, and Bexley, sent in their resignations (Walpole ii. 351–4).

[50] In South Cave, 2 churchwardens were chosen annually on Easter Tuesday to serve for the ensuing year. If re-selected, they might serve for the following and subsequent years. (Willy Atkinson served as churchwarden for 4 successive years, 1833/4—6/7). It was customary for one of the pair to be chosen by the Vicar, the other to be elected at a parish meeting.

[51] The gift was in accordance with Jobson's Bread Charity. Samuel Jobson, who died in 1687, left property to the churchwardens of S. Cave on condition that they provided an annual sum of 20s. for an anniversary sermon every Easter Tuesday, and 25s. for the distribution of white bread to the poor on the same day. By at least 1826 (see entry for 9/10/26), sufficient income had accrued from Jobson's 'bread lands' to provide in addition 20s. each for a dinner at Cave Fair and another in the workhouse at Christmas plus 30s. for the distribution of penny bread rolls on the last Sunday of every month (Hall, J. G. 54–5).

afternoon and measured it, it is one which Mr. Levitt sold to Mr. Briggs. 3a–2r–30p Robt. Marshall trailed the Chain; came back and got tea with him.

Wednesday 18th. Apl

A Methodist missionary meeting here today Eliza and her mother have been there, there are a lot of sturdy beggars persuading the simple to give them their money. This has likewise been the Tansy Day,[52] at Newloves but what company attended I do not know, there was dancing when I went to bed. I recollect my Father talking of having Tansy pudding to dinner on the Sunday called Tansy Sunday, he was brought up a Shepherd and continued so as long as he was able, he aspired to nothing but honest rural manners.

Thursday 19th. Apl

A man at Mr. Atkinson's last night the same I mentioned once before, says that the Government is nearly up, he says the Corn Bill is about as forward as when it was begun. O' says he here is a fine subject for Cobbett now, I must look about me when I go to Hull to see what he says, there is no doubt, he says but the Ministers and others too read Cobbett for instruction but they will not own it; but for my part says he, I retail out what I hear from him not caring whether it be known that I have gained my instruction from him or not; for I do not think it any way at all degrading; for men must have their knowledge from some source, and there are few like Billy who is self taught, and capable of teaching others, providing they have the capacities for learning.

Friday 20th. Apl

Recd. 2 Examiners this morning there was not one came the last week at all, John Turk is at Liverpool a traveller for a Sugar house. I have not seen him since he went. I was at Mr. Tinsdill's last night he is very full of the new ministry,[53] saying there certainly can not be one more disagreeable to the Country than the last one. I suppose the great object with most is to gratify their own ambition, and look close to their own interest, there may perhaps be some solitary exemptions, but such men are looked upon like a white Crow in a rookery. — Thos. Marshall has had an old Shepherd this winter with whom he had a great deal of discourse. There is one Word that the old Man used, which Tom looks upon to be so full of meaning that he intends making use of it himself, it is Swab or Swabhead, a name for worthless fellows who sit at a public house minding other people's business and at the same time neglecting their own. These persons Tom intends honouring with the name of Swabheads.

Saturday 21st. Apl

I saw a Swallow yesterday the first time this Season, but as the Old proverb says One Swallow does not make a Summer, it appears to be verified now as the weather is extremely cold. It is said that a Vessel loaded with Bones sunk this

---

[52] Tansy cake and tansy pudding were dishes traditionally associated with Easter and possibly recalled the 'bitter herbs' of the Passover. According to the *OED*, a tansy was a 'merrymaking or festive gathering; a village feast held on Shrove Tuesday'. RS mentioned the tansy being celebrated in South Cave on 5 occasions but always on the Wednesday following Easter Sunday.

[53] Canning's newly formed ministry of liberal Tories included Palmerston and Huskisson and enjoyed the support of many Whigs (Walpole ii. 354–8).

afternoon not far from Brough, The master of which had his wife and 7 Children on board 4 of whom could not be Saved,[54] A sudden squall took the Vessel and made her heel on one side when she immediately filled with water. The Old Cardinal at Mr. Atkinson's tonight telling of a variety of Spirits which he has seen in [his] life time.

Sunday 22nd. Apl.

The Parson at Church declaiming violently against any persons preaching to draw away people from the Church, but he might have spared himself the labour of saying any thing on the subject for let him and his brethren preach as they do, and there will be no occasion for any endeavours to be used to thin the Church congregations. The ignorance or selfishness of many Clergymen is truly wonderful, they must certainly fancy that the Church of England came down from Heaven, with a Bishop to bear it company and a prayer Book in his hand, but the times are gone by for convincing people that Christ's Church is confined to the National Establishment in England. In fact it is downright plagiarism to Rob the Church of Rome of its first superiority.

Monday 23d. Apl

John Gardam has pulled down the House where Joshuah Cade used to live his (Gardam's) Sister having bought it, he is now building a new house; Joshuah has now got through all his Property, and is a sort of Butcher's Cad[55] to his Son William. Joshuah is a man who has seen sometimes that when Fathers have saved for their Children, it has been wasted, and in cases where Children have had to cut out their own living some have done very well, so he thought it was for the benefit of his Sons that he had nothing to give them, and this squared so exactly with his conduct, that he cries come another glass more, what a single glass cannot hurt much, but then one to another swells up the reckoning, as "Mole hills often heaped to Mountains rise" he had forgot or never knew the sage maxim

"Weigh every small expence and nothing waste

Farthings long sav'd amount to pounds at last"

Tuesday 24th. Apl

A Coroners inquest was held yesterday at Brough on the four Children who were drowned in the Vessel on Saturday last, the oldest was about 12 years old, they were all Girls, they have got the Vessel into Brough, it is a lamentable accident. A Good deal of Snow last night and snowed fast this morning, it has been a very long winter from the beginning, and has been extremely cold for a few days past.

Wednesday 25th. April

Recd. a parcel from Wm. last night, glad to hear he is well, I just peeped into Cobbett last night but had not time to read much I looked over the

---

[54] The vessel was the sloop, 'Ebenezer', commanded by Captain Pennington. The 4 children who drowned were all below at the time of the accident; the master, his wife and remaining 3 children and mate were on deck and survived (*HP* 1 May 1827).

[55] The *OED* defines 'cad' as 'an assistant or confederate of a lower grade, a bricklayer's labourer'.

Dialogue between the King and the seven sages. Cobbett thinks he must be Minister at last, otherwise the Nation which is now out of joint, will not be able to move, it is a curious concern is this same Dialogue, and managed with a good deal of humour.[56] I am fearful Wm. will lose his Five pounds which he lent Mrs. Warwick, I am sorry to hear that the old woman is getting so bad in the world, but he must endeavour to get his money again, he ought to have remembered Poor Richd's saying which is He that goes a borrowing, goes a sorrowing, And he adds, <u>so does he that lends</u> when he goes for his own again, — But as it is truly said

"The tender feels anothers woes
The unfeeling but his own"

I shall see by the Catalogue the rarity of some curious books, it is a sort of reading, I am very partial to.

Thursday 26th. Apl

A Gentleman was in Mr. Atkinson's one night when I was there and began as is commonly usual with many people to praise the accommodation with which the public are pretty well provided, in having Notes instead of Gold in circulation, not forgetting to mention that there are amongst the Sovereigns many counterfeits. I told him I was partial to Gold and would always prefer it before Bills of any kind; he (Mr. Robinson was the Gentleman) said he would let me have Sovereigns for Bills whenever he had any; but I must mind and not take any bad ones. I told him it was a bargain, whenever I had any Rags I would accommodate him and to begin with, he gave me five fine Sovs. for a dirty piece of Paper.

Friday 27th. Apl

At the Mill last night collecting, the first Salute when the honest Miller saw me was an Oath, saying if he had known I had been going he would have been no nearer home than Broomfleet; well says I, I told you I should come; whya but says Tom did not I say you need not trouble yourself, I would come up and settle with you; What it seems I am not to be depended upon; Why I replied not entirely when there is money to pay. Now says he Curse all them Feals that says they pay money with as much pleasure as they receive it, I dean't believe any body that says so, I hate to pay money myself. Well now says his wife if I was you I would always pay one Sessment before another was due, and not drive to so much, then you would not be so vexed when you had it to pay—Heark you there says Tom there's wisdom What the D—l, I should always be vexed if I was to pay every time they were due; Now I get over for 2 or three times a year. So at the last we proceeded to business and got all settled except one Poor Rate which he could not think of paying yet, as it was only lately laid. I then got a Glass of Gin and Water, and in stirring the Sugar that was in it I broke the Glass, and spilt the Mixture most of it on the Table, but as our friend is famed for carefulness, he held his Glass under the edge of the table, and scraped all he could from the table with a knife and caught it in his glass, saying it was a pity

---

[56] An imaginary dialogue between the King and his ministers in *CPR* 62, iv (21 Apr.) 1827, 215–46.

to waste it. He complains of being very poorly in a Cold; but bad as he was he did not give up his custom of setting me a bit of way home. He came as far as opposite Mr. Turk's & I arrived at home a little before ten O'clock.

Saturday 28th. Apl

I have been at Beverley this day paying in Taxes, I never saw so much Gold paid, One Man paid 210 Golden Guineas, another 170 Sovereigns, and several smaller Sums, I myself paid 39 Sovereigns, never before having taken so many whilst collecting[.] I did not stay dinner, as I had a Close to measure for Wm. Loncaster in the Ruffham field which I did after I arrived at home it measured 7a–3r–33p. I got tea at Robt. Marshall's, Rode his Horse to Beverley

...

Monday 30th. April

A very fine warm day; the first day this Season without a fire in the School; had a long Conversation with the Curate this evening at his Lodgings, he is so bigotted to the Church of England as to believe that it is the only true Church. I did not spare him in pleading for the cause of dissent but this in his mind is so heterodox, that he could scarcely listen to it patiently. I recommended him to read the Works of some of the eminent dissenters, he said he had some of them, but he is so delighted with Church Canons, and the Articles of the Church, that there is very little hope of his being any more liberal than he is at present. He says Sir John Nicholl's judgment is a wrong decision, but I told him it was the decision of a judge therefore entitled to full credit. No paper this day.

Tuesday 1st May

This is the delightful season of May, when nature appears to rejoice that winter is cast into oblivion, But I have been pestered with, (what, aye I wonder what!) three Parsons this afternoon pretending to look over and examine the School, they know not how much I detest their officiousness. Old Kit told my wife on Sunday last that Edwd. Barnard would not pay his Subscription any longer to the School, so I told their Reverences if that was the case I should certainly give it up, but the Curate assured me it was not the case.

Wednesday 2nd May

Mr. Nicholas Sykes died on Sunday last, as I have heard from a mortification proceeding from his great toe, he walked to Hull on Saturday well as usual, but a small stone or Flint got into his shoe and hurt his toe, to such a degree that it inflamed and mortified past the power of Medicine to afford any relief.

Thursday 3rd May

At Ellerker last night measuring, as they are in hand with making a new poor Rate, and several parcels of Land that have not been rated at all, they want to bring into charge. I measured last night about 23 acres, after that went to settle with Barnard Cook for the Church dues, as this is the tithe rent day, he wanted his money, and I was ready for him, which suited very well. This day we have got three Waggon load of Coals, Ths Marshall, Richd & Robt each of them brought a load. It is a hard job getting them in, but we managed pretty well, so that we have Coals sufficient for 1 year.

Friday 4th May

Last night was the Club night, I was very tired before I went, with the Coals getting in, got home about ten O'clock. The Club has lent £120 on Mortgage to Geo Lester of Broomfleet on some Land belonging to him. 2 Papers this day, I hope Canning & Co. will not take any notice of the party who have given up their places[57] to make room for their Successors. I think the Country has one comfort, that affairs cannot be conducted worse than they have been.

Saturday 5th May

Measured the Land at Mount Airy which is in the Township of Ellerker, part of it goes down into Woodale, there is about 18 Acres. It came on rain while I was there a smart shower I got wet, but it soon cleared up, then went to Mr. Pickerings with a few Ellerker People to make a new poor Rate, got one drawn up which I have to Copy out.

Sunday 6th May

Thos. Marshall who complains of being ill went to Hull one day last week to have the advice of a Physician, which he got without paying for which was some relief, what advice he got I know not, but he got drunk before he arrived at home, but to make amends the next day he came to the town to get some Medicine, but he took to his old Medicine Rum and water which he swallowed in such a quantity that he could not walk home by himself. I suppose it has loosened his Skin so much that he can wrap his hand in it, he thought he might as well take the Medicine he liked as one which he knew nothing about.

Monday 7th May

Sarah Ringrose's house at Brantingham was broken into one night last week and robbed of plate to the value of £50 or more and about 35 Pounds in Money, the robbers have not yet been heard of. Suspicion is attached to two rat-catchers who were there some time since. Old Kit is very ill with a swelled Knee, he is confined at Home which will be sufficient to kill him if he cannot get about Mr. Barnard's business.

Tuesday 8th May

Mr. Barnard arrived at home today, when the merry Bells rung round on his arrival, perhaps not so much for joy at his presence as for the ringers receiving a Guinea from him, which they seldom omit to beg of him, after he has been from home any time. James Hairsine of Faxfleet had a son buried this day about 23 years of age, he has had twelve Children, eight of whom have died after living to be Men & Women; one daughter who was married died the last winter leaving a family of ten Children.

---

[57] i.e. the old Tories, formerly led by Lord Liverpool. Attacks had been made on the new government by, among others, George Dawson, who had been Peel's under secretary at the Home Office, and by Sir Thomas Lethbridge. More seriously, his ministry was under attack in the House of Lords from Lord Grey, who had joined the old Tories in denouncing the Whig-liberal Tory coalition (Walpole ii. 361–3).

Wednesday 9th May

Newspaper from Wm this morning without a word said by him. Also two Examiners the last week and this, so that I revel in news this day. The Old Ministers seem very sore at losing or giving up their places, but they will not meet with much sympathy, not a single reason do they give for the step they have taken, I suppose because they have no reason to give, well their Services it is hoped can be dispensed with, if they can only be quiet without the sweets of office.

Thursday 10th May

Rd. Marshall complaining that the Frost a night or two ago has cut some of his Wheat so much that there will be no chance of a Crop of it, indeed the frost at this time of the year has been very severe. Beverley fair yesterday, Stock of all kinds particularly Sheep sold very badly, and should this weather continue there will be little chance of improvement in the prices, as no grass can grow, and Winter Fodder is in a great measure exhausted. No Paper this day, it was only on Monday last that all the London Papers missed coming and it is the same again this morning; there must be gross neglect somewhere.

Here is Old Willy's receipt for propegating [*sic*] or creating Eels. Take a Stone trough and pour Clean water into it, then procure some hair from a Horse's mane and cut it into small pieces 3 or 4 Inches long, put it into the trough amongst the water cover it up and these hairs will turn to Eéls, but when neither I nor he knows!!! ...

Friday 11th May

"For Forms of Government let fools contest".[58]

Of all the forms of Government an absolute Monarchy is the best adapted to schools, there are no circuitous forms, nor special pleadings to put off the fate of the Culprit, but punishment follows the commission of Crime immediately on being discovered; No Juries to empanel to prove that boisterous behaviour is praise worthy. The laws are in general so well known and so sure to be executed that there never is any complaint of ignorance on this head, Whoever transgresses does it at his peril, and knows it at the same time. No representative Government for me in this case.

Saturday 12th May

No Papers again this day this is the third time this week they have not come to hand, a complaint must be made at the proper quarter for this neglect. — Wm. Cade had a Beast taken from him at Hull yesterday and burnt for being unwholesome. It was the Flesh of a Cow which he bought of Wm. Purdon of Broomfleet. Old Mrs. Purdon died last night she is about 82 years of Age. I hear Mr. Lockwood of Beverley is dead. It is reported that they have taken two Men at Hull for breaking into Mrs. Ringrose's House at Brantingham, they have found most of the Plate, and a twenty Pound note on one of them. One is a Milkman of Hull and the other of the name of Moor who comes from North

---

[58] Quotation from Alexander Pope's *An Essay on Man.* (Epistle 3 (1733), line 303): 'For forms of government let fools contest: / Whate'er is best administr'd is best'.

Cave, a very bad character indeed. I am glad they are found out. At Ellerker a meeting this afternoon there respecting the new poor rate, there was some opposition to it and threats of appealing against it. Got tea at Mr. Leason's and arrived at home between nine and ten at night.

Sunday 13th May

Robt. Marshall had a Mare died this morning she only began to be ill on Saturday afternoon, she had a fine Colt foal in her. A Very dusty windy day the weather uncommonly dry with cold winds and generally frost at nights. Recd the Paper today which should have been here yesterday, so that all arrears have now come to hand.

Monday 14th May

The affairs of Portugal seem to be in a sad disjointed condition, I think the Government is not vigorous enough with the Rebels, I expect at the last that the present constitution will be put down, they seem to be overrun with Superstition, and guided by a set of bloody minded priests, and whenever they are allowed to interfere in public affairs, there is sure to be nothing but discord and misrule, they ought not to be suffered to interfere at all.[59]

Tuesday 15th May

... Weighton fair yesterday uncommonly cold, things sold for very low prices on account of the weather being so dry and grass so scarce.

Wednesday 16th May

At West end last night, Two of Mr. Carter's of Howden had been here yesterday shooting Crows; there were two Men at Robt Marshall's wanting to buy his Sheep but they did not agree[.] I think there was about a Shilling apiece between them. Heard from Wm. this morning that he is well, he has been at Windsor, the Seat of Royalty—Old Kit keeps very ill yet, I think myself he will not get better, altho' the Dr. says he will, but as he takes but very little support, and is very sick, and his knee swelled, and his body is in such a state that he has no passage without forcing, I therefore think he stands very little chance of getting well again.

Thursday 17th May

Richard Marshall succeeds Old Kit in the office of Steward or <u>Ratter</u> [?] to Mr. Barnard, there is a Court this day where he will enter on duty and Cry "Oyes! Oyes! All <u>mander</u> of Persons who have business at the Court Leet, Court Baron and customary Court of H.G. Barnard Esq. come into Court and do suit and Service or you shall be amerced" <u>meased</u> was the old Bailiff's word, then the Steward of the Court Mr. Spofforth dismisses the Court with God save the King & the Lord of this Manor, to which the Old Bailiff always added "and the

---

[59] Dom Pedro had succeeded to the throne in 1826 but his younger brother, Dom Miguel, made a counter claim to the succession. Dom Pedro renounced his own claim in favour of his 8-year old daughter, Donna Maria, and promised to grant a liberal constitution to Portugal. The rebel monarchists under Dom Miguel were receiving arms and equipment from Spain, obliging the legitimate government to appeal to England for assistance. Dom Pedro was allowed to raise troops in London, and a fleet with 4,000 troops was dispatched to put down the rebels. His forces soon gained the upper hand but the revolt was not finally crushed until the decisive defeat of Dom Miguel's fleet off Cape St. Vincent in 1833. (See n.16 (1833)) (*AR* 1826 Hist. 310–22 and 1827 Hist. 248–81).

Steward of this Court["]. — It is now said that Mutton will be Sixpence a pound next week at Hull; then the sellers of Sheep will draw in the Corners of their mouths as though they would not admit a bit of their favourite fat down their throats. It was expected that Old Kit would not live over the last night, but he has survived, still he cannot I think continue long, his Constitution has been very strong, but it is certainly nearly worn out.

Friday 18th May

Since writing my Journal yesterday forenoon, Mr. Corner has died between twelve and One O'clock yesterday, it was the Court day which he had been giving notice of for a month past; he has not held up his head since he was so gratified with telling us that Mr. Barnard had given up his School subscription; his death gives me no pleasure, neither do I feel sorry as for the loss of a friend. he is about 77 years of Age. — Measured an Ash heap last night at Peasy dales for Wm. Fisher. Called to see Mr. Robinson last night he has been very poorly but is getting better again. — Old Willy was at Court yesterday, they had tea before they came away, so that Barnd. Cook would be quite lifted up as he generally is when he has a good meeting. No Paper again this day.

Saturday 19th May

At Mill this afternoon assisting Thos. Marshall in making out the Executors' accounts under James's Will, none of the Annuitants have yet received their Annuities, altho' it is rather more than two years since he died; we did not get the Accounts finished. It was about eleven O'clock at night when I got home, but Tom set me nearly as far as Wm. Thornam's—we spent a great deal of time talking, he in explaining matters and I in listening to him; then I pointed out some accounts where objections might be raised; so then my old friend had them to look over, and he admitted that he had not taken the same View of them before, which was a strange odd thing, as he thought he had them all off, but then says he I am so badly and so harassed in my mind with this cursed business, that I believe I am fast dropping into the Earth. There are two things which Tommy dare not do, one is he dare not make his Will, and the other he dare not give up business.

Sunday 20th May

A Love feast this afternoon at the Methodist meeting[60] which has caused a good deal of Company in the town, I had forgot to mention or note yesterday that the Paper which missed on Friday came yesterday. it had evidently been taken out and kept, it was very dirty and torn in two places. I do not think James Marshall will be found to be worth so much as he valued himself at, which was £800 in ready money, exclusive of a small Estate at Newbald which

---

[60] The love feast was introduced into England by John Wesley and soon became an established feature of Methodist worship. The service included hymns, prayers, the distribution of 'bread', circulation of a two-handled loving-cup, an address by a presiding minister, and spontaneous (often emotional) prayers and verses of hymns contributed by those in attendance. Love feasts were described by a contemporary writer as 'the most popular and exciting of our social meetings', and were adopted also by the Primitive Methodists who held their first one in Yorkshire in 1819 at Hull (Baker *passim*).

lets for ten Guineas a year—Very fine weather, the fine rain a day or two ago has and will be found very beneficial.

Monday 21st May

Kit Corner's funeral this forenoon, he was taken in a Waggon, Miss went in the Chaise, Farmer's on horseback, Beggars on Foot. Hangers-on, waiting about the door for a drink of ale: but as I did not belong to any of these Classes, I staid at home and did not attend at all. Bearers were chosen and Gloves given them so that they were hired, but as I had no retaining fee I was a free agent, and was pleased not to give my attendance, but left the mourning department to those who were paid for it.

Tuesday 22nd May

It was expected from the Rain last week that Sheep would have sold readily at an advanced price, but there was a fair at Caistor in Lincolnshire last Saturday, when they were nearly unsaleable, many of them being brought back again, it seems that there is a larger Stock than can be profitably turned into money. Recd. a parcel from Wm. this night, when I opened it out Eliza called to her Mother and said here are some Mint drops from Wm. "O, that Good lad" she replied, I have not had a good mint drop since the last he sent. Yes says I those I brought from Beverley were very excellent. Nay they were not to be compared with these; they do me so much good, I do not know how to do without them, then he is so thoughtful.

Wednesday 23rd May

Recd. a letter this morning with the Statement of the Funds & names of the members of the Schoolmasters' Association[.] The Amount deposited in the savings Bank is £340–14–0. In the treasurer's hands £3–10–7 and Arrears of Subscriptions £31–11–6 so that the whole Stock is £375–16–1. There are 41 Members. I hope it will be found beneficial. — Thos. Marshall & Richard will not come at each other to settle James's affairs, so that I expect I shall have to act the part of Mediator amongst them for there is Robert too, who would willingly meet either or both of them at any place; I hope to see all comfortably settled. Cobbett and Hunt it seems are friends again, they will it appears both join to convince the Westminster Electors, that Sir Francis Burdett[61] has abandoned Parliamentary reform. It is a hard matter to be in a public Situation and give unbounded Satisfaction, then it appears from Cobbett's reasoning which on this subject is none of his best; that Mr. Canning is not to be supported by the Whigs on their own principles, so far as Mr. Canning travels the same road. Now I do not admire him for setting himself against the repeal of the Test & Corporation Acts;[62] almost before it was mentioned to him.

---

[61] See n.104 (1827).

[62] The Test and Corporation Acts, originally passed to curtail the rights and liberties of dissenters, had become little more than a formal grievance since annual acts of indemnity had for some considerable time provided safeguards from penalties for breach of the law. The main clauses of the Acts were repealed in 1828.

Thursday 24th May

I have read in the Times this day with great satisfaction the proceedings of a meeting in London, to protect and defend the rights of the Welch Cottagers.[63] How I wish that an end could be put to the Monopoly of Land, and that farms were not allowed to be so large as they generally are, where one great Farmer lives in wealth while all his neighbours are in comparative poverty; I am delighted with the prospect of an uninclosed Common where the Cottager has a right for a Cow, and woeful policy it was that they were ever deprived of this right. Formerly a Farmer's man who had saved 30 or 40 pounds had an opportunity of renting a small farm and bringing up a family in a comfortable way, but now there is no stimulus for saving; for a man of this description must become a labourer to some overgrown Farmer who had sufficient to keep himself independent, without engrossing as much land as would bring up a Dozen families in a comfortable manner. Prodigality and Penury rule the land, while misery everywhere attends. Old Mrs. Ayre died this day in the 83rd year of her Age.

Friday 25th May

I heard Cuckoo one night this week for the first time this Season, Eliza & her Mother took a Walk last night as far as Everthorpe thinking to hear the welcome sound of "Cuckoo" but they came back without being gratified, however this morning while I & Eliza were in bed her mother heard it in our Garden, and fortunately, as luck would have it, she had three halfpence in her pocket, for it is very unlucky to hear Cuckoo the first time without money,[64] and indeed it is unfortunate at any time not to have money.

Saturday 26th May

Went to the Mill this forenoon about ten O'clock to finish the accounts which were left undone last Saturday, I staid till four O'clock in the afternoon, having finished the work in hand: Got weighed today[;] I have not varied 2 pounds for 10 years past, I weigh just about 13 Stone. I was never heavier. Went to Mount Airy between five and Six O'clock to measure a Sod heap burnt to Ashes, got home soon after nine.

Sunday 27th May

The weather now is particularly propitious the Country never had a more blooming appearance, the fields are dressed in living green, excepting the abundance of flowers which spring up amongst the grass—I shall not say who it was a short time ago that sat down to read and smoke a pipe at the same time, but thought so little of what he was doing that he attempted to light his Spectacles instead of the pipe.

---

[63] This meeting, chaired by Henry Hughes, was held in support of a group of Welsh cottagers threatened with eviction by a bill of enclosure for Llandwrog and Llanwnda currently before Parliament (*TM* 21 May, 1827, 5 c and 22 May 1827, 4 c).

[64] 'If when you hear this bird you turn a penny over in your pocket, you will never be without one till you hear him again'—Cited in Gutch 36.

Monday 28th May

While Cobbett has been at the Crown & Anchor amongst [the] Philistines,[65] they would not suffer him to speak which to say the least was very ungracious; these reformers ought to reform their own Manners, but Billy will button them pretty tight. I can hardly have any Conception of such a reform meeting, it beats a parish meeting, when all kinds of discordant speakers or bawlers are shouting together. There are things more wanting than reform in Parliament. One is to let every Country labourer have at least half an acre of Ground for a Garden & Orchard at a moderate rent say a pound a year, which is as much or more than is given by the great Bull-frogs for their land, but if in every parish a piece of land was laid out as Common for a poor man to keep a Cow in the Summer with paying a trifle for, this would cause comparative happiness to thousands. Is not this more to be devoutly wished for than reform? I answer without hesitation it is.

Tuesday 29th May

It was reported yesterday in the Market that the Corn Bill had passed the House of Lords, but in what manner was not known.[66] Some of the Farmers were certain it would not be so good for the Country, (that is themselves) as the present law, they are anxious that the Duty should be either paid or charged at the time of importation, this I combatted with all my might. They said wheat would soon be at 50s.; nay some of them went so far as Cobbett and said it would be 40s. very shortly, saying that wheat could be brought from abroad 23 or 24s. pr. quarter. Now says I you shall have foreign wheat given you without paying a Farthing for it or the freight and if English wheat get to 2 pounds, it is impossible to bring foreign Corn into the market for at this rate it will have to pay 3 pounds duty!! now should this be charged at the time of importing, you are very sure it is a prohibition. our English warehouses will be found empty and Hamburgh and other near ports abroad will become the Depots for Corn for the English market until the price be such as to remunerate the holders for bringing it out.

Wednesday 30th May

Mr. Robinson and Mr. Tinsdill were quarrelling a day or two ago. Tinsdill went to Robinson's house and called him all he could think of in a vulgar way, got up Mr. Robinson's Poker and vapoured[67] with it to the fear of the lawyer; at length Mr. Robinson's man got the Doctor down and the Poker from him, and walked him out, the Doctor Spat at the Lawyer. I know nothing of their Difference or who is right or wrong. this is not my business.

---

[65] Cobbett printed his own personal account of the Westminster election anniversary dinner, presided over by Sir Francis Burdett, which he had attended at the Crown and Anchor Tavern in the Strand on 23 May 1827, and immediately following it, a reprint of the account of the same event which had been published in the *Morning Chronicle* issue of 24 May 1827 (*CPR* 62 ix (26 May) 1827, 513–64).

[66] The Corn Bill of 1827, in its original unamended form, permitted the importation of foreign corn at a 20s. duty when the price stood at 60s. a quarter. See also n.72 (1827) (Walpole ii. 364–5).

[67] 'To bluster or to declare or assert in a boastful or grandiloquent manner' (*OED*).

Thursday 31st May

It is wonderful that the Farmers are now so much set against the Corn Bill when they at the first were such great advocates for it, they have got some Vague notions into their heads that Corn will be low, but what grounds they have for it I believe they cannot say, for my part I think as I always did with respect to the Bill that the Duties are too high. Several of our neighbours have their last year's Wool & their Sheep which should have been sold long ago, so that they now cry out they cannot sell scarcely at any price.

Friday 1st June

In this Age of Chemistry when boarding School Misses attend Lectures on Chemical subjects, and hear a deal of jargon on Hydrogen and Oxygen and Gasses of all kinds but sweet smelling Gasses, for some of them are enough to suffocate one with their abominable stinks. Then all the primmy Creatures can talk of Alkalies and Acids, and I know not what, but is there any real use in the knowledge thus bandied about? certainly a Balloon can be blown up with Gas, but this is of no practical benefit. Is there nothing can be invented to blow up the intolerable nuisance of Bugs? of what use are Discoveries if not applied to the purposes of life? I would myself recommend cleanliness as a great means for subduing these intolerable creatures; certainly there may be some remedy found to vanquish them, if some person of ability would turn his thoughts to this subject.

Saturday 2nd June

Been engaged writing out the Water Jury Pains for Holme Beacon[,] Wilton Beacon & Hunsley Beacon, for Mr. Bridgman who is the Foreman this year. Went into the Old Cardinal's Close up Porter hole where amongst other things he has Swedish turnips growing, I told him I had read of a person getting larger crops than any of his neighbours by sowing them in Rows at 4 Feet distance from each other, but I had as well told him I could touch the Moon for he would believe the one as soon as the other.[68] So it was of no use saying more on this head. He then began telling of a nephew of his who was left worth £1800 who came to see him with an intention as he really believes of taking in his poor old Uncle (viz himself the Cardinal) the Nephew said to him Uncle if I had £100 which I could spare out of my business, I could make it pay remarkably well in a partnership concern. The old Cardinal replied why Thou ought to have £500 to spare out of thy business if Thou art doing any good. This silenced his application so he went home and failed immediately without any further Ceremony.

Sunday 3rd June

A very fine day. Old Mr. Popple of Welton has been preaching here at the Church this forenoon, — Mr. Champney of Ellerker is going to Southampton with his family for some time, he has not his health well here: I was at Ellerker

---

[68] According to Strickland, writing in 1812, the sowing of turnips in rows 'about 26 inches between the rows and 9 inches between the plants' was only just coming into use. He went on to say that 'it will probably be long before old prejudices and practices with the generality of farmers, will give way to conviction' (Strickland 143–4).

yesterday and saw him; he generally enquires after Wm when I see him, which makes me have a respect for him; — A sort of argument with Old Willy last night respecting the situation of Southampton, as usual he referred to his Authority which in this case was a <u>Song</u> made when the good Old King went to see a naval review at Portsmouth; he got it into his head that it was north of London, by his geographical Ballad. I believe his memory fails him very much, and at present [he] has a bad cold. No paper came this day.

Monday 4th June

There is an evil which I have seen and experienced. I lent a person £20 on the first of March for a few days, about two months after he paid £12 back, the remaining 8 pounds still remain unpaid. I shall give up accommodating such persons as this, who purchase or put out their Money to the best interest, then they run about and borrow of their friends without paying any interest as they borrow through friendship, but what business have I or any one else to lend money for nothing, and they reap the benefit of it? I have had other applications, but I shall hold close. The paper which missed yesterday came today, along with the other, it was a good deal soiled.

Tuesday 5th June

It was strongly talked yesterday that an amendment as it is called (such amendment as was done at Old Walker's bellows which were worse for mending) was moved in the Committee on the Corn Bill by the Duke of Wellington, not to allow the Wheat which is in bond to be taken out until the Average be 66s. pr. quarter, which was carried by a majority of four. So that the hereditary lawgivers have carried their point—they might as well have prohibited Corn altogether, or made an Act for not allowing wheat to be sold under three pounds per quarter. The wise farmers cry out if wheat can only be prevented from being lower than 60s. we can live. It is certain they had rather pay high rents than sell at a low price; — Let us say no more about free trade, when the population are prevented from purchasing the first necessaries of life but at such prices as the Land owners or as they are called Agriculturalists think proper to lay on them.

Wednesday 6th June

... Swab, the word which our old friend the long Miller was so charmed with, is a sort of Sea term, Smollett puts into the discourse of Capt. Crow when his face was so swelled that he could hardly speak, but the waiter heard the word Brandy, he brought some in and was going to fill a Glass, but the Old Captain said "Never mind the Glass — you Swab, hand me the Noggin".[69] I cannot fancy myself that it is very elegant. I must write something to get this Sheet filled up as far as I can.

On Sunday mornings, I get up about eight O'clock then I shave and wash and dress, then get my breakfast, and after that a pipe of Tobacco, and give a peep at

---

[69] The words, in a slightly different form, were spoken by Captain Sam Crowe, the seafaring uncle of Thomas Clarke, in chapter 7 of Tobias Smollett's *The Adventures of Sir Launcelot Greaves*, first published in 1776.

the Paper when I have one, then between nine and ten I go out, always calling at Richd. Marshall's before Church time, then about half past ten I go to the Church when the Bells cease ringing and the Organ Grinder blows up his bellows to greet the Parson as he stretches down the Aisle; he then looks over his Book to see if his assistant the Clerk have found the right lessons then he commences reading, which lasts until between twelve and one O'clock, when I go home, get my Dinner and read awhile, then I walk down again, always in the afternoon calling in at Hannah Levitt's; then the same service again in the afternoon when I return home, borrow the Rockingham put off my Sunday Coat and put another on to save it, go no more out this day, and then to bed about ten O'clock.

Monday morning I pay the Poor, then to School until Noon, begin again at One O'clock, and leave about four this day, then go to the Market and hear what is going on in the Neighbourhood, collecting what money I can, then come home and get some Supper then to bed.

Tuesday the same as Monday, until night when I go to Mr. Atkinson's, hear the news good or bad as it happens then return and so this day is finished.

On Wednesday nights I always go to the west end except something particular prevent me, Smoke a pipe with Robt. Marshall and talk over the state of the Markets and the prospects of the Country, Rd. Marshall generally attends to hold on a little. About eight O'clock I come back then read until bed time. I ought to say which may apply to every day that in the morning I look over the Newspaper with a good deal of gratification, but this day it is doubly welcome as I hear from William on it.

Thursday same as yesterday excepting not going to the West end at night, I never go out until after School time at nights. On this night if I have anything to collect, I usually try to get it, then perhaps go on to old Willy's a short time and thus this day is finished; One day is so much like another that there is but little variation in my time.

On Friday at School as usual on other days, then after School time, we Sweep the School, then I shave and go out not to any certain place but generally to Old Willy's, I do not know how the old Gentleman will be spared or how his friends will find another house so convenient, as there is none to find fault with the Company, which he know behaviour much better than to do so.

On Saturday morning I prepare Change to pay the Poor with, which I get at Mrs. Pinder's, after that I walk to the West end; and if no other Company offer, I talk to <u>Awd Beck</u> a little then call at the Blacksmith's Shop and if anything new be going on it is there to be heard; this is the day which if I have any measuring or other employment that calls me from home I attend to it; I generally have a job of some kind which I contrive to get done on this day. Such is the Course of my life with as little deviation as possible. I had forgot that I write my Journal regularly every day, sometimes very little to the purpose, but I never miss a day so that it is here to refer to if wanted.

Thursday 7th June

So it appears that the great Captain[70] has had a conflict with the Corn Bill, it appears I think that he has given it a Blow of which it will not recover, indeed it had better die, than be suffered to shew its head with the Captain's wound on it; I never had any faith in the benefit it was to confer, but I viewed it differently from the Farmers who at the first were so warm in its praise; I always suspect any thing to be far from impartial, when one party looks upon it to be of great advantage; not considering any thing but their own benefit. At west end last night it rained very fast, I was witness to Curds preparing for Cheesecakes for Wm. at Robt. Marshall's and Mrs. Richards, it was made from flowing Pails of new milk so that is genuine. This day Eliza & her Mother very busy in making and baking to be ready for sending off at night. What a piece of work there will be for Wm. when the Box arrives what with Cheesecakes and Tarts eating and what with reading of the Journal, he will be fully employed; when he takes this up and begins to turn over the Sheets, he will begin to think what can all these contain, then when they are read he will perhaps think they contain nothing worth wasting the paper for. But he will be convinced that they (the Sheets) contain an Epitome of my thoughts and the manner in which my time is spent. — I would willingly fill up this page but I think I am nearly exhausted of matter. Now if I say it is a dull day at present, and that it is a fine growing time, that it is expected Cattle will sell better at the fair, as Jobbers are riding about trying to buy[,] that is something. Robt. Marshall had money bid for six of his Beasts last night, a better price than he has been offered for them before, but he was not willing to sell, as he thinks he can make more of them at the fair. — all this is by the way of drawing to a Close—Oh! I had forgot!! this Wellington what a Clever fellow he is to understand the Interests of the Landlords and farmers so well, the Men who prefer an Old rag, to a picture in Gold of his most gracious Majesty are praising the great Captain with all the fervour they can, but I tell them he has overshot the mark, and as I have better intelligence than they can procure, I tell them plainly he has killed the Corn bill, indeed I think it is worth as much dead as alive; all its first advocates are sick of it, though in every progress it has made the alterations have been in their favour: still they are unaccountably out of love with it. So much for consistency.

Friday 8th June

Went this forenoon with Richd. Marshall to measure a piece of Land on the Wold in the Close which he bought of Mr. Levitt, a very hot day. In the afternoon went to the Mill once more to look over Thos. Marshall's Executor's Accounts, got all done he would have given me them and the Money he had in hand to settle with the two others, but I would not accept of the offer but persuaded him either to go with me to them this night or otherwise I would attend him tomorrow, to which he agreed, but face them himself he would not for he says they are two against one, so I must attend to see all fair.

---

[70] The Duke of Wellington. (See n.72 (1827)).

Saturday 9th June

By appointment I was to meet Thos. Marshall at the West end this afternoon between one and two O'clock, but he did not come till about three; then we went down to Robert's having met with Richard he went with us; when we had been set little time, Now says he I have brought these accounts, and I'll be quit of this business, so he feels first in one Pocket and then another, until he at last found them, when he laid them on the table for examination, nothing was objected to but one account, on which they (viz) Thos. & Richd. began quarrelling, when I by Authority of my office as Mediator reminded them they had come to settle not to quarrel; which pacified them a little, and they talked more moderate so at the last they got through and he paid down all the Money in his hands, swearing he would not be called without occasion any more; then a fresh difficulty arose, neither of them would have the money, they all wished me to take it but I told them that I could not, as any one of them was competent to take care of it, beside I told them I should look upon it as offending them if I meddled with it; we then got tea the Money and Accounts laying on the table, and about six O'clock we all came out and left it there, but after a little persuasion Richd. turned back and took it up.

Sunday 10th June

At the Church in the forenoon when a Sermon was preached on the subject of keeping holy the Sabbath day, but it was such a curious composition, that it almost surpassed all human understanding; Amongst other things it was said that a day was too long a time together to be engaged in religious exe[r]cises, and that a little innocent pleasure was allowable: So I expect most of his hearers took the Parson at his word and enjoyed the innocent pleasure of breaking the Sabbath.

Monday 11th June

Cave fair commenced this morning, with Cattle lowing, Dogs barking, Asses braying, Boys whistling, trumpets blowing & every other characteristic for a Country fair; — It was very dusty all the day, Cattle sold best in the morning, they were rather dull after, Robt. Marshall sold 6 Beasts for two shillings a piece less than he had bid the last week, — I expect Wm. would eat Cave fair Cheesecakes this day in London. No Company this day but John Read.

Tuesday 12th June

A very fine day abundance of Company in the Town this afternoon, we had three Sits at tea, some of them whom we never see but at Cave fair time which is quite often enough, these two days have passed over without any disturbance, I was called on at Night by a Man who had sold two Silk handkerchiefs, which he did not get pay for, but before I arrived the Customer was gone.

Wednesday 13th June

This morning commenced with a poor Woman coming for me to assist her in getting pay for lodgings she had let this fair, but the Man who took them said he had no money so he said we might take his Carcase, so I desired some of the Crowd who did not need much encouragement to turn him out of the Town, which was instantly put in execution. He was run a piece of way up Porter hole and landed safely in the Beck, where he had a cool Bath not very clean; but it seemed to have some virtue in it; for he soon after treated for payment and found 3/6d the amount he was charged & thus the affair was settled.

Thursday 14th June

Most of those who came to eat up their friends are now marching off with ugly long faces, when there is no more work for them to do in the Gormandising line. Expected a Semicolon on the direction of the Paper from Wm. this morning as a sign that he had received the Box but there was none, so whether he had forgot, or not received it time must determine.

Friday 15th June

At the west end this forenoon, dined with Wm. Loncaster he is the Constable, he had been taking a Man with a Warrant for an Assault at the Fair; Old Lonc is going with him tomorrow to Melbourne before a Justice there (viz) General Wharton[71] who I understand is a sort of Tyrant, and as is usual with this Species, very arbitrary in his decisions. Very dry and dusty, rain is again wished for and in some places wanted.

Saturday 16th June

Lord Wellington on the second reading of the Corn Bill has carried the starving clause by a majority of 11.[72] All the stir that has been made must now be given up, and the Bill be consigned to oblivion instead of being entered in the Statute Book as a monument of Folly, at the first it was not very good for the interests of the Consumers who in the end have to pay, but most of its usefulness in the different stages it went through was ~~were~~ frittered away, till at the last it received the Coup de grace from the hands of the great Warrior; Peace to its shades; and may the great Duke interfere no more with the interests of the Country, except indeed he confer upon it, the giving up some of his Perquisites which I think is not very likely.

Saturday 17th June

Wheat beginning to shoot fast into the ear, I saw one today fully out. Mr. Barnard's man who has been with him at London and several other places, thinks himself I doubt not qualified to talk nonsense without control[.] He was lately in a Company where I was, and he was telling that he had seen a Cart and a Gig come into <u>Contract</u> with each other, I suppose he meant Contact but the other part of the Company I suspect knew nothing of the word, most likely thinking it was a fine one; however I ventured to ask him how the agreement

---

[71] Lieutenant General James Wharton, of Melbourne near Pocklington, in addition to being a Justice of the Peace was also the Commissioner of Taxes for the North and East Ridings.

[72] In the House of Lords, the Duke of Wellington had introduced an amendment to the Corn Bill to prevent foreign corn from being taken out of bond until the average price of corn should have reached 66s. per quarter. This amendment, which effectively stopped the Bill, was carried, largely on account of government incompetence and a misunderstanding that had arisen over a carelessly worded letter to the Duke by Huskisson. The ministers attempted to salvage the Bill, but Wellington's amendment, the 'starving clause', was re-affirmed by 133 votes to 122 (Walpole ii. 364–5).

went on after the <u>Contract</u> was made, but he did not find himself out, for he said there was nothing but hurry about it !!!

Monday 18th June

No newspaper this day, the Farmers all alive now they think there is nothing to hinder them from obtaining their own prices which surely will not be low if they have the fixing of them. A fine gentle showery day. I hope there will be so much plenty that prices cannot be kept up extravagantly. Lord help this Great Duke who is no more than a Puppet in the hands of others; I suspect he has never acted but by advice & counsel.

Tuesday 19th June

The Paper which missed coming yesterday has not arrived today. I wish I knew where to lodge a complaint, that a remedy could be adopted for the evil; I am convinced it is done purposely or it could not so frequently happen; except indeed that the Post office is in such a state as to be governed by chance. Made out the Expences of the Poor for the last year for So. Cave and Broomfleet, to be sent to the House of Commons, where it may happen they will never be looked at.

Wednesday 20th June

Heard from Wm. this morning that he had received the Box on Tuesday last, all safe, the Paper came this morning which should have been here on Monday. The Marshall's are gone to Hull this morning with the Executor's accounts to settle at the Stamp Office. It is amazing what trouble and expence there is, in cases of this nature where Property is left. The Accounts of all Receipts and payments I have arranged excepting some trifling Sums which they have to settle this day. Tom Turk has taken Old Sam Ayre's house for a Country house, so that he must have done pretty well since he commenced measuring Yards of Cloth;[73] I have not dealt with him a good while, as I do not like to be imposed upon, even by those who pretend to be my friends.

Thursday 21st June

At Weedley last night measuring some Corn land which had been weeded at the rate of 10s. pr. Acre; it was a very fine night. I believe it was a very bad year last year for Tindale who lives there, he must have lost a good deal of money; — He is of opinion that no laws will much longer protect the Agriculturalists that is will allow them large rents, and to live in affluence while the rest of the People are reduced to poverty and incapable of supporting themselves. Indeed I think myself the wisest thing that could be done would be to allow a free trade in Corn, which would tend to equalize the price all over the world so that one Country would not have the advantage of Provisions at half price, when another paid as much more. This is the longest day. Thos. Fisher's Bean Close just at the bottom of the Round Plump sent out sweet perfume, being in full flower.

---

[73] Thomas McTurk's woollen drapery business was at 2 Market Place, Hull. He was said by RS to be worth £10,000 in 1830 (18/8/30). The family is known to have had connections with Bradford, a celebrated woollen district.

Friday 22nd June

A Smart Shower of Hail this morning. I see by the Paper this morning that Mr. Canning is going to allow all Corn in bond before the first of July, to be brought into the Market before the first of May next. I hope this will counteract the Old Walker amendment of the Great Duke. I find that the Editor of the Examiner has been convicted of a Libel on a kind of drunken Carpenter, dubbed Captain,[74] and Author, had I been in his the Captain's place I would have even kept myself quiet and not have been exposed to the whole Country, but some Men glory in their Shame, and certainly this Captain thinks it to his honour to be exposed for his drunkenness. I know men who glory in the name of drunkards and boast how much they can drink, looking on drinking as a gallant exploit.

Saturday 23rd June

In those Countries such as Holland where but little Corn is grown, I believe the prices are more regular than in this Country which boasts of being the very first in Agriculture. The more I consider this Subject the more I am convinced that to permit or make the Corn trade free, would be for the benefit of the whole World, (but I dare not say anything of this doctrine where I am situated, for I should be looked upon as worse than an incendiary) in times of Scarcity we should not have to pay such enormous prices as have been realized. No fear that foreigners would not supply us: Do we ever want a supply of that Villanous Cotton? Is Tea or Tobacco in peace or War ever at such enormous prices as Corn has sometimes been? Are we not always plentifully supplied with Sugar? And even in the time of War when supplies of Hemp were not to be had but from enemies, I never heard of the supply being cut off, then away with the idle talk of being dependent on foreigners.

Sunday 24th June

Recd. the Paper this morning, I think the direction was not Wms. Mrs. Pinder yesterday received a parcel of Blacking from 54 Lamb's Conduit Street, so that it must be the next door to where Wm. lodges. — At Church this forenoon and tiresome work it was, for the Parson had three Children to Christen which he will not do at any time but in Service time. I wonder where the institution of what is called Christening was first invented, the Church of England undoubtedly had it from Rome; I cannot find the smallest trace of it in Scripture. It is nothing more than Man's invention, (perhaps some old <u>Women</u> may have first begun it;) It is a shocking mockery of Religion to make people promise for others what they cannot do for themselves.

Monday 25th June

Some new Potatoes to dinner this day, the first time this Season; what complaints the farmers are making of the badness of the Oat Crops, which has

---

[74] The libel action was brought by William Parry who had served as a major in Lord Byron's brigade in Greece and had published on his return *The Last Days of Lord Byron* (1825). This work and its author had been savagely attacked in *The Examiner*, edited by Leigh Hunt. The jury found in favour of Parry awarding damages against Leigh Hunt to the sum of £50. Parry was said to have become subsequently insane owing to excessive drinking (*DNB*; *TM* 15 June 1827, 8 a).

arisen it is supposed from some frosty nights soon after they came up; but I take very little notice of their croaking, indeed they cannot make each other believe their own tales.

Tuesday 26th June

Saml. Shaw was saying last night that he has some Wheat which has cost him 34 Shillings an Acre weeding, it was overgrown with Corn Poppies commonly called Cop-roses[;] this has been a very prolific Season for Weeds of most descriptions, The farmers praising the Duke of Wellington & cursing Mr. Canning with whom a short time since they were so highly lifted up.

Wednesday 27th June

Recd. a parcel from Wm. last night, with an account that he will not send his Box so often as he has done; glad to hear that he is well. I think the Holderness Agricultural Society[75] has made the Duke of <u>Waterloo</u>, a member of their Society, for his gallant stand to raise the prices of Corn. I expect before long that these Patriots the Agriculturalists will be presenting a Petition, praying the Legislature to let them have the sole right of feeding (or famishing) the whole population of this Country, they will have no objection to feed those well who will give them their prices if they can only get a monopoly established; they would likewise have no objection to Clothe in their own Wool, all the outside of the Male population, and what in fact would insure them a better market for their Wheat and Wool, than this populous Country of which they say they are the support?

Thursday 28th June

Mr. Barnard's began to mow the Park yesterday, which is Meadow this year, a very great Crop. A man called this day with Penknives and other Articles for Sale from Sheffield, he told me he thought he had seen me in Sheffield, I said nay I thought not; I really thought says he that I had heard you <u>preach</u> in our Chapel at Sheffield, but I told him I had never been there; then he said he must have been mistaken however it was a Gentleman very much like me. I bought a pair of Scissors of him. Made out my quarterly account of Stamps, and sent to Hull by Carrier £72–18–6 for this quarter.

Friday 29th June

A Good deal of Rain yesterday, grievous complaints now that the Wheat will be laid that it will in a manner be wasted. I sincerely believe that the Weather is never right for a single week together for the muttering farmers; upon the whole I think it as fine weather as need to be wished for. But they want dry & sunny weather for their Wheat, Rain for Oats, and rather moist for Turnips, so how are they to be suited? Bought 8 Mackarel for 1s/2d. We have had our ears so stunned of late with Waterloo, that it really grows disgusting to hear the Word mentioned so oft. There is the Waterloo Duke, the Waterloo Bridge, Waterloo place[,] Waterloo Coaches, Waterloo <u>Jack Asses</u> &c &c and last of all the Waterloo amendment, to fill the Bellies of the Poor by denying

---

[75] Based in Hedon, the Holderness Agricultural Society was founded in 1795 and lasted throughout the 19th c. until *c.* 1900. It held regular meetings and was responsible for organizing annual cattle shows.

them food. Certainly the Waterloo frenzy must be past height. — I see Mr. Hunt is appointed an Auditor of the City Accounts, and as his Colleague has refused acting with him, it appears he will have the business to himself.

Saturday 30th June

At Brantingham last night collecting Ellerker Church dues I got a Glass of Rum & Water at Mr. Atmar's. I enjoyed the Water more than the Liquor, being fresh from the Spout Hill Spring it was delicious. — I hope the Corn Bill for permitting the bringing to Market the Bonded wheat will pass, but for my part I am for no half measures; I should like to see the trade thrown open without any prohibitory duties, — it might for a while put down some of the great landed Nabobs, but what matter would there be of them, are they to be supported at the Expence of all the industrious Community? what is it to me in whose hands the land is in, would it not be equally as well cultivated, if it was to change owners tomorrow?

Sunday 1st July

A Rainy morning, nothing to do at Church this forenoon. Lord Grey surprises me by his high Aristocratic notions, this Man who formerly was such a friend to the people that he was looked on as a downright radical, is now turned round and making such a stir for the privileges of his order; I see that for the encouragement of Agriculture he wishes to have Tobacco cultivated in England;[76] I doubt not but in a short time some Wiseacre will move for the cultivation of Cotton, Tea, & Sugar, then we shall be nearly "Independent of Commerce". I see very little use of reform in the Commons house, when the Lords can nullify any of their Acts they think proper, What a woeful falling off in those Lords we looked upon to be Patriots, Bedford, Fitzwilliam &c,[77] leagued with Waterloo and some sorry Bishops. — Green Pease to dinner this day.

Monday 2nd July

It must be labour that makes things valuable, the land is cultivated by labour, the abominable Cotton has its value chiefly from labour, it is labour that converts the Clothing of the Sheep to the valuable clothing of the rich, and of the Poor too; then how would the great Aristocrats look if they were to be deprived of the labour of those whom they want to keep down with the smallest allowance, the men who work and sweat to procure large Crops, merely that the Owners of Land, and Power Looms may live in all manner of Luxury.

Princes & Lords may flourish and may fade,

A Breath can make them, as a breath has made,

---

[76] The cultivation of tobacco in England was banned in 1619, and the ban reiterated for England and Ireland, except on a small scale for medicinal use, in 1660 by the Act for Prohibiting Setting or Sowing of Tobacco in England or Ireland (12 Charles II c. 34). The object was always to protect the American colonial tobacco trade. The ban was subsequently lifted for Ireland but not for England (Thirsk 259–85).

[77] William Wentworth Fitzwilliam, 2nd Earl Fitzwilliam (1748–1833) and Lord John Russell, 6th Duke of Bedford (1766–1839) were both aristocratic Whig politicians. Fitzwilliam, although in principle in favour of a Whig alliance with Canning in the coalition government, had been publicly reluctant to give his approval to the acceptance by Sir James Scarlett, one of his own members, of the office of Attorney General in that government (Smith, E. A. 384–5).

But a bold Peasantry, the Country's pride
When once destroy'd can never be supplied.[78]
Tuesday 3rd July

Visitation held this day at So. Cave, but what is the use of it I cannot say, except for Churchwardens and Parson to get drunk and spend the Parish money.[79] I think it is very badly spent money is four pounds allowed by the Town for this purpose: but it has been customary so long that it makes it sacred. — Thos. Marshall had got very drunk last night, he was in the height of his wisdom, he is full of noise and as he thinks wisdom, when in fact his sense has taken flight, this is generally the case with drunkards. I believe our old friend would indulge in drinking, did not his avarice prevent him, for much as he loves liquor, he still likes money more, so that one vice (avarice) keeps down the other (drinking).

Wednesday 4th July

I went last night after School time, to the Visitation, but did not dine there, there was the Vicar of Howden,[80] in the place of Mr. Barnard who was not there, and there was a Proctor from York of the name of Askwith,[81] one of the proprietors of the Yorkshire Gazette[82] commonly called the Soot Bag, they had been drinking the health of the Waterloo Duke before I went, and after I got there his health was proposed again, as a friend to the Country; I eluded drinking it, and observed it was a sort of ambiguous kindness conferred upon the Country, as it was from the weakness of not understanding Mr. Huskisson's letter that this benefit was conferred upon the Country. The Vicar said something about there being no comparison between the Waterloo man and Mr. Huskisson, it appeared that some 30 or 40 years ago Mr. Huskisson was a member of some Society not very friendly to tyranny indeed the Vicar branded him with the name of liberal. After all I think the Parson had something liberal in him but he was like Goldsmith's hard hearted man, who shewed off before Company and practised Charity in secret.[83]

Thursday 5th July

This is Beverley fair day, all the idle the careless and thoughtless are gone in Crowds to it, as it is a time of the year when there is but little night, it makes it pleasant. Young Barnard Cook was giving his Man orders and instructions how to conduct himself at the fair and of all things mind to be at home in good

[78] This is a very slightly misquoted excerpt from Oliver Goldsmith's 'The Deserted Village' (*EP*)

[79] Once a year, the archdeacon of a diocese held his court in the parish church. The visitation was the occasion for a dinner attended by the incumbent, the churchwardens, and other officers and notables of the parish (*EB* ii. 359).

[80] Revd Thomas Guy.

[81] William Askwith of Gillygate, York (Baines ii. 74).

[82] See n.11 (1836).

[83] i.e. the 'Man in Black', a covert philanthropist who featured in letters no. 26 and 27 in Oliver Goldsmith's *The Citizen of the World*, a collection of 119 letters purporting to have been written by, or to, an imaginary philosophic Chinaman, Lien Chi Attangi, resident in London (Drabble 200).

time at night, "it is for thy own good thou knowest", says the sage drunkard for he could not speak plain he was so drunk, upon the whole he is a most disgusting fellow is this same Young Barnard. — Old Barnard is ill his complaint is cramp in the Stomach, I went to see him last night but he was in bed.

Friday 6th July

A very hot day, last night was the Club night which is the busiest in the year, as all arrears are obliged to be paid up the night before the feast: Got done about 11 O'clock there were two drunken Men quarrelling in the Street who had been at Beverley fair, but I did not go out to hear them.

Saturday 7th July

At West Ella this day my Mother is very well in health but lame as ever she was. She can see to read without Spectacles[.] I think she is about 82 years of Age. I came by Swanland and Ferriby home again, I felt very poorly as I came between Welton and Cave, perhaps from the heat of the Day, it was about half past ten when I got home. I had a blister on one of my heels with walking.

Sunday 8th July

Heard something at Church this forenoon which I suppose would be called a Sermon; as it sometimes happens, the text was the only part of Scripture which it contained. The words were "A wise Son maketh a glad Father". I have an old Book of Plato's which contains full as much Religion and a good deal more Morality.

Monday 9th July

There were the Minister of Swanland and his wife, called one day at West Ella, with some tracts which the Lady had swinging in her hand. My mother thought they were going about with quack medicines. The Gentleman asked my mother if she could read, she told him yes, well he says reading is nothing at all, without praying & hearing preaching, she says I am safe from hearing preaching as I can scarcely walk; well would you like to have preaching in your house, no says she I cannot say I should like it at all. Then the Lady asked her whether she could like to go to Heaven or to Hell. My mother told her she might have spared herself that question; and asked her if she ever knew anyone who wished to go to Hell; then the man said he would leave a tract if she would promise to read it, she told him he might either leave it or take it away as he thought proper. — I wish I had been there, I think from his own words I could have fixed him, as if reading was of no use what was he distributing his tracts for? And I take it for granted that he collects for the Bible Society, and what are Bibles for but to read?

Tuesday 10th July

Beverley Sessions begin today, there are five Jurymen from this town, viz. Robinson of Mount Airy, Thos. Fisher, Giles Bridgman, Thos. Leaper, & Robt. Arton commonly called Dab, — It has for about a week back been very hot weather it is very fine for the Hay making. It is said that the field Pease are infected with Insects, how true it is I cannot say as I have examined none of them, but I know they are destructive Creatures. I know Jn. James once had six Acres entirely wasted by them.

Wednesday 11th July

Recd. a parcel from Wm. last night with the project of his Tour into Wales. Swansea is more than 200 Miles from London. We should have liked better had he come here, I doubt he will find it an expensive excursion. Recd. the index for the last years Examiner. I have two years of them to bind now. The Literary Gazette[84] which likewise was inclosed, I wished much to see, and promise myself much gratification from the perusal.

Thursday 12th July

Club feast day, it was at Newlove's where they had a Booth fixed in the yard, and the Members all dined together, at two tables set the whole length[;] there were about 120 members, a very good plain dinner, and good order kept, Mattw. Smith towards night got very drunk and some Boys got some Soot, Tallow & Reds, and daubed his face all over, making him look wilder than an American Savage. I expect Wm. is at Bath this night, the seat of Gaiety, if indeed a National Hospital can look gay.

Friday 13th July

Wm. I doubt not will be thinking of Old Willy Atkinson today when he arrives at Bristol, of which place the Old Gentleman is a Freeman, he gained his freedom there by marrying a Freeman's daughter. Bristol is a place of great trade, but I think at the present second to Liverpool, though it was formerly accounted the second place of trade in the Kingdom. — I have read the Literary Gazette; the Notice of the Life of Bonaparte[85] is quite entertaining, some of the Names of the French, Revolutionists who were quite familiar about 30 years ago, are now almost forgotten or only remembered with horror. I recollect reading the following lines on the death of the Bloody Marat.

Marat is dead and gone to Hell,

That seat of Sin and Evil:

Ca Ira, the foul Demons Yell,

And Gullotine [*sic*] the Devil.

Saturday 14th July

At Newbald this afternoon there was a Sale of some land and a Cottage & Garth, it none of it was sold. I took a view of Newbald Church, it is part of it very ancient, there are two very fine Doorways in the South front, but one of them is disfigured with a paltry porch built before it. there is over this door a figure in Stone, greatly obliterated, which is said to be St. Nicholas, to whom the Church is dedicated. It is said that these door ways and four noble Arches in the Church are of Saxon Architecture, but I rather think they are Norman, they

---

[84] A famous weekly literary review, published from 25 Jan. 1817 to 26 Apr. 1862. It was founded by Henry Colburn, but its principal editor for more than thirty years (1817–1850) was William Jerdan, who attracted many famous contributors, including the poet, George Crabbe (*DNB*; Watson iii. 1821).

[85] Sir Walter Scott, *The Life of Napoleon Buonoparte, Emperor of the French, with a Preliminary View of the French Revolution*. By the Author of "Waverley". 1827. The reference here is to an advance notice for this work.

are Semicircular and adorned with Fret work. The Steeple is in the middle of the building supported by four very fine Arches; and to improve the look of them they are painted blue. So much for a fine taste.

Sunday 15th July

This is called St. Swithin's day, but the Saint has dropped no tears, but smiled in Sunshine all the Day. A preacher who was coming from Hull to preach at the Methodist meeting this afternoon, had a fall from his Horse and cut his head very much so that he was obliged to be put to Bed at Old Richd. Milner's; I am sorry for his misfortune.

Monday 16th July

Thos. Marshall on Saturday night last, aggravated the Parish Clerk very much, by telling him amongst Company, that there were two Men in the town, which he could make fonder than ever Jacky Thornton was. One of them was the Priest and all he would do to him would be to take his Book from him, then what would he know? why hardly his right hand from his left, nay he might take his Clerk to back him & he (Tom) would meet him and argue with him on any ground in England. The other of his wise men was Teavil Leeson and if he had his money taken from him he would be as fond as Priest without his Book. The Poor Clerk was sadly exasperated, but Tom threatened to trample him under his feet. He says he has paid ten pounds this year to the Priest and never heard him preach but once, and that was too oft.

Tuesday 17th July

There was a Water Jury Supper at Wm. Cousen's last night I was there, came home a little after ten O'clock, all the talk was about Becks and Drains, some of them not done in a sufficient manner and others of them not done at all. Mrs. Forge died this morning she was taken with a fit about three weeks since and has been very ill from that time. Mr. Williams of Swanland is likewise dead he had a fit on Wednesday last and only lived two or three days after, it is said he has left Miss Tapp One hundred pounds.

Wednesday 18th July

A few drops of rain this morning, the Pastures are very much burnt up again, and should rain not come shortly there will be very little Fog, it has certainly been a fine Hay time and a good Crop. I expect Wm. is now at Swansea, which is a great distance from Swanland.

Thursday 19th July

London Porter is now much in request, as being they say a fine cooling drink, for my part I had rather be warm than be cooled with such a sluggish mixture, when poured into a Glass it has much the appearance of a mixture of laudunum and much the same effect. Had the Waters of Lethe been bottled off, they would not have been more disgusting than this somnific compound.

Friday 20th July

Old Anthony Burton died yesterday forenoon, and as there was no one saw him die I expect the Coroner over him either this night or tomorrow; Just when I had written thus far Old Lonc. the Constable came to tell me the Coroner had come (4. O'clock) and that I was to attend on the Jury, so I went with him, the

Verdict was "died by the Visitation of God". After that I went round the Town to invite the members of the Club to the funeral tomorrow afternoon at 3 O'clock for which I receive a penny each, there are in the town 61 members.

Saturday 21st July

Attended at the Club Room this afternoon to call over the names of members present, those absent are subject to a fine of sixpence. A very heavy shower of Rain between 4 & 5 O'clock, the Gutters run down like a Beck, the Shower extended a very little way. Robt. Marshall & James Levitt came at night and smoked a pipe with me. James is now the Landlord of the Bay horse since his mother's death.

Sunday 22nd July

I am just wondering where Wm. is today, I expect somewhere on his return perhaps at Oxford, that City of Domes & Steeples the delight of man, a Churchman who has there been educated and looks with contempt on all who have not had a University education, there are some of these Gentry who think they know more than their neighbours merely by having been at Oxford or Cambridge. I suppose a good deal of their learning consists in seeing the beautiful agreement between Church and State; and their hatred to liberals & Dissenters of all descriptions.

Monday 23rd July

On the Paper I recd. this morning there was written near the Seals "Billy's away" and a sketch of some kind of a head, who it was meant for I cannot say. The Papers have come very regular since Wm. went out not having once missed. There is scarcely any thing important now stirring; The Prosecutors for libels have Reaped but little benefit lately, as in two or three instances they have not recovered more than so many farthings.

Tuesday 24th July

My brother came last night it was nearly ten O'clock he walked from West Ella, he appears to be very well. I have written again to Wm. this morning expecting he has arrived back after having seen the sights in the West of England. Farmers as usual complaining of the Weather[,] they say Barley is ripening very unkindly, some parts of it turning colour while others are quite green, this is what they call getting night ripe or Moon ripe.

Wednesday July 25th

Went down to the West end last night with my Brother, we called at Mr. Turk's, Robt. Marshall's & Richard's, it was very hot & Sultry yesterday, but a little rain last night has cooled the air. My Brother has gone away this morning to West Ella, he is going to Hornsea & Burlington before he returns home again. He has brought me a present of a Sermon from Mr. Pool the author, I have not yet read it, it will be an exercise for Sunday, as I do not often hear of any thing of the kind worth remembering. I always feel low & depressed when any friend has been here, at parting with them, but this World is so constituted that the best friends cannot always live together.

Thursday 26th July

Our old friend Mr. Atkinson made a slight mistake when preparing for his tea, he poured the Water into the tea Cannister instead of his Teapot, so that he has it ready mashed for sometime to come. Bought four score Quills last night of Awd Beck for which I gave 10d. I saw an Account of a Storm which was experienced by the Steam packet from Chepstow to Bristol, I suppose it would be about the time that Wm. was there. Two young women who had been at Tintern visiting their Mother, were drowned in a small Vessel loaded with Bark.

Friday 27th July

I was at Ellerker at Watson Arton's at tea yesterday, Eliza and her Mother were to have been there, but it came on rain in the afternoon and prevented them; I cannot say that it was very delightful, as there were nearly half a score Children, shouting and yelping about, all spoiled to as great a degree as possible; I think there is nothing so disgusting as witnessing a number of children in a Company, behaving with the greatest rudeness, while their parents think they are showing off in the most engaging manner; however I was no wise taken with the exhibition of the young Dabs yesterday.

Saturday 28th July

Measured some Turnip land this forenoon for Ths. Marshall and Teavil Leason: in the afternoon I went to Ellerker to settle with Mr. Ths. Leason for the Ellerker Church sess. I had been collecting for him: He told me he had seen in the post Bag today an account of his Majesty turning indignantly from his Counsellors, the inference of which was that Mr. Canning was out of favour; and the Duke of Wellington, was afterwards sent for by the King, &c &c, but I told him I believed that there was not much truth in it. I think it will prove so.

Sunday 29th July

Recd. the Paper this morning with the direction written by Wm. so that he has got back again. I examined to see if there was any thing written, but it was all a Blank, I hope he is well after his Journey. — A very hot day but rather cooler towards night, the wind has got into the East and blows rather strong, we have had the wind westerly a long time this season.

Monday 30th July

A Violent thunder storm last night or this morning, it rained very heavy; with abundance of thunder & lightening. Miss Cooper had all her week's butter stolen a night or two ago out of the Churn; Ellerker Miller had likewise most of his Poultry stolen on Friday night last, but the thieves in neither case were found out. I heard a Man this day affirm that Cheap Bread would be the means of a Revolution; for my part I do not understand this kind of Doctrine, nor how it can happen that a man has more interest in paying a Shilling for the same quantity of Bread as he might have for Sixpence; but this is one of the Agricultural cries, and an ugly sound it has.

Tuesday 31st July

Wrote out the Jury list this day which is to be carried before the Justices sometime in September next; it may happen they may commit it to the house of

Correction, as it is a place they are very partial of letting lodgings in. These Country Justices are the masters in general, for if a case come before one of them in his individual Capacity that cannot be satisfactorily settled, it is then taken to the Sessions where the Bench settle it according to the view taken of it before their Brother magistrates; so that it had been better settled at the first, and the Fees saved to the simple parties who are so fond of appealing.

Wednesday 1st Augt.

Recd. from Wm. this morning an account of his return from his Welsh expedition. I hope it has been pleasant & profitable to him. — Measured some Turnip land of Wm. Loncaster's last night 8a–1r–30p. The Sand has blown so much in his new field Close that is has covered 3 or 4 lands like drifted Snow, he says the Turnips will grow through it, but I think there is a very poor Chance of their showing their heads through the load of Sand with which they are encumbered. Went to Richd. Kirby's to settle with him for Rates & taxes, got a Glass of Gin and water there. Turnips look remarkably well this Season.

Thursday 2nd Augt.

A Meeting last night at Barnd. Cooks to balance the Church accounts for the last year, there were only 5 persons there, so that there was no opposition to the accounts. This is Mr. Barnard's Rent day. Some of the tenants cannot want money much, to keep their Wool unsold for two and some for three years together. I wish they may keep it for a Market, lower than they could have sold it for when it was first clipped. They should have such a Customer as Cobbett, as they complain they could not sell it at <u>any price</u>, but any price with them means the highest prices that is going; they will still keep if they are bid less by 6d. per Stone than what they ask.

Friday 3rd Augt.

It appears that the wise Men in Portugal have a Corn law in operation, to hunger the Poor much in the same way, as that sort of business is carried on in this Country. I think very little of Charters and cries of Liberty, when the poor are kept under the Bondage of hungry Bellies; Surely there will a time come when this odious tyranny will be put away; the non-importation of Corn into certain Countries must make it cheaper in those Countries who have it to export, but for want of a Market, they can neither sell it nor purchase other Articles for the want of such sale.

Saturday 4th Augt.

Recd. a parcel from Wm. last night with an account of his route to Wales and back again. I shall examine it when I have a little leisure. At Brantingham this afternoon measuring some small Closes belonging Mr. Nelson's Estate which is advertised for Sale in the Hull Papers. I likewise saw it in the Times. Drank tea with Mr. Shaw. I saw a single Stook of Wheat as I came home, the first I have seen this year it was in Thos. Robinson's Close near the Ring Beck, a very fine Crop, as wheat appears to be in general.

Sunday 5th Augt.

Thos. Marshall came up this Evening a little after five O'clock and staid till after seven, after getting up several times to go away, he is beaten with this life, he says he cannot understand it; there are so many <u>feals</u> he is almost sick of every thing; but what troubles him the most at present his Cattle have been in a Wheat Close of Laverack's; and he Laverack talks of having a Jury tomorrow to view it and lay on the Damages done; now it will be very hard he says to lay much on him when Laverack Cattle have so often trespassed upon him.

Monday 6th Augt.

Mr. Walker[86] here today exam[in]ing the Assessors to see if any more taxes can be compelled. Upon the whole he is a very fair Man not wishing to take undue advantage. Mr. Canning appears to be going to make some alteration in the Military and to economise by reducing the establishment. There can be nothing said against this excepting by those whose perquisites it will diminish, but the payers of the burdens need not care anything for that.

Tuesday 7th Augt.

There was some quarrelling and fighting in the Street last night after bed time, when publicans let the Rabble get drunk in their Houses, they then begin fighting, then the Constable is called upon to make peace, however I did not get amongst them till all was about over. Mrs. Pickering the Landlady said the Company they had in the house had only been drinking Porter; I then made no wonder of the madness with which they were inspired caused by sitting so long pouring down their throats the worse than beastly mixture.

Wednesday 8th Augt.

Very Dull and low spirited today.

Thursday 9th Augt.

Fine harvest weather most people have begun. I see by the Paper that Mr. Canning is very ill, indeed from the accounts of him there seems to be but little prospect of his recovery, his death I doubt would throw the late arrangements into disorder again. I suppose some of the Oppositionists would be glad to hear of his death, while on the other hand his friends would be much alarmed, as he seems to be the Key-Stone of the building, which can scarcely stand without him.

Friday 10th Augt.

Recd. the Courier this morning with an account of the Death of Mr. Canning, it is what I anticipated for in talking of his illness last night I said I doubted not but he was then dead, which now appears to have been the case; I wonder who will be found to fill his place as an individual, whether any or none; or will a fresh set of Men be appointed for the loss of this single master Spirit? I must acknowledge there were some things belonging to Mr. Canning which I did not much like.

Saturday 11th Augt.

Busy this day sorting cut Quills, I have 13 hundred which I am going to send to Mr. Craggs at 2/6d pr. hundred all picked seconds and thirds very good ones, they are not so valuable as they were some years ago for I used to get 3/6d

---

[86] John Walker, surveyor of taxes, 9 Mason Street, Hull (Baines ii. 312).

pr. hundred, but I must be conformable to the times, as others are forced to be.[87]

Sunday 12th Augt.

> And what is Friendship but a name,
> A Charm that lulls to sleep;
> A Shade that follows wealth & fame,
> But leaves the wretch to weep.[88]

If I stood in need, I wonder whether any who call themselves my friends would use any exertions in my favour; I think I may venture [to] say no such exertions would be made. By the favour of heaven I have so long got on my way without any thing but my own endeavours; how long I may so continue is not for me to say, but I will put my trust in that providence who watches over even the smallest concerns in the world.

Monday 13th Augt.

A very small market this day it being fine harvest weather. I saw Bell's life in London with a Portrait of Mr. Canning[,] it is a strange rough concern, the only consolation is that it cannot be his likeness, — I see Cobbett has been calling the Toll Collectors to account for their extortion and negligence, it appears he has tied them over pretty tightly to their good behaviour.[89]

Tuesday 14th Augt.

It was said yesterday that Sheep had risen in price 6 or 7 Shillings a head, which elevates the sellers of Sheep very high. The Courier (Mr. Brown said) reported that Wheat had fallen in London on Friday last 3s. pr. quarter, but this was not credited by the holders of Corn; so apt are all people to believe according to their own interests. I had such a pain somewhere about my Collar bone last night that it prevented me from sleeping, but it is now better. A good deal of rain last night and this morning, which will prevent harvesting this day.

Wednesday 15th Augt.

Yesterday and today very wet, this afternoon a great deal of thunder but mostly at a distance, I think there has been more Rain these two days than at any time for two years past, should it take up and be fine now it will have done much good especially to the grass land which wanted rain much.

Thursday 16th Augt.

A fine morning but no wind to dry much, it still looks cloudy but I hope it will clear up and be fine, the Farmers are already saying it will have an effect on the Markets and make Corn dearer; but I hope they will be deceived. Settled Accounts with Wm. Loncaster the Constable last night.

---

[87] RS referred on several occasions (28/8/26, 26/7/27, 9/1/36) to buying quills from farmers. He presumably cut and graded them before selling them to John Craggs, a Hull stationer. RS paid 10d for 80 quills on 26/7/27. If the remaining quills in the batch had all been bought at the same price, then he would have profited by more than double his outlay in this particular transaction.

[88] Quotation from Oliver Goldsmith's poem, 'Edwin and Angelina; or, The Hermit (1766)' (*EP*).

[89] Cobbett had accused the lessees of the Surrey New Roads turnpike of charging illegal and extortionate tolls (*CPR* 63 vii (11 Aug.) 1827, 438 and 63 viii (18 Aug.) 1827, 480–93).

Friday 17th Augt.

It was fortunately a fine day yesterday, but a good deal of rain in the night time. There are some people not content with the Weather let it be what it will for 3 days together, when it rained this week, they cried another such day and all the Wheat will be sprouted; last week it was such dry weather that they said Wheat knocked out of the ears upon the land thicker than it had been sown; so let the weather be as it will there is nothing right for these grumblers.

Saturday 18th Augt.

Went to the Common this afternoon to measure two small Closes of Wheat for Robt. Marshall, I saw in several places people examining the Stooks, and seeking in the middle of the Sheaves for Sprouts, and when they found one they cried out as lustily as if they had found something extraordinary, Saying look here sprouts as long as my finger, however I saw none but I daresay there is without doubt some sprouted, a fine working day but no Sun; not a single load of Corn yet got home.

Sunday 19th Augt.

"Blessings on his head said Sancho Panza who first invented Sleep",[90] but what shall we say of the Character of the French which I lately saw in "Moor's France"[91] after describing the amusements of different Classes he says "all in a careless oblivion of the past, thoughtless of the future, and totally occupied by the present". Now I should wish for no more oblivion than what Sleep affords, for there are some pleasing recollections of past times; I must admit there are many anxieties for the future, but still I think the present is not the only time to occupy us. A very dull day but no rain.

Monday 20th Augt.

A very thin Market this day most of the Farmers throng with harvest, it came on rain at night, great complaints of the wet weather, Corn appears to be all ready, and fine weather is only wanting to get forward with it.

Tuesday 21st Augt.

Wrote out the Jury list for Ellerker; a fine morning. Lord Goderich I see succeeds Mr. Canning, how by the bye is his Lordship's name sounded hard Gode-rick or soft Goderich? as I hear it frequently pronounced both ways but whether is right I cannot say. Mr. Canning seems to be generally lamented, I hope his successor will not set himself against reform so much as he did.

Wednesday 22nd Augt.

A Cold high North wind, which is very suitable for the Wheat, the sharpness of the wind will dry it and prevent its sprouting. People are leading today for the first time. Wm. says Cobbett rejoices at Mr. Canning's death, he generally either finds an opportunity or makes one, for being in Opposition to the general sentiments of the Country.

---

[90] Quotation from Miguel De Cervantes' *Don Quixote*, part 2, chapter 68: 'Blessings on him who invented sleep, the mantle that covers all human thoughts, the food that satisfies hunger, the drink that slakes thirst ...' (*ODQ* 138–9).

[91] John Moore, *A View of Society and Manners in France, Switzerland and Germany* ... 6th [i.e. 9th] ed. London: W. Strahan and T. Cadell, 1800. – 2 vols.

Thursday 23rd Augt.

A very fine morning the Sun shines brightly, yesterday it was uncommonly cold but very fine for the Corn. Mrs. Sonley died last night about seven O'clock, she has been ill a long time, Capt. Waller succeeds to her house and the Farm at Drewton. I dare say he will be much gratified to hear of her death, he is now at York, but it is expected he will come to live here.

Friday 24th Aug.

Mr. Atkinson has pulled his Pears, and sold part of them to Merchant Moody at 18d. pr. peck, he will make about one pound of them. Wrote a letter for Robt. Marshall to Howden in answer to one from a Corn factor enquiring if he had any Wheat to sell; he has about 30 Quarters which he has offered at 63s. pr. Qr. I see there has been new Wheat in the London market, indeed it must be nearly all got home in the South, I think it is in general a good Crop this year ...

Sunday 26th Aug.

I and Eliza were at Tea at Mr. Tinsdill's today, the Dr. is full of Politics and retrenchment, but what Mr. Canning proposed is just nothing at all he says. He has an Aunt with him who knows all Sir Johns and Lord James's on the old establishment but so many of the late new made Lords rather nonplus her.

"The Rascals thus enrich'd he call'd them Lords,

To please their upstart pride with new made words."

—Great families of yesterday we shew,

And Lords, whose Parents were the Lord knows who!"

Monday 27th Aug.

A fine harvest morning after a frost last night, which will most likely bring on rain in a short time. Mrs. Sonley buried this forenoon at Brantingham she is 75 years of age. I slept very ill last night caused I think by drinking tea stronger than common, and a Glass of Brandy & Water after; how it is I know not, but common living agrees best with me. Great talk today of sprouted Corn. I have seen no new Samples, but it is inquired after for Seed by those who want to sow in the Wolds.

Tuesday 28th Aug.

Heard two Bakers conversing on the construction of Ovens arguing whether high Crowns or Flat were the best, and whether Square, Oblong, or Oval was the best form, it came to this at last, that was the best which baked best.

Wednesday 29th Aug.

Recd. a parcel from Wm. last night containing 6 Boxes of Pills which were thankfully received. At the same time recd. a letter that my Mother had been taken very ill on Sunday night or Monday morning, it therefore put me off reading anything that Wm. had sent. I went this morning to West Ella and found my Mother much better than she had been the day before. She was in Bed being unable to sit up, the Dr. says he thinks she will come about again. Got a ride in a Gig with Robt. Ramsdale to Riplingham who had been at West Ella.

Thursday 30th Aug.

My Sister told me yesterday that Mr. Sykes[92] will not take any more of Cobbett's registers for the abuse heaped on Mr. Canning and for the observations made on Mr. Brougham's speech at Liverpool.[93] Cobbett will not mind this if he knew, and if he knew that it was a Parson he had offended, it would make him more fierce.

Friday 31st Aug.

Sent last night to Wm. a Basket containing a Ham, and some Pears, after that amused myself by reading in the Spectator the Account of Sir Roger de Coverley, it really is an entertaining description of the old Knight. Robt. Marshall was here last night when the Basket was packed up, he smoked a pipe of Tobacco, he complained of having been put off leading in the afternoon by the rain, he has nearly got all his wheat home.

Saturday 1st Sepr.

I had some land to measure today but as it is the first day of Partridge shooting, I did not know that I should be safe from the Sportsmen, so I measured it last night, there was a Covey of Partridges in the Close; went down to Robt. Marshall's to meet Mr. Levitt of Ellerker respecting the following Crop of some wheat on the Land which he sold to Teavil Leeson.

Sunday 2nd. Sepr.

There are at this time swarms of Lady Birds, what we generally call "Cushy-Cow Ladies". They are a pretty little insect, favourites with Children and it is said they are perfectly harmless from destroying the produce of the Fields, their support is derived from smaller Insects which they destroy with avidity. In some places they are so numerous that it almost seems as if they had come in showers: I avoid all I can setting my feet on any [of] them, as I have a kind of regard for them which perhaps has arisen, from what I and others have heard repeated from the earliest remembrance

"Cushy Cow Lady, hie thee away home,

Thy house is burnt & thy Children's gone" ...

Tuesday 4th. Sepr.

The Stack yards this year will be abundantly filled, all that the Farmers now fear is that prices will come down. (this is not my fear) They have been crying out a long while that Oats were so bad there would scarcely be seed again. Now at the time of reaping they admit the Crop to be better then was expected. In fact Oats were the only article on which they could raise the cry of

---

[92] The Sykes family of West Ella Hall were Whigs and generally supported reform, unlike their Conservative cousins at Sledmere. It seems very probable that the Revd Richard Sykes (1756–1832), Rector of Foxholes, was the disabused parson-subscriber to Cobbett's *Register*. He was the father of Major Richard Sykes (1783–1870), who had inherited West Ella Hall on the death of his grandfather in 1805.

[93] Henry Peter Brougham (1778–1868), later Baron Brougham, was a leading radical politician and law reformer, well known for his oratory and political writings in *The Examiner*. The speech referred to here, which was substantially an attack on Canning and his ministry, was made at a public dinner given in his honour at Liverpool on 18 June 1827 (*DNB* and *TM* 20 June 1827, 2 f).

scarcity; and here they are disappointed. I never saw more Stacks than there are this year.

Wednesday 5th. Sepr.

I saw on Sunday last two old Men meet each other and shake hands, who had been acquainted in their youth (they were about 87 years of age each) Richd. Milner was one, and Mr. Outram the other; they remain like two venerable trees in a forest grown round with young plants. Richd. has been a member of the Methodist Society considerably more than half a Century. He remembers his Mother taking their part from the very first, but his Father was very much against them. Richd. is a very worthy old Man.

Thursday 6th. Sepr.

John Tapp called yesterday to say he had seen Wm. about a fortnight ago, when he looked very well, he talks of staying about a fortnight before he returns. I see Wm. has been dining with Mr. Hurst at Highgate. My Sister said he was in business in Regent street, but I have seen some advertisements of Books from Ths. Hurst & Co. in St. Paul's Church yard; I hope he will be successful, I see another young Man who succeeded Dunn at Messrs. Sewel & Cross's has been robbing his employers to a great extent. They appear to be particularly unfortunate in this respect.

Friday 7th. Sepr.

Corn Laws restrict importation, and increase the price of Bread nearly one fourth; whether Are the growers of Food, or the consumers to be considered the great body of the people? Then why should the Consumers pay for dear bread to encourage the tillage of inferior Soils, when they can be accommodated so much cheaper from abroad? Why cannot the Manufactures of this Country be exchanged for Corn? merely because a Monopoly is allowed to the Landowner, who has the address to make the simple farmers believe it is for their interest to pay high rents and sell dear Corn.

Saturday 8th. Sepr.

All the ministerial places appear to be now filled up: it appears Mr. Herries[94] has been appointed Chancellor of the Exchequer after it having been offered to two others, with what ability Mr. Herries may fill the situation, time will tell; it is a great thing in any ministry to be unanimous.

Sunday 9th. Sepr.

A very rainy afternoon, the last week was in general very cold and gloomy without any Sun, most of the harvest is in excepting Oats and they are as well out yet, as many persons have led them in an unfavourable state and have had their Stacks to turn over on account of their heating. I hope there is no prospect of Corn rising in price as the harvest is very abundant.

Monday 10th. Sepr.

Directed a letter for Mary Bentley to her Son Joseph who is a Corporal in the 40th Regt. at Cork. He is going to Van Dieman's land. Wrote a Certificate

---

[94] John Charles Herries (1778–1855) was Chancellor of the Exchequer in Goderich's ministry from 8 Aug. 1827 to 8 Jan. 1828 (*DNB*).

for Jno. Stather of Hotham who is going to try to get licence for a public house there, at the next Brewster Sessions.[95]

Tuesday 11th Sepr.

Not any great quantity of new wheat at Market yet here, Mr. Brown bid 55s. pr. quarter for some yesterday, if the Seller would warrant it to weigh 4 Stone pr. bushel, but the Seller did not seem to fall in with it. I think there will be a good deal of work this year for thrashing Machines. Henry Arton has one today, he has not so much corn that he need hurry, but he is always in want of Money, and when this is the case people must do as they can in a fair way.

Wednesday 12th Sepr.

Recd. a letter last night from the Stamp Office stating that complaints had been made to the Office in London that in several parts of the Country charges had been made for the Paper on which receipt stamps are printed, I can only say that no charge of this kind was ever made by me. Heard from Wm. that he had recd. the Basket safe which I am glad to hear. An uncommon heavy shower accompanied by a dreadful wind came on last night about six O'clock ...

Saturday 15th Sepr.

Old Brag Watson's Sister has been here from London, but she is so disgusted with the Poverty of poor Brag that she will do nothing for him, for the reason that the Worldly generally give, namely that the distressed stand in need of assistance. Now if the Old man had stood no need it is probable she would either have presented him with something, or at least made large promises of kindness to him. This sort of kindness is akin to that of those persons, "who have seized on the <u>Common</u> lands, inclosed them, cultivated them, and have a Corn Bill to force the poor to buy the produce of them".

Sunday 16th Sepr.

Measured some Land yesterday afternoon for Watty Arton in the Warren near Brantingham, then went to Ellerker and drank tea with him & <u>Mudda</u>, here I was told how much they had eat and drunk this Harvest, they had devoured 7 Sheep in six weeks and swallowed about 70 Gallons of Ale, besides small Beer, all which conversation was very edifying, I had very little occasion to say any thing as they seemed overflowing with the subject; so I filled a pipe of Tobacco and appeared pleased & surprised to hear them; and no doubt but they were as much satisfied with the subject as I was.

Monday 17th Sepr.

Eliza went to West Ella on Saturday afternoon to see her Grandmother, (she got back last night) she is much better. Eliza says she looks as well as she has seen her for a long time. We have pulled our Pears, and asked Merchant Moody what he would give for a Peck, he said 7d. or 8d. but he shall not have them at that rate, we will eat part of them ourselves and give the rest away, as

---

[95] Brewster Sessions, which took place annually in Sept., were meetings held by Justices of the Peace for the purpose of licensing public houses. The Justices were required to exercise control over the conduct of licensees and ensure that they did not permit gambling or unruly behaviour on their premises.

we can be generous in this case at a small expence, so the Merchant may try where he can fall in at his price for it will not be here.

Tuesday 18th Sepr.

Yesterday the prices for Wheat were lower that the week before, by 4 or 5 Shillings a quarter. There are so many persons thrashing with Machines that the market appears to be glutted at present, and what is now thrashed must be sold, as it will not keep. Rd. Marshall & Robt. had the Machine both of them the last week. There were more than 10,000 Quarters of Wheat at Wakefield market last Friday. I have got the Examiner for 1825 bound, likewise the Vol for 1826. They are very neat, but I do not think they are good to bind being printed at different times, and the margins not all alike.

Wednesday 19th Sepr.

Some persons on Monday night robbed two Orchards, and also pulled up some young fruit trees by the roots and committed other depredations, the offenders are not known, but there are strong suspicions of them. — Michael Clegg's wife died yesterday in Child birth of her twelfth Child, she only lived about three hours after being delivered, the Child is living. — A Cold day having been a frost last night.

Thursday 20th Sepr.

Bought 6 Quire of letter Paper of a travelling merchant last night, after that went to the West end being throng collecting Composition money for the Highways as the Accounts are to be made up in a few days. I dislike Horse racing almost as much as any thing, this is Doncaster race week, and there is scarcely any other subject of discourse than this ...

Friday 21st Sepr.

It appears by the Times that there are several dreadful houses in the Neighbourhood of Bow Street, where the unthinking are robbed of their property with impunity. These receptacles seem to emanate from the Play houses, it is a very pretty kind of morality that is taught at these sinks of iniquity, when the Managers allow free admission to prostitutes. It is high time that the Police exert themselves with more vigour than they have hitherto done, and at once break up the Flash Houses, and punish the frequenters of them.

Saturday 22nd Sepr.

This is my Birth day, I was born in the year 1773, so that I am now 54 years of age.

Sunday 23rd Sepr.

There were 3 Christenings at Church this afternoon which appears to be equal to a tune on the Organ, there is no conception how tired and disgusted I am of all that belongs to the Church, I cannot much longer put up with it.

Monday 24th Sepr.

Wrote 2 notices for Rd. Marshall the Steward, for 2 of Mr. Barnard's small tenants at Broomfleet; at the Market this day wheat was lower than it has been, nay some are thinking that it will be at Cobbett's price before Martinmas, namely 40s pr. quarter, then what grumbling on the part of the growers there will be; I have never been persuaded yet that dear Corn is to the advantage of the purchasers altho' this doctrine has been preached a long time.

Tuesday 25th Sepr.

Ths. Milne one of James Milne's Sons preached at the Methodist meeting last Sunday night, and as I have been informed he acquitted himself very well; indeed such preachers as he is, have proved themselves more useful than M.A.s & D.D.s from the Heathen Colleges where more of their study consists in the fables of the Pagan Gods, than in understanding the mysteries of the Gospel of Jesus Christ. How is it possible but their hearers must be still in ignorance.

Wednesday 26th Sepr.

Heard from Wm. this morning that he is going to send his Chest in a few days time. It is now a long while since it was here, we shall be glad to receive it. Yesterday at Weighton fair Sheep sold for low prices, it is the opinion of several people that they will not yet advance in price, the account of the Turnip Crop in the West riding is very bad, so that there will not be any call for Sheep in that district to any great amount, and that is the great Market for this part of the Country. Brewster Sessions today at Beverley , where many of the Landlords generally contrive to get as drunk as they conveniently can, both to indulge themselves, and likewise for the benefit of the Excise.

"Let mirth and music sound the dirge of Care!

But ask thou not if <u>happiness</u> be there?"

Thursday 27th Sepr.

All the Publicans in this Place except Barnd. Cook had their Licenses refused at the Brewster Sessions yesterday. It is supposed to have been the meddling parson who has informed something or other against them, however he has the <u>honour</u> of it; if it can be called honour, in his own eyes, with all impartial observers not of the clerical order, such dirty proceedings are called odious. The Landlords are to appear again before the Justices on Wednesday next, when I think there can be nothing against having their Licenses renewed, after having the Scandal of being refused.

Friday 28th Sepr.

Cooper Tindle the Landlord when coming from the Brewster Sessions a good deal "<u>hellewated</u>" as the Watchmen say, fell from his horse and when he was laid down, he swore to his horse to be quiet and give him fair play and not strike at him when he was down, but let him get up again then they would try, but begged of his horse not to be cowardly and strike until he was fairly up. He was no worse for his fall.

Saturday 29th Sepr.

Measured 11 Acre of Beans for Robt. Marshall at the Ings this afternoon, got tea with him. Old Lonc. came with an order to serve on Wm. Cade for fighting with Val. Tindle, I don't know which of them are the worst.

Sunday 30th Sepr.

Ths. Harper is here now, he has been selling his House and Close to a man of the name of Dennis who lives at Ferriby. The Close is up Porter Hole about 3a–3r–0p the Garth about an Acre, all the property is Copyhold the price is

£500, which I think a very good price for it, I should think the fine which is 2 year's rent and the writings will cost fifty pounds more.

Monday 1st Octr.

There is great talk of a new Act which passed the last Sessions respecting Maltsters and making Malt,[96] from what I have heard of it, it seems to be made up of Penalties, some of which are as high it is said as £500. Some Maltsters I heard talk of it seem to think it will be almost impossible to carry on their business under it.

Tuesday 2nd Octr.

Wrote a notice to quit and delivered the same to Daniel Foster yesterday from the Executors of Jas. Marshall, to give up possession at Lady day next of a Cottage & Garth and a small Close of land situate at Newbald, they talk of selling it, it lets for 6 Guineas a year, they think they can sell it for 300 Pounds, but I think it is over-rated, at that price.

Wednesday 3rd Octr.

Expected Wm's Box last night but it did not come. Recd. a Rect. from the Stamp Office for £74.12.6 sent yesterday, heard from my Mother that she is much better than she was. — A meeting at the Bay horse last night to balance the Highway accounts, I came away about ten O'clock there was nothing particularly interesting going on. The Landlords are gone to Beverley again today to try to get their Licences. A very fine day.

Thursday 4th Octr.

All the Publicans got their Licences again yesterday after having had an extra Journey to Beverley; the Parson has denied that he was the cause of their being before refused, but some of the Justices gave them to understand yesterday that it was through his meddling that they did not get their licences the last week. Such conduct is detestable.

Friday 5th Octr.

Mr. Atkinson the inspector of Stamps from London has been here this morning taking an account of Stock, I was at Barnard Cook's with him last night, he is a well informed man on several subjects, he is an admirer of Goldsmith and repeated several lines of his deserted Village, this brought us immediately acquainted. He is likewise an advocate for a free trade in Corn, and generally he says speaks his sentiments freely upon it. This Gentleman tells me his Father in Law was the Editor of the Courier in the French War, I think he said his name was George Thomas Street, he sold his Part in the Paper for £20,000. I have before heard of his name.[97]

---

[96] An Act to Consolidate and Amend Certain Laws Relating to the Revenue of Excise on Malt Made in the United Kingdom ..., 8 Geo. IV c. 52, passed on 2 July 1827.

[97] One of London's principal evening daily newspapers, *The Courier* was published, from its foundation by James Perry in Sept. 1792, until 6 July 1842. RS's memory seems to have let him down here, or he was misinformed, for the editor from 1811 to 1822 was one, Peter Street not George Thomas Street. Before Street, from 1803 to 1811, the paper was edited by its then proprietor, Daniel Stuart (Watson iii. 1792).

Saturday 6th Octr.

Mrs. Wood of Drewton who has been in a melancholy way a good while, took some poison this morning when her husband was boiling some mercury (arsenic) to mix amongst seed wheat;[98] in his looking for something which he wanted she took a Cup and drank some of the fatal mixture and died sometime towards night. It is a melancholy affair.

Sunday 7th Octr.

I saw Tommy Harper today it is said he is married but whether it be so or not I cannot say; he looks very thin he says he is going back to London in a short time, he expects getting payment for his Property he has sold some time the next week. He says it is a long time since he saw Wm. probably four or five months. He proffered to take a letter if I had one to send.

Monday 8th Octr.

Mr. Leeson of Ellerker brought us a Brace of Partridges today. Wheat today is worth little more than two Guineas a quarter, so that it has nearly got to Cobbett's price, but as the Crop is so large it may perhaps nearly make as much money as though it had sold higher; but then to hear the complaints of the Farmers is quite amusing but nothing out of the common way.

Tuesday 9th Octr.

Sometimes when I first see a little Boy in Button Clothes, I give him a penny to put in his Pocket, which I know from experience is very gratifying. I can remember very well the first time that I got on Coat and Breeches Roger Pinder gave me a penny, I know the place to a yard where I then was; what scenes have passed over since then, which is half a Century ago, most of all that were then Men and Women are far removed from the cares and trifles of this world, but some of their memories are fondly cherished by me. — An old Man who keeps the Kelthorpe toll Bar at Drewton had his house robbed one night last week about nine O'clock by three Men whom he did not know, they got in Money and Goods to the amount of ten pounds.

Wednesday 10th Octr.

We have looked for Wm's Chest the two or three last Carrier days[;] last night when it did not arrive we were afraid it had miscarried, but this morning we find it was to leave London only yesterday, so that it is yet safe. Old Mrs. Akam has lost some money out of a Chest in her house to the amount of fifty pounds or more, but when it was gone she does not know, as the Chest continued locked, and was so when she discovered her loss, her suspicion is on a Girl that she had, there were 28 Golden guineas in a Nutmeg Grater, which she has had for more that thirty years!!! and about 20 Sovereigns, and some

---

[98] As a preventive measure against smut, the soaking of cereal seed grains in brine, often with the addition of urine and other substances to the solution, had long been practised by farmers. In 1812 Strickland reported that some farmers in East Yorkshire were steeping their wheat seed in urine and drying it by using quick-lime, but others used a solution of arsenic in water for the same purpose. He commented that 'the use of so dangerous a drug in the hands of careless and ignorant people should ... be discouraged' (Mingay vi. 312–3; Strickland 123).

loose money she does not know how much, there were some seven Shilling pieces left in the Chest.

Thursday 11th Octr.

An uncommon stormy rainy night and continued so this morning. As this is Hull fair day it will make it unpleasant, we are none of us there — In the Times there is an Order from the Magisterial Gentlemen of Beverley at the last Sessions, to secure to the Office of Justice such Gentlemen as are agreeable to the Great Dons now in power.[99] I have an account or list of the Magistrates in the East riding for 1824. The number then was 41 — seventeen of whom were Clericals, so that there appeared no want of those who ought to have been studying their Sermons, instead of protecting Game, and committing Poachers to the tread Mill.

Friday 12th Octr.

Yesterday being Hull fair the Carrier was there when we desired him to call to see if the Box had come from Wm., we were gone to Bed before he came back, but on enquiry this morning it had not arrived, so that we shall not receive it before Tuesday next at the soonest, as he does not go to Hull any more this week, therefore we must wait patiently.

Saturday 13th Octr.

Measured some Land in Ruffham Field, and the Ings and a little Close of Mr. Turk's down Goose Croft's lane which Wm. used to call Dead man's lane. — The newspaper missed coming this morning.

Sunday 14th Octr.

The Paper which missed yesterday came this morning. The weather keeps remarkably fine, since the storm last week. Mr. Craggs has let his land at North Cave, but keeps the Mill in his own hands, the land only 32 Acres will be but a poor thing for a living and some of the land very ordinary.

Monday 15th Octr.

Newspaper missed again this morning; I am sorry when it happens so. Js. Levitt told me yesterday that T. Harper would have to send for his wife before he can give a title to his Property which he has sold, as it will be necessary for her to sign before the Conveyance be legal.

Tuesday 16th Octr.

I have seen an abstract of the Malt Acts, particularly the last one, it is a bundle of Penalties, there is one on the Maltster or other Person who promises any gratuity to the Excise officer to induce him to defraud the Revenue, this is the greatest Penalty in the Act which is £500. It is like other acts not adapted to the understanding of those who have a little of that Article called common

---

[99] An order had been made at Beverley Quarter Sessions on 9 July 1827 to consider at the next (Michaelmas) Quarter Sessions a proposal that no recommendation for any new East Riding magistrate should be made unless proposed by 2 magistrates of the division in which the vacancy had arisen nor should a new magistrate be appointed without the support of three-quarters of those magistrates present on the first day of the Quarter Sessions. Reproducing the text of this order, *The Times* was scathing in its condemnation of the proposal, arguing that it would give undue influence to the Beverley members of the East Riding magistrature (*TM* 6 Oct. 1827, 2 c).

sense, whether such things edify Metaphysicians or not I cannot undertake to say.

Wednesday 17th Octr.

The Chest arrived last night all safe with its contents, the Handkerchiefs are very much admired. All the old Cloaths will be useful,[100] there is the great Coat which will make me a Coat I dare say very well, and the trewsers make excellent Waistcoats, then there is a Hat which I am told will make a Man of me when I wear it ...

Thursday 18th Octr.

A Jury Supper last night at Tindale's there were thirteen at Supper, I came away a little after ten O'clock, when there was no preparation making for breaking up the meeting. Recd. a letter from the Stamp Office inclosing a ten pound Bank of England Post Bill, for not being properly indorsed, there is an expence of 3s/8d upon it besides the letter from Hull. — If this had been paid in Gold instead of the Rag there would not have wanted any indorsing. I had nothing to do with the indorsing as it was not made payable to me.

Friday 19th Octr.

I have read Cobbett's account of the Petticoat Speculation in Bonds[101] which is very amusing, likewise his account of his bidding for the Whig Club Chair which it seems he could not get at his price as he only wanted it to burn at the feast of his Gridiron. He has however purchased some of the Crown and Anchor Staves,[102] which he talks of dressing up as Shey Loys.[103] The Paper missed again this morning, not one London paper having come. I wrote a letter yesterday for Barnard Cook in answer to a complaint made by Mr. Todd of North Cave on the frequency of his Papers not coming regularly, but it appears our Old Postmaster was not to blame as the letters and Papers for North Cave do not come here.

Saturday 20th Octr.

Cobbett is unnecessarily severe on Sir Francis Burdett,[104] and some of his former friends if indeed he ever knew what friendship meant. He is frequently abusing those who do not think as he does himself; and he is not much less liberal to those who happen to reason in his own way, for he immediately turns round on them and accuses them of stealing his very words; He appears to be

[100] The trade in second-hand clothing flourished in London. It was concentrated in certain districts, notably around Monmouth Street, and Holywell Street in the Strand (Dodd 398).

[101] Discussed in his article, 'Mexican Bonds' (*CPR* 63 xiii (22 Sept.) 1827, 769–88).

[102] See his article, 'Chair and Wands' (*CPR* 63 xiii (22 Sept.) 1827, 788–94).

[103] 'I shall, I think, take some of mine [the staves] to my gardens, and use them, to put old clothes upon and dress them up as shoy-hoys [i.e. scarecrows]' (*CPR* 63 xiii (22 Sept.) 1827, 794).

[104] Popular Whig politician and defender of free speech, Sir Francis Burdett (1770–1844) was a stern critic of parliamentary corruption and was twice imprisoned on political charges (in 1810 and 1820). He was a strong advocate of parliamentary reform and other liberal causes but after the passing of the Reform Act of 1832, he inclined towards the liberal Tories and served as Conservative MP for North Wiltshire for the remainder of his parliamentary career (1837–44). Cobbett frequently attacked him in his writings (*DNB*; *CPR* 64 ii (6 Oct.) 1827, 65–84 and 64 iii (13 Oct.) 1827, 159–75).

much exasperated against Baines[105] the Editor of the Leeds Mercury, who is looked upon to be very liberal in his principles, and I understand has an excellent character at Leeds and in the neighbourhood. He (Cobbett) is very humorous on the Petticoat Speculation in Bonds.

Sunday 21st Octr.

Yesterday and the night before was very wet, a great deal of rain having fallen, it has nearly given the Farmers who have not got their Wheat sown the Cholic, for they make very wry faces, all does not seem to be right within. I always have said that the weather for a week together is never right for them, but twenty four hours or less rain puts them into grievous quandaries. I had forgot to note that the paper which missed on Friday came to hand yesterday morning.

Monday 22nd Octr

Wm. Green of Brantingham had a Son killed on Saturday last by a Cow Shed falling upon him, he was about 15 years of Age. Farmers all on a very flat key today, partly on account of the wet weather, but chiefly the low prices affect them. One Man who is a methodist preacher a farmer and owner said no good would be done for the farmers unless Foreign Corn was absolutely prohibited from being imported into this Country. I have not a very high opinion of the Legislators at present, but should such an insane proceeding as this take place, let them be supplied by Barbers' blocks.[106]

Tuesday 23rd Octr

Wm. Loncaster had 5 or 6 Lads up at Riplingham yesterday for robbing his Walnut trees, they were fined 2s. each and had the expences to pay, they all prepared themselves with Gew-Gaws (Jews-Harps) and played old Lonc. a tune all the way home he is generally in hand with something to defend himself against the insolence of silly lads who call him "Cuckoo" which he abominably detests, nay it is almost wonderful he does not get an Order for the Cuckoo herself when she cries.

Wednesday 24th Oct

Wm. says he did not receive a paper the last week, it must have been stopped somewhere as it was regularly sent, I never heard of it miscarrying before, there certainly is great negligence somewhere regarding the conveyance of Newspapers. It appears the Hull Packet is going into fresh hands, it is to be published by Topping for the first time on the 13th. Novr. next.[107]

---

[105] Edward Baines (1774–1848), proprietor of the *Leeds Mercury*, publisher, and prominent Whig politician, being MP for Leeds 1834–41 (DNB; *CPR* 64, ii (6 Oct.) 1827, 84–90 and 64 iii (13 Oct.) 1827, 147–59).

[106] i.e. rounded wooden blocks on which wigs were made and displayed (*OED*).

[107] The *Hull Packet*, published 1787–1886, was a Tory newspaper. It was taken over by Thomas Topping of Lowgate in 1827 and published by him until 1831, when it was acquired by William Goddard and Robert Brown, who continued to print it together until 1838. At first the paper appeared weekly on Tuesdays but from 1832 onwards it was issued on Fridays (*VCHYER* i. 428).

Thursday 25th. Oct

Another complaint has been made by Mr. Popple of Welton on the irregularity of the arrival of the London Newspapers. I have written a letter to the Postmaster of York on the subject for Old Barnard: I hope there will be some regulation made, from the number of complaints which take place. The weather this week since the rain has been fine as summer. Ths. Harper's wife is here, he talks of setting off for London on Monday next. I have heard that he has taken a Shop at Hull in Silver Street, where he intends commencing business.

Friday 26th. Octr.

There has been a sort of justification from the Globe[108] of the Country Bankers, endeavouring to prove that they have been of benefit to the Public by advancing their Rags to the holders of various articles that they might be enabled to keep them from the Market, and raise the prices; thus the great Frog-bellies were enabled to hold Corn from the Poor, but the Curse of God is upon them.

Saturday 27th. Octr.

It is now said that there is too much Stock (Cattle & Sheep) bred in the Country, as the Markets are so stocked they can scarcely be turned into Money; but I think little of this sort of reasoning, because high prices cannot be obtained all those who can afford to keep will not sell; I know that if the poor had but the means of procuring Flesh meat, there would be a far greater consumption; it is Poverty which makes them go with empty bellies; they are obliged to submit to necessity.

Sunday 28th. Oct

No paper again this morning. A very Stormy rainy night last night. Went to Mill yesterday afternoon, for some Money of the long Miller but he could not think of paying, as when a Bill is presented there was three days grace allowed so he promised to pay before Wednesday.

Monday 29th. Oct

A Cold frosty morning but fine and clear, I have just been looking out for what Cobbett's I have as we are going to send off the Box tonight. The paper which missed yesterday came this morning it had evidently been detained as it was folded in a different manner to what they in general are, and the wrapper was much torn.

Oct. 30 Tuesday

Sent off Wm's Box last night, the first stage to Wm. Cousen's. Robt. Marshall was summoned to Riplingham yesterday for pay for some Stones for the Highways supplied by W. Bullock who lives with Mr. King he charged one Shilling a load when they were buying as good stones for five pence a load, the

---

[108] Published 1 Jan. 1803 – 28 Dec. 1822. Continued as: *Globe and Traveller* 30 Dec. 1822 – 5 Feb. 1921. *The Globe* was London's oldest evening newspaper, and was owned during the period of the diary by Robert Torrens. It was eventually incorporated into the *Pall Mall Gazette,* and shortly afterwards merged into the *Evening Standard* (Watson iii. 1792).

Justices would not interfere, but told Bullock he must go to law for his money if he could not get it without.

Wednesday Oct. 31st.

I have had a pound note of the Craven Bank returned to me this morning with information that it is a forged one,[109] this is not pleasing, but I know I never paid it, I had one of the same Bank which I paid to Wilkn. Ayre on Monday night. I know who I took it of, but I will sooner put [it] into the fire than carry it back and say it is the Bill I took; I have sent word to Wilk. that it is not the note I gave him and I understand he says he is positive I gave it him, but this I will always deny, the worst is the loss of it. Confusion attends this ragged System, there was a Gentleman told me only on Monday night that he would rather have Paper than Gold, I told him I had a very poor opinion of any person who preferred Rags to pure Gold, this Man I believe is a half pay officer, so I was not so much surprised.

Thursday 1st Nov.

Measured last night some land at Ellerker of Mr. Levitt's which he has sold to S. Ringrose; it was very cold and not pleasant working and walking amongst the Turnips, there are 17a–2r–3p at I suppose 80 pounds or more per Acre. I said yesterday that I should always deny that I had paid the note to Wilk. but I find I have been mistaken in taking it for another which I had, when I was convinced, which I was in a satisfactory manner I admitted that I had been wrong, I knew from whom I had it and returned it, so that there is no loss to me. I might have verified the Spanish Proverb "a fool never changes his mind" but it is added a wise man will.

Friday 2nd. Nov

Court today, Old Lonc. was thrown out from being Constable, he was very ill vexed about it, had I been in his place I would not have had it at any rate, if there had been any objection to me. Robt. Tindale who lives at Weedley was appointed in his room, and I as usual stand Deputy. I think it very inconvenient for the Constable to be far out of the town.

Saturday 3rd. Nov

Went down to the Mill this forenoon to see if the Miller had had sufficient days of Grace before payment, but he was out at Ings sowing Wheat so I did not see him, he came a little before ten O'clock at night and paid as much he said as ever he could which was about half, as he did not wish to put me about!!!

Sunday 4th Novr.

The hum-drum Curate and his dreaming Clerk, spent a full hour and half this morning at prayers, one would think to hear them that it was a trial of

---

[109] Forgery of both provincial and Bank of England notes was widespread in the early 19th c. In the private ledger of the Craven Bank of Birkbeck and Co. (founded 1791) of Settle, there is an entry: '31-12-1827 N.B. from forged Craven notes we have incurred expenses over the last six months of £6-0-10d.' (Cited in Hartley, p. 27).

Skill, which of them could, draw out their words at the greatest length, it is far from "Links of sweetness long drawn out".[110]

In the afternoon two Christenings and two or three tunes on the Organ, and about fifteen minutes talk, by courtesy called a Sermon. I have been tied for years to a pillar and attempted to be fed with what is worse than pure water; it is a mixture of something derived from Rome, but perhaps adulterated. I am heartily tired of it.

Monday 5th. Nov

Wm. Lundy the Carrier of North Cave was buried on Friday last, he had been ill about a week before he died. This is Beverley fair day, Cattle and Pigs have sold very dear, but Horses very low. No Factor at the Market today, wheat does not rise to the wishes of those who have it to sell.

Tuesday 6th. Nov

I saw in the Hull Advertiser that Newspapers to be sent by Post must be put in within seven days of their publication I do not know whether this be right or not. The Packet I send on that day week after it is published, and as I have not heard but all is right, I shall continue doing so, they say that a paper not sent within the time is liable to be charged as a single letter. Ordered the Chronicle of the Cannongate.[111]

Wednesday 7th. Nov

Saw by the Direction on the Paper this morning the ; as the mark that Wm. had got his Box; At west end this evening the Farmers complaining that much of the Wheat which has been sown on low land has not come up thick enough, so that they are already crying out it will be a bad Crop the next year, but they still keep sowing, but seed time is nearly finished for this season; except as they say some of what is sown should be ploughed up again.

Thursday 8th Novr

This is a very fine day, clear and sweet as spring, there have been Hare feasts at all the public houses this week, I have not been at any of them; all has been very quiet — Most of them were on Monday night. Cousens had theirs last night they had about 20 at Supper. What a falling off in the appearance of Tommy Harper, who can recollect the blooming boy and have any idea that he is the same person. I am afraid he has been living very freely, that is he has been plunged in Vice; I have been told that while he has been here, he has drank almost every night two or three or more Glasses of Spirits, or mixture.

Friday 9th. Novr.

I was settling the Constable's Accounts with W Loncaster last night, he is terribly exasperated at being deprived of his office he talks of not giving up the Book until he is obliged to do it, which I should think will not be long past. The most of his vexation proceeds from being told that he is not fit for any parish

---

[110] 'Such as the meeting soul may pierce, / In notes with many a winding bout / Of linkéd sweetness long drawn out.'—John Milton, *L'Allegro* (1632), lines 138-40.

[111] Sir Walter Scott, *Chronicles of the Canongate*. [First Series. *The Highland Widow. – The Two Drovers. – The Surgeon's Daughter.*] By the Author of Waverley ... Edinburgh: Cadell and Co., 1827. – 2 vols.

office; he was even told of it at Beverley fair so that his incapacity for a Constable has travelled from home; he is not much regarded.
Saturday 10th. Nov.

Measured 8a–2r–26p of Potatoe land at Provence which Mr. Shackleton has sold for 10 Guineas pr. Acre, he is at the expence of taking up and delivering at Crabley, there are many of them rotten, part of the land being very wet, I do not think it will be a very good speculation for the buyer; I cannot learn how many Pecks there are on an Acre, but from what I hear I think there may be 1200 Pecks. They are of various kinds some of them uncommonly large, I saw several as large as a Quart Pot.
Sunday 11th. Nov.

Ths. Harper has arrived from London, he saw Wm. on Wednesday week, he says he looks as well as ever he saw him. — Richd. Goldwell died today about noon, he had not been worse than usual, he has walked about nearly until the time of his Death; Mr. Barnard had taken the Trancledale Closes which the old man farmed, into his own hands at Michaelmas last, so that he has not long been without them; he is about 86 years of age, and it is said he has never been at Church since he was christened, nor any other place of worship. I have known his house for 20 years and never knew it washed in that time, nor perhaps long before.
Monday 12th. Nov.

Nothing done in the Corn Trade this day, as the prices do not seem to advance; the Maltsters, I think are rather nonplussed with the new Act, as it appears they will be more strictly looked after, for there has been so much roguery in the trade that at Wakefield Malt has sold generally at 10d. pr. quarter lower than here so that it is impossible to send Malt there for a market.
Tuesday 13th. Novr.

The Rockingham of last week says that the paragraphs in the papers last week, do not refer to Newspapers sent by post in this Country; but they may be sent at any time after the day of publishing. So the world goes, one says one thing and another contradicts it, so that they both find a subject for those who may read their news.
Wednesday 14th Octr. ['Nov' is written in pencil on this date and all until 19th]

Recd. a parcel from Wm. last night, and are sorry to hear that his Linen was in such a bad state in the Box, it is the more provoking as it was got up with so much care. — Cobbett has put forth his address to the freemen of Preston in which he tells them what he intends doing. He has so much work in the Planting and Gardening line, that he can spare but little time to be amongst the Electors, how then should he be elected will he find time to attend in Parliament? He promised in one number that in the next he would shew up the Turnpike trusts, but not a word has he said about it since.
Thursday 15th Nov

Sittings day today. There were many Servants to hire, but few I suppose were hired, as the Masters do not wish to give such high wages as they have done. There was a Constable meeting at Newlove's 23 dined and the Company broke up about five O'clock in a peaceable manner as meetings of Peace officers ought always to do.

Friday 16th Nov

What will be the consequence of the destruction of the Turkish fleet?[112] we shall perhaps hear how the Sultan relishes it, I suppose it will not go down very quietly, it appears that the Turks fought with great desperation, the loss of the English is large, but here it is talked very little about many persons scarcely knowing that there is such a Country as Greece.

Saturday 17th Nov

Mr. Kelso who lately preached at the Chapel and now lodges in Mrs. Gillett's parlour, had his Room broken open on Thursday night last and a Chest stolen out containing Money to the amount of nearly five hundred pounds chiefly in Sovereigns, the Chest was found the next morning in Mr. Ayre's Ruffham field Close without the property in it. It is a most serious loss.

Sunday 18th Nov

A very dull November day such a thick mist that one could see a very little way. There is no suspicion that I hear of any person getting Mr. Kelso's money,[113] he has suffered by hoarding Gold, he had better have laid it out in land even if he had bought it somewhat high.

Monday 19th Nov

As soon or very likely before a parson enters into orders, he commences running a race for lucre, he is no sooner a Curate but he is endeavouring with all his influence to procure a living, then when this is obtained, he is trying for some Prebendary or something more valuable than he possesses, and if we look at the Bishops, where is there so much scrambling for advancement as amongst them, they are never satisfied until they reach the topmost ladder of the good Church which they support, because it supports them ...

Wednesday 21st Novr

There is a long notice in the Hull Packet this day of a Tea Company, which it appears Ths. Harper is going to sell for, by Commission I suppose. I heard it mentioned before that he was going to sell for some London House by Commission, it is a safe way, if he can only command a Sale for his Goods, and the way for this, is to sell low and have them of prime quality.

Thursday 22nd. Nov.

This is Cave Sittings day but a small company here it being only the day before Martinmas; a very cold frosty day came on Snow towards night, very stormy, all pretty quiet.

---

[112] This was at the battle of Navarino fought on 20 Oct. 1827, when a combined British, French and Russian fleet under the command of Sir Edward Codrington decisively defeated a joint Turkish and Egyptian fleet. Three-quarters of the Turkish and Egyptian ships were destroyed with great loss of life; British losses were 75 killed and 197 wounded (*AR* 1827 Hist. 316–20 and Chron. 410–6).

[113] Revd Seth Kelso (1748?—1831) succeeded Mr Nettleship as minister of the South Cave Congregational chapel in 1824. As a young man he had been a weaver, but in 1796 he sailed as a missionary to Tahiti (where he was ordained) and later to the Friendly Islands. He returned to England in 1800. Before coming to South Cave, he was the first pastor of the Congregational chapel at Dent near Sedbergh in the Yorkshire Dales from 1809 to 1818 (Trout 11–13).

Friday 23rd. Nov

A good deal of Snow, and very cold which makes one to take badly to it as the change has come so sudden. I see that the young man of the name of Powell who robbed Sewell & Cross is left for execution,[114] it makes me shudder to think of it.

Saturday 24 Nov

I see there is a person of the name of Smith a Grocer who lives in the Corner Shop of Myton Gate and the Market place who has answered T. Harper's Advertisement for Cheap Teas and has offered his own full as low, he charges Tommy or the Company with publishing direct falsehoods, so amongst them be it.

Sunday 25th. Nov

It began to thaw rather this morning and so continued all the day but the Snow has wasted away very slowly. They say Old Lonc. is more put out by being thrown out of the Constable's Office, than the poor old preacher is in losing his money.

Monday 26th. Nov

Went to the West end today with Mr. Atkinson to settle some affairs which he had of the late Joseph Purdon's, he said he was glad he had got an end made of the trust he had been in, but I think he is out of Pocket by the Office he has held, which was to pay for the funerals of Joseph Purdon and his wife, for which the Old Man left thirty pounds in the hands of our Old friend before he died, it is thought he has laid out more than the Sum by five or six pounds but he has only Bills for about 26 pounds, he thinks he has more Bills but he cannot find them, so I persuaded him to take a little more time, that they may be looked for.

Tuesday 27th. Nov

Our old friend Mr. Atkinson had an Attorney's letter sent him last night by Thos. Clegg who is Mrs. Purdon's son in law to make him pay the balance of his Account which he was always willing to do as soon as he could be convinced that it was right, but he was so fearful of law that he settled I believe in his own wrong to the amount of nearly ten pounds, but he thinks if he can find his Bills that Thos. Clegg will pay him the money, so do I not think.

Wednesday 28th. Nov

A long discourse last night at West end on the Beauty of Fox hunting, and what an honour it is for a Gentleman to be first in the Chace, I maintained that he had no merit in it, for if there was any merit it belonged to his horse. Oh, but it showed a man to be a good rider to be the first, but this did not fall in with my ideas, so I told them to set the good rider upon a slow going horse, then if he could come in first there would be some merit due to him.

"The Squire is proud to see his courser strain,

---

[114] John Powell, aged 23, succeeded Henry Dunn (see n.43 (1826)) as clerk to Messrs. Sewell and Cross, silk merchants and haberdashers in Compton Street, Soho Square, London. Like his predecessor, he was caught stealing from his employers, but unlike Dunn who was sentenced to transportation, Powell was executed by hanging, on 22 Nov. 1827 (*TM* 19 Nov. 1827, 3 d).

"Or well-breath'd beagles sweep along the plain,–
"When his sleek gelding nimbly leaps the mound,
"And Ringwood opens on the tainted ground;
"Is that his praise? let Ringwood's fame alone;
"Just Ringwood leaves each Animal his own."[115]

Thursday 29th. Nov

No newspaper today. A dull dark November day, last night very stormy and a good deal of rain. There is a new Parson of the name of Horne who is it is said Brother to the Chancery Barrister of that name who has been appointed to the living of Hotham, he has commenced operations by raising the tithes, very much from what they were in Mr. Stillingfleet's time.[116]

Friday 30th. Nov

The paper which missed yesterday came this morning, but that which should have come this morning has not arrived, how the neglect is I cannot tell. Wrote a letter for Mr. Atkinson to send to York with £10.5.0 to pay for some Leather.

Saturday 1st Decr

A very stormy rainy day, the complaint now is that land is overset with wet, — two papers this morning both packed together, it appears that no tumults at Constantinople have ensued from the destruction of the Turkish Fleet, and I hope all will remain still.

Sunday 2nd Dec

I think there is no profession that requires so little talent as Church of England parsons, they have only to read, what they ought to have off by rote viz. the prayers and then to shew that some of them even cannot read a few disjointed remarks called a Sermon. No paper today.

Monday 3rd. Decr.

The paper which missed yesterday came this morning, but that which should have come this day did not arrive. This wet weather is all against Wheat being in good condition. 3 pounds a Quarter was asked for Old Wheat, and a sample of new this day was offered for 36s. it was very bad in quality.

Tuesday 4th. Decr.

The paper which missed yesterday did not arrive this day. I understand Ths. Marshall had got too much liquor last night and was quarrelling with Abm. Barff calling him about his Sparrow picked wheat. When Abm. was a farmer in his younger days about Gilberdike he gently thrashed over his wheat and then stacked the Straw, the Stack of which I understand was sold, but the Wheat that was left in it was so small and so little of it, that he said Sparrows had picked it, so it has been since then when any person has any thing against him to call him Sparrow picked Abm.

---

[115] Quotation from the the poem, 'To His Grace the Duke of Dorset' by Edward Young (1683–1765). In the original poem there are 4 additional lines between the second and third lines of the quotation (*EP*).

[116] The Revd James Stillingfleet, who died on 19 Dec. 1826, had been Rector of Hotham for nearly 56 years. His successor, the Revd William Horne, was the Rector there until 1844 (Hall, J. G. 139–41).

Wednesday 5th. Decr

The paper which should have come on Monday came packed up with the regular one this morning, with an account that two new tippetts[117] were coming, they were the very things that were wanted, and have caused much pleasure in the thoughts of receiving them on Friday next. John Wray of Brantingham died yesterday, he had been ill a long time.

Thursday 6th. Decr

Mr. Barnard has sent Teavil Leeson a notice signed by his tenants, not to shoot any more upon his Grounds. The west end self-stiled Esquire it is expected will be much galled by this proceeding. We are in the town at present not all on the most amicable terms. Old Lonc. for losing his Constable's Office, Mr. King for not getting pay for his Stones at his own price; and Teavil out of pure folly, these are the opposers of every thing not their own, but there is one comfort they are so perfectly silly that they are despised.

Friday 7th. Dec

Teavil Leeson when he got his discharge for shooting told the Keeper that he would send Mr. Barnard a challenge to fight him a Duel, which when he Mr. B. was informed of went down to see his adversary and met with him in the Street, and talked to him while Teavil stood like a post without saying any thing. Mr. B. told him he would shun such Characters as him as he would a Mad-dog.

Saturday 8th. Dec

The Box with the Tippetts arrived safe last night and were joyfully received, they are very nice ones and much liked. Measured some Turnips for Mr. Robinson of Mount Airy this afternoon in two lots about 12 Acres, staid and got tea and a pipe after[,] arrived at home about seven O'clock, a dark night.

Sunday 9th. Decr

I do not approve of Cobbett's plan of paying his Workmen in Provisions,[118] notwithstanding he says so much for it, yet he seems to know that there are more things than meat wanting, as House rent, Groceries, Clothing &c. &c he offers each Man 12lb. of Bread a Week which at the London prices is 2s.3d[,] 12lb. of Meat at 6d. is 6s. the Cheese he does not specify the quality, but we will suppose it to be worth 3s. pr. Wk. I think there is too little bread in proportion to the Meat & Cheese but I am sure money as wages would be preferred.

Monday 10th. Dec

A Very dark gloomy day, nothing scarcely done at the Market today, — Lord Muncaster who lives at Mr. Barnard's house at Brantingham keeps a few hounds, with which he goes out by himself alone frequently and blows his horn

---

[117] The tippet, often of lace or lawn, was an article of light female neck-wear worn around the neck and shoulders like a cape and distinguished by long hanging ends. It was used generally for day or evening wear, although there were heavier outdoor versions (Cunnington, C. W. and P. 360).

[118] Outlined in *CPR* 64 x (1 Dec.) 1827, 583–601.

to keep the Dogs together, but he generally contrives to lose some of them, then his Whipper-in has to range about after them and take them home if he can. This is fine employment for a young Lord!!

Tuesday 11th. Decr

Mr. Atkinson had seen a man today who had filled him full of knowledge, respecting a Steam engine for travelling Carriages,[119] which had been tried in the <u>Regency</u> park at London on Thursday last, moving at the rate of twelve miles an hour with 6 inside passengers and 15 outsides, he expects soon to see a full account in the newspapers, but has not much expectation that it will answer the purpose of travelling.

Wednesday 12th. Decr

No news yet of a satisfactory kind from Turkey, but I cannot think they will be so mad as to declare war against the Allies, it seems that some of the late Tories who were at the head of Government continue to exclaim against the destruction of the Turkish fleet, they are like the harriers of Lord Muncaster who yelp about and find themselves lost now that they are not in their Cribs.

Thursday 13th. Decr

For equanimity of temper commend me to old John Hallowell late of Ellerker, one day when he came in his wife Peggy contrived to hang herself up, which when old John saw he said, Peggy what is thou hanging thyself, then with great composure he looked for a knife to cut her down, which when he had found he strapped a few times on his old greasy leather breeches, and then proceded leisurely to cut the string which when he had accomplished, he said now Peggy if ever thou hang thyself again I will not cut thee down any more. The old Woman was gasping for breath but came about again.

Friday 14th. Decr

Richd. Marshall has got settled with Mr. Levitt for the Wold Close which he bought of him the last Spring. Mr. Levitt has likewise sold the house at Cave where his mother lived to Mr. Hill a Doctor who came the last year, he is a young man his father was a Builder at Cottingham. A very Stormy dark day, yesterday was very fine.

Saturday 15th. Decr

Old Billy Dunn had once been drinking at Brough, where he met with an old Parson of the name of Summers who formerly lived at Brantingham who had got himself very knoppy, they set off together and after many reels and full stops were tolerably fair on their way; when old Billy found out he was in Company with a Parson so he asked the learned Man if he would tell him who was the Father of Jethro? Jethro, Jethro, says the old Parson where dost thou come from? from So. Cave was the reply, then says his Reverence ask Garnons,

---

[119] Invented by Goldsworthy Gurney (1793–1875), this vehicle, although not the first of its kind, was remarkably successful, and incorporated Trevithick's design for a high-pressure steam jet which had been used to double the original speed of Stephenson's Rocket. Gurney's carriage made a particular virtue of safety and was designed to carry 21 passengers. In July 1829, this coach made a memorable journey from London to Bath at an average speed of 15 m.p.h., which was the first such long journey at a maintained speed made by any steam locomotive on either road or rail (*TM* 11 Dec. 1827; *DNB*).

ask Garnons, Garnons will tell thee who was Jethro's father. — Now this was a conscientious Clergyman who would not meddle with matters not in his own Parish.

Sunday 16th. Decr.

One would think to hear some of the Church Parsons that what they aim at is to explain away the meaning of the sacred Scriptures, they are in general the most worldly and tyrannical Sect that ever disgraced the Country they are nearly all rank Tories their principles if they have any are worse than the Radicals ever pretended to.

Monday 17th. Decr.

When Old Willy was in London he had a companion who bought a pair of Silk Stockings of a Jew, but when he attempted to put them on they all broke in pieces, they watched for the Jew and at last found him somewhere about Charing Cross when the man who bought the Stockings seized him by the Collar threatening vengeance against him if he would not return the money, but the Jew told him he had no money, and was an honest tradesman and did not want to take in the people, and if they would go with him to Leadenhall Street he would give him the money back, so off they walked with the Jew, who told them he was not the manufacturer of the Article and if they were bad, he had been taken in himself, all this went on very fairly till they arrived at a Court in Leadenhall Street entirely occupied by Jews, where they entered a house, the Jew said a few words to some men in the house and went up stairs. One of the men went out and soon brought in more of the same fraternity but the Stocking merchant they saw no more; the man then ordered them out, and began striking them when our two heroes turned again and defended them selves in the best manner they could, but they were soon overpowered by the Israelites, and after receiving a pretty good thumping they secured their retreat; and never saw either the Stocking selling Jew, the Court in Leadenhall Street or their money from that time to this.

Tuesday 18th. Decr

Going around town this Evening with Robt. Tindale the Constable, taking down names for the Militia, the Constable got a Brace of Pheasants given by Mr. Barnard's Gamekeeper, one of which he presented to me as we came home, it will be a fine treat for Wm. it is a beautiful Bird.

Wednesday 19th. Dec

Recd. the Paper with an account that the reading of the Cover could not be made out last week, I do not know how it has been, as I am always as careful as I can to have good Milk, I never heard of the like occurence [*sic*] before. A Poor blind Fidler came about today playing he said a Christmas tune or Hymn, I gave him a penny not to play it as I am not very fond of scraping of that kind; he went down stairs where Eliza and her mother gave him a halfpenny to play and sing his tune; I expected I had quitted him without any of his music but it proved otherwise.

Thursday 20th. Dec

I see by the Paper this morning that Lord Goderich[120] has tendered his resignation, it appears that he does not feel comfortable with his new honours upon him. — Rd. Marshall was thrashing with the Machine on Monday, and Thos. yesterday, they have no objection to Machines if they think to gain by them, I told them of the new Steam Carriage when they exclaimed against it as being an invention to ruin the Country especially Agriculturalists, as there will be neither horses nor corn wanting for it, their hearty wishes are that it may be blown up, — I have the Money to send tomorrow to the Stamp Office for the last Quarter which is £112.17s Busy in making out the Militia list which has to be put on the Church door on Sunday next. I have likewise the Ellerker list to make out for Watson Arton who is Constable.

[120] Frederick John Robinson (1782–1859), a Liberal Tory politician, was created Viscount Goderich in 1827 and Earl of Ripon in 1833. While Chancellor of the Exchequer from 1823 to 1827, he was known as 'Prosperity Robinson' because of his fiscal reforms including the abolition of many assessed taxes. As Lord Goderich, he was briefly and unsuccessfully Prime Minister, after Canning, from Aug. 1827 to Jan. 1828 (*DNB*).

1829 Jan. 1. Thursday

The year Rolls round and steals away,

The breath that first it gave.[1]

I think I have seen time represented in Hieroglaphycs [*sic*], by a Serpent biting its tail, to shew that time moves in a circle, which is a very just allusion. It advances rapidly, tho' one of our Poets says, "Flight in a circle urged advances nought". — My wife has been very busy in securing good luck this morning, taking care to get a Boy into the House at one door and walk him out at another, but while she was doing this a <u>Girl</u> got into the Kitchen but she was ordered off in a hurry, and might think herself happy to escape without a kicking for showing her <u>unlucky</u> face this morning.

Friday 2nd. Jany

Went to West Ella this morning, walked to Mount Airy where I borrowed Mr. Robinson's great Coat, brass ended riding whip and Horse, and left my Umbrella until I returned. My Mother looks remarkably well, I had not been there since July last having been so poorly, but I hope my illness is entirely gone, as at present I feel very well.

Saturday 3rd. Jany

This forenoon I had the Stamp Account to write over again it having been returned for the alledged [*sic*] mistake of one penny which they say I sent too much, altho' I do not think so myself, but I thought it was of no use remonstrating so I wrote the whole over again to please the Master, the Account contained 3 Sheets. Went at night to settle with Robt. Arton he being the Overseer. Young <u>Dab</u> the darling appears to be the Master at Castle farm, the Old Lady his Grandmother wanted to put him in a Slip which he did not choose to have on his person, so there she followed him about with it in her hand seeming as much afraid as though she were going to bag a Fox, but all would not do. So then the young Gentleman took up a pair of new Steel Scissors and opening them as wide as he could he took another pair of large ones and hacked the edges until they appeared somewhat like two handsaws, so when his mother wanted to use them, behold they would not cut, which I was not at all surprised at having seen the Actions of young Dab all along.

Sunday Jan. 4th

We had a fire in our little six cornered parlour which was very warm and comfortable, greatly in contrast to the open Air, which was very cold, as on the last night it had been frost, Snow, rain and a high wind, all these properly mixed up I think will make a Storm. I was reading an Old Magazine for 1773, where there is an account of a "Shirt ordinary": in a Street near Charing Cross, where Gentlemen might have their Shirts washed, a Cup of Coffee and two

---

[1] From the poem, 'Frail Life and Succeeding Eternity' by Isaac Watts (1674–1748) (*EP*).

Slices of Bread and Butter all for one Shilling and be dispatched within an hour with a clean Shirt.

Monday 5th. Jan

Politics with us are little attended to, the people have some Idea that Roman Catholics are strange formidable Creatures that would count nothing of running red hot pokers into the Bodies of the Holy protestants. I have asked some of them if they wish for a better neighbour than Billy Dodd of Ellerker, as he is one of the frightful bugbears, this sometimes rather nonplusses them but they get over it by saying it is for want of power in his party. He is a very quiet fellow and will take a glass with any Heretic and be as merry as any of them, caring no more for them than they do for the Pope. A very cold day.

Tuesday 6th. Jan.

At the Market last night, I think it has become a Custom with the Publicans to have Bread and Cheese on the table, at the commencement of the year, for the accommodation of their Customers. I can say nothing against it, if it do not encourage the partakers to have an extra Glass, then they might as well have purchased eating for themselves. Last night the buyers of Corn not very anxious to purchase, altho' the farmers took all the pains they could, as they have long done to persuade the factors of the deficiency of the Crop, but this seemed to have but small effect. The Farmers but ill conceal their joy at the high prices but say the price is not adequate to the deficiency, however all the poor know that it is far too high for the wages they receive.

Wednesday 7th. Jany.

A Party of Poachers on Sunday night last, made an attack on the Game belonging to the Duke of Devonshire at Londesborough[2] near Market Weighton, when they were discovered by a party of the Keepers and helpers, and a Scuffle ensued in which the Poachers fired on the keepers and dangerously wounded two of them, one of whom died on Monday the other has lost an eye and [is] not expected to recover; the Poachers were finally overpowered and three or four of them committed to York Castle, one of them it is said is a Man of the name of Sellers who was working at Mr. Barnard's last year, I do not know him, another of the name of Clark whose Father lives upon Wallingfen, and a third is the son of a Publican at Market Weighton of the name of Sturdy. This is the Current report perhaps it may be magnified. When will these bloody game laws be mitigated,[3] and the sacrifice of human lives cease from being offered to them?

---

[2] The Londesborough estate was owned, but rarely visited by, the Dukes of Devonshire from 1753 to 1845. In 1829 its owner was William George Spencer Cavendish, 6th Duke of Devonshire (1790–1858) who was responsible for demolishing the old hall and modernizing the estate (Neave (1977) 18–20; *DNB*).

[3] From the 14th c. until 1831, no-one was allowed to kill game, or certain other animals including rabbits, unless qualified to do so by the ownership of land worth £100 or more per annum, or by social status. At this time, the game laws were embodied in more than 2 dozen separate acts. Two years later, however, they were brought together under a single umbrella, the Game Act of 1831 (1 & 2 Will. IV c. 32), which enacted that the right to kill game should be conditional on the possession of a game licence (EB xi. 440–3).

Thursday 8th. Jan.

The Man I mentioned yesterday as dead who was shot by the Poachers is still living, so that common report in that instance as in many others is a common liar, I am glad it is not true, I am not like the Editors of Newspapers who with their fingers twisted up begin to make an awkward apology for some false report which they have published generally taking care to say that they had it from a correspondent on whose veracity they could <u>re-ly</u>.

Friday 9th. Jan

Last week I was gardening, setting Cabbages, cutting Gooseberry trees, planting daisies &c. but this week has put a stop to all work of that kind; as winter in his white robe has paid us a visit, I am not partial to his Company but as in other cases so here one's own choice cannot always be had. Some people say they are very fond of frosty weather, but I never cordially believed them: as to its being more healthy I am rather sceptical, for in winter it has been observed that more old people die than at any other time ...

Sunday 11th. Jan.

A very cold day. Only prayers at Church in the forenoon, and a thing by Courtesy called a Sermon in the afternoon only preaching once a day, that is the same as once a week; How can a man who is ignorant of the first principles of any Science be supposed capable of explaining the difficulties in the more abstruse parts. The Organ is ground as usual. In the 21st. Chap. of Job the Organ is mentioned along with other sounding things of the same kind, but in no praise worthy manner. I count no more of the great bellowing, blethering, bellweather, than the honest Irishman did of the Church Clock, who set his watch by it in the morning, and at night returned to see how they had kept time together, when taking out his watch he said "Och and is it you ye great Braggadocia my little time piece made by Mr. O Callaghan has beat you three hours this blessed day!!!" ...

Tuesday 13th. Jan

Mountebanks were here yesterday, inveigling people to put in their Shillings in hopes of getting prizes. At night it is said they were acting some kind of play: these sort of actors are at the fag end of the profession; but Thespis who was the first of this Class was much such another as these runagates, witness the following

"Thespis the first professor of this art,

At Country wakes sung Ballads in a Cart."[4]

Wednesday 14th. Jan

Wrote a letter for Richd. Kirby to his Club at Etton to take himself off, he has been very ill a long time, but is now getting better; his wife died sometime last Summer, he spoke to me to make his Will, for which purpose I shall shortly

---

[4] This is very slightly misquoted. The correct quotation, which is from John Dryden's 'Prologue - Sophonisba' in his *Prologues and Epilogues* is: 'Thespis the first professor of our art, / At country wakes sung ballads from a cart.'

attend him, with my treatise on Wills,[5] this is the only law Book I ever had and I find it useful, the last will I made was for Rd. Thornton's wife, who died a short time since.

Thursday 15th. Jan

There was a miniature edition of Plough Boys with their usual attendants of Fools with black faces and hump backs from this town the last two days, consisting for the most part of Boys from 10 to 12 years of age, dressed as fine as they could be made in Ribbons with most enormous paper Caps on their heads covered over with tinsel, which made them look as if they had extinguishers on their heads, then the little imps had swords in their hands not too bright; and sung and danced like their betters, if indeed they had any; the last night after paying the Fidler, they met to spend their money, while some of their Mothers were obliged to fetch them home, this must be the march of Folly.

Friday 16th. Jan

Dr. Johnson in his Journey to Scotland,[6] says the people have a method of polluting the Breakfast table with Slices of Cheshire cheese, had I been there I should have thought it rather a treat than been polluted with it, but the tastes of People are so various that there is no standard of government; there would be neither Cucumbers nor Oysters eaten had every one my taste ...

Sunday 18th. Jan

At church today where the Meritmonger held forth about twenty minutes, he tells his hearers there is no such thing as Conversion, and they need not look for any change of heart, as there is no other change than what they recd. at their Baptism when according to him they were regenerated. I do believe there never will be any change in his hearers if they believe this doctrine. These high Churchmen who exclaim so much against Popery are the greatest Slaves to the Popish doctrine of Churchly supremacy: they either know or may know that they enjoy the Spoils of the old Lady of Babylon and proud they are to wear her cast clothes.

Monday 19th. Jan

Mrs. Rd. Marshall has been and is very ill, and I think pride has brought much of it on, for they have got a Parlour fitted up with a good Carpet, the Walls painted, fine Window Curtains, polished Irons, grand Glass &c.&c. but fine furniture like fine Clothing is of no use to the owner except it creates the envy of those who cannot afford to be ridiculous. But the Lady about Christmas thought she was not very well so she adjourned to the Parlour and sat in state,

[5] Thomas Wentworth, *The Office and Duty of Executors;or, A Treatise of Wills and Executors ...* To which is added an appendix by Thomas Manley. London, 1676. The earliest edition of this work had been published in 1641 and numerous other updated editions continued to be published well into the 19th c. Although RS does not specifically cite this work, it is likely that it is his 'treatise on Wills ... the only law Book [he] ever had'. He also cites Thomas Manley as the author of William Leybourn's *The Compleat Surveyor ...* (1674) so that it is possible that he was confusing the authorship of 2 almost equally old works in his possession.

[6] Samuel Johnson, *A Journey to the Western Islands of Scotland*, with remarks by the Revd Donald McNicol ... Glasgow: R. Chapman, 1817. Pp. vi, 504. First published London: J. Pope, 1775. Pp. 268. Also 'New ed.' Edinburgh, 1819.

where her neighbours had an opportunity of seeing her and her furniture together; but, lo & behold! she really grew ill from the dampness of the Room, and the Doctor was obliged to be had, and her display brought down by bleeding and blistering, and she now has a Screen put up to keep the cold off. O, Vanity many are thy Votaries.

Tuesday 20th. Jan

John Ramsdale was here yesterday, he has quite a Farmer look, I had not seen him lately, so that at the first I scarce knew him. Peter Foster of West Ella is dead, and James has taken his farm, and is going to it in a week or two; John is quite elevated at the thought of it, as he will have the Company he likes which are Horses, they will keep Chaise and Post horses as usual, and John says he will be bound for it he can drive them as well as any Post Boy on the Road. Recd. the Examiner & Cobbett of the 11th. Jan. I wish people were capable of writing a paper direction, and not say <u>South Cave – Hull</u>.

Wednesday 21st. Jan

I have read Cobbett's Register of the 11th. inst. which he says is printed on paper made from the husks of his Corn; this certainly is a valuable discovery. As to the quality of the paper for writing or even printing, I cannot say much in favour of it, but as it is a first essay it is to be recommended. I should like to have a few Grains of his Corn, I think I could find a little room to plant them in, they would at least be a curiosity. Cobbett talks of holding or shewing up Mr. Waithman, his hands must be nearly full of this kind of work, he pulls O'Connell pretty well in pieces,[7] it is like Dog eating Dog, however I do not care if he worry the Irish Demagogue; Cobbett seems to be like Ishmael, whose hand was against every man and every Man's hand against him.

Thursday 22nd. Jan

A Man of the name of Wainman who lived at Anlaby, and came here twice a week with Fish, hanged himself in his own Stable on Tuesday last; I have heard no cause for the rash act, it is said he had not a good Character, he always appeared remarkably cheerful and talkative. — The Postman who took the letters from Cave to Welton and back every day has been charged with secreting, purloining or in plain English stealing a letter containing a five pound Note and it is reported he has been committed to prison for the Offence it is said this is not the first time that money has been missed out of the letters which he had entrusted to him; he is likewise accused with keeping back post paid letters, he is an old Man & indulged in drinking.

Friday 23rd. Jan

There are various Opinions on the quantity of Corn in the Country one party which includes the Farmers in general, say the Crops are so bad, that Wheat does not yield half the produce on an Average, which it ought to do, yet with this scarcity staring them in the face, they in general deprecate the importation of foreign Corn; but they know not, nor care how the people are to

---

[7] In his articles, 'Decline and Fall of the "Member for Clare"' and 'Decline and Fall of Big O' (*CPR* 67 i (3 Jan.) 1829, 25–32 and 67 ii (10 Jan.) 1829, 42–59).

be fed, only they get enormous prices for what they have to sell. Another party which consists of Old Women, or men as silly—assert that there is plenty of Corn, and to spare in the Country, so that the price of Flour ought not to be above 2s. pr. Stone. It is in my opinion certain that Corn is wanted, and without doubt the Harvest has been greatly deficient, and I think we shall stand in need of all the foreign Grain that can be had, a few thousand quarters are like nothing. One hundred thousand quarters which has a great sound would not be a supply to the Country for the half of one week; but if it be as the Times says that there will be an importation of 1,500,000 Quarters, it may supply a population of 12 Millions for about six weeks ...

Sunday 25th. Jan

There has been a meeting of the East Riding Clergy at Beverley to petition against any further concession to the Catholics, the Revd. Jn. Gilby L.L.B. Rector of Barmston[8] with a thousand a year for scarce ever preaching was Chairman. These letters L.L.B. for any thing I know signify a person learned in the knowledge of boiled Turkies. The Archdeacon it appears refused to call the mercenaries together by his authority. This shewed a little sense.

Monday 26th. Jan

A most dreadful Stormy day, it has been a great deal of Snow and dismal starving weather for most of a week past. This morning the Snow was so much drifted one could scarce get in and out of the Cross. I think we fell in for more than our portion, this snowy weather is my aversion. It has frozen very hard, but I think I have known it more severe as all our Ink has been at times frozen.

Tuesday 27th. Jan

It is a long time since I have said any thing of the long Miller; I lately heard that Willy Milner had been down to settle with him, but he was not at home, so he left word for Friend Tom to meet him at Jem Levitt's that night and as he is not often backward to attend where he can fall in for Rum and Water he attended, when Willy presented his Bill for Walling, Jobbing, &c. So the Miller looked it over and said this is a strange great Bill of thine Willy, it is right was the reply, Aye very like says the Man of Dust it may for ought I know, but I tell thee it is a great one, So Tom produced his which struck little Willy comical for when he saw it he said I am sorry I cannot settle with you tonight. Whya what the Devil did thou call me here for then? Willy complained he had no money. So the Man of the Mill the first time he came called at Willy's house and enquired of his wife for the Master, but he was not there, but says she perhaps I can do as well, Whya says Tom I called about settling, Aye replies she but your Bill is not right, you have set down more Flour than we have had, for I have been at my Father's so long. O D—n it says he are you up to that, then its ower. Then Willy just arrived, Now my lad says Tom I have just called to settle with thee, as I want a little Money why says the little Waller what has my Wife

[8] John Gilby was Rector of Barmston from 1790 until his death in 1829. According to the Diary entry for 1/8/29, he was said to have left an estate of £120,000.

said to you. Curse thee for a feal to ask me when thou teld her what to say, now I mun be hobbled with you beath.

Wednesday 28th. Jan

The Edinburgh Murders[9] which were attrocious [*sic*] as any that could be committed, as they were entirely for the basest interest without any malice against the unfortunate victims. I think that the Surgeons were as guilty as the murderers, for with all their <u>subjects</u> they know but little of their profession, if they are unable to distinguish between a person who has died a natural death, and one that has come to a violent end. Were a few of the Doctors handed over to the hangman, it might be a means of making the remainder study something better than hacking up human bodies, but I believe it is dispensing with Study that makes them in love with this worse than barbarous employment. — Some person has told Old Willy that there are six Resurrection men in this town he seems to credit it, but cannot conjecture who they are!! If he was told that Six Indian Jugglers would swallow the Church, Steeple, Parson, Clerk & Churchwardens, it would alarm him as he is one of the latter Officers.

Thursday 29th. Jan

There is some talk of the Mail from Hull to Weighton coming through here, there are at present two Mails go through Beverley, and since the new Road from Hull to Ferriby has been made through Hessle,[10] it is reported it is much better and easier than the old one by Swanland field and Anlaby, therefore it is thought it would be an advantage for one of the Mails to come this way; it is proposed to change Horses at Welton which is about half way between Hull and Weighton.

Friday 30th. Jan

The Hull Packet man says he has had complaints from some of his sage subscribers that his paper is too large, seeming to think that they were obliged to read all that it contained; so he made it less, and to shew his wisdom published a sort of supplement on a half sheet printed on one side containing something about a Gas trial at Beverley Sessions,[11] this was the second week after he used a less paper. The Times on the contrary has published a Paper

---

[9] The murders were committed in Edinburgh in the previous year by 2 Irish labourers, William Burke and William Hare. This was the period of the resurrectionists, who illegally and secretly disinterred newly buried bodies and sold them to surgeons for dissection. Not content simply to disinter the already dead, Burke and Hare had murdered at least 15 victims by suffocation. They sold the corpses to a certain Dr Robert Knox at prices varying from £8 to £14. After their arrest, Hare turned king's evidence thus escaping the death penalty. Burke was found guilty and hanged on 28 Jan. 1829, the very date of RS's diary entry (*AR* 1828 Chron. 365–85 and 1829 Chron. 19–20).

[10] The Hull–Hessle–Ferriby turnpike Bill was sponsored early in 1825 by, among others, the Hull solicitor and historian, Charles Frost, and received widespread support from several owners of estates in the district. Despite stiff opposition from the Hull–Anlaby–Kirk Ella turnpike trustees (inaugurated 1745) who rightly recognized in the proposed new trust a serious rival to themselves, the Act was duly obtained and tolls instituted on the new road on 28 July 1825 (MacMahon 36).

[11] The supplement covered the proceedings at the Quarter Sessions at Beverley concerning a dispute between the British Gas Lighting Company and its former agent, Mr Hill (*HP* 20 Jan. 1829).

double the size; for my part I shall not complain of any of them being too large, for what I do not like to read I can omit ...

Sunday 1st. Feb

Now for a little of the march of intellect in the Country. A Cave Man W. Cousens bound his Son Apprentice to a Shopkeeper at Howden, but as he always was allowed his own way at home I suppose he did not think himself under any obligation to obey his master, neither did his Master wish to submit to the behaviour of his Apprentice, so they came to some kind of agreement, and the Indentures were given up when he had 8 or 9 Months to serve. So his Parents to shew their love to the Son who had unexpectedly got his time out, made a Supper to celebrate the auspicious event. This shews that some people are more simple than one could expect to find them. Many Persons would rather have mourned than rejoiced on such an occasion; for what kind of recommendation can he have to any place of respectability?

Monday 2nd. Feb.

I was very poorly last night, having got something I think that did not agree with me, but I am quite well & hearty this morning for which I am very thankful. — I think some parts of my Journal may be compared to the intelligence in the Court circular which begins with telling us the news and ends with saying the result of the conferences is a secret, however I find something every day to notice. As for example this morning it is a very hard frost and has been so for three or four days past; there is a great deal of Snow on the Ground, and last night it was a strong Rime or hoar frost.

Tuesday 3rd. Feb

The Bishop of London it appears is shewing a great share of intolerancy, if as it is reported, he has refused his Churches for Sermons for Charitable purposes where Dissenters are joined in the same cause with Churchmen:[12] so the Bishop in an authoritative manner is resolved to put a stop to Brethren living together in unity — I doubt not but the Dissenters are more liberal subscribers to Charitable institutions, than the Church monopolists in general are, with all their pomp and Authority: there were some of old who professed a great deal for the purpose of being seen of men; and there is the same spirit at work in our days.

Wednesday 4th. Feb.

Paid Abraham Barff for a Pig weighing 20 Stone 4 pounds at 7s. per Stone. — Bought another Pig of Frankish Cress 13st. 8lb at 6s–7½d pr. Stone. As we are Bacon sellers[13] we shall have something to begin with. We sell Flour, Barley meal, Pollard,[14] Bran, Bacon, white pease, Cheese, Herrings, Bread,

---

[12] Charles James Blomfield (1786–1857), Bishop of London, was severely censured in *The Times* for his decision not to allow sermons to be preached, in any of the churches in his diocese, in support of charities or religious societies which were managed by committees with one or more dissenters among their members (*DNB*; *TM* 29 Jan. 1829, 2 d; 31 Jan 1829, 2 c; 3 Feb. 1829, 2 b).

[13] The Sharps had recently started to run a shop, near the market hall, selling food and general stores. It did not prove to be particularly successful, and they gave it up in the spring of 1833.

[14] i.e. fine bran sifted from flour; also flour or meal containing fine bran (*OED*).

Butter, Same, &c., &c. We have sold nearly 200 Stone of Flour, Barley meal &c. within the last month, but as it is a critical time for Flour selling, some of it has been without profit. We keep Capital Tea, Sugar, Tobacco &c. — indeed all our Articles are of the best quality, which indeed they ought to be, as we are under no obligation for Credit to any Person we deal with, So that what we want we can purchase where we please, without any fear of having inferior Goods. May Providence give us prosperity.

Feb. 5 Thursday

The following was related to me as a fact which occurred some time ago. The Vicar of St. Mary's Church in Beverley[15] is what is called a high Churchman, he keeps a Journeyman parson and as Masters generally choose the lightest work, he read the Prayers at the end of which his Lacquey mounted the Pulpit, when the Master sat down, and put his hand before his face as if musing or meditating, but after leaning in this manner some time, he threw back his head when it was evident he was fast asleep, and so he continued till the end of the Sermon, and there he was left after the Congregation had gone out, when some who had a little Compassion and part boldness went back and shook the Revd. Gentleman by the Collar and really awaked him.

Friday 6th. Feb

That far famed building the Minster at York by some means caught fire on Sunday night last,[16] and was not discovered until Monday morning when soon after part of the Roof fell in. It was still burning on Tuesday, the accounts we have had are full of confusion respecting the Accident[.] My Opinion is that the stinking Gas had caught fire, but this is not the general belief. The damage done has been estimated at from 70,000 to 300,000 pounds, the lofty Columns, lengthened Aisles and painted windows, are one mass of ruins—It is one of the largest buildings in England the length from East to West is 524 Feet, the Breadth of the Body and Aisles 100 Feet and the height of the Lantern tower 235 Feet ...

Sunday 8th. Feb

What a great many officers, belong to York Minster, the names or titles of whom have no foundation in Scripture. First the <u>Arch</u>. Bishop, then the Dean, then Canons residentiary, Precentor, Chancellor of the Church, Sub-dean, Succentor of the Canons, Arch-Deacons, Prebendaries, College of Vicars, Organist, Clerk of the Vestry, Singing men, Boys and Vergers. Then there is the Ecclesiastical Court (which is a sort of Protestant Inquisition) with a

---

[15] i.e. Revd William Robinson Gilby, son of Revd John Gilby, Rector of Barmston. He was instituted as Vicar of St. Mary's Church in 1823 and later held the office of Mayor of Beverley for 1834/5 (Oliver 365; *VCHYER* vi. 205 and 274).

[16] The fire was started deliberately by a certain Jonathan Martin who, after evening service on Sunday, 1 Feb 1829, concealed himself in the north transept until after midnight when he set fire to some music books that he had placed under the organ. He was subsequently captured, found to be insane, and detained in an asylum. The fire was not discovered until the Monday morning and not extinguished until that night. It did a great deal of damage: the choir was gutted, much of the glass in the windows broken beyond repair, and the roof collapsed. A restoration fund was established and on 6 May 1832 the choir was re-opened for service (*AR* 1829, Chron. 23–4, 43–4, and 301–6; Knight 600–1).

Chancellor, Commissary and Deputy Registrar, and a host of Proctors and Apparitors. — Now if any man can prove all or any of these to be necessary, or consonant to the Gospel, I will give him credit for seeing further than I can do. The Simplicity of the Gospel is overrun with Pomp and Shew ...

Friday 13th. Feb

Most of the talk here is of Jonathan Martin the poor Maniac who set fire to York Minster it appears he left York, immediately on his committing the crime and made the best of his way into the North, where he was taken at Hexham in Northumberland, and brought back to York. On his examination he tells some of his Dreams, and confessed it was himself who set fire to the Building. He seems to have great Antipathy to the Black Coats, from what cause he does not say, however he set their <u>God</u> on Fire, he has silenced the 5000 piped Organ. It appears he ought to have been confined in an Asylum instead of being at large, he is without doubt as crazy as ever Peg Nicholson was ...

Monday 16th. Feb

Four Men for assaulting Tindale (of the three tuns) and his wife were taken before the Justices this day and fined one pound each and 4 Shillings a piece expences, this will be a means of stopping great headstrong fellows who get drunk and think they will have all things their own way. Rd. Kirby was also there on a Summons to shew cause why he did not maintain his Son John, without applying to the Parish for work, but he came off without having any thing laid on him.

Tuesday 17 Feb

Grievous lamentations at the Market yesterday, on account of Corn getting lower, it was fully expected that before this time wheat would have been Five pounds a Quarter and now it is worth little more than three; I hope the price will be kept down, as the spring puts in there will be more importations from abroad, indeed I am surprised that Wheat should come from such Countries as Spain & Italy, but it appears very plain we can have it from almost any place at high prices; Our Merchants are to be praised for their exertions. although they do it for individual profit yet it is a national benefit.

Wednesday 18th. Feb

Measured Mr. Cook's Turnip Land, Ryland Hill 8a–3r–14p top of Wold 11a–0r–21p. these Turnips were not eaten, and it came on a heavy shower, which made it very uncomfortable among the Turnip tops, got done just before dark, then came home and got some tea, which quite refreshed me. Frost this morning.

Thursday 19th. Feb

Writing Copies of Affidavits in Chancery for Mr. Robinson in the matter of Barney Gelder of Cliffe a Bankrupt, but they are so unintelligible that I can hardly guess at the meaning. It seems that the Assignees under the Bankruptcy had sworn that the Auctioneer was drunk at the Sale, then he comes with his Affidavit and some of his friends to contradict it, and swears that he only drank one Glass of Gin and Water at the said Sale and this occupies nearly eight Sheets of Paper.

Friday 20th. Feb

Wrote a letter to Mr. Coltman of Beverley[17] in answer to one from him, desiring me to make enquiries respecting the Family of Mr. Wakefield who formerly lived at Rowley, Mr. Coltman is the Grandson of the late Mr. Wakefield, and wanted to know the maiden name of his Grandmother likewise what Children she had besides his Mother, and whether they died married or unmarried. There were two Sons and a Daughter besides his Mother who all died unmarried. One Son I understand was a great Companion of Stephen Forge when in his Prosperity on a Farm at Riplingham and was as drunken as old Steen himself.

Saturday 21st. Feb

Copying some deeds for Mr. Robinson not quite so unmeaning as the Chancery affidavits, they were attested Copies. At Brantingham this forenoon at Miss Wrottesleys School. She has nine or ten young Ladies[,] rained as I came back got rather wet, very uncomfortable day.

I see the Catholic Association has dissolved itself.[18] I think it is a wise plan, I never liked such headstrong meetings. It seems now that the Catholics will get some redress; the Tory papers are absolutely mad about it, but if it be a Government measure they will soon come round again and show their loyalty!!!

...

Monday 23rd. Feb

The Editor of the Yorkshire Gazette, alias the Soot Bag is about as insane as Jonathan Martin, he cannot call the Duke of Wellington in a decent way, but lets his Pen off ~~at him~~ so choaked with filth both at him and his Colleagues that its characters are nearly illegible. Nay I do not know whether he will suffer the King to reign if he does not keep himself within bounds, This is one of the rank Tory papers which has all on a sudden, begun to cry out for popular rights and an appeal to the People, not a month ago no flattery was too gross for the Duke and the Ministry, but I have no fear that this wise man will long continue to bawl out against the Government, this true supporter of the Church will like all Church Weathercocks when kept properly oiled turn with the wind, for his Paper is in a great measure supported by high Churchmen.

Tuesday 24th. Feb

I met with a man last night by name John Waltham of Newbald who was Collector of the Property tax and Assd. taxes the first time I was at Beverley on that Account; he has been assessor for 21 years, and says he is a Scholar for he went to School for 15 years together; he told me that when the consolidated Bill for the Assd. taxes was passed he had some sharp work with Mr. Smelt respecting the manner of making out the Bills. Mr. Smelt told him they were completely wrong, but Waltham told him he was worth 8 or 9 thousand pounds

---

[17] See n.24 (1836).

[18] Peel's bill for the suppression of the Catholic Association introduced on 10 Feb. 1829 was passed almost unopposed since the Association's aims were to be fulfilled in the forthcoming legislation for Catholic emancipation embodied in the Relief Bill scheduled for 5 Mar. that year (Walpole ii. 406–7).

and knew as well how to make out the Bills as he did. Mr. S. thought otherwise and returned them for correction, for which Waltham said he was a silly fellow, for says he I made them out in the consolidated form that is <u>all separate</u> for consolidate says he means to keep separate; after this Specimen of his Scholarship I was satisfied that he might have gone to School until now, and had lessons yet to learn, but he still stands to it that he is a Scholar, which many Farmers are not and find themselves at a loss: but he has learning at his fingers end.

Wednesday 25. Feb.

Lord Muncaster who lived at Brantingham in Mr. Barnard's house has left it in disgust, but for what I cannot say, it is reported he wanted a lease of it, which they were not willing to grant, So his Lordship and his yelping Dogs are all gone together; this does not seem a congenial Soil for Sprigs of Nobility to flourish in. He was married a few weeks ago to a Daughter of Sir John Ramsden who is the owner of all the Town of Huddersfield except one house which belongs to a Quaker, which he even cannot purchase.[19]

Thursday 26th. Feb

Eliza fell yesterday in going out of the Kitchen, and broke a Bone in her Elbow, which is very painful, we got Mr. Tinsdill to her yesterday who bound it up, and she slept tolerably well last night, and feels easier this morning. I hope it will be better soon, Mr. Tinsdill says it will be a fortnight before she be better. She is obliged to attend the School with her Arm in a sling.

Friday 27th. Feb

A Vestry meeting was given notice for on Sunday last by the Overseers, for laying a rate for the Poor, the time was six O'clock but the Overseers did not appear so at the end of half an hour the meeting dissolved, the Overseers were then just coming at the Church Steps, but the Churchwardens would not return to sign the rate, this is the second time the Churchwardens have put off the Overseers; about a week ago the Overseers got a Summons for the Churchwardens for not signing the Rate, but the Justices, ordered a meeting to be called for the purpose, and this is the result, — Here is nothing but contradiction and Opposition going on in the Town.

Saturday 28th. Feb

I do not know how it is but I am generally in the Opposition and frequently in the Minority, here they are all mad against any relief to the Catholics; whether it be a natural Sympathy that causes me to wish well to the oppressed

---

[19] Sir John Ramsden (1755–1839) initiated a number of large-scale speculative building development projects in Huddersfield. Among the many stories that circulated about him, is the one relating to the Quaker and the sovereigns. According to this story, Sir Robert, as Lord of the Manor, was the owner of the entire town of Huddersfield with the exception of a small house belonging to a Quaker blacksmith called Tommy Firth. Wishing to purchase this property and thus become the owner of all Huddersfield, Sir Robert approached Tommy who asked him what he would pay. 'I'll cover the kitchen floor with sovereigns', said the Baronet. 'Will thou lay them edgewise?', asked Tommy. 'No, I'll cover your floor with them, but I'll lay them flat', replied the Baronet. This offer was refused, and the Quaker blacksmith ended the conversation by saying, 'Ah, well then, Sir John, Huddersfield belongs to thee and me' (Ahier i. 63–5).

or a spirit of contradiction in Argument that urges me to oppose, the domineering Spirit at present abroad I cannot say, perhaps it is a little of both.

Sunday 1st March

A Lady (Mrs. Wrottesley Mother to the young Lady who keeps the School at Brantingham) asked me yesterday how the people at Cave were affected to the Catholics, I told her they were nearly without exception stanch protestants, which she was very glad to hear. I did not think it worth while to Volunteer my own Opinions, but suggested that persons of any religious persuasion ought not to be debarred from Civil rights, when she immediately said but what will become of the Church and its ministers. I now saw that she thought the Tythes were in danger, so contented myself with hoping the Clergy would if possible be more pious than they some of them are at present.

Monday 2nd. March

The following two placards were stuck on the Cross sometime last night. One was "To the Poor, beware, look about you Sheep heads are a Shilling a piece at Val Tindales" the other "Glorious news for the Farmers, Sheep heads a Shilling a piece, what is a fat Sheep worth?" I have no idea of the writer or who it can have been. — Two papers this morning, not having had one yesterday.

Tuesday 3rd. March

I am not sure that Pall-Mall has always been pronounced Pell-Mell, for I have the following lines in recollection which makes wretched metre, if always sounded as they are now, the lines allude to Kitty Fisher an infamous Courtezan[20] who fell from her horse in the Park.

> "Poor Kitty had thy only fall,
> Been that thou met'st with in the Mall
> It might deserve our pity;
> But long before that luckless day,
> With equal justice we might say,
> Alas! Poor fallen Kitty."

Wednesday 4th. March

I am in the midst of moral Sentences, and short pithy instructions: for any person who perused a parcel of Copy Books will at once perceive that they are well qualified to instruct, if indeed they be at all noticed: they appear to be a collection from various Sages, and in general are excellent for their brevity, so that the memory may not be burthened by thinking of too much at a time.

Thursday 5th. March

The Anti-catholic meeting at Hull on Monday last has gone off in the manner I expected, the requisitionists had all their own way, not one word from the Opposition against the Petition, it was in fact a meeting, where there would not have been any chance for Argument; I am informed that it was at one time

---

[20] Kitty Fisher, born Katherine Maria Fisher or Fischer, was a famous courtesan in mid-18th c. London. She posed as a model for several paintings by Sir Joshua Reynolds and was the subject of numerous lampoons and satires published around 1759 and 1760. In 1766 she was married to John Norris, MP for Rye and owner of Hemsted Manor near Benenden in Kent, but died of consumption the following year (*NQ* 3rd ser. viii. 81–2 and 155; 3rd ser. x. 375; 10th ser. xi. 245–6; *DNB*).

the intention of the Vicar of the High Church to have offered some Arguments in favour of Conciliation, but this was abandoned before the meeting took place. The Irishman O'Neil is the man they adore at present, and our friend Dan[21] I doubt will stand a poor chance of being returned at the next election, except the Government carry the measures they intend into execution, then indeed things may be materially altered, and Dan will be again the Man of the People.

Friday 6th. March

Mr. Barnard's Rent day yesterday. We got Mr. Carter who is one of the tenants to look at Eliza's arm, he said it was going on very well and that it had not been broken, a bone might have been dislocated, but he says it will be some time before it be well; he lifted her arm to her head which caused much pain. I hope it is in a mending way.

Saturday 7th. March

I once called at the Malt Shovel,[22] this is a real hedge Alehouse I suppose they were more frequent formerly than they now are. I called for a pint of Ale, and desired the Old Woman to be as quick as she could, but she said, "Whya pray you Sor sit down a bit while I wash my hands for I have been sweeping Chimler this morning" so I thought I might as well exercise a little patience until the Old Lady was ready to appear clean washed; in the mean time I took a view of the Room; Chimney piece there was none, therefore it stood in no need of ornaments; in one of the Corners was a Shelf on which was placed that useful article a tinder Box, and a Shoe brush or two in a recess, commonly called a hole in the Wall. In the other Corner was turned upside down to hinder the dust from entering, a tin Can, used for airing the Ale of such Customers who chose that indulgence; two or three Laths nailed to the joists displayed a collection of old black Tobacco pipes, one of which the good Woman would have accommodated me with assuring me they were superior to clean ones, which I did not in the least doubt or wish to try. — I will say no more on this head as the Old Landlady is lately dead. Peace be to her memory.

Sunday 8th. March

There was an Anti-catholic meeting at Beverley on Thursday last, at the New Sessions house, but as there were some Gentlemen of liberal Opinions, the Protestants as they proudly call themselves adjourned to the Market Place that they might not be disturbed by the Opposition. The liberal Gentlemen were Mr. Bethell of Rise,[23] the Revd. J. Coltman[,] Mr. Beverley[,] young Mr.

---

[21] Daniel Sykes, whose staunch advocacy of Catholic Emancipation was not popular in Hull at that time, decided not to stand for the town in the 1830 election. He did, however, stand successsfully for Beverley. (See also Appendix 2).

[22] Situated near Riplingham toll bar about 3¼ miles east of South Cave on the North Cave–Kirk Ella–Hull turnpike owned by the Beverley, Hessle, North Cave Trust. It is featured on the O.S. 6 in. map of 1855.

[23] Richard Bethell (1772–1864) was a member of a local landowning family, active in politics, whose seat was at Rise in Holderness. He held the office of High Sheriff in 1822 and was for many years chairman of the East Riding Quarter Sessions. He served as a liberal Tory in the Reform Parliament of 1830–1 and represented the East Riding as a Member of Parliament from 1832 to 1841 (Ward 39).

Beverley[,][24] Mr. Schonswar[25] & Mr. Popple who witnessed the <u>Rebellion of the Beasts</u>. Mr. Peters of Hotham who now calls himself Burton[26] ordered his tenants and dependants to attend, and gave them their Breakfasts before going—their Dinners at Beverley and Suppers when they came back, he provided a Waggon to take a load of his Worthies; Kemp the Lantern maker & Kettle mender, and Val. Tindle the fat Butcher were there from Cave. — After Supper at Hotham every man was allowed half a Bottle of Wine; Poor fellows when they were drenching themselves with Sloe water which they mistook for Rough Old Port, it made them grin so horribly, that their mouths involuntary opened and out came Huzza Burton for ever!!!

Monday 9th. March

The feeling of the Country is certainly against concession to the Catholics. I dislike their Doctrine and mummery as much as any one, but at the same time I would not debar them from having the same privilege as their fellow subjects, for I do not consider that the Religious Opinions of any ought to be held up as marking them out to execration by the Vulgar.

Tuesday 10th. March

Botanists say there are some hundred sorts of Roses, but Poets have made some thousand Similies on Roses, in fact there is no Poet pious or profane but what has pressed the Rose into his Service; in some Works they bloom in full vigour, in others they appear dry and withered. The first time I read a small Poem called the Pilgrim I think, (which in former times with others used to be sold by old Robin Stubbs, who used to cry out "Beuks and Ballads and fine Pictures", my Uncle used to allow him to open out his Pack in the School as he was a sort of Townsman coming from Skipsea). This Pilgrim contained the following beautiful lines which I have never since forgot

"The blushing Rose smiles with the morning Sun,

Just then looks gay, now withers, and is gone"

Wednesday 11th. March

I have got a very bad cold, indeed colds are very prevalent here at this time. I have seen Mr. Peel's Speech this morning, he has said something worthy of praise, as the abolition of civil distinctions and the equality of political rights. I don't know how his new Oath will be relished by the Catholics, but I think not very well. All the hopes of the persecuting Zealots are

[24] These were William Beverley and his son Robert Mackenzie Beverley. William was an American who had come to England in order to study but never returned to his native country. He eloped with a rich heiress and, on her death, inherited Norwood House in Beverley. He held the office of Mayor from 1806 to 1807, stood (unsuccessfully) for Parliament at the elections of 1812 and 1818, and was appointed a JP and Deputy Lieutenant of the East Riding. He was a man of strongly liberal views and an ally of William Wilberforce. His son Robert Mackenzie Beverley, like his father, was a staunch liberal and campaigned against corruption in the Anglican Church and in the Universities. His writings on these topics achieved national fame and provoked furious debate. Both father and son seem to have spent large sums of money with the result that in 1833 William was forced to flee the country as a debtor (Tucker 1–2).

[25] See n.32 (1831).

[26] See n.17 (1831).

now on the House of Lords; these stedfast friends to no innovation, however much for the better.

Thursday 12th. March

Out last night collecting with the Overseer. I cannot say that we were very successful, either money is scarce or else those who have it do not wish to part with it; but I think a good deal of it is contradiction to the overseers. — My Cold yet very bad my Nose runs so fast that it is difficult to keep up with it ...

Saturday 14th. March

Mr. Copeland, Mr. Barnard's Butler is going with his Master to London, I intend sending these Sheets with him, I thought he would have been off before now, but he is here yet. I think he will commence his Journey before I write a fresh Sheet, as this is full here will be no waste or at least Blank paper so the next remarks will serve for a future time.

Sunday 15th. March

Yesterday afternoon inviting the Members of the Club in Cave to Matthew Smith's funeral this day, for which I have one penny each. He hanged himself on Friday morning in Grace Holborn's Garret where he lodged. A Coroners inquest was held on him yesterday, when the Jury of which I was one brought in the verdict temporary insanity, he has been ill and in a low way for nearly a year past.

Monday 16th. Mar

A very hard frost last night, — Mr. Fleming of Elloughton who has lately been employed to collect the Taxes and Rates has stopped payment being nearly thirty pounds bad in his accounts, without Sixpence to pay it with, he is so ill off that the Parish is obliged to relieve him, I am sorry for him. He was well situated when we first came to Cave, having many Boarders, but his wife died and he married a young Woman, and had a second family in his old age, for which it appears he is not able to provide.

Tuesday 17th. Mar

Kemp the Lantern maker was married this morning to a Daughter of Mr. Robinson of Mount Airy. — A Woman from Newbald here today enquiring when she was to receive the Money from the Club for her husband's funeral who was buried on Sunday last, he was a young man, and had been ill about a year. As he has been a member for a less time than three years, his widow will be entitled to £3–8–6 which I told her she might receive the next Club night.

Wednesday 18th. Mar

I suppose this time is called Lent; it is a time for mortification and affliction in Popish Countries, as if one were called to repentance for a few weeks in the Spring more than at any other time. What a folly is this! in general the most ignorant are the most superstitious, great observers of set times. Measured some Turnip Land for Mr. Leeson last night in the new field very dirty it was.

Thursday 19th. Mar

Old Willy in hopes of an Election as he has no doubt this Parliament will be dissolved if the House of Lords do their duty and turn out the Catholic relief

Bill, even if this should not be the case he is fully persuaded the King will not sign it. How little such persons know of the history of their Country, neither King nor Queen has refused to sign any Bill past by both houses for more than a hundred years, and surely the King is better advised than to refuse signing what he has recommended. The freemen of Boroughs are a venal tribe [This last sentence is in larger writing for emphasis].

20th Mar Friday

I was gardening last night, setting some early Potatoes. I think I had worked rather too hard, as I had a pain in my back before I went to bed, but a night's rest has brought me round again and I am quite right this morning. Mr. Tinsdill has sent me his bill for the Parish last Year which is £32–6–6. this will drive the Catholic question out of the heads of some of the stanch protestants[.] I look for stormy debates on the Doctor's bill when it becomes known.

Saturday 21st. March

I think I have little to remark this day. Saw the Doncaster paper which I seldom look at, as it is not one of the most enlightened and found the Majority on the second reading of the Catholic Bill 180. went to Barnard Cook's and got notice to call a meeting next week to lay a Church Rate ...

Monday 23rd. March

Crows very busy making and repairing their nests, they are full of noise and quarrelling, I looked at them one day when two of them were very throng building, but their proceedings did not seem to be approved by others of the Society, for eight others set to and pulled the nest all down even though one of the builders had sat down in it, when they had committed this devastation, they set up a triumphant shout, and told the poor sufferers not to offend in like manner again. So I interpreted their cawing.

Tuesday 24th. March

Heard yesterday that the Duke of Wellington and Lord Falmouth* had been fighting a Duel,[27] that the Duke shot and missed his Adversary; when Lord Falmouth fired his Pistol in the Air, and thus the matter was over!! — Heard also that the Duke was hissed on leaving the House of Lords on Friday night, the Mob thus showing their true Protestant Spirit which is that of Persecution to all opposed to their view. — No wheat to be seen at the Market yesterday on account of the advance in price.

*[In the margin] This was a wrong information, it was Lord Winchelsea ...

Thursday 26 Mar

A Meeting this Evening to lay a Church rate and a poor Rate, very few attended, the Expences of the Poor this year are great; indeed the maintenance

[27] Shortly after the presentation in Parliament of the Bill for Catholic Emancipation, Lord Winchilsea, one of the leaders of the Anti-Catholic party, had publicly accused the Duke of Wellington of personal dishonesty in a letter published in *The Standard* newspaper. Failing to win an apology from him and unable to resort to law as the courts were closed until May, Wellington demanded the satisfaction of a gentleman. The duel, which was the only one ever fought by Wellington, took place on 21 Mar. 1829 in Battersea Fields. Neither party was injured as the Duke shot wide and the Earl of Winchilsea fired into the air (Greig 462–4).

of the Poor under the present system must increase. — I have a Scheme to make the expence less, and that is to let every Man with a Family have at least an Acre of Land at the same rent as the Farmers, then I will stake my veracity that none but the idle and careless of this Class will ever apply for any relief.

Friday 27th. Mar

Making out the Stamp Accounts for the last Quarter, amount of Sales in that time £87–6–6½ which is now paid monthly. Since the allowance has been less, the trouble has been greater; as in most cases they who do the least work are the best paid. All these sort of Gentlemen understand the Rule of Three inverse: where less work requires more money and more work requires less money ...

Sunday 29th. Mar

I have been looking over the Report of the Society for promoting Christian knowledge,[28] which is preceded by a Sermon of John-Banks Lord Bishop of St. David's[29] in St. Pauls 5th June 1828. It contains about 12 pages 8vo. it seems to be of fashionable shortness: he intimates that Ignorance & Idleness are the main source of misery that prevail amongst the poor. Now I think that Poverty and want of employment are fruitful sources of misery, and I can think as I please without asking the Bishop. What fine pickings there must be from this Society. Messrs. Rivington's Bill from last audit (I expect 1 year) is £55,382–6s–1d. For printing 15,250 annual reports £730–10–0. For sewing the annual report 2 years £235–19–0. Salaries to Clerks &c. £1296–3–10. This does some persons good, so the Parsons shall have my consent to subscribe their annual Guinea very few subscribe more.

Monday 30th. Mar

This Catholic business makes friends quarrel. Mr. Levitt of Ellerker and Geo. Hodgson have split and called one another after having been thick as thieves for seven years past. Geo. called Levitt's friend George Coulson the Mayor of Hull,[30] a great Leather nose, and Levitt got to hear of it, but George would not deny that he had called him, and repeated that he was nought else but a great Leather nose, and did not know what Catholic emancipation meant, neither did he know what the principles of Protestantism were for which he is such a stickler. But what says he to Levitt did you say about Dan Sykes? did not you say you wished he was thrown into the Dock? No no such thing, I only said if he had been at the meeting at Hull I should not have been surprised if he had been thrown into the Dock. Now says George that is a d—d lie. The reply to which was you are a scurrilous fellow. And so they went on in language not becoming either Protestant or Catholic.

---

[28] Society for Promoting Christian Knowledge. *The Annual Report.* 1814— . Continuation of: *An Account of the Origin and Designs of the Society* ... 1733—[1813?]. All the Society's earlier reports were prefaced by printed sermons.

[29] John Banks Jenkinson (1781–1840) was consecrated Bishop of St. David's, formerly the most extensive of the Welsh dioceses, on 23 July 1825 (*DNB*).

[30] George Coulson was elected Mayor of Hull in 1825 and again in 1828 (Sheahan 234).

Tuesday 31st Mar

Spent part of this Day in looking over the Poor Book accounts for the last year. I have added them all over again for fear of a mistake occurring, which I should not wish to be the case, but now I am [in] no fear about it. Recd. the Examiner for the 22d. March on Saturday but the one for the week before, viz. the 15th. never came to hand. I often think of one of the Wards in St. Thomas's Hospital which I visited when in London. I confess I did not like the looks of it. A passage in the middle of a long Room with Beds on each side without hangings. Some patients seemed to be almost in dying Circumstances, others recovering, some taking refreshments of different kinds, but all exposed to one another and to every visitor. I may be singular but I am certain were I in their situation I should like to be private; but then this occurs where is the means to be had to provide for such numbers except in a public hospital. It appears by a Writer a Surgeon of course that to learn Anatomy six subjects, that is dead bodies are necessary, and that it is <u>impossible</u> to be an adept in dissecting without cutting up ten or twenty more; This is hacking with a Vengeance!! What a pity that such writers as these are not confined in a Lunatic Asylum. I am sure want of sense would qualify them for the situation.

Wednesday 1st. April

At Beverley this day getting Sworn in Assessor for more than the twentieth time. It was a very cold day, and snowed very much as I came home with the Storm full against me; I had tooth ache dreadfully after I got home, I have not had it some years before; but I have suffered so much with it that it terrifies me. At night there was a meeting to let the lanes which I was obliged to attend, but left as soon as possible, but

"Tis a poor relief we gain

To change the place, but keep the pain."[31]

Thursday 2nd. April

Filling up the Notice papers for the Assessed taxes, it does not appear that there will be any reduction for the present in this species of taxation, indeed Economy appears only a secondary consideration at present. Club night done before ten O'clock.

Friday 3rd. Apl

Mr. Robt. Arton going to call on me this Evening to collect the Poor rates as he wishes to see who pays. I gave him the Slip the other night and went without him. Dab I tell you what, must pay now, time out, have all cleared up ...

[*Sunday 5th April*

There is no entry for this day, which was the day after Eliza's wedding. The entry for the previous day, which has been omitted, consisted of an instalment of a serialized moral tale by RS; it contained no mention of his daughter's wedding].

---

[31] Quotation taken from Isaac Watts's *Hymns and Spiritual Songs*, book 2, hymn 146 (See Appendix 3).

Monday 6th. Apl.

At Riplingham this day to meet a Man who wanted to swear me out of paying his Sess (viz. Jack Smith) but he got no good there excepting it would be any comfort to him to be told that a Distress Warrant would be granted for the amount, which would have been done then, had there been two Magistrates.[32]

Tuesday 7th. Apl.

Very busy this day in making up the Poor Accounts, a meeting at James Levitt's where I was kept until 10 O'clock at night before the Accts. were settled on account of the negligence of the Overseers in not bringing in their disbursements sooner[,] Giles Bridgman & Richd. Marshall Overseers for next year, that is from this time.

Wednesday 8th. Apl

Copy'g Abstracts of Titles for Mr. Robinson, One of the Parties formerly lived at Swansea in the County of Glamorgan, his name was Wm. Padley an Ironmonger who became a Bankrupt there about 1794. His Estate was sold consisting of Land at No. Cave to Geo. Holborn.

Thursday 9th. Apl.

There are yet left some few old houses furnished as in former days. A Brass Mortar & Pestle in the Centre of the Chimney piece, & in one Corner a Salt Box; in the other a pair of Bellows with Shining pipes and Sparkling nails. But even here Fashion is making encroachments, for I observed an Italian Iron hung by a Brass faced Warming Pan. — Sent a Box with a Ham & some of Cobbett's Regs to Wm.

Friday 10th. Apl.

A paper this morning not directed in Wm.'s writing[,] my wife uneasy all day for fear he should be ill. — The first Sunday I was in London I expected to have heard the Bells ringing merrily from the Scores of Churches, how great then was my disappointment to hear nothing of the Kind—I have often wished I had gone into the Chapel into which we looked, I think it was in Cannon Street

...

Sunday 12th. Apl

At Church as usual to hear the Prattling parson, but as there was no Gospel in his talk I even gave up the thoughts of any good, and surveyed Bobby Thornton's head. — Bobby has a head and face nearly the length of a tether; but to speak seriously from his Chin to the top of his head seems longer than a foot Rule, if this is not a long head I wonder what is!! then Bobby has his topping twined up to lengthen his Visage still more, and as he appears to be Whiskerless he has his hair frizzed out at each ear, that an Irishman's wig in disorder would be elegant to his matted hair. Then Bobby has got I suppose a fashionable Coat the Collar of which is so far from his neck that it might well hold a Sixpenny loaf, for at this time a Bread loaf is not very large for sixpence. — Then in walking Bobby is very circumspect he always sets down his heel

---

[32] A distress warrant issued by 2 magistrates empowered the seizure of an offender's goods and chattels to the value of the money owed by him, in this case the sum of the unpaid assessed taxes.

first, and gets on "the light fantastic toe", as well as he can; Bobby thinks himself a Dandy especially on Sundays.

Monday 13th. Apl.

I made some remarks on Bobby Thornton's head and likewise his feet yesterday, & now just by way of finish, I will complete him, I believe Bobby sucked after he got into Breeches, if indeed it could be said he ever got into them; for Old Nanny his Mother would have no new fashioned things called Trowsers, so his first Breeches were made to button at the knees, but Bobby either grew longer or his Breeches shorter (and that was needless) when his buttons were fairly above his knees, so the next pair was made in the Slop Fashion to come down to his Calf if he had any, but they work'd themselves up and appeared in the end like a pair of Breeches without any Buttons at the knees. Who would have thought that a creature of this description should now be a Country Sunday Dandy.

Tuesday 14th. Apl.

I lately carried a Note for Sess.ts. to a wise man who lives in old Sam Ayre's house[,] the sum was £2–18–1½, he looked at it and said this is a deal of Money to pay, two pounds eighteen Shillings and a penny <u>threehalfpence</u>, I told him I thought it was not so, he looked again and repeated it in the same manner, I told him he did not know a half penny from three halfpence. Such is a specimen of the Fools I have to do with.

Wednesday 15th. Apl.

A most terrible stormy day, the Wind dreadfully high. — I see the Catholic Relief Bill was carried on the third reading by a Majority of 104. I hope it will be the means of healing many griefs, but I here enter my Protest against the Doctrines and practice of the Catholics, but as Fellow Subjects, I know they have the same right to Civil liberties and eligibilities as others who hold a different belief. It has been a tedious subject and all has been said on it that can be said except the same Arguments be repeated.

Thursday 16th. Apl.

A Parish meeting last night to consider of a proposition made by a Man who has a Wife and 3 Children belonging the Parish who wishes to go to America, he proposed taking 16 pounds which was at length agreed to, the Passage money will be £8–10–0 and he has his Victuals to find for the Voyage[;] he is going to Quebec[,] the time of the Voyage is estimated at 6 weeks so that the Poor fellow will not have much left to establish himself in a foreign Land.

Friday 17th. Apl.

Our old friend the long Miller got a County Court Summons for Willy Milner the little Bricklayer, for his Bill, and got what is said to be called an Attachment to take his Goods, but Willy contrived to remove his furniture and nothing was to be had. So Tom's man of Law came to an agreement with his Adversary, with which Tom is highly displeased, he swears he would freely have spent Five pounds rather than have been beaten with such a little underhanded Devil as he is, Curse him he says I should have catched him sometime, a <u>lahtle</u> nasty beggar to be done with him is almost past biding. Heard from Wm. that he had got the Box safe. May God preserve him & his family ...

Sunday 19th. Apl.

I have been pestered with that pitiless complaint the Tooth Ache since the 1st. Apl. I have not had it for several years before, my face has been swelled by it, but I hope it [is] now about leaving me. — This is Easter Sunday, a very cold uncomfortable day.

Monday 20th. Apl.

It is a great folly to let small matters put one out of temper, but I know it is hard to avoid it; yet after a little time we wonder we should have been so ruffled about trifles. One would think some people have a delight in making themselves miserable, and because some misfortune may happen to them at a future time they begin to lament it long before it is actually felt, and suffer more in apprehension than they very possibly ever would in reality. Can this be Wisdom?

Tuesday 21st. Apl.

Easter Tuesday, this day the Churchwardens are nominated[,] Wm. Loncaster in the Room of Barnd. Cook appointed by the Minister and Mr. Atkinson by the Parish, a long noisy Contest between two Candidates Old Willy and Robt. Tindale it was at last put to the Vote when there was an equal number on both Sides. Then the Chairman as was his Right should have had the casting vote, but he declined and one of the opposition gave way and our old friend carried the day. I do not like this same Tindale for there has been nothing but disturbance in the Parish since he came into it, and he wanted this appointmt, just for the sake of creating more. I voted for Old Willy.

Wednesday 22nd. Apl.

I did not attend the Easter Dinner yesterday for old Barnard had not pleased me the day before very well. Some of the Company I understand got very full of old <u>Bant Cuck's</u> wine, indeed I saw Jno. Reynolds who could scarcely walk, this is the Parish Clerk, who had only the Sunday before recd. the Sacrament. I really durst not degrade myself in this manner. There were only 11 in Company and 3 Guineas is alld. by the Town which I think was quite sufficient both for eating and drinking, but they had to pay 8s. pr. piece more; I wonder the Clerk did not cry, from such feasts Good Landlord deliver us ...

Friday 24th. Apl.

I think there is scarcely a place in the British dominions where reading is so little thought of as here. Books in many houses are nearly obsolete, or at least some few people have a few Books for them, but they would as soon think of reading them as Goldsmith's Irishman would think of eating his Bacon kept for a Shew.[33]

---

[33] See n.2 (1837).

Saturday 25th. Apl.

At Brantingham as usual this forenoon, but as it was my Lady's Birth "we did keep Holiday" so I came back and made an attempt to collect some Assd. taxes, but I was not very successful.

Sunday 26th. Apl.

My Wife very ill with Sick Headache today I have not known her so ill for a long time past. She has been afflicted with this complaint ever since I knew her and has suffered severely, she was very sick all the day but a great deal better before bed time.

Monday 27th. Apl.

When I was at Hull (some time since) I went into a Public house (I think it was called the London Tavern)[34] into a sort of Parlour where there was a decent looking Company, but as little was said, I ventured to ask if any fresh News had arrived from Turkey; I was referred to a Newspaper about a week old, besmeared all over with Ale and Tobacco, which was laid on the table, which I took up and being seemingly engaged with it, the discourse of the Company was renewed as I thought it had been interrupted on account of my entrance. It seems they met at that place every night to enjoy each other's Company and quaff their pipes over a Cup of Nut brown Ale but the last night some strangers had intruded into their Company, and a quarrel ensued when the Landlord was called for to dismiss the Strangers, but he took their part, so it appeared their gravity this night proceeded from what they looked upon to be a slight put on them, and they vowed they would meet at some other house; I soon laid down the Paper and bidding the Gentlemen good night, I left them to settle the matter as they thought proper.

Tuesday 28th. Apl.

I think Abm. Barff is drunk almost every day, he is one of the Surveyors of the Highways and as full of Mastership as any petty officer in any public office can make himself. Last night he had been exchanging a Horse with Ths. Brigham of Brantingham and was so drunk he scarcely knew what he was doing. I happened to go into Cousens's where they were when he would have me to look over the Money he had to pay he is uncommonly purse proud, and generally talking about his money.

Wednesday 29th. Apl.

A very strong report here that the King was dead, I never gave any credit to it and the more I enquired the more I was satisfied that there was not the least truth in it. Old rumour that notorious liar had been very busy in spreading the report.

Thursday 30th. Apl.

Had to send a special Messenger to Hull today for some Stamps which were wanted for Surrenders at Weighton Court tomorrow the lad I sent went at 10 O'clock in the morning, and got back about five in the Evening.

---

[34] The 'London Tavern' was located at no. 20 Queen Street, Hull (Baines ii. 332).

Friday 1st. May

The Weather more like February than May-day, very cold high winds. At Brantingham this Evening instead of tomorrow as I have to pay in the Taxes at Beverley tomorrow. Money very bad to come at for them.

2nd. May Saturday

The Old Cobler at Walkington has got a notice in his plantation that no Papists nor Popish Priests will be suffered to enter there: it happens that he is always opposed to the Parson, and in this case he the Minister was of the liberal Party, which with Tithe eaters has not been very common. I think this Plantation cannot be more than 4 or 5 yards square!!

Sunday 3rd. May

A Cloudy morning some weather wise people saying it would be nothing but rain, these weather sages are generally great Fools. So in this Case Providence to confound them favoured us with a finer day than common, to shew them if they have sense for it that they knew nothing of the matter.

Monday 4th. May

Barnard Cook has made an Assignment to his Daughter in law, and her Brother, her name is now over the Door, and what Old Bant is going to do does not appear very plain. I should think he has gone on as far as he can, and this is like putting on a Cloak to cover his dirty Cloaths.

Tuesday 5th. May

There have been some Soldiers here the 4th Dragoon Guards they had come from Exeter and were going to Beverley. But o what looking and gazing and admiring and wondering and conjecturing and arguing, at seeing the Men in Red Coats or rather waistcoats, and their Horses and trapping. Such a sight as Soldiers with us is rare.

Wednesday 6th May

Measured a Turnip Close at Everthorpe for Wm. Hudson 12a–3r–16p. This was a finer day than we have had for some time past, the Sun shone all day, but the wind blew strong. Called at Js. Pearson's on my return and got a Pint of Ale, the poor old Duke on the outside looks very much weather beaten, and the tail of his Horse which appeared so stiff has almost disappeared.

Thursday 7th May

I had a Note given me when I balanced the Constable's Accounts one Item of which was "Horse and Cart eating 1s/6d". I enquired if the person had eaten the Horse and Cart for the small Sum of 1s/6d or whether the Cart had eaten to that amount. This was the Club night I got home about half past nine. I have been very throng this week in writing out the Tax Bills, a great deal of work for a very little money.

Friday 8th. May

Yesterday was Mr. Barnard's tithe Rent, Mr. B. is in London his Steward Rd. Marshall recd. the Rents, this money as tithe is paid to a Lay Rector, but it makes little difference to those who have to pay it whether the Receivers be Lay or Clerical. Several of the payers it appeared liked Mr. Barnard's strong Ale, amongst the rest the low Miller, who I am informed got so much that it fairly knocked him down in the Street.

Saturday 9th. May

A Foot Ball play[35] in the Ings adjoining Provence Ground, between 6 young Men of Cave and the same Number from Ellerker, the Ellerker Men were complete conquerors having beaten their adversaries in a very short time, the match was for 5 Shillings each.

Sunday 10th. May

Yesterday and today the Weather has been delightful. Cowslips and Daisies bespangle the Ground and vegetation has made a surprising progress even in two days. My wife went to what is called Dickey Straker's Close on the little Wold Lane to see the spring visitors the timid Cowslips. Heard the Cuckoo yesterday for the first time this Season.

Monday 11th. May

The Methodists had a Missionary meeting here today,[36] there were several fine preachers from Hull and other parts who on these occasions are transformed into Beggars to entice the Money from some who can ill afford to spare it. I understand the Collection was not very large perhaps about five pounds.

Tuesday 12th. May

The weather in the day time remarkably fine, but very cold at nights. I was rodding pease last night, and doing other little jobs in the Garden, — There appears to be dreadful work in the Manufacturing districts, misery and Poverty are there united. These Engine Spinners have brought such a mass of People together that under adverse circumstances they cannot be maintained, and when men are hungering there is nothing so desperate that they will not undertake.

Wednesday 13th. May

Old Willy almost hopeless that the Parliament will not be dissolved, he glories in the hurry of an Election but it is with a view to self interest, as the Freemen contrive to sell themselves for the best price they can.

"Hark to the Roar, the hubbub and the Din,
  Some bawl for liberty and some for—Gin."

Thursday 14th. May

This is Weighton fair Day and a sweet day it is[,] this dry weather is very favourable for Wheat. Old Barnard Cook was arrested on Saturday last for which I understand he has given Bail, they are taking several Articles of Furniture out of the House, and have had them away to Wallingfen to young Barnard wife's Father's. I am afraid there is a good deal of tricking and Roguery going on.

---

[35] Football games, either impromptu small-scale affairs or matches involving large numbers and held on festive occasions, were common at this time. They frequently involved village against village (Malcomson 34–5).

[36] The Methodists had been established in South Cave since the 1780s. Their first purpose-built chapel was erected in Church Street in 1816. The numbers were not large at that time and missionary meetings were held to recruit new members (Neave (1984) 48).

Friday 15th. May

Newlove who lives opposite to us at the Bear is I think as idle a fellow as any we have in the Town, but yesterday he thought he would do some work so he got two lads to help him to set Potatoes in his Garden, which with a Wheelbarrow was the whole force he mustered. So he set the lads to work and set himself down in the Barrow to look at them; he most likely thought (if he ever heard of it) of Poor Richard's assertion that a Master's eye does as much work as both his hands.

Saturday 16th. May

Now for a Remark or two of my own. I have heard much talk by Persons who say they cannot pay because they cannot get their debts in, these I invariably set down as having little or nothing owing to them. When I hear a Person talking of his having much money, I am certain he is in want of it all; When I hear People extolling their own honesty I know for certain they are (or would be if they had an opportunity) Arrant Rogues. When I hear a Person talking he would do nothing and wants nothing but what is right, I am sure he would take advantage if he could, and say that was right. When I hear Persons say they prefer Banker's Rags to Sterling Gold, I know them to be fools double distilled. Heard from Wm. last night.

Sunday 17th. May

I was at West Ella yesterday my Mother is very well in health for her age she was born the 7th. day of Old May 1745 so that she is now just about 84 years of age, she can see to read a Common print without Glasses, she is uncommonly lame and has got a Crutch, yesterday was the first time of using it, she did not seem very perfect in its use as the Corner of it hit her under her Chin. I thought to have seen Mr. Sykes about the Post office but he was at Billing.

Monday 18th. May

Wrote to Wm. this day to desire him to see Mr. Barnard about the Post office, it is currently reported that I am to have the place by those who know nothing of it. I do not contradict them as it is as well to let them have their own way, as it is in my favour.

Tuesday 19th. May

Sowed some Carrotts this morning as we had forgot at the proper time; however the weather is fine and the Ground warm that I expect they will be soon out of the Earth then I will encourage them all I can to get on with those who started before them; as is the case with myself at present where three or four had made application for the Post office before I knew anything of it, so there is nothing left for me but to apply myself with more diligence than if I had had a fair start with them. I think some of them are already distanced.

Wednesday 20th. May

Some time ago before Goole was dignified with the name of a Port, I have been informed that it was the most wretched place of any almost in this Country. The houses were built with Sod walls at the expence of the Occupiers and when any tenant left a habitation he thought himself well off if he got 10

Shillings for his dwelling house!! 20 or 30 men on a Sunday (better day better deed) set to when a house wanted erecting and finished it off the same day.

Thursday 21st. May

I had a letter from the Surveyor of the Post office saying the application should be made to the Post office at Market Weighton as his recommendation would have great influence. I therefore wrote to Mr. Holmes to day begging for his interest.

Friday 22d. May

Recd. a letter from Mr. Holmes saying that he had had a previous application, but in case of a Vacancy he should not forget that I had applied; I had likewise a letter from Mr. Barnard very flattering and assuring me of doing all in his power to procure me the Situation, as I am the only person he should wish to have it, and he will oppose, all in his power any person whose integrity or ability is not unimpeachable. My Character so far has always been my Sheet Anchor ...

Sunday 24th. May

I saw James Levitt today and told him if he had let me know that he was going to apply for the Post office I would have started fair with him, but as it was I had to Gallop to overtake him, but I doubted not before this time I was before him, he did nothing but laugh.

Monday 25th. May

Exerting myself this day in getting the Certificate signed, which I have done very respectfully. There was not one who signed it but did it cheerfully. I hardly expected that Tindale would have signed it as I voted against him being Churchwarden, but he was satisfied I had done right in voting for our old friend Mr. Atkinson. This shews more liberality than I expected to find.

Tuesday 26th. May

Court at the west end yesterday at the Bay Horse[.] Old Barnard has given up the Closes called Flatts and the Tolls and left half a years rent unpaid. It is expected that Jem. Levitt will take them as he has bid a rent for them, but I think they will be rather inconvenient for him, but of this he must judge himself.

Wednesday 27th. May

Sent my certificate to Weighton yesterday to desire the Post master there to sign it but he declined on account of there not being an actual Vacancy, should that occur he will take the matter into consideration, this is but a sort of genteel denial, I have done what I could and if I do not succeed I have not myself to blame for any neglect. In all I have said I only desire the Situation in case of a Vacancy.

28 May Thursday

Mr. Oddy one of the Inspectors of Stamps was here yesterday taking the Stock and examining the Accounts, which he found all correct, he says I have the Stamps in the best order of any he has found, he has been a Month on his examination he was going from hence to Hull, the Account he had from Hull was wrong cast two pounds which he immediately corrected when he saw mine, which he commended for their accuracy.

Friday 29th. May

This is what is called or sadly miscalled King Charles' martyrdom.[37] I don't know what pretence there is for calling such a Tyrant as Charles was, a Martyr, except he was a Martyr to his tyrannous arbitrary and unjust proceedings, England then found men to vindicate her rights, and may she never want Patriots who prefer their Country's good to their own private Interest ...

Sunday 31st May

John Dunlin died this day about Noon at the age of 85 years, he was a peaceable harmless old Man; when we first came to Cave he was a thrasher for Wm. Tindle, he has long been a Pauper, but well respected as he was no impostor.

Monday 1st. June

Mr. Shackleton has taken the Farm of Scatcherd's lately occupied by Ths. Fisher, he has therefore now two farms, namely this and Provence, he has removed into the house here, and a Brother of his called James has taken the Chapel house where Mr. Tapp lived. — There have been four Persons at this Farm of Mr. Scatcherd since we came to Cave, Wm. Tindle, then Wm. Akam, then Ths. Fisher and now Mr. Shackleton. It is accounted a good Farm.

Tuesday 2nd. June

In a late Bankrupt list I saw Richd. Wells of Nottingham, Paper dealer, I am inclined to think this is the fine Mr. Wells, the best Shopman in Hull.[38] I doubt he will not make so much of this affair as of the Packet Speculation when he made so much money as to furnish him with means to range over the three kingdoms, and find how easily he could spend it ...

Thursday 4th. June

I saw in the times today a witness on a Coroners inquest on the Body of a Druggist apprentice; where the witness said he found him weltering in his Blood but he was quite dead. Now I am at a loss to know how any person quite dead could welter in his Blood. He might indeed be laid in it but for a dead man to wallow in it, is surprising to me who live in the Country, but they understand these things better in London.

Friday 5th. June

Uncommonly cold and dry weather, yet the Country looks very blooming, I believe this is very fine weather for Wheat; though the Farmers who are never content are continually wishing for Rain, but should rain come three or four days they would immediately cry out surely there was never such weather as

---

[37] Oak Apple Day or Royal Oak Day was celebrated on 29 May in commemoration of the restoration of the monarchy and the return of King Charles II; it was the anniversary of the day on which he re-entered London in 1660. It was customary to wear oak leaves in memory of the occasion when the king was compelled to hide in an oak tree to escape his pursuers after his defeat at Worcester (Hone i. 356–7).

[38] Richard Wells is recorded as the printer and publisher of the *Hull Packet* in Scale Lane in Hull in Jan. 1819. In Sept. of that year, however, he was succeeded by Thomasin Peck (*VCHYER* i. 428).

this, at this time of the year; this dry time I know suits them (and so do they know it too) for working and cleaning their Turnip Land. John Ramsdale has been here for a Load of Oats this week that came from Weighton ...

Sunday 7th. June

A very sharp Frost last night, it was so severe that it has injured the Potatoe tops a good deal in several places, it is very unseasonable to have such frosts at nights at this time of the year. I remember an old man who was a Butcher who used to come to Barmston, who once said in the Summer time that he thought it was a frost air, he was laughed at for being so silly as to talk of Frost in the Summer but now it is well known, long after old Butcher Croft has had done with all kinds of weather.

Monday 8th. June

A Pleasant Shower of Rain this morning, which has made things look very lively. Old Barnard brought a letter from Wm. this morning, he looked uncommonly gruff. It appears the Post master of Weighton has the disposal of the office here, I must endeavour to see him and try to make him my friend, — I have not myself nor my Friends to reflect on for not doing the best in our power. — Wm.'s letter was written on paid, but not being marked with Red Ink, I suppose it had not been paid.

Tuesday 9th. June

Yesterday at Market time attending the sale of Jno. Dunlin's Goods, the amount of the Money raised was 15s–2d. including Bedding, Chairs, tables. &c, &c. Now this man with his few Goods was very Content, he had 2s. pr. week from the Parish but he had good friends who took care that he wanted nothing; when he was ill the Overseers asked him if he wanted any thing, but he replied he had plenty of every thing and was not in want, indeed he seemed hurt at being asked if he could be assisted

"Man wants but little here below"

Nor wants that little long".[39]

Wednesday 10th. June

Recd. from Wm. this morning the Hull Rockingham and the York Herald. I had not seen either of them before, so that they were new to me. It appears the Parliament will shortly be prorogued, they have done nothing but settle the Catholic Question. Corn Laws, distresses of the Country, and all other things are left to the Chapter of Accidents. The Game laws it appears are to remain as they are; but this is nothing to me, I never killed any Game in my life, and I think I shall not begin now, it is an idle employment, which some persons exert themselves more in than by working.

Thursday 11th. June

I have seen the Post master of Market Weighton, but as no alteration is to take place at the present, he did not promise neither deny his Support in the event of a Vacancy, should this occur I think I could bring him to favour me, but I may be deceived, he says my recommendation is very strong, and certainly

---

[39] This quotation is taken from Oliver Goldsmith's *Edwin and Angelina, or The Hermit* (1766).

he would not oppose it, he is under no promise to any one; but has been applied to by others as well as myself.

Friday 12th June

All busy in preparing for the fair, a great deal of bustling and cleaning and sore disturbing the poor Spiders, who without doubt, thought (if they thought at all) themselves secure in their habitation, but the merciless broom came upon them at unawares and frightening some and killing others made strange havock in the Community.

Saturday 13th June

Very busy in the Shop most of this week particularly amongst Currants, Raisins, and other things which are in demand at this time, for people will have them at the fair let them want at what time they will besides, but so it is and so it has been, and I think will be.

Sunday 14th. June

No company at all for the fair with us, so that we got our dinners very comfortably on a piece of Roast Beef, we had no bustle, therefore enjoyed it the more, for where there is so much Company there is but little enjoyment in general; at tea the same, Eliza has got some Company, but with that we do not interfere, let them have it who like it, we have had our Share for nearly thirty years past.

Monday 15th. June

We had John Baitson and his Son to Breakfast this morning and James Ramsdale and his Son Robt. to dinner. James had been buying a horse, it was uncommonly dusty and dry to day, people had their Coats so much covered with dust, that the Colour could scarcely be distinguished.

Tuesday 16th. June

This is the great day of all the days in the year with us for display. I dare say not many good Clothes would be left at home, there were shews as usual. Mary Martin and the Red Barn, and the murdering of Daft Jamie[40] all by the way of amusement!! It was a very fine day, but nothing like the number of People which I have seen before on the like occasion.

Wednesday 17th. June

Horse Racing, Ass Racing, Foot racing, Blobbing for Oranges in a Tub full of Water, Running Wheel-Barrows blinded and other Rustic amusements, concluding with getting drunk by those who could afford it and those who could not pay were thankful to others that would afford them the gratification.

---

[40] *The Murdering of Daft Jamie* and *The Murder of Maria Marten; or, The Red Barn* were popular 19th-c. melodramas based on actual murders. The 'shews' referred to by RS may have been either enactments of the melodramas, or (especially in view of the recent date of the events) static tableaux or displays depicting the crimes. 'Daft Jamie' was James Wilson, murdered by the notorious Edinburgh resurrectionist, William Burke, who had been recently hanged for the crime, on 28 Jan. 1829. Maria Marten was murdered by William Corder in a red barn at Polstead, Suffolk in 1827, and Corder was executed the following year (Rayner and Crook v. 209–16).

Thursday 18th. June

A very fine Rain last night, and the same again this day, which will be of great benefit to the Country. All the Fair loving throng making long faces now that the frolic is all over. I had forgot to mention that my Sister and Mary were here on Tuesday from West Ella.

Friday 19th. June

The Parliamentary proceedings are now drawing to a Close, and all the important business of the Country is to be left as it was at the beginning of the meeting, surely some methods might be found for at least alleviating if not removing the distress which is so very prevalent.

Saturday 20th. June

This morning commenced with a misfortune. A Miller who had been bringing us some Flour let his horse run the Cart backward into the Shop window which completely dashed in four Squares and the Wood work along with it, the Miller seemed the most unconcerned, he said it was the first accident that had happened by him; so he will pay for it, but it is conjectured amongst the knowing ones in Family affairs that his wife would not be quite so easy with him as he was with the horse.

Sunday 21st June

This understrapping Parson of ours has been to Cambridge the last week to vote for who? why for Mr. Bankes.[41] I hope the Petty parsons and Mr. Bankes along with them will be taught that they cannot dictate who and what sort of a Person they will return for the university of Cambridge, but these Black Coats swarm like Locusts and are nearly as destructive, they care for nothing but themselves. I hope Mr. Cavendish will be returned, although I have some fears on the occasion.

Monday 22nd. June

Newlove's had a Man for Hostler at Cave fair, who at night got so much liquor as to make him quarrelsome, but as he could not get any one to fight with him in the house he went into the Yard and challenged out a Jack Ass. Jack made no reply, so the Hostler let fly at him, but Jack did not take it quietly but putting himself in a posture of defence began beating the poor Hostler over his legs, in such a manner that the victory was soon given to Jack; so the man went limping into the house with his Ancle so bruised that he could scarce set it down: he told the Company he had been quarrelling with his brother, who had used him very ill.

Tuesday 23rd. June

I find that Mr. Cavendish, has succeeded in putting down the Corfe Castle Gentleman,[42] all liberal minded persons will be glad that Bigotry has been cast into the back ground. — I think Cobbett in his Register of the 13th. inst. has a

---

[41] The candidates were W. Cavendish and George Bankes (1788—1856). The unsuccessful Bankes was the son of Henry Bankes, MP for Dorset, and brother of William, another sitting Tory MP The family held the close borough of Corfe Castle (*DNB* and *TM* 16 June 1829, 2 d).

[42] i.e. George Bankes. See preceding note.

better cause for his abuse of Sir F. Burdett than he had before, if it be true what he (Cobbett) asserts that Sir F. left the house that he might take no part in the motion for Reform, for which he formerly clamoured so much.

Wednesday 24th. June

Mr. Holborn has two tame Pigeons in a Box at the back door set against the wall, they breed several times in a year and have now two young ones, which they talk of taking and either making a pye of them or having them roasted. I could no more think of eating them than I should think of eating our two Cats, after I had been a long time intimate with them; but every one to their taste.

Thursday 25th. June

I have been waiting in the Shop at the Fair week, and did very well, while at last some envious Sprite, with mischief in its mind, attacked me when I was weighing two Ounces of Snuff, and made me fairly throw it all down behind the Counter; which made me get into disgrace ratherly, but there was no such thing as talking much there; for with whisking about the Snuff soon showed its virtue and a fit of sneezing succeeded to finding fault with my miscarriage.

Friday 26th. June

Here is very fine weather now, it having been a good quantity of Rain which will be of very good use to the growing Crops. The Farmers complain that Wheat shoots with small ears, but this discontented race even God himself cannot please; for the Season could not be finer even if they had the wishing for it, and their wishes fulfilled to the utmost.

Saturday 27th. June

Here has been so much Street Music lately what with singing weavers and tawdry Italians that to me it is quite disgusting. But this afternoon in going to the west end I met a Flock of Sheep newly shorn with their lambs bleating in concert with the Dams, it was quite reviving. How many former recollections it brought into my mind. The thoughts of Clippings long since gone and to me never to return. When my father used to attend the Clippings, there was I to accompany him, at Barmston (he was the best Clipper of his time) then—about eleven O'clock in the Forenoon hot Cheesecakes were brought into the barn, with Butter sufficient for them to swim in, if the eaters thought proper; even now I remember the delicious taste of them; then when the work was done the Rustic's sang their songs in plain intelligent language, — Scenes of my boyish days ye are all, all gone.

Sunday 28th. June

A Sort of wet disagreeable day. The wheat I think is most of it shot it is accounted not to be backward if it be round shot by Midsummer, this will be the case the present year, and I hope Providence will be favourable, and confound all grumblers.

Monday 29th. June

Old Bant looks so gruff at me and lifts up his elbow in such an illnatured stile, that I have not been at his house for a Month past, and this day I believe he had no Company at all at the Market. All of us who used to attend there went with one Consent to another house, so he may look as grim as he pleases to attract fresh customers. I will let him see that his ill behaviour shall not make me subject to him.

Tuesday 30th. June

This is one of my most inanimate days, having no Newspaper on Tuesdays; then I have no letters to write to Hull this day, Mondays being the chief day for that purpose. I have been amusing myself with reading Sir Jno. Carr's travels[43] which are very fine light reading. I never read them before, having heard and seen so much said against them by the slanderous Critics that I never looked into them before, so that they are all new to me.

Wednesday 1st July

Heard from Wm. that he intends being here the first week in August, I am sorry to hear that he is unwell, I hope a Sea Voyage will be of benefit to him.

Thursday 2nd. July

A Letter from Wm. this morning saying that he intends leaving London on Saturday next by the Steam Packet, so that we are anticipating the time of his Arrival with his wife and Child which we are anxious to see.

Friday 3rd. July

Club night last night the last meeting night before the feast, when all arrears and fines are paid, it was Eleven O'clock before the business was done, which is not very pleasant amongst such a confusion of noises.

Saturday 4th July

Walked to Beverley and back today, it very often happens when I walk any way, that my feet are sorely blistered but this time they had not the least blister in them[.] I arrived at home between six and seven in the Evening very hungry, as I did not dine at Beverley.

Sunday 5th. July

Been wondering and talking this day several times whereabouts the Steam Packet would be at certain times, but it is all pure conjecture. A very high west wind which will be against the passage up the Humber but it is fine and dry so far, five O'clock in the Evening.

Monday 5th. [i.e. 6th] July

Wm.'s avaunt Courier Jno. Hall has arrived bringing an account that they arrived at Hull last night about seven O'clock all well, and will be here tomorrow in the afternoon. I thought yesterday they would be up late as the Wind was so strong against them.

From the 6th. to the 23d. July Wm. and his family were here.

---

[43] Sir John Carr (1772–1832) was a prolific travel writer and published numerous books of his journeys in various parts of Europe (See Appendix 3).

Thursday 23rd. July

Wm. went away this morning for West Ella, and I was left at home Shopkeeper, My harp was hung all the day on the Willows.[44] I went out at night to Old Willy's when first one and then another asked me what was the matter with me that I looked so ill, I suppose it proceeded from my short illness yesterday. But I soon came home not caring about much interrogatories. So got my Supper and a Gill of Ale which disagreed with me, but not very much.

Friday 24th. July

Went up to old Bant's Sale a little while tonight. Ned Coates had bought some things and got them away and would not pay for them, the Auctioneer got down and tried to put him in the Gutter but could not accomplish his purpose. Mrs. Cook turned Ned headlong out of the house, she was drunk as Ned was. Robinson of Mount Airy and Old Tim. Dunn were quarrelling Tim gave him a good sisserara[45] on the side of his head which quieted him.

Saturday 25th. July

This afternoon very winter like it blew hard with a Dense fog which wetted nearly as much as though it was rain. I was afraid that Wm. on the outside of the Coach would not be comfortable, but before night it cleared up again. At west end this afternoon.

Sunday 26th. July

A very fine day hope that Wm. his wife and the sweet little blue eyed creature have arrived safe at home. I have been very dejected, but pretty well in health. These parting Scenes are more painful than the pleasure of first meeting. No paper today.

Monday 27th. July

Two Papers the Times today both together, so that there had not been one sent to arrive yesterday. Went to the Sale after School time, bought two old Sheets for which I was very little thanked. Conder bought two Canisters which will hold about 4 or 5 lbs. of Tea each, we wanted these the price was 2/6d. — Bound a Lad Apprentice to a Shoemaker at Welton.

Tuesday 28th. July

My Brother came last night about eight O'clock, he told us that Wm. was only just in time to get on board the Packet for Barton as she was on the point of Sailing when they arrived. Ben. Tapp saw them safe on board all well and cheerful. I wonder whether he got the Hamper with the Fowls. I hope he did.

---

[44] This is a reference to the biblical quotation 'By the rivers of Babylon, there we sat down; Yea we wept, when we remembered Zion. We hanged our harps upon the willows in the midst thereof'—Psalms, 137, lines 1-2.

[45] 'siserary' is a popular corruption of the Latin 'certoriari' as in a 'writ of Certoriari' and has the connotation of suddenness or promptness. The term was used variously to denote: 'a severe rebuke or scolding'; 'a sharp blow'; 'a loud clanging noise' (*OED*).

Wednesday 29th. July

Recd. a letter from Wm. giving an account of his dreadful Journey.[46] My wife is so agitated that she does nothing but fret I am truly thankful to God for sparing them with life and limbs[.] I hope his wife will be better, I saw the Hull Packet just before the letter came giving an Account of the Accident, but I little thought that they were there, not expecting they would leave Barton until Saturday morning. Here is abundant cause for Gratitude that God has been so favourable as to save them in such imminent danger. My Brother went away this morning between five and six O'Clock. — I do not think there was any thunder here on Friday night last.

Thursday 30th. July

Wm. Turk's wife is dead at Bradford, there was an Account on Sunday morning that she was very ill. I suppose she has always had some complaint on her, in the Spine, but whether she has died of it or not I cannot say. A meeting last night to consult of what was to be done respecting Langricke.[47] It was agreed that I should draw up a sort of certificate to be signed by the Inhabitants to be laid before the Grand Jury. I told them it would be of no more use than sending my Umbrella. — I think Reynolds wants to make the affair up.

Friday 31st. July

Recd. a Bristol Paper with a long account of the meeting of Reformers of which Hunt was the Chairman. Wrote a Petition for Ths. Wiles to beg for the loss of his Pig which died, it was worth about 50 Shillings.

Saturday 1st. Augt

Mr. Gilby the late Rector of Barmston it is said, died worth £120,000. he is scarce regretted by any one, it is not much to his credit to leave the world, with the Poor saying that he scarcely ever did a generous action. However he is now where his money can be of no avail, nor what the world says can either benefit or harm him.

    "Princes this Clay must be your bed,"

    "In spite of all your towers;

    "The high, the rich, the Rev'rend head,

    "Must lay as low as ours".

Sunday 2nd. Augt

A Sort of meeting today at Mr. Bridgman's respecting Langricke. Reynolds had agreed by his Brother last week that he would not appear against Langricke to prosecute, but yesterday he came and said Genl. Wharton would not allow him to make up the affair. It was therefore agreed that Langricke

---

[46] On the Friday night of 24 July 1829, the express coach to London, on which William Sharp and his wife and daughter were travelling, had overturned as a result of the horses being frightened by sudden lightning about 3 miles north of Peterborough. No-one was seriously hurt (*HP* 28 July 1829).

[47] William Langricke was committed to York Castle, charged with stealing a yellow-bay mare from George Reynolds. He was later released without trial (see entry for 6/8/29) and it appears from remarks made by the president of the court on that session's cases of horse-stealing that it was more a case of disputed ownership than actual theft (*HA* 24 July 1829, 3).

should be defended and the Parson has volunteered his Services to go to York tomorrow to endeavour to prevail on the Grand Jury to throw out the Bill.

Monday 3rd. Augt

Wm. Turk's wife was buried here this afternoon at five O'clock. I was Shopkeeper while Eliza and her Mother went to the funeral. After that I went to the new Landlord's David Morley's, where there were a few old acquaintances, I had not been at the house since before Cave fair, but as Morley's have been Customers I went and got a glass there, then came home, and the long Miller came in and had a long discourse respecting the Chancery business,[48] he has put in appearance and has them so fast that they cannot stir an Inch he says until November; and before that time he will endeavour to have all settled. He says it would take a Summer's day to tell the whole of the usage he has met with. These Clout-headed Sisters of his he says have been prompted on by that damn'd Poll Corner, curse their silly heads.

Tuesday 4th. Aug

Geo. Petfield, Jn. Barratt & Jno. Reynolds are subpenaed [*sic*] to appear at York by Geo. Reynolds they are going off this morning, there has been a letter from the Parson from York, he says he expects the Bill against Langricke will not be found by the Grand Jury.

Wednesday 5th. Augt.

It can scarcely be thought, that the Editors of Newspapers who seem zealous for the good of the Nation, can be really in earnest; for they discuss the Merits of these Vagrants, (male and female, by Courtesy Ladies and Gentlemen,) called Players, with as much seeming feeling, as when engaged in pointing out the fitness or unfitness of various individuals who are at the Helm of Affairs. It seems to be as much a serious affair to have a fine Singer or Ear-tickler in the Theatre as to have a wise and good Man to guide the Destinies of the Nation. — The Old Cobler from Welton who is a customer of Mr. Atkinsons, calls the Government for their extravagance. The Villains he says who are in power, want to make the Country Bankrupt, in a secret manner then what says he will be our Situation? This poor fellow then had but a single Halfpenny left after paying for his leather!!!

Thursday 6th. Aug.

Langricke has got home from York Castle without being tried, the Grand Jury not having found a Bill against him, so that he was immediately discharged, how the Prosecutor Reynolds will come on for his Expences I cannot say. I was at Ellerker last night drinking tea with Watson Arton, got home about nine O'clock, the Tea was so strong that it made me sleep very uneasy all night. — Reynolds sent a Letter yesterday to demand the Mare of Langricke, but how he can have any right to her after Langricke has suffered

---

[48] The suit probably arose from the recurrence of the dispute over James Marshall's will, which RS had earlier noted (11/11/26, 19–20/5/27) as causing a rift in the Marshall family, with one sister, Mrs Bellard from Hessle, not speaking to her brother, Thomas, for a month. The Court of Chancery would have been the appropriate court for dealing with the administration of the terms of a will or an appeal against a settlement.

the Law on that account, and nothing being found against him, is not easy to understand. I think he will not get the Horse at least until he pay all the expences that have been incurred. — I wonder how the Paper missed which I sent to Wm. the Tuesday after he went away, as I never neglect to send one.

So. Cave, 6th. Augt. 1829.

Dear Wm.

I hope this will find you well as it leaves us at present. I have been very well in health since you left, but at times rather pensive. I hope your wife has got well again. It was a most merciful providence that you were not either killed or disabled in your limbs. I am glad that the dear little Child escaped without any injury, and hope your wife will be no worse. It has been to you a most disastrous Journey. Your Mother has sent you a Pot of the very best Butter she could buy on Monday last, it is dearer than when you were here being 1s. pr. lb, but think on we are not going to charge you for it. You will also find a Bottle of Raspberry Vinegar which I have labelled according to directions from your Mother, and likewise a Couple of Fowls which were living today. Your Mother has been alternately fretting, then making the Raspberry Vinegar, and enquiring for Fowls; &c. &c. She will make you some Elder Syrup when the Berries are ripe and if you want any thing else only she knows, you shall have it. — She had the misfortune last night to be stung by a Wasp in her mouth, which was in a bit of Sugar she took out of a Pot just when shutting in the Shop, she rubbed it well with Treacle, it was very painful and much swelled, but she slept pretty well, and is much easier this morning. Our best love to you all, likewise Eliza's and her husband, — When you have an opportunity you may send back the Basket Hamper &c but not the Pot—if your wife mix a little Salt in boiling water and put it on the top of the Butter when cool it will make a fine Pickle for preserving it and changing it every day or two.

from your loving Father,

R Sharp

Friday 7th. Aug.

Sent off last Night a Basket to Wm. containing Butter, Fowls &c. which we hope will arrive safe. I know it will be gratefully received. Club night last night, a very thin attendance, Soon got done. Newlove accommodated the Members with sour Ale, but as I am not very partial to that sort of Liquor, I got a Glass of Gin and Water.

Saturday 8th. Augt.

I sometimes give a few Crumbs to Mr. Holborn's Pigeons, of which they are very fond; but our old Cat who will scarce eat any thing that is given to her, always contrives if she can to either pick up the Crumbs or keep away the Pigeons; I believe it is pure Contradiction in her, but some creatures that are called rational, will frequently act in the same manner. At Brantingham again this day the first time since the Holidays.

Sunday 9th. Augt.

Conder had got his Sunday Coat rather stained with an Orange and as it was only new a few Weeks back, he thought it spoiled the <u>mense</u> of it. So there was a Runagate came about who could take spots out of any kind of Cloth, he engaged to renovate this said Coat, which he took I think to Cousens's. he has made a complete cure of it, for it looks as if it had Vitriol spilled upon it; he has likewise set a piece in on one of the Sleeves, and cut away the Elbow of the Coat, and the facings on one side, so that the Pocket is seen, the fellow made away as fast as he could without Conder meeting with him; He went to No. Cave yesterday to see after the fellow on purpose to give him a dressing but could not find him. So there the matter ends.

Monday 10th. Aug

Got two new Penknife blades put in by a travelling Cutler, one into a haft that was Jane's, it is not of much value but a great favourite on account of having belonged to her. No business doing at the Market today.

Tuesday 11th. Aug

My wife at Hull this day she has not been there before for more than a year and a half, very well looked on where she had money to pay, got home a little after nine, very tired. Cousens was there and got drunk coming back so that he had to lay down in the Waggon and a little Boy to drive; He is very subject to get Liquor when he goes to Hull, but never at home.

Wednesday 12th. Aug.

A Parcel and letter from Wm. this morning dated the 31st. July, he says he did not get the Newspaper. I cannot account for it, as it was regularly sent: glad to hear that his wife was recovering, hope she is quite well before this time. I have written with the Papers for the last three weeks, but unfortunately forgot I think on them all to make a Semicolon on the outside. I must try to do better.

Thursday 13th Aug.

I was at Ellerker last night, and got a single Glass of Rum and Water, which I believe was not good, as I was very unwell after I got home; But after a good night's rest I am very well this morning. — Some freeman of Beverley has been telling Old Willy that there will surely be an election in October, as the Duke of Cumberland is going to take the King under his protection, and dismiss the Duke of Wellington. I told him I would believe it when I saw it but at present there was not the least appearance of the Beverley freemen being called upon to exercise their means of extortion.

Friday 14th. Aug

Heard from Wm. this morning that he had received the Basket on Tuesday last, all good except the Chickens. I blame myself for not marking the Paper, I think he had not seen that it was sent, which on my part was very forgetful. A very rainy day yesterday and all last night and still continues wet though not so excessive as it was. It is very much against the Harvest, as it was about fit to begin with.

Saturday 15th. Aug

At west end collecting this afternoon. Robt. Marshall could not be easy in any position on account of the Rain, he is very soon cast down, but there are some Farmers highly elevated at the prospect of a wet harvest, as they think they will be able to sell their old Wheat for an extravagant price. I hope providence will confound them.

Sunday 16th. Aug

After three days of dreadful rain, it is now fine weather the Wheat is in general laid, but I think not damaged as the weather has been cold which will prevent it from sprouting, the Harvest would have generally commenced the last week had the weather been favourable. Heard the parson today in reading the 84th Psalm pronounce Sparrow (Spay-row) and Swallow (Sway-low) It is disgusting such affectation as this.

Monday 17th. Augt.

Richard Milner died last night between six and seven O'clock in the 85th year of his age. He was born at Flamborough, but shortly after his birth his Father removed to Burton Agnes where he was employed by Sir Griffith Boynton, and in his old age I remember him living in one of the Hospitals at Barmston. Richard formerly worked for Mr. Barnard, but having more Zeal than humility he offended Mr. Barnard and lost his situation; He has done much for the cause of Methodism, and has not left a better man behind him, he was respected by all, even those who had no sense of Religion could not help esteeming him.

Tuesday 18th. Aug

Dr. Turnbull has lost his trial at York,[49] for a Will made in his favour at Beverley by a man of the name of Stephenson, it appears to have been conceived in fraud by the Doctor, but it is surprising that a Gentleman one of the attesting witnesses should have witnessed and signed the Will as did the other attesting witnesses before the Man whose will it was had signed it himself. The Doctor I think had best cross the Tweed as Soon as he can, as it is up with him here, sae he may gang back again.

Wednesday 19th. Aug

Very indifferent harvest weather, but as it is ready the work is going on but not with much Spirit. Last night collecting for the Highways with Abraham Barff, he drank three Glasses of Rum and Water in less than half an hour while I stayed with him at Newlove's. I then left him, but whether he had any more or not I cannot say, but I think he then had had a sufficient Quantity, and if the Liquor was strong he ought to have been drunk. — I lately read the following in

---

[49] Alexander Turnbull, a Hull doctor, was the plaintiff in a trial at York on 14 Aug. 1829 (Turnbull v. Shepherd and Watson) in which he was represented by Sir James Scarlett with Brougham as the defence lawyer. Dr Turnbull had inherited the bulk of the estate of an elderly Beverley patient according to the terms of a will which was made under the guidance of the chief beneficiary without the presence of a lawyer and signed by a witness who attested that he had not realized that he was witnessing the signing of a will. It was admitted at the trial that Dr Turnbull had earlier inherited a large legacy from a previous patient (*TM* 17 Aug. 1829, 3 b; *HA* 14 Aug. 1829, 3 and 21 Aug. 1829, 3–4).

a Book of travels. "We passed a mountain covered with white Goats & Sheep; the latter are most of them <u>black</u>"!!

Thursday 20th. Augt.

Mr. Tinsdill is going away in a very short time; there is a Person here who is to succeed him, but I neither know his name nor where he comes from. I think there is no occasion for two Doctors in this place, but it is so in most businesses and professions, they are overstocked.

Friday 21st. Aug

My wife and Eliza with other Company were yesterday at Mr. Tinsdill's, the Gentleman was there who is going to succeed him. He was talking of his coming from London in the Steam packet, which makes me think that it is the same person that came down when Wm. came. His name is I understand Stewpart, I think I have seen him, he has pretty large whiskers, and about the size of Mr. Barnard.

Saturday 22nd. Aug.

It is reported that Mr. Barnard is going to leave Cave and live in the Neighbourhood of York, it is said he is going to let the Gardens, and the Gamekeeper is going to live in the House. I do not know what his motive can be, nor whether it be true, but time will tell.

Sunday 23rd. Aug

A great deal of Rain yesterday afternoon and this day I am afraid that the Wheat will be damaged, the rain has come so heavy; had it been fair weather there would have been wheat, lead in a few days. Let us put our trust in providence and hope for the best. There are plenty of Croakers to take every advantage.

Monday 24th. Aug

A great deal in the Papers respecting the new Ministry in France,[50] to us it is a matter of as little moment, as the change of Scenes in a playhouse. The French press seems very violent on the occasion, it seems to be ridiculous to think that the Ministers have been appointed by English influence.

Tuesday 25th. Aug

A great outcry this day that Wheat is sprouted some say it grew half an inch yesterday in Corn that was not cut; others say it will be but little worse if the weather comes fine. Flour has advanced in the Neighbourhood, but I think not here but is as they say within a crack. Matty brought us none yesterday he said he had no wheat but I believe he with his brethren intend raising the price tomorrow. I cannot see very clearly that for two or three rainy days, Corn should advance, because there is no less quantity, nor will be now, but it may be inferior in quality, and when Corn is worst it <u>generally</u> sells higher than when it is a good year.

---

[50] The centre-right ministry of the Viscount de Martignac and his colleagues had become increasingly ineffective and was dissolved by King Charles X on 5 Aug. 1829. Four days later, on 9 Aug., he appointed an ultra-Royalist cabinet with de la Bourdonnaye and Polignac holding the key posts of Ministry of the Interior and Foreign Office respectively. Later, in Nov., Jules Polignac became Prime Minister (Leys 162–6).

Wednesday 26th. Aug.

Mr. Barnard has given his Servants and Labourers notice to quit; it is said he is so annoyed with the complaints of his tenants that he cannot live amongst them. Had I been in his Place I would have given them notice to quit (instead of his Servants) and threatened them with their Rents being raised, they should have found that they were not permitted to live in the Stile of their Landlord, with their Carpets, and Floor Cloths, their Mirrors and Table Covers, their Cut Glass Decanters, and abundance of Liquors, which they cannot support even if the farms were their own. Then some of the Boobies would fain be polite, and make about as graceful a Bow, as a rugged Oak when bended by a Storm.

Thursday 27th. Aug

The person who is going to succeed Mr. Tinsdill is he who came down at the same time as Wm. he is a North Country man, but has married a wife in the neighbourhood of London who is said to be very rich, I think he has not made a good choice to come here, for if he be attentive to his business he will find it very laborious. Mrs. Tinsdill and her Sister are going to Buxton for the Season.

Friday 28th. Aug

Yesterday afternoon and night were very stormy with a great deal of Rain, the weather is such as might be looked for about Martinmas, it is really very dreadful harvest weather, in low lands there is a deal of Corn under Water. In the Carrs it is said the Crops are wasted, but this land was never meant by nature for Corn, but the high prices of Corn caused it to be changed from bad Grazing to worse Culture.

Saturday 29th. Aug

A Fine day this, the Farmers very busy leading Wheat which I understand is very little injured, although some of the indefatigables seek for sprouted ears, and they seem to be very happy in finding one, for they bear it either home or to some public house, where they take a pleasure in shewing it, and crying out how the crop is spoiled. I wish they could be accommodated with nothing else but sprouted flour as it seems to be a favourite with them.

Sunday 30th. Aug

Richd. Marshall was at Beverley yesterday with the return of Lunatics in the Parish,[51] but there happened to be none; when the Gentlemen asked him if there were no lunatics in the Parish he said no, but if it had been a rainy day there would have been more to put in than the paper would hold, they smiled at him.

Monday 30th. [i.e. 31st] Aug

Mr. Barnard it is said will leave Cave this week, he has dismissed all his Work people, he is only going to keep a Gamekeeper for the Season, so that all his Pheasants and Game which he has been so anxious about will be destroyed.

---

[51] According to section 36 of the 'Act to Amend the Laws for the Erection of County Lunatic Asylums, and more effectually to Provide for the Care and Maintenance of Pauper and Criminal Lunatics, in England' (9 Geo. IV c. 40) passed on 15 July 1828, the Justices of the Peace were required at the first petty sessions after 15 Aug. each year to issue warrants to the overseers of the poor in the parishes under their jurisdiction to return detailed lists of all insane persons chargeable to their parishes.

It has not transpired what he is going away for, the house they say is to be shut up. It is said there are but two persons who know the reason of his going away, but if it be so, there will soon be three, then out comes the secret.

Tuesday 1st. Sepr.

This is the day when the Murderers of Hares & Partridges sally forth according to law,[52] to wage exterminating war on defenceless animals. I should not much wish to be near some of them; was it not more for the Dogs than the Bipeds, the poor Creatures would be very safe. — Misfortunes attend me, for when I try to make myself a little more useful than common, some disaster generally befals [*sic*] me, last week I made a mistake and mixed Brimstone amongst Starch, from which I did not escape very easily. This day the Oatmeal pot fell down when I was in the Shop, and who was blamed for it but unfortunate me, but it is said I shall now be better as I have been three times unfortunate, so now I have brighter times before me.

Wednesday 2nd. Sepr.

Last night we recd. the Parcel from Wm. with the Cow Cabbage seed.[53] It is an amazing plant, I will sow some of the seed and try it. I have not yet seen the old Cardinal, but have given Miss Catharine some of the seed and lent her the Book with the description of it. We are all very glad to hear that Wm. and his wife are well, and little Mary we hope is only suffering a little with her teeth which will only be temporary. I believe the laxity of the Bowels is very favorable to Children when in this Situation. Conder sold a new Saddle and Bridle to the new Doctor today.

Thursday 3rd. Sepr.

A Beautiful day a great deal of Wheat got in, in fine condition. Matty the Miller called yesterday with some Flour which my wife would not take in as it rose last week, and he wanted as much for it as we are selling for 2s/8d, he has been this morning to say that he will bring some on Saturday at 2s/6d; last week we could scarce get any Flour. I hope it will soon be lower.

Friday 4th. Sep

Tailor Waudby once coming from Broomfleet, saw a Partridge limping on just before him, which he thought he could easily catch, so he ran after it, but it still contrived to keep before him on the road, and thus they went on for nearly a Mile, when it popped through a Gate into a field of wheat, he thought he then had it secure, but he soon completely lost it, when getting over the Gate to come back he saw a neighbour who asked him what he was after. He said he had been running after a lame partridge to which at times he was so near as almost to touch it. But the man who knew the habits of these Birds better than the Tailor,

[52] The dates of the open seasons for taking game remained unaltered by the Game Act of 1831. Of the 3 main categories of game protected during their breeding seasons, grouse could be taken from 12 Aug., partridges from 1 Sept., and pheasants from 1 Oct. There was no close season for hares (Bell 56 and 65–7).

[53] Strictly 'a kind of cabbage for feeding cows', it was probably a variety of large open-headed cabbage or kale (*OED*).

told him that it had only been drawing him off from its young brood. Confound it says the Tailor I'll be burned if ever I run after a lame partridge again.

Saturday 5th Sep

I have read Cobbett's Emigrant's Guide[54] which is very amusing, the letters he has published from the Sussex Emigrants appear to be written without the least art, and no doubt give a true account of the feelings of the writers, some of whom have gone through incredible hardships, such as I should not like to encounter; Our Emigrants do not trouble themselves to write home, or if they do their letters do not come to hand. Rd. Padgett and his Brother Willy have not been heard from of some years. Neither has Robt. Dunn who went to Quebec and it was reported was doing well by keeping a Livery Stable, but his friends think that he is now in the United States, but this is merely conjecture.

Sunday 6th. Sepr.

Very fine weather the last week, almost all the wheat is got in. Loncaster was threshing yesterday with a Machine so that I expect it will be soon lower in price, but the Millers are very reluctant to settle the price, but as the Farmers in general want money many of them will be obliged to bring their wheat to Market with as much expedition as possible.

Monday 7th. Sepr.

Plenty of new Wheat in the Market this day, but the buyers were very shy of purchasing; we settled Flour this night to 2/6d. we were the first to bring it down, Pennington brought us a load today at 2s/4d from new wheat, we have had new flour last week very good: there is nothing but Machines at work: they are sure to bring down the price.

Tuesday 8th. Sepr

It was rain last night, and very dull this morning; I have been taking a Voyage towards the South Pole and have just stopped in Latitude 71° 10' South and Longitude 106° 54' west, the most southerly point that was ever sailed to. The Climate towards the South Pole is a great deal more severe, than the same Latitude towards the North; indeed the Sea is so covered with Islands and Mountains of Ice, that it requires the greatest perseverance to navigate it. — My Cow Cabbage seed which I sowed last Wednesday is coming up, indeed it made its appearance yesterday, so that it has laid a very little time in the Ground, which proves that the Seed is good and fresh. Mr. Holborn's is not so forward as mine as his is only just peeping this morning, he thinks he has sown his deeper than I have done.

Wednesday 9th. Sepr

A travelling Match seller was about yesterday with his goods, offering them for Sale, when I told him we could have more for money than he offered, on which he said that those I spoke of were <u>Engine</u> made matches, I asked if engines were used in this department of trade, O yes he answered and they run

[54] William Cobbett, *The Emigrant's Guide; in Ten Letters, Addressed to the Tax-payers of England; Containing Information of Every Kind, Necessary to Persons who are about to Emigrate ...* London: published by the author, 1829. A new, and extended, edition was published the following year (1830).

the prices down so much that a poor Man by <u>manual operation</u> (formerly called hand labour) cannot compete with them. I do not know whether they are made by steam engines or not.[55] — I was lately at Beverley when a person gravely asserted before the Company that he had seen persons to the number of 50 or 60 shaved by steam in the twinkling of an eye; it was laughable to see the open mouths, and stroking of Chins that this Orator produced on his hearers. Wheat 10s. pr. quarter lower at Hull.

Thursday 10th. Sepr

That great Stronghold of Vice Covent Garden Theatre appears to be in a very pretty situation at present,[56] the lovers of the Drama as it is called, either cannot afford to pay to keep up the establishment, or they love their money better than they love the Drama, for it appears the Playhouse folks are nearly fixed; I have some hopes that this amusement of Play going is on the decrease.

Friday 11th. Sepr

An uncommon deal of Rain last night, it had run down Porter hole across the Street, but we heard nothing of it—Mrs. Holborn got up she was so much alarmed, she thought that a Cloud had burst it poured down so rapidly, it has been very fine weather today.

Saturday 12th. Sepr.

I was at the West end this afternoon collecting. Mrs. Robt. Marshall got an Apple to eat but she says she is not much of an apple eater: but I found there was something more, for it was attended with a little display, she pulled a small case out of her Pocket in which was a silver fruit knife, this was enough! It has been so much rain that the water has run through the Barn of Ths. Marshall.

Sunday 13th. Sepr

Mr. Popple of Welton who was the Curate here sometime since, was found dead in his Study yesterday morning. I am very sorry for him, for he was a very excellent Character, feeling and humane. His father will feel his loss severely, it is said he had only got his text written which was "What shall I do to inherit eternal life".

Monday 14th. Sep

We have settled Flour this morning to 2s/4d pr. Stone. Pennington sent word he would bring us some at 2s/2d but we did not order any. Hotham Miller came to see if we wanted any, we bid him 2s. pr. Stone for 20 Stone, but he

---

[55] The match-seller would appear to have been intentionally misleading the diarist. Matches were then, and continued to be for some decades, made by hand. A 'match' at that time was usually a splinter of wood dipped in sulphur and used in conjunction with a tinder box, although some friction matches might have just begun to become available as their invention is generally credited to John Walker of Stockton-on-Tees in 1827. The large-scale manufacture of matches by machine does not seem to have occurred in Britain until the second half of the 19th c. Bryant and May set up their factory in London in 1861 but at that time the manufacture of matches was described as a 'laborious practice involving fifteen to twenty operations, most of which had to be done by hand' (*DNB*; *EB* xvii. 876).

[56] The theatre was experiencing a period of financial difficulty and had been compelled to sell off some of its assets, including costumes and scenery. The first of a series of meetings of creditors took place on 7 Sept. 1829 (*TM* 27 Aug. 1829, 3 a and 8 Sept. 1829, 2 d).

could not take it, he is to bring 20 Stone for £2–1–0. we shall then settle it again, I hope it will keep reasonable.

Tuesday 15th. Sep

I think that Wheat yesterday could not be sold for more than 50s. pr. quarter, altho' I heard a Miller say that 52s. had been refused. I think flour might at these prices be afforded for 2s. for if a Quarter make 27 Stone it will pay well at that, including the offal.[57] Recd. the Examr. & Cobbett this morning of the 5th. Sepr.

Wednesday 16th. Sepr

Mr. Davenport's traveller was here yesterday, we paid him and gave fresh orders, — Wm. Cade is removing to Hull today, I am afraid old Joshua will not be well provided for, he has got through a deal of money—he used to say when at a public house, "Come dan it another Glass, a single glass more cannot do much" ...

Friday 18th. Sepr

A very rainy day; Some of the Weather sages said yesterday that the Glasses were so high, we should have no rain for some time. Now I do not pretend to foretell with any certainty what weather we are to have a day beforehand, Yet I venture to say when these Glass gazers are expatiating how wonderful clever they are, that I should not be surprised if we have Rain shortly, when they prophesy nothing but fair weather, and vice versa, and I am as oft right as they are.

Saturday 19th. Sep

I was at the Mill last night for Money but could not come on for any—Tom Leak had been out one night and taken one of the horses without leave of the Miller his father in law; but he found it out the next morning, when they quarrelled as they often do. Tom Leak told long Tom he would be safe to go to the Devil, why he says what, that will not do thee any good neither will thou be hurt by it, but thou hast done me an injury by taking my horse, so what satisfaction will it be to thee if I go to the devil, mind thou does not come there, for we shall not agree if I be there when thou comest.

Sunday 20th. Sep

A very fine day, some of the Farmers I doubt not muttering that they cannot work, but for all the weather has been so often wet, yet the harvest has often been far more injured for the Wind has generally been sharp and strong, which has kept the Corn from sprouting.

Monday 21st. Sepr.

It is said that Robt. Arton has given Mr. Barnard notice to quit his farm, it has been said some time that Rd. Marshall wants it either for Norrison or Tom Levitt but it is generally thought for Norrison; they are so selfish and so worldly minded that they wish to have every thing in their own hands. If Robt. Arton has given Notice I think he has shewn a becoming Spirit; he told Mr. Barnard at the Rent day that Rd. Marshall wanted his farm, but Mr. B. said no such

---

[57] i.e. the waste material, dust, or scourings from the corn (*OED*).

thing had ever been mentioned to him, but he (Arton) still said, you may depend on it Sir what I say is true, so there it ended for that time. <u>Flour 2s/2d pr. Stone</u>.

Tuesday 22nd. Sepr. [This entry written in red ink]

This I am resolved shall be a Red letter day with me. It is my Birthday. I was born the 22nd. Septr. 1773. I never have any feasting or rejoicing, and it was in the Evening this day when I mentioned it, or else we should have had a Spice Cake.

Wednesday 23rd. Sepr.

Bobby Thornton now attends fairs with his Shoes his father Old Dicky says lad can do better than he could himself and he did not think himself a Bad Salesman. But Bobby beats him hollow What he talks away says Dicky so much and gets company about him, that young Lasses buy of him like <u>Smack</u>.[58] Now Bobby is not famed for Oratory at home; but abroad he really is surprising!!

Thursday 24th. Sepr

Old Willy Atkinson says that in a kind of Riot at Doncaster with some of the low Gamblers the Duke of Wellington seized some of them. I and Giles Bridgman told him that his Grace was not there on that day, but he said he had his information from a Man that saw him. We found it useless to reason with him longer, indeed I think it is of little use to endeavour to set a person right, when he is so confident of what he asserts. I am sure it was of no moment to me whether the Duke did this feat or he did not.

Friday 25th. Sepr

The Parson was examining the Candidates for Confirmation on Wednesday last, when he asked one Girl what was her name which she told him, he then asked who gave you that name? "I seer I dont know" was the answer, what not know who gave you your name, No my Mother never told me Indeed I never ax'd her. So the Parson was fairly at his ne plus ultra. This was told to me I did not hear it.

Saturday 26th. Sep

At Ellerker this afternoon settling with Mr. Leeson for the Ellerker Church Sess, got tea there and a Glass of Brandy and Water. I think I have not tasted Spirits for more than a month before; I feel always best when I take the least.

Sunday 27th. Sep.

The Parson has found out a new method of preaching for instead of explaining the meaning of Scripture, he explains what it does not mean, so that his discourses may be called negative. He is a poor Creature.

Monday 28th. Sep

Howden Shew is at this time for Horses. I never saw so many come through here; at Weighton fair last week there were great complaints of Stock selling very low, for my part I am glad to hear it; for the great Bull frogs have had their day, and they may now croak as they please, they are not much minded.

---

[58] Used colloquially in various dialects to mean 'very quickly' (Wright).

Tuesday 29th. Sep

Horses it is said sell very badly at Howden shews, several have had horses there and were never asked the price. I have a little pleasure in hearing the Loggerheads mutter so much but as to their general complaints it is all my eye and Betty Martin, let prices be what they will they are never content.

Wednesday 30th Sep

Robt. Arton has not given notice of his Farm neither will he yet he says; He cares nothing for the Steward and this he told Robt. Marshall which nettled him not a little, he knows he says that they want his Farm, and I do not dispute it. Out last night collecting Highway Sess. Money very bad to get. I see in the paper this morning that a printseller has been before the Magistrates for selling prints before their publication. It does not appear how he has become possessed of them but honestly he cannot.

Thursday 1st. Octr.

Mr. Ingram the Surveyor of Taxes was here today, seeing if he could not find out some ground for surcharges, he seemed although this was his first visit to be as well acquainted with what Articles the different persons have as I am, nay he told me of one person (Fenwick the Carrier) having a Dog[59] which I did not know of, but I dare say it is true from the enquiries I have made.

Friday 2nd. Oct

Club night last night, very throng as it is what is called the third night, when if the payments are not made they are fined the next meeting night— Newlove has been employing young Teavil Leeson to get some small debts for him some of about 3 or 4 Shillings, and some of the Poor debtors have been put to the expence of as many pounds by this limb of the law.

Saturday 3rd. Oct.

Abm. Barff called me into Tindale's this day where he was drinking. I never saw him so drunk before, he wanted to go out and got into the Closet instead of out of doors, he was fairly made up, he seems to mind nothing but drinking.

4th. Octr Sunday

I really think I have nothing to remark this day, nothing particular to notice, — I put up a Notice for a meeting on Tuesday next, and I wrote April instead of October but it just answered the same end, and I think there were very few that discovered the mistake.

Monday 5th. Oct

Long Tom was here today, muttering as hard as he could, we had an Apple pie on the table, and asked him to have some, which he got and said it was a

---

[59] Taxation on the keeping of dogs was first introduced by Pitt in 1796 (36 Geo. III c. 124). This Act taxed dog owners on a rising scale according to which of 3 classes they belonged: persons keeping one dog only and that not a sporting dog — 2s.; persons keeping a sporting dog or more than one dog — 5s. for every dog; persons keeping a pack of hounds — £20. In a series of Acts, over the next 16 years, the rates for the 3 classes of dog owners were raised to a maximum of 8s., 14s., and £36, but in 1824 sheep dogs belonging to farms of under £100 p.a. were made exempt from taxation (5 Geo. IV c. 44), a privilege extended in 1834 to all working farm dogs irrespective of ownership (4 & 5 Will. IV c. 73) (Dowell iii. 263–4).

very good pie, there was a piece left and he was invited to eat it up, but he excused himself, however Tom who knows how to behave asked if we really wanted it eaten, we told him certainly for if he did not eat it we should have it to eat ourselves. Whya then if that be the case I will try for I do not like to set anybody to work at what I can do myself, I will try, so he set to and finished it in a neighbourly way.

Tuesday 6th. Octr.

The Newspaper missed coming yesterday. I thought it would have been here this morning, but it did not arrive. So I must wait patiently (if I can) without it. — Found half a Quire of best gilt edged paper behind some drawers on the Shop Floor, which was entirely spoiled, having turned all Colours but the right one.

Wednesday 7th. Oct.

A meeting last night to balance the Highway accounts, but one item of A Barff's the Surveyor for £3–10–0 was unintelligible when he brought his accounts to enter in the Book. I could not make it out what it was for neither could he who was the writer give any explanation of it. The consequence was that his accounts were not allowed by the meeting, as he would not have the £3–10 struck out, the entry was as follows

Paid   7 May 1829—£3–10–0   in the Blank in his own account was some kind of writing, he came this morning and said he expected I had entered it the same as his Copy, but I told him I could not think of entering an account I could not read, so he said he would write it himself, and take it to Beverley for the Justices to allow. I asked what he would say if the Magistrates asked him what it was, he said it showed that it was for something. I believe myself that he may have paid the Money but not for the Highways. The Paper which should have come on Monday, came this morning it had been at South Shields. Notice in it that all were well.

Thursday 8th. Octr.

At Brantingham last night measuring some land belonging Mr. Nelson, it was very cold, and this morning the Ground was covered with Snow, the Winter has come upon us very soon, but I hope the Weather will not long continue so severe as it is at present.

Friday 9th. Octr.

Ab. Barff did not get his Highway Accounts allowed by the Magistrates on Wednesday last, he is to attend again on the 24th. Octr. after having called a meeting of the Parishioners when he is to establish his claim for the £3–10 or have it disallowed, the latter I have no doubt will be the case. Teavil Leeson and Richard Marshall are appointed Surveyors for the ensuing year. It was expected that Robinson of Mount Airy and Mr. Shackleton would have been chosen as their names were first on the list.

Saturday 10th. Oct.

Our Baskets and a Besom were left out last night after it was dark, and the Besom was gone, just after our friend Nanny Hordale had been in the Shop. She soon came again when Mrs. said to her, Nanny the lads in the Street were shouting that you run away with our Besom, but Nanny knew nothing of it, but she said she heard them shouting so, but the Besom was there when she went away, but she would make enquiry after it for she knew someone who had always two new ones, and if they had three it was sure to be there, but nothing transpired to get it returned, and poor Nanny is hurt with hearing the cry of taking the Besom away.

Sunday 11th. Oct

Henry Arton has got the Bailiffs in his house, they seized on Friday last, it is Brother Watson who has put them in, but for what I cannot say, some say he is bound for the Rent and he wants to secure it while there is sufficient on the Premises. I doubt some trickery is going on amongst them. I am afraid we shall be losers on the occasion as he owes for Schooling between two and three pounds for a long time past,[60] he promised last week to let us have some Wheat for it, but this has put all out.

Monday 12th. Oct

Michl. Clegg as Bum Bailiff to Teavil Leeson, got into Tommy Shaw's house today with an Attachment, when he was saluted by Tommy's wife with Fire poker and tongs, he defended himself with a Chair, and he got another of his Companions in, on which Jenny had locked the door after Mic. entered, he having gone in to beg a pipe. Mic. did not like his reception.

Tuesday 13th. Octr

I have heard that Newlove wants to let his house, I think it has been evident some time that he is not making a living, for he never does anything, excepting in fine weather lolling against the Sign Post, besides he is a noisy ignorant fellow, and not many Persons like to go to his house.

Wednesday 14th Oct.

Wrote a Notice to the Surveyors of the Highways for Ellerker to remove a Clough which they have in the Mill Beck by which they turn the Water into Crabley Drain near Swan Neck, which they have no right to do, as far as I can understand, however the Ellerker people are of a different way of thinking, and they are stupid and insist on it as their right. — But I well remember the Clough being first put down, so that they have no claim of Antiquity to support them.

Thursday 15th. Octr.

Recd. with the Paper this morning a notice to order Cousens to call at Mr. Redford's for a <u>Packet</u>, which I shall not forget to do; a letter from the Stamp Office requiring me to return some Parcht. Skins of 4s. which are going to be discontinued and 3s/6d ones, to be used instead, likewise 2s/8d Skins instead of 3s. as formerly. I shall therefore return all the 3 and 4s Skins I have. This has been a very fine day, yesterday was uncommonly stormy; it blew some of the thatch off our old Stable top. Mr. Holborn will mend it when we get some straw.

---

[60] See *Introduction* for the scale of fees charged to parents in 1818. Subscriptions may have increased by 1829. Henry Arton and his wife had a large family, so that it is probable that they had more than one child attending the school at this time.

Friday 16th. Oct

Robt. Marshall was here last night it is a long time since he was here before, he had two horses at Howden Fair of which he was not asked the price; he had money bid for them before the fair 28 pounds for one and 25 pounds for the other, he would be glad to take it now, but it is too late. He lost a Cow in calving yesterday. He complains that times were never so bad as they are now.

Saturday 17th. Oct

Recd. a parcel from Wm. last night, we are glad to hear that they are all well and that little Mary is so lively. I have read the Monthly Magazine, but it shews a strange Change of Principle from what it was in Sir Rd. Phillip's time, it is outrageously Tory, here Mr. Sadler's[61] speech to the Blubber-men at Whitby is extolled to the Skies, while the Leeds Mercury and the Times, execrate it as the very ravings of a distempered imagination.

Sunday 18th. Oct

Mr. Barnard's Groom says his Master has left the House because it is haunted. This man appears to be rather weak and the lad or under Groom one day dressed up an image of a Woman which he fixed over a trap door above the room where they slept, the lad got into bed first, and when the groom was just getting in the lad pulled a string which he had fixed when the Woman shewed her head, but he had scarcely time to look when she bolted head foremost into the Room and the poor Groom run out naked, and made his way to the Girls' chamber which was fastened as they were in the secret, he expected the lad after him, but as he did not arrive and the Man did not know where to turn, he ventured back, and asked the lad if he was not frightened, the lad asked what must he be afraid of, he said the Woman that came through the trap door, but the lad told him he had neither heard nor seen anything of a Woman for he had got all cleverly out of the way before the man returned—the lad dressed up a Cat in paper one night and had her shut up in the Room, which met the poor Groom when he went to bed. — so that he is now certain that the house is haunted.

Monday 19th. Oct.

We have had two or three very fine days, which is quite reviving after so much severe weather, — Geo. Scott from Newbald has been selling Flour in odd Stones at 2s. pr. Stone, so we have settled ours to that price—Pennington says he will come and take a room and sell it at the same price as he is selling to Shops, but before we will be beaten in this manner we will sell it for a time as we get it. I think he can be checked.

Tuesday 20th. Octr.

Shop goes on much as usual, at this time there is but little Flour sold, as the Poor people have gleaning Corn, but then they have their money to lay out for other Articles, so that we take nearly the same as we did. Indeed I believe

[61] Michael Thomas Sadler (1780–1835), a protégé of the Duke of Newcastle, was Tory MP for Newark at this time and an opponent of free trade and supporter of the landowners. He later became an active social reformer, introducing a bill to regulate the conditions of young persons working in mills and factories (*TM* 23 Sept. 1829, 2 d; *DNB*).

we sell more, as the last winter Flour was 3s/4d pr. Stone, so that the same Sum taken weekly now, requires more things to be sold for the same money. We have no occasion to complain. My wife is an excellent Shopkeeper, and she says she never undertook anything but she was favoured by providence.

Wednesday 21st. Octr.

Lord Muncaster has been at Brantingham this week, some say he is going to live there again, it was said last week that he was in a Lunatic Asylum, but this appears not to have been the case. Geo Holborn who was his Gamekeeper, has been discharged from his Service. I suppose his Lordship is much like some other Lords and Commoners too, he contrives to live <u>elegantly</u> above his income. When people get forward in this manner they are without doubt Candidates for the Company of Jonathan Martin. Flour 2s. pr. Stone.

Thursday 22nd. Octr

I have had Abraham Barff this morning, he says the Accounts which I settled with him are not right; but when I know that they are I could not for a moment entertain an idea, that any thing was wrong; in fact he does not know his receipts from his Disbursements; so that it is idle to try to convince him. There was a Sum of £31–7–8 which he had laid out, and he took in his head that it was charged to him as money he had from me, I showed him his own book where he had entered it himself, but I think he knew nothing about it. He is quite disagreeable to do any business with. There will be à meeting tonight to call him to account for the £3–10–0 which he could not make out.

Friday 23rd. Oct

A meeting last night but Abraham could not make out his £3–10 so he did not get his Book signed, last night he was charged with paying too much for other things, he said he did not pay the money but it was paid by me but this is shuffling, they are his accounts and not mine, nothing was paid by me without his approbation. I told him this morning it was his duty to take all the responsibility upon himself and not to try to involve me with him, it is the first time that ever an officer blamed me for paying money to his order. I am heartily tired of him. Tom Marshall told him the £3–10 should not serve his turn he would have as much more taken off.

Saturday 24th. Oct

Went from Brantingham to Ellerker to Mr. Levitt's where I wanted some money but he was gone to Howden, from thence I went to the Mill but the Miller had gone to Broomfleet, so that I was out here again[.] I then went to Teavil Leeson's but he was out shooting, so that all was disappointment to me this day.

Sunday 25th. Octr.

Old Mrs. Akam died yesterday she is 85 years of age and will be buried at Brantingham, she has been ill some time, the House goes to Wm. Akam's Children and the Holland toys[62] are going to live in it. Both her Sons have done

---

[62] Apparently a collective sobriquet, the origin of which is lost, for Mrs Elizabeth Akam and her sister, Rachel. (See Appendix 2).

as ill for themselves as possible. John has a great overgrown extravagant wife which he cannot manage within bounds, and as to poor simple Willy, (as Cobbett says by Castlereagh) he cut his throat and there was an end of him.

Monday 26th. Oct

The Politicians know not what to say of the Peace between Russia & Turkey.[63] The Russian is certainly a great overgrown State but still grasps at more, and keeps adding Country to Country without almost opposition; as to the Turks their Indolence and Tyranny have long been proverbial, but as they were tolerably quiet they were tolerated, more for fear their fine Country should pass into more enterprising hands, than for the sake of themselves.

Tuesday 27th. Oct

We had Hannah Martin washing yesterday, a Sister of hers came to see her, she had been to her house, and told Hannah that her Girls were at Dinner when she was there, they had made a fire in the parlour, and indulged themselves with Apple Dumplings—at the sound of Apple Dumplings and parlour fire Hannah broke out quite outrageous. Od rot 'em says she but I will give 'em something else when I get home, I'll strap 'em to some tune I'll mak 'em remember Apple Dumplings. My wife said why you grow the Apples, and have gleaned the Corn for flour so that it costs you very little; but Hannah could think of nothing better for them to a Supper than the Leathern Strap.

Wednesday 28th. Oct.

Court yesterday the Dinner was at Cousens' I was there, about twenty dined, Geo. Petfield & Ths. Levitt again appointed Constables and Michl. Clegg the Pinder these are all the Officers that are appointed. There formerly was another officer called "Flesh Greaves" whose duty it was to examine the Butchers' meat and to seize what was bad. Old Billy Dunn was the last officer of this kind he used to attend in his official Capacity at the Court since I first came.

Thursday 29th. Oct

Abraham Barff got his accounts settled last night, he was allowed 3s–10d instead of £3–10–0. and if he can make out what the remainder is for he is to have it; I would have lost it all sooner than have compounded for 3s/10d. There were but two who signed the Book, viz. Teavil Leeson & Mr. Gardam.

Friday 30th. Oct.

A Letter from the Stamp office to enquire if Watson Arton and his Mother yet lived at Ellerker, and whether they were in good circumstances, to which I gave an answer in the affirmative. I suppose that they want to make some further charge on their Duties, on them as Executors of Jn. Arton's will, but this is only my own thought.

---

[63] The Treaty of Adrianople, signed on 14 Sept. 1829, granted favourable terms to Russia including full liberty of navigation and commerce in the Black Sea. Both Britain and France were worried by the increase of Russian power in the area and the weakening of the Ottoman empire (*TM* 19 Oct. 1829, 2 b; *EB* xxiii. 904).

Saturday 31st. Oct

Measuring some Wheat reaping for Robt. Marshall this afternoon at the Ings adjoining Provence Ground, a very cold day, got a Blister on my heel with walking, staid Tea at Robt. Marshall's, then came home and helped a little in the Shop, though my help is sometimes little better than hindrance.

Sunday 1st. Nov

A Very severe frost last night, but this day was bright and Sun-shining— Called at the Mill yesterday when the Miller was in a severe fit—of swearing, the lad had been pulling Apples and broken a new ladder, which was a copious source for Tom to vent his rage. These folks he says are the greatest fools that ever existed to offer to pull Apples at all, when they can neither sell them nor give them away, they lay under the trees and nobody will pick them up, and still they will be such fools as to pull them, and to break his ladder.

Monday 2nd. Nov

A Good deal of Barley shewn in the Market today, the Market had been higher at Wakefield on Friday last, so that, the sellers were stretching out their necks like a little Bantam Cock crowing. I believe there were but few buyers. We are selling Barley meal for Pigs this Season at 13d. pr. Stone, it was 17d. pr. Stone last year.

Tuesday 3rd. Novr

Very busy this week collecting the half year's taxes which are to be paid in on Saturday next, it is a troublesome concern as in many Cases money is scarce, and very bad to get hold of. Wheat appears to be rather advancing in price, but Flour remains at the same price, we got 40 Stone of Barley meal and 22 Stone of Flour today from Hembrough of Hotham.

Wednesday 4th. Nov

The Gamekeeper and Newlove have been out today for hares for the Hare feast on the 5th. Novr. Newlove has got two they have likewise got a load of Ale in so that they will be quite ready to entertain their Customers. I think they are not in a very good way for last week they got a single Cask of Ale only.

Thursday 5th. Nov

Mr. Hill the Doctor has had an execution in his house and this day a Bailiff from Beverley came with a Waggon and took away all his goods, I happened to look out and saw the Waggon loading, but I was not long before I was there to secure the Taxes due. So I demanded them of the Bailiff who ordered me to shew my Authority, and as it is folly to go to fight without Arms, I shewed him a Warrant, when he immediately agreed to pay the demand for half a year, I wished to have the taxes for the whole year, but I put up with what was now due. — The Seizure was for borrowed Money about £60 which with the Expences has run to about £83.

Friday 6th. Nov

Yesterday the fifth of Novr. was kept up as usual with the ringing of Bells, Bonfires and Hare feasts at the Public houses. I attended none of them. Indeed I was glad that I had not an invitation, as it did not put me under the necessity of giving a denial—It was Club night, got done about nine O'clock and came home. Conder was at Newlove's feast.

Saturday 7th Nov

The Churchwardens had ordered three new Bell Ropes against the 5th. Novr. they were sent down to James Levitt's, and when they were wanted there were but two left, some person had taken one away in sport[.] Old Lonc was terribly exasperated, but I suppose they know where it is, but he says he will not have it again.

Sunday 8th. Nov

I was at Beverley yesterday paying in the taxes, I wanted about six Guineas of Mr. Levitt of Ellerker and had been four or five times for it on purpose on Wednesday last he promised to pay before Saturday morning, but he then sent a note beginning with "I am sorry" I read no further for I did not want his Sorrow but his money. Shackleton above Five pounds did not pay a penny.

Monday 9th. Nov

Both my Customers I mentioned yesterday and some more promised I should be paid today but I have not seen one of them, nor got one Farthing of the money. It is very tiresome to be thus put off and to advance money for people to whom I am not under the least obligation.

Tuesday 10th. Nov

Pocklington fair was yesterday, for Sheep, the prices were higher than they have been, and the Farmers enjoying the prospect of exorbitant prices once again. I hope they will not be realised, for every one knows that even at the present prices the poor can have but very little flesh meat. The motto of these Dung heads is "High prices and no free trade".

Wednesday 11th Nov

I went last night to Robt. Arton's for some Rates, and he was telling of his Adventures at Malton fair; when he was there who should I spy says he but Mr. Atkinson aye dere he was sure enough, got to him before he saw me tipp'd him on the Shoulder like a <u>Bull-Bailiff</u>, looks about and found it was me, aye I was dere safe enough, then saw Mr. Bridgman tell you what, wondered to see them, but recollecting a little, I knew they went every year.

Thursday 12th. Nov

Burton Sittings day, held here, a terrible rainy morning and forenoon, in the afternoon rather better, but still wet, which prevented many persons from attending[.] Mr. Smelt was here, I was as usual at the Constables' dinner, it was at Newlove's there were 18 dined. After that went up to Morleys to settle with Barnard Cook, Ths. Wride and David for the half years taxes, which they paid amongst them, thought I had done very well then came home, and soon after went to bed so thus ended the Sittings day.

Friday 13th. Nov

The Farmers still anxious for a monopoly, either for feeding or starving the Country, to them it is immaterial provided they profit by it. High prices for Corn is the end of every harangue. For my part I hope that instead of the monopoly being made over to them, that it will be discontinued and we shall be permitted to purchase where we can to the most advantage.

Saturday 14th. Nov

Had to send to Hull today for a Stamp the Carrier not bringing what I sent for yesterday, and the one that did not come was wanted for a purchase to be completed on Tuesday next. I gave the lad 2s/6d for going. Settled with Teavil Leeson for the Highway balance for last year. I had to receive £1–6–1½ so that it was soon paid.

Sunday 15th. Nov

Mrs. Holborn has lent me Sewell's History of the Quakers.[64] I have read a good deal of it this day. The first persons of this persuasion suffered incredibly. I have a great respect for many of the Quakers, I think it proceeds from being acquainted with two old Women of this Sect who lived at Burlington, they had a good many Books, and I was allowed and invited to ransack amongst them as much as I liked, where I could get amongst Books it was always a treat to me. One of the Old Women whose name was Ruth used to tell a deal about Oliver's wars, and either her Father or Grandfather had then suffered persecution, she was then I think about 80 years old and this is—40 year since. Thus our time passes away.

Monday 16th. Nov

Farmers looking dull today as the Factors were bidding lower prices, indeed they did not seem inclined to buy at all, Barley was offered but could not be sold, as the Maltsters say they have plenty of old Malt—Newlove was begging for the Sittings last week, my wife offered him a Shilling, but he would not take it, for which I am not at all sorry, so he says he will not use the Shop, then I will not use his house. His custom was worth very little, and had it been better, I should not have liked to buy it. Now I will prophesy, I fully believe I shall see him out and I think not long first.

Tuesday 17th. Nov

Marshalls have got their Chancery business settled the expences were about 17 pounds, a very moderate Sum for a Chancery suit. Tom says he has been in all Courts in England; Mr. Garnons once put him in the Spiritual Court for some tithe of Flax which he once grew, he got out here for about half a Guinea. Robt. & Tom differed, Tom brought up his wife to prove Robt. a liar. Robt. is so out about it that he says the Miller shall not grind for him any more, this to him is the unkindest cut of all, he can bear calling, if he have the <u>Poke</u> only it is some consolation, for Tom finds such a pleasure in Moultering as none but Millers know, he can forgive almost anything if he can only have the Bag confided to him.

---

[64] The reference is to Willem Sewel's *The History of the Rise, Increase and Progress of the Christian People called Quakers*, of which several English editions had been published in translation from the Dutch original, first published in Amsterdam in 1717. Probably the most recent edition available to RS was the 5th ed., published in 2 vols., in London in 1811.

Wednesday 18th. Nov.

Recd. this morning a parcel from Wm. with an order for Ducks Fowls and Geese which will be attended to, glad to hear that they are all well. Returned the paper as desired where there is an account of the Coroners Inquest, when Wm. was a witness, was the man on whom the inquest was held the Druggist, with whom he was acquainted at Hull? I almost think it was the same.

Thursday 19th. Novr

This is Cave Sittings Day, very cold and frosty, a good deal of Company in the town, but I think not much hiring. Dancing at Newloves I dare say most of the night, if the house were mine I should be afraid of them dancing it down.

Friday 20th. Nov

A very hard frost again, looked into the Picture of Australia,[65] New Holland[66] is an amazing Island, I think the Emigrants to Swan River, are too sanguine in their expectations, for I do not see what immediate benefit they can derive from their situation,[67] I believe it is a general observation that where the Land is nearly clear of Wood the soil is generally ungenial.

Saturday 21st. Nov

Wm. Dove died last night shortly after having had a palsy fit or stroke of some kind, he has been employed by Mr. Barnard and his Ancestors for 60 years, but discharged a short time ago, and presented or was to be with £20. He has recd. £10 of it. Saml. Leighton was ordered to have the same.

Sunday 22nd. Nov.

Yesterday I had to invite the Members of the Club to Wm. Dove's funeral at 2 O'clock this day they met at the Club room I have a penny each for letting them know, there are in the town 61 Members, they met at the time, and after that they went to the funeral, but after I had called over the names I went home, and came no more out this day.

Monday 23rd. Nov.

On account of a small advance in the price of Wheat last week, the Millers not to lose anything by being too late, have raised the Price of Flour. Pennington brought some this afternoon which he would take no less than 2s. pr. Stone for, and as we were out we took it in at that price, although none of the Shops have yet raised it ...

---

[65] Robert Mudie, *The Picture of Australia, Exhibiting New Holland, Van Diemen's Land and All the Settlements, from the First at Sydney to the Last at the Swan River*. London: Whittaker, Treacher and Co., 1829.

[66] New Holland was the older name for Australia.

[67] Following a favourable report on Swan River, on the western coast of New South Wales, by Captain Stirling, R.N., in 1827, a syndicate was formed to purchase one million acres from the government and exploit the area as a colony. Captain Stirling was appointed governor in May 1829 and the first settlers arrived. Unfortunately the venture proved to be a failure partly due to lack of preparation and organization by the speculators, and partly because fewer colonists than expected were forthcoming, and many of them had little experience of farming and were ill-prepared for pioneering life in virgin territory; in addition, the land proved to be infertile by English standards. The population in 1830 was 4,000; in 1832 it had fallen to 1,500 (Barnard 196–200).

Wednesday 25th. Nov

The old Cardinal called me out today to look at the Cupola[68] which he said was leaning to one side viz. next the Street and that the Wall had budged out, he took me to his place of observation, where something of the kind appeared, but upon looking more attentively I found he was mistaken, I then went up on the inside to examine it, but could not find anything amiss. A very wintry snowy day.

Thursday 26th Nov

America and Swan River Mania is very prevalent here at present. James Milner and most if not all of his family are attacked with it, but I think if he has a mind to Americanise he cannot raise the needful to get him there. Robt. Nicholson they say talks of Swan River, he married one of Matthew Pickering's daughters, and his wife will not hearken to his folly. There is a Joiner who served his time with G. Petfield and married his Sister who talks of emigrating, as the sure way to independence.

Friday 27th. Nov

This is a very dull Martinmas week, the weather has been so stormy and cold, I was going past Morley's last night, there was a great noise, which I suppose was called singing, but it had no charms for me. Ned Coates came to borrow a pack of Cards of us, but such articles we never had therefore could not supply him.

Saturday 28th. Nov

There is a Farmer at New Village who has been sold up, his Landlord loses £400 by him, they say it is excellent land, but wretchedly managed and not too high rented. There is likewise another in the same neighbourhood who has failed with a loss to his Landlord of £180. Let them go say I, they have looked high enough, so now is their time.

Sunday 29th. Nov

Heard there was no Paper this morning so did not get up till about nine O'clock. Saw the Leeds Mercury[69] in the afternoon, the Editor fights hard to persuade his readers that trade is improving, while the other Leeds papers on the Contrary assert that their [*sic*] is no improvement at all, that prices and wages are ruinously low.

Monday 30th. Nov

Got up this morning about seven O'clock as I expected 2 Papers, but behold there was one came and that an old one eight months back, entirely filled with advertisements, so that all in the News way was nothing this day.

---

[68] The market hall and school was built in 1796 to the design of the then squire, H. B. Barnard. The building is surmounted by a cupola resting on a turret which served as a bell tower for the school (Pevsner (1995) 701).

[69] Published from May 1718 to 25 Nov. 1939, when it was incorporated into the *Yorkshire Post*. Originally weekly, and for a time thrice weekly, it became one of the foremost provincial daily newspapers, especially under the proprietorship of Edward Baines (senior),who ran it single-handed from 1801 until 1827, and in conjunction with his son, Edward Baines (junior), from 1827 onwards, throughout the period of the diary. See also n.105 (1827).

Went to Riplingham to swear to the delivery of Surcharges, got back about One
O'clock.

Tuesday 1st. Decr.

Nothing doing at the Market yesterday, higher prices are asked for wheat,
but the buyers not very free to give it. Barley very dull, and ordinary qualities
scarcely looked at. At London on Friday it is said the Market was very dull.

Wednesday 2nd. Decr.

I had 2 papers this morning both packed together, the one that should have
come on Sunday has not yet arrived. — There has not been (says Mr. Shaw) a
good crop in Swanland field since the inclosure, before that time it was noted
for fine crops of Wheat, the last year there was not more than 5 loads on 4
Acres; but this is not the worst, for in the open state the land was about 15s. pr.
Acre with the privilege of 500 Acres of Common land for no rent. But now the
rent is from 50 to 55s. pr. Acre, so that this improving is like the improvement
of the Irish Captains company, who improved in growing worse and worse.

Thursday 3rd. Decr

I must here close my Journal for this time, as we are throng making ready
for sending off a Basket to Wm. We have Hannah Martin dressing Poultry and
where she is there is generally plenty of noise. She has got one of her Girls
hired to Jackson's at Ellerker Sands.

S. Cave, 3rd. Decr. 1829

Dear Wm

   As I have sent you my Journal, (which I have no doubt you
will esteem more than two or three Letters !!) I have but little to write about
except in the trite stile of "all well and hope you are the same". The first
opportunity you have which I expect will not be before the Spring you must
mind to send all Boxes, Baskets &c you have, as we are quite out of sorts—I
sent a Paper this day which will apprise you to be on the look out for 1 Goose,
two Ducks and 4 Fowls we hope they will all come safe and good[,] the Goose
and Chickens we got from Mount Airy, and the Ducks from Mrs. Arton of the
Castle farm, so from this you may judge of their breed, Seed, and generation.

   Shop goes on very well, your Mother really is excellent in that line,
and delights in it we all give our best love to you, your wife and little Mary, so I
conclude with my best wishes for all your welfare

      Your affectionate
      Father
       R Sharp

[On reverse of sheet] Mr. W Sharp
      London

Friday 4th. Decr.

Got a Box packed up for Wm. last night and sent off, which we are in
hopes he will receive on Saturday night, as I gave the Carrier particular caution
to be sure to get it off to Barton as soon as possible. — Club night also last
night there was £120 taken out of the Box to put into the Savings Bank.

Saturday 5th. Decr.

At Brantingham as usual this forenoon, it was very thick and foggy, but cleared up rather about noon, when I packed up my Poles & Chain and set off to Edwd. Usher's at Drewton, to measure some Turnip land, both he and his wife had gone to Beverley Market, so that I did not go to the house, but made the best of my way home, tolerably tired.

Sunday 6th. Dec

This is the second succeeding Sunday that the Paper has missed coming, I have no doubt but it is purposely stopped, or in plain English stolen, for stealing is appropriating other people's property to one's own use, I wish they might not be easy all the time of reading it.

Monday 7th. Dec

Heard at the Market this day that Jno. Smith the Schoolmaster of Welton, who has long been Collector of Taxes, has been committed to York Castle for not paying in Money which he has received, I doubt the poor Man is in a bad way, as both the Commissioners who have sent him away, are Priests; — How it would gratify these merciful Men if they had me in their power; they would recollect the Natl. School, but Satan I defy thee.

Tuesday 8th. Dec

Old Willy is more and more learned in the Science of Geography, he says there is a Canal cut made from the Swan River to New York, which is a convincing proof that the Country is settled. I told him it was a branch of the same that led from England to each of these places!!

Wednesday 9th. Decr

Heard from Wm. this Morning that the Basket with all the hollow meats arrived safe and good, little Mary he says has been ill, but is now better again. Old Willy was at Hull yesterday, he speaks largely of the improvements which are in progress, by reason of the new Dock.

Thursday 10th. Dec

I have had a travelling Schoolmaster from Beverley to examine what he calls the national School, but I told him I had nothing to do with those who had sent him, he sent a letter last week, which I never opened so he took it with him and paid the Postage. He wished me to write to Mr. Gilby, but I told him I had nothing to write about, I could only say in the words of Scripture "Answer him not a word".

Friday 11th. Decr.

A Parish meeting last night respecting the Highways, Teavil Leeson and Rd. Marshall, the Surveyors, could not agree but called each other pretty heartily. One wants to proceed one way and the other another, they are like two awkward hounds coupled together, when one is pressing forward the other with all his strength is pulling back.

Saturday 12th. Decr

A very rainy day; at Brantingham in the forenoon the young Ladies break up for Christmas as the next week, joy sparkled in every eye with the prospect of home and the anticipation of pleasure; so that my attendance there is for a while suspended.

Sunday 13th. Decr

Rd. Marshall and his wife with Mrs. Hodgson (Mr. Barnard's housekeeper who came last week) have this morning gone to York, on a Visit to Mr. Barnard or at least to accompany the Housekeeper, they may sing as they go

We three, — Loggerheads be;[70]

Aaron Robinsons mother was buried on Friday last

Monday 14th. Decr

I went last night to fetch some Papers out of the back Chamber, when I hit my head most dreadfully against a Beam that goes across, which for a time stunned me amazingly, the Skin was not broke, nor any swelling raised, but I could eat no Supper; neither could I sleep much in the night, but this day I feel no effects from it any more than the place being rather sore.

Tuesday 15th. Dec

A Beautiful day the Sun shining very bright which is quite reviving after so much gloomy weather we have had of late. — Wrote a notice for a transfer of a Publicans licence at Wilberfoss, for Robt. Stobbart who lately kept the Malt Shovel near the Riplingham Bar.[71]

Wednesday 16th. Decr

Wrote notices for several persons this day to cut their hedges and dress out the Gutters on the road side. Felt very dizzy this forenoon, which I imagine proceeded from the blow which I gave my head on Sunday, but I have felt nothing of it after dinner, and hope I shall experience no ill effects from it.

Thursday 17th. Decr.

A Young Man here last night from Davenport's the Grocer at Hull, he had been as far as Selby, and expected to receive something more than £400, but out of that Sum he had scarcely received £50. We paid our Account which was £12. — He had sent us a side of Bacon which tasted so strong of Smoke, that made it quite disagreeable. And some tea which was not very good being highly coloured, and looked like extract of Iron. — The young Man said he could not afford to have Suppers. I told him if we had known of his coming he should have had a Rasher of broiled Bacon, and a Cup of his own tea; then he would not want any more Supper for some time to come. — However we gave him an Order for several things, but not for Bacon, nor his horrid tea.

Friday 18th. Decr

We have this morning got a Pig of Abraham which was killed yesterday, it weighs 16 St.–8lb. it appears to be a very good one[,] I expect the price will be 5s. or rather more a Stone, it has a rare fat head, the report is that Pigs are on

---

[70] A reference to the traditional 'Three Loggerheads' inn sign, which depicts 2 silly-looking faces with the legend, 'We three loggerheads be'. The reader of the sign is left to puzzle out the identity of the third loggerhead (Hackwood 301).

[71] Riplingham Bar was situated about 3¼ miles east of South Cave on the North Cave–Kirk Ella–Hull turnpike administered by the Beverley, Hessle, North Cave Trust. It is featured on the O.S. 6 in. map of 1855.

the advance. — We had a very full house at Old Willy's last night there being no fewer than eight pair of us sat on Chairs, three on a Bale of Leather and the host himself perched above all, on the Flour Bin. There were likewise 2 large Dogs of Mr. Bridgman and the Landlord's Cat.

Saturday 19th. Dec

I think I know hardly how I spent this day—only I know it was very cold; O' now I recollect, in the forenoon I was weighing and assorting goods that came from Hull by the Carrier—Conder went to Warter yesterday to see after his Bill he wanted of Lord Muncaster, but his Lordship would not be seen so that he was obliged to come without his Money which is £28. I persuade him to put it in the hands of an Attorney, and not be kept out of his money by a titled Creature who pays little better than George Dunn and that is not at all.

Sunday 20th. Decr

Very cold and wintry—David Dennis who married Robt. Todd's lahtle lass, last week swallowed an Ash Tree and consumed 150 Pecks of Potatoes; now you Conjurors hide your dimished [*sic*] heads and knock under to King Pepin, (as he is commonly called) but this was not all for he felt so powerful after having the tree within him that he went home and knock'd down his Father in law Bobby, who was a fool for suffering him [to] do so, I would have soon silenced the drunkard.

Monday 21st. Decr

This is the shortest day, and a short one it is, for it has never been light, the weather is frosty with Snow at times. We have got Sausages and Black puddings made ready to pack up for London where we hope they will arrive before Christmas day, that they may then enjoy the same.

So. Cave 21st Decr. 1829.

Dear Wm.

Herewith we have sent you a Basket of such Articles, as generally appear at pig killing time, we hope they will arrive safe for your enjoyment on Christmas day. We are all very well and hope all you are the same. I think I have nothing particular to say, only Eliza has taken pains to make the Pork pies as good as she knew how. I hope they will prove more agreeable than Old Willy's Yorkshire pie which he once purchased in London for a treat, when he cut it open it smelled so strong that it could not be eaten. — If I was to tell you that Billy Langricke (Land dealer) and his wife, and his Son and his Son's wife, and his daughter and the Man who is going to marry her, have all fallen out, and fought, it would afford me little amusement, so I will conclude with my and all our best love to you all and remn. your affectionate Father

R Sharp

Tuesday 22d. Decr.

Sent off the Baskets last night to Wm. which we hope will arrive safe and sound. Newloves had what they called a Ball last night. Cards were sent round to the Simpletons, with notice of 2d. each for admission; the scheme did not answer as but very few attended; but the Fidler was kept scraping most of the night.

Wednesday 23rd. Dec

The weather uncommonly cold—George Dunn and young Tim have been had before the Magistrates today for obstructing a Bailiff who wanted to seize George's goods. I have not heard positively the result, but I think they are bound to appear at the Sessions.

Thursday 24th. Dec

This morning I recd. a double packet of Papers which was quite satisfactory. There is a great deal of examinations respecting Davis the Tea dealer, how it will terminate I can not say, but I think there has been enough said already to make him mad if he was not so before.

Friday 25th. Dec

This is Christmas Day, I have not been out, as I had a slight Cold and so I staid at home, — Plenty of Boys and Girls too running about for Christmas Boxes, this is an old Custom and will be kept up as long as there is any thing to bestow.

Saturday 26th. Dec

My Wife has been more affected with the Cold this winter than I ever knew her before, her feet have been very bad, but I think they are something better. She has rubbed them with Salt and Onions.

Sunday 27th. Dec

Heard by the Paper yesterday that Wm. had recd. the Basket safe. Hannah Martin sent a Basket at the same time to her Aunt in London, but does not expect to hear from her in less than three weeks.

Monday 28th. Dec

Christmas Holidays now. Spent part of this day at Old Willy's, and part of it collecting Poor sess[.] Money not very plentiful, the Farmers complain as usual, but it is so natural to some of them that they really cannot avoid it.

Tuesday 29th. Decr

Eliza has gone to Hull with the Carrier today, and very cold it is, — I think I never felt it colder than it was yesterday, it was unusually severe, but today it is more moderate, although it is very cold yet.

Wednesday 30th. Decr

Yesterday and the day before the Plough Boys were out, last night they had a Supper at Morley's, where I dare say they staid until they had spent all their Money, they had got something more than seven pounds, which is not a very bad sign of the times.

Thursday 31st. Dec

I was at West Ella today, My Mother was very glad to see me, she had been very uneasy and thought I should not get there as the weather was so bad, indeed it was very bad walking. My Mother I think looks very well for her years but she complains that she gets very little sleep, she is very cheerful but exceeding lame. I think her memory is very little impaired.

1830 Friday 1st Jany

We are now entered on another year, but who can say they will live to see the close of it. Numbers of all ages we daily see are called away and to them the cares of this world are as if they had never been. The last year is now with the time before the Flood.

Saturday 2nd. Jany

We have had a Coach come through for the last week from Hull to Booth Ferry on Account of the Frost, the Rivers being so frozen that the Packets cannot make their usual Voyages.

Sunday 3rd. Jany

Very few people at Church this day, indeed the preaching there is not calculated to keep any body warm.

Monday 4th. Jany

At the Market today there appeared to be no purchasers for Corn, the Factors would not give 50s pr. Quarter for Wheat. Butter was 11d. pr. lb. which at this time of the year is very low. I have known it as much more. I am glad that prices of the necessaries of life keep low.

Tuesday 5th. Jany

Another set of Plough Boys this day they came from North Cave and made a great noise, it might for any thing I know to the contrary be musical, but this sounding science is out of my knowledge.

Wednesday 6th. Jan

Joseph Barratt has applied to the Overseers for relief they have allowed him 5s. pr. Wk, which amounts to the same thing as if he had put out £250 to interest. Geo. Dunn after all his spending and extravagance and running into debt has likewise applied for Relief and has had some money given him. I am sorry to say that he is about 3 pounds in our debt which may be put down to the Debtor side of the Profit and Loss account. Sent on Monday last 2 pounds for Ths. James who lives at Wentworth near Rotherham, he has a family of 7 Children.

Thursday 7th. Jany

It began to thaw last night and continues this day, but it is very cold. The Newspaper which came this morning was not of Wm's writing neither of his wrapping up, but there was no writing in it.

Friday 8th. Jany

Last night was the Club meeting. James Milner made a proposal to take 12 pounds (which is what is allowed at a member's funeral) as he intends going to America in March next; I think if he will take this and exclude himself that he will have it given to him.

Saturday 9th. Jany

Very cold and frosty with a good deal of Snow. There has been a dumb Man in the town telling Silly people their fortunes, for which he receives 2

Shillings each. But some of the Heroes of So. Cave true to their breeding, abused him a good deal. But he blacked up Cottam's face in a superior manner.
Sunday 10th. Jany

I went to Church this morning, as the Scotchman said "to have some cold Morality cluttered about my Lugs, but nae Gospel to keep ane warm". I staid at home in the afternoon, we had a fire in the parlour where I contrived to keep myself very warm and comfortable.
Monday 11th. Jany

Nothing doing at the Market today it seems that there is no wheat wanting, although Flour does not settle in price. Conder has got a letter to go to Warter tomorrow to receive his Bill of Lord Muncaster; the fellow had got to such a pitch that he would neither answer a letter when sent to him, or be seen by any Person who wanted Money of him. But the Law has arms long enough to reach, and an Attorney's letter, has let him see that nothing but payment will serve the Tradesmen he has so long put off.
Tuesday 12th. Jany

Old Willy has got hold of a marvellous Story which had been transacted at Paris, of a young Lady having been walled up on a Wall; he said he never heard of such a thing, and has appealed to the Company whether they had or not, was answered by most of our members in the same manner as himself. I said it was without doubt a most cruel punishment but it appeared to be as old as some of our Nunneries, where such places in the Walls were purposely made, for "immuring" the Nuns who had been found faithless to their Vows of Chastity. Then the cry was turned on the Cruel Papishes!!!
Wednesday 13th. Jan

This has been a real stormy snowy drifting day[.] Condor got his Bill yesterday of Lord Muncaster's Steward, so there is a finish with his Lordship. I do not expect he will come to Brantingham again.
Thursday 14th. Jan

Geo. Dunn and Timothy (Son of Robt.) have been tried at Beverley Sessions this week and convicted of obstructing and assaulting a Sherriff's officer, and sentenced to 6 Months imprisonment in the House of Correction, to learn proper behaviour.
Friday 15th. Jan

Whether Tim Dunn ever read Shakespeare or no I cannot tell, for Tim, encouraged George to Rip up the Bailiff as it is said, but this is denied as George he says had not a knife in his hand, but just then instead of ripping up the Bum he ripped up a bed, so this amounted to proof that he had a knife at the time, "Will says"

"Away, Varlets: draw Bardolph; cut me off the Villain's head."[1]
Poor Will! I think his readers in general are not much better for his "wise saws".

---

[1] Sir John Falstaff to Bardolph, in Shakespeare's *King Henry IV, Part 2*, act 2, scene 1.

Saturday 16th. Jan

I was at West end this afternoon and very sloppy and dirty it was being a kind of partial thaw, after that I went and settled with Cousens for carrying, we have had about 2 tons weight of goods the last three months, he has risen the Carriage from 10d. to 1s. the Cwt.

Sunday 17th. Jan

We have had a fire in the parlour today, it was very warm and comfortable. Eliza and her husband are gone to Swinefleet, and I think a poor errand they have to go at this time of the year, I know it would not suit me.

Monday 18th. Jan

I had a letter for some money from Malton which I paid in July last by sending a pound note, I wrote to the person saying he only wanted pay from that time 1s/6d pr. week so I sent 2 pounds and recd. a letter from him acknowledging the receipt of the former pound.

Tuesday 19th. Jan

Complaints about the badness of trade and the low prices of Agricultural productions. Peter Gardam a Rope maker of Mkt. Weighton who generally contrives to get drunk whenever he has an opportunity, said yesterday that there are not half so many Rogues hanged as formerly but now in general they are transported to the manifest detriment of the <u>Halter manufactory</u>.

Wednesday 20th. Jan

I was at Old Willy's one night smoking a pipe, and his Cat set on the Table, and the old Gentleman in a sort of half Doze, when I blew a quiff up the Cat's nose—which made her jump clean over his head upon the Flour bing, and then off again, in a crazy sort of way. Bless me he says how my Cat jumps about, it must be a sign of bad weather.

Thursday 21st. Jany

Yesterday was dreadfully Stormy. A very high wind and a great deal of Snow which drifted very much. Recd. this morning the Foreign Literary Gazette[2] No. 1. I have not yet read it, therefore I have the pleasure of anticipation, it is on very fine paper. I wish the times Gentlemen would procure their paper of a little better texture, for they are frequently much torn.

Friday 22nd. Jan

Billy Kirby who is a Ranter,[3] provokes his wife at times with his talking and shouting, which makes her sometimes not too mild, she was calling Billy one day, when he says the Devil came to his Elbow and whispered in his ear "Knock her down she deserves it, there will not be a bit of Sin in it", but Billy would not agree to the tempter but turned about and ordered him not to interfere, so he got fairly quit of him and rejoiced in his Victory.

Saturday 23rd. Jan

If you say anything to the Farmers of the times now, they exclaim almost in the words of Wills Justice Shallow, "Barren, Barren, Barren, beggars all,

[2] London periodical, 6 Jan.–31 Mar. 1830.

[3] i.e. a Primitive Methodist.

beggars all".[4] So now their complaints are they are all going to wreck and ruin but when they meet in the Market Room there appears no want, but encourage one another to "Be merry, Be merry".

Sunday 24th. Jan

I have been rather out of order in my Bowels, but it is I may say a common complaint with me, and on the whole I think rather beneficial; but I have not had such a fit of it for a good while past; and it is very cold turning out in the night time.

Monday 25th. Jan

John Akam has advertised all or most of his Property for sale preparatory to his going to America; the Emigration fever is pretty high here at present, but it strikes me that all will not go who talk of it. There has been a favourable letter from a Man who went from Newbald last year, which makes them more anxious to see the land of Milk and honey. He is about 700 Miles from New York.

Tuesday 26th. Jan

Very cold weather the Streets are a complete Sheet of Ice. I am very tired of this Cold weather, but some and indeed the Wiseacres in general say it is fine healthful weather, but I observe there are generally more people ill in cold weather than at other times when it is fine and genial.

Wednesday 27th. Jan

James Milner and the other Emigrants talk of going to near the Lake Mitchigan in North America to a place called St. Joseph's land, I see by the Map there is a River called St. Joseph's River that runs into the So. East part of that lake, not far from Detroit. I think James will be hard set to raise Money to get himself and Family there.

Thursday 28th. Jan

I think I feel better in my laxative Complaint today after taking almost all that has been prescribed by my Friends, One recommended Rice Milk, another toasted Cheese, another Mulled Ale, I thought myself I would take a little Rhubard [*sic*] which I did; last night and this morning I dare say I eat half a pound of fine Cheese each time, called a Welsh Rabbit; last night I was very bad, I went to Old Willy's but could not sit, neither can I smoke much. But now I hope it is leaving me.

Friday 29th. Jan

My Friends very ready in prescribing gratis for me, One recommended Fine Chalk or whiting which I took last night, another Flour and Milk made like Child's meat, which I had last night instead of Tea, and this morning I had three Eggs boiled hard as part of my breakfast, so that I shall certainly soon be better. Mr. Turk is very ill, it appears to be a complete breaking up of the Constitution he is very weak.

---

[4] From Shakespeare's *King Henry IV, Part 2*, act 5, scene 3, line 8.

Saturday 30th. Jan

All the Specifics which I have taken have done me no good, so that today the Doctor has given me Draughts and Spoonfuls of Medicine, which I hope will be of use to me, but he does not wish to stop the evacuation too soon. I am heartily tired of it. The Doctor says Mr. Turk is better, his Son Wm. I understand is here.

Sunday 31st. Jan

The Doctor (Mr. Stuparte) has ordered me not to go out today, and as it snowed fast, I was easily persuaded, he has given me a powder of some kind to take, I feel a good deal better. Two papers today the one yesterday did not come, indeed it had not been sent out as they were both packed together.

Monday 1st. Feb.

This month has come in very stormy. Some of the Prognosticators say we shall yet have 7 weeks of hard Winter weather; I hope it will not be the case, I am tired of it now; but that is no rule that we are not to have it.

Tuesday 2nd. Feb.

Some of the knowing ones have got in their head that Cobbet is a clever fellow, he told his Auditors in Leeds, such a fine tale of his having Sheep to sell, which he expected to get 60 pounds for but when he came to the fair he could only get 30, then the Rencontre with the Taxgatherer who wanted £20, which Cobbet offered to pay with £10, but that would not do. All this they believe to be literally true!! God help their numb heads; Cobbet would be as great a fool as themselves if he expected as much more for an Article as it was worth.

Wednesday 3rd. Feb

This morning a letter from Wm. with the Edinburgh Review[5] 2 Nos. which now are a Novelty to me. It appears the Weather in London is as severe as it is here and that is wintry enough. My Complaint is quite removed and as it is troublesome I hope it will not suddenly return.

Thursday 4th. Feb

James Milner this night at the Club received £12 to exclude himself he is resolute of going to America, he says he can buy 40 Acres of good land for his 12 Sovereigns, I wish he may find all according to his expectations. — Newlove would not pay his Annual payment to the Club due last night as a free member, so that I think he will hardly have a chance to have it again, indeed he wants to go away, for I think he has staid as long as he can get on. If any one wants the picture of an Idle fellow, let them peep here and they will in fine weather see him lolling against the Sign Post. Idleness is generally noisy and silly withal.

---

[5] *Edinburgh Review, or, Critical Journal*: Oct. 1802 – Oct. 1929. Important literary quarterly attracting many famous writers, including (briefly) Sir Walter Scott, Lord Brougham, Carlyle, Hazlitt and Macaulay. It was first edited by Sydney Smith, who remained as one of its regular contributors, but was quickly succeeded as editor by Francis Jeffrey, under whose management (1803–29), it acquired its pronounced Whiggish character (*EB* xxi. 151–2).

Friday 5th. Feb

Richd. Thornton thinking he could like some Vinegar to his Cold Beef at Dinner, came with an intention of getting some, but when he saw me he asked for Ink, imagining I suppose that I was more used to Ink than Vinegar, however Rd. did not find out his mistake till he poured the Ink upon his Beef, he thought it looked black, then he recollected he had asked for Ink, thus was he baulked of Beef & Vinegar.

Saturday 6th. Feb

Very cold again today, at West end this afternoon we have I think nothing but confusion, one of the Surveyors Teavil Leeson, will have the Rate laid one way and Rd. Marshall the other Surveyor will not agree to Teavil's method.

Sunday 7th. Feb

I was not from home again today. I believe I was never two Sundays at home together since I came to Cave before; as I was not very well and the Weather very stormy I thought it beneficial not to venture out.

Monday 8th. Feb

Nothing comparatively doing at the Market today, the Factors will not make but very little advance in the price of Corn; It has thawed most of this day, and a good deal of Snow has disappeared, but it will take a long time to make a clearance.

Tuesday 9th. Feb

A Fine day and the weather much softer than it has been. James Milner says he is obliged to go to America as there is no work here, I think if he had used Economy he might have had something to have helped him until the Cloud which overshadows us shall pass away.

Wednesday 10th. Feb

The King's Speech, and debates or talking which followed are conspicuous in the Paper today; that distress exists in the Country there can be no doubt, but what is called Agricultural distress wants defining, I believe the Landlords think that they will be obliged to lower their Rents, and the Stupid tenants wish for high prices as much as their masters, not considering that Rents will rise with the price of produce.

Thursday 11th. Feb

I had not read Lord King's amendment[6] when I wrote yesterday. He has told some bold truths, what he has said goes to the very bottom of curing the present distress; these great monopolists want paring down. — I am likewise glad to find that the grand Duke will not countenance an unlimited paper

---

[6] The King's Speech presented in the House of Lords on 4 Feb. 1830 was ill received by the Whig country gentlemen in the House because it represented the current state of national economic distress as being only partial and caused mainly by unseasonable weather and other factors not amenable to legislation. Unusually, amendments to the speech were proposed, the first by Lord Stanhope, and the second by Lord King (i.e. Peter King, 7th Lord King, Baron of Ockham, 1776—1833), who attributed the country's economic problems to excessive taxation and the monopolies of corn, beer, sugar, tea, and other commodities (*TM* 5 Feb. 1830, 2 b; *DNB*).

Circulation; for which he will get pretty well railed against, by those who like bits of Rags, better than the King's picture in Solid Gold.

Friday 12th. Feb

The cry here with the Farmers is to keep up the Country that is as they mean; to have Corn at prices, impossible for the Poor to pay for it. They cry out against the Poor Rates not knowing that if they paid none, their Landlords would soon advance their Rents. In fact the Poor Rates are a part of the Rent, but say they only let us have corn 10 or 20s. a Quarter higher, then Rent is no matter.

Saturday 13th. Feb

Now that the Occupiers of Land wish for 10s. pr. Quarter more for the Produce, than for a lowering of 10 or 20 pr. Cent in their Rents is perfectly reasonable on the principal [sic], of every man making the best he can for himself. Suppose that 100 Acres of Arable land to be let for £150 pr. year or 30s. pr. Acre, and that it produces on an average 3 Quarters pr. Acre, then an advance of 10s. pr. Qr. would be equal to the whole rental, but a lowering of 20 pr. Cent would only be £30, this is self evident.

Sunday 14th. Feb

A meeting at the Church on Friday night last to choose Assessors for the ensuing year, when I & Robt. Marshall were again nominated. I got a bad cold for there was no fire, and the Clerk did not want our Company there; — but my Cold did not prevent me from going out this day.

Monday 15th. Feb

Nothing doing at the Market today, I did not see a single Sample of Corn offered for Sale, the Factors seemed not to be anxious to purchase, but the Millers say that they are asked higher prices; which is an excuse for them to raise the price of Flour if they can, but I hope that will not be yet.

Tuesday 16th Feb

John Akam had an Auction Sale last Thursday at the Duke of York at Everthorpe, preparatory to his leaving this Country for America, but nothing was sold, as the prices he wanted were high as in the most flourishing period of land buying. All was bought in at extravagant prices.

Wednesday 17th. Feb

A Stranger, it is said of the name of Smith has taken Newlove's house so that the town will not be much longer encumbered with the Idle fellow's presence, they are going to value the Furniture tomorrow. I think it is a very poor Speculation. There have been six different persons at it since we came to Cave, and this will make the seventh.

Thursday 18th. Feb

Read over today Sir Js. Graham's[7] Speech on his motion for Economy and retrenchment, which was answered by Mr. Dawson, a sort of Secretary or

---

[7] Sir James Robert George Graham, bart. (1792—1861), born into a Tory family, was himself a liberal Whig. He was MP for Hull in 1818, St. Ives in 1820, and Carlisle from 1826. He later served twice as First Lord of the Admiralty (1830–4 and 1852–5) and was Home Secretary from 1841 to 1846. His speech on 12 Feb. 1830 proposed a general reduction in the salaries of all public servants. He withdrew

something of the kind, he assured the Honble members that Economy had been rigorously enforced, which quite charmed them and made them cheer the Speaker, he told them of one department where the Expences were reduced from £64000 to 48000 pounds, which he gravely assured the House was a saving of 30 pr. Cent, with this they were delighted; proving to the world that they knew no difference between £25 pr. Cent and 30: Send some of them to School to learn the Rule of three, then they will not be so easily gulled.

Friday 19th. Feb

What a dangerous thing it is for such men as the Secretary Dawson, to say any thing where figures are concerned, but I suppose he knows his Auditory. Let him talk nonsense by the Hour, and according to the length of his Speech he will be called a fine Orator, but beware of these stubborn things called figures ...

Monday 22nd. Feb

The Overseer has been at Riplingham today with Thos. Shaw's wife's daughter, who said she was married some time ago, but the last week it transpired that she was not married. She has been this day to swear to her Settlement, when an order of removal was granted to remove her to Ellerker.

Tuesday 23rd. Feb

A good deal of Snow again last night, this winter has already been, both long and severe. This is Pancake Tuesday, but as I now write in the morning or forenoon, I know not whether we shall have any or not, for I never enquire what we are to have to Dinner, neither do I ever find fault with any thing.

Wednesday 24th. Feb

We had no Pancakes yesterday, we had a fine Pease Pudding. John Watson, commonly called "Brag" was buried this afternoon, he died on Sunday night or Monday morning last, he has laid in bed a number of years. The Woman who was removed to Ellerker on Monday had a child there that night, so that she was only just quitted in time.[8]

Thursday 25th. Feb

Ministers have said they will make retrenchment to some amount, but it does not seem that they will take off any of the taxes, so of what use will their proposals be, if the same amount of taxes are to be paid? what will they do with the Surplus? Mr. Hume I think does what he can, and Colonel Davies who appears to be made of stern stuff, says they may dismiss a number of the forces and be all the better for it.[9] But for my part I can see no benefit in Economy if the People still have the same to pay.

---

his proposal when the government put up Dawson, Secretary of the Treasury, to propose an amendment pledging the House to every possible saving (*DNB*; Walpole ii. 437).

[8] Children born to unmarried mothers who were not themselves resident in a parish would become by law the responsibility of the parish in which they were born and thus a lasting burden on its poor rate. For this reason, overseers of the poor were always very prompt to remove such women before they could give birth. Sometimes their keenness to perform their duty in this respect could result in great harshness and inhumanity (Henriques 108).

[9] In a debate on the military estimates in the House of Commons on 19 Feb. 1830, Colonel Davies, MP for Worcester, argued for retrenchment and proposed that the estimates should be voted for only 3 months and that an inquiry be set up to investigate the practicability of reductions. His motion was

Friday 26th. Feb

I am afraid the hard weather has killed my Cow Cabbages, they are only just to be seen, I doubt they will not recover. Mr. Atkinson last night had a very learned discussion on the Voyage of St. Paul, I asked him the name of the Sea, where the Voyage was performed, but all he knew of it was it was the Sea to be sure; who would ever ask such a question but for contradiction, this did not put me down. I knew my way.

Saturday 27th. Feb

Measuring a Close of Turnips this afternoon at Brantingham for Mr. Wray. There have been two Sheep stolen out of the Close this winter they belonged to Mr. Hopkinson, a reward was offered for the apprehension of the Thieves, but without finding them out; it appears they knew the Value of Mutton.

Sunday 28th. Feb

Mr. Barnard is coming against Thursday next which is the Rent day, they have got fires made to air the House and have been brewing—It is said he is going to do some thing for his tenants, which on his part does not shew much wisdom, there are none but what live in comparison as well as he does: but these Agriculturalists are in general capital complainers.

Monday 1st. Mar

This month has come in fine and moderate, the Farmers now can get on with working their land. Pennington has risen his Flour 2d. pr. Stone. I am rather afraid that the price will get up. It was reported last week that young Teavil Leeson was sent to York Castle for Debt, but he was here today so whether there was any truth or not in the report I cannot say.

Tuesday 2nd. Mar

Wrote this day to Wm. to ask him if he could fall in for a little pocket Globe second hand; It will be useful to shew the Situation & distance of one Country from another; I do not know that such a thing is absolutely necessary for me; but if I can be gratified for a few shillings, it will not be very dear.

Wednesday 3rd. March

One of the Lords in Parliament I think made a very just observation on the distress of the Country, he said it was not the abundance of the Supply which caused it, but the want of Consumption of the Articles. This I think is true, for the poor instead of being able to purchase, are in a state of starvation, May there be quickly a remedy.

Thursday 4th. March

This is Mr. Barnard's rent day, he is here himself. Mr. Bridgman came in at dinner time, it appeared from what he said that his Landlord had given something again today. All these Landowners are uncommonly backward in settling their Rents, they put off their tenants with a scanty per Centage.

defeated by 225 votes to 93, and although he again deplored the government's extravagance on 22. Feb., he declined to make any further proposals as he believed that those with vested interests in the military were too numerous in the House to be opposed (*TM* 20 Feb. 1830, 4 d and 23 Feb. 1830, 1 f; *AR* 1830 Hist. 42–3).

Friday 5th. March

A Travelling Paper merchant was here to day, of whom I have bought some Paper and Copy Books, he came from Hull yesterday, and did not take a single Penny; he thought he had made a good beginning this morning as I laid out on him 10 or 11 Shillings, and I thought I did not make a bad bargain.

Saturday 6th. Mar

Measured some Turnip Land for Rchd. Marshall at Willows Flatt, a very fine day, but the Close had lately been very wet, and being strongish land was very much trodden with the Sheep.

Sunday 7th. Mar

Crows very throng building their Nests today it being fine they worked away, as though they had taken the job, and not by days work. The first day this Season that I heard the croaking of Frogs in the Fish pond by Scores.

Monday 8th. Mar

Richd. Marshall has recd. from Mr. Barnard a printed Protest and Petition to the House of Commons[10] to get signed by the respectables here, some of whom will be overset to read it, much more to understand it; I believe the chief purport of it is to keep up the price of Corn, and consequently rents.

Tuesday 9th. Mar

A Gentleman whom I happened to fall in with yesterday, and seemed a profound politician, said all the Miseries & Distresses of the Country proceeded from the Currency, but he could soon remedy all, I told him I understood very little, I thought of the Currency question and many people who talked of it seemed to know little more than myself. He said he would raise the Value of the Sovereign to 30s. I told him that if that was to be a cure it would entail misery on Creditors, who would be afraid of having their debts paid in two thirds of the amount; — How I detest these Quacks.

Wednesday 10th. Mar

Planted some Cabbages yesterday, the plants are very small and puny, having been nipped so much by the severe weather—Likewise set some Potatoe Onions.

Thursday 11th. Mar

A Gentleman of the name of Grimstone, it is said has bought the House at Brantingham Thorpe, which belonged to the late Mr. Barnard.[11] So that we are not to have a Lord any longer in the neighbourhood. Indeed from the Specimen

---

[10] The formal petition framed according to precise rules was at this time the generally accepted means by which sections of the public could draw the attention of Parliament to particular issues and exert some degree of pressure in support of their interests. A petition had to be presented by a member who until 1842 could insist that it be debated in the House. The early decades of the 19th c. saw a steep rise in the number of petitions presented; in the 5-year period ending in 1831, there were 24,492 (Walpole iv. 341–3).

[11] Revd Edward Barnard lived at Brantinghamthorpe Hall from 1819 to his death in 1828. There is no evidence that a Mr Grimstone bought his house, but it was sold by Barnard's devisees in 1832 to Captain Richard Fleetwood Shaw, an army officer. In that same year, Shaw also bought Brantingham Hall from the Revd James Simpson who had been arrested for debt in 1831 (see entry for 8/12/31) (Allison 49).

we have had, his absence will not be lamented, at least by me. Sowed some Marigold Seeds today.

Friday 12th. Mar

Farmers throng sowing Beans, it is a fine time for them. A Man of the name of Moss called yesterday to see if we wanted any Mustard, he is in a Mustard Mill at Hull. He was master of the National School at Beeford; but the Patrons & Parsons contrived to dismiss him; as they would have done to me if they could have had their own wills and ways. But I remain not by their permission but in spite of them.

Saturday 13th. Mar

There is land at this town which now lets for nineteen pounds a year, which ought to be applied in putting poor Children to School; but there is only £9–10s applied to that purpose; the Property was laid hands on to buy the creaking Organ, for which no one gave a Shilling voluntarily, but £100 was borrowed to pay for the grinding instrument and half the proceeds of the Land is kept back to pay the Interest, and for what else I have never learned.

Sunday 14th. Mar

James Milner has adventured his Goods for Sale on Monday the 22nd, previous to his leaving for America. — Very dry and windy so that the dust blows about, which is not very Common at this time of the year. Sowed some Onion Seeds, and Pease yesterday.

Monday 15th. Mar

Richd. Marshall with his Petition in his Pocket today again for Signatures. He only wants it signing by Freeholders. I am fortunately not one of that Class, therefore I shall be spared the trouble of signing any thing for the advance of Landed property. None of the Farmers here I will be bold to say will give up their Farms, even at the present Rental.

Tuesday 16th. Mar

The Man who had taken Newlove's house, it appears has considered otherwise, and will not enter upon it, such is the report; I think he has determined wisely.

Wednesday 17th. Mar

Wm. Thornam (the elder) had been at Hull yesterday with the Carrier; and in getting out of the Waggon, just coming down the Hill at Weedley Pitt, his Foot slipped and he fell, and the Waggon went over him, his Arm was broken and he is otherwise injured: It is said he had got more Liquor than he ought to have had.

Thursday 18th. Mar

Thos. Glasby who has been Gardener to Dan. Sykes for some years has gone to live at Hull, their Goods went this day, his old Master has procured him a place in the Sugar House,[12] and will further allow him five pounds a year, which is a very Gentlemanly action to an old Servant.

---

[12] The principal sugar-refining company in Hull at this time was Messrs. Thornton, Watson, and Company. Originally founded between 1726 and 1731 by Godfrey and William Thornton, its sugar

Friday 19th. Mar

My wife has been examining the Covers of the Papers every day to see if there was any thing written on them but nothing was discovered, she thinks it a very long time since she heard any thing.

Saturday 20th. Mar

This town has been highly gratified this day by a piece of Scandal which has occurred. A Daughter of Matthew Pickering's has had a Child, who was never suspected by her own family or any other to be in that prolific situation. Old Betty her mother who has 5 or 6 Daughters, was telling a Gentleman not long since, "We have not a <u>hoor</u> in our family, not one single <u>hoor</u>;["] but how is it now? The Exr. did not come this wk.

Sunday 21st. Mar

I was going past Ab. Barff's last night, when he had got his Windows shut in it was about four O'clock, he had got drunk in the morning and gone to Plough, but his lad loosed off the Horses and brought them away; he sat down in the house at Night, and said what a Dark morning this is I think it will never be light, he then asked his lad if the horses were fed ready for work; the lad told him it was night; neet Abm. says, wounds I think it does grow darker and darker; what have I been deen all day, why very little his man says; Aye says he I thought so.

Monday 22nd. Mar

James Milner has been selling off by Auction today so that at present there is every probability of his going to America; he has taken his Passage in a vessel from Hull called the Wilberforce,[13] which is to sail on the 9th. or 10th. of April next. Robert Nicholson Junr. has also engaged a passage in the same Ship.

Tuesday 23rd. Mar

Betty Pickering (Matthew's wife) said to a Man who went in to her house, "what do you think has happened; (but you have heard,) we have got a Bastard in our Family, aye we have a Bastard in our Family now, Such a thing was never known in our Family, since the world began O, dear, O dear, we have begun to breed Bastards.

Wednesday 24th. Mar

Old Jemmy Hurst of Rawcliffe, had such an antipathy to paying taxes of any kind, that he had a Carriage made of Basket Work, and no Leather about it as it was an excise Article: this Carriage of his was drawn by a Bull instead of a Horse, as the horned Animal was Duty free. At an Election for Yorkshire one of the Candidates applied to Jemmy who was a freeholder for his Vote. Jemmy

house was situated near the river in Lime Street, close to North Bridge, Drypool, Hull. The building, which was illustrated in T. Gent's *History of Kingston-upon-Hull* (1735), was an imposing 9-storey edifice. The premises were extended in the mid-18th c. and the firm continued to operate until about 1843 (Baines ii. 251 and 310; Jackson, G. 196–7; Sheahan 326–7).

[13] The *Hull Packet* in its issue for 9 Mar. 1830 (and other issues) contained the following advertisement: 'FOR QUEBEC, The fine A.1. Ship, WILBERFORCE, Captain Gowland Clark; (A general Trader; 395 tons Register). She has superior Accommodation for Passengers, and will sail early in April ...'

says thou Maut's (Malt) me, and thou Saut's (Salt) me, and thou peeps in at my Windows, I'll not vote for thee.[14]

Thursday 25th. Mar

Flour has risen 2d. pr. Stone it is now 2s/4d. and the Millers say it will soon be 2s/6d. The Farmers are all animation at the prices of Corn rising, though many of them have but little to sell. Rd. Marshall delivered a load this week 12 Quarters at £3 pr. Quarter.

Friday 26th. Mar

The Holland Toys Mrs. Akam and her Sister Rachel are fitting up the House of Old Mrs. Akam for their reception. — It is said that Wm. Cousens has taken old Jemmy Levitt's Farm, whether it be so or not I cannot tell; but I know he had offered to let it to Ths. Fisher ...

Sunday 28th. Mar

A very fine day this; I had my great Coat on in the forenoon but in the afternoon I went without it, so that I shall scarce have it on any more this Season. The Old Painter who delights in Green has begun his work, which looks very well, but in a short time he intends studding it with flowers of various hues.

Monday 29th. Mar

Robt. Nicholson has his Sale today in old Mrs. Akam's Yard, he seems resolved to cross the Atlantic, with his Family.

Tuesday 30th. Mar

Some of our Senators appear to be as ignorant of the Nation's distress (I had very near written National, but it is a word I hold in utter detestation) as Thos. Marshall is of taking Pills for when he has them to take he chews them before swallowing and then swears they are made of Stuff that would poison the devil.

Wednesday 31st. Mar

Robt. Marshall and myself at Beverley today to be sworn in Assessors we came home without our Dinners, but got a gill of ale I think two each for which we were charged 3d. pr. gill, so I think I shall have no more fine Burton ale suddenly.

Thursday 1st. Ap.

Cousens has taken Old Jemmy Levitt's farm for a certainty, but the old Gentleman will still reside in the House; and Cousens live where he is.

Friday 2nd. Ap.

A parcel from Wm. containing the Umbrella well wrapped in waste paper, which came very opportunely. The Umbrella is much admired and came very safe and quite perfect.

---

[14] The wide range of assessed taxes, which had been imposed by Pitt, was much reduced in the 1820s by the reforms of 'Prosperity' Robinson. Many of the articles taxed were essential to daily life, such as candles, leather, and salt. Carriages were taxed according to type (2 wheels or 4 wheels), and standards of utility and comfort. Farm and trade carts were exempted if they were used only for those purposes. Horses were taxed, as were dogs (see n.58 (1829)). Leather was freed from tax later in 1830, and candles in 1831. Salt had been exempted in 1825 (Dowell ii. 341).

Saturday 3rd. Apl.

Busy with filling up the Notice papers for the Assess'd taxes and getting a few of them out. I was at the West end this afternoon. I made Richd. Kirby's will and he signed it on the 30th March. The old Man is very poorly.

Sunday 4th. Apl.

Richd. Kirby had a physician from Hull which I believe was Dr. Chalmers[15] the same I think who was at Beverley. From what I can learn Rd's complaint is Ossification of the Heart, that is the Heart turning or forming into Bone. I think the complaint is not curable but the Patient may continue a long time.

Monday 5th. Apl.

Great talk today of the Markets being higher so that the Farmers ask as is common as much more than the advance, which makes the Factors very shy of purchasing.

Tuesday 6th. Apl

A Meeting this Evening to Balance the Poor Book the Expences this year were 441 pounds odd, and last year the Expences 586 pounds odd so that there is this year less expence by 145 pounds than the last year, which does not shew much distress here among the Poor, indeed there have been but few Labourers out of employment.

Wednesday 7th Apl

Richd. Marshall was at Beverley to day with the Poor Book to get allowed by the Justices. Thos. Marshall & Wm. Cousens are appointed Overseers for the year from this time ...

Friday 9th. Apl.

I think I have finished sowing Garden Seeds I sowed some Pease today, this is what is called Good Friday but not in general kept as a Holiday by the Farmers, and the Shops are open as usual.

Saturday 10th. Apl.

I have been very throng today but on summing up all at Night, I find I have done but very little, part of the day I spent in making Paper Bags, not being at Brantingham today as it is Easter Holidays.

Sunday 11th. May [i.e. April]

This is Easter Sunday which has long been noted for Children to have on their new Clothes, if they have been so fortunate as to have had any prepared. — James Milner and his Family and Robt. Nicholson's wife and 4 Children left here for Hull yesterday to Ship themselves for America in all 17 Persons and Robt. Nicholson himself and a Son of John Gardam's who went it is said from Liverpool on Tuesday last.

---

[15] Dr Matthew Chalmers was the physician at the General Infirmary in Hull. He became active in local politics in the Whig interest, served as a Justice of the Peace, became an Alderman and was elected Mayor of Hull in the year before he died at the age of 61 on 3 Mar. 1842 (*HA* 18 Mar. 1842, 5).

Monday 12th. May [i.e. April]

Amongst the 17 Emigrants was Mails Moody, Matty's Son, who generally calls him our Mails, this same Mails did at School the thing he ought not to have done, like Danl. Porter's young Master whom he took to Church with him one Sunday, Danl. said he did the thing he ought not to have done[.] He —— himself and so did Mails.

Tuesday 13th Apl.

Measured the Flatts 2 small Closes belonging to Mr. Barnard which James Levitt has taken[,] they contain about 7 Acres these with the Tolls are lett together[.] I suppose James has taken them for the sake of having the Rent days' and Courts' dinners at his house.

Wednesday 14th Apl

Yesterday according to Custom there was a Sermon (or what is called one) at the Church, after Service on that Day a penny loaf is distributed to all who hold out a hand for one, there is no lack of Children and their Mothers. — Giles Bridgman and Wm. Loncaster were appointed Churchwardens, — and a Church rate for the last year was laid at one penny in the Pound.

Thursday 15th. Apl.

Our Old Cat poor faithful Creature is dead, she had lived so long that she could scarcely walk, she got out one day and a Boy brought her in as near dead as possible, so I gave him a piece of String to hang her, and put her out of pain, I also gave him a halfpenny to bury her in a decent manner which he said he did.

Friday 16th. Apl.

South Cave Township (exclusive of Broomfleet, Faxfleet and Oxmardyke which are in the Parish of So. Cave) contains about 4000 + Acres; the amount of the Poor Disbursements including the Constable's expences and County rates was £441—odd, the last year ending at Lady day.

[In margin]: + this from a late calculation RS.

Saturday 17th. Apl.

Last night measured some Turnip Land of Mr. King's in the Cave Gate Close, it was a very fine evening, there were plenty of Palms there being several Willow trees at the low end of the Closes there has been a new fair at Howden.

Sunday 18th. Apl.

This has been a fine day—several wondering how far the American adventurers have yet got, they left Hull on Tuesday morning, and as I have been told they go North about that is round Scotland, which they have perhaps hardly cleared yet.

Monday 19th. Apl.

As to the relief that will be afforded the Poor by the taking off the duty on Beer,[16] as the old saying is they may put it in their eyes and see no worse for it.

---

[16] 'An Act to Repeal Certain of the Duties on Cider in the United Kingdom, and on Beer and Ale in Great Britain ...' (1 Will. IV c. 51) was subsequently passed on 16 July and came into force on 10 Oct. 1830.

But for all this I maintain that so far as they have gone they the Ministers have done right. I have no objection in the least for the Malt duty to be taken off, they shall likewise have my approbation if they suppress the brewing altogether. The farmers say if the Duty had been taken off from Malt Barley would have advanced, then they who brew for their own use would have double advantage having neither Malt nor Beer duty to pay.

Tuesday 20th. Apl.

I resume from yesterday. The growers of Barley do not wish for Beer to be any lower; what advantages the Pint purchaser expected the farmers intend putting in their own pockets; maintaining with unblushing front that it is for the relief of Agriculture and to force Barley up in price to put more money in their Pockets at the expence of the revenue. Barley has already risen from 5 to 10s. pr. Quarter.

Wednesday 21st. Apl.

A meeting last night at James Levitt's to let the lanes there were hardly any Tenants for them they were let for £6–13–0 last year £7–15–6 the year before that for more than £20, so that here is a decline of Rent nearly two thirds, if this decline were general in Rents how the Landlords would lengthen their faces; Cobbett has been at Hull[17] the last week applauded by some and censured by others. Acts Chap 28 Verse 24th,[18] so it was in the time of the eloquent Apostle Paul.

Thursday 22nd. Apl.

Heard that the Hamper sent to Wm. had been recd. on Saturday night, it ought to have been there on the morning of Friday, glad to hear they are all well; — A mad Bull, A mad Bull, was the cry yesterday it was said a mad Bull was about to pay the town a Visit being at the North end of the town, Shop windows were clapped up and the public and other houses shut in their windows, we were not bitten with fear so did not shut in. But if the Bull would not come here, a deputation met him and Obed Martin shot him dead, and Val Tindale dressed him, and Bull Beef it will be for Hull. We had Goat mutton in the town last week!!! ...

Saturday 24th Apl

A very rainy stormy day, I was at Brantingham in the morning, it was very tempestuous, went down with an intention of going to the Mill at afternoon, but met with the Miller ploughing in his Close opposite the Sheep dike, he promised to come up at night if possible; but I saw no more of him he is forced he says to work rain or fair weather and all will not do.

Sunday 25th. Apl

This is a fine dry day tolerably sunny such weather is wanted very much as a great deal of the Land is so wet that it can scarcely be sown in the state it is in. Great talk of the fresh licensing System for selling ale, I have not heard who

---

[17] Cobbett described his visit (which included nightly lectures to several hundreds of people) to Hull on 15–18 Apr. 1830 in *CPR* 69 xvii (24 Apr.) 1830, 517–21.

[18] 'And some believed the things which were spoken, and some believed not'.

are likely to begin here, but some without doubt will, I think John Smith for one, and perhaps Merchant Moody for another.

Monday 26th. Apl

Very throng now this week collecting taxes. Money is very scarce which makes it very troublesome[;] a very fine day again, I think I saw nothing particular at the Market today.

Tuesday 27th. Apl.

Young Crows are about fit for Pies now, the keeper was shooting some today, we never had one last year and perhaps shall not this, as the keeper sells all he can and I hardly think them worth buying.

Wednesday 28th. Apl.

At west end this Evening, out of at least £100 I did not receive two pounds so that I was not much more forwd. with my work when I left off than when I began.

Thursday 29th. Apl.

I am as throng this week as one of Will's men who caught a Cold "with ringing in the King's affairs",[19] not on his coronation but throng collecting money to uphold his State; I have not like him caught a Cold; but I have as yet caught very little money.

Friday 30th. Apl

This busy week is drawing to a Close, I have done pretty well today; it is nearly labour in vain to begin collecting a week before hand.

Saturday 1st. May

John Murgatroyd of North Cave was going to Beverley this morning just as I was setting off so we went on together; He had to go by Little Weighton and I went with him, it is the first time I was ever there—got my taxes soon paid; staid to dine at Beverley and got home about six O'clock, I rode Cousens' Galloway.

Sunday 2nd May

I have only heard the Cuckoo twice yet this year, it is in general a welcome sound, for it tells us of the time of Spring—Yesterday there were some Crow shooters, when Cottam the Butcher was hawking his meat, he pulled up there and left his meat to itself staid all the day at J. Levitt's and all the night too being so drunk that he did not get home before eight O'clock this morning.

Monday 3rd. May

A new Miller has come to River Bridge of the name of Wilson, we had some flour from him last week and he has sent some more: Pennington & Matt. Turner would not bring a Stone for less price than we could sell it; on these terms trade is worth nothing.

Tuesday 4th. May

Pennington has sent 30 Stone of Flour today at a penny a Stone under Wilson; yesterday he said he would rather keep it than sell it for less than 2s/4d

---

[19] Bullcalf to Falstaff: 'A whoreson cold, sir,—a cough, sir,—which I caught with ringing in the king's affairs upon his coronation day, sir.' —*King Henry IV, Part two*, act 3, scene 2, line 194.

but he says he had bought some Wheat accidentally so that he could afford it at 2s/2d. I believe my wife is a match for the Millers she can fight them off one against another.

Wednesday 5th. May

I was at Brantingham last night instead of Saturday last when I was at Beverley, it was very pleasant, but I never take a walk for pleasure purposely; But when I am on business if pleasure falls in with me we keep company until either pleasure is tired of me or I think little of her which is the case with most parties of pleasure at times.

Thursday 6th. May

The farmers say that Wheat (growing) seldom looked worse on strong land such as Wallingfen than it does at present; I can only say that on the Land near the town and indeed on all the Land I have seen it looks remarkably well, of a fine dark Green and healthful as can be wished; this they admit, — but the exceptions are more looked at than the Rule.

Friday 7th. May

Mr. Levitt of Ellerker by whose Interest I know not had been valuing some Crown land; amongst others that of Sunk Island[20] in Holderness, which I understand contains about 7000 Acres, the present Lessees under the Crown have it for a very trifling Rent as is the Case with most Crown lands. This land is of the most excellent quality, superior as much of the Holderness land is, this is in the superlative degree most superior.

Saturday 8th. May

Wm. Cade who left this town some time last year and went to live at Hull, left his taxes unpaid, I wrote twice for the Amount, the last time he sent the letter back unopened and told Cousens to take it back and be d—d. I immediately wrote to the Surveyor, and this day the Money was paid to Robt. Marshall at Beverley.

Sunday 9th. May

A very stormy day ready to blow Umbrellas away. I was at the Church where the parson said that there was not much difference between the least degree of punishment and the lowest state of happiness—which I understand if he meant any thing that the best place in Hell was nearly equal to the worst in heaven. Was ever such a Sentiment (doctrine I will not call it) stated before?

Monday 10th. May

Conder has taken a Shop at Market Weighton to which he intends going once a week viz on Wednesdays the Market days. Nothing particular at the Market prices much as usual.

Tuesday 11th. May

John Read came from Hull today in a Gig with Mr. Buckton who was going a Journey, he looks pretty well [a] good easy man. He has brought an account that Old Obadiah has lost his money, I believe he was only to have had

[20] See n.11 (1833).

the interest of it for his life; he married my wife's Aunt and at his death there was to be £10 each to her and her Brother. Thus perish the hopes of gain.

Wednesday 12th May

It is amazing but not very surprising that Parliament should do so little to try to benefit the Country. There is the small debts bill for instance, I think it would be better if they would pass an Act, and tell the Shopkeepers that if they gave Credit it should be at their own Risk, they should have no assistance from the law to lose four or five times as much as the debt.

Thursday 13th. May

Jed Dean was here today receiving £140 from the Club on Mortgage of his Property at Hotham a House and Garth; he had a former mortgage of £100 to pay off—very cold weather yet for May.

Friday 14th. May

Yesterday was the Spring Court at Js. Levitt's. There was not much Company I never attend the Court at Spring. There was a good dinner and moderate charge. Our old Friend Mr. Atkinson was there, he got home in good time.

Saturday 15th. May

Weighton fair was yesterday. Conder has got enough of his Weighton Speculation, having fetched all his things back today, they are such a raffling drinking set he saw no prospect of doing any good amongst them. He has paid a Sovereign for his Rent so he has bought wisdom.

Sunday 16th. May

Mr. Bromby[21] the Vicar of the High Church at Hull preached here today, he spoke uncommonly low, but I understand this is not his manner at Hull, he most likely thought it would do here without much exertion.

Monday 17th. May

I went down to the Mill on Saturday afternoon and found the Miller loading with the help of his Man a Cart with fire Wood. He began calling his Trashy Cold sandy Clung land (nay says I thats a contradiction) I have says he both sorts of that Rubbish. The Cuckoo happened to be crying out. I said you have the pleasure of hearing the Cuckoo, almost any time; Aye and what the devil good does hearing her do me? do I get ought by her crying and roaring out? O I says I like to hear her that tells of the Season of Spring, why then she tells a lie for we have no Springs now, do you call this weather Spring? Wheat! I shall have no wheat this year. Naebody sud luke at Wheat on sike land as this of mine, except he have £500 in his Pocket and a Bottle of Brandy in his Belly, then he may face it. I am said I acquainted with one who says with Usquebaugh

---

[21] Born on 18 Oct. 1770, John Henry Bromby came from a distinguished family of Hull merchants. On 28 Nov. 1797, at the age of 27, he was appointed Vicar of Holy Trinity, Hull's largest church, and retained that office for 70 years, not retiring until 1867, at the age of 96. He was suspected of High Church leanings by the evangelical wing and was criticized for his refusal to allow any division of Holy Trinity's very extensive parish in order to create smaller parishes for the new churches being built in Hull around mid-century (*VCHERY* i. 239 and 290; Sheahan 379 (note) and 501).

he would face the Devil.[22] Husky, Husky what, but if it be Husky at all he is a feal, if he said a <u>Bottle</u> of good liquor he would have been nearer truth!!!

Tuesday 18th. May

Letter and a small parcel from Wm. last Saturday I am sorry to find that they have had a breach of trust, It is a dangerous thing ever to take liberties with other people's property, but the fact in most cases is that people want to appear something superior to their circumstances, so they go in inequity until they tumble headlong into disgrace & poverty.

Wednesday 19th. May

A little old fashioned looking lad about the height of Conder's Shopboard came into his Shop, for some trapping for Mr. Simpson of Brantingham, and as he had them to wait for he was asked to sit down, when he pulled out a Pipe about the length of his finger and black as <u>a Reckon Creak</u>; he set down in the great Chair, and fell into a fit of musing, (which is common to smokers) until it broke out in words. I think says he it is better to be married than not, for then Parish is obliged to find one work, — well it is a wonder you don't marry. O I have been wed a good while, but I have not got an Arm Chair yet, I should like one like this it is so easy, (<u>quiff</u> <u>quiff</u>) there the little fellow sat not so high as the Chair back; but says he an Arm Chair I will have—well you must buy one when you get your furniture, <u>fonniterry</u>, I fancy I have as good <u>fonniterry</u> as a deal of folks, I laid out eight pounds to furnish my house so I will leave you to judge whether I should not have some capital <u>fonniterry</u> !!!

Thursday 20th. May

Now for the wife of the little fellow with the black short pipe. He said he was above having a Common Fårmer's lass, his wife was Mrs. Simpson's Nurse maid, they are very fond of her and she is very clever at needle work, she gets a deal of good work at Mr. Simpson's, — well what kind of work does she get, <u>O she washes there</u>, she is rather better than Labourers' wives in general. (How I admire this fellow's Simplicity).

Friday 21st. May

Mr. Atkinson this morning Recd. a packet of Papers directed to the Registrar of the Peculiar Court[23] of South Cave relative to the Ecclesiastical Commission, but as our Old friend is the Church warden, and these officers are not mentioned, I gave my Opinion that he had nothing to do with the Query's therein. However as it was a kind of Church affair, I advised him to apply to the Curate who most likely would afford him <u>his Opinion</u>. I have not seen him since he went.

---

[22] From Robert Burns's 'Tam O' Shanter: a tale': 'Inspiring bold John Barleycorn! / What dangers thou canst make us scorn! / Wi' tippenny, we fear nae evil; / Wi' usquebae, we'll face the Devil!'. Usquebae is whisky; tipenny is twopenny ale.

[23] The ecclesiastical court of a 'peculiar', which was a parish, or church, exempt from the exclusive authority of the bishop in whose diocese it was situated (*OED*).

Saturday 22nd. May

Very cold rainy weather most of this week. — I have not been at Brantingham today as the Ladies are gone from home. Conder went to Swinefleet this morning. I think it would rain before he got there.

Sunday 23rd. May

There were two or three Christenings today of Pat Fwokes Children. One of the Women came about noon, to my wife to buy Flour, Currants, Sugar, Tea, Butter, &c, but she told the Woman she did not make a practice of selling on Sundays—Nay now Mrs., God will forgive you this time I'll be bound for it, so she got eight or nine Shillings worth of Stuff and some good Cakes she said she would make at Tindales, about 5 O'clock she set off with her good Cakes and 15s. worth of Liquor to their Camp at 4 lane ends on the Drewton Road. Tindale the Publican and Ned Coates went as Visitors and Partakers of the good cheer ...

Tuesday 25th. May

Our Old friend improves in Geography, he knows that the East Indies are further than America, but thinks there will be a passage by land from Swan River to America; He has even heard tell of the Cape of Good hope, nay he has something vivid in his mind regarding the East Indies, for a Tailor of his Acquaintance made the Voyage when he was in London.

Wednesday 26th. May

At west end this Evening with the Overseers, looking after a Man of the name of Hallowell, who with his wife and Family are in the Poor house; his Father has taken his passage to America in a Ship now in Hull Dock, and this Man had made preparation to go with him and leave his Wife and 3 Children to the parish the youngest of whom is not 3 Weeks old; however at last they agreed that the Parish would pay the Passage of the Wife & Children, they are to go to Hull on Friday next.

Thursday 27th May

My wife was at Hull today she went with the Coach there is one runs daily from hence to Hull, it was very cold and at times wet but she got home safe and well they go about 7 in the Morning and arrive here a little before eight at night, it is a very good conveyance.

Friday 28th. May

Thos. Marshall who is one of the Overseers went to Hull yesterday to agree for the passage of Hallowell's family to America. Cousens who is the other Overseer expected him back at nine O'clock but I knew he did not move so quickly especially if he had a Rum Bottle before him. I told Cousens I was almost certain he would not leave Hull before ten O'clock at soonest. Well he arrived at Cousens' about 12 O'clock at night and called them up, he had been so raffled and put about with this plagy nasty troublesome business but he had got all arranged, and the Poor Woman who has not been laid in 3 weeks, & has 3 Children the eldest of whom is not 3 years old took their Journey this Morning by the Carrier to Hull.

Saturday 29th. May

Ths. Shaw brought me a letter to read over, which he had this day recd. from Hull which for him contained good news as it was to let him know that he had got £300 left by the death of an Uncle, "Whya says Tommy it is better than a Slap ower yan's head".

Sunday 30th. May

Yesterday was the day called Royal Oak day, which is kept up by a display of Oak leaves or branches stuck in the Hats of the Loyal friends of Charles the Son of the <u>Blessed Martyr</u>, but many of these who wear Garlands know nothing of either of the Charles's but merely it is Royal Oak day!!

May 31st. Monday

What with Colouring and Painting on the outside of the Houses and covering dirt within, we (the Inhabitants) are at present generally employed, to welcome the approaching fair; for my own part I should be gratified if there was no fair at all. I do not like such hurries.

Tuesday 1st. June

Wilson the Miller of River bridge called yesterday to receive a trifle for some Flour he had sent, he had before taken some back to exchange, and brought the same kind instead of it. My wife was more put out with him than I ever saw her before and told him she would not pay him; he might get his money as he could a <u>Villain</u> as he was. Well then says I, I will pay and have no more of this connection, for I thought I saw in the fellow some indications of awkwardness. I told him he might have his flour back for 2d. pr. Stone less than he charged for it, but this would not do. So having the fear of the <u>Law</u> before my eyes I paid him, and my wife says if ever he comes again she will order him out, and if he will not go she says she will turn him out, he is but a little fellow and she knows she can manage him.

Wednesday 2nd. June

I have been rather remiss with my remarks, as the approaching fair ingrosses all the attention of our friends at present, very busy selling Currants Raisins &c for the good cheer to be provided.

Thursday 3rd June Friday 4 & Saturday 5

Now here are three days together of which I can say but little; what with baking bread Cheesecakes, tarts &c the whole town is in a Stew. On Saturday according to Custom we had Mrs. Arton & her relations at tea together with Watty the wise, who is just as usual.

Sunday 6th. June

We had John Read and his Son today from Hull they went away at night as we could not accommodate them with a Bed, Eliza and her husband sleeping here they having some relations and friends from Swinefleet.

Monday 7th. June

This day we had James Ramsdale and his Son Robert from West Ella they went away at night; A throng fair for Cattle and I dare say sold pretty well, very few went away unsold.

Tuesday 8th. June

John Ramsdale and his Sister Mary were here today, it began to rain yesterday and has rained nearly all this day. Mary went away in a Cart in which we sent some Cheesecakes & other things for my Mother, who is much better than she has been, what time John went I cannot tell.

Wednesday 9th. June

A Thorough rainy day, it was attempted to get up some racing but it was abandoned and the Races were cried to take place tomorrow at five O'clock.

Thursday 10th. June

Rain again all the day, about eight O'clock there was an Ass Race for a tin tea kettle when a long eared Animal of old Lonc's carried off the Prize—after that a Race with two Galloways Rd. Marshall's & Robt. Arton's. <u>Dab</u> won the first heat, but the Gallant grey beat the two last heats and had the honour of taking away the prize which was a bridle.

Friday 11th. June

This has been a very fine day so far, (3 O'clock in the afternoon) upon the whole this has been the most gloomy fair I ever knew, having rained almost incessantly from Monday afternoon to Thursday night, without the least glimmering of Sunshine, the Company consequently has been very thin.

Saturday 12th. June

The funeral of the Vicar of North Cave Mr. Robt. Todd came through here yesterday, he died on Saturday last, he will not be much lamented as a preacher there was a hearse and four Coaches and a Gig to attend him to his silent abode.

Sunday 13th. June

James Ramsdale's Brother John who lived at Market Weighton died on Wednesday last, he had been ill some time, I did not know him nor whether he has left a family or not. I think he has not as James expects to receive something by his Will.

Monday 14th. June

Very little Company at the Market today, and what there was looked almost as gloomy as the weather. I never saw a single Sample of Corn shewn this day. The Farmers have got it into their heads that prices will shortly advance, some of them have not much to sell; but there are others who have yet Wheat Stacks to thrash.

Tuesday 15th. June

Wilson the Miller came yesterday with what he called an amended account for a further claim of 13s–8d. I was not at home when he called, but he threatened my wife with the Law; but she told him, she would never pay him he might Law all he liked. I afterward met with him at Cousens's I shewed him the Note he had brought and told him I believed he was paid the whole as I paid him myself; but he was not convinced until I shewed him the account settled by himself. This was a stunner, in fact nothing further could be said by him, he offered to treat me with a Glass, but I would not compound with him for his Liquor, I would not have it so I turned from him and left him to his meditations or ruminations.

Wednesday 16th. June

I should like to see the second Volume of Cobbett's Reformation,[24] containing a list of Abbeys, Priories &c I am rather in ignorance of these things.

Thursday 17th. June

Very cold wet weather yet, it is not at all like Summer, but so cold that fires cannot be dispensed with; at this time of the year I have known every pond dried up and water very scarce, but now every gutter is full of Repletion.

Friday 18th. June

Turnip land is in such a state that it cannot be got cleaned for sowing, here is plenty of work but not a season for having it done.

Saturday 19th. June

I have not been at Brantingham today the Ladies have broken up for Midsummer—Old Willy has been told of a Cow speaking at Broomfleet, he hardly believes it.

Sunday 20th. June

Nothing to do at the Church this afternoon as the Parson said in the morning he was going to perform Divine Service at North Cave; and as he is an Actor perhaps he could not have found a more appropriate term than performing; but I do not like the word perform when used for Religious Services, no more than I like the name peasant or peasantry for the Rural Population.

Monday 21st. June

Barnard Cook it is said is in the Fleet Prison. I thought he was in the King's Bench prison, but it appears he is not. Ben Tapp and his Partner Mc.Bride are the Creditors who have sent him there, the Debt is for Liquor, it was tried at York and undefended ...

Wednesday 23d. June

Recd. the Hamper last night with its contents, they are very useful, there is some good reading amongst it which I must look over before it be condemned; I have the Hamper safe under my Desk, where I can refer to it as opportunity offers.

Thursday 24th. June

There are Societies of all kinds I think at present, One I see is called the Temperance Society,[25] which is to prevent drunkenness; as for Gluttony it is

---

[24] *A History of the Protestant "Reformation" in England and Ireland ... Containing a List of the Abbies, Priories, Nunneries ... Confiscated ... by the Protestant "Reformation" Sovereigns and Parliaments ... In a series of letters ...* London: the author, 1829. – 2 vols. Originally published in parts by Charles Clement, 1824–6. Also part 2, containing a list of the abbeys, etc., was separately published by Cobbett in 1827.

[25] The temperance movement, which had begun in the United States in 1808, expanded rapidly throughout Britain and by 1830 it had reached Yorkshire and Lancashire and supported some 127 societies with 23,000 paying members and 60,000 associated abstainers. Its nationally most important society, the British and Foreign Temperance Society, was founded in London in 1831. The movement owed much of its success to the strong backing given by the Anglican clergy, which may well account for RS's somewhat dismissive attitude (*EB* xxvi. 579).

pretty well provided against; as many poor Creatures can sorrowfully witness, who cannot get Food sufficient for the cravings of hunger. Now Drink is a Luxury and these temperance people, for what I know to the contrary may wish to enjoy it themselves, and not let the Poor have a Share with them. As for those who can afford to drink and cannot guard against its abuse, it is quite unnecessary for any such foolish Societies to interfere, with any chance of reforming them ...

Monday 28th. June

Recd. the Globe this morning with an Account of the Death of his Majesty[26] on Saturday morning last. This occurrence interested me very little, knowing that we shall, (nay we now) have another and a gracious king, — How some Old Women and some Men much weaker cry out, what Calamitous scenes we are to witness shortly.

Tuesday 29th. June

Electioneering is all our old Friend's discourse at present, he is a Freeman of Beverley, & Bristol and a Freeholder of Yorkshire: and he is so possessed with the Election Mania that his little knowledge of Geography which I have formerly noticed, appears most astonishing. Windsor he says is in Oxfordshire; and Austin Friars (this beats us both) is in Teoly Street in the Borough, there I know it is not ...

Thursday 1st. July

A Gentleman it is said (Mr. Beverley Junr) has said we are not to have more than three fine days together this Summer—and some Old Woman says that we shall have no fine Weather until September; I hope both the Prophets will be deceived. Yesterday was very fine and this day so far. I planted some Broccoli last night.

Friday 2nd. July

We had King Wm. 4th proclaimed in the afternoon, the several publicans attended, and gave away Ale in the Cross, which was paid for by Subscription there was no lack of Customers; all ended quietly after 3 times 3 loud Bawls, led on in loyalty by the Curate, who pulled off his Hat and shouted as much like the Town's Crier as the Parish Priest.

Saturday 3rd. July

A fine Day till towards night, I went with Mr. Holborn to his Close and it came on such a shower that we took shelter in his little Shed in the Close where he told me some marvellous tales of Spirits how the Devil got up on horseback behind a Quaker preacher and how the Quaker said to him when he got up, "Thou art a bold fellow" and how he rode behind him till they came near the Eight and Forty house[27] on Wallingfen, and how the Devil then left him in a

---

[26] King George IV died, unlamented, after a lifetime of libertinism and profligacy, at the age of 67 on the morning of 26 June 1830 (*TM* 28 June 1830, 1, 1).

[27] Reputedly the meeting place of the governors of Wallingfen Common, on which the commoners of 48 townships and hamlets had rights until it was enclosed under an Act of 1777. The 'Eight and Forty House' was still standing at the end of the 19th c. (*Hall* 151; *Hull Times*, 26 July 1924).

flame of fire and entered the Eight and forty house, and <u>how</u> he said much more to the same purpose.

Sunday 4th. July

The Church; that is the Pulpit and the Priest's and Clerk's apartments hung with black Cloth, the Sign of Mourning, that God has taken away the <u>Head of the Church</u>; as I seldom look at the Vain fellow, it was some time before I saw the sombre look that presented itself.

Monday 5th. July

Old Mr. Barnard once found Sam Leighton rather late at his Work one morning, when he said well Sammy what makes you so late this morning; Sammy said I have [been] doing a job for myself Sir. Job for yourself, what Job have you had to do? I have been easing myself Sir, says Sammy.

Tuesday 6th. July

My Brother came last night, he is very well: his friend Pool is very ill he has had an Apoplectic attack and is so ill that he cannot get up from his Bed, his wife is likewise so ill that she keeps her Bed.

Wednesday 7th. July

Cousens throng today fixing the Booth for the Club feast which will be tomorrow. My Brother went away this forenoon for West Ella.

Thursday 8th. July

A fine day for the Club feast there are 138 Members it has cleared something more than £28 the last year. A very good dinner and all in good order. Music playing all the afternoon.

Friday 9th. July

There are many (what are called) Anecdotes of his late Majesty, some of them disgusting in the extreme, I think the less said the better, for very little comes out to his credit.

Saturday 10th. July

Extract from Ned Coates' Gazette "There has been terrible work in London, Lord Wellington has been killed by Prince Leopold, and all is in confusion, nobody knows what will be the result, nor who will take Lord Wellington's place".

Sunday 11th. July

George Dunn and Tim arrived at Home today, having suffered their six months imprisonment; they appear not to look much worse for their confinement; whether it will have any effect as to their future conduct remains to be proved ...

Tuesday 13th. July

Acupuncturation, a Surgical Operation originally peculiar to the Japanese & Chinese, and now (1821) introduced into European practice,[28] called by the Japanese & Chinese Zin, Hing.

---

[28] Acupuncture was known in Europe since the 17th c. It was used occasionally in the first half of the 19th c. to relieve lumbago, rheumatism and similar disorders but was regarded as unorthodox and not taught in hospitals (Smith, F. B. 378–9).

Wednesday 14th. July

At west end last night turning over and examining the award of South Cave inclosure,[29] to see if the Ellerkerians, cannot be stopped in some of their attempts at claims of which we the Cave-ists think they have no right, I gave my opinion (Gratis) that they ought to be opposed; today the Drains are to be viewed, where the claim is depending and on Saturday next the Court (of Sewers) will be held at Howden, where complaints of incroachments of <u>our</u> Rights will be made.

Thursday 15th. July

There has been an Account of the Arrival of James Milner and his Family, and the other Emigrants arriving at Quebec, after a very rough passage of eight weeks, they arrived there on Cave fair Monday. This is St. Swithin's Day, but for my part I saw none of his tears fall here, though some say they saw some few drops. Such weather as we have had the last two or three days is very reviving.

Friday 16th. July

We have not had a single flower in our Garden of either Lilac or Laburnum this year; the Blossoms of Laburnum have been particularly scarce this year; indeed I do not know that I have seen any; but I have heard some say that there have been but odd flowers in very few places.

Saturday 17th. July

Eliza got her bed this morning between 7 & 8 O'clock of a Girl,[30] she had been ill most of the night but nobody was called till about 3 O'clock in the morning, she is as well the old Women say as can be expected. My wife did not go till the morning as she wished not to be called on in the night time; there was old Betty Pickering there in a twinkling after she was called, and as soon as it was over, she set on and got breakfast ready in a <u>jiffy</u>.

Sunday 18th. July

Our friends who were at Howden Court yesterday did not meet with the support they wished for as the Court thought they had no right to interfere, but recommended them if they felt aggrieved to apply to the Law; whether they will or not I cannot say; but if they do they will certainly have then cause enough for grief.

Monday 19th. July

At the Market today some farmers saying that the Crops are the worst they have ever seen, while others more honest or more fortunate say they never had their Crops look better than at present. I hope Providence will confound the growlers.

---

[29] South Cave was enclosed under an act of 1785 (25 Geo. III c.5 (Priv. Act)). The award (ERYARS RDB. BG/139/12) was signed in 1787. Mill Beck and Crabley Beck formed part of South Cave's eastern boundary with Ellerker. In 1787 a rate was imposed to maintain sluices on Crabley drain which carried the water from Mill Beck and Cave Beck into the River Humber (*VCHYER* iv. 39).

[30] i.e. Ann Conder (See Appendix 2).

Tuesday 20th. July

Our old Stable fell down one day last week about noon fortunately without doing any harm; the Old Cardinal has been very busy clearing away the Rubbish, he reckons himself very clever at this kind of work, he is Surveyor general of the old buildings, and I think under his care they will all come to ruin.

Wednesday 21st. July

Mr. Burton of Hotham (formerly Peters) was waited on by some of the Freemen of Beverley on Monday, in order to put him up as a Candidate for that Place. He went with them that day; it is said he will have no objection of becoming a Candidate provided they will not put him to any expence. But if the Freemen of Beverley undertake to return a Member without expence it will be the greatest sign of reform I have yet heard of!!!

Thursday 22d. July

Barnard Cook has been at home some time, having it out of durance vile. He appears to be very little concerned but looks rather in a torn down manner, how he has got settled I do not know.

Friday 23d. July

I see by the Paper that some simpleton who has been preaching a Sermon on the late King, and has the very essence of Popery in him, has begged of his hearers to pray for the Soul of a Dead Man—I see it remarked in the Paper with Red Ink.

Saturday 24th. July

Went to West Ella this morning, found my Mother looking well, she complains that she sleeps ill at nights, but on the whole she is better at her age than could be expected. My Brother was there he intends leaving on Monday or Tuesday next. It is said Dan Sykes is going to put up as a Candidate for Beverley, indeed I believe he is gone there today, — he is so disgusted with Hull that he will not suffer himself to be proposed there.

Sunday 25th. July

This is one of the very hottest days we have had this Summer it is indeed a charming Summer day. If it please God to send us such weather I hope it will make a great change for the better, as the Crops require fine warm weather now.

Monday 26th. July

My Brother has got a large brass Tobacco Box of Dutch Manufacture, of an old Friend of his at Burlington of the name of Cowling, who has lived until he is beholden to his friends, he offered this Box to my Brother as a token of Friendship, but he would not take it without giving him something for it, the Box has an engraving (a rough one) of Amsterdam on the lid of it; it was found after a Storm somewhere on the Coast.

Tuesday 27th. July

Mr. Sykes or his Committee has sent a Letter to Old Willy soliciting him for a Vote at Beverley, the Election is to be on Saturday next, he thinks he shall favour Mr. Sykes with one Vote, — One he has promised to Mr. Burton, but it is said he will not get returned. Capel Cure Esq. the Present High Sheriff for Essex is a Candidate, they say he pays £100 every day in expences, this Man will certainly suit the Beverlonians.

Wednesday 28th. July

Broiling hot weather, I have seldom known it hotter than it has been three or four days back and still continues Stephen Thomas a labourer who lived here has left his wife and Family and gone to America with young Teavil Leason & George Mantle a Nephew of the late Mrs. Sonley.

Thursday 29th. July

Wrote a letter for my old Friend Mr. Atkinson this morning to York, he had a tradesman yesterday to whom he paid some money, and this morning he found out that he had paid 2 five pound notes instead of one. So I have wrote to the Person to have it corrected.

Friday 30th. July

Last night at M. Pickerings was appointed for the Sale of Geo. Hodgson's property at Ellerker, there was only one lot put up which was bought in by the Owner, a Man was there who lays claim to either all or a part of the Property, which caused a shyness amongst those who intended to bid.

Saturday 31st July

Geo Schonswar Esqr. & a Gentleman of the name of Wrightson near Doncaster have been elected Members for Hull and Dan. Sykes and Mr. Burton for Beverley.

Sunday 1st Augt.

It is with extreme Sorrow what I am going to write today as Eliza was burned out of Bed and brought over to our house about 2 O'clock this morning. The nurse set the Bed on Fire by having the Candle on the Bed. It is the greatest Act of Negligence I have known. The hangings were entirely consumed not an Inch remaining The Sheets & Counterpane also, the Blankets and Bedstead much injured, The bed tick burned in two or three places, the Mattress on fire in such a manner as nearly to suffocate any Person who entered the Room. The best Room so full of Water on the Carpet, that I got wet shod, — It is a trying circumstance for her, just laid in a fortnight and forced to run down stairs naked to escape from the flames; none of the other furniture is damaged except by the Water thrown on it, — the ceilings and Painted Walls black as though Sulphur had been burned against them. The infatuated Nurse who would not call any person has her hands burned (had it been her head I should not be sorry) Eliza was obliged to get up to call for assistance. Conder slept at our house. The suffering is painful the Child seems no worse.

Monday 2nd. Aug

"They have set the Bed on Fire", still sounds in my ears, these were the words Conder told us when he was called up. O dear O dear, my wife said that Creature will burn them all to death (She was not long before she was there) I knew said she there would something happen; for this same Creature broke Eliza's looking Glass last week, and now she will be the destruction of her and her goods and all.

Tuesday 3rd. Aug

All the Gangs and Gang-rails & Pepper Gangs of all degrees hasted away to Hotham yesterday where it was said Ale would flow in Rivers & Beef rise up like Mountains, but it was a take in; the Gang & Gangs were whipped off the Premises; Experience will <u>not</u> make Fools wiser.

Wednesday 4th. August

I am glad that Alderman Waithman is returned again as member for the City, and as well pleased that my old friend Dan is returned for Beverley; tomorrow is the day of nomination and Election for the County of York, Mr. Robinson has gone, he is agent for Duncombe, I think from all that transpires that Mr. Brougham will be sure of his Election.

Thursday 5th. Augt.

France seems to be in a terrible turmoil at present, the infatuated King has it appears been obliged to fly,[31] John Bull will receive him, but last night at our Old friend's we voted unanimously that he should be sent back he is of no use to us.

> "A curious War John Bull where the whole gain,
> "Is grinning honour for the thousands slain,"
> "Tis false say our allies for John shall get"
> "A hundred millions more in debt".

Friday 6th Augt.

Last night was the Club night, a noisy meeting, for the most part by Newlove who refused in February last to pay his Subscription, he now wants to pay it provided David Morley is not taken in as a free member. He was but little attended to, and nothing decisive was done. I wish he may be excluded from any privilege or benefit that the Publicans have in the concern.

Saturday 7th. Aug

Saw in the Paper this morning that there was a contest for Bristol, which I shewed to our Friend the Freeman had he known before that there was likely to be an opposition he would have gone on the strength of it, but as it was so long since as last Saturday that the account was made up to, he thought, before now it was over. I believe he could have liked to have gone.

Sunday 8th. Aug

Heard from Wm. this morning that little Mary was not well, her Grandmother says she wishes she had her, now that she can run about.

Monday 9th. Aug.

If a Person wish for China & Crockery not to last long Employ a Nurse. — If you have a good stock of Liquor and wish it to be lowered—Employ a Nurse. If you wish to be worse attended to than common—Apply to a Nurse. If you wish to hear Lies and Scandal in abundance—Have a Nurse beside you. If you

---

[31] King Charles X of France, who had reigned since 1824, had been forced to abdicate after the successful revolution in Paris in July 1830. He was allowed to retreat to Cherbourg, where he embarked for England on 16 Aug. He lived for a time at Holyrood Palace in Edinburgh, which had been once more placed at his disposal, but subsequently retired for reasons of health to Goritz, where he later died in 1836 (Beach 403–28).

wish to be ignorant of what is going on in your Family by all means have a Nurse. If you wish to hear your Children fret, Employ a Nurse.

Tuesday 10th Augt.

The Exciseman who surveys here and to whom I sometimes lend an Old Newspaper, is a relation of Sir Robt. Wilsons,[32] (by this time I expect a Member again for the Borough) begged one to send to his Mother who lives at Newark upon Trent, and is Sir Robert's own Cousin; — I think there are a good many liberal Members returned this Election.

Wednesday 11th. Aug.

The Person I wrote to for Mr. Atkinson has sent word that he did not receive the five pound which the Old Man thought he had paid him; he knows he is so much wanting but I think not positive that he paid it to the Person in question.

Thursday 12th. Augt.

There was a special Court at Newlove's yesterday, I was one of the Jury I believe the Court was to receive a Surrender from Newlove to Mr. Carter of a Mortgage of his Property, to secure his Debt, most likely. I and Abraham Barff and Matty Moody came away without spending a penny, the Jury have a Shilling each: had it been another house I should have either spent it or left it for the Company, but I will not come at the House unless compelled by business so long as he stays at it. — He would not have our Shillings so I will have none of his.

Friday 13th. Aug

I had a bad sore Throat last night and now I am so hoarse that I can hardly speak. I took some Raspberry Vinegar which I think was of service. I am no otherwise ill as at Old Willy's last night arranging the Church accounts, there is to be a meeting tonight to balance the accounts of the Churchwardens, it is to be at Tindales.

Saturday 14th. Aug.

I have had a most <u>audacious</u> Sore throat and bad cold for three or four days, with such a hoarseness that I could scarcely speak, I hope it is beginning to be better. We have got a Ton of Flour from Beverley today, this is the third load to that amount. I have heard that Pennington is taken to York Castle for Debt, but do not know for truth.

Sunday 15th. Aug

There has been a letter from James Milner in America (this morning.) He is at a place called Kingston in one of the Canadas, he and all his family have fallen in for work at good Wages (of course) he does not intend to proceed to Michegan this Summer. Some of his Companions have gone on there.

---

[32] Sir Robert Thomas Wilson (1777–1849) had a long and distinguished military career culminating in his appointment as general and governor of Gibraltar in 1842. His career was temporarily disrupted when he was dismissed from the army for his action against the mob at Queen Caroline's funeral in 1821 but he was publicly re-instated by King William IV with the rank of lieutenant-general in 1830. He was elected MP for Southwark in 1818, 1826, and 1830 (*TM* 27 July 1830, 2 b; *DNB*).

Monday 16th. Augt.

After the meeting at Tindale's on Friday night Jno. Gardam went to call Val. Tindale the Butcher. Val thrust him into the Beck, and a pretty hurry[33] there was, but I did not see or hear it. — Rob. Marshall would not sign the Church accounts because there had been six pounds spent in putting the Pulpit in mourning. Abraham Barff would not sign because the ringers have £1–11–6 on the 5th. Novr. Wm. Cousens objected because the Visitation was at Morley's. I signed but protested against two pounds being charged for Confirmation, viz in conveying the Candidates to Beverley and treating them with their Dinners. I have no objection to any Persons being at their own expence for this mummery, but to make the Parish pay for it is too bad.

Tuesday 17th. Aug.

My Cold still continues though not so inveterate, last night I took some Vinegar and Treacle when going to Bed, I have taken some Camomile tea, which with us is a favourite family medicine. — Pennington the Miller is certainly sent to York Castle, for £100 borrowed for which he has paid no interest for 6 or 7 years his Son was here yesterday, it is expected he will be able to go in with the business.

Wednesday 18th. Aug

Thos. Marshall was here on Monday night saying that Tom Turk has cleared or saved near £10.000 pounds since he began business. I know he was a famous charger therefore if he had custom, he was sure to clear a good deal of money. I said he should be called Tom of ten thousand.

Thursday 19th. Aug

I have received the following Notice from the learned & clever Mr Newlove, (a true Copy)

> to the sessers of the parrish of South Cave
> I doo here by give you notice that I shall
> Apeal at the Appel day menshioned in your list
> delivered to me for the sesment of of house duty
> yrs Richard Newlove

this is nearly a fac simile & verbatim et literatim

Friday 20th Aug.

My Cold I think is very little better than it was. I have taken many things for it, some tolerable palatable, and some not much to crack on. I think a little Spanish Juice is as good as any thing I take. I feel no ill effects, any more than being hoarse.

Saturday 21st. Aug.

Notice has come for the Publicans to appear as usual at Brewster Sessions which will this year be on the 8th. Sepr. next. I think the new Beer Act[34] will

---

[33] 'commotion or agitation, social or political disturbance' (*OED*).

[34] The Beerhouse Act (i.e. 'An Act to Permit the General Sale of Beer and Cider by Retail in England', 1 Will. IV. c. 64), passed on 23 July 1830, had the dual aim of weaning drinkers away from spirits, especially gin, and counteracting the trend towards 'tieing' public houses to breweries. It permitted any rate-paying householders to sell beer from their own houses on the purchase of a licence from the Excise

not be of much benefit, it is almost as bad to understand as Adam Martin's Book, which he found out a day or two ago, had two last ends in it, one of which was in the middle of the Book, this was a poser, Adam could make neither head nor tail of it.

Sunday 22d. Aug

We have tolerable fine Weather, several have begun harvest; I saw some Stooks yesterday, for the first time when going to Brantingham. Should the Weather keep fine the Wheat will be of superior Quality, and the Crops very good especially in the land hereabouts. I understand the Strong land Crops are not so promising, but let the Farmers alone for complaining.

Monday 23d. Aug

The old doating King Charles of France I see has arrived in England; John Bull suffers all sorts to come to see him but I hope he will shew him no familiarity. Adam has a got a Book this morning which has not a last end at all, it is like the Irishman's Rope which had no end, he said somebody had cut it off

...

Wednesday 25th. Aug

Ths. Marshall says he is very poorly, he never looks jolly but I think he is thinner than Common. He has had a <u>cursed old Sow</u> get into his Wheat Close and wasted he says a Quarter of Wheat, which may have some effect on his health.

Thursday 26th. Aug

My Wife has been at Hull today and I have been Shopkeeper and thought I did very well, until somebody came in and said "Your butter is melting" and Sure enough there was half a Pound in the Window of fine Melted Butter, not such as is met with at Inns to spoil Potatoes and Greens with; as this was genuine.

Friday 27th. Aug

So the "old foolish King that would not be admonished" has arrived in England, I think he would have been as well away; but this land of ours refuses nothing.

Saturday 28th. Aug

A Fine Harvest day, but had been part rain the last night, or there would have been throng deed today leading wheat, I dare say the Crops are very good in general.

Sunday 29th Aug

There is one thing Rd. Marshall said to me this morning that wants doing for the good of the Country and that is reducing the taxes. I told him he was very right, but there were two things wanted doing first; Rents wanted reducing and tithes abolishing, but as he is both Steward and tithe Collector, he did not exactly agree with me. He thought a Gentleman ought to have the worth of his Land. I thought so too, but he should not have War Rents in time of Peace.

at a cost of 2 guineas a year and without any prior requirement to obtain authorization from a magistrate.

Monday 30th. Aug

Now here is a little bit of calling which was going on this morning, between Val. Tindale the Butcher and Cooper Tindle—Val. Thou was at York Castle; Coop. Aye and I got home again but if thou ever gangs there, thou will be hanged, thou will never get yam again. Now look at that great Tup Mutton fellow, he went to Mr. Scholefield's and could not drink so fast as he wished, so he was taken out and laid in the Yard, and liquor was poured into him with a Beast Horn. For Sham of theesen thou great ugly Beggar. Now look at that great Val. there he is ...

Wednesday 1st. Sepr.

This day the War begins against the defenceless Game, several Lords of Manors and many not Lords, wish to transfer the Partridges from the Stubble fields, into their own hungry maws. I have not been out and therefore not seen a single Sportsman, whose Play is death.

Thursday 2 Sepr.

No Paper this morning; so that I have not had my accustomed treat. I took down an Old Magazine to amuse myself with, as I cannot dispense with reading—and made myself as comfortable as I could. — Pennington has got home again.

Friday 3rd Sep

I have had Geo. Petfield this morning putting on a new Bell Rope, it has been nearly a week unrung as the Rope was broken. Recd. two papers this morning, so that I have plenty of news this day. It appears the Revolution has taken place at Brussels. I do not think that the French are yet in any thing like a settled situation.

Saturday 4th. Sepr.

A good deal of Rain last night which has prevented the leading of Wheat this day to any great extent; — Revolution and Change seems to be the order of the day—I remember the beginning of the French Revolution, at that time it was confidently said there would not be a King in Europe in 6 years from that time So mad were the Republicans with frenzy.

Sunday 5th. Sep

Some person has inserted a letter in the Hull Packet of last week respecting North and South Cave, what it was when Domesday Book was compiled I have not an opportunity of knowing, neither do I know that a person of the Name of Jordanus took the name of De Cave, but I do know that there is not a single monument in the Church of that family, altho' the writer says there are several.[35] The oldest inscription on a pillar is as follows

    "Sacra Haec Aedes
    Dei Structa Fuit
    Ao Domi 1601 Thoma
    Flinto Eiusdem =

---

[35] The unsigned letter appeared in the *Hull Packet*, 31 Aug. 1830, p. 4. Its author referred to monuments in the church at North Cave, not at South Cave, as RS mistakenly believed.

Tunc Vicario".

If I interpret this right it appears to say that this sacred temple of God was built at this time 1601. — but I think the Church is likely to be older. There is an old Gravestone in the Church yard recording the death of a Man Ricardus Danby who died in 1602. There is also an inscription or tablet in the Faxfleet Aisle saying that this Aisle was repaired at the proper Cost and Charges of the Worshipful Garwaies Alderman of the City of London in 1633. There is not in the Church a single Monument of any kind, so how the writer of the above could say there are several to one Family, is such a sort of even down lying that I am at a loss to conceive his motives for so saying. — In the Chancel there are two small marble tablets or remembrances for Mr. Barnard and his Son Charles.

Monday 6th. Sepr.

This has been a very dull day, we have had a Young Man from Beverley today paid him £31–9–0 — part of which Sum was for 200 Stone of Flour, he is going to send us a load tomorrow which he says is excellent, we have lately got a good many Groceries from him (Mr. Oxtoby) as we save Carriage which 1s. pr. Cwt. Salt cost 2s/6d when we have it from Hull we pay 1s. for the Carriage so that here is a saving.

Tuesday 7th. Sepr.

When Cumberland the Author[36] was buried in Westminster Abbey, the Dean after his interment delivered an Eulogium on him, in which was the following, "May God forgive him his Sins", this is praying for the Dead, plainly—Some of these Deans and Church officers (whose names neither I nor the Scripture knows any thing about) have a natural liking to Popery, and not to the best parts neither ...

Thursday 9th. Sepr.

I see there are Pens called "Perryan Pens"[37] advertised which they give out will never want mending. Now of what kind of materials, or in what manner are they made, that this is said of them? For my part I do not believe it, for how can such an Article as a Pen be used without requiring mending? I should like to have one of these kind of Pens as I am rather difficult with mine and spend a good deal of time in mending them.

Friday 10th. Sepr

Rain again today, It is tedious Harvest weather, there is a good deal of Wheat lead, but more that is not. There is but little either wisdom or knowledge

---

[36] i.e. Richard Cumberland (1732—1811), a minor dramatist. He was buried in Westminster Abbey, in Poet's Corner, on 14 May 1811. The service was conducted by his childhood friend, Dr Vincent, Dean of Westminster (Mudford 588–90).

[37] The *Hull Packet* for 7 Sept. 1830 contained an advertisement for 'Patent Perryian Pens'. They were steel slip pens manufactured by their inventor, James Perry, and sold in Hull by Thomas Topping, the printer and publisher of the *Hull Packet*. They were still being advertised, at least as late as 1836, by which time they had been refined to incorporate 'an india-rubber spring' to make them more flexible in action.

in continually muttering about the weather, it is wisely ordered by a gracious providence for the best.

Friday 11th. Sepr. [i.e. Saturday 11th Sept.]

At Ellerker this afternoon putting in or entering the Highways Accounts in the Book for the Surveyors.

Saturday 11th Sepr.

I was at Mr. Robinson's this morning, when he told me that he was going to London on Monday next, and offered to take a letter or small parcel; I shall therefore embrace the opportunity of sending my Journal, so far, and here for the present I close my remarks.

Sunday 12th. Sepr.

I went to Mr. Robinson's today to carry the Parcel for Wm. but he did not know whether he was going tomorrow or not until the Post came in the next morning. I left the Parcel with him, as a day was no great matter, So this is again the first day I recommence my Journal.

Monday 13th. Sep

I have had a Gentleman from London today taking an Account of my Stock of Stamps, I do not know his name, I had no previous notice of his coming.

Tuesday 14th. Sep

Mr. Robinson and his Man Robert, went by the Coach this morning on their way to London, I expect they will be in London, tomorrow night, Mr. R. is going to stay at Camberwell.

Wednesday 15th. Sep

Wrote a Notice for Mattw. Pickering, to quit a Close on Wallingfen, which he only entered on last Lady day, so that he is soon tired, it belongs to a Person named Jepson a Painter at Hull, who married Miss Sissons, it was her property, she has been dead some time.

Thursday 16th. Sep

The Flour Sellers viz. Collinson & Pinder, last week settled the price of Flour, just when we had got a large load in, which I believe was their contradiction, they being willing to lose twopence if they could make us lose a penny, but it appears they are tired of this scheme for the present, as they have this morning risen it again; — Now they may hang themselves if they will, they shall not influence me to do the same.

Friday 17th Sep

I expect Wm. has recd. the Parcel by this time which I sent by Mr. Robinson; the weather is tolerable today for the harvest.

Saturday 18th. Sep

At Brantingham in the morning as usual, and in the afternoon at Ellerker; I was at Mr. Allison's a Farmer who lives where Heslewood's did, he says he has an excellent Crop this year of all kinds. From thence I went to Mr. Leason's to settle with him for the Church Sess I collected for him, got tea there, and came home about 8 o'clock.

Sunday 19th. Septr.

A Stormy day, a kind of Equinoctial gale—Ths. Marshall says he would have written a Notice to his Landlord to quit, on Saturday night, but it got dark before he had done, this forenoon he was busy he could not get on with it; but this Evening he thinks he shall finish it.

Monday 20th. Sep

Ths. Marshall came this morning to get me to seal him a letter, to send to his Landlord; but I told him as to giving notice that was one of the things he durst not do: the other two were he dare not make his will, nor buy any Land, — he swore two of these he would do, and the other he could not viz buy land whether he has given notice or not, I am not satisfied; for I told him he ought to Post pay the letter, which stumbled him, but he said he would do it, so he went to the Post office.

Tuesday 21st Sepr

At our old Friends last night, he was as he thought entertaining the Company with "Recollections" of London some 50 years ago or more; Lord George Gordon's Riots in 1780, he was then a house keeper in Long Acre; his wife had been out, and came back and told him that Newgate was burnt down, he said he would not credit it, if all the people in London told him so; He then set off to see and sure enough it was consumed, and demolished; he had 17s. to pay as his share of the Expences incurred by the destruction of Property.

Wednesday 22nd. Sep

At the late election at Hull there was some Window breaking, and other depredations to the amount of 72 or 73 pounds at Sculcoates, a Rate has been made for the payment, in the Division of Hunsley Beacon. South Cave has to pay £3–12–0 as its proportion.

Thursday 23d. Sep

I recd. Cobbett's for last Sunday, this morning. It has come very irregular of late indeed some weeks not at all, "What the reason is I cannot tell", this is the fact.

Friday 24th. Sep.

The Continent has got a little warm, the lower Classes feel themselves, rather heated, and I believe they will not cool till some of the Countries are in a Broil, there is in my Opinion no likelihood, that the Belgians will be still yet, let them Rule or be Ruled as they like, only do not let us interfere.

Saturday 25th. Sep

Four of Mr. Barnard's tenants it is said have given notice. Ths. Marshall of the Low Mill, — Leaper at the Sands[,] Robt. Arton the Castle farm, and another tenant at Walkington. I am not at all sorry that some of the proud, ignorant, overbearing fellows are beginning to feel what has been long felt by the Poor, viz that their Expences are above their incomes.

Sunday 26th. Sep

Mr. Atkinson has got cold and is very poorly, he looks very tottering, one day last week he could eat nothing, some sent one thing and some another. I prescribed <u>Camomile tea</u>, he took some and thought he was better for it, as he had been sick, and it settled his Stomach.

Monday 27th. Sep

I have written a Notice for Watson Arton to give Mr. Collinson the Landlord of Henry Arton that he will quit his farm at Lady day next, then what will become of Mr. Henry I cannot tell, — Mr. Ellerker has given two of his tenants at Ellerker notice to quit their farms, they intended it is said to give him notice; but he is before-hand with them. Jackson of Ellerker Sands is one and Thos. Robinson the other.

Tuesday 28th. Sep

There was formerly a Wind Mill at So. Cave on or near Willy Wardell's plump facing the Castle, this was called the high Mill, and where Thomas Marshall lives was and is still called the Low Mill. We have this day got another load of Flour a Ton from Beverley, along with other goods ...

Thursday 30th. Sep

As a matter which concerns me very little, I had forgot to notice that the little Quaker Jn. Pinder, and his Brother's widow (the late Tommy), went to Hull last week and were married as the report is, I know nothing to the contrary but think the thing would have been as well undone[.] They have been calling in their Customers, and treating them with liquor, (Bramble wine) they say & Bridecake But <u>me even me</u> they have not called in. Do I grieve for it? No not I!!

...

Saturday 2nd. Oct

At Brantingham as usual in the forenoon. In the afternoon collecting along with Mr. Leeson the Composition money for the Highways, we did not get much. I believe the Surveyors will be on the wrong side viz their Rects. will not cover the Expences.

Sunday 3rd. Oct

I came from the Church with Mr. Robinson's man, he was telling me of his adventures in London, he had attended the Service at St. Pancras's new Church (I do not know that there is an old one) one Sunday, he had walked from Camberwell to Highgate, and only lost himself once; he made a successful Journey from the said Church to Blackfriars bridge without any mistake, this will serve Robt. to amuse his friends.

Monday 4th. Oct

Met with a Man today Mr. Purdon of Newland the Surveyor of the Turnpike roads, who told me that one of his Children which he said had been <u>Vakkinated</u> had after that the small Pox, but in a very favourable manner.

Tuesday 5th. Oct

Very little doing at the Market, but the Prices did not seem to be so high for Wheat as they were lately, many threshing Machines are rattling away, and Cause an artificial Supply, which had it come to the Market in the regular way of Flail threshing, would have been a means of keeping up the Prices, but it appears the farmers must have money.

Wednesday 6th. Oct

There was a meeting at Js. Levitt's last night to balance the Highway accounts. I have been so absorbed in Highways, and Drains that I am glad for a season to escape from the turmoil of Composition, Statute Duty, Acre money, Lands Gate money and all etceteras, and this morning I sat down comfortably, to the Newspaper, and a Pipe, with the Savour of Welsh Michaelmas Goose, and the Pleasure of hearing that little Mary is better.

Thursday 7th. Oct

There has been a meeting at Beverley called the Beacon Club in honour of Mr. Burton being elected for Beverley, it seems his Crest is a Beacon, these Clubs are got up for the most part, as an opportunity for spouting, it seems as if some or one of the Orators, wanted the Proprietors of Hotham Hall to be hereditary Members for Beverley; they who are so outrageous, will most likely be the first to cry out for a third man[38] at the next Election, except the Hotham Hall member will pay the best.

Friday 8th. Oct

When I hear of any thing with the word National prefixed to it, I am almost seized with a shuddering fit,[39] — The National Guards of France are much cried up, but not one word of Approbation shall they have from me, I am not at all in love with these kinds of Citizen Soldiers. We have the National Debt, is that a comfort? then there is the National Church, this is a source of comfort to those who divide the Spoil, then there is that other ominous "National" I have a good mind not to write the word, School [written in small letters with a line of dots underneath] it has or had an old Woman as instructor General viz Mrs. Trimmer,[40] and this old Dame has under her many more, some in Lawn Sleeves, and some that aspire to them, to keep the People in ignorance not to instruct them. I myself I, nearly fell a Victim, to this species of National Craft, but no more Friendship with National priests for me as friends they would have ruined me, why then need I value their selfish kindness.

---

[38] It was customary in Hull elections before 1832 to have an outsider, known as a 'Third Man', to stand in opposition to the local candidates. Such men often spent lavishly in their attempts to gain a seat thereby increasing the cost of elections for the town's regular MPs (Markham (1982) 18).

[39] RS's diatribe against everything 'National' reflected his deep dislike of the National Society for Promoting the Education of the Poor in the Principles of the Established Church, which had been formed in 1811. For a time his own school had been conducted on the principles of the National Society, apparently against his wishes. (See Introduction).

[40] Mrs Sarah Trimmer, herself a devout Anglican, was instrumental in the development of the rift between Joseph Lancaster and Andrew Bell, who had independently set up schools based upon a system of monitorial supervision. Lancaster, a Quaker, had established non-denominational schools, whereas Bell, an Anglican minister, had introduced the system into existing parochial schools. In 1805, Mrs Trimmer accused Lancaster of copying Bell's system and of failing to teach the catechism. The Church of England withdrew its support from the schools set up by Lancaster, and the subsequent division between Anglican and nonconformist schools proved very damaging to the cause of national education (Curtis 201 and 207–8).

Saturday 9th. Oct

Cobbett has commenced in fine Stile with the musical Bishop, and the Play house Singers,[41] these Raffle Caps, whose calling is of no earthly use to any, but themselves, but if Fools will support Knaves, I cannot help it; I know they never had a Shilling of mine to encourage them in their idleness; and I think they have not had much of Cobbett's money.

Sunday 10th. Oct

Our old friend and Mr. Bridgman set off in a Gig yesterday morning according to annual custom for Malton fair, — Barratt's Cart set off this afternoon for Hull fair with a load of Gangrails, the town is well quit of them; No shews have come through from Howden to Hull fair this year, sometimes there have been crowds of them.

Monday 11th. Oct

My cold is not yet entirely gone; I have a piece of Flanel on my Breast and a Plaster on my Back, so that I am stuffed before and stiffened behind, I feel very little inconvenience from the long continuance of this cold; I have often suffered more, from a shorter attack. My wife has had a bad eye, which has looked as black as though she had had a stroke over it, she put on two Blisters a day or two ago, and is now rather better. — This is Hull fair day none of us there—indeed I never was at Hull fair.

Tuesday 12th. Oct

Several advertisements for places, say that salary is no object; certainly it cannot be for the sake of employment, for there must be more satisfaction in being the masters of one's own time than being under the controul [*sic*] of others, and all for nothing. I will not believe that those who account wages as nothing, are serious in the want of places.

Wednesday 13th. Oct

I have had Ths. Marshall this morning with a lengthened visage, Laverack has pounded 10 or 12 of his Cattle, and will not let him have them out of the Pinfold without Tom pays a Guinea for their liberation, as Laverack pretends to claim something for an old Arrear of the same kind which occurred four years ago. The poor <u>injured</u> Miller says that his Opponent cannot stop his Cattle for the old arrears, and as he has a good deal of Real Bullism in him he has set off to lay his case before Mr. Robinson, he cares nought about his cattle nor the expence neither, only he can keep clear of giving that Rascally Laverack any of it. — Our long friend says he has been in all the Courts in England, Civil and uncivil, Spiritual & temporal and if he had only money he would always be in law, he would make some of the Slinking beggars know what was what.

Thursday 14th Octr.

The time that Mr. Atkinson has been away has been employed by Mr. Bridgman's housekeeper in giving his house a thorough cleaning and painting,

---

[41] Cobbett had attacked a sermon preached by the Bishop of Rochester at a 'music meeting' in Worcester Cathedral on 14 Sept. 1830. The Bishop had incurred his wrath by defending the use of the cathedral as a venue for the music festival (*CPR* 70 xiv (2 Oct.) 1830, 417–26).

which has put the old man to as much inconvenience as if a Revolution had happened amongst his Nails and Leather, he could have liked to have gone on his old way.

Friday 15th. Oct

Set off from home this morning between 7 and 8 O''clock to measure the Ellerker Sands farm, but I need not have been so early, as the morning was so misty that there was no seeing more than a few Yards round; but before noon it cleared up and became very fine, I got done a little after Sunset finishing at Brough Haven, we were three of us and went into the Public house and got a Pitcher or two of Ale, which was very refreshing, I was very tired and a Blister on one of my heels, but I got home about eight O'clock, The Farm contains 161a–1R–10P.

Saturday 16th. Oct

This morning I was very stiff with my work yesterday, there is no harder work than measuring land, going over Stubble of all sorts and ploughed land, — however I got very well to Brantingham and back; in the afternoon I did not go out.

Sunday 17th. Oct

Another very fine day, the weather now is much more pleasant than it was in the Summer. The poor Creature of a Parson concluded with saying that of all persons the Christian had most cause to be proud. I hear such things at times, that I am ready to conclude the driveller has not read the Scriptures, of which he is, or should be an expounder.

Monday 18th. Oct

Mr. Barnard's farm at Walkington of which the present tenant gave notice to quit is let to a Man of Sancton of the name of Rotsey—Tom Robinson of Ellerker has again taken his farm, and Jackson of the Ellerker Sands wants to try to agree for it again as soon as the Landlord gets the measurement, which I have got made out.

Tuesday 19th. Oct.

Some of the Publicans have reduced the Price of Ale to 2d. a pint. I heard a man say last night that there was one house he knew that had but one tap (Cousens) selling at 2d. — 2½d and 3d. all the same kind, I suppose there is all sorts but good selling at all prices, Sweet, Sour, Bitter, in fact all kinds but good, — Now I do not care one farthing what the price or the quality is; I get a Pint once a month at the Club night, this is my greatest consumption.

Wednesday 20th. Oct.

There are two new public houses at Ellerker under the new Beer Act. Wm. Dodds is one of the new Landlords, and another of the name of Reed opposite to where Mr. Levitts did live, here is not one house of the kind opened here.

Thursday 21st. Oct

I signed two Petitions one to the Lords and the other to the Commons for the abolition or Suppression of the abominable Slave trade, I would have no gradual abolition, but let liberty burst upon them at once, I signed these with the more pleasure as the person who brought it, said that the Curate would not sign it as he thought Slavery was right; I wish the fellow was one of these same Jamaica Slaves he could be spared from here without loss.

Friday 22nd. Oct

Yesterday was the Court day, it was at Js. Levitt's I was at the Dinner as usual where, I always before today had half a Guinea, but as Mr. Spofforth who is ill, sent his Son to officiate for him, he had no orders to pay it, but said he would mention it to his Father, however I comfort myself with being no worse for what I never had.

Saturday 23rd. Oct

I had no paper yesterday, neither did it which was wanting arrive today, — When going to Brantingham this morning, I met with Mr. Shackleton's Brother, who lives in Mr. Tapp's house[,] he is rather flighty, but he talked remarkably sensible and on subjects much out of the comprehension of our Bacon eating neighbours. He had been reading Milton's work on Christianity[42] lately discovered in the British Museum, he was well acquainted with the works of this delightful author. — By the way when I first read Paradise Lost which was when I was about 13 years of age, I was enraptured with it, not so much perhaps for the Languages as the incidents it contained, I was in strict fact a Miltonist.

Sunday 24th Oct

The Paper which should have come on Friday, was brought this morning, it was not directed by Wm. and was addressed near Hull, and my name was Wm. Sharp on it. No better direction than South Cave, Yorkshire.

Monday 25th. Oct

As for the Market today I have seen very little done in the Corn line. Wheat I think is much as usual. Barley seemed to be enquired after, — The farmers and Growers who are not of the most intelligent order, wish that the Whole of the Malt duty was taken off, that they instead of the Government might put the amount of the advanced price in their pockets they do not wish for Malt lower, but Barley higher.

Tuesday 26th. Oct

Richd. Marshall has had the threshing Machine at work today, but from the appearance of his Stack yard one would have thought he need not have been in such a hurry, as he has certainly a very poor appearance of Stacks this year.

Wednesday 27th. Oct.

We Diarians or Journalizers, are tied to no manner of Stile, or method, in our remarks, Narrative, Dialogue, Anecdote, Rhyme (when we can fall in for it,) and any other art matter, or manner of jumblery together a few lines every day, seems no very hard task, but to follow it up every day requires, some little time even if imagination and thought be kept at a distance.

---

[42] John Milton, *A Treatise of Christian Doctrine* ... Translated from the original by C. R. Sumner. Cambridge University Press, 1825.

Thursday 28th. Oct.

Some old Women and some young ones are in a terrible quandary expecting nothing but a Revolution. Our neighbour the old Cardinal is the trumpeter on the occasion; a Revolution is inevitable, it is nearly at hand, then Old Mother Shipton's prophecies come in to back on the argument for the time is nearly at hand for their fulfilment, — (These I know nothing about,) Some people have strange ideas, What said the Jailer of Newgate, when inflamed with liberty, and he was going to lose a Prisoner (Peveril), I quote <u>authentic</u> history, to be taken from him to the tower, What says he "Free born Britons to a Military prison, as if we had neither Bolts nor Chains here"!!

Friday 29th Oct

Two of the intelligent farmers Leaper & Rt. Arton want to take their farms again, their Landlord will be as simple as they are if he lets them again to them without raising the Rents, now observe the wisdom of these tenants to give notice to quit, and want to take on again; certainly all the parties concerned are not entirely void of that essential article called Common Sense.

Saturday 30th. Octr

Now, I believe that the troubled state of France is far from being ended, nay I think it has scarcely begun. The King of the Citizens or the Citizen King, may be a good King Log, but he has so many discont[ent]ed Spirits about him, that he must to secure his place, be something more resolute than he has till now shewn himself or his masters will put him down, if he does not put them down.[43]

Sunday 31st. Oct

The Parliament I see by the Paper this morning met on Tuesday last, No speech from the King, which many are so anxious to see, and for which I am in no anxiety at all; The Old Speaker is chosen; he seems to be commended by all parties, and as far as I know he is quite worthy of his Situation.

Monday 1st. Novr

The weather commences very fine, for what is called the gloomy Month of November; — I have recd. from the Surveyor of taxes today no fewer than 13 surcharges for different people in the town; I hate these Surcharges.

Tuesday 2nd. Nov

The Old Cardinal has been about with two Petitions, sent to him by Mr. Sykes for the abolition of Slavery. He went to the petty Curate, but he likes Slavery so well that he would not sign them; the Old Cardinal says he is fit for nothing but a Slave whipper, but here I think he is not exactly right, I would rather have him flogged than make a flogger of him; I would make him <u>passive</u> and not <u>active</u>.

---

[43] After the July Revolution of 1830, the Duke of Orléans, Louis-Philippe, succeeded to the throne on 9 Aug. 1830 as a constitutional monarch with the title 'King of the French' in place of the traditional 'King of France' to signify the monarchy's new status. The transition proceeded with relative smoothness, although there was continued agitation in Paris for some months afterwards, and the reports of rioting and disturbances there had a bad effect on France's reputation abroad (Leys 176–87).

Wednesday 3rd. Nov

I have seen long and said often that the rage for enclosing open fields and Commons, was one great cause of the Ruin or poverty of the rural population, this opinion seems to be gaining ground but whether it will be for the better or not I cannot say, but I think it will not raise a poor labourer into a small farmer. These great farms are the very bane of England; here is one of the great bloated Gentleman farmers as they call themselves surrounded with Crowds of labourers, who now as a boon ask for employment and cannot have it, but at such a Rate that hunger, is always in their train.

Thursday 4th Nov

When the late Mr. Barnard wished for a Rookery he had no Crows so he sent for some I think from Lon[d]esborough, and got some sticks in the form of Nests put in the trees, with plenty of Branches and sticks strewed about as materials for the future Colonists, but they were shy a long time ere they began at last one or two of them begun building but not a stick would they use of those prepared for them. They are now a goodly Colony.

Friday 5th. Nov

Busy all this day or rather night collecting the Assd. taxes. It is a tiresome time, I have however got the Money as well as I expected.

Saturday 6th. Nov

Went to Beverley this morning in Mr. Robinson's Gig, his Man was going to fetch two Ladies[.] I walked back, and got wet through, It came on to rain very heavy. when upon Weedly ground I came back with Dr. alias Joe Galland, at some future time I shall give a Sketch of our conversation.

> Exit omnus as Will says or
> those who came after him

Sunday 7th. Nov.

I think I left off the last Sheet on Saturday, the day I had been at Beverley paying in the Taxes. I came back with Joseph Galland who professes some little Doctoring in which he says he is very skilful. Our talk (or his at least) was of the Patients he had had. One Woman and her Daughter came to him, the Woman with some complaint quite in the Doctor's way, either of the Liver, Lungs or Limbs, Joseph it appears uses alliteration without knowing its meaning. He had in a great measure cured the Mother, when she said I never told you of my Daughter's illness, You need say nought about [it] he says I see what is the matter with her, let me get you well, and you shall take her underhand. I will give you some medicine for her, it will be very nasty, and very like she will not take it (she was about 12 or 13) but never mind her mak her tak it, Gang you tiv her, and throw her down, get a stride on her, nip her nose and team it intiv her, Od rot her never mind her noise, nip her nose well and team it in, tak no notice of her roaring and screaming &c &c

Monday 8th. Nov

The Old Cobler at Walkington I saw on Saturday had got a fresh sign which was "May I keep Master of my Currier, Friendly to my Customers and be at home when wanted",

Tuesday 9th. Nov

Sent a Hamper this day by the Carrier to Hull for Wm. it is to leave Hull tomorrow in the Steam Packet containing my <u>interesting</u> Journal to last Saturday, and what is more substantial a fine Goose, a Couple of fine lovely Chickens as much of a Ham as we could get in, 2 lbs of Jn. Baitson's butter which is famed above the famous, some Flour without weight or measure, and a bit of Cheese for Mary who keeps up the family taste.

Wednesday 10th. Nov

Mrs. Arton of the Castle farm has been telling us that Tom Levitt who married Nancy Marshall is to have their Farm, so that the Marshall's spread and occupy farms here like a hungry Colony in a new Country—Tom is a Shopkeeper at the Westend, and it is said that the Gamekeeper who married his Sister is to succeed him in the Grocery and Bacon line, so thus they play into one another's hands, — I have seen such things before.

Thursday 11th. Nov

This is the first Sittings Day here, Mr. Smelt was here at the Constable Meeting; he was married last Tuesday week—his wife was with him. I do not know at all what kind of hiring there was. My Sister was here from West Ella, my Mother she says continues ill, but from what she says, I think not in immediate danger. — I was at the Constable's dinner as usual.

Friday 12th. Nov

Thos. Marshall has had a Labourer a number of years, and the last week he was discovered Robbing his Master of Flour, they did not indeed catch him with the Bag in his possession, he is likewise suspected of stealing Bacon and other things, his name is Watson, Tom thought he was ower fond to be a thief, but here he was mistaken—he has dismissed him and how he will get work is not easy to say.

Saturday 13th. Nov

This afternoon measuring a Close for Cousens, which had a following Crop of Wheat of Mr. Js. Levitt; he the old Man told him there were 11 Acres, but Cousens wished to have it measured, and it is very near 12 Acres so that he will lose by the trouble.

Sunday 14th. Nov

Went to West Ella this morning by the Coach to Ferriby, got there about Breakfast time, found my Mother looking much better than I expected, as from the Accounts we had had, I looked upon her to be dying. She was in Bed she has not been up lately, she was very cheerful, her seeing, hearing, and faculties are very good, She has not much pain, but appears to be short of breath—I got home about half past five walked back by the way of Riplingham.

Monday 15th. Nov

My Sister at West Ella has 3 Cats a Dog and a Nanny Goat these are Domestic Animals, Robt. said they had some Ferrets, which he wished me to see, but I made an excuse, as these fierce fiery Creatures are no favourites with me.

Tuesday 16th. Nov

I am extremely sorry that the work of burning the produce of the Farmers in the Southern Counties still continues,[44] this is certainly the most wicked and abominable course that can be taken for a redress of Grievances, even to destroy the very means of subsistence, the Vile incendiaries deserve severe punishment, and sooner or later their "Sins will find them out".

Wednesday 17 Novr.

A meeting at Js. Levitt's this Evening to consult on the Rate of Composition for the Highways,[45] there was not many there, these sort of meetings are of very little use except to the Publican at whose house they are held.

Thursday 18th. Nov

Recd. the <u>Standard</u> this morning with an Account of the resignation of Mr. Peel & Co.[46] I think it a matter of very little moment who take their places, I said I did not like Ferretts a day or two ago, and these same Ministers are of the Blood sucking tribe

> "For forms of Government let Fools contest,
> For what is best administer'd is best"

Friday 19th. Nov

Mr. Smelt left some Petitions with me for the Abolition of Slavery, One of which I carried to the Revd Mr. Simpson of Brantingham, but he declined signing it, although he said he was quite an Advocate for the Abolition "<u>But</u>" in short he would not sign, Revd Mr. Thompson of Riplingham declined signing on account of as he said it being made a party concern. Now in my Opinion the Clergy ought to be of the Party who shew mercy ...

Sunday 21st. Nov

Conder had got a Hare given at Newbald the last week, and had it roasted to Dinner today we went to dine there, which is the first time since Eliza was married.

---

[44] The outbreak of agricultural unrest in the autumn and early winter of 1830, usually known as the Swing riots, occurred chiefly in the rural districts of East Anglia and the southern counties of England. It was for the most part an unco-ordinated response by agricultural labourers to their distressed condition resulting mainly from low wages, poor harvests, unemployment and the operation of the old poor law. The disturbances were characterized by arson attacks, riots, the destruction of threshing machines, and threatening letters. East Yorkshire was largely unaffected (See also n.49 (1830)) (Hobsbawm and Rudé *passim*).

[45] According to legislation enacted in 1555 and 1691, every parish became responsible for the state of its own roads, and all the able-bodied men in it were required to work on them for 6 days per annum. By 1830, many parishes had commuted this statutory labour obligation for a money payment, and the Highway Act of 1835 made the practice universal.

[46] George IV died on 26 June 1830 and in the ensuing election which followed the *ipso facto* dissolution of Parliament on the death of a sovereign, the Tories lost some ground. Wellington attempted to form a new government, but, largely as a result of his outspoken and complacent attitude to parliamentary reform, it lasted only a matter of weeks and after being defeated, for the second time, on 15 Nov., the Duke resigned and Lord Grey was invited to form an administration, thus inaugurating a long period of Whig supremacy after many years of Tory rule (*AR* 1830, Hist. 162–3).

Monday 22nd Nov

Heard this Evening that Mr. Brougham was made Lord Chancellor, Lord Grey Prime Minister, and ending with Mr. Bickersteth, had it been Bickerstaff, I could have recollected honest Isaac,[47] Lord Hill it appears is over the Host; Sir Js. Grahame, first Lord of the Admiralty; some say it is better to have a Landsman than a Sailor in this Situation, as the Seaman is acquainted with Rocks & Shoals, which never hinders the orders of a Land Shark.

Thursday 23rd. Nov

This is Martinmas Day, the Servants with us receive their wages and are their own Masters for one short week, — which is longer than their good Behaviour entitles them to.

Wednesday 24th. Nov

Went to West end this Evening to settle Mr. Leason's accts. for the Highways the last year he being one of the Surveyors, he said he was out of Pocket £26 but when his Accts. were examined it was found that he was at least £10 wrong in his expectations. I left him to correct his Accounts, which he said he would do in a day or two.

Thursday 25th. Nov

Rd. Marshall went to York on Monday to see Mr. Barnard and has not yet arrived back as his Master it is supposed has not yet got from London. Robt. Arton is seeing about taking the Ellerker Sands farm, where he and his Father formerly lived, but I have not yet heard whether he has succeeded.

Friday 26th. Nov

John Allison says none of the Marshalls are good managers of their Farms (they never employ John) Tom's farm he says is so run out, that a Man ought to have it two years without paying any rent, Whya a Feal Tom says that is the varry state I wanted to leave it in—and Bob begins to be nipped so that there is no living with him; and as for Dick the Steward he just does as he likes, putting what Stock he has a mind into the Park, but says John they are all nought.

Saturday 27th. Nov

Our old Friend Mr. Atkinson made a mistake last night, he went to bed about nine O'clock, and got a sleep, when waking he heard talking in the Street he got out of Bed and dressed himself thought he had slept too long, when he came down he asked what time of the morning it was, when he was answered Eleven O'clock at night!! he could not believe it at the first; but after some time, he went to bed again and slept until the real morning.

Sunday 28 Novr.

Rd. Marshall said Tom Coulson's wife (who lives on Robt. farm at the Common) was so fat that they would be obliged to get a Horse and Cart to bring her to the town, she says he is as fat as her, and will get an order for him and take him to Riplingham, that the Justices may decide which of them is fattest!!!

---

[47] 'Mr Bickersteth' probably refers to the prominent liberal Whig lawyer, Henry Bickersteth (1783—1851), later Lord Langdale. Isaac Bickerstaffe was a minor late 18th-century dramatist. Lord Hill was appointed Commander in Chief of the military (*DNB*).

Monday 29th. Nov

Mr. Atkinson & myself have each of us bought a handkerchief which the dealer told us was real Indian silk we gave 2s. a piece for them, and now we are told they are Cotton, worth nothing at all, but I remembered Moses (Vic. of Wakefield) with his gross of green Spectacles[48] when his mother would destroy them because the Rims turned out to be of an inferior metal to what Moses expected; but the old Vicar was wiser and said that Copper Rims were worth something. So I say Cotton handkerchiefs are not to be wasted, though I really believe they are silk, and those who depreciate them, are sorry we have them so cheap.

Tuesday 30th. Nov

We having got a Stock of Pipes, some of them were broken which were laid a side for my own particular use, "good as ever when fresh tipped" So I tipped them with Sealing wax, and I believe I used as much Wax as would have bought good pipes, but never mind, the Pipes were useful, — This is Domestic economy.

Wednesday 1st. Decr.

This is a dark gloomy morning, Decr. appears with a Shroud before his face, indeed he is a sort of personage that does not like much Daylight, very grave he appears now, and so solemn one would think, he was not akin to Merry Christmas.

Thursday 2nd. Decr.

A meeting was held last night at the Church (alias the Bay Horse) for the purpose of petitioning for the Repeal of the Assessed taxes, the Committee at York, having sent a Copy of their Petition, I am to write out fairly two petitions, one to the Lords and another to the Commons.

Friday 3rd. Decr.

Last night was the Club night; after the Hours of business were over Ths. Wride and Mattw. Leaman quarrelled, and called each other liars and Robbers it was no affair respecting the Club, but Ths. had had Mattw. employed to drill for him, and as he said paid 2s. a day instead of 2s/6d.

Saturday 4th. Dec

Went to Brantingham this morning by the way of Ellerker, I wanted 6 pounds of Mr. Levitt, I only recd. a Single Sovereign; and a few Pears was given me by Mrs. Levitt.

Sunday 5th. Decr

We have had no Swing Letters here yet, but it is said that at Walkington they have, threatening the Farmers, that if the Labourers have not their wages raised they must abide by the consequence.[49]

---

[48] An episode in Goldsmith's *Vicar of Wakefield* in which Moses, the son of the impoverished vicar, Dr Primrose, sells the family colt in order to buy fashionable clothes for his sisters, but instead spends the money on a 'bargain' of a gross of green spectacles.

[49] There was surprisingly little agricultural disturbance in the East Riding compared to what was happening in other parts of the country. Some threatening letters purporting to come from Captain Swing had been reported by the press in the neighbourhood of Beverley (which would include Walkington).

Monday 6th. Dec

At the last Parish meeting, I endeavoured to impress upon the Farmers that it would be most advantageous to the Labourers to let them have a small quantity of Land at the same Rent as they were giving themselves, I told them that it was my firm belief, that an industrious Man with half an Acre of Land, would never want any help from the parish; The long Miller swore and said good Labourers wanted no land and the bad ones curse them wad not be a bit better for it, so the matter ended.

Tuesday 7th. Dec

The Castle farm where Robt. Arton lives is let to a Man from Bubwith or the neighbourhood[;] Leaper has taken again the Sands farm, so that there is but the Mill farm unlet, but I do not expect the long Miller will leave it.

Wednesday 8th. Dec

Wm. says he shall give up Cobbett's Shillings worth[50] I think a single dose for 6d. was as much as could be properly dispensed with in a week, for all his writing and prating and prophesying is the same thing over again. So I think it is wisdom to discontinue the concern ...

Friday 10th. Decr

We have got a load of Flour &c today from Beverley 301 Stone, — about 3 Cwt of Rice, Sugar, Currants, Salt &c besides smaller Articles; paid £32–8–0 on Wednesday for the last load of Goods which we got 3 Wks since.

Dec 11 Saturday

There was a meeting on Thursday Night last at Cousens' it was canvassed, whether a person that was ill could not be got into the Hull Infirmary[51] as a patient. There were many observations made, not indeed very learned Ths. Marshall said "These Infirmities I understand is for Persons who are endowed with complaints, that require more skill than one Doctor is possessed with, where they try various experiences with them that are sent there.["]

Sunday 12th Decr

I always on a Sunday afternoon before Church time call at Js. Levitt's, if I miss calling viz if I be not at Church, he comes up on Sunday night to see what

---

The *Hull Advertiser* (3 Dec. 1830) announced that "measures were taken at the Post Office" and a young clerk was arrested. In the *Hull Packet* (21 Dec. 1830), it was reported that some Skidby schoolboys had been detected as the authors of some threatening letters. Both newspapers implied that any 'Swing letters' sent at this time were the work of 'mischievous and wanton individuals' rather than genuine threats sent by aggrieved labourers. There were some isolated cases of threshing machines set on fire, for example at Etton (*HA*, 3 Dec. 1830) but no reports of damage on any larger scale.

[50] The price of Cobbett's *Weekly Political Register* increased from 7d to 1s. with the issue for 30 Oct. 1830.

[51] The Hull General (later Royal) Infirmary, established in 1782, was located in Prospect Street. Persons wishing to be admitted to the hospital had to have the recommendation of a governor or subscriber. Categories of patients specifically excluded from admission included: persons 'able to support themselves and pay for their Medicines', persons recommended by subscribers in arrears with their subscriptions, women 'in a state of pregnancy', persons 'suspected to have the venereal disease, itch, or any infectious distemper, or any apprehended to be incurable'. Notwithstanding these restrictions, however, 'persons who [met] with accidents' were admitted at any hour of the day or night, without a recommendation (Greenwood: 113–6).

is the matter, but as I do not matter Company at all on a Sunday I seldom omit calling, that I may not have the <u>pleasure</u> of his Company at night.

Monday 13th Decr

The long Miller came to town one day last week before dinner, and went to Cousens's (they are Overseers) when Cousens asked him to have a drop of summat but he said he had not got his dinner, it was over soon to drink, but they brought him a Glass which he drank and as he does not like to be <u>scrubby</u>, he called for another; then went down to the West end, where he found his Waggon had been bringing Frans. Ruston some Potatoes, so he got in there, and a full bottle of Rum set before him, but he says he only drank two <u>varry</u> moderate Glasses, then he went to Js. Levitt's, and got two glasses more, which was <u>nobbut</u> six in all. Jem asked him when he went away if he could walk, walk, aye what was 6 Glasses to hinder him? when he got a little way into the street he <u>thought</u> he should be drunk, when he got out of the town he <u>fand</u> he <u>was</u> drunk, for he could not hit the road, at last he falls right into the Beck, and says to himself aye now here thou <u>ligs</u>, but he soon got up, and presently after falls in again, and loses his hat, but bad as his legs were they saved his hat, so then he says to himself here thou is again mind and keep thy head out of water, never mind it running over thy legs, thou knows thou cant get up yet so lig still, what thou always did rise, and thou knows Scripture says there is a time for all things, I'll warrant thee thou will get out here, but thou need not try yet for thou cant stand but thou will rise again innow, — and so he did the muckiest devil that ever was plastered over with mud with his wet hat running down his back but he got home and all gone to bed however they got up and pulled of his Cloaths got him to bed and very comfortable he was. All this he suffered because he had got nothing to eat; else half a Score glasses would have been nothing to him. The above he told at our house but begged I would not tell it at Old Willy's, so I have put him down here nearly verbatim.

Tuesday 14th Dec

There is an order come to the Constables to summon a number of the Inhabitants to appear at Riplingham on Monday next, for the purpose of being sworn in as Special Constables.[52] — This is a work which may be called as the Catholics do their good works when they have more than a sufficient quantity they call the remr. Supererogation, So swearing in Special Constables here is more than enough.

Wednesday 15th Dec

Old Willy has bought a little ham a good deal too dear. Mr. Bridgeman said if he would boil it, he would give him a Couple of Chickens, and I promised to find stuff for a Rice pudding, Matt. Pickering offered two or three Bottles of Porter, so that all this looks like something, but I believe it will come

[52] Similar *ad hoc* contingency measures were being taken in many parts of the country to deal with anticipated outbreaks of violence by agricultural labourers. Fifty special constables had already been sworn in at Beverley, and a meeting of the magistracy of the East Riding was held there on 13 Dec. 1830 'to consider measures for preserving the peace of the Riding from being interrupted by proceedings like those which have disgraced the southern countries' (*HA* 3 Dec. 1830; *HP* 21 Dec. 1830).

to nothing, as our friend wishes more to save his Bacon, than have a feast held at his house.

Thursday 16th Dec

We have it hand ganging that Prince Leopold's house with all the Outbuildings are burnt down,[53] Mr. Leeson of Ellerker says it is in Bell's Messenger[54] (I did not hear him tell it), but I have almost pledged my veracity that it is not so, for I think I should have had a Paper from Wm. if this had taken place, so here is my reason.

Friday 17th. Dec

Ned Coates says they have sworn in 150 Special Constables at Market Weighton, he happened to be there and was one amongst the rest. 50 it is said have been sworn in at Welton; Mr. Raikes has had some threatening letters, he has offered a reward of £50. for the discovering of the writer.

Saturday 18th. Decr

I have not been at Brantingham today, the Ladies having left off for the Holidays, I was employed part of the day making Paper bags, this was a very stormy cold day.

Sunday 19th Decr.

The Parson at the Church this afternoon had forgotten his Sermon, so after the Prayers were read over he said he was sorry that he had not brought with him the Lecture, which he intended to have delivered, he therefore was under the necessity of dismissing his audience without any more to say. Now when he publishes he may for the title of this Sermon have "a Lecture that might have been delivered in the Church of South Cave on Sunday the 19th. Decr. 1830".

Monday 20th. Decr

Yesterday Mr. Smelt's Clerk came to say that the persons who were summoned as Special Constables to attend this day at Riplingham, were to attend on Thursday next, but this morning there was a letter that they need not attend at all. The Magistrates will not swear in any special Constables except five respectable Inhabitants of any place first make Oath that there has been a disturbance, or that there is danger of it. So this is over; for here is no likelihood of disturbance with us I am sure ...

Wednesday 22nd Decr

I have I think almost as little to say as the Parson had on Sunday last when he forgot his Book. I fancy the Apostles did not travel about relying on Sermons in their Pockets; these idle Priests ought to be taught at least to speak grammatically for a Quarter of an hour at a time. Do the members of Parliament read their Speeches? No, a written Oration would have but little effect; — I will take the methodist preacher who travels from one place to

---

[53] Prince Leopold of Saxe-Coburg (1790–1865) was later, in 1831, elected as the first King of the Belgians but at this time was still resident in England. There is no evidence that his house was burnt down so that RS seems to have been correct in rejecting the news as a baseless rumour.

[54] Probably an abbreviation for *Bell's Weekly Messenger* published 1 May 1796 – 28 Mar. 1896 and continued as: *Country Sports and Messenger of Agriculture*, 4 Apr. 1896 – 31 Dec. 1904.

another, and he shall be better understood without his Sermons written down than a lazy Reader with his bad writing before him.

Thursday 23rd. Decr

Our old Friend Mr. Atkinson went with Robt. Dunn a tenant of his to M. Pickering's to treat him when he paid his Rent; he was full of cold and got some Rum and treacle, his tenant was so full that he was led home; — the Old Gentleman got home and fastened the Door, and by some means fell against the Corner of a Chair or table and cut his head, he would not open the Door but went up stairs and got into Bed, — M Pickering broke open the Doors accompanied by Mr. Bridgeman's housekeeper, and the old Man got a plaster put on his wound, and now he seems to be no worse; he would not tell me, but Mr. Bridgeman said I should know, so he told me.

Friday 24th. Decr

This is the day before Christmas day when both Scholars and Masters, rejoice at the thought of holidays, yet for my own part, I think I am generally most busy when not at School.

Saturday 25th Dec

Plenty of Boys & Girls running about this morning for Christmas Boxes; Some I quitted with telling them they were too soon, and others with being too late, and some few got a halfpenny apiece.

Sunday 26th. Dec

This is a tolerable fine day, for the Season of the year, I can say that I have not got either bite or Sup as a Christmas Box; it is a satisfaction to know that I am not in the least obligated to any one for what I have had, and but to few for their offers.

Monday 27th. Dec [1830] to 3d. Jan 1831

Here is a week together without much remarkable, on Wednesday we had another load of Flour from Beverley, and paid £35–odd. — on Thursday I was at Edward Usher's at Drewton measuring some Turnip land, it was a very thick misty day; this kind of weather accompanied with crooked fences are some of the miseries of Surveyors. On Friday measuring some Rape land at Ellerker for Charles Rudd, it was very dirty and pretty well I was daubed. On Saturday I think I did not do much except weighing tobacco—On Sunday at the Church twice as usual, and met with the same comfort, viz. none at all.

Tuesday 4th. Jany

I shall probably now that the Holidays are over get into my old method again, and write some occurrence or thought regularly every Day: I cannot bear being put of out of my regular Way.

Wednesday 5th. Jany

Plough Boys have been running about all this week the Set belonging this town, are to have a Supper this night at Newlove's—One of the Fools asked our old friend Mr. Atkinson for a halfpenny, but he said he had not one, could he (the fool) change him a Penny, O' yes, so he gave him hold of a halfpenny before he got the Penny; now says the old Gentleman I find you are a natural fool, but as I will not take advantage of your folly, come again at Cave fair and I will give you a Penny; so he kept him for some time longer, and then gave him a Penny, such catches as these are just calculated for the Meridian of our Friend's capacity.

Thursday 6th. Jan

The Hull Packet has not come this week it ought to have been here yesterday, I suppose it has been sent wrong. Beverley Sessions are this week, there is to be a Man transported for stealing a Box from a Cart in Tindale's Garth (here) at the Sittings it contained hardware &c.

Friday 7th Jan

Last night was the Club night, there was a sort of Revolution, they will not have any longer any Publicans as free Members, Merely for the purpose of having the Feast and meetings at their houses, but those Publicans who are members are to have the Box, yearly in rotation, beginning with the eldest member, which is Matty Pickering. The Hull Packet arrived this morning having been sent to Burlington.

Saturday 8th Jan

Measured a Close at Sweety Hill this forenoon 11a–1r–5p what this place is called Sweety Hill for, I cannot positively say, perhaps it may have been for its producing in a State of nature quantities of wild Thyme, growing amongst the Whins, — which was a great deal more picturesque than now when all or most are grubbed up, growing bad Turnips and worse Corn; — I do greatly admire to see ground with Whins all in beautiful flower, and linnetts hopping about, they delight in Cover of this sort to breed in, some are called Whin Linnetts.[1]

Sunday 9th Jan

The Vicar Mr. Creyke was here today, and a poor Creature he appears for a preacher, he was they say reading himself in,[2] I suppose he read over the 39 Articles, but I am certain I did not hear ten Words, — I hear he has got another living and was therefore to be again inducted here.

Monday 10th. Jany

A man who stole a Box out of a Cart in Tindale's Garth, here at the Sittings, was tried at Beverley Sessions last week for the theft, and found guilty and sentenced to 7 years' transportation. (I see I have noted this before)

Tuesday 11th. Jan

Mr. Creyke the Vicar left on Sunday last Five pounds to be laid out in Coals and given to the Poor, they have been distributed to day, and as usual in such cases there are more displeased, than satisfied with the distribution. So difficult it is even by a good action to give satisfaction.

Wednesday 12th Jan

We have at last bought a Pig, we were not at all anxious to buy this year, but we have fallen in for a large one of Barnard Cook weighing 20½ Stones at 5s–1d pr. Stone. So that we shall fall in for Black puddings and Sausages, Spare Rib & accompaniments.

Thursday 13th. Jan

I have had an Account with Mr. Atkinson late Church warden long unsettled, last night we got all comfortably settled, and the Book delivered over to Mr. Bridgman the new Churchwarden. We had a Quart of Ale sent for, which is somewhat extraordinary with us.

Friday 14th. Jan

A Letter from Ths. Milner in America they are at Kingston in Canada, the Account it said is very satisfactory, but highly Coloured, James by his business they say clears 4 or 5 Acres of Land in a week so that if he goes on in this way for a year (half year) he will have a snug farm of his own.

Saturday 15th. Jan

I think I have not been from home today at all, I have been weighing Tobacco & Leaf which I can manage very well.

Sunday 16th Jan

A Sermon at Church this day on the love of Country but where the love was said to consist I never knew. There was what Goldmsith would have called part Rigmarole, about supporting the Rulers &c, and paying every due.

---

[1] RS seems to have used the word 'linnet' to denote finches generally. The name, 'whin linnet', was used in the north of England and Scotland to describe the particular species, the Linnet (*Carduelis cannabina*). In Yorkshire this bird was also known locally as 'song linnet', 'thorn linnet', and 'bent linnet' (Jackson, C. E. 53–4).

[2] 'to enter upon office as an incumbent of a benefice of the Church of England by reading publicly the 39 Articles and making the Declaration of Assent' (*OED*).

Monday 17th Jan

Now I close this shut as tonight we shall pack up a Box for the great City, of some small share of the good things of this world; — I believe there are many who care little for the Country because they cannot have a belly full.

Tuesday 18th. Jany.

Last night we packed up a Basket for London, and sent it by Cousens, to go with the Barton Coach, we hope it will be soon there and in good condition. — I now resume my daily scribbling; — Sometimes I meet with a Sheet of Paper very small at other times a larger one, and sometimes I have scarce one at all, — but here I am fortunate in a tolerable large one; whether it be Demy, or any other name belongs to it I know not; neither is it of any consequence, so long as it is sufficient for my purpose—the name of Foolscap would perhaps be as good as any other.

[Note: The paper used in this section is about 1¾" longer than what is used generally elsewhere in the diary, with the consequence that the bottom of each sheet is folded over making it difficult to read the writing in places].

Wednesday 19th. Jan.

Writing Notices this day for the Surveyors of the Highways to Robt. Arton & Mr. Shackleton to cut their hedges adjoining the Beverley Road, within 14 days from this time.

Thursday 20th. Jan

There have been letters from America by some persons who went from Elloughton, I understand they speak highly of the plenty they find there; Robt. Nicholson had bought 2 Geese for 3d. Matt. Pickering says there are Geese & Ducks by Thousands & Millions—Pig heads feet & hearts they sell by the Bushel measure, when they have not a Bushel they throw them away; he talks of a River 200 Miles long (no great length in America) and 40 Miles broad, I cannot find where it is; he must mean one of the Lakes.

Friday 21st. Jan

Richd. Kirby died on Tuesday last, and was buried yesterday, I made his Will, and was there and read it over after the Funeral, his Children all but one were satisfied with it, that is Robt. who has been rather flighty; he is left the same as his Sisters; and the other two Sons have the houses and Land; except a small Close of an Acre which is left to his daughter Hannah, who has been his Housekeeper.

Saturday 22nd. Jan

A very stormy day, I intended to have gone to the west end but it rained so fast and blew so strong that, I got no further this day than Mr. Atkinson's, and my Shoes were as dirty as though I had walked 10 Miles.

Sunday 23d. Jan

Heard this morning that Wm. had got the Basket safe, we are very sorry to hear that poor little Mary has been so ill, we all hope she will soon be better.

Monday 24th. Jan

I have seen a letter from a Man that went from Elloughton to America he is at a place called Detroit, it is a sort of rambling letter, giving an account of a great number of Fish being caught, and numbers of <u>wild</u> Ducks ...

Tuesday 25th. Jan

After all that has been said about the Castle farm being let it appears that some of the Marshalls will have it, as they have begun ploughing it: Robt. Arton had taken the Provence farm, but Shackleton does not seem inclined to give it up; so that there will be some disagreement here.

Wednesday 26th. Jan

Recd. with the Paper this morning a Pencil Scrawl from little Mary informing us that she had been ill, but had got better again, (this we were glad to find) and that she is shortly going out with her Mother on a very important mission viz to choose a Cap for her Grandmother, who says the little Creature how considerate she is.

Thursday 27th Jan

Tindale of the Three Tuns, has left his house to Fenwick the Carrier who lives at the West end; Tindale is for America. Fenwick is to enter on the House on Saturday week ...

Saturday 29th Jan

Very cold frosty weather, it has from the beginning of the winter to this time, been very disagreeable; — great meetings for reform seem to be taking place in different parts of the Country.

Sunday 30th Jan

A very rainy ragged morning, and exceeding cold, my hands in going to the Church were never so cold this winter. Wm. Woolas was buried this afternoon he was 83 years of age.

Monday 31st Jan

I saw nothing done at the Market today. Abm. Barff was in Morley's Market Room drunk and quite talkative, he knew more than anyone, but it was generally thought by the Company that he was the most simple noddy there.

Tuesday 1st. Feb

This Month has come in with such a Storm of Snow and Wind as we have not had ~~before~~ this year before, (I think this is the most correct, perhaps the other would have been understood) the Snow drifts terribly, our Passages, Cross & Shop almost drifted up that there is scarcely a passage in and out, I think the wind is Southerly, and sometimes when a Storm comes from this Quarter it is very severe as is the case at present.

Wednesday 2nd. Feb

This Evening taking an Inventory of the Goods of the late Richard Kirby, It is expected that he died worth in Money (exclusive of his real Property) £1100, there will be I think £200 each to his Children.

Thursday 3rd. Feb

Club night, the last nights arrangement entirely altered and the Box as usual is to go to the houses of those Publicans who are free members, after the next month it will go to David Morley's.

Friday [4th Feb]

Great news and glorious!! Prince George walked out with his Tutor, Prince George had three of the Lord somebodys to dine with him [illegible word] Prince George was shooting in the Garden. O what news is here.

Saturday 5th. Feb

While others talk of reform, cannot a Smoker put in a word for the repeal of the Duty on Tobacco; I have heard it advanced that it pays £1100 pr. Cent, but if it pay £600 pr. Cent there is no doubt but the poor man whose only luxury is a pipe, has to pay a great deal more in proportion, than a Winebibber who indulges in the Choicest wines, — then the Old Women and young ones too are taxed 100 pr. Cent for their beverage of tea—besides 40 or 50 pr. cent for their Sugar, — then the poor Laundresses who endeavour to keep the Shirts of their Customers clean have to pay a duty of about 2d. pr. Ct in every pound of Soap they use; and the poor Mechanic must pay a duty of a penny a pound on his Candles, do the Rich pay any duty for their Gas lights? Will no one in power attend to the hardships of the lower orders?[3]

Sunday 6th Feb

Mr. Day the Doctor is now at Cave at James Levitt's the Bay horse, I have not seen him, he is going to practise as a Physician somewhere North of us, I have heard at Richmond. The weather of all sorts but good, Rain, frost, Snow &c all together.

Monday 7th. Feb

I saw Bell's Life in London today, but I think there is nothing particular in it, it seems the Minister will bring forward some plan for Reform, which is conjectured will vex the thorough paced Tories, for granting too much, and the Radicals will be displeased for it doing so little, so that perhaps moderate persons may in a degree be satisfied.

Tuesday 8th. Feb

It appears we are favoured with two Prince Georges viz. of Cumberland and he of Cambridge;[4] which of them par excellence is Prince George? both

---

[3] The duty on unmanufactured tobacco at this time was 3s. in the pound. Althorp in his budget of 1831 had proposed to reduce duty on tobacco by half but was forced to withdraw this and other measures in the face of the strong opposition to his proposals. Tea was taxed at 96% per pound when costing 2s or less but at 100% when above 2s. The duty on foreign sugar at £3 3s. was higher than the duty on colonial sugar at £1 4s. per hundredweight. Duty on hard soap remained at 3d per pound and on soft soap at 2d until 1833 when it was reduced on each by half (Dowell iv. 25, 225, 258–9, and 321).

[4] Prince George of Cambridge and Prince George of Cumberland were grandsons of King George III. Prince George of Cambridge (1819–1904) was the only son of Adolphus Frederick, the seventh son of George III. Born in Hanover, he settled in England and had a long and distinguished military career, commanding a division in the Crimean War and serving as Queen Victoria's chief personal ADC. Prince George of Cumberland (1819–78) was the only son of Ernest Augustus, the fifth son of George III, who later (1837) became King Ernest I of Hanover. Although totally blind by the age of 14, George

these Princes lately visited the Duke of Devonshire at Kemp-town. I observe the progress of this George or these Georges, for I know not one from the other, — One of them shoots (at Sparrows) in a Garden, this must be a gallant Prince.

Wednesday 9th. Feb

At west end this Evening taking an Inventory of the Goods in the Workhouse. — Paid Mr. Oxtoby today £48–0–0 for Flour and other goods received on the 22nd. Jany last—fell in with Mr. Day at the Bay horse, he has been travelling in France, Guernsey and Jersey &c.

Thursday 10th. Feb.

Mr. Day said last night (when Ths. Marshall, W Cousens and I were at Js. Levitt's) to Ths. well I see you just the same the old Philosopher of So. Cave, do you get drunk as you used to do? No Sir I can't bide it; I said there was a greater hindrance though that he could not afford it (by his own talk), he lives very hardly now no longer since than Monday night he laid down on the Cross Steps, — I know nought about Cross Steps says the Philr. but this I know they are awkward on a dark night; — aye when you get more than you can carry you lay down there. — O'dear O'dear says the doctor.

Friday 11th. Feb

A very fine Spring looking day. — I was at Jem. Levitt's one night, when the Company were talking of a Man whom I do not know, called Peter, a sort of itinerant tradesman, who writes down every day what occurs, viz he keeps a Journal, which was laughed at by most of them; I said it was a kind of relaxation, — I did not tell them that I was a Journalist, but I thought this would serve me to notice, I dare say not one of those who censured the Poor man, would find themselves qualified to notice daily what comes under their observation—I still persevere and find something daily, which helps to fill up my paper.

Saturday 12th. Feb

What news now? My Prince Georges [have] been fighting with the Son of a Dancing master!! a terrible degrading account this, only think of their Royal hands, chastising the Son of a Dancing master!! — but indeed who can they fight with but such Company as they keep? this dancing master's Son may account himself fortunate in having received a Royal drubbing. Well done Prince Georges, — at the dancing master himself next, and drub him that he come into your presence no more; for he will never be of any benefit to you, you appear to be complete dancers, so cannot want a Master.

Sunday 13th. Feb

The Organ at Church this forenoon, made some such music as Val. Tindale's Sheep Rack, when trailed on the Street and the Rusty Wheels and axles, crying out for Grease. — something like a Concert of Pigs, with a Bull bellowing for the Bass: the Poor Parson was sadly mortified and rose up and said "Let us pray" so there was an end of the noise for this time.

---

succeeded his father to the throne, becoming King George V of Hanover. Largely as a result of his unwise foreign policy, Hanover was invaded and annexed by Prussia in 1866 (*DNB* and *EB* xi. 746).

Monday 14th. Feb.

I have a knee rather painful at times, by a fall I had at Christmas last, when measuring at Drewton, — then I have had a Plaster on my heel which has fairly worn off and left that place without pain, then I have a great toe nail which I believe will come off in a short time, it has a little pain in it. I have had my great toe nail come off before; now all these grievances have been on one foot and leg.

Tuesday 15th. Feb

Made a Bond today for David Morley for security of the Club Box, John Gardham is bound with him in the Sum of One hundred pounds.

Wednesday 16th. Feb

I have been employed part of this day in arranging names for the Militia list. — I generally fall in for a long Job when there is nothing gotten by it, but so it is & has been ...

Friday 18th. Feb

So the Chancellor of the Exchequer has agreed to abandon the tax on the transfer of Stock, and to continue the duty on Tobacco and Glass as usual.[5] I hope the Repeal of the Duty on Coals will be found beneficial, as to the tax on Timber I know nothing what will be the result; I was most concerned for the Repeal of the Duty on Candles, as we have 20 or 30 Dozen lbs. but as it will be the 10th. of October before it takes place, we shall have a chance of quitting some of them, although the Candle light time is fast passing away.

Saturday 19th. Feb.

Now what am I to write today? Oh I have been making out the Militia list, there are nearly 90 liable to the ballot here, a hard case it is on the Poor Men who are called on for their Services to defend &c. &c.

Sunday 20th. Feb.

The Militia list was on the Church Door today, and plenty of Criticks and informers were examining it, some of them found out that there were two men whose names did not appear, and as they wished to do their neighbours a kindness, they gave in their names without any scruple, as it happened I had one of the names in my Pocket which I had just received after the list was made out, this was very satisfactory to the fault finders.

Monday 21st. Feb

Merchant Moody talks of going to America with all his Family he was telling Tom Levitt, he should go to Queensbeck and from thence to Meretrop hall (Montreal) and then to Lake Tally O (Ontario), and where then I know not nor him neither. I think Tom helped it a little, — but Matty says bless you there are thousands of Acres of fine Grass which any man may mow, — what will he

---

[5] Lord Althorp's ambitious budget had sought to pay for the repeal of a number of unpopular taxes on various commodities such as sea-borne coals, candles, calicoes, and glass and for the halving of the taxes on tobacco and newspapers chiefly by the imposition of a tax of 10s. per cent. on the transfer of all real or funded property. His proposals raised such a storm of opposition both in the House, from Goulburn, Peel, and Sugden, and also in the City that he was forced to suffer the humiliation of withdrawing them (Walpole iii. 202–5).

do with grass? perhaps he will be at a loss to tell. — Prince George has been coursing, what a fine Prince this is!!

Tuesday 22nd. Feb

A meeting this Evening at Jem Levitt's to choose Assessors of the taxes for the ensuing year, Robt. Marshall would not stand any longer, so it was left to me to choose a partner. I thought I would have none of the Marshall's so I chose Robinson of Mount Airy. Adieu to Friendship I wish I had my money.

Wednesday 23rd. Feb

Several Surcharges at present under way, Cousens for an extra Gig, Billy Langricke for Horse dealing, Henry Arton for 2 Dogs—and two of Laverack Sons a Game Certificate each, as they have been it [is] said out shooting.

Thursday 24th. Feb

A Fire last night at Val. Tindale's, the Bed got carelessly set on fire by an old foolish Nurse, who is attending Mrs. Scholefield she has been a long time ill, and is there for convenience of Medical attendance. The Bed and several kinds of wearing were burned, it was about Eleven O'clock at night, we had been a Bed a short time, I got up but it was then nearly over. The Windows in the Chamber were all broken, so that the old Cardinal fell in for a job.

Friday 25th. Feb

The Constable has gone with the Militia list to Sculcoates today, it being the appeal day there instead of being at Beverley, there are 85 not exempt and 51 exempt from various causes, so that there are 136 men between 18 and 45 years of age.

Saturday 26th. Feb

Measuring a Close of Turnip land this afternoon for Mr. Popple of Ellerker; it was very wet and stormy in the forenoon, but cleared up in the afternoon I found when in this Close, I had measured it before, by remembering a Spring in it.

Sunday 27th. Feb

There were 13 Men went to appeal when the Militia list went in, 12 of whom were exempted, some lame in their legs and some in their heads, but they can put up with slight aberrations so long as they are clear.

Monday 28th. Feb

Merchant Moody has advertised his house for Sale previous to going to America, but if his Emigration depends upon his selling it, at what he asks, he will not go yet.

Tuesday 1st. Mar

Robt. Nicholson, and Cooper Tindale have been at Hull today to engage their places in a Vessel for Quebec the Name of the Ship they are going in is the Westmoreland,[6] the same which was mentioned in a published letter in the Newspapers, by a Man who went from Bempton near Burlington.

---

[6] The 'Westmoreland' was advertised as 'the well-known fast sailing ship', which carried a surgeon and offered to 'take Cabin and Steerage Passengers on moderate Terms, for which she has excellent Accommodations ...' She was registered at 400 tons and her captain was Thomas Knill (*HP*, e.g 22 Feb. 1831)

Wednesday 2nd. Mar

Paid Mr. Oxtoby this day £44–2–7 for Goods recd. the 11th. Feby last. Ordered another load which we are to have in a few days—we are all anxious at our meeting house to hear the Report of the Ministers plan of reform, — but I believe our old friend the Freeman, had rather hear tell of Parliament being dissolved than any plan of reform carried into execution.

3rd March Thursday

Sir James Graham has made some curious disclosures respecting the Public money, being applied to different purposes for which it was appropriated. I think the accounts must be kept in a most lamentable manner or else it would have been seen, by them how the money had been applied; but are the readers of such accounts, any quicker than the writers? No the same dulness reigns throughout, and they are satisfied that "Whatever is, is right".

Friday 4th. March

Last night at the Club, Robt. Nicholson sold all his right and title for five pounds. Robt. Smart the Mole Catcher for £2–19–3 and Cooper Tindale for £1–6–0 they are all for America (if it so happen) I believe more of the members would be glad to take money and be excluded. This is no great sign of the popularity of benefit Societies.

Saturday 5th. Mar

Measured a Close of Turnip Land for Mr Robinson (Airey) at the Bottom of the Steep hill Road, — Richd. Kirby's Sale was this day I went down in the afternoon but did not stay long as it rained, and they were selling in the Garth, I think several Articles were bought in.

Sunday 6th. March

Matthew Moody who has been talking of going to America was at Hull last week viewing the Vessels laid on, and as Tailors may be judges of Ships, Matty gave his Opinion that the <u>Roarer</u> (Aurora)[7] was the finest vessel going she was he said better than the Tighten (Triton) and some other names not easily distinguishable, Matty makes strange havock amongst proper names.

Monday 7th. Mar

Matty Moody put up his house for Sale this day by Auction but there were no buyers so that he cannot quit his House I think his talk of America is only "Fudge".

Tuesday 8th. Mar

There was to be a Sale of Land this day at Morley's it is situate near Ellerker Mill and formerly belonged to it, there was not a single bidder, consequently no Sale; it belongs to a Man called Clark who went to America the last year. Land does not appear to be so much valued as it was some years ago.

---

[7] RS may have been wrong in his interpretation of Matty's 'Roarer'. The name, 'Aurora', does not feature in the regular advertisements of ships' sailings, which appeared in the weekly *Hull Packet*. There are however advertisements for a ship, bound for Quebec on 2 Apr. 1831, named 'Almorah'. She was commanded by Richard Ward and registered at 423 tons. The 'Triton', also sailing for Quebec, was commanded by Captain Robert Keighley, jun.

Wednesday 9th Mar

Wm. hopes we have received a Basket from him, but there has none yet come to hand, Cousens had not heard of one so where it is or what way it has been sent we cannot tell, we certainly wish it safe here, with little Mary's present whatever it may be—it will be very acceptable.

Thursday 10th March

The Reform meets with Opposition from several of the Speakers who wish things to remain as they are, but I think they will be thrown into the back Ground—It seems to make little impression here, indeed here are very few who know any thing of the Matter—Mr. Shackleton who is perhaps as well informed or rather better than many amongst us, is delighted with the proposals of Lord John Russel.[8] — Hedon appears to be the only Borough in our neighbourhood which is to be disenfranchised, and by Accounts which I have heard it merits its doom.

Friday 11th Mar

I think I noticed before that Wilkn. Ayre had sold all his land and Houses at S. Cave and Ellerker, a person at Hull of the name of Hudson has bought it; and it is now to let[.] Mr. Levitt of Ellerker has been about taking it, but whether the bargain be closed or not I cannot ascertain. I am not sorry that Wilk. has done here.

Saturday 12th. Mar

The Basket and Hamper arrived last night from Wm., my wife opened the Basket and said ["]here is nothing in it but old papers; O'Yes here is a nice little Box", it was brought out and the Cap displayed, O' what a Beauty, what a nice Ribbon it is; the little Creature, give me her letter, it is mine, Bless her, I'll send her some more Raisins, and some fine Bacon too when it is ready.

Sunday 13th. Mar

The Crows my old Acquaintance whom I have not noticed for some time are now busy building and Repairing, they seem to be making a reform, for they are Rooting out all their Old Rotten boroughs, which age has in a manner Rendered useless. — I saw a tree today full of Palms.

Monday 14th. Mar

At Riplingham this forenoon swearing to the delivery of two Game Certificates. Mr. Egginton had got an Anonymous letter which he let me look at to see if I knew the writing, but I assured him I was ignorant of the hand, I saw it was badly spelled, writing was begun with an R. I did not read it over.

---

[8] Lord John Russell on behalf of the newly elected Whig government of Earl Grey introduced the Reform Bill to the House of Commons on 1 Mar. 1831. Its proposals included the abolition of 60 'rotten boroughs' with a population of less than 2,000, a reduction in the number of MPs returned by small boroughs of less than 4,000 from two to one, and 55 more seats being allocated to the counties, 8 to London and its suburbs, and 34 to provincial boroughs. In addition it provided for a uniform franchise in boroughs of £10 per annum and in counties, the franchise was extended to £10 copyholders and £50 leaseholders (Walpole iii. 205–10).

Tuesday 15th. Mar

Robt. Nicholson's Sale was yesterday previous to him and his Family going to America, I did not attend, but I understand there were several Articles not sold they talk of going at the beginning of April.

Wednesday 16th. Mar

As I like to understand as well as I am able, the several public topics brought forward, I endeavour to inform myself in the best manner my means will afford. I am rather lost with respect to America as I have not a good Map, nor a Gazetteer of that part of the World.

Thursday 17th. Mar

I was told by a person who had a relation that was going to the Illinois, that he would have to travel 2950 Miles for New York. I was amazed at this Ignorance, and as what I do know is generally correct, I said there was but about 18 degrees of Longitude in the Latitude of 42° where the length or extent of a degree is under 50 Miles that it could not be more than 900 Miles, so that 2000 Miles could well be spared in this case!!

Friday 18th. Mar

My wife was at Hull yesterday, and I was the Shopkeeper and managed pretty well, I daubed pretty well amongst the treacle then powdered myself with Flour, and where these two came in contact, I was tolerably pasted. I found every thing that was asked for, excepting a tape needle which was wanted, I could not find the place where Needles was kept. I say was not were, as place is the Nominative case.

Saturday 19th. Mar

The Judge comes into York this day. Teavil Leeson is summoned on the Jury to attend the 28th inst. — I have been gardening today setting Potatoes and Cabbage plants, and Potato Onions[9] I have likewise sown some Poppy Seeds. I expected I had some Marigold Seeds but could not find them, as I have taken such good care of them that they are out of my reach.

Sunday 20th. Mar

This has been a very fine moderate day. George Hodgson of Ellerker died yesterday, he is only a young man, the last year he set off to go to America, but fell ill at Hull and came back, he has not been well since; but only about three weeks he has been laid up his complaint was the Gravel.

Monday 21st. Mar

I did not see a single Sample of wheat shown this day at the Market; there were some Beans, but the buyers did not seem keen of purchasing, 68s. this is wrong I forget the price pr. Quarter was asked but it appeared too much as they were soft.

---

[9] A variety of onion (*Allium cepa* var. *aggregatum*), also known as the underground onion, which produces, beneath the surface of the soil, numerous small lateral bulbs from the parent bulb (*EB* xx. 112).

Tuesday 22nd. Mar

Spent part of this day in entering an Assessment for the Highways, as there is to be a meeting tomorrow night, I always like to be beforehand with my work, I do not like to put off till tomorrow what I can do today. — This is the Motto of some. Do nothing today that you can put off till tomorrow. [The last sentence is written in larger letters for emphasis].

Wednesday 23rd. Mar

Heard from Wm. this morning that he had got a Son, may heaven bless the Child, and the Parents and all the Family, we wish we had little Mary with us, but this distance keeps us separate, yet we are equally interested in their welfare.

Thursday 24th. Mar

I was a day in Arrear with my Journal yesterday, therefore the first thing this morning was to note the Birth of a Son to Wm. it is antedated a day; however it may stand—We had a meeting last night, when Thos. Marshall said the Churchwardens were just like Par-lee-ment men, for the devil a bit wad they try to save ought, he offered to take their Accounts this year by contract and would engage to save half the expences, but he did not succeed in his proposal.

Friday 25th. Mar

Recd. the Paper this morning containing an Account of the Division in the House of Commons on the second reading of the Reform Bill the numbers were very near being 302 for it and 301 against it; how zealous the Gentry are who think and say that all is right, but will this be right with them?

Saturday 26th. Mar

A very stormy day, I went to the west end this afternoon but it rained so fast, I borrowed an Umbrella and came back again, when just as I arrived the Sun broke out and remained fine. I was then told that I ought not to have gone in the wet, but staid for a fine night, this was by way of comfort, but I found no relief from it.

Sunday 27th.

I got the Rockingham this morning to take with me to the west end, but it was a baulk, only the first and last pages were printed the two middle pages being blank. I suppose it had been a mistake, I sent it back to Hull, so they will see it as it is—I never saw anything of the kind before.

Monday 28th Mar

A dull market today for Corn, a few weeks since there was no wheat to sell, and now they cry out they are taken in with keeping it in expectation of better prices, may all who withhold the necessaries of life be thus rewarded.

Tuesday 29th. Mar

Went to Everthorpe this Evening for some Sessts. due by Jno. Akam, but no better he was at Hull, he and his Family are going to America, and I believe most of those who are going have a smack of Roguery in them, some of them say boldly get your Money as you can I am now your master!!

Wednesday 30th. Mar

At Beverley this day with Robinson of Mount Airy in a Gig getting sworn in assessors we got very well there I walked back as far as Walkington leaving him drinking at Beverley. I waited at the Public house till he came, he was drunk as possible, got into the Gig with him, he drove his Poor mare which is heavy with foal, in the Jehu Stile,[10] and at Weedley gate threw over, we were no worse, but he swore he had never been out of the Gig since he got in; he drove full Gallop down the Plump hill, and coming down Porter hole crossed the Road in all directions, which quite terrified me. I prepared to get out, and the first opportunity jumped down having fixed both my feet on the Steps, I got out pretty well but rather hurt my Ancle Bone of which I dare not complain. Bad news travels fast, when I got to the door Tom Leason was telling my wife I was almost killed, but I soon put this tale aside. Before I go in a Gig again with this driver I had rather walk all the way barefoot.

Thursday 31st. Mar

My Ancle is very painful and swelled, about the outside joint it is on my unfortunate Leg, I was lame rather with a Bad great toe nail, I hope it will soon be better.

Friday 1st. Apl

This is good Friday, and the day noted as all fools' day, but for what Reason I know not, I suppose this appellation is not peculiar to the Country of John Bull.

Saturday 2nd. Apl

Several people have gone to Hull to see the Rogues go on their Voyage of transportation, not one scarcely but left something to pay either to one or another, I know not how they think of being prosperous. A very rainy day.

Sunday 3rd. Apl

This is the day when Children are glad to put on their new Cloaths if they have any, as to those who have none all times and seasons are the same to them.

Monday 4th. Apl

This is generally a busy day here, many idlers come to see the Horses showed. I wish some of them would stay at home and mend their Stockings and make themselves useful in a domestic way.

Tuesday 5th. Apl.

After Service at the Church this day the Churchwardens are chosen, the old ones stand again Mr. Bridgman & Loncaster, the Easter dinner was at Newlove's I was not there, I have not attended for some years, and think I shall go no more, there were only nine at the feast.

Wednesday 6th. Apl

Making up the Poor Accounts today to pass the examination of the wise ones, the meeting was at Cousens' Thos, Wride & Robinson of Mt. Airy are the first two on the list but Robn. does not want to stand, I shall write to Mr. Smelt not to put him on, whether he will or not remains to be seen.

---

[10] 'The driving is like the driving of Jehu the son of Nimshi: for he driveth furiously'—2 Kings ix. 20.

Thursday 7th. Apl

John Cousens has taken Hewson's Shop, they are now busy decorating it; if he do no better for himself than he has done, he will not do very well, I expect he could not get a place, so here is, to sell us down, well let him try, he will have a bitterish Pill.

Friday 8th. Apl

John Akam who is gone to America owes some Money about £25 to Thos. Fisher, and some more to a Man of the name of Bullock, he has paid neither of them, but I think he will pay or cause them to be paid, he told me last Saturday nobody should lose a penny at him, he paid up all his Sessments very honourably.

Saturday 9th. Apl

Measured part of a Turnip Close for Mr. King adjoining the Brough Road, it was ploughed which made it not very comfortable to my Ancle, which still remains swelled, but without pain, I have got some Verjuice[11] to rub it with.

Sunday 10th. Apl.

Thos. Wride and Ths. Robinson are the Overseers of the Poor. Recd. Papers last night for taking the Population which is to commence on the 30th. May next, miserable Specimens of Skill they are; I will be bound I could make such forms as any Overseer who can read would be able to understand, but as for these they are out of the question for being understood!!

Monday 11th. Apl

A great shew of Horses today, which brings together all the neighbouring rabble, Men, Women, and Children. I am no ways fond of the exhibition, and hope it is over for this Season.

Tuesday 12th. Apl

There have been 4 meetings cried for Subscriptions to the Militia[12] at 4 different public houses, but it was contrived to set them all aside and a meeting was called at the School Room this Evening at half past 7. There were 31 subscribed 8s. each, and to have out of the Subscription to those who may be ballotted £5 each if the Subscription amount to that Sum; if it does not the whole money to be equally divided amongst those who may be ballotted.

Wednesday 13th Apl

I have seen nothing lately of either of the Princes George, where are they? or what are they doing? certainly they are not forgotten. Newlove and Robt. Marshall who had the Church Land have given it up and James Harper has taken it.

Thursday 14th. Apl

A meeting this night at Jem. Levitt's to let the Lanes, they were let by Auction, Constable (formerly the partner of Boyes) the Auctioneer, there is only

---

[11] 'the acid juice of green or unripe grapes, crab-apples or other sour fruit, expressed and formed into a liquor; formerly much used in cooking ... or for medicinal purposes' (*OED*).

[12] 1831 was the only year in the period covered by the diary, when a muster of the East Riding's militia regiment was held. See also n.93 (1826).

3s. difference in the Rent between this year and the last. — The Subscription for the Militia closed this Evening with 59 Subscribers out of 74.

Friday 15th. Apl

I have seen an account this day in the Paper that Divine Service was performed before Prince George, it does not say whether it was a private or public exhibition. How I detest this word performed when used for Divine Service. — performing in the presence of Almighty God? No, No, before my Prince George and a Duchess.

Saturday 16th. Apl

What will the reform come to, I think the ministers are rather wavering, they give away too much to the corruptionists. I think they the ministers have not sufficient resolution; they have frittered away every thing they have proposed—these stinging nettles must be grasped tightly, that they may not be felt.

Sunday 17th. Apl

Alice Padgett was buried this afternoon, she came from London (as it is said) about three weeks ago very ill, in a Consumption, she was here two or three years ago and said she was married, she had a Child with her, which she has left behind, it appears she was not married.

Monday 18th. Apl

Heard from Wm. this morning, that the second Wm. is very clever for his age, I doubt little Mary will be put out of her place; We could wish to have her a while.

Tuesday 19th. Apl

I have been making out the Land tax Bills for the year commencing Lady day 1831. — Our old Friend Willy knew a German when in London who like other foreigners found it difficult to pronounce th, he was asked his age, he said he was dirty and his wife was dirty two, this is one of our old friend's standards which he occasionally draws from the treasures of his memory.

Wednesday 20th. Apl

This is like yesterday a very cold day, it is washing day with us, we have Hannah therefore do not lack want of noise. She never has a topic to seek for discourse, — My Ancle does not yet get well it continues rather swelled, I rub it at nights with Verjuice and Saltpetre.

Thursday 21st. Apl

Thomas Pashley of Ellerker has been sent to York Castle for Debt, his Brother has arrested him for about £50. He Pashley has made all over to his Landlord, who is going to sell his Farm Stock on Saturday next for Rent, only one half year of which was due at Lady day last, it is said that Tom Robinson has taken the Farm, so that the poor old Man will be broken up ...

Saturday 23d Apl

Pashley's Sale was this day the Goods were sold until sufficient was raised to satisfy the Landlord, the old Man was expected back this night but not to his home, for he has no home to come to. Tom Robinson is going to live in the

House and has taken the Farm, and this is he who was such a friend to Pashley!!

Sunday 24th. Apl

Recd. the Sun (Paper)[13] this morning with very near an Acct. of the Dissolution of Parliament, the old General has out generalled the Ministers, but it is hoped it is only to make way for more liberal minded men than the Ratters and Tories, — Soon the Country will be tried, so shew not your diminished heads, you who are so fond of ——

Monday 25th. Apl

Our old friend is delighted with the thoughts of another Election, he as one of the non residents had received notice to quit, but as he can hold on a little longer, he is anxious to shew his friends he is yet alive, I think that he and many more in his situation will not consent to die quietly; — there must be means used for stifling their voices, then their calling is gone.

Tuesday 26th. Apl

There was a Sale by Auction last night of Land at Broomfleet belonging to Geo. Lester, it was at Matty Pickering's there were 2 lots both bought in again, as the price was not sufficient for the Seller. Poor George he is about done Idleness, Sloth, and drinking, let his house come down, he has his land mortgaged, and if he sell it or keep it; he will be beaten to live, I think there is no prospect but the Parish before him.

Wednesday 27th. Apl

There were two persons from Beverley canvassing the Freemen on behalf of Mr. Marshall who I suppose is Son of the late member for the County, our old Friend is in the height of his Glory, it almost appears a pity to attempt to abridge his pleasure for the short time he will to all human probability enjoy it[,] he is 82 years of age.

Thursday 28th. Apl

I think the Hereditary Legislators, have been very near fisty-cuffing each other; they some of them are so arbitrary that they will scarcely allow the King to exercise his undoubted prerogative of sending the Commons to get new Instructions, I think his Majesty has acted very properly; — as to a new Parliament, I suppose interest will make a return of many who without the Gold would not readily enter the Chapel of the Saint-Stephen.

Friday 29th. Apl

Mr. Burton has it is said signified to the Electors of Beverley that he will not be at any expence to secure himself a Seat; but if they have a mind to put him in nomination and support him he will have no objection of serving them (himself he means) Some of the wise men (Fools) of Beverley set off to fetch him on Wednesday morning from London; thus Beverley has to beg for a member—Confusion attend the Shallow Brains.

---

[13] Daily London evening newspaper published 1 Oct. 1792 – 15 Apr. 1876. Proprietors: Patrick Grant, Apr. 1826–31; Murdo Young, 1832–50.

Saturday 30th. Apl

It appears from what was said at a meeting in the Borough that Col. Jones is the writer of the letters in the Times signed Radical,[14] they are written in a fearless Stile, and from their appearance, the information they contain, appears to be for the most part true.

Sunday 1st May

Sweet Mayday, it is very pleasant not indeed much sunshine, heard this morning from Wm. that they were all well, Wm. 2nd—very lively. — Prince George I see has been dancing with a Countess with a terrible name Bjornstj— there are some more Consonants in it which I cannot now make out.[15] What a delightful prince this is that can dance

2d. May Monday

I had Mr. Atkinson an Inspector of Stamps from Sculcoates here on Saturday last. I was charged with a Consignment that I had not recd. to the amount of £29–10–8 I wrote to the Office at Hull and had an answer today that by mistake it was entered to me when it belonged to Howden; so there is an end of this, only I have to write to Mr. Atkinson to inform him of the result.

Tuesday 3d. May

A Schoolmaster at Welton who was employed to collect the Assd. taxes and who collected to the amount of more than £100 some say near £200 has set off with the Money to America. He was one of the <u>National</u> patronised by Mr. Raikes, adieu to him and all such Rogues.

Wednesday 4th. May

Mr. Schonswar & Mr. Wrightson[16] the two old members for Hull have been returned without opposition, they are both reformers. Mr. Marshall and Mr. Burton[17] for Beverley, a Reformer and a half at least if not two if Burton be stanch of which there is a little doubt. Our old friend has arrived at home again with Orange & Blue Ribbons, he thinks they are as good Ribbons as he ever got, he had about 10 yards. He is highly lifted up. — He tells a rambling story about losing his favours and had given them up, when it appears they (like Sterne's

---

[14] Colonel Jones was proclaimed as the writer of a recent series of letters to *The Times* under the pseudonym 'Radical' by one of his supporters at a meeting of the electors of Southwark, where he was standing as a candidate for election (*TM* 27 Apr. 1831, 3 c).

[15] Countess Bjornsjerna, wife of the Swedish Ambassador (*TM* 29 Apr. 1831, 2 e).

[16] George Schonswar (see also n.32 (1831)) and William Battie Wrightson had both been elected as members for Hull in 1830, the former having been put forward by the freemen of the town and the latter nominated by the then outgoing member, Daniel Sykes, who described his nominee as 'a good Liberal'. Both candidates, supporters of parliamentary reform, were returned unopposed in the 1831 election (*VCHYER* i. 206).

[17] William Marshall of Leeds was a prominent Whig industrialist and a staunch supporter of parliamentary reform. Henry Burton had been first elected for Beverley in 1830. He had strong local connections, being the son-in-law of General Burton of Beverley and brother-in-law of R. C. Burton, a former Tory MP of Hotham Hall in North Cave. Despite his Tory background, he was an avowed supporter of reform, although RS seems to have had some reservations about the sincerity of his commitment to the cause (*VCHYER* vi. 130).

Ass) had been seeking him as much as he sought them even discovered themselves in his Side pocket when he went to bed, this was really fortunate.

Thursday 5th May

Mr. Atkinson and five more of the "free and independent" Burgesses of Beverley met last night at Newlove's to spend half a Sovereign on account of the Election of Mr. Marshall; Old Rd. Rickle is one and Tom Wade an old drunken Butcher is another, the whole 10s. would be a trifle in their way. I do not know how long they were about it. — In the course of my reading as some Scholars say, I met with the following "When a body of Men pay for their folly all out of their own Pockets, we need not fear that it will be a Folly of very long duration".

Friday 6th. May

This has been the Day for swearing in Men for the Militia, there were plenty of men to hire at various prices from 3 or 4 pounds to 7 or 8. Ned Coates has hired and been sworn in for a Man of North Cave he will scarcely be sober so long as his money last; but this is his enjoyment.

Saturday 7th. May

Yesterday was Snow and Sleet and cold as winter, and at night a hard frost, which has cut down Potatoe tops which were above ground, they are black as if burned; there was Ice a considerable thickness, I am afraid it will injure Fruit trees.

Sunday 8th. May

The Cause of Reform seems in general to go on prosperously, Yorkshire has returned 4 Stanch friends to it. I believe there were none of the Freeholders went from here; and perhaps but few of them either know or care what reform means. Enquiries would have been made who are likely to pay the best.

Monday 9th. May

Prince Georges have been at a Juvenile Military Review, (what Lads here call playing at Soldiers,) I believe these Georges will be qualified for several callings as Dancing, Sparrow Shooting, Reviewing ...

Tuesday 10th. May

I went to Brantingham this afternoon after School time to measure two Closes for Mr. Simpson about 28 Acres they were on the Wold; I met with Mr. Geo. Marr or Atmar he told me [he] had never been a week out of Brantingham together in his life; he had been once three days and 4 nights this was the amount of his sojourning from home; he had never been further than Howden on one hand and Beverley on the other, but had been in Holderness from Hull and at York I think.

Wednesday 11th. May

This Evening was appointed for the Subscribers to the Militia to have the remaining money divided amongst them, but on meeting it was considered advisable to let it remain until all be settled, as it is thought the town will have to be ballotted over again on account of Robt. Kirby.

Thursday 12th May

I have been making out the Assess'd taxes Bills and have got them finished and packed up, I intend sending them to Hull tomorrow, Saturday is the day appointed to return them at Beverley, but as my Ancle rather lets me down I shall beg to be excused.

Friday 13th. May

Eliza & her husband & Child set off yesterday for Swinefleet feast[.] I did not know till after they were gone, they walked, the forenoon was very fine, but came very cold in the afternoon. I think it poor employment to go so far to a feast; but different People have different Opinions. Got a load of Flour and other Articles today preparatory for the fair; Paid Mr. Oxtoby on Wednesday last £42 18 for good recd. on the 21st. Apl.

Saturday 14th. May

I have been making up Paper Bags today in expectation of their being wanted against the fair, — Weighton fair has been today I understand Sheep and lean Cattle sold low, may they keep so.

Sunday 15th. May

I have neither heard the Cuckoo nor seen a Swallow this Spring. My wife went to walk up little Wold lane last night on purpose to try to hear 'Cuckoo' but was not gratified with her voice.

Monday 16th. May

Recd. this Morning an Irish Paper of the 12th. May called the Freeman's Journal,[18] it appears to advocate the cause of Reform. Upon the whole the liberals have not much reason to complain there are but few places like Cambridge which I think I have heard called the "Whig University" but now they are resolved all the Country shall know; that they think the present order of representature works well. These Parsons are generally the last that open their Eyes to any improvement.

Tuesday 17th. May

At west end this Evening, as Saturday is the final day fixed upon for the payment of the Assess'd taxes, they were ordered to be paid on the 7th. inst. but on Account of the Elections, even the Tax receivers could not make it convenient to attend at the time so it was put off a fortnight.

Wednesday 18th. May

Where Mr. Turk's old Farm house was; down the Lane, they are building a new one, it belongs Mr. Earnshaw of Hessle, I suppose they have nearly finish'd it, the Old Cardinal has been glazing the Windows, Jem Levitt does the Joiner's work and Jn. Smith the Bricklayer's.

Thursday 19th. May

This has been the Court day at J. Levitt's I was not there indeed I never was at the Spring Court; and as to the other I think I shall give it up.

[18] 10 Sept. 1763 – 20 Dec. 1924. Irish daily newspaper published in Dublin and originally entitled: *Public Register; or, Freeman's Journal.*

Friday 20th. May

Very busy this Evening in collecting, as the taxes are to be paid tomorrow. Money is not good and easy to obtain, but I believe many put off to the last when they could as well pay sooner.

Saturday 21st. May

I walked to Beverley today and back again, I took my time and was never less tired, I was rather afraid of my Ancle but it is no worse it remains rather swelled but without pain, which is one comfort.

Sunday 22d May

I rather think from what I heard yesterday that the Receivers of Taxes will be abolished very shortly,[19] it is to be hoped that other useless offices will share the same fate. It behoves the Rulers to save all that is possible, and then we may hope for better times ...

Tuesday 24th. May

Henry Bentley's wife from Hull was here this morning for Relief, her husband Henry is gone to America and left her and a family of 4 or 5 Children to the tender mercy of the Parish. As far as I can find it has been made up between them, and I believe she wants to be sent after him at the Parish Expence I relieved her this morning with six Shillings; Hal was a great Ranter and a preacher; he wanted the town to give him £15—but they would not oblige him, neither indeed would they offer him any thing.

Wednesday 25th. May

The first Swallow I have seen this year was yesterday, one came into the School in the afternoon, I think they are very scarce this Season, the Cuckoo I have not yet heard, although on Saturday last I had a fair opportunity in going and returning from Beverley.

Thursday 26th. May

What Colouring & cleaning here is going on now, in preparation for the fair, — Cheesecakes tomorrow will begin to smell very strong—I could like to have the Parsons turned over to my care to Regulate, I think I could teach them to be a little more liberal or at least I would put it out of their power to hurt the Community by their arbitrary measures; they appear to be the most bigotted of the Tories.

Friday 27th. May & Saturday 28th

Here is nothing but preparation going on, Saturday is the Market day before the fair, Butter which was 1s. pr. lb. last week, is this day 1s/5d an extravagant price.

Sunday 29th

John Read and his Son John came last night to be partakers of the good things to be found here, and the Junior plays his part excellently, he is never absent if there [be] any thing good stirring.

---

[19] RS's information proved correct, for the office of Receivers General of the Land and Assessed Taxes was abolished, and their role assigned to 'persons executing the offices of Inspectors of Taxes' in an Act passed later that year on 6 Sept (1 & 2 Will. IV c. 18).

Monday 30th. May

This is the Fair Day for Cattle & Sheep, which both went off languidly, I cannot say that the Stock was very numerous. We had James Ramsdale and his Son Robert today.

Tuesday 31st. May

The weather this fair has been delightful, and it was expected there would be a full assemblage of Company, but the fair was very thin, whether it be that people get tired of it, or that they are short of money I cannot determine, but so it was, the Company was very small, we had Watty Arton and his Sister Mrs. Stephenson at tea.

Wednesday 1st. June

This was a full Boat day to me, I had no less than three Newspapers, besides the Packet which I always get before Mr. Bridgman, the Aberdeen Observer[20] I have looked into and find Reform triumphant in Scotland, or at least much more of it than could have been expected.

Thursday 2nd. June

Preparing a Hamper for Wm. a fine Ham and some Super fine flour such as has been used for Cheesecakes, here by the way we have not made one this fair, being so throng, but Eliza has furnished us with a supply, we have not had many Cheesecake demolishers this fair which is one comfort. Paid Mr. Oxtoby this day £35 for goods had about 3 Wks ago and have given another order for more.

So Cave 2nd. June 1831

Dear Wm.

With this you will receive the Hamper filled as well as we could store it, first a very fine Ham with which you will I hope be gratified, and some very excellent flour the same as Cave fair Cheesecakes were made of, a little of our best tea, and some Raisins for little Mary, as to Wm. 2nd. I don't know what you will find in it for him. We understand your Aunt Mary is coming to see you this Summer, your Mother has therefore sent the fine tea and some Sugar that you make her a very good Cup of tea, she particularly wishes you to look on her in the best manner, although we have no intercourse, we rejoice to find that she is glad of your welfare; So make her as comfortable as you can. — Your Mother is gone this day to West Ella. I am the Shopkeeper, and as this week is a slack time I can manage pretty well, we hope you all keep well as we are all at present, — Herewith you will receive 2 Sovereigns for the bonnet which is really highly esteemed, after paying yourself for it you must give Mary the remainder for being so kind as buying the Cap and writing to her Grandmother. When you send the Hamper or anything else Send half a Dozen Boxes of the genuine Hooper's Pills. Now I don't know what I can say more except that I am very drowsy, and that may well be an excuse for saying no more, indeed you

---

[20] *Aberdeen Observer: a commercial and political journal*, Mar. 1829 – Mar. 1836.

will most likely find in my <u>very elegant</u> Journal enough said; Eliza said she would write with this I have not yet got her letter, her little Girl can nearly run

    I remn. your
           loving Father
           R Sharp

Saturday 4th. June

The Hamper for Wm. will leave Hull this morning, I hope it will arrive safe, and be satisfactory—We that is the town very gloomy this morning, last Saturday all was anxiety and expectation for the fair; now it is past like the "baseless fabric of a Vision",[21] it is a hurrying disagreeable time at least to me, for I am heartily tired of <u>hurrying</u> Scenes. This is the first day of my additional lucubrations, there has been a good deal of Paper scribbled over since I commenced.

Sunday 5th. June

A fine moderate Rain began about noon, the weather has been very dry and dusty for some time past; this rain will be very acceptable; the Farmers say they have prayed for Rain, but their prayers are all selfish, and for their own interest, if they pray at all, which I am sure many of them never do.

Monday 6th. June

We have often heard of the Pleasures of Memory, which doubtless are great; but is there no pleasure in forgetfulness? yes, surely when one has read an entertaining Book and forgot its contents there is the pleasure of reading it over again without any anticipation aye or recollection either, now is there not a pleasure in forgetfulness? Certainly there is.

Tuesday 7th. June

I have finished taking the Population[22] and here is the result. 173 inhabited houses, 181 Families. 1 house building. 9 houses unoccupied. 109 families engaged in Agriculture. 49 in trade and 23 other classes. — There are 407 Males & 426 females Total 833—In 1821 the numbers were 885, to account for the deficiency, several have gone to America, and Mr. Barnard has no Servants nor himself here now as he had then.

Wednesday 8th. June

At Ellerker this Evening assisting, or rather taking the Population there are about 280 Persons; whether they have increased or not since the last Census, I have not at present the means of knowing.

---

[21] 'And, like the baseless fabric of this vision ...' —Prospero in Shakespeare's *The Tempest*, act 4, scene 1, line 151.

[22] Censuses of England and Wales were taken at 10-year intervals. The census of 1831 was the fourth in the series, following those for 1801, 1811, and 1821. Each census at this period required authorization by a specific Act of Parliament, and in England the inquiry was entrusted to the overseers of the poor. Names of individuals were not recorded by the enumerators until 1841. The 4 earlier censuses were restricted to basic questions concerning the number of houses in each parish or township and the population of each family, by sex and occupation. The 1821 census had attempted to get a detailed breakdown by age, but this experiment was not repeated in the 1831 census which concentrated on collecting more detail on the occupation record (EB v. 663).

Thursday 9th. June

Heard from Wm. this morning that he had recd. the Hamper safe and glad to find they are all well. — This "hearing from" I think is not altogether correct for what did I hear? I saw from him by his writing, but as it is the customary method of speaking, I must not criticise ...

Saturday 11th. June

I saw yesterday a letter from Charles Barff[23] a Missionary at Huahine, he gives an account of a Voyage he had made to several Islands, the names of which I never heard before. He has seven Children the eldest a Boy, he is going to send to London to learn the art of <u>Composing</u>, I suppose in plain English he means a printer; he likewise thinks of sending a daughter or two to Newbald, to his Parents to be educated. I think myself he is only a poor Creature, I am certain his writing is no credit to him.

Sunday 12th. June

I think this must be nearly a Blank day. My wife went to the West end this afternoon intending to go to the Chapel, she called to see Mrs. Marshall (Rd.) who has been very ill a long time, she staid the afternoon with her, Mrs. M. would have her to stay tea which she did, as she thought it might be the last time.

Monday 13th. June

The Market very thinly attended today, indeed from Cave fair until after Harvest very few people come to the Market, it is a time of the year that there is but little to sell.

Tuesday 14th. June

The Visitation is this day at Cousens' I am not there, I have not attended for some years past they are meagre meetings except for eating and drinking, and I am very thankful that I have sufficient at home, and need not desire expensive banquets; indeed I always feel best with my own every day way of living.

Wednesday 15th. June

This afternoon we had thunder, not particularly heavy, but it rained as fast as ever I saw it, for a short time, between four and five O'clock; in about an hour after it was very fine weather again. — The Emperor of Brazil I see has <u>run away</u> from his business,[24] it seems that the trade or calling of Kings is in a

---

[23] Born in South Cave in 1791, Charles Barff was brought up by his grandparents at nearby Newbald. In 1818, Barff and his wife settled as missionaries on the island of Huahine in the Pacific, where they remained for the next 47 years with only a short break for a few months' leave in 1847, and a spell of sick leave from 1855 to 1859. Apart from his missionary activities, he founded schools for the islanders' children and encouraged the production of coffee, sugar cane and cotton. In 1864 the Barffs left the island to retire to Sydney which they eventually reached after a delay of some months on account of their ship being wrecked on Danger Island on 16 May. Charles Barff died and was buried in Sydney at the age of 75 in 1866, his wife surviving him by 5 years (Richardson (1914) 89–95).

[24] The Emperor of Brazil, Dom Pedro, faced with insurrection at home, was forced to abdicate the throne in favour of his young son. He embarked with his family on board a British frigate on 7 Apr. 1831, leaving the country without any effective government. He and his daughter, Donna Maria the Queen of Portugal, sailed for Europe where they raised a fleet which eventually defeated Dom Miguel,

poor way at present, for first one and then another declines or are forced to give up business ...

Friday 17th. June

Norrison Marshall was at Hull yesterday on business, I think buying bones for Manure, he set off for home between five and six O'clock in the Evening, when it came on a thunder Storm, he took shelter under a tree just at the end of the town of Hull when a flash of lightning struck both him and his horse dead: this is an alarming stroke of Providence; we feel much for his untimely fate, he and our poor dear John were like Brothers and of the same age within a month; In the midst of life we are in death. He was an excellent Character.

Saturday 18th. June

I walked to Beverley this day and back again, I took my time and felt very comfortable, I got home about Six O'clock without any dinner, indeed when I am from home I seldom feel much disposed for eating; I can drink cold Water the best of any thing, but as I was too warm I called at Walkington and got a glass of Ale and a pipe, which refreshed me.

Sunday 19th. June

I went this morning according to Custom to Richd. Marshall's it is indeed the house of mourning, he was not in the House but walking about the Garth like a distracted Man, I went to him, O'dear! O'dear! he says and got hold of my hand, I have been wondering and telling our folks that you had never been here, since this sad event happened, but could I be pleased with ought, I should be pleased with your coming to see me; well you know the reason I said; I do, I do, he says, he meaning Norrison was of your own bringing up, you taught him all he knew, I thought it would affect you so much you could not bear to come, but thank you for coming, thank you; I walked about with him perhaps half an hour, and desired him to be resigned as possible—Norrison was buried this afternoon at four O'clock, My wife and I were there having had Gloves sent last night; I never saw so many People at a funeral here before; the Church was crammed full, and many shed tears; — we did not stop tea, I cannot eat and drink at funerals, I took a single glass of wine not to appear singular. He Rd. Marshall told me he would give up business and have no more bother with this world; but this I opposed and said what will you do? you cannot spend your time without some employment; now think with yourself what a state you would be in giving yourself up to idleness; No, No, you must have business, Why if I have I will not set my heart on the World as I have done, but perhaps I should not be right without something to do; — Now do you think Norrison is happy he says? I hope he is and believe he is, — aye he says I hope he is in heaven making intercession for me and many more; in the state he was in I did not wish to show him the fallacy of this Popish Doctrine, but I must at some opportunity, let him know that there is no intercession between God and Man, but Jesus Christ.

the Emperor's brother and rival claimant to the throne of Portugal (See n.16 (1833)) (*AR* 1831, Hist. 460–4).

Monday 20th. June

This day the few Farmers who were at the Market, looked rather blue, at the news of Corn being lower, and should the weather prove favourable they were assured that it will be still lower. All Kinds of Grain look remarkably well, the Wheat a great deal of which is shot; it is calculated the Harvest will be very forward; some say Wheat in places will be ready before the end of July.

Tuesday 21st. June

I went down to the West end this Evening to see Rd. Marshall, he is far from being resigned to his loss, I went to the Water Close with him, with a few Sheep, he had a Dog which was Norrison's which he says is so daft since he lost him, that he cares nothing about attending to the Flock as he did, though I thought he did very well, running to turn the Sheep as he was ordered; it will take some time to make the Father submit to his loss.

Wednesday 22d. June

With respect to the War in Poland,[25] I am fearful that the Barbarians will either crush the Poles or harrass them so much, as to make them succumb to their late Masters but, still there is hope, for a whole nation is not easily overpowered.

Thursday 23rd. June

I this day saw a funeral pass by, there were a Hearse and two Mourning Coaches. I heard after that it was Mrs. Craggs they were taking to No. Cave to bury; whether she has been ill or died suddenly, I do not know, as I have not heard her mentioned in any manner for a long time past.

Friday 24th. June

Mrs. (Rd.) Marshall died this afternoon about four O'clock after a very tedious illness, she is all worn away. I called last night to see them, the shock of her death is nothing so alarming as was Norrison's last week, for it was long seen she could not recover; but whenever death comes the most callous, seems to be softened. She is 53.

Saturday 25th. June

The Campaign in the two Houses has commenced, instead of attending to business, there are some that seem to diverge as far from it as possible, and spend their time in talking and others in hearing, of illuminations or no illuminations, I think several of them know little of the public business, so what they lack in knowledge they make up in words; if they can find nothing else to set them a gabling, they say the old Chancellor wanted manners, when he threw down his hat or took it up, (it is immaterial which) and left their Lordships, to wonder at his want of breeding. Now had he been instructed by a good clever French dancing master, he might have retreated with dignity.

---

[25] The sector of Poland under Russian domination proclaimed its independence under the leadership of Prince Adam Czartorisky in Dec. 1830. Russian forces invaded Poland at the beginning of Feb. 1831, and there followed a series of fierce engagements which lasted until early Sept. when Polish resistance was finally broken with the fall of Warsaw after which the rest of the country was quickly subjugated (*AR* 1831, Hist. 422–36).

Sunday 26th. June

Saw Mrs. Marshall in her Coffin this morning, as much display as could be, the Coffin covered with Black Cloth, and a large breast plate, with the usual armaments for the dead. My wife went in the Evening to see her, there appears to be no change in her looks, she seemed as if a sleep.

Monday 27th. June

Matthew Pickering told me today that he had sold his house preparatory to his going to America. Some Man from Bishop Burton has bought it, he wants to let it, — Matthew had £200 on Mortgage on it, it is sold for about £350, so that he will not have a great deal to spare for his Voyage and Journey.

Tuesday 28th. June

I have been writing and making out all the necessary documents, — against the approaching Club feast, there have been 13 members excluded the last year, and not one fresh one entered, there has not been the last year the death either of a member or his wife the total worth is £580–4–1½ it has cleared or increased the last year £9–13–3 there are 125 members.

Wednesday 29th. June

I have read the opening speech of the Campaign on reform, the Ministers I think to their credit are resolved to persevere and Sir Robt. Peel will persevere too, but it is in contradiction; Now what will the <u>born</u> Legislators do with this same reform measure, they will for their own sakes I think pass it; I do not know they can do any better.

Thursday 30th. June

Our Old Friend the Freeman of Bristol, is afraid that he will be disenfranchised, he is fearful he must bid adieu to the pleasures of another Election. — He has been reading Mr. Beverley's letter to the Archbishop,[26] he hardly knows what to make of it, but thinks he has gone rather too far, though he thinks there wants a <u>reform</u> amongst the Clergy, so do more people besides him.

Friday 1st. July

Thomas Marshall was here today, he had been getting a drink for a Cow— he said he had made up his mind when Norrison got killed that he would give up swearing, and he thinks he should have kept his resolution, had not their Servant Girl, left the Garden Gate open and let in the Pigs, which had destroyed all his Potatoes and Cabbages; he was obliged to break out and swear at her with authority. — Now I said to him as your Garden stuff was all destroyed, there was very little occasion for anyone to weed your Garden on <u>Sunday</u> last, Ha, what, what do you say? I say I was told <u>you</u> were weeding your Garden on Sunday, you were seen coming out with an armful of weeds; I deant kno wha the Devil tells you all these lies, well was it true—No I say it was not; — I say I heard so.

---

[26] Robert Mackenzie Beverley, *A Letter to His Grace the Archbishop of York, on the Present Corrupt State of the Church of England.* Beverley: W. B. Johnson, 1831.

Saturday 2d. July

There have been two Men of North Cave tried at the Sessions last week at Beverley for stealing beans, and sentenced to be transported for seven years each. One of them Tom Constable is an old offender; Lundy the Carrier of North Cave was taken with them he having received the Beans and sold them at Hull; he was admitted Evidence and thus saved himself; he is supposed to be as bad or rather worse than the others.

Sunday 3rd. July

This has been a very fine warm day, there was what was called a funeral Sermon for Mrs. Marshall at the Chapel this afternoon, I did not know or I should have gone, my wife was there; but she said she never heard such a sleepy discourse so I do not much regret not having heard it.

Monday 4th. July

Ths. Marshall was talking this Evening of the funeral Sermon on Sunday last, but such a Sermon he says as gave him <u>Belly wark</u>, he says he would as soon take a <u>Cow drink</u> as hear such Sermons, from a proud sleepy headed fellow, he wishes to go to the Chapel, but he cannot put up with such preaching as there is, a fellow to mutter for an hour, and he thinks he has his hearers safe (he says) and there they are like Cattle in a Pinfold watching to be out as soon as possible.

Tuesday 5th. July

Matthew Pickering told me last night, that Barnard Cook has taken his house; I think it may be the means of a livelihood for him; Matthew cannot get off before the 13th. August, as it is the first day for transferring the Licence, he seems in good Spirits, with the prospects before him; he says there is a place engaged for him in America, a public house and Blacksmith's Shop, so he expects he will be at home again, as soon as he arrives there.

Wednesday 6th. July

My Brother came last night, he walked from Market Weighton to Cave with his great Coat, and Umbrella, which was not very comfortable on such a warm day. He looks very well and is very well, he is going to West Ella this Evening, we that is I and He are going to tea at Eliza's.

Thursday 7th. July

This is the Club feast day this year at Morley's, there were just 100 members present; dined in the Barn, I came away before 4 O'clock, all was quiet so far as I saw; the Musicians playing about, all the afternoon, for their own benefit if not to the amusement of others.

Friday 8th. July

Two Men who went to America this Spring have returned back again, (they went from Cottingham) they have been 12 Weeks away and travelled in the Country 700 Miles; it seems they were not satisfied so came back, I doubt not with a bundle of lies.

Saturday 9th July

Matthew Moody who was accounted the best man in the town at throwing the hatchet,[27] is now in the back ground for it is admitted that Ned Coates is his master. Matty says Ned is such a liar there is no believing a word he says, the old adage remains true, "two of a trade cannot agree".

Sunday 10th. July

So the reform Bill has passed the second reading by an overwhelming Majority, one would think that the Antis might be convinced, that they are engaged in a hopeless work, the Country is against them, this is certain, now for the incurables, if they see their own interests, and they appear to know it, they will fall in and swim gently with the stream. I think they will.

Monday 11th. July

Mr. Brown (who takes Bell's Life in London) says that the Jury in Cobbett's trial[28] did not give a Verdict but that a Juror was withdrawn, I think he was hardly right as, at the Conclusion of the trial in the times, there was written "Not Guilty": but I shall soon know if I live; One thing which he said that the Lord Chancellor was not examined and sworn on the trial to give evidence was not true: as I fully proved.

Tuesday 12th. July

Tuesday with me is a sort of listless day, I have got so used to the Paper in the morning that it feels rather dull without one; but I contrive to get on without, for what cannot one do or suffer when they are forced!!

Wednesday 13th. July

This afternoon it rained very fast and thundered; — A Gentleman has taken Frog Hall and come to it, his name is Nicholson as I have heard; he comes from Hull, but I do not know him; he has been here about the Window duty, he wants to stop some of the windows up, but I told him he was too late for this year.

Thursday 14th. July

I have been pulling some Currant-berries to make wine I am not very partial to the job; we have some very fine ones, but, we have often had more, Goose Berries are very Cheap, Sixpence a Peck; Caterpillars have made much havock amongst our trees this year.

Friday 15th. July

This is the day of the weeping Saint Swithin, we have had a few of his tears, but what he has to do with the Weather, is past my Comprehension. Saint Sathan as Adam Woodcock calls the Old enemy; has just as much to do with

---

[27] To tell lies or make exaggerated statements (*OED*).

[28] Cobbett was suspected by the Whig government of having encouraged the Captain Swing disturbances in the southern counties in the autumn and winter of 1830 and was prosecuted for an article published in the *Political Register* of 11 Dec. 1830 which was alleged to have been written with an intent to incite farm labourers to acts of violence. Cobbett conducted his own defence, subpoenaed several cabinet ministers, and called Brougham, the Lord Chancellor to the witness box, forcing him to admit that he had asked Cobbett for leave to reprint an article written by him in 1816, 'Letter to Luddites', as a means of dissuading the rioters from acts of violence. The case against him collapsed: the jury failed to reach a verdict and Cobbett was discharged by the judge (Sambrook 172–4).

the rain as the Winchester Saint; nay perhaps more for he is called the Prince of the Power of the Air; I wish all these sort of Saintish fables were forgot.

Saturday 16th. July

This morning recd. a letter from Wm. and some Boxes of Pills glad to find they are all well, should like to see them, I told Rd. Marshall this afternoon how sorry Wm. was for his loss; he says it is consoling to find himself so much sympathised with, but all this brings him no comfort, I went to the Clover Close with him, they were beginning to lead; he says had his wife been spared she would have been the means of dispelling his melancholy: but he must submit, to Providence.

Sunday 17th. July

There has been no little stir in the Commons on account of the reform bill, but Ministers I am glad to find are determined to persevere; Sir Robt Peel in his wisdom went home to bed, I expect in a little time he will come round in support of reform, he has not much to say against it at present; and that is not a trifle.

Monday 18th. July

Mr. Burton one of the Members for Beverley, it is said has sent a letter to his Constituents, that he will never more appear there in the Character of a Candidate for Parliamentary honors it is owing to his having been promised at the last Election to be brought in free of expence, and he has had a Bill made out for him to pay of 1000 or 1100 Pounds!! this is clever.

Tuesday 19th. July

The two Simpson's Farmers and Sheep stealers at Wold Newton have been sentenced at the York Assizes to transportation for life. One of them was a Methodist preacher, and the morning he was taken; he was going to preach; It is lamentable that a man of this description should have been a teacher; when he ought to have known better; but why should the Methodists be blamed and exulted over, by those who are always glad to find a flaw in Religious professors. Christianity is no less true because Judas was one of the Apostles or disciples.

Wednesday 20th. July

My Brother came this Evening on his return home, he had been at Burlington; he intends walking to Market Weighton in the Morning, he will start about five O'clock that he may be in time for the Coach. Danl. Porter he says is very lame and asthmatical.

Thursday 21st. July

I am no great Gardener, but I have some very fine Marygolds those old fashioned Garden flowers; I must have some London Pride if I can fall in another year; I like such flowers as these, which were the flowers of my Youth, & admired by my Children, I would not give them up for the most gay exotics, I like the smell of Southernwood but at present have none, but I will try to get a Root of it.

Friday 22d. July

Mr. Beverley has published another Pamphlet which he calls a lay Sermon entitled the Tombs of the Prophets;[29] My Brother had bought it, but his stay was so short, I had not an opportunity of reading it over; I should like to peruse it, most likely I shall be meeting with it shortly.

Saturday 23d. July

This forenoon measuring part of a Close of Turnips for Ths. Wride on the little Wold, (what is called the little Wold is on the left side of the Road going to Beverley;) it was very pleasant, there is a fine Prospect from it, but not equal to that from Mount Airy.

Sunday 24th. July

Instead of the fine Old Roses which bloom in June and July (and have been pressed into many a ditty;) we have now what are called Monthly Roses,[30] which may if the Weather be favorable flower twice in a year: but what flowers!! they are like a fly flap, thin and single like a rag of Muslin; — the Improvement as it is called in the Culture of Apples is nearly akin to this, for nearly all the fine old sorts are banished or forgotten and new varieties are introduced but with no advantage either to the fruit or the trees; for after standing a few years they decay and then there is an end of the matter; they are no more like the fine Old Apple trees which I recollect of my Grandfather's, than the flapping roses are to the fine old fashioned English Cabbage roses.

Monday 25th. July

I think there was nothing doing at the Market today, most of the Farmers are throng with their Hay, and a fine Season here is for it.

Tuesday 26th. July

Hedon I see is to be placed in the Company of other Condemned Criminal Boroughs;[31] I think it would have been better and saved time had they all been knocked down together, without the ten times twice told lamentations of their lovers.

Wednesday 27th. July

Mr. Schonswar[32] one of the Members for Hull has stopped payment, his debts are to a very large amount it is said £150,000 his Brother is in the Isle of France, has been speculating in Sugar plantations, which is one cause it is said of the failure. I was at Ellerker this Evening at Charles Rudd's, who is tenant to

---

[29] Robert Mackenzie Beverley, *The Tombs of the Prophets: a Lay Sermon on the Corruptions of the Church of Christ.* Beverley: W.B. Johnson, 1831. Also 2nd ed. 1831.

[30] China roses, varieties of *Rosa indica*, were first introduced into England in the 1790s. They were also known as monthly roses from their capacity for repeated flowering (*EB* xxiii. 730).

[31] The second Reform Bill, introduced on 24 June 1831 after the general election had strengthened the position of the reformers, was substantially the same as the first. Hedon was the only East Yorkshire borough to be included in Schedule A, which listed those boroughs with a population below 2,000 which were to be wholly disfranchised (Walpole iii. 216–22).

[32] George Schonswar, a prominent Hull merchant and shipowner, had twice held the office of Mayor of Hull, in 1811 and 1817. He had been elected MP for Hull as a supporter of parliamentary reform in 1830 and was returned unopposed in the election of 1831 (Sheahan 233; *VCHER* i. 206).

Mr. Schonswar, his farm is about 240 Acres; he is a good deal depressed, on the occasion.

Thursday 28th. July

My wife was at Hull today and I was Shopkeeper. It came on here about five O'clock in the afternoon a dreadful Storm of thunder, & lightning, hail & Rain, but nothing at Hull, a Boy a Son of Mary Bentley's who lived near Beverley, was killed by the lightning, when going home from the Hay field, there were two others with him who escaped.

Friday 29th. July

I had forgot to notice yesterday that the Boy of Mary Bentley who was killed by lightning, lived the last year with Richd. Marshall, which Renews the grief for Norrison, he cannot yet get up his Spirits.

Saturday 30th. July

I was at Ellerker this afternoon, met with Mr. Leason, we went and drank tea with Watty Arton and Mudda, the Discourse was not very intellectual, we staid till about eight O'clock when I returned home.

Sunday 31st. July

The weather is remarkably hot and sultry, scarcely a breath of air, — heard today that a Man of the name of Thurlow, who lived at Welton, and formerly was at lodgings at Brantingham had hanged himself last night; He was I believe a stranger here; a sort of sulky half melancholy look he had.˙

Monday 1st. Augt.

A very thin attendance at the Market today, some of the Farmers talk of beginning harvest this week, indeed Allison of Ellerker has begun, having reaped some wheat, which is a good crop, I think there is more old wheat than was expected, or at least was talked about, here are several Stacks in the neighbourhood to thrash yet; since I can recollect the Farmers always contrived to have all threshed out by Mayday, but now they have threshing all the year round.

Tuesday 2nd. Aug

I was at Everthorpe this night, Mrs. Tomlinson has taken the house where Francis Ruston formerly lived, I suppose for the Summer, and wants me to go and teach her Children—I have engaged to attend twice a week.

Wednesday 3rd. Augt

Measuring some Turnip land for Mr. Lockwood the person who has taken Scatcherd's farm; it was in the Close on the left hand side of the Road going up the Steep hill leading to Mount Airy, a very thick fog this night.

Thursday 4th. Augt.

This is Mr. Barnard's Rent day, he is not here himself, there has been a dinner for the tenants at Js. Levitt's, I have not yet heard what sort of doings there was, but I doubt not but some would be merry enough, amongst the rest the Man of Meal. (No he was not there)!!

Friday 5th. Aug

Last night was the Club meeting, there were not many members present, indeed there was not much to entice them there, nor to keep them when there; Sour Ale is not so very exquisite as to keep a Company long together.

Saturday 6th. Aug

A very hot day, went this afternoon to measure some Turnip land at Ellerker Wold, about 15 Acres, it was warm work. I was very thirsty but there was nothing to be had to quench my thirst, until I got home at tea time ...

Monday 8th. Aug

Mr. Oxtoby has been here today we have paid him £38–10–0 and ordered another load of Flour and Groceries, which will come this week, — I saw no wheat at Market today.

Tuesday 9th. Aug

I was out this Evening in the Market place collecting Poor Sess and very little I got. — Several farmers have begun harvest the weather is tolerably fine, we had some rain this night.

Wednesday 10th. Aug

This Journal of mine serves me in the place of an Almanack, to know the days of the Month, I do not know that I have bought an Almanack, for the last thirty years. There has been a letter from a young man who went from Broomfleet last year to America, which only gives a very poor account of his prospects, he says the Roads there are worse than at Broomfleet; if they are they need not be called Roads at all, at all.

Thursday 11th. Augt.

I was at Ellerker this Evening settling with Mr. Leason for the Church Sess which I had been collecting for him—Harvest work going on very briskly and so far fine weather for it. I hope it will be got together in a good state.

Friday 12th. Aug

I have been pulling some Gooseberries perhaps about half a Peck, to boil for preserves: this year Berries are scarcely worth pulling, I made myself sweat pretty freely it being very warm, and when I got them pulled I dare say they were not worth more than 4d. Saw some fine Apples today at 18d. pr. peck, a cry was raised a short time ago that there would be no Apples, but the croakers are deceived, I hope there will be plenty at a reasonable rate.

Saturday 13th. Aug.

I was at Everthorpe this forenoon at Mrs. Tomlinson's, one of her Sons has the very look and Actions of his Uncle John, and appears to have not much greater inclination to a Book, his Mother says he is, surprisingly happy in his Ignorance; one of the Girls brought in some Turnips; he wished he had one of them—but not one was to be had: so he was forced to handle his Pen, and con over the Multiplication table.

Sunday 14th Aug

Heard this morning that Wm. had been two days ill, with a Bowel Complaint; it is what I frequently have; we have had but a dull day, hope he will soon be better.

Monday 15th. Aug

Mattw. Pickering or Barnard Cook, I don't know which of them, has had a sale today, Barnard enters tomorrow on Matt's house, Mattw. has removed into a house of Mr. Bridgman's, until he takes his departure across the Atlantic. I think he is to blame as he appears to live here as well as any of his neighbours.

Tuesday 16th. Augt

Mr. Bridgman has got a few loads of Wheat home, if the weather keeps fine the harvest will be very short; old Barny has got removed to Matt's house, so that we have the Post Office very near us at present.

Wednesday 17th. Aug

This Day we got a load of Coals, it was warm work carrying them in, I filled and the man that brought them carried. There has a Man or two come back in the neighbourhood who went to America last year, they give dismal Accounts of the Country, neither work nor money to be had, no more of America for them.

Thursday 18th. Aug

Wheat this year they say will be light, the Sheaves do not weigh so solid as if the corn was bold; here are complaints of Mildew, but I have seen none of this kind; it came on a very heavy rain this afternoon about three O'clock with much Thunder and lightning, we have had a great deal this Season.

Friday 19th. Aug

Tailor Wauldby and David Dennis were lately making hay, but the hay happened to be rather too wet, and they were too dry, so they left the hay to dry, and took themselves into the town to steep themselves, and both got so full that they could scarce Walk; the Tailor got himself laid down in a stable and got a sleep, when he awaked he wondered where he was, and thought he would go home, but when he got up he could not stand, then he wondered what was the matter, until somebody told him he was drunk, and he was glad it was no worse for he thought he had lost the use of his legs!!

Saturday 20th. Aug

This day from about Eleven O'clock has been a real storm, much rain and a high wind, it has settled the harvest working for this week so that the Labourers will have a half holiday.

Sunday 21st. Aug

This has been a very fine drying day with a brisk wind, if it continues so until tomorrow the Farmers will be very throng leading home their Corn. — Mr. Barnard came home yesterday, how long he is going to stay I do not know but suppose not long: Rd. Marshall thinks two or three weeks, he has been in London since Lady day last.

Monday 22d. Aug

My wife desired me a few days ago to pull some Berries for boiling in my own Garden, I told her there were very few to pull, as I had at times eaten most of them, which I thought was a saving as if they were boiled there would be the expence of Sugar, but my economy was not very well liked, so that a reform in this case it appears will not answer, as it would keep us without tarts at Cave fair, however I found as many Gooseberries left as were sufficient, when all was well again.

Tuesday 23d. Aug

I have been making out the List of Persons qualified to serve on Juries which is annually returned in September. I think I have done little else today.

Wednesday 24th. Aug

Old Barnard has got the Post office removed so that we have it very near, I for the first time put a Newspaper in, to go to Swinefleet.

Thursday 25th. Aug

Very fine weather for the Harvest, I think most of the Wheat about us is safe at home in good Condition. Not an idle person scarcely to be seen in the Street. Eight or ten Irishmen I saw go past today, there are none employed here, nor ever were.[33] Poor unfortunates.

Friday 26th. Aug

There has been a letter today from America giving an Account of the Death of James Milner's wife, poor Woman it was against her will that she went, and she has not long survived it; It is said that James has been not in his right mind since his Arrival in America.

Saturday 27th. Aug

I was left to mind the Treacle tin today being filled, and did not look at it until it was running over, which was a discovery that I got very little credit for; "That awd newspaper is all you mind" was shot off at me, as I happened to be engaged with the Dublin Election, which I believe was not quite clear to understand even in a meditative mood; but with Treacle in the Shop floor, not a thought more was to be wasted òn it ...

Monday 29th. Aug

Heard from Wm. this morning that he had got quite well, which was very cheering to us. Are glad to find they are all well that the little Wm. is so much like John we are pleased to find, how much we could like to see them. Eliza's little Girl can walk over the Street, and get up stairs into the School to me. — The fellow who has made a noise lately with his Chin Music, is not an original. In No. 283 of the Spectator, a Boy beats the Grenadier's March on his Chin, he maintains himself and his Mother, and lays up Money every day. January 24th. 1711–12.

Tuesday 30th. Aug

I cannot for the life of me understand this Reform Bill from the little Sketches of the Clauses which I see; and perhaps if I saw the whole of it I could not comprehend it

> "It is so vast, so wide, and deep;

---

[33] Irish farm labourers regularly migrated in large numbers to England for the summer harvesting season. They were generally popular with farmers and employers (though not with their English counterparts) on account of their skill and willingness to work for relatively low wages. They usually travelled in small gangs, each under a gang-master who negotiated their wages with the local farmers. The gangs stayed in England for about 3 months following a regular circuit and initially working at the harvesting of the hay crop, then corn, and finally potatoes (Mingay vi. 681–3).

So powerful and commanding:
That like some other things; tis past
All human understanding".[34]

Wednesday 30th. [i.e. 31st] Aug

Mattw. Pickering has engaged a Passage in a Vessel called the Freak[35] to New York, which is to sail on the 7th. Sepr. so that his time now grows short here.

Thursday 1st. Sepr.

Mr. Watt has taken the several Manors and Royalties of South Cave &c of Mr. Barnard to shoot over, he has hired Mr. Barnard's Gamekeeper, but I think he has not yet been here sporting.

Friday 2nd. Sep

Last night was the Club night, Mattw. Pickering wanted to have some money out and be excluded, but he could not accomplish his purpose, indeed I think there will be no more money paid to Members for excluding themselves.

Saturday 3d Sepr.

My wife was at Hull yesterday buying Bacon, and I was Shopkeeper, I dare say I did very well; but as it is such a throng time harvesting and gleaning I had not a great deal of Customers, tho' nothing to complain of.

Sunday 4th. Sepr

There was a Woman came with a Child from Broomfleet to the Church to have it baptised today but the stupid parson would not baptise it, without it being christened, and she was not prepared with sponsors, neither would he let her stand for it herself; so she was obliged to return as she came. This Priest is an intolerant fellow.

Monday 5th. Sepr

Heard from Wm. this morning that he is going to see his Aunt at Liverpool for a fortnight; I hope he will have a pleasant Journey, Poor little Will he said when he wrote was "happily a sleep", which is to say the least; being comfortable and knowing nothing about it ...

Wednesday 7th. Sepr

I had Ths. Marshall here today to settle some accounts with Mr. Pickering of 5 years standing, they have not been friendly lately, Mattw. lent Ths. an Iron Crow or Gavelock some 6 or 7 years ago which Ths. by some means or other forgot to return, so now that he has made his Bill out he > Mat has charged for the Gavelock £1 and as Matty's Bill was the least poor Tom has had to pay for the Gavelock £1; and losing two Traps of his own which he carried to Matty to

---

[34] This is a slightly misquoted excerpt from the poem by Edward Ward (1667–1731), entitled 'The Ambitious Mercenary; or, The Climbing Lawyer' which was published in his *The Modern World Disrob'd; or, Both Sexes Stript of their Pretended Virtue* ... (London: printed for G.S. and sold by B. Bragge [etc.], 1708). The original lines read: 'It is so deep, so wide, so vast, / So powerful and commanding, / That, like God's Grace, tis almost past / All human understanding' (*EP*).

[35] Advertised as the 'fine A.1. coppered brig' of the 'New York Line of Packets', the 'Freak' was commanded by Captain James Bouch and registered at 201 tons. Her sailing date was advertised as 28 Apr. 1831 (*HP*).

mend and never got back again; but upon the whole he has come off better than he expected as he had £1–16–2½ to take. Let me ha my <u>Traps</u>: D—n it where's my <u>Traps</u>, I want my <u>Traps</u>, was poor Tom's cry.

Thursday 8th. Sepr

The unfortunate Miller who so often comes off with the burnt side of the Cake, has just been to tell me that he has been weighing the Gavelock, it weighs 22½ lbs which at 4d pr. lb he finds comes to about 7s/6d for which he has paid 20s. so that the Balance and loss of his <u>Traps</u> makes him about the loser of a pound, he swears he is the best natured fellow alive and the easiest defrauded for he never has any thought of ought <u>but what is right</u>, and these <u>shifty Devils</u> take advantage of him and Rob him and keep his Traps, yan a Rabbit trap and tudder a Rattan Trap which he values at 5s. for beath <u>Traps</u>.

Friday 9th. Sep

We had an illumination last night,[36] the first I have known here, we to shew our loyalty and <u>save our</u> <u>Windows,</u> stuck Candles up and all went off peaceably, the Musicians as usual parading about with their Whistles and Drum, some of them were drunk in good time, and obliged to be led home; amongst whom was the leader or Master of the band; so that not much more concord was to be heard.

Saturday 10th. Sepr

This afternoon measuring some land for Ths. Pashley at Ellerker on which his following Crop had grown, 13A–1R–34P. Went after we had done to a new Beer house at Ellerker (Dodd's) where we had a pitcher of Ale, in a snug little Room, which has been fitted up for Customers; I think a House of this description or a public house was wanted at Ellerker. — It is surprising that the Magistrates should be so offended at their not having power to grant licences for these poor Beer Shops.

Sunday 11th. Sepr

I think the Parson today in his Sermon said something to the purpose; for he desired those who had taxes to pay, to be sure to pay them regularly and cheerfully, unfortunately there were but few to hear him; and those few I dare say will pay no more attention to what he said than to a common Sermon.

Monday 12th. Sepr

Mr. Turk came to the Market last Monday after leading & stacking Some Oats, when he thought he would go home and cover the stack with straw, as it looked like Rain; but some of the Weather wise gentlemen being in Company, they told him it would be no rain, as the Glasses had risen a good deal, so he, as he says like a Feal (took their advice or) relied on their Wisdom, but it came on rain notwithstanding the Glasses and the Oats got so wet that he had them to lead out into the Close again. A lot of Fools he says with their Weather Glasses, and he as great a fool to believe them.

---

[36] This 'illumination' and the attendant celebrations were in honour of the coronation of King William IV.

Tuesday 13th Sepr

Got up at (nay, before) eight O'clock, rung the Bell that the town might know I had arisen; then breakfasted, after that got a pipe, then wrapped up the Newspaper to send to Wm. — from 9 to 12 at School nearly by myself as but few of the Scholars have arrived from the Harvest yet. As soon after 12 as possible dined then another Pipe until between 1 and 2; then in the afternoon, school as usual, read in some Book till about 5 when I got my tea, and went to Mr. Atkinson's about 6: Settled there that Wakefield market will be lower on Friday next. About 8 or a little after came home, got some Supper; shut up the Shop, went quietly to bed, and so no more for this day, it being one of my Idle days.

Wednesday 14th Sep

Some of the Sportsmen, who it appears have a little of the Cockney in them, have been out Shooting in Ellerker Lordship, but instead of hitting Game, they have shot a Bullock belonging to Allison, when it was found it was quite dead; but the Sportsman has not been discovered.

Thursday 15th. Sep

John Akam has arrived from America but what account he brings I have not heard, but it will soon be known, he was at the Old Cardinal's today so that we shall soon hear the report.

Friday 16th. Sepr

Very fine weather yet, the Farmers are leading their Beans home, so that the Harvest will soon be finished.

Saturday 17th. Sper

I think the Parliament get very slowly on with the business this Session, I wonder what Mr. Hunt wants to do with the Corn Laws, let it be what it will, I do not think he will be attended to, I think it would be as well if they were all abolished ...

Monday 19th. Sepr.

Heard this day that the Russians had entered Warsaw,[37] for which I am sorry, I have been fearful for some time that the Poles would be obliged to give way, whether all be over or not with them time will tell.

Tuesday 20th. Sepr

Here has been a Mountebank in the Town today, making a Fool of himself as is usual, to get Money from those who are more simple than he is; a great hurry in the Street before Fenwick's Door; but more lookers on than had money to spare.

Wednesday 21st. Sepr.

I had a grand Field day today viz. I was measuring most of the Day[.] I began in a Close near to the Sands house; and ended besides Riplingham, it was S. Shaw's following Crop, it was a beautiful day we got nothing to eat all the

---

[37] The Russian army under its commander-in-chief, Count Paskevich, entered Warsaw on 8 Sept. 1831 after 2 days of heavy fighting (*AR* 1831. Hist. 435–6).

day—but called at Mr. Beaumont's at Brantingham and got a drink of Beer, which was very gratifying. (67a–2r–23p)

Thursday 22d Sep

Went out with the Overseer this Evening to collect the Poor Sess I did not wish this time to be very successful, and certainly in that I was gratified, for we were over all the West end and only got about 23s. so we must wait a little longer, before Money becomes more plentiful.

Friday 23d. Sepr.

John Akam has bought 170 Acres of Land about 15 Miles from Philadelphia, 60 Acres of which are cleared the rest Wood-Land, he brought with him some Ears of Wheat which grew on the Land, which I suppose was much like other Wheat.

Saturday 24th. Sep

Eliza this morning between twelve and one was delivered of a Boy, what his name is to be I have not enquired.[38] Hannah Levitt it is said is in a Family way to Norrison Marshall, and I think it appears to be true.

Sunday 25th. Sep

Here has a deal of Horses come through for Howden Shews, which begin on Tuesday; the Judges in Horse Flesh have had a busy day in examining and looking on; and without doubt making many sage observations. This is Company I have no relish for.

Monday 26h Sep

Nothing doing of consequence at the Market today.

Tuesday 27th. Sep

Mr. Levitt has been valuing Sunk Island in Holderness,[39] and I have been arranging the Particulars, there are about 6000 Acres, 5000 of which on an average he has valued at 35s–6d pr. Acre annually and 1000 Acres at 20s. — It is Crown Land, let out to Lessees at a low Rent. (This is a secret)

Wednesday 28th. Sep

It is said that Horses have not sold well at Howden Shews this year.

Thursday 29th. Sep

John Baitson's Daughter of Broomfleet who was married about a year ago, was buried yesterday having died in Child-birth.

Friday 30th. Sep

I have seen an American Newspaper, called the Port Hope Telegraph, Feb. 15. 1831. The Publisher is one of Jn. Furby's Sons of Burlington, the Price of the Paper small Folio is 12s/6d a year ready money and 15s. Credit. The Place is in upper Canada, Newcastle District. Wheat was then 5s/4d pr. Bushel.

Saturday 1st. Oct

Measuring about 5 Acres of Beans in the Trancledales, it was very dirty having been much rain the night before, I had on a pair of new Shoes which I was glad to pull off as soon as I got home; My Great Toe nail which I expected

---

[38] Thomas Conder (See Appendix 2).

[39] See n.11 (1833).

would have come off in February last, has not yet lost its hold; it makes me not bear pinching on my Foot.

Sunday 2d. Oct

I have been this day reading Shrubsole's Christian Memoir on the Plan of the Pilgrims Progress,[40] I think it must be 30 years since I first read it, it is both amusing and instructive. It is well worth reading.

Monday 3d. Oct

A very thin attendance at the Market to day, it being Howden fair day.

Tuesday 4th. Oct

This Day making up the Highway Accounts, as the Book goes in tomorrow and new Surveyors will this night be nominated, a list of ten Names goes before the Magistrates out of which they choose or appoint two.

Wednesday 5th. Oct

Recd. last night a letter from Wm. giving an Account of his Travels to Liverpool, Dublin, Manchester &c: I enjoyed the Description of the Rail Road perhaps more than some who travel on it, are satisfied with its appearance in Reality. Sorry to hear that Wm. has again been ill with the Bowel Complaint. I think I have before said that this with me is a very common complaint, but seldom any sickness with it. I have in general with it a good Appetite.

Thursday 6th. Oct.

I am glad to see the Nos. of the Englishman's Magazine.[41] I had seen it advertised, but did not know that it was our Mr. Moxon[42] who was the Publisher. — These new Magazines at least what I see of them, are as much on the Plan of Quarterly Reviews, as they are of the Old Magazines; I know I used to be much entertained with some of the Old ones, when I could get an Odd No. but a Volume set me up. My Uncle used sometimes to lend us one, with a Charge to be careful of it as it was only lent to him.

Friday 7th. Oct

A Son of Laverack's at the Common last week stole a Pig and had it to Beverley Market last Saturday to sell, the Man from whom it was stolen went to Beverley and found the Pig which had been sold three times over in the Market. The Owner was to have the Pig; and Laverack paid the Money, the Lad has run away and it is said he had drowned himself in the Dock at Hull, I think it is not true.

---

[40] William Shrubsole, *Christian Memoirs; or, A Review of the Present State of Religion in England, in the Form of a New Pilgrimage to the Heavenly Kingdom of Jerusalem* ... Rochester: the author, 1776. – 3rd ed., with the life of the author [by his son, William Shrubsole, the younger]. London, 1807.

[41] *Englishman's Magazine*: vol. 1–2, no.2, Apr.–Oct. 1831. Published in London and edited by Edward Moxon.

[42] Edward Moxon (1801–58), verse writer and successful publisher, came to London from Wakefield in 1817 and joined the staff of Longman's publishers in 1821, the same year in which William Sharp entered their service. The 2 new employees would have had much in common as regards their situation, age, and county of birth. Edward, however, left Longman's in 1830 to set up as an independent publisher. He married Charles Lamb's adopted daughter, and was associated, both socially and professionally, with many important 19 c. writers, including Wordsworth. His first book of his own poems was published in 1826 (see Appendix 3), whilst still in the service of Longman's (*DNB*).

Saturday 8th, Oct

We have had another Thief in the Town, of the name of Langrick, who has stolen three Sheep Nets from Robt. Usher of Drewton and had them to Hull and sold them for 2s/8d. he the thief says Ned Coates told him where the Nets were and advised him to go and get them.

Sunday 9th. Oct

Here is part talk of Hull fair, a good deal of Geese have died to give fresh life to the Revellers, very fine weather.

Monday 10th. Oct

Recd. the Morning Chronicle[43] of Saturday last giving an Account that the Reform Bill was lost in the House of Lords, by a majority of 41. what the result will be we must wait to discover; I suppose our old friend the Freeman of Bristol & Beverley and formerly a Voter for Westminster will be pleased at the Result.

Tuesday 11th. Oct

Hull fair today, Hannah Martin who thought she would do a little good, bought some Geese and took them to Hull and I think will lose about 18d. a piece at them; She was very full of her exploit last week but that was before the unlucky Geese were offered for sale—I have often (said she) wanted our John to begin to Huckster, but he has nea Spirit for ought to dea ony good, but however I will try mysen, and a poor beginning she has had!!

Wednesday 12th. Oct

I have not had the times of Saturday last, I suppose the Morning Chronicle was in its Room, I sent it to my Brother when I had read it; the Rejection of the Bill by the Peers makes no stir at all here; I believe the objects of the Bill in the Country mostly to be mistaken, for they (the People) imagine that Reform was to abolish all duties and taxes, when it appears to me to be only the mode of choosing members.

Thursday 13th. Oct

This Evening with the Overseers collecting Poor Sess Ths Wride one of the Overseers had laid out about £20 and very fearful he was he should not get it again, however this night I managed to pay him so that he would sleep comfortably; there is only one drawback I gave him two Howden Notes of £5 each, and there is a Rumour of a Run on the Bank;[44] but I cannot trace it to any authentic source. — These vile dirty Rags I do not like; I shall not be at all surprised at a Run on the Banks, in the present state of the Country.

Friday 14th. Oct

I have not seen Ths. Wride since I gave him the Howden notes, and as I have heard no more of the Bank, I suppose the "Promise to pay" will yet be current as Sterling Gold!! nay we have Fools who prefer paper as being

---

[43] London daily morning newspaper published 28 June 1769 – 20 Dec. 1862. Proprietors: James Perry (1789–1821); William I. Clement (1822–34); John Easthope (1834–). It was edited from 1819 to 1843 by John Black.

[44] In 1831 the Howden bank of Schofield, Clarkson and Clough (founded 1809) was taken over by the newly established (1830) York City and County Banking Company (Hartley 155 and 163).

convenient, when it is well known they never had nor are likely to have so much Gold as to put them to the least inconvenience.

Saturday 15th. Octr.

Measuring land this Afternoon at Brantingham Wold, 52a–1r–30p. in the Morning and forenoon I was very unwell, with the Bowel Complaint and presages of Sickness, my throat was as full of corruption and as disagreeable as though I had eaten Rotten Eggs; in the afternoon I was much better, but could not smoke a Pipe.

Sunday 16th. Oct

I take the Rockingham down to the West end every Sunday morning to Ths. Levitt's, by which means I have an opportunity of reading it, — this morning it did not come so that I was disappointed; it often happens that Papers miss when there is anything particular ...

Tuesday 18th. Oct

I am sorry to find that the rejection of the Reform Bill has been the cause of Rioting in some places, a proceeding which is sure to be attended with evil, and from which no good can arise. I remember an Old Man who had spent much of his time in London, and who was there in the time of Wilkes' Riots,[45] saying he would go five Miles out of his way rather than come in contact with a Mob. I believe this a very wise resolution.

Wednesday 19th. Oct

John Akam's Property has been put up for Sale this day, at the Duke of York at Everthorpe; it was I believe all bought in, Purchasers for land are not so brisk as they were some years ago, in the glorious times of Paper money, when the Land holders were all life and fortune men; now the Chields[46] hold back, but they are not yet sufficiently down.

Thursday 20th. Oct

There is a Set of some kind of Men in London, called the Lumber Troop;[47] what are they? I think the appellation applied to them cannot be called "Honourable", a set of Lumber to be called Honourable; if not an absurdity, it is something like it.

---

[45] John Wilkes (1727–97), MP for Aylesbury, was a radical politician, whose turbulent career provided a focus for popular unrest, in the later 18th c., which united under the banner cry of 'Wilkes and Liberty!' In 1763 he received strong support when he was imprisoned for a violent attack on the King's Speech in his newspaper, the *North Briton*. After his release, he escaped to France, and remained in exile until 1768. On his return, he was elected MP for Middlesex, but was re-arrested and unable to take his seat, which led to an outbreak of rioting by his followers. The worst riot occurred on 10 May 1768, at the Massacre of St. George's Fields, when the mob stormed his prison and several of their number were killed or wounded by the soldiers who were guarding it (Stevenson 81–5).

[46] Fellows or chaps (*OED*).

[47] The Ancient and Honourable Lumber Troop, which seems to have been founded as a society in favour of political reform, drew its membership from prominent Whigs and radicals. At an anniversary celebration held on 17 July 1832, those in attendance included the Lord Mayor of London and the radical politician, Joseph Hume (*TM* 19 July 1832, 3 c).

Friday 21st. Oct

Heard from Wm. this morning that his Aunt Milcah is going to have her Breast cut for a Cancer, this is the very first time I have heard of her having the Complaint, but as I am only an Outside passenger I know very little of the privy Counsel.

Saturday 22d. Oct

Measuring Land this day on Wallingfen, I measured 3 Closes in Laxton Township which joins So. Cave, at the outside of the Common and one Close in So. Cave Lordship. It came on to Rain so fast I was obliged to leave one Close undone the best to measure of any of them, it being Grass about 18 Acres; I got wet through, and clogged up with Clay ...

Monday 24th. Oct

We had this Day a new fair or Cattle shew here, which is intended to be held annually as this day the 24th. James Ramsdale and John were here. My Sister has had her breast cut off and is doing very well. I hope she will get better, she suffers most by being obliged to lay so long in one position.

[At top of page]: Small Paper Edition, as I have no large.

Tuesday 25th. Oct

Measuring some land at Trancledales and the little Wold this Evening, it belongs to Mr. Popple 35a"3R"21P, it was dark when I got done.

Wednesday 26th. Oct

Howden Bank has shut up, it has not been opened this week, I am very fortunate in not having any of the Notes; several People I think will be sufferers.

Thursday 27th. Oct

I have this day planted some Cabbage Plants for the next year, they are very fine ones and if they stand the Winter well, we shall have a prospect of their being ready early.

Friday 28th. Oct

This is the Court day, it is the first that I have not attended since I came here, I recd. 10s/6d always before the last year, so I thought it was time to decline attending, I might have dined gratis I dare say, but nobody cares less for a good dinner than I do.

Saturday 29th Oct.

I was at Brantingham this afternoon, I went about one pound of Mr. Simpson the Parson for measuring, he has got as far as he can, and his goods are to be sold; I am afraid, I have sweat myself on the Hills for him for nothing.

Sunday 30th. Oct

The Parson at Church gave notice that he has recd. a letter to beg for the Bartlett's Building Society alias the Society for propagating the Gospel;[48] he

---

[48] The Society for the Propagation of the Gospel founded in 1701 did not become a distinctly missionary agency until 1821 when it began to be active in India, Japan and Africa. It is unclear why RS should have referred to it as a building society, although an ecclesiastical one had been established under the Additional Churches Act of 1818, in order to raise subscriptions to build new churches coincident with a government grant of one million pounds for the same purpose (Soloway 268–90). Bartlett may be

will preach to exhort his hearers next Sunday, to give liberally for the good of the—Church—I think I shall be out of my Duty if I give any thing; No not one Copper farthing from me for this Cause.

Monday 31st. Oct

Allison of Ellerker this evening accused Wm. Green of Brantingham with being in Company with the person who shot Allison's ox some time since; he (Allison) was <u>drunk</u> (this is English, no mincing in saying he was fresh or merry; <u>drunk</u> he was) he struck Green with his Stick[,] Green threw him down the Company interfered and got Allison out of the Room, so I dare say it is over.

Tuesday 1st. Nov

Another thing beginning with "a National" Political Union[49] no National's for me; what good will it do? has any National been any thing, but—Humbug!! I am sure I will never sanction any such a scheme.

Wednesday 2nd. Novr

I have a good mind to write Recollections of Barmston, or its Inhabitants 40 or 50 years ago. I know my remarks will be no manner of use to any one, they will be very brief (for Instance.) Francis Wilson the first farmer in the Village who rode in bright Stirrups, and polished bridle bits and was the cause of Rents being raised, there were two Sons and four daughters not one of whom I think is now living. This family was not very sociable with their neighbours.

Thursday 3d. Nov

Another Sketch. — Boynton's (town end) Farmers, good kind of Folks, very intimate with the Sons, I do not know whether one out of four be living or not. — If he (Frank) was rather backward at sowing or in the harvest, and any of his Neighbours offered to help him; he always dispensed with their help (as he always got done at some time) as he never helped them so he wished no help, and thought he was best served who served himself.

Friday 4th Nov

Last night was the Club meeting, there was but a thin attendance.

Saturday 5th. Nov

A very wet forenoon, Beverley fair day, it cleared up in the afternoon. Sketch 3d. Barmston. — Roger Pinder and Caty his wife, how I revere their names, with Peter their Son, who had a head for any invention, but hard work was his Aversion. I believe he now lives near Selby. Roger was a Capital Shooter, formerly he was Game keeper to Sir Griffith Boynton,[50] then for Fishing and Shrimping none could excel him. What Pleasant times have we had at their house, they are all no more.

Thomas Bartlett (1789–1864), rector of Kingstone, near Canterbury, from 1816 to 1852 and a noted evangelical writer (*DNB*).

[49] The National Political Union, or Grand Central National Political Union as it was known officially, was one of a multitude of similar organizations set up at this time to support the cause of political reform. Foremost among them, and serving as a model to many, was the Birmingham Political Union founded on 14 Dec. 1829.

[50] In the 18th c. 3 Sir Griffith Boyntons followed each other in succession at Burton Agnes near Bridlington: the 5th baronet (b. 1712, inherited 1739, d. 1761); the 6th baronet (b. 1743, inherited 1761, d. 1778); the 7th baronet (b. 1769, inherited as a minor aged 8 in 1778, d. 1801) (Imrie 62–88).

Sunday 6th. Nov

The begging Sermon put off until next Sunday, — Mr. Haydon of Swanland preached at the Chapel today. A wet uncomfortable day.

Monday 7th Nov

Now must I give separate Sketches, or as the Painters say group them? No another Sketch, which shall be our own loved dwelling; I even now long for it with regret. My Father was the last Cottager I believe who had a small Close about 3 Acres, which grew Wheat, Potatoes, Grass &c. This Close had a hedge on one side hung with Woodbine, or Honey-suckle, I just now fancy I see it; how often have my Brother and I wandered to it, hand in hand; one part of the Close was in the Spring, thick set with Cowslips—but those days are gone never more to return.

Tuesday 8th. Nov

Next to our House at Barmston, lived Saml. Sharp (no relation) he was the man who killed the Pigs of the Cottagers, for then every Cottager kept a Pig, Sam liked Ale too, and when the Pig was killed it was a time of rejoicing & a Boy or Girl was dispatched with a Pitcher to the Village Alehouse for the accustomed Beverage; then how happy were the owner of the Pig and Old Sam, over their Brown Ale.

Wednesday 9th. Nov

Old Isaiah Clifton commonly called I–a, and his wife Peggy who kept the Village Public house hearty as good nature could make them, their Sign was the Bull and Dog, they both died in a good old Age, Peace be with them.

Thursday 10th. Nov

I am busy collecting taxes that I cannot go on with my Recollections. Recd. Notice that nothing will be taken for taxes but Bank of England Notes and Gold!!! Smack go the Country Banks; and all their Promises will be no better than the promise of a Customer who buys goods and never intends paying.

Friday 11th. Nov

I have taken some Beverley Notes and if the Banks keep open till tomorrow I shall have the pleasure of getting his Majesty's Pictures in Solid Gold for the bits of dirty paper.

Saturday 12th. Nov

Paying in taxes today at Beverley, when I got there the Receivers were taking Beverley Notes, I told them I had been a Collector 24 years, but never knew any thing of this kind before, to send a Notice on Thursday as dated above and on the Saturday taking such money as before they had rejected, O they had made an arrangement with the Beverley Banks, I had two five Pounds of Raikes'[51] they would not take, I got them changed for others; Confusion attend every Bank there is in the Nation.

---

[51] Country banks continued to issue their own banknotes, but from 5 Apr. 1829, they had been legally obliged to withdraw all notes with denominations under 5 pounds. The bank of T. and R. Raikes and Co. of Hull was founded by Sir Christopher Sykes of Sledmere. It was taken over by Robert Broadley in 1801 in partnership with Robert Raikes. Known as the East Riding Bank, it had branches in Beverley and Malton until 1811, when they were taken over by Messrs. Bower and Duesbery. The Hull business

Sunday 13th. Nov

We had the Sermon or rather the reading over the Report of the Old Venerable Society, (who have Estates in the West Indies and keep Slaves themselves) to beg for money to propagate the Gospel and keep the Poor Negroes in bondage. Nothing from me.

Monday 14th. Nov

(Barmston) James Blakestone, and his Wife Old Mally, she was a Midwife (before Doctors were so much in Fashion) and fetched to the neighbouring Villages, and was very clever in her way, when she went out she dressed in a Green Joseph,[52] this was before Riding habits and Pelisses were christened.

> Jemmy shall tickle the Coal,
>
> And Jemmy shall skim the Bowl
>
> (Barmston Lyrics)

Old James used to keep Geese, and he had an old Gander, that was the terror of all the Children; once I recollect being afraid of him (the Old Steg) for he would not suffer any Children to walk on the house side—Old James saw him and took him by the neck and swung him off; and said to me thou sud handle him sea. — When the Old Blacksmith was on his Death Bed, he told some who were with him, not to screw him down in his Coffin when dead, as a few Sprigs would be cheaper which they could <u>drive in</u>.

Tuesday 15th. Nov

Tristram Holder, (I carry my recollections as far back as I can) had 2 or three little Closes about a Mile or perhaps more from his house, and his wife every time she went to Milk the Cow, took some Ashes or Manure of some kind in a Bag, which made the Land in fine condition; The Closes at their death were swallowed up in a Farm, and no longer occupied by the tenants of the Cottage. (more the Pity I say)

Wednesday 16th. Nov

Richd. Skinner after old I–a died kept the public house[.] When Dickey was a Boy, he went to School but could never learn any thing; a Man once said to him, Dick thou dost not know thy letters; yes says Dick, I know them very well by eye-sight thank God, but I do not know what they call them!!! He had three Sons, one of whom the youngest Frank, was as great a Dunce as his father, as he could never learn to read: I hired him as my Substitute for the Militia; after that he volunteered and went to the West Indies, and came home safe back again, — whether any of them be living now or not I cannot tell—My Uncle used to say that the Skinners had been a disgrace to Barmston School for fifty years.

---

gradually declined in its latter years and was finally forced to close in 1861 (Hartley 95–6; Pressnell 345).

[52] The joseph or green joseph was·a woman's green riding coat or surtout fashionable in the 1760s but already old-fashioned in the 1780s. A pelisse was a capacious outdoor cloak with 2 vertical slits for armholes (Cunnington, C. W. and P. 153, 339, 342–3).

Thursday 17th. Nov

Sittings this day, a very severe Frost and Snow the last night. I never knew the Winter so early, it is like the weather about Christmas or after; the Ice is a great thickness. — a Very thin attendance at the Sittings.

Friday 18th. Nov

(Barmston) Thomas Marshall, a Farmer very respectable, he had a Son, who after leaving Barmston, took a Farm near Pocklington I think at Grimthorpe, and died a few years ago; they had at Barmston an Image fixed up in the Farm Garth, the Figure of something like a Man, it had been the Figure head of a Ship—(and we I recollect had another Figure of a Woman in our Garth, just against the Orchard Gate; but now there is neither Figure nor Orchard, all being levelled)—Ths. Marshall lived at Burlington Quay after leaving Barmston: I believe he was blind before he died.

Saturday 19th. Nov

Mr. Samuel Ingmire, an old Custom house officer who lived at Barmston, to look after Smugglers but I never heard that he took any; indeed in my time there was little of the kind going on there; but formerly a good deal was done in this way; the <u>importers</u> wishing to give as little trouble as possible to the Custom house officers, — Mr. Ingmire's wife was called <u>Madam Ingmire</u>; they made some Shew of Gentility.

Sunday 20th. Nov

Extreme cold and frosty weather, I was twice at Church but there was nothing to keep me warm. No more this day.

Monday 21st. Nov

We have had Justice brought to our Door,[53] and a poor Creature she is. She came in a covered Cart shut in a Box, accompanied by an officer called a Chief Constable, an understrapper, and a rough Cartman—her Ladyship was brought out and set on the Counter, Scale in hand, our weights tried by her, and what were not heavier than herself she seized and took away with her (bad luck to Justice) One weight of 2 Drams she seized and took with her like a thief—but to be serious 5 of our weights were seized or stolen the heaviest a lb which was about a balance to that it was tried against, but if not heavier they were seized and taken away, all our Flour weights and some of the small ones, weighed more than Dame Justice could put in her Scale. However some > viz 5 as I said before < were Seized, and I was summoned to appear at Beverley, to hear what I was to pay for being innocent, several more were summoned to appear. I had a great mind to go, and give the Magistrates to understand, that I cared not what fine was levied on me as I was entirely innocent and had no guilty intention; but

---

[53] The Weights and Measures Act of 17 June 1824 (5 Geo. IV c. 74) attempted to standardize English weights and measures by the introduction of the Imperial system based on the Gallon and Troy Pound. It did not introduce any new penalties for infringement of the law or make alterations to the system of inspection then in force, but merely confirmed the existing legislation embodied in the Acts of 35 Geo. III c. 102 (1795) and 37 Geo. III c. 143 (1797) and 55 Geo. III c. 43 (1815). These Acts empowered examiners, appointed by the Justices, to enter shops and examine all weights and measures; if a shopkeeper were convicted at Petty Sessions of using a false or deficient measure, it would be seized, and the shopkeeper fined not less than 5s. or more than 20s. for each defective measure.

I was persuaded to write to Mr. Smelt who seized the weights, and desire him to act for me (this I did much against my own inclination, but it appears that it was for the best, for I was never called on). Several in the town went, and were fined some 10 and others 15s. each for deficient weights which they had bought for good ones. Some whose weights were seized were not summoned. Can this be Justice? No, let all be made alike. I must have the Act of Parliament relating to this business, and see to what the fines are applied, and what becomes of the stolen weights.

Tuesday 22nd Nov

(Barmston again) Mr. Dade[54] was the Rector, the living is worth a thousand a year at the least: He was a worthy man; he was an Author, and wrote the History of Holderness, but died before it was published, his Brother who was the Rector of Burton Agnes, has the Manuscript; but I believe it never was published. Mr. Dade was succeeded by Mr. Gilby a Clerical Magistrate, a morose and sour look he had; but he is gone, he was a Gormandizer, and eating Green Pease at the beginning of the Season, two or three years ago proved fatal to him: his Son is now the Vicar of St. Mary's at Beverley, and so well beloved, that at this very time, he has three Men to watch his House every night at half a Crown each, with plenty of Meat and Drink, perhaps he never did a better Action in his life.

Wednesday 23d Nov

This is Martinmas Day when the Servants here leave their places, and have a week to enjoy themselves and spend their Money; The Farmers at Barmston used to join their Servants the night before, and had Spiced Cakes and Ale, amongst them, whether they were hired again, or had got a fresh place, they parted in peace. I think the Custom is not kept up now; all good Customs are forgotten or not practised, which is much the same.

Thursday 24th. Novr

(Barmston) Henry Hammond a plain old Farmer commonly called "Awd Herry"; He had a daughter about my age; her Father bought some land at Frodingham; the Daughter was married to a Farmer >who went to live on it< with not too much wisdom, as the following will shew; He had been looking at his Stock, and saw some Calves which he did not know, so he took them to the Pinfold; when an enquiry was made for the Owner of the Calves, it was found they were his own which he had pounded. It is long since I heard of poor Grace but the last Accounts were they had a large Family, and were very ill off; the Children obliged to go out to Service.

Friday 25th. Nov

(Barmston) Gregory Milner lived at the Hall, his wife was the Daughter of Ths. Marshall; He gave up business and went to live at Burlington Quay—

[54] William Dade (*c.* 1740–90), F.S.A., was the Rector of Barmston from 1766 until his death 24 years later. He had intended to publish a history of Holderness and had accumulated an extensive collection of manuscripts and commissioned numerous original engravings for that purpose. His collection formed the basis of George Poulson's *The History and Antiquities of the Seigniory of Holderness* ... Hull: Robert Brown, 1840–41.– 4 vols. (Ross (1878), pp. 53–4).

where he and his wife both died, they had no family. The Hall is surrounded by a Moat, it is said that Sir Griffith (now Sir Francis) Boynton's Ancestors lived here before the Hall at Burton Agnes was built;[55] and in the list of Baronets, Boyntons are designated of Barmston; there was one Close near the Hall walled round a great part of it, — which was said to have been a Garden, and in which when I knew it were some old Fruit trees[.] This Hall like most others was said to be haunted, it stands near the Church.

Saturday 26th. Nov

I had some particulars respecting Barmston but cannot at present lay my hands on them; I have somewhere the names of every Close and the Quantity of land in each, and the whole Parish. — Barmston is called in writings Winton-cum-Barmston; there is now no place in the Parish called Winton; there is some Land called Quinton-Garths, which perhaps should be Winton Garths; however this is the place which I think was Winton, it appears that there have been buildings on part of the land it is situate at Stonehills; I think it may be two Miles from the Town, there are or were 2 Farms at Stonehills, but very like they are swallowed up in one; there lived at one of them an Aristocratical Farmer whom I will neither name nor notice ...

Monday 28th. Nov

I was at Riplingham this forenoon swearing to the delivery of Surcharges, before a Magistrate; this is Martinmas Monday, a great hurry in the Town of Servants—On Saturday last I was at Drewton measuring some Turnip Land for Edwd. Usher, very dirty it was.

Tuesday 29th. Nov

Ed. Usher lost himself lately when going from Market and got into his Landlord's Garden, and cried out lost; and offered 5s. for any one to shew him way home, he did not know where he was, I suppose he had got more in his head than he could carry straight home, his Landlord called a servant to go with him, and charged him to get the five Shillings.

Wednesday 30th. Nov

Rel[ieve]d. several Soldiers wives & Children under a War office pass[56] from Liverpool to Hull, the money paid to them to be recd., again of the Collector of Excise.

---

[55] The Boyntons inherited the manor of Burton Agnes through the female line from the Griffiths in 1654. Until then the family seat had been at Barmston. The Boyntons were an old-established East Riding gentry family with extensive landholdings (Imrie 44).

[56] In accordance with the provisions of 'An Act ... for Enabling Wives and Families of Soldiers to Return to their Homes' of 10 June 1818 (58 Geo. III c. 92), overseers of the poor were instructed to relieve the wives and families of soldiers who were returning to their own homes, either because their menfolk had died in service or had been posted abroad. The returning women were supplied with passes by their husbands' commanding officers for presentation to the overseers, who gave them sufficient money to stay overnight if necessary and an allowance per mile (up to a distance of 18 miles) according to the rate specified on the pass to enable them to travel to the next village or town on the journey home. The overseers were reimbursed by the local excise collector.

Thursday 1st. Decr

This is the Club night, a very thin attendance, got done before nine o'clock, the night very dark and damp it has been a great deal of wet lately.

Friday 2nd. Decr

Mrs. Newlove (of the Black Bear) died this morning about three O'clock she has been ill some time not much of a neighbour to us, so that we shall feel no loss of her.

Saturday 3d. Decr

I recollect the beginning of a Tory effusion in the time of the French Revolution it commenced with

> "Go sow your Corn go plow your land;
> "And by King George's Interest stand;
> "Cast prejudice away;
> "To abler heads leave state affairs,
> "Give railing o'er and say your prayrs,
> "For store of Corn & Hay.

It concluded with (I think)

> All hail to liberty Reform & Riot;
> Adieu to Peace Content and quiet."

Sunday 4th. Decr

Mrs. Newlove was buried this day at Rowley, my wife was not invited, but they had the assurance to come to borrow some Towels, and she was so weak as to lend them; had I been at home they would have been denied, or refused.

Monday 5th. Decr

This and two or three of the following days, the Effects of Barnard Clarkson late of the Howden bank are to be sold by Auction: I have not heard what sort of a dividend there will be amongst the Gulls; who prefer or preferred empty promises to Solid Gold.

Tuesday 6th. Decr

Old Willy has been favoured with the Loan of a Book by me of Anecdotes which he calls Antidotes—they are very much in his way of reading, but not so low as many he is master of; a standing question with him is: Do you know where the first Candle was lighted? perhaps the answer is how should I know—O—but I know—Aye do you? — Yes it was lighted at the end first, you could not think any person so foolish as to light a candle first in the middle!! the reply I once heard ["]you old fool I know that".

Wednesday 7th. Decr

When I finished my Recollections of Barmston, I did not express that it was complete; Some there were that I will not give the honour of appearing in my Foolscap. Some upstarts that I can neither forget nor yet remember; — I said nothing of South Field where my Father for more than forty years, spent the greatest part of his time with his Flock; he was no Arcadian Shepherd; but up late and early attending to the wants of his charges; there are no such Shepherds in this Country as we find painted or described in the Poets; their Pastorals are what poor Shepherds never experience.

Thursday 8th. Dec

There is a Sale today at the Revd. Mr. Simpson's[57] at Brantingham; the Parson is now in the King's Bench. Saml. Ringrose was one who gave Bail for his appearance; but the Parson got out of the way, and was found somewhere in Lincolnshire; and Sammy set off with him to London, and delivered him up safe; a <u>nasty beast</u> Sammy says; He (Sammy) was badly before; and his Journey has not done him good.

Friday 9th. Decr

No Paper this morning; it is a good while since one missed before, and soon enough now.

Saturday 10th. Decr

This morning there were two papers which made up for the one that missed yesterday. There was an account of the trial and execution of the two Burkers,[58] those hardened villains whose trade is blood and Death. I think the Surgeons are far from being guiltless. I hope they would cut up these wretches with pleasure ...

Monday 12th. Decr.

There lived at Barmston a farmer whom I have omitted (at Hamilton Hill or the Odd house) his name was John Boynton, and his Mother lived with him; they had a bible with the Apocrypha, where I first read the History of Bel and the Dragon.[59] Their Door was never opened to any Person on the morning of Christmas Day or new Year until my Father had called which he made a point of not missing, in his way round to see his Flock. — This Poor Man died of the Small Pox.

Tuesday 13th. Decr

(Barmston) When I mentioned South Field, I said nothing of the number of Tufits, (Grey Plovers)[60] which frequented the place called South field bottom; how often have I caught the young ones and carried them home, they are exceeding sprightly looking birds, — My Mother has frequently carried them

[57] i.e. Revd James Simpson (Baines ii. 170).

[58] This was the trial of John Bishop, Thomas Head alias Williams, and James May, which resulted in the execution of the 2 first named on 5 Dec. 1831. Bishop and Williams confessed to the murder of 3 persons but were tried and convicted specifically for the murder of a 14-year old Italian boy. The pair lured their victims by the offer of hospitality and plied them with rum and laudanum until they were unconscious, when they were hung by their heels upside down in a well, and so drowned. The bodies were sold to surgeons for dissection (see also n.9 (1829): Burke and Hare). In the course of the trial, Bishop admitted to having been in the 'resurrection' trade for 12 years before resorting to murder and claimed to have disinterred between 500 and 1000 corpses, which he had sold to London anatomy schools (*AR* 1831 Chron. 316–35).

[59] The story of Bel and the Dragon constitutes the 12th book of the Apocrypha. It relates how Daniel first outwits the priests of Bel (or Baal) and proves to King Cyrus of Persia that the god is only a lifeless idol, which he is allowed to destroy. He then goes on to demonstrate the mortality of yet another of their deities, a large snake, which expires shortly after consuming a noxious concoction of pitch, hair and fat prepared for it by the resourceful Daniel.

[60] i.e. Lapwings (*Vanellus vanellus*), not Grey Plovers (*Pluvialis squatarola*), which do not breed in Britain.

back to their breeding place for fear they should be destroyed, (was not this trait worth recording? Yes there was pure feeling here.)

Wednesday 14th. Decr.

We have had Mr. Oxtoby today and paid his account 17 pounds, ordered another load of Goods which are to come on Friday next, — I think he deals in everything, we used to get our brushes at Hull, not thinking he sold Brushes, but when we enquired today whether he sold them or not, — "O yes the best Sheffield Brushes", — however, we ordered none; we wanted some Sand Paper, and he had so many different kinds that one would almost suspect it was his particular calling.

Thursday 15th. Decr.

I must say a little of the Clippings (Sheep-Shearings) which used to take place at Barmston—The Clippers all Sweating at work, while peaceful Jokes went round, About 11 O'clock in the forenoon hot Cheesecakes with Butter, were brought into the Barn along with Ale, for the Clippers—When the Sheep were stripped of their Coats what bleating with the Ewes—and the Lambs seeking about for their Mothers, (sweet Music!! I love now to hear it) When the work was done a good Dinner was served up in the house, and every face beamed with Joy; then Rustic singing took place (or was performed) which if not very musical, was vastly entertaining. — My Father was the best Clipper of Sheep in the Country; he could Clip a Sheep better and sooner than any Man he ever wrought with.

Friday 16th. Decr

Newlove wants to let his house, there is a Man they say about taking it; I think there is a poor prospect of making a living at it; as the idle Fellow who had no rent to pay, has continued to let his Brewer have a Mortgage of it for I hear £200. So how must others live who have Rent to pay?

Why they must exert themselves, and not loll so much against the sign Post.

Saturday 17th. Decr

I had a Gentleman from Cottingham this forenoon, to enquire who paid some Money to a Man of the name of Carr, who was employed to do the Parish business of Cottingham, he Carr it appears has proved a Rogue and cheated the Parish to the amount of nearly a thousand pounds; the Money the Gentleman was enquiring after was paid in March 1822 I believe by Rd. Marshall, there has been a Bill of indictment found against Carr, and he is to be tried either at the Sessions or Assizes; he is now out of the way, but they know where he is[.] The Gentleman said it was probable that I, and Rd. Marshall would be Subpened to appear, at the trial. I have no desire for it but rather the contrary.

Sunday 18th. Decr

A very fine day, we had employed Hannah Martin to get a Goose for us, which was to be such a Goose as is seldom seen; but we were deceived in receiving it; we are to have one of Rd. Marshall's which I have bespoke this morning.

Monday 19th Decr

Packing up the Hamper for Wm. two O'clock we have not yet got the Goose, but shall have it this evening, we have got three Fowls which I expect will be very fine, we shall get a Pig in about a fortnight's time, and then we must send some Spare Rib &c Heard from Wm. this morning, little Mary says she will come to see her Grandmother, but as that cannot be done her Grandmother will not forget her, she will send her some Raisins and a piece of Cheese; of the very best she has.

I am going to Copy over some of my former Work, it appears to have been in the Condition or Situation of the Works of some unfortunate Authors, whose writings find their way into Cheesemongers' Shops, and greasy they come out again for Butter has an Antipathy to Literature.

Tuesday 20th. Decr

I believe I wrote down in my last Sheet yesterday, so this is the continuation, or as the Publishers say a New Series; I shall not like them make large promises of future improvement; but I think I can say the work will be carried on with the same application as before; and I shall be satisfied if my Reader can be pleased with it.

Wednesday 21st. Decr

This is the shortest day—but not much shorter than yesterday; we have been saying, I wonder how far the Basket is on its way to London; the answer to the wonder, for these "I wonder" are sort of questions which require astonishing answers; these answers generally fall to my lot; and I get very well through with them.

Thursday 22d. Decr

I have not I think mentioned my Uncle, in my Recollections of Barmston. But let me not forget him. No never so long as Memory holds her seat. He spent his time at Barmston from the time that I, and my Brother were fit to go to School; until the time we both left, when he went to either Skipsea or Ulram. He never went into Company: I never knew him go to a Market Town. Whatever I know, the foundation of all was laid by him: He was the last male of the Family, and of the same name: Robert Harrison, which Robt. Harrisons have succeeded each other, from Father to Son, since the time of the Commonwealth & perhaps before. The following is the Account of the time when he died.

"My Uncle Robert Harrison died 2nd. August 1812 aged 75 years.

I walked from So. Cave to Barmston on the 4th. August to his funeral, but his Grave was about half filled up, when I got into the Church Yard; he was buried at the Steeple end in Barmston Church Yard:

R SHARP

Friday 23d. Decr

All the old women and young ones too, with their Children are running about <u>Gooding</u>.[61] Mrs. Baron of Drewton[62] gives the Women 2d. and Children 1d. each. I dare say she does not want Customers; many who go would rather spend half a day for twopence, as work at home for threepence.

Saturday 24th. Dec

We have had some Furmity as usual on Christmas eve, aye and we have had a Youle Clog, burnt in the best manner.

Sunday 25th. Dec

This is Christmas day, all the young Gangrills in the Town, running and shouting a merry Christmas; but they are not contented with all the noise they make, except they be paid for it, how they get supplied, I cannot tell, as Money is a scarce Article now a days.

Monday 26 Decr

Very fine moderate weather; it is a Green Christmas, which the Old Proverb says makes a fat Church Yard. Very little doing at the Market today.

Tuesday 27. Decr

(Barmston) John Holder was a Wright and Spinning Wheel maker, (when the Women were industrious, and every Family had at least one Web of Cloth spun in the Winter) John's wife Old Betty was the greatest Snuff taker in the Town, and at times scarcely knew how to obtain it. — He went to live at Burlington to carry on this business of Wheel making but this branch of domestic Industry failing he died in want. In their Parlour at Barmston they had the Shell of an Ostrich Egg hung up, this was something extraordinary, I never saw but it.

Wednesday 28th. Decr

(Barmston) Ralph Day was a Labourer and had a wife too idle to dress the Meal which came from the Mill; My Mother used to buy Bran of any who had it to sell, and Mall Day brought more Bran out of a Bushel of Wheat than any one else. My Mother used to dress it over again, and used to get as much Flour as would make a small bread Loaf.

Thursday 29th. Decr

This morning we had a letter franked from Wm. pleased to hear that little Mary was so delighted with the Basket, happy as a Merchant with the safe arrival of one of his rich Vessels from the further Ind.

Friday 30th. Decr

This day I was at West Ella; when I went in I found my Mother in Bed reading in the Prayer Book, she can see to read without Spectacles (I ought to say Glasses) formerly they were called Barnacles (as may be seen in the

---

[61] 'Going a goodin' meant going around to farms and other houses at Christmas time, begging for money or eatables. It was called 'good-tahming' in some parts of the East Riding (Ross (1877): 69).

[62] Sarah Baron of Manor House, Drewton, was the mother of George Baron, the antiquary, who later identified a Roman coin for RS. See the entry for 20 Aug. 1833 (Allen 92–3).

Fortunes of Nigel)[63] viz in the Reign of the first James—My Mother would fain be thought older than she is, she is in her 87th. year with her Memory very good. My Sister is greatly recovered, and looks as well as usual.

Saturday 31st. Dec

The Overseers would go with me this day to collect, I think by way of amusement, as they neither of them wanted any thing: however our success was not very good, but quite sufficient for me.

[63] Sir Walter Scott, *The Fortunes of Nigel.* By the Author of 'Waverley' ... Edinburgh: A. Constable and Co., 1822. – 3 vols.—2nd ed., Edinburgh and London, 1822. – 3 vols. Also published in his: *Novels and Romances* ... Edinburgh: A. Constable and Co., 1824. – 7 vols.

1832

Sunday 1st Jany

This is the entrance of another year, what it may bring forth, but few will even guess, (except Francis Moore Physician: who knows the taste of his Readers:) of what will be seen and done: I have seen one of his Almanacks for 1832. but like the Heathen Oracles, it may admit of more than one interpretation.

Monday 2d. Jany

Almost every day there are parties or sets of Plough Boys, going about with their trumpery Music, and Rattling Drums, and what they get given they spend for the good of the Publicans and for their own ill—there wants a Reform here.

Tuesday 3d. Jan

Castle building is an employment in which I sometimes indulge; many a fair fabric have I raised without the least foundation. I have paraded in my fanciful building from one room to another, and seen in prospect various things, as if present; namely how I would live had I the means of such and such persons; when I have been sat down in the Library of my Airy Castles I have considered how I could do the most good to the deserving, who lived near my Castle Walls; but I need say no more to those who know any thing of this sublime Science. Call this employment, Contemplation, or Meditation, then you pass for a wise man; but Airy Speculations will mark you as a fool.

Wednesday 4th. Jany

Mr. Oxtoby has been here today, we have paid him £30 and ordered another Freight, which is to come on Friday next, so we go on as well as we know how, we always keep up our Credit, and contrive to have the money ready against the time. Bought a Pig this day of Ths. Grasby, it weighs 15 Stone at 6s. pr. Stone.

Thursday 5th. Jany

Recd. yesterday the Pills and a letter from Wm. all safe, — Wm. asks if Frank Wilson's riding in Polished Stirrups was the cause of the Farms being raised at Barmston? I have no doubt of it as the Rents were certainly raised at the time, and this was stated as the cause. The farmers are no wiser yet, for some of them have Pianos for their daughters. Do not their Landlords mark this? yes, and certainly they deserve punishing for their folly. — After all the cries that the Landlords will be ruined, I think they are yet in a prosperous way; their Rents they will not lower, and what they consume, is much lower, than when they let their land at War Rents.

Friday 6th Jan

Carr of Cottingham who was tried at the Sessions at Beverley on Tuesday or Wednesday last, has been cleared of the charge against him, for defrauding the Parish: the Magistrates after the trial was begun would not suffer it to proceed: it appears that the trial was got up more from private Malice than the public good. However the Man's Character is gone: but as it is so many years since the transaction took place he was favoured.

Saturday 7th. Jany

(Barmston) There was an old Woman, who when we were Children, used to go about with a Vessel Cup and sing a Christmas Carol. I had quite forgot her name, until my Mother when I saw her last week and was talking of bygone times, was mentioning this old Woman's name and her employment at this time of the year. Her name was Mary Newsom the conclusion of her song was,

> God bless the Master of this house,
> The Mistress also;
> And all the pretty Children,
> That round the table grow, *

I cannot say much for the Poetry, but it has one merit at least; the meaning was well known for at the Conclusion the Singer was rewarded, and her Vessel Cup shrouded under her old scanty Cloak, and she departed with many thanks, to cheer others with her song.

[Written along margin:]   * And all your Kin & Kindred born far and near
                                 So I wish you a merry Christmas & happy new
                                                year

Sunday 8th. Jan

I think I have little to remark this day, only that it is very dirty. Hannah Levitt calls one of her Children Norrison Marshall, and the other Marshall Norrison.

Monday 9th. Jan

We have got a Hare given which we shall send to Wm. it was a present from Mr. Nicholson who lives at Frog Hall. — I did see a live Hare on Saturday last: they are very scarce; it is long since I saw one before, I was measuring some Land at Ellerker Stone Pitts.

Tuesday 10th. Jany

There were formerly more Farm Houses here than there are at present, where Rd. Goldwell lived was one, and an old House Barn & Stables, which Giles Bridgman has was another, where Ths. Wride lives was a Farm house where Ths. & Rd. Marshall lived. The house where John Grasby lived was a farm house, and there was one near St. Helen's well; another where Joseph Purdon lived; the House at or near the Pinfold was another and at the west end where John Crathorne lived was a Farm house; (Mr. Barnard's Castle farm house has been built in lieu of the St. Helen's farm stead.) besides numerous Cottages with their Garths which are now swallowed up in farms.

Wednesday 11th. Jany

Richd. Marshall has three farms one where Fenlay Robinson lived, and Joseph Purdon's and the Castle farm. Robt. Marshall has two Farms viz one where his father lived, and the Common farm where Rd. Kirby lived, then the Farm at the west end where Jn. Crathorne lived is divided amongst Ths. Marshall, Rd. & Robt.* so that Rd. has 3 Farms and one third of another, Robt. has 2 and one third and Ths. has one & one third of another in all 7 amongst them.

[In margin:] * I think Robt has none of this farm.

Thursday 12th. Jan

Frans. Wood has had some Sheep worried at Riplingham by a Dog strongly suspected to be Cousens' but as there is not positive proof; they >Cousens'< will not suffer the Dog to be destroyed neither will they pay for the Sheep, 2 Ewes worried dead with 2 Lambs each in them, and 2 more bitten so ill they were obliged to kill them, besides some others not so bad.

Friday 13th. Jan

I think much benefit would be found; by letting the Labourers have some land at the same Rent as the Farmers give for their Land, from half an Acre, to not exceed an Acre, but perhaps ½ an Acre would be sufficient, to make them better Labourers and less Expence to the Parish, 1/8 of An Acre planted with Potatoes which is 605 Sq. Yards, would produce well managed and tolerable land 150 Pecks. — 1/8 for Fruit trees & Vegetables a very pretty piece near 25 Yds. long and as many broad will grow sufficient for a family, and have something to spare for a Pig: — a Pig he must have, and he will have 100 Pecks of Potatoes which will go a great way towards feeding it (notwithstanding what Cobbett says of the worthlessness of Potatoes) Now I have only allotted half of my Land, if the other 1/4 of An Acre could be managed to have Wheat I should not fear having a Quarter of Wheat on it, — this would be something at Martinmas time, a Fat Pig and a Quarter of Wheat!! for the rent at most of a Pound, we must not give higher Rents than Common, as we want the land for use not for Convenience altogether. I could like to be employed to lay out about 20 Acres, which I would willingly undertake to do gratis—This is a little in the Castle building line ...

Sunday 15th. Jan

One of Hannah Levitt's Children is dead, and the intolerant Priest will not bury it because it was baptised by a Dissenting minister; it is a decided case that Church Parsons are compelled to bury all Persons that have been baptised no matter by whom; I advis'd them to make a complaint to the Vicar, and if he would not attend to it, to lay the case before the Archbishop, whether they will or not I cannot say.

Monday 16th Jan

Heard from Wm. that the Box had arrived and all the Contents spoiled; where the Fools had set the Box to melt the Butter I can't tell, we are grieved at the mischance it is entirely waste instead of doing good it is nothing worth, I wish it had gone by the Coach.

17th. Jan Tuesday

I have found the Particulars of the Land in the Parish of Barmston. I think the particulars are dated 1739 there Quinton Garths are called as I before noticed Winton Garths containing 18a–3r–36p there is likewise Winton Moor 61a–0r–0p. South field contained 133a–2r–15p. I will in a little time put down the Estate of Sir Griffith Boynton about the year 1725 or 1726 to 1739.

Wednesday 18th. Jan

The following is the Quantity of Land which I said I would make out belonging Sir Griffith Boynton—No greater man than he was ever thought about at Barmston.

	A	R	P		A	R	P
Burton Agnes	1549	2	18}				
Do. Garths	41	3	1}		A	R	P
Small piece		1	20}		2261	1	3
Burton Moor	669	2	4}				
Barmston	2284	3	36}				
Do. Garths	36	0	27}		2321	0	23
Rousby	1076	2	25				
Haisthorp	1096	2	0				
Thurnholm	26	2	3				
Boynton	238	3	8				
Rudston	689	2	35				
Swanland	684	0	14				
Hassel tenants	69	3	35		(Hessle)		
Ferriby	134	2	27				
Melton	200	2	6				
Woldby	91	0	2		(Waudby)		
Riplingham	212	0	21				
	A9103	0	2				

A very pretty Estate; Rousby has been long sold neither have the Family any Land at Swanland Hessle, Ferriby, Melton, Waudby or Riplingham and I think none at Boynton.

Thursday 19th. Jany

I am very sorry to hear of the miserable end of Col. Brereton,[1] he was not made of Stuff stern enough for his situation, I heard on Monday night he had shot himself, from what I have read of the Evidence on his trial (& I have read the whole of it in the Times) I have not the least doubt he would have been found guilty; he had too much compassion for the misguided mob, to give orders to fire on them.

Friday 20th. Jany

Wm. Milner and Sadler Tommy had been at North Cave and both got <u>drunk</u> (English) however they got home and the little Sadler helped Willy to pull some hay out of his Stack for the Horse; when Willy's Dog bit Tommy's

---

[1] Colonel Thomas Brereton (1782–1832) shot himself on 13 Jan. 1832 pending his trial before a court martial on a charge of neglecting his duty as commanding officer of the military during the Bristol riots in Oct. 1831 (*AR* 1832, Chron. 14–15; *DNB*).

hand, so Willy to comfort him gave him a Glass of Brandy, which so elevated him, that Willy was glad to get him out of the House; when Tommy was at the right side for running away, he disdained such a thought, but stripped and challenged Willy's dog to fight for a Sovereign; as the Dog he said was a Coward and had bitten him without any notice, but he would fight him fairly if the Coward would come out; However Willy was wiser than to let out his Bull Dog, and the little Sadler vapoured about as long as he thought proper, then retreated with honour.

Saturday 21st. Jan

Barmston. I now give the Names of the Tenants, with the Quantity of Land they farmed in 1739.

	A	R	P	
James Taylor	330	1	25	
M. Dumbleton	124	3	36	
T. Hudson	115	1	39	
C. Maimpus	87	0	18	
Robt. Jordan	98	3	33	
Wm. Frost	108	2	4	
Geo. Wharton	124	2	20	
Jno Hickson	46	0	29	
Wm. Boulton	36	1	24	
Jno. Brown	3	3	4	
Wm. Milner	34	1	28	
Henry Clark	12	3	9	
Mary Grainge	19	3	3	
Benj. Rattle	14	3	16	
Jno. Anthony	6	3	28	
Jno. Milner	9	3	13	
Ja. Kemplin	8	3	0	
Ed. Fox	16	1	24	
Wm. Wharram	13	0	6	
*Eliza Hutton	3	1	5	my Father had this Close for more than 40 years *mark this
Wm. Dook	25	2	17	
Wid. Farding	8	3	23	
Wm. Sharp	58	0	1	no Relative of ours
Ja. Robinson	64	3	36	
M. Boreman	130	0	0	
	1504	0	1	

Farmed jointly	453	1	20	
North Field	194	0	0	since inclosed
South Field	133	2	15	
	2284	3	36	

Saturday 21st. Jany

The Names of the Closes, together with the tenants names, of what they occupied jointly

	A	R	P
Horse Carr			
Maimpus, Boulton, Brown & Topcliffe	26	1	16
Great New Close			
Brown, Gration & Hudson	63	3	14
Rift Closes			
Speck & Clark	49	3	6
Bartingdale Close			
Brown & Speck	12	1	24
Little Stone Hills			
Hickson, Boulton & Farding	47	1	14
Water Mill Grounds			
Dumbleton, Hudson & Jordan	91	0	0
Winton Moor			
Taylor, Hudson, Maimpus, Jordan & Speck	61	0	0
North Warren Close			
Taylor & Frost	42	2	20
Beck Ground			
Taylor & Frost	59	0	6
	A.453	1	20

Ja. Taylor who farmed so much, lived I think at Barmston Hall, there is not one name in the list but perhaps Dumbleton left in the place now. I recollect the names of Dumbleton & Speck, on some Grave Stones in the Church yard.

Sunday 22d. Jany

A Fine moderate day, so was yesterday when I was measuring a Close of Turnips for Ths. Robinson at Ellerker near the Ring Beck, it was very dirty but the weather as mild in comparison as Summer—as I have put down the names of the tenants and the quantity of Land they farmed at Barmston some 90 years ago or more, I may perhaps do the same at the present time of the Occupiers of So. Cave, as no one knows it better than myself, as I know all the Closes in the Parish, and what they contain.

Monday 23d. Jany

Heard from Wm. this morning that the Clock will be here on Tuesday next (tomorrow) we are all anxiety for the sight of it.

I will begin at Weedley the extent or Eastward boundary of So. Cave.

	A	R	P	Tenants
Weedley Arable & Grassland	336	0	0	
Weedley Warren	284	0	0	
Owner Jn. Broadley Wilson	A620	0	0	Robt. Tindale

Esqr. I think he resides at Henley
on Thames. He is a religious Character I think a Baptist

The next will be Mount Airy

	A	R	P	
Sweety Hill	10	0	0	
Sweety Hill. West	15	–	–	
Woodale	16	–	–	
Cliffs	32	–	–	
Remr. of Mount Airy	171	–	–	
Beverley Plump	2	–	–	Tenant
Owner H.G. Barnard Esqr.	246	0	0	Ths. Robinson

I think it will be best to take the Farmers in alphabetical order, now to proceed

	A	R	P	
Little Wold	9	2	28	
Ryland Hills 5 Closes (top)	25	3	30	
Ryland Hills. bottom	10	–	–	
Sands	5	3	26	
Tofts (Tillage)	3	–	–	
Tofts Swarth	2	–	–	
Wallingfen late Kirkman	3	3	10	
Jarratt Hills	8	1	30	Tenant Henry Arton
Owner Mr. John Collinson	68	3	4	

Tuesday 24th. Jany

	A	R	P	
Stray	1	1	10	
Porter hole Close late Cade	3	2	–	
Common	3	2	33	Tenants
				Robt. Dunn
				G. Bridgman
				& B. Cook

As I find I shall put myself to a good deal of unnecessary trouble, in making the Changes, which have taken place since 1828, I will for the future, Copy the Valuations I have made, if I proceed any further with the Quantity of Land in So. Cave. To me it is all known; to Wm. he may like to see the names of some of the Closes; as I liked to see those at Barmston.

Wednesday 25th. Jany

Last night arrived the Box containing the Clock, it is a beautiful Colour, the very thing itself; it pleases uncommonly, there is nothing against it except it be too fine, this is not often found to be a fault. Mary's Grandmother almost saw her riding on the Chair to see her. Eliza's little Girl is very apt at climbing Chairs and Tables, but what amuses her the most is blowing out the Candle and lighting it again, when she sees a Candle she begins saying Canla, Canla. glad to hear that little Wm. has got so many of his teeth.

Thursday 26th. Jany

Richd. Marshall is (or was) much taken with Hannah Levitt's Children; when both living: no affection is wanting for the one which is left. He is very much exasperated at the petty priest for refusing to bury the innocent babe. I persuade him all I can to proceed against this intolerant fellow, but I am afraid the love of his Money is above the love of Justice. I wonder how the fellow had the Hypocrisy to say he durst not bury it, or he would have done it, but his duty would not allow it. And this in the face of a decided Case "Kemp ver. Wickes.["] Sir John Nichols as well as the Rubric say the Ministers of the Church are not to refuse Burial or reading the Ceremony over any Persons that have been baptised; no matter by whom only they have been baptised in the name of the Father and of the Son & of the Holy Ghost. After the Legislator have admitted all to equal Civil Rights, such Puny persecutors as this still hanker after Exclusion, confound their Malice.

Friday 27th Jany

It is said that Mr. Barnard has let the Castle here to Lord Stourton, he is a Roman Catholic either he or his Brother lives at Houghton near Sancton. His Father lives at Holme. I think the family name is Langdale. I am wrong there. Mr. Danl. Sykes died on Tuesday morning last, I am sorry for his death, he was a kind Man and very useful Magistrate, & will be greatly lamented.

Saturday 28th. Jany
South Cave again.

	A	R	P	
Stone Pitt.	7	2	30	opposite
Beverley plump				
Weighton Poor land	28	0	0	belongs Mkt. Weighton poor
Glebe or Great Wold	25	0	34	I think this should be A35
Medd Garth	2	–	–	
Little Wold	15	3	2	
Remr. of Castle farm	122	1	14	I think there is too much here
Owner H G Barnard Esqr.	201	0	0	Robt. Arton was the tenant in 1828. it is now occupied by Rd. Marshall

Sunday 29th. Jany

	A	R	P	
Common	12	2	0	Jebson owner
Sands	6	0	16	Akam own.
Common	20	1	36	Do.
Little Wold	5	–	–	Do.
Blakehows	8	1	24	late Wm. Stather's
Shepherd well Close	1	–	–	Akam's own.
	53	1	36	

I think the above will be as plain and intelligent as I can make it.

Monday 30th. Jany

In one of the Spectators (newspapers) which Wm. sent; in looking over the List of Lords, I see that one of the Ancestors of Lord Stourton >Charles the 7th. Lord, in 1557< was hanged for Murder at Salisbury, but on account of his being a Lord, he was favoured with a Silken Halter to swing in. Old Willy tells of two Gentlemen who were crossing a Field where a Man was sowing; & said to him, Aye you sow but we shall reap the benifit [*sic*] of your labour, the Sower said aye varry likely; "I'se sowing Hemp".

Tuesday 31st. Jany

In coming out of Cousens's last night, there was a Cart loosed out, I stumbled over the Shafts, and cut my thumb, hurt my knee, and raised a bump on one of my Eye-brows; but this morning I felt no worse, only rather stiff.

Wednesday 1st. Feb.

South Cave again

	A	R	P	
Stray	1	0	28	Ab. Barff owner
Sancton Lands	13	1	32	Vicarage
Vicarage Garth	3	2	–	Do.
Ings Vicarage	9	2	12	Do.
Garth	2	–	–	Ab. Barff owner
	29	2	32	Ab. Barff occupier ...

Friday 3rd Feby

So. Cave

	a	R	P
Wold Close	13	1	18
Ruffham field	27	2	35
Ings & Sands	14	0	28
New Field	13	1	24
Common	11	0	8
Audas Ings	4	2	10
Garth & Orchard	2	–	–
	a86	1	3

The above was Wilkinson Ayre's, but now all sold, together with the House where old Sam his father lived ...

Sunday 5th. Feb

Yesterday I was measuring some Turnip land for Mr. Atmar at Brantingham, one Close on the Wold and another adjoining the Brough Turnpike; it was very clean on the Land the Turnips eaten off and the Land not ploughed; it was a pleasant day; and I thought I could discern some appearance of the approach of Spring, several small Turnips which had been left in the furroughs (I believe the word should be furrows) were putting out Green Sprouts; some Nettles I observed shewing fresh leaves; they are generally forward as most in welcoming the Spring.

Monday 6th. Feby

So. Cave.

	A	R	P	
Porter Hole Close	2	0	14	G. Bridgman's own

Tofts	2	2	0	H G Barnard owner
Sand hill Close	9	3	13	Do.
Ellerker lane land & Grass Close	80	1	36	Do.
Stone Pitts	3	–	–	Do.
Common land Closes	11	1	33	G. Bridgman as own.
New field or Sheep Dike Closes	2	1	34	Do.
	111	3	10	G. Bridgman tenant of the above belonging H.G. Barnard Esqr.

Tuesday 7th. Feby

How the Court Martial at Bristol (on Capt. Warrington)[2] will terminate is not for me to say, but I know if I was in the Captain's place I should think the odds against me; it is very certain that either the simple Sawneys, called Bristol Magistrates must be called to an account, or the Capn. be condemned. They have already had one Victim. I hope they will be disappointed in a second; they hardly appear to be fit for Costermongers.

Wednesday 8th. Feb

I had a travelling Paper merchant here this night, I bought some Copy Books and Paper of him, and his whole stock of Black lead Pencils which was 13 for which he asked 8d. I bade him no less, so it was a bargain; the Copy Books very good at 3s. pr. Dozen 5½ Sheets Foolscap.

Thursday 9th. Feb

The great Fidler that has astonished so many Simpletons in the Metropolis, and other parts of this gullible Country, is to appear at Hull, to pick up half Guineas from those who have been, and are crying out on the hardness of the times, who will endeavour to make them harder still, by subscribing to have their ears tickled, and their eyes gratified by the working of a Fidler's Elbow.

Friday 10th. Feb

A meeting this Evening to choose Assessors of the Taxes for the ensuing year, when I and Mr. Robinson of Mount Airy were again chosen. I believe I have been about 25 Years in this Office; a troublesome one it is, and but little profit attached to it ...

---

[2] Captain Warrington had commanded a troop of the third dragoons at the Bristol riots in Oct. 1831. He was the second officer, after Colonel Brereton who committed suicide (see n.1 (1832)), to be court martialled for inaction and dereliction of duty during the riots (*AR* 1832, Hist. 51).

Sunday 12th. Feb

I was at Church as usual, but as to what I heard I say—nothing at all. But what did I see? why Ralph Martin with a new Wig on, he looked as wild in it as though he had escaped from some Lunatic Asylum, and was afraid of again being caught. I surveyed the few heads there were, one of which was Mr. Champney's of Ellerker, which seemed as though he had mounted a Mop above his shoulders, but there is not one for a long head like Bobby Thornton, no, no.

Monday 13th. Feb

I believe it is 28 years this day since I came to Cave, a pretty long time, but now it is gone it seems to be very short. 28 Years in advance seems a very long period.

Tuesday 14th. Feb

If I get no faster forward with the Valuation of S Cave I shall be a long time in getting through with it now to proceed.

	A	R	P	
Beverley Road & Wold Closes	10	1	14	Fras. Ruston owner
Stray	1	–	–	Wilmot owner
Close late F. Harper	3	–	26	Dennis owner
2 Paddocks	1	1	0	H.G. Barnard Esq. do.
Nunnery	13	–	–	Mr. Robinson of Muskam owner
	28	3	0	

Wm. Cousens tent. in 1828

We had Mr. Oxtoby today to whom we paid £41–15–11 and ordered more Goods, which he says he takes more pains to send them good to us than to any other Customer, for this Reason that he has never been put off in the payment.

Wednesday 15th. Feb

So Cave again

	A	R	P
Wold Close (where the Spring is)	20	0	0
Trancledales	17	3	24
Garth end Close	8	1	35
Townend Garth	1	2	–
Ryland Hills	14	0	32
Bagletts	15	–	–
Bagletts (Leonard's)	15	–	–
Flatts	9	–	–
Blakehows	18	3	32
A	120	0	3

Barnard Cook tenant in 1828

Thos. Wride the present tenant—Mr. Todd of Swanland the Owner of all except Leonard's Bagletts which have been sold.

Thursday 16th. Feb

This is a very cold Frosty day, but no Snow although it is quite cold enough for it. Mr. Earnshaw's farm at this place (which Mr. Turk formerly occupied) is to be put up for Sale this day at Hull, I have not heard of any one going to bid for any of it, it will be put up in Lots.

Friday 17th. Feb

I see by the Paper this day that it is rumoured Capn. Warrington is to be Cashiered, but recommended to Mercy;[3] the mercy I am afraid will be but small—Corporal Trim did right as a Soldier but wrong as a Man, when he stuck close to the Orders of Uncle Toby—Now it appears that the unfortunate Capn. has done right as a Man but wrong as a Soldier—I will take on me to assert that the Old Grim General with an outlandish name, has done what he could to get the Capn. found guilty.

Saturday 18th. Feb

I see it is reported that the Cholera has shewn itself in London,[4] but as there are so many different Opinions whether it be really that complaint or not, I think there is no certainty in saying. However there appears to be some kind of disease which has carried off some Persons in a very short time after being afflicted with it. I hope it will be checked.

Sunday 19th. Feb

Farmers here are afraid that some alterations in the Corn laws will be attempted as soon as the Reform Bill is settled; they say that lower Rents will not do for them, for Rent is nothing to high prices.

Monday 20th. Feb

I think I have nothing particular to notice this day, only the Farmers exclaiming against the import of Corn from Ireland, which they in their wisdom, say is the Ruin of this Country, viz. in plain English the Prices are kept lower than they wish for.

Tuesday 21st. Feb

So. Cave

	A	R	P
Wold	18	0	0
Ruffham field	18	2	35

[3] Captain Warrington was sentenced to be cashiered, but, on the recommendation of the jury, he was allowed to retire from the service by selling his troop. The prosecuting officer was Major General Sir Charles D'Albiac (*AR* 1832, Hist. 51).

[4] A severe outbreak of cholera occurred in 1817, in British India, where the disease was endemic. Throughout the 1820s it spread westwards, and by 1830 had reached Persia and the Russian Empire, where it assumed plague proportions. It first appeared in England in Sunderland in Oct. 1831 and broke out in London in Jan. 1832; by the end of that year it had spread to most of the larger towns and cities in Great Britain. Its first appearance in Hull, which escaped the worst ravages with only 270 victims, was on 8 Apr. Cholera continued to be an intermittent scourge in this country until almost the end of the century (*EB* vi. 264; Sibree 79; Smith, F. B. 230–2).

Sands	25	1	–
Park	6	–	–
Common	19	0	20
Garth	4	–	–

Mr. Earnshaw of Hessle	91	0	15

the Owner & Occupier

The above was put up for Sale at Hull last Thursday but nothing of it was sold—Mr. Turk formerly occupied the Farm.

Wednesday 22nd. Feb

Newlove has left his house and another Man has taken it; it is said he comes from Beverley I doubt he has a poor prospect of making a living however I am glad the idle fellow is off.

Thursday 23d. Feb

I have not for some time said anything of the long Miller merely because nothing had come to my knowledge, but a few days ago he got so full of Rum and Water that he was judged by one learned in the mystery of liquor not to be capable of travelling home so the little man (to wit, Jem Levitt) undertook to lead home the Man of the Mill; they managed pretty well, having only had two or three falls, before they arrived in Tom's fold Garth; when plump he went partly on the Middin partly in the Middin pit, — aye now he says to Jem D—n thee hast thou led me here thou lahtle shifting devil and thrown me down upon my own Middin so he pulled Jem beside him, and well they were both bedaubed—The poor Miller cried out, O dear I wanted to gang to Hull tomorn, and now thou's mucked me sea, me Clease is a sham to be seen beside stinking so damnably, why Jem says good night to you Thos.; I have got you safe home, safe! safe! what does thou call this safe, safe in a Middin Pit; get away with thee I sud hae been nae worse without thou, thou had no casion to come here wi me.

Friday 24th. Feb

Rd. Marshall is gone to York today, he will enquire of a Proctor whether the petty Curate here can be justified in refusing to bury the Child of Hannah Levitt's, I will help him all I can to bring the Parson to a hearing, as I know he has not the law on his side.

Saturday 25th. Feb

This afternoon measuring (or rather setting off) some Turnip Land for Mr. Lockwood, it was very dirty having been a Frost the night before, the Close was what is called the Far Wold, which is chalky, the afternoon was very fine ...

Monday 27th. Feb

I see Capn. Warrington has been found guilty, but recommended to Mercy; and will be allowed to sell out; the Scripture says "the tender mercies of the wicked are cruel".[5]

---

[5] Proverbs xii. 10.

Tuesday 28th. Feb
So. Cave

	A	R	P	
Wold	48	3	13	
Cow Pasture	23	1	12	
Garth end Closes	18	–	–	
Ings & Sands	2	2	12	
Ings Swarth	13	3	8	
Tofts	12	2	–	
Pease Dales	9	–	–	T. Fisher's own
Garth & Garden	2	–	–	
Garth & Paddock	1	2	0	T. Fisher's own
Common	3	2	33	Do.
	161	0	38	

The above Farm except those marked as T. Fisher's own belongs to the Heirs of Mr. Scatcherd. John Lockwood is the present tenant.

Wednesday 29 Feb

There was an old Man who lived in one of the Hospitals at Barmston, called Thomas Mitchell who I think had formerly been one of Sir Griffith's Servants and afterwards a small tenant. In summer time he used to keep a Bucket of clean Water with a tin besides it for the Scholars to drink of when thirsty (he lived near the School). But had any one gone and begged a drink of him, it was an affront, for he would say thou knowest where the Water is thou need not ask me. I think I can just see the Old Man with a Break[6] hung across his shoulders and a Bucket at each end, fetching the Beverage for those he would not allow to ask for it. Tommy Mitchell was in those days noted for making a healing Salve.

Thursday 1st. March

I will if I can put down one of Old Willy's Stories, which he tells regularly, when he has any Company that does not know what time he spent in London. It begins as follows—"I have seen two Clergymen hanged, one was Dr. Dodd for forgery, and the other the Revd. Js. Hackman for Murder,[7] he shot Miss Wray when she was coming out of the Playhouse, and after that he attempted to shoot himself—Miss Wray was taken to the Shakespear tavern where I saw her, she was dressed in White Satin, she was nearly all covered with Blood it was a sad sight to look on—There were 30,000 Persons signed a petition to his Majesty King George the 3rd. to save Dr. Dodd's life, but his Majesty could not pardon him because the the two Perreau's had been some time before executed for forgery, so that if the King pardoned the Dr. he had murdered the Perreaus so

[6] From RS's description, a 'break' is presumably a 'yoke' or carrying frame, although this meaning is not given in the *OED*.

[7] For Dr Dodd, see n.37 (1827). Revd James Hackman was executed by hanging at Tyburn on 19 Apr. 1779 for murdering Miss Reay outside Covent Garden Theatre (Rayner and Crook iv. 139–41).

the Dr. was hanged that the other might not have been murdered; I saw him go in a Coach to be hanged. I saw 40,000 Persons go with a Petition to the Parliament with Lord George Gordon at their head, every Man having a purple Ribbon in his hat or on his breast I forget which; they met in St. George's fields in the Borough, and came over London Bridge and through the City, — and I was in London when there was not a single prison left standing, they all having been fired or pulled down by the Mob;[8] "O, the sights that I have seen!!" — when I first went to London there were three heads on Poles at Temple Bar, the heads of some of the Scotch Rebels. This may be called a long tale about nothing.

Friday 2d. March

Club night last night; it is the annual night on which the Landlords who have the Box pay up their yearly Subscriptions of 12s. each, it is now at Morley's and was to have been removed to Cousens's last night, but he would not pay; so that the Box is to remain where it is another year; so that he Morley will be entitled to all the rights, profits and immunities of the said Club for another year at the least.

Saturday 3d. March

Robt. Arton's Daughter Mary and John Robinson of Mt. Airy, set off this morning or some time in the night to get married, a runaway wedding; Bobby set off after them as soon as he was acquainted with it but was too late to prevent the marriage. — Some Man saw him going and said to him where now Mr. Arton in such a hurry is some of your family badly, — badly no worse dan dat, lass run away, what your Servant lass, never mind you will soon find another, no Servant lass, my own lass run away to be wed; — who with pray you Mr. Arton, why they tell me young Robinsons the man. Dod, Dab, only think of that, mak a man mad ...

Monday 5th. Mar.

Heard today at the Market that Mr. Sykes of West Ella died yesterday morning; I think there is some truth in it ...

Wednesday 7th. Mar

Saw in the Hull Packet this morning that Mr. Sykes died on Sunday morning last aged 77 years. Robt. Arton after all his vexation (if he had any) for his daughter running away: has this day got both her and the young man to Provence in a friendly way. So much the better; not to have envy hatred or malice ...

Friday 9th. Mar

The Man who has come to Newlove's house has got his name put on the Board above the Door, his name is Edward Fewson; but who he is and where he comes from I know no more than I did before, he appears to break Horses.

---

[8] On 2 June 1780 an estimated 60,000 supporters of the Protestant Association assembled in St. George's Fields, London, and marched on Parliament after being harangued by their leader, Lord George Gordon. In the widespread anti-Catholic riots which took place in London over the next 7 days, more than 210 people were killed outright and 75 died subsequently in hospital (Stevenson 94–113).

10th Mar Saturday

Ths. Marshall was harrowing one day, when he swore to his Horses that they did not understand him, they had for ought he knew learnt a fresh language, as they neither knew, <u>Hove</u> nor <u>Gee</u>; whether the Miller's Horses have been studying the March of intellect or not he cannot tell, but they have got so learned that they do not understand honest English.

Sunday 11th. Mar

The Castle it appears is let, to the Honble Chs. Stourton,[9] either his Father or Brother is Lord Stourton but I think his Father, as Rd. Marshall says this Honble will be, Lord Stourton at I think his Father's death. He is to come the 1st. May.

Monday 12th. Mar

Very little attendance at the Market today; the Farmers throng sowing Beans & Oats, it is a fine time for them, the land being in fine order.

Tuesday 13th. Mar

So. Cave, again

	A	R	P	
Sands —	6	2	10	
Moors —	11	2	7	
Cave Gates —	10	–	–	
Goose Crofts —	6	–	–	
Goose Crofts & Common— 2	2	–		
Hogmanpit	12	–	–	
Land behind hse —	1	–	–	
Dalby Garths —	2	–	–	
	51	2	17	Revd. Jno. King. Owner and Occupier.

I think Mr. King has forsaken Cave, it is a long time since he was here; he has a Man who manages the Farm; he has more land at Ellerker & Broomfleet.

Wednesday 14th. Mar

Mr. Simpson's Son of Brantingham came yesterday to pay me the Sovereign which I wanted of him for Land measuring; I was afraid I should not get it, as he offered five shillings in the pound to his Creditors; it was not offered to me, and if it had, I would not have taken it.

Thursday 15th. Mar

I was at Ellerker this Evening at Charles Rudds, posting up his Books, he is Overseer of the Poor and Surveyor of the Highways. I got tea before I went and got home about 8 O'clock.

---

[9] Charles Stourton was the son of William Stourton, the 18th Lord Stourton, who was the owner of Allerton Park in the West Riding and the head of an old aristocratic Roman Catholic family. Charles had lived at nearby Holme Hall before taking up residence at Cave Castle. He subsequently inherited the title from his father to become the 19th Lord Stourton. His uncle, Charles Langdale, also a Roman Catholic, was MP for Beverley from 1832 to 1834 (Ward 36).

Friday 16th. Mar

Hunters and Hounds came through here about Noon, they were to meet this morning at Brantingham and it seems they had found nothing, as they rode very leisurely through here, shewing their Red or Scarlet Coats; where they were going I know not, indeed I dispute whether they knew that themselves.

Saturday 17th. Mar

I was Gardening today, it was very stormy, sometimes Hail, sometimes Rain, sometimes Sunshine. I set some early Potatoes, planted some beans, and sowed some Carrot seeds.

Sunday 18th. Mar

Rd. Marshall shewed me this morning, a letter from Mr. Creyke the Vicar of So. Cave respecting the Burial of Han. Levitt's Child; the Vicar says he entirely differs from the Curate: he certainly had he been here would not have refused burying the Child; but as the Curate is licensed, he cannot turn him out. The letter of Complaint which was sent to him, the Vicar, will be laid before the Archbishop, to have his Opinion of the Case. I hope he will visit the delinquent Curate with Ecclesiastical censures, I shall be rejoiced if he send him a packing.

Monday 19th. Mar

Various Opinions on the Reform Bill, and as to whether it will pass the Lords or not, for my part I hardly think it will; but it gives me very little concern ...

Wednesday 21st. Mar

This is the day appointed for a fast; there were here at the Church this morning, more people a great deal, than on Sundays, I dare say some people think there is more holiness in a day thus appointed than keeping holy the Sabbath day: I am not one of these, — mind that.

Thursday 22d Mar

Robt. Kirby one of Rd. Kirby's Sons who is rather flighty, this day took it in head to abuse his Brother and Sister; they got the Constable to take care of him, but what he is done with I have not heard; he and the Constable were together at the Black Bear.

Friday 23d. Mar

> "And half the Ease & Comfort he enjoys
> Is when surrounded with Slates, Books & Boys"[10]

Such are the enjoyments according to the Poet (Crabbe) of a Schoolmaster. I shall not controvert it, for my best days have been spent in this employ.

Saturday 24th. Mar

The Overseers of the Poor are to make up their Accts. on Tuesday next, they are uneasy, but for what? I think they have never been five Pounds out of Pocket the whole year, and at this present time one of them only wants 26 Shillings and the other nothing: there certainly is a good deal of money to come in, but I have little fear of getting it.

---

[10] These lines are taken from a poem by George Crabbe (1754–1832): *The Borough: a Poem in XXIV Letters* (1810), letter 24: Schools, lines 93–4.

Sunday 25th. Mar

A very fine day; the Frogs croaking in Mr. Barnard's Pond close by the new Road, and the Crows very active in Building rebuilding and repairing their abodes; young Lambs begin to appear, all looks here quite rural.

Monday 26th. Mar

The farmers expected that Corn would advance at this time of the year, as Seed is wanted to sow the Spring Corn, but the trade appears to be stationary and but little doing.

Tuesday 27th. Mar

A meeting this night at Barnard Cook's to balance the Poor Books—all very quiet. Robt. Tindale of Weedley, & Jn. Lockwood were appointed or nominated overseers for the ensuing year.

Wednesday 28th. Mar

I was at Beverley this day with Robinson of Mount Airy getting sworn in as Assessors. I walked and got there and back very well; the last year I got my Ancle hurt which I can feel at times yet.

Thursday 29th. Mar

The reform Bill I see has got through the House of Commons favoured by a great Majority, now for its ordeal in the Lords; It is my own Opinion that it will not pass the born Legislators, but I may be mistaken: so may others who are sure that it <u>will</u> be passed by their Lordships.

Friday 30th. Mar

Young Billy Thornham got drunk on the Fast day and lost ten pounds out of his Pocket Book there were 3 Sovereigns left in it, he never missed it till the Saturday following: he has been at Barnard Cook's, and blamed young Barnard's widow for it he summoned her before a Magistrate, but he had a sort of Rigmarole tale to tell; so that he could make nothing of it. Some people say that his wife had got it.

Saturday 31st. Mar

This afternoon measuring some Turnip Land, two Closes at Everthorpe and one of Rd. Marshall's the whole about 26 Acres; a very fine day, got pretty well tired, as the land was sandy and some of it fresh plouged [*sic*].

Sunday 1st. April

Eliza and her Mother were at West Ella today. My Mother looks well as can be expected; she did not know them when they first went, she never gets up but to have her bed righted.

Monday 2d. April

There were some Horses shewn today, but my fancy does not incline that way at all. I do not like to be near them, nor even in the Street when they are there. But to Horse fanciers this is a great treat.

Tuesday 3d. April

So. Cave. I proceed a little further with the Quantity of land

	A	R	P	
Loyd' Com. land —	9	2	16	Mr. Robinson of
Do. ————	2	2	30	Muskam the

				owner
Park ———	6	–	–	
Water Close & Hall Garth	9	2	–	Do.
Garth & land below				
Rd. Kirby's house	4	–	–	Rd. Kirby owner

31	3	6

The above was occupied by Rd. Kirby, there formerly was an Old Hall called Loyd's Hall or West Hall, the Place is called Hall Garth, it is nearly opposite to where Mr. Turk lives.

Wednesday 4th. Apl

So. Cave

	A	R	P	
Sands ——	6	3	15}	
Ings ——	30	–	–}	
Common —	12	1	14}	Mr. Craven of
			}	Hull the Owner
Land near the house	63	–	–}	
New field —	17	–	16}	

129	1	5

Wm. Laverack tenant. & Laverack's house at the Common.

Thursday 5th. Apl

This morning a letter from Wm. with an Account of his Aunt's will, what she has left him, will I hope with his endeavours, set him above any fear of want. The £400 I am convinced will come to him at the decease of his Uncle.

Friday 6th. Apl

This Evening the lanes were let at Fenwick's there was a good deal of Competition they were let for £13–11–6 last year the amount was £6–16–0. I got a bad cold the Room when we first went in was damp and a fire just lighted, it is a small room and was so much crowded that before we left it was like being in a Stove.

Saturday 7th. Apl.

Nothing I think particular this day, so I shall proceed with So. Cave,

	A	R	P
Sands ——	12	0	8
Cardales—	24	2	4
Pigdam—	9	–	–
Hilldales –	13	2	20

59	0	32

The above belongs Mr. John Levitt of Ellerker who occupies it himself.

Sunday 8th. Apl

It is very dry weather generally cold & snarling wind but the Spring makes progress notwithstanding; the trees are full of Buds, but few of them yet in leaf.

Monday 9th. Apl

"Shall the Lords be called upon to determine the rights and privileges of the Commons? They cannot do it without a flagrant breach of the Constitution". these are the words of a celebrated political writer viz. Junius,[11] and I think the above is in his letter to a King.

Tuesday 10th. Apl

There is a Gentleman come to Brantingham-Thorpe[12] who has bought the House & Land of the late Revd. Mr. Barnard's he has also bought all the Estate of the Revd. Mr. Simpson he is making great alterations and has a number of Labourers employed, which is a great relief to the Poor men both at Brantingham & the neighbouring Parishes.

Wednesday 11th. Apl

This Evening my wife went to Ellerker to buy some Flower Seeds, she laid out 6d. in various kinds, so that we are in expectation of having a showy Garden in the Summer at present the Weather is very cold.

Thursday 12th. Apl

I recollect or remember (I hardly know which is the most proper expression) the victory of Admiral Rodney over the Count De Grosse;[13] that same Summer there were Songs of the Victory; Old Robin Stubbs crying out here's your new Rodneys, I was not then 9 years old, but I recollect the very place where I heard him, but my Memory goes farther back than this.

Friday 13th. Apl

Our Old Friend who is afraid of losing his right of voting at Beverley is very much against the Creation of any new Peers—and I am resolved to have them made provided the measure cannot be carried without. But he says it will be an arbitrary act. But all he is afraid of is that Corruption at Elections will cease.

Saturday 14th. Apl.

I think this day I have little to notice; it is a very fine day; a letter or writing from Wm. saying that I had not filled up the Sheet on which I wrote to him; this was perhaps for want of something to say; what if I had babbled of Green fields, and noisy Rooks, it would have been something certainly; but

---

[11] Anonymous author (generally identified as Sir Philip Francis, 1740–1818) of a series of politically motivated letters written to the London *Public Advertiser* from 1769 to 1772 (*DNB*, *EB* xv. 557–9).

[12] Richard F. Shawe (d. 1872), an army officer (Allison 49).

[13] RS is here referring to the victory of Admiral Sir George Rodney over the Comte de Grasse off Dominica on 12 Apr. 1782. This was a critically important naval victory at a time when England was beleagured by her enemies. It saved Jamaica and dealt a crushing blow to French naval prestige while earning for its author the status of a national hero (*DNB*).

when he receives this Mass of <u>Foolscap</u> he need not complain, of any thing being left out that is of <u>consequence</u>.

Sunday 15th. Apl

Measles very prevalent here and have been for some time, Eliza's Children have not yet had them indeed we think she has never had them herself.

Monday 16th. Apl.

When I was in our Garden today, I heard a Tufit crying out; I was immediately in Southfield Carr at Barmston, running after the pretty sprightly Birds, where I used to run more than 40 years ago.

Tuesday 17th. Apl

Workmen are painting the Castle; (this I think is as proper as saying the Castle is <u>being</u> painted) for the Reception of the Honble tenant, who is to come to it the first May next.

Wednesday 18th. Apl

My wife was at Hull today and amongst other Places at a Druggist's Shop where she wanted something, the Master was a steady knowing Man and knew almost everybody; he was asked if he knew Wm. Sharp who was with Craggs', O'yes no one better, he was a worthy young Man; well he is my Son; the man was overjoyed when he heard he had got so much left him, and his Mother (Wm's) pleased as if she had found a treasure.

Thursday 19th. Apl.

Yesterday I was Shopkeeper, I had Mr. Oxtoby here and paid him his Account £39–5–8½; he said he would send another load of Goods today but they have not arrived.

Friday 20th. Apl

This is what is called Good Friday, but why it is any better than another Friday I have yet to learn; there was Service at the Church, but very few people were there as I am informed. Old Mr. Barnard once said on Good Friday that Mr. Garnon's might say, Dearly beloved Harry (old Harry Bentley was the Clerk) instead of Dearly beloved Brethren: as the Parson and Clerk were the greatest part of the Congregation.

Saturday 21st. Apl

This forenoon I was planting some Potatoes, and sowing some Sun Flower Seeds, and Kidney Beans of the Scarlet running kind, more for the Flowers than the Pods, as I am no great admirer of them for eating.

Sunday 22d. Apl.

Easter Sunday; It appears to me not [to] be comprehended that this should be called the day of Christ's rising from the dead; it is no particular day of the Month in each year, but varies sometimes nearly a Month: but the Church clings to the Reliques of her Old Mother.

Monday 23d. Apl

This has been at times a very throng day here but this day there was very little Company, there were no Horses shewn; and scarcely anything doing.

Tuesday 24th. Apl

This is the day on which the Churchwardens are annually chosen here; Mr. Nicholson of Frog Hall and Giles Bridgman were chosen; and an Assessment of one penny in the Pound was laid to defray the last years Expences.

Wednesday 25th. Apl

This was a real Rainy day it rained all the day; it came very moderate and will do much good, should it be succeeded by warm weather. As this day there used to be what is called a Tansey at some one of the Public houses: but there is none this year; all things are subject to change.

Thursday 26th. Apl

Measles have come out on little Ann this afternoon. She has been sick and ill all the week, we hope she will get well over them, we are naturally timid of them remembering, we lost little Mary by them at the age of one year.

Friday 27th. Apl

Old Willy begins to tremble at the thoughts of the Reform bill passing, and he says he should quite despair but he thinks the next reform will be in the Church, and hopes the Parson Justices will be dispensed with.

Saturday 28th. Apl

I had a Gentleman called to look at the Plan of Ellerker Lordship, and for the examination he gave me a Shilling, which is the first and only gratuity I ever received; for any thing of this sort; I wish there would be an inspection every day at the same price.

Sunday 29th. Apl

There was to be a Christening this day, and the Persons had come from Broomfleet with the Child, likewise another Christening belonging to Parents in the Town; but the Parson sent them both back without having the idle Ceremony read over, and as I am informed told them to come again the next Sunday; but I know if it was my Case I would trouble him no more on that score. Heard from Wm. this morning that he had been ill, which added nothing to our Comfort this day. We hope he has recovered again.

Monday 30th. Apl.

Fanny Langricke (Billy Langricke's wife of this Place who goes about selling Clay Balls &c) was at Beverley on Saturday last; and most likely was preparing for Cave Fair; as she had stolen about a Stone of Currants, with which she was taken; and committed to Beverley Jail, to lay there till the Sessions at Midsummer next; it is surprising that anyone should be so far gone in Iniquity as to steal the Luxuries of life which could very well be dispensed with; but Fanny has been noted a good while for Spice Cakes & Currant Puddings.

Tuesday 1st May

This is May day and very cold it is. — The information I had on Sunday respecting the Parson refusing to Christen two Children was a fabrication so that I must make an apology for inserting it, which is here

"Bad as he is, the Devil may be abus'd
Misrepresented & falsely be accus'd:

Bad men unwilling to bear their faults alone,
Lay those on him that truly are their own."

Wednesday 2d. May

This day I was very unwell, so much so that I was obliged to go to bed as soon as ever the School left: I suppose I had got cold, as I was quite listless and all my bones felt sore.

Thursday 3d. May

This morning I felt nearly quite well again and have so continued all the day; Yesterday I could neither read the Newspaper, nor smoke a Pipe. Club meeting this night, had it been yesterday I could not have attended, but I am thankful that I am better ...

Sunday 6th May

This is really a pleasant day, fresh and fine Green & Gay—it is quite reviving, we have had very little fine weather yet this Spring—Eliza's little Girl has got over the Measles, but they have made her look very thin and pale, the little Boy has not yet caught them.

Exeunt

So. Cave, 7th May, 1832

Dear Wm.

I do not know that I have any thing particular to write <u>about</u>, Your Mother has sent a Ham, which you may get a Slice at a time for your Breakfasts, Some Butter & a Piece of Cheese for Mary, the Raisins she thinks must be for Wm. the 2d. She has sent you some Arrow Root which is very good, I have taken it almost daily for some time past, I hope all will arrive safe and not spoiled as the last was, You will receive my Journal with additions and Corrections to the present time, All our best love to you all, I need not say sincerely, for never a day passes but you and your family are talked <u>about</u>

I remn. your
loving Father
R Sharp

Tuesday 8th. May

This day sent off the Basket for Wm. which we hope will arrive safe, and have no doubt but it will be gratefully received.

Wednesday 9th. May

The Churchwardens & Overseers received a letter of which the following is a Copy.

Page Z. A. 2114

The undersigned is able to inform you of something considerably to your Advantage, Yearly and for Ever on receipt of Twenty Shillings by Post Office order or otherwise for his trouble

Respectfully
Joseph Ady
No. 11 Circus Minories

near Tower Hill

40 years Resident in same Parish

& known to Alderman Copeland M.P.

of London who will be answerable

for my Integrity as far as £1000

March 24th. 1832

No Letters received unless Post Paid.

The letter appears to be lithographed, and this same Joseph, I believe to be a Swindler, for I think I have seen his name before the Magistrates in the Police Report for attempting to receive Money under false pretences.

Thursday 10th. May

Thomas Leaman died today, he had been long troubled with shortness of Breath, he was 77 years of age, I made his Will 14 years ago.

Friday 11th. May

Mrs. Hodgson, Mr. Barnard's Housekeeper set off for London today; she had taken lodgings before she went at Mrs. Akam's but has not been there more than a fortnight or three weeks.

Saturday 12th. May

This day I walked to Beverley & back in Company with Wm. Purdon of Broomfleet; we took time and did not tire ourselves: it was a very cold blustering day, I dined with him at a Cook-Shop at the expence of Sixpence: we got well home.

Sunday 13th. May

I was sent for last night after I got home to read over Thomas Leaman's will; he has left his Close 2 Acres on the Common to one of his Sons who is to pay out of it £10 each to two of his Brothers.

Monday 14th. May

This is Weighton fair day, which has caused a very thin Market here; I understand it was a very dull fair for Stock; — viz. Sheep & Beasts;[14] when we speak of Stock it is not [to] be understood in the London meaning of Stock-jobbing.

Tuesday 15th. May

This is no News day with us here, so that we are ignorant of what is going on, — Ministers or no Ministers, — Soldiers or Civilians, we will wait for when we can do no otherwise it is as well to be resigned.

Wednesday 16th. May

I have just seen the definition of what a Philosopher is; I have most likely seen it before; — it is in <u>Audam Smeeth's</u> Wealth of Nations. —

"The trade of a Philosopher is not to do any thing but to observe every thing".

— According to the above we have abundance of Philosophers.

---

[14] i.e cattle, not animals in general.

Thursday 17th. May

Heard this Evening at Mr. Atkinson's that the Ministry of Lord Grey is again in Power;[15] it is seldom that I mind any thing of the ins or the outs but I think at the present the recall of Lord Grey is a healing measure: all the Antis may see that if there be no reform, there will be confusion worse confused.

Friday 18th. May

Busy collecting the half yearly taxes; there is no obstruction in paying, except some who are short of money, I think I seldom ever got the Money in better.

Saturday 19th. May

This day I went down to the Common, for Wm. Laverack's taxes; but he was not at home, and I was informed that if he had been there he had no money: I believe the Man is honest, but he has been hardly used, he has promised to pay the 28th May.

Sunday 20th. May

Mr. Haydon of Swanland preached at the Chapel today; he is I understand a very good preacher I did not hear him myself.

Monday 21st. May

I walked to Beverley and back today in Company with Wm. Purdon of Broomfleet; I neither eat nor drank at Beverley so that the town was no better for my presence; got home about four O'clock, in time for the Market, quite well.

Tuesday 22d. May

Jack Cade was a Reformer as he said and here is part of his Speech,

"Be brave then, for your Captain is brave and vows reformation. There shall be in England Seven halfpenny loaves sold for a Penny: the three-hoop'd pot shall have ten hoops and I will make it felony to drink small beer." Shakespeare's King Henry 4th: — I have part of Shakespeare's Plays, perhaps the worst Edition that was ever published; from which I have extracted the above.

Wednesday 23d. May

Mr. Stourton now occupies the Castle, I have not yet seen him, but I have seen his old Popish Priest and spoken to him, he seems a sort of liberal man he is one Frenchman.

Thursday 24th. May

This is the Spring Court day, it was held at James Levitt's, there was a good Dinner I understand; there was not one Surrender of any Copyhold

---

[15] Charles, Lord Grey, leader of the Whig party had resigned his ministry earlier that month, when King William IV had gone back on his promise to create new peers in order to enable the Parliamentary Reform Bill to go through the House of Lords. The King had contrived to get the Tories to take office and pass a less radical bill of reform. For the space of a week, the political life of the country was in crisis—the famous 'Days of May'—but with massive popular support for 'the Bill, the whole Bill, and nothing but the Bill', the King was forced to give way, and Lord Grey was returned in triumph on the condition of the surrender of King and Peers and the guarantee of free passage for the Bill of Reform (Walpole iii. 240–5).

Property which seems to indicate that the Possessors of this kind of Property do not feel that the times are so hard as to oblige them to sell.

Friday 25 May

Another letter today from Joseph Ady in the Minories word for word same as the last: no notice will be taken of it.

Saturday 26th. May

This day I had a travelling Paper Merchant, I bought some of him, but he says he can scarcely get any thing by me, as I know the Quality and Price of Paper as well as he does—perhaps better.

Sunday 27th. May

Mr. Bromby Vicar of the High Church at Hull preached here this forenoon, — in the afternoon there was no Service; but as it was the Bread day a Congregation of old Women (and the Churchwardens) attended for the Loaves.

Monday 28th. May

Very thin attendance at the Market today; I did not hear how the price of Corn was, a fine mild day with Rain towards the Evening ...

Wednesday 30th. May

We have had Mr. Oxtoby today and paid him £39 and ordered another load of Goods against the fair which will be here in a few Days.

Thursday 31st. May

Mr. Robinson (Lawyer) has begun to pull the old thatch off his house, he is going to put on a new Roof, which is to be slated; Mr. Mountain of Hull[16] has the direction of the work.

Friday 1st. June

There was a Man came from Hull who belongs this Parish; he said to Ths. Marshall you and I are Cousens; Tom was then Overseer but nothing would he give his Cousen Grasby—well then he says I must go without, but Tommy thou knowst I am thy Coz. Whya says Tommy as to Relationship it is as it is, and must stand sea, but the Devil of ony Money shall thou Coz. out of me, No no thou shalt not Coz. me to get ought from me.

Saturday 2d. June

Had the Romans Clocks? Caesar says what is it a'clock—Brutus says, Caesar 'tis strucken eight. — Shakespeare's Julius Cesar.

Sunday 3d. June

Conder, Eliza and Children have gone to Swinefleet Feast, a Brother of Conder's came for them on Friday last; they are to come back tomorrow.

Monday 4th. June

Old Loncaster has given notice to Billy Bullock that he Lonc. will keep Bullock's Rattens no longer; why Bullock says they are no more my Rattens than yours. I say says Lonc. they're yours and I weant keep them; whya, whya

---

[16] Charles Mountain (1773–1839) was a prominent Hull architect, who, after succeeding to the family business in 1805 on his father's death, was responsible for the design of a number of public buildings in the city in the style of the Greek Revival (Hall, I & E. 105–6).

then send 'em back—Damn the Rattens they've eaten me a new Riddle bottom out but I did not know they were mine before ...

Wednesday 6th. June

Our Old friend Mr. Atkinson comforts himself that he will still have a Vote left for the County or part of it; if he be cut off from Beverley,[17] where he will lose all rights—privileges, immunities and bribery; he will not he is afraid have an opportunity of again selling his Vote.

Thursday 7th. June

What preparations here are going on for the fair, White Washing, yellow washing and Colouring of various descriptions, which makes me wish myself almost out of the way of it.

Friday 8th. June

The new tenant have [sic] got the Bear fresh painted but it is Brown this time it was a Black Bear before and a ravenous beast it was, for it has devoured or worried all who have had any thing to do with it.

Saturday 9th. June

Eliza's little boy has the Chicken Pox, they appear to be very favourable, he does not appear to be unwell with them: little Ann I think has not had them.

Sunday 10th. June

Charles Jenkinson has a Daughter very ill with a bad knee, she is perhaps 12 or 13 years old; her knee has been cut, but it is no better, they talk of having her leg cut off; but in the state she is in I think it will not be necessary she cannot to all appearance recover; I have not seen her, but my wife saw her this day.

Monday 11th. June

I think I never saw more Pot Carts at the Market than there were today; and seldom more fighting both with Men & Women; all drunk alike; one Girl who broke another Man's Pots, was knocked down and hurt; she was afterwards blooded, but not capable of being removed this night.

Tuesday 12th. June

A Standing Joke of old Willy's is when a person wants a pennyworth of Nails, for him to ask them whether they want Iron or Horn nails—they reply generally they never saw any horn nails; he assures them they are saying what is not right, but they still persisting he shews them his finger nails and triumphantly asks if these are not horn nails. He has often the satisfaction of being called an old Fool, which he sets down to his quickness ...

Thursday 14th. June

The French are at their old business again of murdering each other;[18] they have followed this calling far too long, but they cannot forget their old habits; They are both Fools and Madmen.

---

[17] The Reform Act of 1832 reduced Beverley's electorate by disfranchising those freemen who lived more than 7 miles outside the town. Old Willy Atkinson would have been included among them as South Cave is 9 miles south west of Beverley (Markham (1982) 10).

[18] Considerable unrest prevailed in France at this time, under the newly established monarchy of King Louis-Philippe, which was under pressure from both the reactionary, royalist forces and the progressive

Friday 15th. June

Customers coming in to the fair, all anxious to eat up their friends, or at least their provisions ...

Sunday 17th. June

At Church this forenoon but not in the afternoon as I have never gone in the afternoon on Cave fair Sundays.

Monday 18th. June

This is the Fair day the Street as usual full of Beasts, we had James Ramsdale and his Son Robert to dinner, that was all the Company we had. I think they went away before tea, Robt. went out to see a Shew for which he paid 2d. but after staying a good while there was nothing to be seen, so he recovered half of his money and came away not very well satisfied. A very fine day.

Tuesday 19th. June

A Rainy morning which did not augur well for the influx of Company, but it rather cleared up, but continued dull all the day. There was a tolerable appearance of pleasure seekers but not so many by a great deal as I have seen. John Ramsdale and Mary were here this day.

Wednesday 20th. June

This afternoon there were some races by Asses for a teakettle, and a Hat for running Footmen; likewise Ribbons for others, all very pleasant for those who delight in them.

Thursday 21st. June

Longest day. But this week with us Time is not reckoned by the length of the Days, but by the amusements going on; I think there was no fighting in the town, but one or two matches went out of the Parish to try their hands at each others faces. (very rainy)

Friday 22d June

Visitors with lengthened faces now leaving the Town, having mostly eaten out their friends, and sorry that there is no more gormandising for them; well let them go.

Saturday 23d. June

This Evening there was a Horse race for a Bridle, and lads blinded running Wheelbarrows for Oranges, as a finishing stroke to Cave fair.

Sunday 24th. June

A very great Wind this day, which made it very disagreeable, indeed windy weather is never pleasant; towards evening it became calmer.

Monday 25th. June

The Market this day very thinly attended, indeed one could scarce see that there was a Market; but so long as a few come from Broomfleet it will continue.

---

liberal and republican elements. After the death of Casimir Perier in 1832, the agitation which he had successfully held in check in Lyons, Grenoble and La Vendée, again began to erupt in violence, whilst at the same time the republicans were organizing themselves into armed secret societies (*AR* 1832 Hist. 314–342).

Tuesday 26th. June

Visitation today at Morley's what Company there is I cannot tell, but I think there are not many People there: a fine day.

Wednesday 27th. June

I have been making out the Quarterly Accts. for the Stamp Office this day; and taking the Stock in hand which is £169–17–10½ ...

Saturday 30th. June

Old Saml. Leighton died this afternoon, it is said to be a Case of Cholera; it may; but he was an old Man and I understand some Persons had given him some Porter some day this week, which not agreeing with him; the Doctor was sent for on Friday night but he could not save him; Geo. Petfield who made his Coffin, says he was as much like himself as ever he saw a Corpse.

Sunday 1st. July

This forenoon I had (as Clerk to the Club) to invite the Members in Cave to Saml. Leighton's funeral to meet at the Club Room at four O'clock this afternoon, and from thence proceed as is customary in such cases to the house where the deceased Member lay and accompany the departed member to the Church: there are about 50 members in the town of which I receive 1 penny each, — after the funeral the Club Box was opened and 12 pounds paid to the Widow.

Monday 2d. July

The Farmers beginning generally to mow Clover and Grass, of which there are large Crops, it having been a very favourable time for their growing; The Earth seems clothed with plenty.

Tuesday 3d. July

My Brother whom we expected last night, arrived this day at dinner time; he is very well, I have desired him at Wm.'s request to see Dr. Chalmers, and have the matters in the Will settled, which he will do when he goes to Hull—he says Mr. Richardson has informed him that nothing can be settled in less than six Months, but I have pressed on him to desire the Executors to get the Effects into their hands immediately.

Wednesday 4th. July

My Brother went away this Evening, I went with him as far as the Fox Cover, on his Road to West Ella; it was a pleasant evening but very warm and tiresome walking up the Hill.

Thursday 5th. July

Club night the Settling before the feast day there are 121 members—2 having died this year and the wife of a member, there has been paid to sick and aged members since the Feast last year the Sum of £57–11–9d — the whole of the Contributions since last feast is £121–10–3

the Expences have been 112– 9–3

Cleared the last year   9– 1–0

Friday 6th July

There was a meeting this Evening of about half a Dozen People to establish what they call a Board of Health which is to keep up the Alarm of Cholera amongst us; some (or one viz the Parson) maintaining that Saml. Leighton died of that Complaint, and others declare he had no symptom of it; it is generally believed that the Porter or Ale disagreed with him, he having been so greedy of it.

Saturday 7th. July

Fanny Langricke was tried at Beverley Sessions this week for stealing Currants from a Shop at Beverley, she pleaded guilty and is sentenced to three Months imprisonment.

Sunday 8th. July

A Smart Shower of Rain this afternoon, which will be beneficial to the Turnips lately sown ...

Tuesday 10th. July

There is a great deal in the Papers on the commission of Lunacy on Miss Bagster:[19] one of the Mad Doctors I think says it is a sign of unsoundness of Mind or Lunacy for a person not to understand figures, now here is a young person who has never been taught Arithmetic and because she does not understand it she is to be accounted insane or of unsound mind. I might as well be called a lunatic because I do not understand "Heathen Greek".

Wednesday 11th. July

The weather in general wet, which makes a very precarious Hay time, it is also too wet for the young Turnips.

Thursday 12th. July

This is the Club feast day at Morleys, there were 93 members at Dinner a good Dinner and all comfortable. John Bentley a member from Welton, had a little Girl who was coming in the Evening to meet him, and on her way between Welton and Elloughton dropped down dead on the Road, it is said by the bursting of a Blood vessel.

Friday 13th. July

I believe there was not one person drunk at the Club feast yesterday, which is more than can be generally said; whether the Liquor was mixed so as to favour sobriety or not I cannot say.

Saturday 14th. July

A very rainy day, I intended going to Ellerker this day, but the Rain prevented me, I went out towards night to collect the Poor Sess ...

---

[19] Miss Rosa Matilda Bagster, otherwise known as Mrs Newton, was the granddaughter of Alderman Crowder (see n.63 (Letters)), former sheriff and mayor of London. On his death and the death of her uncle, she had inherited a substantial fortune of £5,000 as well as an annuity of £4,000 a year. Apparently simple-minded, she had fallen prey to an adventurer, Raymond Newton, who had induced her to elope with him to Gretna Green, where they were married. The investigation into her sanity had been instigated by her mother in an attempt to reclaim the family's fortune from the hands of Newton. The case received extensive coverage in the press with the jury finally reaching the verdict that Miss Bagshot was of unsound mind (*TM* 4 July 1832, 6 b and daily thereafter until 16 July 1832).

Wednesday 18th. July

My Brother has seen Mr. Richardson respecting the Will, who says the Articles cannot be got in less than 6 Months. The Money they are calling in and lodging it in Smith's Bank,[20] there is £300 wanting of which there is no account, and I wish nothing else be wanting.

Thursday 19th. July

Mrs. Tapp and her daughters are here, one of them Mary (now Mrs. Perks) lately saw Wm. in London he had a Flannel on his face; but for that looked pretty well; we know he is now better which is comfortable to know ...

Sunday 22d. July

No Paper this morning—yesterday the Overseers recd. the Reform Act,[21] with instructions to give Notice to those qualified to Vote to send in their claims, and one Shilling with each claim; these Shillings are to go in aid of the Poor rates; the Notices are to be put on the Church Doors on the 25th. July.

Monday 23d. July

A Miller out of Lincolnshire has bought Ellerker Mills, and as report says has entered on them today; Mr. Brown bought a Load of Wheat for him at the Market this day at 68s. pr. Quarter.

Tuesday 24th. July

Mr. Atkinson's Cat has bitten his finger, a Dog having gone into his house began to fight the Cat, he wanted to get the Cat away when she bit his fore finger. I dare say it is very painful.

Wednesday 25th. July

I have got a swelled face, it is a long time since my face has been swelled. I have had it rubbed with Marshmallows Ointment; it is [*sic*] has no pain in it but feels very hot and inflamed.

Thursday 26th. July

Ths. Marshall shocked the fine feelings of some one or two who wish to be thought very sensitive, when there was a meeting called to form a board of health. He said when Brandy was recommended, that he would never believe that God had created him to be such a fool as give away his Money to buy Brandy & Tobacco for those who fancy they have the Cholera, when their fancy is for Liquor.

Friday 27th. July

Very fine weather for Hay making & leading, it must be well got this Season, the Harvest it is expected will be forward this year, particularly if the weather come favorable.

---

[20] Smith's Bank (Samuel Smith Brothers and Co.) was located in Whitefriargate, Hull, and lasted from 1784 to 1902 (Sheahan 305–6; Hartley 126–31).

[21] The Reform Act of 7 June 1832 (2 Will. IV 1831–2 c. 45) made the local overseers of the poor responsible for preparing and publicly displaying the lists of persons entitled to vote in county and borough elections. It contained detailed instructions on how the lists should be prepared as well as how to deal with any subsequent objections (sections 37–39, 44, and 47) and included an appendix of sample forms.

Saturday 28th July

At Ellerker this afternoon collecting the Church Sess for Mr. Leeson; I think my face is rather settled. but it is yet considerably swelled.

Sunday 29th. July

A very hot sultry day; I see the wise men of some of the Boards of health have at length found out that ripe fruit eaten moderately is not likely to bring on the Cholera; have they found out this by their own quickness? if they have what a wonderful discovery they have made.

Monday 30th. July

Heard from Wm. this morning, that little Mary is gone into Wales for the benefit of her health; I am no great advocate for sending Children from home; as we have tried it. When Jane was ill she went to Barmston; and I believe the most good she felt was when she saw me when I went to fetch her back. Where can the poor little Creatures be so free or contented as at home?

Tuesday 31st. July

David Dennis' Father who lives with him gave David a Chapter or Section of the Whole Duty of Man on Drunkenness to look over. David found it all right from experience and said nothing, but gave his Father the Book back desiring him to read the Article on Covetousness;[22] his Father took it without saying a word; and David himself thinks that Covetousness is worse than Drunkenness, however he does not like it so well.

Wednesday 1st. Augt

It is rumored that the Man who took the Black Bear, (now a Brown one) at Lady day last wants to quit the house; and I think the sooner he does so it will [be] the better for him, for I am certain he cannot make a living of it; I doubt the Poor fellow will be minus by his Speculation.

Thursday 2d. Aug

This is Mr. Barnard's Rent day, but he is not here himself, therefore his Steward takes the Rents, he got some Rect. Stamps yesterday to be ready.

Friday 3d. Aug

The Registering of Persons eligible to Vote goes on here very languidly, but as there is sufficient time before the 20th inst. there may be more briskness before that time.

Saturday 4th. Aug

Recd. a letter from Wm. this morning with the Edinburgh Review which is quite a treat to me now, as I never see except by chance either a Magazine or Review.

Sunday 5th. Aug

A very warm day, it had been part Rain the last night. Some Persons talk of beginning Harvest the next week; there is a fine prospect.

---

[22] i.e. chapter 8, 'Of Temperance in Drinking ...' and chapter 7, 'Of Contentedness, and the Contraries to it; Murmuring, Ambition, Covetousness, Envy ...' in Richard Allestree's *The Whole Duty of Man* ... first published in 1659 and issued in numerous editions thereafter.

Monday 6th. Aug

Pocklington Lamb fair today which caused very few People at the Market here; the Fair for Lambs by the Report of some who were there was that all were sold at good Prices; Cattle not good to sell.

Tuesday 7th. Aug

I and Eliza walked this day to West Ella to my Mother's funeral she was 87 years old in April last. she was born in the year of the Scotch Rebellion 1745. Her days have been long and peaceful was her end, she seemed only to be in a Sleep, Out of 4 of her Children I was the only one to attend her to her Grave she was buried in Kirk Ella Church yard, in Virgin Mould, not so much as a single bone being thrown out of the Grave. — We walked to Ferriby after tea and waited till the Coach came from Hull, it was so full on the outside there was no room, so we went in the inside, at the outside fare, and arrived at home about eight O'clock at night.

Wednesday 8th. Aug

My Sister is so ill that she is obliged to keep her bed, she is troubled with a Violent pain in her back, and so weak that if she was up she could not stand, she cannot even turn herself in bed.

Thursday 9th. Augt.

Recd. a Letter from the Stamp office with a Memorial which had been sent to the Board from River Bridge by a meeting of Licensed Hawkers— complaining of an Inspector of Hawkers' Licences of the name of Hornsby, and desiring me to recommend a steady person for the Situation. I know of none that I can recommend indeed I do not know what Salary there is for it, or whether there be any.

Friday 10th. Aug

I believe some Persons are about beginning Harvest, it is and has been all the week very fine Weather. The Crops look well and are said to be very good I hope Providence will send a favorable time.

Saturday 11th. Aug

Heard from Wm. this morning that little Mary is better, the Paper was so torn I could hardly make it out but think he said her Mother was with her; if so I am glad of it as the poor little Girl would be happier with her than alone in a strange place.

Sunday 12th. Aug

Eliza and her Mother were at Hull on Thursday last buying mourning for my Mother; we have bought some Paper, to paper the Room as we intend giving up the old Glasner's house at Lady day next, there is no living so near him and old Kate with any comfort.

Monday 13th. Aug

I have the annual Jury list to make out as usual having recd. directions for the same, — Mr. Hudson who bought Sam. Ayre's property has bought Mr. Earnshaw's farm here. I think he (Hudson) is a Draper of some kind at Hull.

Tuesday 14th Aug

I have lent Old Willy the Reform Act, which will exercise him for some time; he was reading something in the Paper about Solicitors which he always calls Solitarys, but which he explains to be the same as Lawyers. He often talks of Algernon Piercy[23] whom he calls <u>Algerine</u> Piercy.

Wednesday 15th. Aug

I have now very little employment as most of the Scholars are harvesting, some making Bands[24] and others at different employment.

Thursday 16th. Aug

The Bristol Freeman says he has found in the Reform Act that he still has a Vote for Bristol but he could not point out the Place to me, when he wanted my Opinion: I believe if it were the case he would gladly take a Journey so far as Bristol old as he is (82) were there to be an Election.

Friday 17th. Augt

To this time very few who are entitled to Vote have sent in their claims to the Overseers, as the time grows short for the return of the Claims, they must either send them or stand excluded from the privilege; it is to save a Shilling that they hold back.

Saturday 18th. Aug

I was at Ellerker making out a return of the Valuation of the Township &c to be sent to the House of Commons. Charles Rudd is a very good Book-keeper his Parish Books are kept in a regular way. When I go he brings them out tied round with a Piece of String, and when done with he packs them up in the same manner until they are again wanted—This is an easy method of Book-keeping.

Sunday 19th. Aug

A very rainy morning, and so much rain yesterday as to put off the harvest work—Last night there was some fighting going on in the Street with some Swabs who had got so much muddy Ale, that for amusement they began to belabour one another.

Monday 20th. Aug

This is the last day for receiving claims of Voters; there are 36 sent in, so that I must proceed in a few days to make out the lists of those who have sent in their Claims ...

Wednesday 22nd. Aug

We had Mr. Pool called to see us a day or two ago he had been at Hornsea & Burlington, he has a Son who was going in a few days to the College at Highbury[25] as a student for the Ministry.

---

[23] See n.31 (1836).

[24] i.e. bands of twisted straw to tie around the sheaves of corn before stooking.

[25] Highbury College in London was one of the principal Congregational academies dating from the 18th c. It was originally founded in 1778, as a training college for evangelists, and was known as the Evangelical Academy. In 1791 it removed to Hoxton Square, and the name was changed to Hoxton Academy. Finally in 1825, it moved into a new building in Highbury Park, and the name was changed, yet again, to Highbury College (Dale 593–4).

Thursday 23d. Aug

As to Don Pedro's Expeditions, I think little of it—this Miguel[26] who is rated as a Rascal by all England almost; does not seem to be so ill beloved in his own Country; so even let the two Dons take their own way.

Friday 24th Aug

This has been a fine harvest day, and part Wheat has been got safe home, I hope we shall be favoured with fine Weather, for completing the Harvest.

Saturday 25th. Aug

A very rainy forenoon nothing to be done out of Doors, I am afraid the wet will be injurious to the Corn, however it is what pleases God and it is folly complaining of the Weather.

Sunday 26th. Aug

Rain again today—I have sent off the Valuation of So. Cave to London which is £6613–8s–0d the Rate at half that amount—the amount of the Poor Rate last year 2s. in the pound which was very low. although there were 3 County Rates to pay out of it which amounted to nearly Seventy pounds.

Monday 28th. [i.e. 27th] Aug

Scarcely any Market today, there was some new Wheat sold at 3 Guineas pr. Qr. and some at 56s. which was badly sold according to the times.

Tuesday 29th. [i.e. 28th] Aug

I have been making out the List of Voters for the Township, and likewise the Broomfleet list, that they may appear on the Church and Chapel Doors on Sunday next; there is one from London, James Smith Scatcherd, No. 2 Oliver Terrace, Mile end Road London. for the Farm occupied by John Lockwood.

Wednesday 30th. [i.e. 29th] Aug

In some Cases one property ~~confers or~~ gives the right of two Votes, as in the Case of the Landlord for a Farm, and also the occupying tenant when above £50 pr. Ann. So says the Act.

Thursday 30th. Aug

Rain every day, Sprouted Wheat is talked about but as the Weather is not hot, I am in hopes there is not much damage yet done.

Friday 31st. Aug

Heard that my Sister is so ill as to keep her bed, I think there is little chance of her recovering again, so as to be healthful.

Saturday 1st. Sepr

Measuring some land for Mr. Leeson on the Little Wold; this is the first day for Partridge Shooting, I saw no Sportsmen out, and I was glad of it, for some of them are rather dangerous to come in contact with.

Sunday 2d Sepr.

A Letter from my Brother this morning which much surprised us, as he talks of resigning his place at Skipton and wants to take our Shop, but as we gave notice last week to quit; we can say nothing to it; only we know by experience that nothing is to be had by it, — We have agreed to give him an

[26] See n.16 (1833).

invitation to come and live with us, in an independent manner, and not to trouble himself with either Shop or any thing else: for it will not do.
Monday 3d Sepr.

Yesterday and today tolerable fine weather, I wish it may continue, — Wheat it is said is much sprouted, so that there will be soft Puddings for those who make them the ensuing year.
Tuesday 4th. Sepr.

This is a delightful day, it was a very thick misty morning, but soon cleared off; all hands busy at the Harvest.
Wednesday 5th. Sepr.

What a great deal of unintelligible matter there is in the Papers relating to the Bank of England,[27] it appears to be the result of the reasoning of the Editor that the affairs of the Bank are not conducted in a manner to benefit the Country.
Thursday 6th. Sepr.

I had a Gentleman called this day to look over the List of Voters, he is a friend to Beilby Thompson, who has been declared a Candidate for the East Riding, I do not hear that any Persons have been canvassing, there appears to be at present, Mr. Bethell & Mr. Thompson so if there be no more, there will be but little to do.
Friday 7th. Sepr.

Richard Marshall has been ill all this week for the most part in bed, it is said he is rather better, what his complaint is I do not know, but he seems to be very languid and weak, one of his legs has much pain in it; indeed when he is ill he generally feels it there.
Saturday 8th. Sepr.

The Farmers very throng leading home their Corn this day it being fine weather, I think most of the Wheat is got in, some of it very well, and some not in very good condition.
Sunday 9th. Sepr.

The Voters' List was on the Church Door this day for the second and last time, many who are eligible have made no claim, merely because it would cost a Shilling; they value their freedom at a very low rate.
Monday 10th. Sepr

Mr. Brown the Cornfactor says that wheat is not worth so much at Wakefield as it is here by 8 or 9s. pr. Qr. he had been at Wakefield Market last Friday and had brought a Sample back of some wheat he had there, and was going to try to sell it at Hull tomorrow.
Tuesday 11th. Sep

The Old Glazier after having had our notice to quit since the 31st. Augt. has put himself to the trouble or pleasure of <u>giving us notice</u>; so that we are in a

---

[27] *The Times*, for example, had been printing lengthy verbatim reports of the proceedings of the Committee on the Bank of England Charter (*TM* 3 Sept. 1832, 3 b and 4 Sept. 1832, 3 d).

fair way of retiring; the last Rain we had water to take out of the old wrecky house by pails full, which had come in through the walls.

Wednesday 12th. Sep

I had a Gentleman from London a Stamp Inspector of the name of Morris; he has not been here before, he soon took my Stock as I was prepared and had all in good order.

Thursday 13th. Sepr

Acland the disturber of Hull[28] was here yesterday in the town, I suppose on his way from York; I wish the fellow was punished for his impudence, as I hope he will shortly be.

Friday 14th. Sep

It has been a very fine week for leading this week, complaints of bad gleaning this year, which will be a great loss to the poor, there is very little to pick up, and that little damaged.

Saturday 15th. Sepr

John Pinder died this morning about seven O'clock he has been a long time ill; he had been at Burlington Quay for the benefit of his health and he thought himself better; he was at the Chapel on Sunday last; and was taken worse; he could scarcely walk home ...

Monday 17th. Sepr

As to the Market today, if indeed there was one for it was difficult to find; there was nothing particular occurred.

Tuesday 18th. Sepr

Went down to the Mill to see the Miller and try to get some Sessts. of him, but he was so busy he could not get time to pay; he said if I had brought him any money he would stop his horse throng as he was, to take it; I said to him you have all that, then about you yet. Aye he says more than ever I had, he swears he knows more ten times over than he ever knew in his life before; He says this weather has saved him some old wheat which he was either going to sell or grind into Flour to sell at half a Crown a Stone; but he will keep it and accommodate the eaters with some new sprouted; D—n their Guts on 'em they never got nean good aneuf, curse 'em they sall ha something to find faut about; it's all good aneuf for 'em.

Wednesday 19th. Sep

Mr. Hudson who bought Mr. Earnshaw's farm, has put out hand Bills for letting it, there is about 73 Acres; the Wold Close near Riplingham and the Sands adjoining the Humber, nearly six Miles from each other ...

---

[28] James Acland was a radical agitator and instigator of popular political disturbances in Hull at the height of the Reform fever from 1831, and afterwards until 1835. He published a weekly newspaper, the *Hull Portfolio*. His main targets were alleged corruption in Hull's corporation, the lessees of the Humber ferry, and bridge and market tolls. His campaign as a radical candidate in the 1831 election was accompanied by violent and disorderly behaviour on the part of his supporters. He was tried at York and in Nov. 1832 sentenced to 18 months imprisonment at Bury St. Edmunds, but continued to publish the *Hull Portfolio* from the gaol (Sheahan 159–61).

Friday 21st Sep

Newlove's Daughter who was married to Jas. Barratt died this morning, she has been a long time ill.

Saturday 22nd. Sep

I was at Ellerker this afternoon, I wanted some Sessts. but got no money: I think Cash is very scarce at present.

Sunday 23d Sep

A very fine day. a Sermon at Church which the Parson said was on moderation; I think it might with more propriety have been called Botheration.

Monday 24th. Sepr.

Children it appears are too hard worked for many Hours in the day, and they have no time for learning but on Sundays, so that Sunday Schools are appointed that they may enjoy a <u>Holiday</u>. On the other hand work is so scarce that Labourers cannot get employment, and Schemes for emigration are to be put in motion to take them from their native land. Had not the Men as well be employed and the Children sent to school instead of to work?

Tuesday 25th. Sep

By the Hull Papers it appears that there are no want of Candidates for Parliament, it appears that at present there are four, viz. Hill, Hutt, Carruthers, and Burke.[29]

Wednesday 26 Sepr.

Yesterday was Weighton fair, it used to be a great fair for Old Milk Cheese, but this year there was but a short supply; — Horses in Droves came through to Howden Shews.

Thursday 27 Sep

This Evening with Mr. Bridgman & Leaper, collecting Composition money for the Highways—I ran against a Scraper and cut the foreside of my Leg which swelled a good deal, but hope it will not be much worse.

Friday 28th. Sepr.

This Evening a meeting at Cousens's to balance the Highway Books, and nominate Surveyors for the ensuing year; Robt. Tindale & Thos. Wride are the first two on the list.

Saturday 29th. Sepr.

This day making up the Quarterly account of Stamps, the value of the Stock I have in hand is £186–15–10. the amount of my Sales for the last Quarter £94–1–9½.

Sunday 30th. Sep

A Sermon this morning at Church on Lying, I cannot say that the parson reduced it into an art; but he endeavoured to prove that Lies sometimes <u>are not</u> <u>Lies</u>.

---

[29] Thomas Burke, who had been the unsuccessful 'third man' candidate at the 1830 election was not a candidate for the 1832 election at which Matthew Hill and William Hutt were elected. The defeated candidates were Carruthers and Acland, the latter campaigning from prison and coming a poor fourth in the poll (See also n.2 (1835)) (Markham (1982) 49; *VCHYER* i. 206).

Monday 1st. Oct.

There have been Mountebanks or Horse Riders this evening in the Yard of the Black Bear with Prizes for those who would venture a Shilling., Conder amongst others put in, and got a little Japanned waiter with a Dog on it which quite pleases little Ann.

Tuesday 2d. Oct

Wrote a notice for Saml. Shaw to his Landlord to quit the House he lives in at Brough. And two notices for Ed. Usher to two of his tenants at Everthorpe. And one for Watty Arton to a tenant who lives in the Warren house ...

Thursday 4th. Octr.

Recd. a parcel from Wm. and an Account that little Mary has got home again, we are afraid from what he says that she is but weak, we wish we could see her and all of them; this Separation is very unpleasant. — I was at Ellerker last night balancing the Highway Book which goes in, or is to go, or be carried in on Saturday next to Howden, as Ellerker is in the Division of Howdenshire.

Friday 5th. Octr.

Sent off a Basket this day containing a Goose &c for Wm. it went by the Steam Packet we wished when too late that we had sent it by the Coach, hope it will arrive safe.

Saturday 6th. Octr

~~Slave Trade~~ Slavery. It appears that the plans of some of the so called friends of the freedom of the Slaves, is to put off their Liberty as long as possible.[30] I am for immediate emancipation, It would have been fortunate had the West India Islands never been discovered; of what use are they? that so many poor creatures from day to day and, year to year; live to be used worse than the very beasts. Let them have their liberty; and let us want Sugar, if it cannot be produced without paying for it the price of Blood ...

Monday 8th. Octr

Wheat which is sprouted is selling at a very low price, even under 40s. pr. Quarter; the good sound wheat bears good prices. Flour from 2s/2d to 2s/6d pr Stone according the quality.

Tuesday 9th. Octr

Mr. Bridgman and Old Willy according to annual Custom, intend setting off tomorrow morning for Malton fair, they generally go in a Gig, which is to be their Conveyance this year.

---

[30] The slave trade had been effectively abolished in British dominions by Brougham's Bill of 1811 which made traffic in slavery an offence punishable by transportation. The leading figure in the campaign against slavery from 1821 was Sir Thomas Fowell Buxton (1786–1845). In bringing the matter before Parliament in 1823, he adopted a gradual approach to abolition by recommending that all children of slaves born after a certain date should be declared free. The movement was given impetus by Brougham in 1830, and became a popular issue in the country and the subject of numerous petitions. Buxton again raised the question in Parliament in 1831, but it was not until 1833 that legislation was passed to effect the emancipation of slaves in British colonies. By the provisions of the Act for the Abolition of Slavery throughout the British Colonies (3 & 4 Will. c. 73), slave owners were compensated by a grant of £20,000,000, and the freed slaves were to continue to serve an apprenticeship to their former owners for a period of 7 years (5 years for domestic slaves) (*EB* xxv. 223–5).

Wednesday 10th. Octr

Richd. Marshall says he will give up some of his land he thinks of keeping the Castle farm, as he says it will be quite enough for him. I think he and his Family are at present very uncomfortable, there is a talk that he is going to marry Miss Kitty Corner, Nancy is much distressed concerning it.

Thursday 11th. Octr

Heard from Wm. this morning that the Basket with the Goose had arrived safe and very fine; glad to hear that little Mary is better, and all of them well; we could like to see them as much as they could wish to see us; hope another Summer if we be spared will bring some of us together.

Friday 12th. Octr.

Yesterday was Hull fair, I have heard nothing at all of what was there going on; I never was at Hull fair: and indeed if fairs did not come to me I should not go to them.

Saturday 13th. Octr

This forenoon measuring some harvesting for Mr. Leeson at Ellerker Wold, and Brantingham Sands; about 18 Acres, I got home about one O'clock tolerably tired I went out no more in the afternoon.

Sunday 14th. Octr.

Ths. Marshall went to Hull fair last Thursday and got home sometime on Friday morning with his Hat wrong side before, and looked quite wild, a Man at Ellerker said he saw him when he came and was asleep on his Horse; but the honest Miller says he has not been asleep so long as Natty Massey (who saw him) for he Natty was never yet rightly awake, Sike hounds as him to talk of me being asleep!! Bud whether I was or was nut he had nought to dea with it. Cusse him I deant want to be talk'd about wi' him.

Monday 15th. Oct

When the Coach came in on Saturday night, Timy. Dunn had the misfortune not to stoop low enough when the Coach went under the Gate way; he was hurt a good deal, about his head & neck; it is a foolish thing to persist in going under the Gate way, where there is not head Room sufficient.

Tuesday 16th. Octr

Our Friends have arrived safe from Malton fair, while they have been from home Mr. B's Servants have new cleansed Mr. Atkinson's house; which has put him to much inconvenience, as most of his goods are mislaid so that he scarcely knows where to look for many things, which before the cleaning he could have found in the dark.

Wednesday 17th. Octr

Yesterday Old Bant said I was too late with the Newspaper, but what he wanted was a penny with it; The Post did not go out ten minutes after, but he says he shuts up a Quarter of an hour before the Post goes out; I once gave a penny for being too late. He thought I would continue to do; but I sent for the Paper back, and have sent it today.

Thursday 18th. Oct

Sent to Hull to the Schoolmaster Association £1–3–6 for 2 Quarters' Subscription at 10s/6d each and 2s/6d as a fine for not attending the yearly meeting; I hope it may be of use to me at some future time. Gave the money to Wm. Cousens. Ed. Usher being present on Monday night last.

Friday 19th. Oct.

This Evening collecting the Poor Rate, I only went over the Market place. I did not receive much; but was desired to call again another time.

Saturday 20th. Octr.

This day measuring some harvesting for Chs. Rudd at Ellerker, part of Cave Gates, and the other at Ellerker Sands 18a–3R — went in the morning and got home about one O'clock. the day very fine ...

Monday 22d, Octr.

Very little doing at the Market among Corn, the Wheat trade not brisk, but the Farmers want more for the Sprouted Samples than the Factors are willing to give, so they must hold a little longer.

Tuesday 23d. Octr

Mr. Burland is going to be Steward of Mr. Barnard's Courts instead of Mr. Spofforth, the Court will be next week on Wednesday and Thursday.

Wednesday 24th. Octr.

This is the day for the new fair here,[31] there were a great many Cattle, more than could be sold; James Ramsdale was here, My Sister remains very ill with very little hopes of recovery. They have recd. some of the Goods from Liverpool amongst others the Gold watch; they have written to Wm. to know how he will have his part sent.

Thursday 25th. Oct

The Belgium and Dutch concerns are as Jno. Gardam used to say "a Bag of Moonshine", sometimes we hear of nothing but war, at others all appears satisfactory and peaceable. My desire is for peace.

Friday 26th. Octr

Recd. a letter this forenoon that my Sister died yesterday morning; and is to be buried tomorrow forenoon. She was called or named Milcah after my Father's Mother, whether there be any other of the name I know not.

Saturday 27 Octr

Went this morning with Eliza by the Coach to Ferriby and walked from thence to West Ella; my sister was buried about Eleven O'clock in the forenoon, She was 49 years of age. Jn. Ramsdale had a letter from Wm. this morning; he said he was well, they are going to send his Goods next week.

Sunday 28th. Oct

Eliza and I walked home last night by the way of Riplingham we got home about dark, she was very tired, but soon got rested again.

---

[31] This cattle fair, also known as 'back-end' [i.e. autumn] fair, was still being held in the last decade of the 19th c., when South Cave's market had ceased to exist (Bulmer 580).

Monday 29th. Octr.

This day paid Mr. Oxtoby — £43–14s–0d we are in debt to no one; therefore are not afraid to look any body in the face; being in debt has the effect of making people pusillanimous & cringing; though I can say this for many who are in debt that they never endeavour to be out of it; but these are thieves & Robbers.

Tuesday 30th. Octr,

Turnips this year do not appear to be so much enquired after as they have been in some Season; I do not think there are many yet sold here.

Wednesday 31st. Octr.

What a deal there is of the trial of the Mayor of Bristol;[32] this is like shutting the Stable door after the Horse is gone, what could the worshipful Mayor do if he had nobody to help him? they will even send him back if indeed he be in London; and if not he may stay at home and be quiet.

Thursday 1st. Novr

Yesterday and today the Courts are held. Geo. Petfield & Ths. Levitt are the Constables. I was not at the Dinner as I found the half Guinea was not forthcoming. Ths. Marshall they say was poorly after Dinner he complained of being blown up, that he could hardly speak, he asked some that were there if he had eaten a deal, they thought he had played his part at the Plumb pudding— however he staid until the last; and at night he began to feel more easy after having drunk about a Jill of Rum which was left in a bottle spared in making Punch; it opened his mouth and loosened his Skin so that it was the happiest part of the time with him.

Friday 2d. Nov.

Ths. Marshall's Cattle had got amongst his Brother Robt. Turnips, which enraged Robt. so much that he vowed to Sue his long Brother; Sue me, Sue me, says Tom let him gang on; — but it will be as weel for me to see what damage has been done, so he took a view and found they had eaten, pulled up, and otherwise injured, One hundred and eleven Turnips—Mr. Turk was to estimate the damage which he did at ninepence, reckoning the Turnips at one Penny a Dozen. The Miller thinks he is entitled on payment to all the Turnips damaged, and not consumed and as he hates to be shabby, he will give the little brantling fellow a Shilling, when he settles with him, he says he will dea ought for quietness but he will settle with Bob, not pay No No.

Saturday 3d. Novr.

A Parcel from Wm. this morning, containing the Ed. Review and one of the cheap Publications. We are glad to hear that they are all well, and were gratified with the Goose &c. We bought it of Lockwoods, who live where Wm. Tindale's lived when we first came to Cave, — I hope he will get his plate the

---

[32] Mr. Pinfold, the Mayor of Bristol at the time of the Bristol riots of Oct. 1831, was tried at the bar of the King's Bench for neglect of his duty, in failing to take the necessary action to suppress the disturbances, but was found not guilty, and indeed recommended for his conduct at that time (*AR* 1832, Hist. 51).

next week, but as it has been through so many hands I am fearful that it may have lost weight.

Sunday 4th. Novr

I have got a Bible from West Ella, which indeed is my own, but had I not asked for it I should not have recd. it. I bought it at Burlington of Mr. Leadley many years ago. There is a Tea board which my Mother had which is ours, but it seems to be owned; however we shall claim it.

Monday 5th. Nov.

A very stormy day, Rain (Snow the first this Season) and very cold it is Beverley fair day, which has made the Market here very thinly attended.

Tuesday 6th. Nov

Beverley Sittings are held this day; it is said there was very little hiring; the day was very rough and rainy.

Wednesday 7th. Nov

It appears that the Fleets of England & France are going to the Coast of Holland, to try to convince the little King, with their strong Arguments that he had better give up Antwerp, than have it taken from him.[33]

Thursday 8th Nov.

This morning I bought some writing Paper and Copy Books of my old traveller, I laid out 9s/6d he was glad to be lightened of his load—though I dare say he would at the first opportunity again augment it.

Friday 9th Nov

Rd. Marshall has either let or agreed to let the Farm, where he lives to a Man of the name of Elgie whose wife is Ths. Marshall's wife's Sister, I think there are about 250 Acres of Land.

Saturday 10th. Nov

A very rainy day particularly in the Afternoon and night when it was very stormy, I was at the West end in the afternoon but got home before it was very bad.

Sunday 11th. Nov

After the Storm yesterday we are this day favored with a very fine Sunny day; so it is with life after a gloomy time, light breaks in upon us, and hope points to happier days.

Monday 12th. Nov

Some of the Farmers at the Market exclaiming against Ireland, because so much Corn is exported from thence that the prices are kept lower than the English producers wish for. Heard from Wm. that he had recd. the Plate which was spared for him, it appears to have been in such Company as the Man who

---

[33] In 1830, the Paris July Revolution had been followed by the revolution of the Belgians against the partnership with Holland, which had been enforced upon them by the settlement of 1815. After negotiations, involving both Palmerston and Talleyrand, a settlement was finally agreed upon in Nov. 1831, but the Dutch King refused to accept it, or to evacuate Antwerp, and was only made to do so by the operations of a French army and a combined Franco-British fleet. The situation was not settled to the satisfaction of all the countries involved until the treaty of 19 Apr. 1839, which guaranteed the independence of Belgium (Walpole iv. 258–60).

journeyed from Jerusalem to Jericho; <u>who fell among thieves</u>—it is very strange that there are no Sugar tongs—I was greatly afraid that it would lose in weight.
Tuesday 13th Nov
I have an old Book on Surveying by "Thomas Manley of the Middle Temple Esqr."—"London, Printed by E. Flesher for George Sawbridge, at the Sign of the Bible upon Ludgate Hill. 1674".[34]
"You may hear of him (the Author) at Robert
"Morden's house at the Sign of the Atlas in Cornhil
"near the Royal Exchange in London, where you may
"have all sorts of Globes, Spheres, Maps, Mathematicall
"Instruments &c"—This Ths. Manley it seems wrote many works. 1. His Arithmetic in 4 Parts 2. Arithmetical Recreation. 3. Compleat Surveyor. 4. Geometrical Exercises. 5 Tables of Compound Interest. 6. Platform for Purchasers, Guide for Builders—7. Use of the Line of Proportion.
8. Art of Dialling
9. Panorganon.
10. Use of the Semicircle, in Surveying Land.
11. Astroscopium. his uses of the two Hemispheres
He had then (1676) nearly finished
 The Use of the Globes.
 Treatise of Navigation.
Second part of the use of the Line of Proportion, or Gunter's Line <u>made</u>
 <u>easie</u>
Wednesday 14th. Novr.
    Mr. Stuparte the Surgeon has left Cave, and a young man of the name of Carter has taken the Situation. Stuparte for the present has gone to live at Elloughton.
Thursday 15th. Nov
    This was the Sittings day, a very unfavorable time being rainy most of the day; Mr. Smelt was not here; he sent a Clerk there were twenty Constables dined. I amongst the rest though no Constable, the Dinner was at Fewson's.
Friday 16th. Nov
    I saw a Print of Saint Luke (I think it was) writing, he held his pen so badly that I could have wrapped his knuckles; his pen was held by his forefinger and thumb; and his three other fingers laid on the Paper; and the knuckle of his forefinger nearly at his nose. — abominable.
Saturday 17th. Nov
    I went to Ellerker this afternoon and in going over the Stonepits; I fell in with the Fox hounds, and several other Animals, some in Scarlet; but the Fox they had had in view had given them the go by. I got on one of the Stone heaps

---

[34] The author of this standard work on surveying was not the lawyer, Thomas Manley, but William Leybourn. RS may have been confusing this work with his 'treatise on wills' which was probably Thomas Wentworth's *The Office and Duty of Executors*, of which the 1676 edition had an appendix by Thomas Manley. (See Appendix 3).

to look after them, and saw them go up the Cliffs to Mount Airy, after that they turned towards Brantingham—and I went on my way and saw them no more.

Sunday 18th. Nov

I read this Evening most of the Book of Job, it is a favourite with me; Job was a favorite of God yet was afflicted in a more severe manner than any other mortal. His friends in their manner of administering comfort, took it for granted that Job was wicked and a Liar, and therefore punished for his wickedness— Miserable Comforters were they all.

Monday 19th. Nov

The affairs of Belgium and Holland are something like the Letter which a Friend of Billy Bullock recd. and could not understand so he got Billy to read it for him which he did, and swore it was nought but "Hawman, Jaw-man. (I believe Billy meant Horam-Joram) Jowl-heads together, all of it nought else,["] so the two Jowl heads agreed it was Hawman Jawman: past all human comprehension.

Tuesday 20th. Nov

Paid Mr. Oxtoby yesterday £43–6–0 he was here about breakfast time, as he had to go to Leeds, so he got his money and I dare say went on his way rejoicing. We expect a load of Flour &c today. This I write in the morning.

Wednesday 21st. Nov

Witnessed Mr. Robinson's will this day, — I think he makes a will every year, it may be to keep his hand in; the present one contains 12 Sheets of Paper. — It has been observed that Doctors do not take much of their own Physic—but here is a Legal Gentleman who has taken a good pull in his own line.

Thursday 22d. Nov

Sittings again today it has been very fine but only a thin attendance. Copied over an agreement for S. Shaw, it is expected he will come to live at Drewton at Lady day next, he having bought the Farm where Frans. Wood lives.

Friday 23d. Novr.

Recd. a letter from Mr. Pool this morning respecting my Brother, from his Account he is in a very bad way, he wishes me to go over to try if it be possible to get him to come to Cave; but at present I dare not venture for I have such a dreadful cold that it would be very imprudent for me to venture from home. I have written to Pool to see that he wants for nothing. This is a dreadful stroke to us.

Saturday 24th. Nov

This morning I went to Walkington to swear to the delivery of some Surcharges, and being so fortunate as to meet with the Magistrate at Home it saved me the trouble of going to Beverley. I got home about two O'clock in the afternoon. A very thick foggy day ...

Tuesday 27th. Nov

There was some disturbance at Fewson's last Thursday night, when the Constable was called in; but he was assaulted by the drunken Squad; he has got

Orders for five of them to appear before the Magistrates on Saturday next, where it is expected they will meet with the punishment they deserve.

Wednesday 28th. Nov

I was at the Castle this Evening and saw the Honble Occupier, who paid me his taxes, he seems to be a decent kind of young man; he is married and has three or four Children, and a Dozen Servants of all sorts.

Thursday 29th. Nov

This is Martinmas week, but here is very little stir going on amongst the Servants, now their own Masters. When I was at Burlington I always as at this time went to Barmston, saw its pebbled shore the loved South field and every Juvenile prospect now how changed, the Sea & Hill indeed remain but the old friends are for ever fled.

Friday 30th. Nov

Sir Francis Boynton of Burton Agnes it appears is dead, his Brother Henry succeeds to the title and Estate, this is the third brother who has succeeded each other.[35]

Saturday 1st Decr

Some unruly lads who were making a hurry at Fewson's the last Sittings day, were this day at Beverley, but it appears there was very little against them, they were discharged with paying the Expences or part of them I do not know which after they returned home they set up three dreadful howls; perhaps meant for Hurrahs, but all was quiet after.

Sunday 2d. Decr

I saw in the Rockingham this morning, that there had been a meeting at Barton of the Candidates for Lincolnshire and their friends, some of the Candidates for Hull were there and made such long speeches, that I had neither time nor inclination to read them over, as I had the Paper to take down to the West end to Tom Levitt who takes it in.

Monday 3d. Decr.

Abraham Barff who seems to take a pleasure in being well called; must have been this night highly gratified; by Peter Gardam giving him a complete dressing down, in words and abuse for Peter is no fighter, but he baited poor Ab, while he left the Room: I did not hear them; but I had the account as official ...

Wednesday 5th. Decr

I wonder what these persons mean who say they would have no objection to put an end to Slavery if the Slaves were in a proper state to have freedom conferred on them; will keeping them longer in bondage, bring them into a proper State for liberty, No, No—let them have their liberty, and they will find means to enjoy it.

---

[35] Sir Francis Boynton, 8th baronet (b.1777, inherited 1801, d.1832), was succeeded by his brother Sir Henry, 9th baronet (b.1778, inherited 1832, d.1854). Sir Francis had succeeded Sir Griffith Boynton, 7th baronet (b. 1769, inherited 1778, d. 1801). All 3 were the sons of Sir Griffith Boynton, 6th baronet and his second wife Mary Hebblethwayte (Imrie 111).

Thursday 6th. Decr

Heard from Wm. & that little Mary had got a Muff and tippet &c. little Ann has been very sick and ill part of the last night and today, I saw her in the morning she said she would come at night and see the Red Book—an Old picture of London which I have, she begins to cry out for her <u>led</u> (red) Book, she knows Newgate.

Friday 7th. Decr

Ann is better today, but she has fallen down and cut her head, and is obliged to have a plaster on it; we expect it will soon be better.

Saturday 8th. Decr.

I am going to Copy for the Parson, a Critique on Scott's force of Truth; in the Quarto Edition of Bishop Heber's life;[36] there are 20 Quarto pages which will be a stiff job, as he wants it finishing the next week; and I have the taxes to collect.

Sunday 9th. Decr

I have begun to copy the long letter, it is the first Volume. Chap. 17. I have written out the title, and ruled some of the paper, as I wish to be correct.

Monday 10th. Decr.

The Siege of Antwerp (old Willy calls it Antewerp) seems to be carried on in a murderous way,[37] War is a rough trade; and a siege is not the most pleasing part of it; especially at this time of the year.

Tuesday 11th. Decr

Beverley election was yesterday, when Mr. Langdale and Mr. Burton (Peters formerly) were chosen; there was a Tory of the name of Winn, it is the second time of his trial at Beverley. He may well come no more ...

Thursday 13th. Dec

I was at Ellerker last night where I went for some money, but all I got was a promise to have some sent on Friday next Tomorrow; now I dislike verbal promises; as bad or worse than paper promises, in both cases, I had rather had sterling gold!!

Friday 14th. Decr

I intended going to the Mill this evening, but the nights are so dark, I omitted it, not I dare say to the displeasure of the Miller, honest Man, who abominably hates to pay money; and he says nobody pays money so freely as they receive it; he does not care what any body says of the pleasure in paying, — there can be no pleasure in it; and they are liars who say they pay with as much pleasure as they receive.

---

[36] Reginald Heber, *Bishop of Calcutta*. 'Critique on Scott's "Force of Truth" [originally written as a letter addressed to Miss Charlotte Dod, 1819]' *in*: Heber, Amelia. *The Life of Reginald Heber ... By his Widow ...*, London: John Murray, 1830, vol. 1, pp. 533–53.

[37] According to the Anglo-French treaty of 22 Oct. 1832, Holland was required to withdraw all its troops from Belgian territory by 12 Nov. When it failed to remove its garrison from the citadel of Antwerp, the city was besieged by a French army under Marshall Gérard. The siege works were conducted by the French military engineer, Baron François Haxo, to such good effect that the citadel capitulated on 23 Dec. 1832, after little more than 3 weeks of besiegement (*AR* 1832: Hist. 367).

Saturday 15th. Decr

I was at Beverley this day paying in the assessed, and Land taxes; it is very little trouble paying when the money is ready. — The Beverlonians are all alive with the Election that is past, and the East Riding Election which is to be on Tuesday next, that is the nomination day, and as it is not expected there will be any opposition it will be finished the same day. As much bribery as ever it is said!

Sunday 16th. Decr

I have finished my long letter from the Bishop's life, where much is said to very little purpose, that is my opinion; but to the Arminians[38] I suppose they highly extol it.

Monday 17th. Decr

Mr. Bethell for the East Riding does not seem to be very popular with the Agriculturalists, they have got some undefined notion that he is not their friend; but wishes for a free trade in Corn; which they cannot with patience hear mentioned.

Tuesday 18th. Decr

The Paper I received yesterday, was not Wms writing. I suppose he had been throng, and given it some other person to write the direction. At least I hope this was the case.

Wednesday 19th. Decr.

I see by the Hull Packet this morning that it is going to be the only Tory paper alias Conservative in Hull; as it is said that Isaac has sold the Property of the Advertiser to a Company of Whigs.[39] Cobbett I see has been returned as a member, from Oldham;[40] I do not suppose he will have much influence in the Senate; he may be amusing, and at times impudent and boisterous.

The Old Cardinal is contrary as his old wife, it is said they have stopped up our parlour Chimney, and I think they have, as we cannot have a fire in it—but when the days get a little longer we will leave it on Sundays. I hear of nobody yet applying for the Shop, indeed if it >the house< were

---

[38] i.e. followers of the Christian school of theology developed by the Dutch theologian, Jacobus Arminius (1560–1609), which opposed the Calvinistic doctrine of predestination and laid stress on free will and salvation by grace, repentance, faith and good works. Wesleyan Methodism owed much to Arminianism and there was an Arminian tendency or wing in the Church of England (*EB* ii. 576–7, xxvi. 781).

[39] Isaac Wilson had been co-publisher of the *Hull Advertiser* with William Rawson and William Holden from 1805 until 1821, when Wilson became the sole publisher. Under Wilson, the newspaper became more vigorously committed to politics, and staunchly supported the Tories throughout the Reform Bill crisis. In 1833, however, it was acquired by George Lawson and in the same year passed to William Kennedy, under whose proprietorship and editorship it was transformed into a Radical organ (*VCHYER* i. 428).

[40] Cobbett had stood as a candidate for both Manchester and Oldham in the general election of Dec. 1832. However he withdrew from the Manchester contest when, on the second day of polling, the Oldham poll showed that he and his popular radical ally, John Fielden, were so far ahead that their rivals conceded defeat. He was duly elected MP a few months short of his 70th birthday, but proved to be less effective as a politician than he had been as a radical publicist (*CPR* 78, xii (22 Dec.) 1832, 705–25; Sambrook 177–9).

examined I think there would be no one very ready to join such sweet neighbours, as they have proved and shewn themselves to us, at Ladyday if we live we shall leave it altogether. — They never lay out a penny with us, indeed I think they are grieved to see we have so much custom. I envy not their dispositions; I will take care he shall mend our Windows no more. If I cannot get another Glazier, I will patch them up with Paper, until I can fall in.

Now I think I have written nearly all I know, and it does not appear to be much; but as this will not fall into the hands of a miserable Critic, I have no fear of having it condemned.

I have not heard of the proceedings at Beverley yesterday, in the East Riding election, If I hear before we pack up the Goose tomorrow, I will note it.

So. Cave, 20th. Decr. 1832.

Dear Wm.

We now send the Basket with the Goose, and some fine Raisins for the Bairns a little Spice loaf &c. and I am sure I do not [know] what else, but it will be found—we are all well & hope you are all the same, our best and kindest love to you all, with the wishes of a merry Christmas & a happy new year. — Your Mother talks of going to Skipton next week to see your Uncle and if possible to bring him back with her; I am not at all anxious for her taking the Journey, but when she sets herself fairly on any work, she has strength of mind to carry her through; she dare not trust me to go, for fear it would make me ill: hoping all will be for the best

I remn. your
loving Father
R Sharp

[On next sheet in pencil]: Let us know as soon as you have received the Basket

Friday 21st. Decr

Sent off a Basket by the Carrier this morning for Wm.which is to leave Hull this day to go by the Barton Coach; so that we expect it will be in London tomorrow night.

Saturday 22nd. Decr

Mr. Robinsons of Mount Airy had a little Boy buried this afternoon about eight years of age he died of a complaint called Croup,[41] he was a very fine healthy looking Boy, and had only been from School a few days: — I was looking for a description of the Complaint, and find it was not formerly known; its first appearance in England was at Wooler in Northumberland in the year 1755 ...

---

[41] The word 'croup' for the inflammatory disease of the larynx and trachea in children had been used in SE Scotland for many years before being first being introduced into general medical use by Professor Francis Home of Edinburgh in 1765, when his treatise, *An Inquiry into the Nature, Cause and Cure of Croup*, was published (*OED*).

Monday 24th. Decr

This being Christmas eve, we had a very thin attendance at the Market; as the Market at Hull is this day on account of tomorrow being Christmas day; We had Furmety this night as usual, and a Youle Clog on the Fire.

Tuesday 25th. Decr

Christmas day, plenty of Lads aye and Lasses too—running about wishing their friends a merry Christmas; for which they expect to be paid ...

Thursday 27th Decr

Isaac Wilson it is said has sold the Advertiser for two thousand pounds to a Company or set of Radicals;[42] how oddly things fall out!!

Friday 28th. Decr

At Old Willy's this night as usual; when two women came in and began to sing a Christmas Carol, but the Old Gentleman stopped them; when one of the Women said, why we sung to you last year; very well he says, I am sure it will be sufficient then for two years. So they walked off with the vessel Cup.

Saturday 29th. Decr

David Morley has a Brother who served his time with him to be a Blacksmith this Brother has been breaking in to the Saddle house at Booth Ferry. He has stolen it is said about 15 or 16 pounds in money, he has been committed to the House of Correction at Wakefield; where he will not enjoy a very happy Christmas.

Sunday 30th. Decr

Another little Boy died in the Croup the last week about four years old, he was Christr. Wood's Child, — We have got our Room papered. — I see Antwerp has surrendered—what next?

Monday 31st. Decr

Mr. Brown the Cornfactor said this day at the Market that there had been Wheat sold last Friday at Wakefield Market for 1s.pr. Stone, which weighed 36 Stone a Quarter. which is a good weight.

[42] See n.39 (1832).

1833

Tuesday 1st January

This Evening the Plough Lads had a supper at Cousens's, which passed off quietly, as I suppose they had not much Money: they got about five pounds today; and yesterday after paying their expences they had only 11s. to spare.

Wednesday 2d. Jany

A Parish meeting at Morley's this Evening, very few attended; it was to consider what wages were to be allowed to the Men who work on the Roads; and others who have no work, want some allowance.

Thursday 3d. Jany

I do not understand rightly the manner of voting by ballott (stop only one t)[1] every man has two Votes and as his name is not to be known in voting, he is to distribute his Balls in what Box, Glass, or Urn he thinks proper: how is he to be furnished with the Balls? are the Voters names to be called over and two Balls each delivered to them?

Friday 4th. Jany

A Traveller called at Mr. Atkinson's, and begged leave to light his pipe; but the old Gentleman, said no I never suffer any one to light his pipe at my fire. The man said it could not do him any hurt; but our old friend stuck to it that he never allowed such a thing; the Man was going away, when old Willy said to him: you are welcome to light your Tobacco, but, I never let any one light a pipe. This will bear talking about and about, for some time to come.

Saturday 5th. Jany

A Letter from Wm. this morning, glad to hear that his health is so good, hope the others who have Colds will soon be better, — we are happy to hear that they were all so delighted with the contents of the Basket.

Sunday 6th. Jan

I cannot recollect whether in my Barmston Recollections I mentioned Old Neddy Hopper >a Farmer< who lived at Allison lane end; I think I should not forget him, he was troubled with the Palsy; so that he could with difficulty get his hand to his head; yet he would try at a tankard of Ale, and when with two or three friends he like Tam O Shanter was in no hurry of starting. He had two Sons about my Age, but where they are now I cannot say. I once had a hard battle with one of them, when my Brother and I were going to Beeford to see our Grandfather, Jem Hopper met us in White Bread lane, and to it we went; until we were both tired; so we gave up and were friends.

---

[1] The practice of dropping balls into boxes to denote choice originated in ancient Greece and has persisted in some clubs to the present day. The term 'balloting' came to be associated specifically with the secret ballot. At the time that RS was writing, voting at elections took place in public with the subsequent publication of poll books. Secret balloting was not introduced until the Ballot Act of 1872, after several notorious cases of bribery and treating had come to light, most notably at Beverley (Kinzer 1–18; Crowther (1990) 17–20).

Monday 7th. Jan

I went down to the Mill one night lately when the Man of Dust set me to the West end as usual; in coming over his land there was a Mole trap set, I asked him who catched his Moles, he says Neabody; well then who sets the traps, whya Tom Coulson, but the devil of a Mowdart does he catch; that trap has been set a month; but the shifty devils weant gang intiv it; or else feal does not know how to set 'em right.

Tuesday 8th. Jan

John Ramsdale was here today to enquire about his Uncle; but I was unable to give him much information; I have written to him but received no answer; I think he is in such a state as to be hardly able to attend to any thing. I want John to go over to see him, which I think he will; and see if it be possible to get him here: when if he cannot come by himself we must go for him.

Wednesday 9th. Jan

Making some Ink today with me it is a sort of dirty job as I have to remove the old Ingredients from one Bottle to another: at the last they are all put together in an old pancheon; where the most inferior Ink is kept.

Thursday 10th. Jany.

This morning only a part of the Paper came to hand, it had been carefully cut: I believe from what was in another's part, that the piece detained, contained an account of the number of Reformers and Conservatives with their names; returned at the last Election as members of Parliament. I can dispense with it.

Friday 11th. Jan

No Paper this morning. I had arranged with Mr. Bridgman last night that he was to have the Paper which came today and I was to have his; I shall send it off on Saturday morning, so that it will be in London on the morning of Monday.

Saturday 12th. Jan

At Ellerker this afternoon at Mr. Levitt's, he is a very slack payer I only got three Sovereigns out of more than ten pounds. I think he will be obliged to sell the remainder of his Land.

Sunday 13th. Jan

John Turk who has given up travelling wants to be a Farmer; he could like to have a Farm where there are good roads. I do not know when or where he will fall in for one.

Monday 14th. Jan

The Parson yesterday gave notice that he should next Sunday preach a Sermon in obedience to a begging letter from the King, in support of the National Society for education in the Principles of the Church of England, — which for any thing I know to the contrary, the Contributions of those who are simple enough to give any thing; will, as Cobbett formerly observed be paid to

Joshuah Watson, Wine Merchant.[2] Now all who are not taxed enough, nor pay Poor Rates enough, nor who pay Rent enough; are at liberty to give away their money, without any let or hindrance from me. — But this sort of Plastering will not do, Let a Poor man have sufficient wages to bring up his Family, and he will contrive to give them Education; without any Society degrading him by a Charitable education.

Tuesday 15th. Jan

There has been a letter from Jn. Gardam who went from here to America; he has got a yoke of Oxen Pigs & some Poultry, and as content as such Articles can make him; he has no thoughts of returning. I had forgot that he has a house and some land.

Wednesday 16th. Jan

Mr. Atkinson was telling how the freedom of Cave might be acquired, I suppose it is an old Joke, but as I had not before heard it, I will note it down. This is the method. If you see three Pigs laying amongst mud in a Sunshiny day; you have nothing to do but pull up the middle one and lay down in its place; then you are entitled to the freedom of Cave.

Thursday 17th. Jan

Wm. said he had lately been reading over my Journal for 1826. It seems I have served the time of an Apprenticeship to the trade: and I doubt with very little improvement: however I still continue in the scribling [*sic*] profession.

Friday 18th. Jan

Thos. Marshall's miller has got bitten by a great Dog of Watty Arton's at Ellerker, but is not incapable of Cadging. Arton's have long been noted for keeping chained up a great ugly fierce Dog. In old John Arton's time, one night some person had placed a Mawker (a Bogle) dressed up like a Man, which when the Dog saw he rung up a merry peal, and disturbed Master & Misses and all the family, they were sure there were some thieves about the premises; One peeped one away and another another way, at length they spied a Man peeping over the hedge; then it was yonder he is, what must we do? Shoot, Shoot, the old Farmer says, then pop goes the Gun, and down comes the thief, there says old John there's down with thee. When they went to see who it was, the poor fellow was found stiff, but turned out to be a Potatoe bogle.

Saturday 19th. Jan

I have read over part of the Evidence on the cruelty practised on Children engaged in the Factories, it is high time that some humane regulations were made and immediately carried into effect, to prevent the poor little creatures from suffering the brutality of their taskmasters.[3]

---

[2] Joshua Watson (1771–1855), a London wine-merchant, was the leader of the pre-Tractarian high-church party and the first treasurer of the National Society (1811–42) (*DNB*).

[3] Before 1833 the only protection afforded to children working in the textile industry was that provided by the Act of 1819, which prohibited child labour under 9 years of age and limited the number of hours worked to (any) 12 in the 24. However its scope was limited to children working in cotton mills and no effective provision was made for the enforcement of its regulations. Lord Althorp's Factory Act of 1833 (3 & 4 Will. IV c. 103) was a more serious attempt to improve the

Sunday 20th. Jan

This day the Parson had what he called a Sermon for the benefit of the— Institution after which a Collection was made. I had a single farthing in my Pocket and I kept it there. I will not encourage them to ruin others as they wished to do to me. No No. no encouragement.

[Monday] Jan. 21

Morley's Brother has been tried for the Robbery at Booth-ferry and found guilty and sentenced to twelve months imprisonment.

Tuesday 22d. Jan

Our old Friend still likes to talk of his former Election pranks, once he came from Bristol to Beverley to vote he thinks it is 43 years since, he voted for the losing Candidate but received fifteen pounds to pay his Expences, Once in London he went to one of the Members House and asked to see Capn. Anderson (I believe the Brother of Lord Yarborough) the Capn, then being Member for Beverley; he knocked at the Door and asked if the Capn. was within? which was answered by another question where do you come from? the answer was from Beverley; — "Oh Capn. Anderson is from home", Our old friend who knew something of Members being from home was not disheartened; but a week after he went again to enquire for the Capn., the question was again asked "where do you come from", from Kilkenny was the answer, Oh walk in, so he walked in and was introduced to the Captain, who soon found his Beverley friend, and asked him why he said he came from Kilkenny. — I am sorry Sir to say that I was obliged to deny my Country because I could not see you when it was known I was from Beverley. The Favour the old Gentleman wanted was a "Frank;[4] half a Dozen were given him with an apology for not having the pleasure of seeing such a respectable Elector when he first came. He was ordered to have both meat & drink.

Wednesday 23d Jan

Hannah Martin was at Hull, and left a Pig to be served and attended on when she was out, but when she came back the first thing she saw was the Pig hung up ready dressed. They had given 30s. for it a month before. I tell Adam her son who is as old fashioned as Old Adam that he hungered the Pig to death, but he says it would not eat when he carried it meat; but Adam's way of serving Pigs is to say to them "Steck thy een and open thy mouth and see what God will send thee". Now Adam is qualified for a Pig lad!!

---

conditions of children working in factories. Its main provisions included the setting of limits on the employment of young persons under the age of 18 as well as of younger children, the prohibition of night-work between 8.30 p.m. and 5.30 a.m., and the introduction of a system of inspection. Unlike its predecessors, the Act applied to the whole textile industry and not just to the cotton mills (*EB* xvi. 10–11).

[4] Certain privileged persons, including notably all MPs, were permitted to post letters free (up to a certain limit on the number) provided that they were identified by their signatures or franks. Since the number of free letters allowed was normally higher than their need, it was customary for them to pass on the surplus franks as favours to their friends and supporters (Robinson 245).

Thursday 24th. Jan

Why should I say that I am delighted with Lord Byron's Poetry? when in fact I do not matter it; I neither like his subjects nor his verse. — I am growing somewhat old fashioned—I do not like his misanthropy for one thing nor his licentiousness for another, so it may be seen he is no favourite of mine. I find no fault with others for being enraptured with his muse; but I have no occasion to join in the cry.

Friday 25th. Jan

Crabbe whose poetry rises just above prose, has a great deal of feeling and an enlarged view of human nature; his subjects are generally low; the tale of Jesse and Colin,[5] which I have just read is in my opinion one of the best; he has no lofty flights; excepting indeed his flattering dedications.

Saturday 26th. Jan

We have not heard of my Brother since Jn. Ramsdale was here; we sent yesterday to know if he had been at Skipton: as we do not know whether he went or not.

Sunday 27th. Jan

The weather still keeps very fine, we had a slight frost last night, but no snow of any Account this winter so far.

Monday 28th. Jan

The Corn trade appears to be very dull, at least the prices are not such as to satisfy the sellers, I only saw one Sample shewn today; for which no price was bidden.

Tuesday 29th. Jan

We are beginning to make preparations for removing and in a little time we anticipate being again at home—It is said the Old Cardinal has two or three applications for the old Shop, but no one has said any thing to us concerning it.

Wednesday 30th. Jan

We have got a few things removed today, we have had Hannah Martin to superintend and David Dennis to act under her direction, we have got a new Arm Chair, to match with the others.

Thursday 31st. Jan

A tolerable fine day, but at night it came on Snow—I had the old Paper merchant again today—he has a Son at Hull a Wood engraver or cutter, Copper plate Engraver and printer; he has been out of his time about 3 Years, and I dare say can hardly find any employment his name is Graham.

Friday 1st. Feb

A Vestry meeting this Evening was called, to nominate Assessors for the ensuing year, but as it seemed to be more comfortable to be at a good fire side, than in the cold Church; the respectable company even resolved to stop at the Bay Horse, when business commenced and was soon over by the appointment of myself and Thomas Levitt to the office. I think this is either the 25th. or 26th. year of my appointment.

[5] George Crabbe, 'The Tale of Jesse and Colin'.

Saturday 2d Feb

We have removed several more things today, and got the Glass put up, the Room begins to look like itself we shall have the consolation of retiring from the <u>Grocery business</u>, without owing any thing, but I doubt we cannot say without some loss.

Sunday 3d. Feb

We never opened out the old house today but as soon as we got up we adjourned to our old home, got a fire made, and remained quite comfortable all the day; and at night went to the old prison to sleep. We had not been an hour in the house in the morning before the Cat came to bear us company, and seemed to be as comfortable as we were, for she like me has always had a hankering after the old situation.

Monday 4th. Feb

I took a retrospective look this day at our old habitation at Barmston—The Garth altogether was under half an Acre. It was divided into the Far-Garth — Pig-Garth, Orchard Garden, and fore Garth. In all 5 divisions. In the Pig-Garth were two Apple trees; a Sweet Apple, and the Awd (Old) tree. In the Orchard the first row contained a fine spread Apple tree and 2 Codlins. In the second a fine large Sweet Apple a Codlin & another called my <u>Mother's</u> tree. In the third row a Tree of the same kind as the Awd tree in the Pig-Garth — a Codlin and a Cow snout tree. In the fourth Row a Russet and two Codlins; at the far end of the Orchard was a fine spread Apple tree, the fruit of which would keep the year round. In all 15 Apple tree, The Codlin trees were in general small, but bore very fine Apples. But now I am informed there is not one tree left nor any fence; it (the ground) is all thrown together. How I deplore such devastation. The Orchard was planted by old John Milner, I just recollect him, I used to sleep with him; — he had a little Shelf at the Bed's head, where he used to put something for me to eat at nights. I used to call him our old John.

Tuesday 5th. Feb

I see Mr. Levitt has advertised his land for Sale I expected he would be obliged to come to this. When he bought the Cardales & Pigdam, Mr. Turk said to him in the sale Room; "are you waring your own Money Mr. Levitt?" Yes I am Mr. Turk; then said he I can only say you are laying out very badly; — I think this part of the Land will be dear enough at half of what he gave for it.

Wednesday 6th. Feb.

Recd. a letter from Wm. together with Pills and Lozenges I find he has been so ill advised as to suffer himself to be distrained on for the Taxes—so long as the Law remains as it is, there is no escaping or evading payment. As far as I can find the Collector has not exceeded his instructions—5s/6d has been thrown away.

Thursday 7th. Feb.

I have heard that Mr. Beverley of Beverley has gone away, it is said so much involved in debt that he can pay no longer; whether it be true or not, time will shew; but it appears to be quite astonishing.[6] He was one of the Magistrates for the East Riding.

Friday 8th. Feb

Last night was the Club night, when new Stewards were appointed for the next six Months. There were three fresh members proposed, who will be voted for the next meeting. It is a long time since any new members came in.

Saturday 9th. Feb

Measuring some Turnip Land this afternoon for Mr. Robinson at Mount Airy, about 15 Acres, it was a very pleasant day; as to the delightful prospect, for the Hill, I need say nothing about it, as it is so well known. — A Young man who was working in a Gravel pit at Brantingham, was killed this day by the Gravel falling upon him; his name is Underwood, his Father is a Carrier and Huckster.

Sunday 10th. Feb

I read the King's Speech yesterday, it contains much matter and but little meaning; however as usual serves for a text to spin out long debates upon.

Monday 11th. Feb

Last Monday I gave a description of <u>our</u> Garth at Barmston this day I will say something about <u>our</u> Close (which was the name we always used for it) It was situated at the Bottom or descent of Hamilton Hill, it was of a triangular form and contained something more than three Acres. — It was divided into two parts, one part for Meadow; but part of this and the greatest part was a sunken Bog, growing nothing but Seaves and Rushes. In the other part was six ploughed Lands perhaps nearly 1½ Acre two lands yearly were wheat, two lands Potatoes and the other two Beans, and on the outside of the ploughed lands was a broad Balk or land of meadow; the Hedge adjoining in Summer time was beautifully hung with Woodbine (Honey Suckle) at the Bottom of the Close there was an old rotten Dike or Gutter which produced Reeds in great plenty, which were much valued, by us when Boys, to make arrows for our Bows. — The land as may be judged was of very ordinary quality; but nevertheless, it was very useful. I believe my Father was the last Cottager in Barmston, who held a little Close. Whether there be any alteration now I cannot say.

Tuesday 12th. Feb

I understand that last night there was some fighting in the Street, by some drunkards; we never heard it which was quite as well.

Wednesday 13th. Feb

Eliza this morning got her bed of another Boy;[7] It is 29 years this day since I came to Cave. I was at the West end this Evening, and very stormy it was.

---

[6] See n.24 (1829).

[7] i.e. Robert Harrison Conder. (See Appendix 2).

Thursday 14th. Feb

Mr. Levitt's land was put up by Auction this day, there were no bidders for any of the Lots but one; which was the Close called Hilldales, Ths. Turk (Tom of ten thousand) was the highest bidder, he bid 53 pounds pr. Acre; it was bought in again at 85 pounds pr. Acre; and at that price it is likely to remain unsold.

Friday 15th. Feb

I find the Irish Church is going to be somewhat re-<u>something</u> done to it; there are to be 10 Bishops fewer than at present; I think they might all be dispensed with—

"Such are the Men, blind Chance—not God has
given,
"To be the Guides of humble Souls to Heaven!!

Saturday 16th. Feby

A letter from my Brother this morning, informing us that he is much better, and has been preaching for the last three Sundays. I hope he will continue to improve; for the present he will stay where he is: may he be favoured with health and strength of mind to support him ...

Monday 18th. Feb

I was at the Justice meeting today at Riplingham being summoned for the Overseer, respecting an old Woman to whom I had paid some Money in the beginning of August last; and had denied receiving it, but when I got there she said she knew she had, had it; she had been at the Overseer to pay her again, and I went to prove if [it] had been necessary that she had been paid by his Order.

Tuesday 19th. Feb

Wrote a letter this day to a man at Hotham of the name of Watson, to make enquiry for the Stamp Office, for the personal representative of a Man named Benjamin Wilson; as there is some duty unpaid in respect of property left by a Sarah Wilson to the said Benjamin Wilson.

Wednesday 20th. Feb

I was at the Castle this Evening collecting—I saw one of the smallest Clocks, that I ever saw before, I suppose it is a Dutch or French Clock, I think the Pendulum is not more than a foot in length and the Face not much larger than a Watch face. Mr. Barnard once when in London, was attacked with the Clock mania, and brought several Clocks of various kinds; this I suppose amongst the rest.

Thursday 21st. Feb

It appears that the Irish are to be placed under coercion,[8] it is a difficult subject to handle, this same Irish disturbance; but the upshot is they either will be masters or otherwise they must be mastered.

---

[8] The Irish Coercion Bill, introduced into the House of Lords by Lord Grey on 15 Feb. 1833, had its second reading on 18 Feb. and passed through committee on the following day. It incorporated a number of extremely repressive measures including a curfew, prohibition of public

Friday 22d. Feb

I think there is some little amendment in the Stupid Article called the "Court Circular", I see that Prince George and others of the Royal family, "attended divine service". It used to be divine Service was "performed" &c. ...

Sunday 24th. Feb

We remove every Sunday morning, I think this will be the last time; as we intend removing our Bed this week; so then we shall only attend to the Shop to sell off what we can. We both feel very comfortable at our old home.

Monday 25th Feb

I saw Mr. Stuparte this Evening, who said he was going to London in a few days' time; I gave him Wm's address, he said he would call on him.

Tuesday 26th. Feb

This day we have been removing our Bed, and we intend sleeping <u>at home</u> this night. So I carry on my report almost as circumstantially as the late reports on the siege of Antwerp.

Wednesday 27th. Feb

Joseph Barratt who married Newlove's daughter, took the opportunity when Newlove was from home of conveying some Furniture away which he said Newlove had given him; but a Warrant was got for Joe, and they have been at Beverley this day and Newlove has got his furniture restored. I do not know which of them is the greatest Rogue.

Thursday 28th. Feb

Jane Wood has seen my wife and told her that she and an Aunt are going to occupy our old Shop and wish to buy the fixtures, which of course we shall have no objection to sell, so we shall shortly get them valued.

Friday 1st. March

We wanted some squares putting into our Windows so to be <u>neighbourly</u> with the Old Glazier, who for the last twelve months and more has not laid out a penny with us; we employed another Glazier who comes once a Week from River bridge; he does not charge so much for our School windows by sixpence a Square as the old Cardinal.

2d March Saturday [written in red ink that has not faded]

I have been making some Red Ink, the first I ever made and this is a Specimen of it. I think I have had the ingredients 10 years; and in seeking for something in the School Closet I found the Brazil Wood (ground) so I set to and made it. I put no Gum in it as I had none, but for the present it seems pretty good, how the Colour will stand time will tell.

Sunday 3d March

An Accident of a serious nature occurred at Newbald the last week; a Shoemaker who lived there was correcting an Apprentice when the lad by some means stabbed him with a Knife, he lived near 24 hours after; the lad was committed to York Castle yesterday.

meetings, and trial by courts-martial. The Bill expired at the end of the session, and was replaced in the following year by a new Irish Coercion Bill, which omitted all the severer clauses of the original (Walpole iii. 376–81, 469–70).

Monday 4th. March

I see I have begun this Sheet on the wrong side, but that will make no meaning as to the matters so it must even go as it is—On Saturday last I was measuring 2 Turnip Closes for Jno. Stather of Everthorpe.

Tuesday 5th. March

Newlove was selling his Furniture by Auction yesterday, I saw a crowd of the thoughtless standing against the Door; we neither wanted any old Riff Raff, nor had any Money to waste in it.

Wednesday 6th. March

Heard this morning from Wm. that Mr. Stuparte had called on him, he has been faithful to his word.

Thursday 7th. March

I was at Ellerker last night posting up the Accounts of the Overseers and Surveyors of the Highways. Thomas Allison (who lives at the Farm where Heslewood lived) who had been at a party one night last week, and who had got his load, but got safe home; had occasion to get out of bed soon after he had laid down, fell against a table which he broke, and likewise broke two of his Ribs, so that he is now confined.

Friday 8th. March

Yesterday was a kind of stormy weather. Club night the Box was voted for to be removed to Barnard Cook's there were only six against him; so the Box was carried to his house: I have been this day drawing a Bond for Barnard and his Bondsman to execute this evening; for the safe custody of the Box &c.

Saturday 9th. March

Mr. Nicholson who lives at Frog Hall has taken a house at Lund not far from Beverley, and is going to remove thither this Lady day; He and Mr. King his Landlord here could not agree ...

Monday 11th. March

Adam Martin when playing at Noon found a Shilling and he had plenty of Companions to help him to spend it, so he spent fourpence of it and his Sister got eight pence from him; and poor Adam when he went home got well "walloped", for being so generous as to treat his friends—but he has made up his mind not to find another Shilling: they may find it who will for him.

Tuesday 12th. Mar

It is said that the Lad who stabbed his Master at Newbald is to be transported for seven years; no great punishment I think for depriving a Man of his life.

Wednesday 13th. Mar

Francis Ruston & Robt. Kemp this Evening valued our Shop Fixtures, so far as each was concerned in his own line; Counter, Cannisters, Drawers &c the valuation is £4–15–9 we have two or three Casks to value yet; we must have a Cooper to them.

Thursday 14th. March

We have got the Casks valued at £1–5–2. There is an Oven and Range in the house and another in the Kitchen which the old Cardinal wants valuing, but which we decline, as we were to leave them for the price we gave for them, and which we shall stand to.

Friday 15th March

Since the old Glazier has got the Account of what the Fixtures Come to, he has been buying some Canisters and other Articles of Timy. Levitt, so whether he intends to have ours or not we know not; but we do know, that if he will not have the whole he shall have no part of them.

Saturday 16th. March

Measuring a small piece of Turnip land this afternoon for Teavil Leason at the west end, a very unpleasant day; got home and went out no more out after six O'clock.

Sunday 17th. March

A wet morning, but the Crows notwithstanding are very busily engaged in erecting and repairing their habitations—when I hear them I am frequently put in mind of a Lad called Billy Tranmer who came to School from Skipsea to Barmston. He said one day "As I was coming to Skeal this morning I saw an old Creakum, Croakum at Willy Foster's Close end". I know we were surprised what it could have been that he had seen; as we had never heard that name for a Crow.

Monday 18th. March

It is as we might have expected, the old Cardinal says he will not have our Shop fixtures—he is busy himself in making some things for the Shop; but only look at the usage; to request of us to get them valued; and immediately when he saw the value to go and try to buy others Cheaper; such behaviour I cannot endure; it is keeping the value out of our Pockets; altho' we have paid for them long since. May I be kept from such friends and neighbours ...

Wednesday 20th. March

I have been writing Barnard Cook notices to the Overseers & Constables of his intention to transfer his Licence of the public house to his daughter in law, the next day for transferring Licences will be the 6th. April, at Beverley.

Thursday 21st. March

Mr. Walmsley was here from Hull one day, with Goddart of the firm of Goddart & Brown Printers of the Hull Packet, he is a young man, he asked me if I ever saw his paper I told him yes every week, I said you are Conservatives he said o'yes certainly, he asked me how I liked the paper, I evaded him and said I saw the Times every day. O he says that spoils you for our Paper. The Times is so violent.

Friday 22d March

Very bad stormy weather, though we had no great quantity of Snow this winter yet on the whole it has been very disagreeable weather, and a long time since it commenced.

Saturday 23d March

I and Tommy Levitt have to go to Beverley on Wednesday next to be sworn in Assessors, he told me if I would borrow a Gig he would find a Horse, I asked Robt. Marshall for his which he immediately said I should have; then my friend

Tom thought they had not a horse that would draw a Gig; so thus it remains: I shall make no application for a horse as I am confident I can walk without putting myself to inconvenience.

Sunday 24 March

Exceeding cold and dirty today, so stormy that my Wife did not go to the meeting this night; a place she seldom misses ...

Monday 25 March

The Farmers complaining heavily of the wet weather which makes the seed time to be put off; Something there must be to find fault with and now the fault is in the unfortunate weather: I think it is very foolish to be complaining of the sort of weather which it pleases God to send us.

Tuesday 26 March

Went this Evening to see Robt. Tindale of Weedley who is very ill, he wished to see me as he is the Overseer, his complaint is an inflammation of the Lungs, he was in Bed; I encouraged him to keep up his Spirits and told him a week would bring him about, whether it will or not I cannot tell but I really thought so.

Wednesday 27th. Mar

At Beverley this day swearing in with T. Levitt as Assessors. I rode Rd. Marshall's white Galloway, it carried me very well, got home about six O'clock.

Thursday 28th. Mar

At Ellerker this evening after School time; there was a parish meeting to Balance the Overseers' Accounts, it was held in the Chapel, and soon over; then we adjourned to the Sign of the Black Horse kept by Wm. Dodds; who opened a Beer Shop, but the last year, he got a regular Licence; and is therefore now a legitimate Publican; and for money can furnish his Guests, with Ale, and Spirituous Liquors.

Friday 29th. Mar

At this time of the year I am always very busy the Overseers are making up their accounts, and I am knee deep in Parish concerns and the Poor and Constable accounts.

Saturday 30th. March

Went this afternoon to collect, I first went to Ellerker where my Customer was not seen by me, I then went down to the Mill; but the poor man had no money: I then went to W Laverack's on the Common, and here I was put off by the offer or mention of a Check for twenty pounds: so that I found I was equally unfortunate, to meet with those who had no money; as well as poor Laverack who had too much for me.

Sunday 31st. March

This is a very fine moderate day, after violent Stormy weather; In the afternoon I did not go out; In fact I did that which I did not like, I had to take the Stamp Account; I do not like so much as to take hold of a Pen on Sundays.

Monday 1st. April

A very stormy day, which kept people from the Market, there has been so much wet that the Farmers cannot get on with sowing; and the wet weather is very unfavourable for young Lambs.

Tuesday 2nd April

A meeting this evening at Fewson's the Bear Inn to balance the Overseers' Books and nominate new Overseers: Robt. Marshall & Thomas Leaper are the first two on the list: there being ten names put down, out of which the Magistrates appoint two; generally the two first on the list.

Wednesday 3rd April

Recd. this morning a parcel from Wm. containing the Penny Magazine:[9] which will be quite a treat for me, at least I anticipate as much; he appears to be rather fearful that he will not be able to get over to see us in the Summer; we should indeed be happy to see him as he proposed and likewise little Mary; it is almost in vain to plan so long before hand.

Thursday 4th. April

We have about got all our furniture removed and tomorrow we shall take away the Shop fixtures.

Friday 5th. Apl

This is Good Friday it is a holiday at School, so we have a little leisure, and to make the most of it we took down the drawers, Counter, &c and removed, Cannisters, Casks and all other articles useful or not useful; so adieu to the Awd hole as Hannah Martin calls it.

Saturday 6th. Apl

At Brantingham this forenoon measuring some Turnip Land for Wm. Fisher, in the afternoon measured a Close for Mr. Popple of Ellerker, and part of a nether Close for Charles Rudd; I called at Mr. Levitt's for some money about dinner time but there was none (viz. money) for me, so I thought I might as well have my dinner as I did not exactly know where to fall in.

Sunday 7th. Apl.

This day I was very unwell in my Bowels, in the afternoon I went with an intention of going to the Church; but I felt so languid and faint, I took a walk towards Everthorpe, and got back about four O'clock and towards night I was much better.

Monday 8th. Apl

This is Easter Monday, a great number of horses were shewn, to the delight of Men, Women and Children who came to see them; as for my part, I abominably hate the appearance of them and the rabble who attend; I am always afraid to come near the horses for fear they should strike.

Tuesday 9th. Apl

I was at Hull this day, I went by the Coach I think it is either six or seven years since I was there before; I went to look after some money for taxes and

---

[9] Weekly periodical, 1832–46, edited by Charles Knight. It was one of the most popular and successful of the 'useful knowledge' miscellanies of the period. (See also Appendix 3).

was so far favored as to receive it £1–18–7. This Journey paid me very ill as the Coach there and back was 3s/6d besides my expences—I got very well there and back again between Seven and eight in the Evening.

Wednesday 10th. Apl

I called to see Mr. Craggs yesterday his Son John was there who they told me was learning to be a Farmer, he has as much the appearance of one as Billy Anson (a ranter Preacher) has to the Archbishop of York. — Mr. Craggs told me that he had had his hopeful Son in London under the care of Wm. who could make nothing of him so he was obliged to recall Mr. Clever home, the Father complains of the trouble he has had with, his spoiled Son. No Paper this day

Thursday 11th. Apl

Wilkinson Ayre it appears has got as far as he can so he has stopped; he has given up what he has on the Farm to his Landlord: such is generally the end of extravagance; Poverty succeeds Prodigality. Well such things we witness every day. 2 Papers today!!

Friday 12th. Apl

Another bit of History. Hume Chap 16th—Edward 3rd—A pestilence. "first discovered itself in the north of Asia, was spread over all that Country, made its progress from one end of Europe to the other, and sensibly depopulated every state through which it passed". Does not this appear to have been like the late Cholera?

Saturday 13th. Apl

At west end this afternoon, Rd. Marshall's removing to the Castle farm, they have been at the house they are leaving, about five years—Wilkinson Ayres Sale I have heard is to be on Thursday next, it is said he is going to live at Hull. He has nothing left of his Estate either here or at Ellerker.

Sunday 14th. Apl.

Our old friend Mr. Atkinson, was reading over, a night or two ago, a piece of Poetry called the "Orphan's tale",[10] he pronounces Orphan, Orphian—but he fairly swerved from both, and in reading the title he said the Scorpion's tail. I wonder what the writer would make of a Scorpion's tail!!

Monday 15th. Apl

This which I am going to notice is known but to few, and I make no mention of it—as I came to know it in a sort of official manner. Sunk Island in Holderness which is Crown Land contains about 6000 Acres, it was leased out and the Lessees gave 3000 Pounds pr. Ann for it, they let it out again to tenants for about £11,000 pounds a year, so that they cleared 8000 pounds a year by it. The Lease is nearly out and the Lessees have made an offer of £9,000 pr. Ann for it; which for the present has not been accepted.[11]

---

[10] It has not been possible to trace any poem with this precise title. The reference may have been to 'The Workhouse Orphan: a Tale' written by John Clare in 1821.

[11] Sunk Island was reclaimed land and as such belonged to the Crown. The lessees, principally the descendants of the first man to be granted the lease in 1669, Colonel Anthony Gilby, were

Tuesday 16th. Apl

I have been applied to, to make an Assessment for the Repairs of the Ellerker Humber Bank, the last Assessment for the purpose was made in 1820—since then there have been many changes; and all the Land is not liable to the rate, but I think, I know as well or rather better than any one else what ought to be charged.

Wednesday 17th. Apl

Recd. a letter from Wm. this morning, he says they have all been ill, it appears with very bad colds; what I would prescribe is to take some Spanish Juice[12] especially when going to bed; it is no nauseous medicine: and will certainly allay the irritation produced by coughing. — (I find I have dated this wrong, the letter not being recd. until Thursday morning)

Thursday 18th. Apl

Being yesterday in Arrear with my remarks I made a mistake; as when I recd. the letter this morning I could think of nothing else, so began to scrawl away for Wednesday instead of Thursday, however there is very little harm done; No more this day

Friday 19th. Apl

This Evening I went to Weedley to balance with Robt. Tindale who was the Overseer last year, he wanted about forty pounds, which I paid him, and we settled very comfortably, he is much better than he was, he has been out once or twice, but he yet looks very ill, a little time will bring him well.

Saturday 20th. Apl.

Rd. Marshall has got <u>flitted</u> to the Castle farm I was there this afternoon. Nancy does not like it, I think it is very pleasant myself; the Crows are very near, and make a great noise now they are busy on family concerns.

Sunday 21st. Apl

I think no Gentleman does less good on his Estate than the Lord of our Manor, he stays in London and seems to hardly know, indeed he cannot of his own knowledge understand any thing of his Estate, there is a negligence here that might be remedied.

Monday 22nd Apl

John Turk was here today he is now a Farmer I was near to him in the Market Room, he says what alteration I see in Cave, some grown proud, some turned fonder than they were, and that is needless; but I see no difference in you, (to me) the very same to all appearance when I was in my happiest days in coming to School; but then it was hard work.

mostly absentee landlords, and sub-let the land to tenant farmers at a substantial profit. Before the then current lease of 1804 ran out, in 1833, the sub-tenants applied to be considered as direct tenants, and the Commissioners instructed their surveyor, John Bower, to make a valuation of the Island. For their part, the lessees proposed a new rent to the Crown of £5,025, but were offered instead a rent of £9,814, which they refused. As a result, in the spring of 1833, the former sub-tenants, who actually farmed the land, became the direct tenants of the Crown on payment of a combined rent of £9,140 10s. 0d. per annum (Whitehead 6–28).

[12] i.e. liquorice juice.

Tuesday 23d. Apl

This has been a delightful day pleasant as Summer. I sat down in the Garden after dinner and smoked a pipe, observing and admiring the flowers, some of which were overpowered by the Sun, and drooped down their heads.

Wednesday 24th. Apl

Letting the Lanes this Evening at Morley's, they were let for £7–11–6. I have known one of them let for more than the whole now raise. A good deal of rain this day: a change from yesterday.

Thursday 25th. Apl

A Letter this morning from a Gentleman at Skipton saying that my Brother had had a Paralytic Stroke on Monday last which had deprived him of the use of his right side: this to us is afflicting intelligence, my wife intends going to Skipton the next week to see him, it will be a great Journey for her, who was never so far from home before.

Friday 26th. Apl.

Rd. Marshall's Servant Girl has gone away, and he will neither take her back nor pay her wages, so that he will have to appear before the Justices on Monday next as the Girl has got an order for him.

Saturday 27th. Apl.

I was at the West end this afternoon, there was a Man had been begging at Rd. Marshall's and had recd. nothing. Tom Levitt was coming out of the back door as the man was leaving the other Door, now Tom had an old Coat on all in tatters, and the beggar took him for one of his tribe, and asked him if he had got any thing given, Tom said no, he thought they gave nothing here; the beggar said he thought it too for he had got nothing ...

Monday 29th. Apl

This day the Brough Road Turnpike tolls were to be let at Morley's; I was there, they (the tolls) were put up at the old Rent but there were no bidders at the old price: so that the letting of them was adjourned for a fortnight.

Tuesday 30th. Apl.

With 4 weights the first being 1 lb the second 3. the third 9 and the fourth 27 lb. any weight between 1 and 40 lb. may be weighed: let those who dispute it make the trial and they will find the above to be correct. In the same manner with five weights of 1—3—9—27—81 lbs. may be weighed even from 1 to 121 lbs.

Wednesday 1st. May.

My wife Set off this morning on a Journey to Skipton. She got a Lad to drive her in a Cart to Mkt. Weighton. This is the most distant Journey she ever undertook. It is a visit of Mercy = I wish she may find my Brother better but at present I have little hope of it.

Thursday 2d. May

I am now my own Housekeeper an office of which I am not much enamoured; I care not how soon I am quit of the situation.

Friday 3d May

Club meeting last night, got done and at home about nine O'clock and as I had no fire I went to bed soon after.

Saturday 4th. May

Expected a letter from Skipton this morning but none arrived, I therefore think my wife will be at home this night; Eliza went to meet her mother this night but after going about a mile she turned back without meeting her.

Sunday 5th. May

My wife arrived this morning, it being after ten O'clock last night when she arrived at Weighton, where she stayed all night. My Brother is very ill indeed so much so that he cannot stir, neither can he talk, he is in a deplorable state, there is no possibility of having him removed here; He will want for nothing; he may long continue in this helpless state, he frets much, and will not take any medicine: his Leg is likewise very bad; he cut it when a Boy with a Whin Bill, and it has never been well; a piece of Bone having lately come out, and more is likely to follow.

Monday 6th. May

Who are the News cutters, that disfigure the paper so much almost every day? is this a new business in London? I know it was carried on by Simon Grindall at Burlington, until nobody would lend him a newspaper—he was not a purse cutter but a News cutter.

Tuesday 7th. May

My wife managed her Journey very well, nay she says she should think nothing of a Journey to London; what put her most out of the way was the impositions of the Coachmen & Guards.

Wednesday 8th. May

I was at the Mill last night and got some Money of the Miller, he is but poorly, and any one asking for Money of him, he says is bad for his complaint, he feels it in his head, and then through all his body tiv his Toe ends; he is surprised that folks has no more feeling for him, now that he is ill, than to ask for money!!

Thursday 9th. May

I have had the old paper merchant again today, I laid out on him 13s/6d for Paper & Copy Books—a very warm day; — the Spring Court is held this day at Js. Levitt's, but I have seen no stir of it as yet.

Friday 10th. May

Thos Marshall has lost all the Sheep he had (which were three;) he had been out seeking for them yesterday. Tom Levitt had told him he had heard they were at Sancton, so off he went to seek his flock, but none of them were there; so he spent all day and came back at night faint & weary having got nothing to eat or drink, for neabody ever thinks that he wants ought or ails any thing.

Saturday 11th. May

I was at Beverley today, I set off to walk and had got between Tim Turner's and Walkington when Hugh Kirby of Bromfleet [*sic*] overtook me, riding on a Galloway: he then got down & I mounted and Rode on to Beverley:

I got home about Six O'clock, sometimes I walked & sometimes Rode in Company with Hugh.

Sunday 12th. May

I do not know that I have any thing particular to say today, only I put the Paper in the Post office for Wm which had been forgot yesterday, as I was from home. So now I have here finished this Sheet which with 6 more makes 7, but here are only 6.

Monday 13th. May

This day packed up a Ham to send to Wm., together with all the News which has transpired since we sent to him the last time: — It will go to Hull tomorrow and leave from thence by the Steam Packet on Wednesday morning.

Tuesday 14th May

This is Weighton fair day and very fine it is, I have seen a good many Cattle come through from thence, Sheep sold at high prices, but Beasts not so well.

Wednesday 15th. May

A Coroner's inquest was held at Ellerker this day on an old Woman of the name of Franklin, whose husband picked her down some time since, and her thigh was broken; I believe it was purely accidental from what I have heard, however the Jury thought otherwise and returned a Verdict of Manslaughter, so the old Man her husband is to be had to York Castle tomorrow.

Thursday 16th. May

Received a letter from Skipton this morning saying my Brother is somewhat better, he begins to have a little feeling on his right side: and his articulation is becoming better; we are glad to find that he is in some measure relieved.

Friday 17th. May

I see there is a new Steam Packet[13] going to start from Hull to London on the 5th. June next—It is rather to be wondered at that there has been no opposition before this time.

Saturday 18th. May

Eliza and all her family went yesterday to Swinefleet feast, Conder's brother came for them, I think they would have been as well at home, but it appears they thought otherwise.

Sunday 19th. May

I was at our old Friend's one night last week when he was making a display of his knowledge of English History: He shot Cardinal Wolsey, nay he said the Cardinal shot himself, which is much the same, I ventured to tell him he was under a misunderstanding, but I might as well have talked to the Town

---

[13] This was the 'Enterprise' steamship, master William Turner. It left Hull for London on Thursday, 6 June with the return trip on Sunday 9 June and was scheduled to continue 'to run in that order'. Passengers were assured of separate beds, and charged one guinea for best cabins and 15s. for forward cabins (*HA* 31 May 1833, 2).

Stocks, so as I did not much value the Cardinal, I told the old Gentleman he might shoot him over again!!

Monday 20th. May

This is again a very hot day, the weather this year has become hot very early. — A Brewer of Mkt Weighton who had been at Pocklington market on Saturday last, had got so <u>drunk</u>, that he knew not how to ride home, but as <u>drunken</u> people are generally more clever than when they are sober; he rode away as fast as his horse could go; when the fellow drunk and a fool, fell from his horse, and thus put an end to his drunken fit and his life together.

Tuesday 21st. May

Ths. Marshall says he never was so badly used as he was by me when I was there, when he said he would not pay neither me nor neabody else these d—d Sessments; so I left him without bidding him good night and what was the highest affront without asking him to come a piece of the way with me. — But badly as he was he says he would have freely ridden 20 Miles if he could have found out a way to fine me 40 Shillings for leaving him in the manner I did.

Wednesday 22d. May

It is a long time since we have had such hot weather in May as we have at the present time and for some time back have had. It is indeed glorious weather, there hardly ever was more Grass at this Season of the year and it is very favorable for the growing wheat Crops.

Thursday 23d. May

I have lately read a good deal of Hume's History of England;[14] how the Infidel blackens the Puritans those founders of English liberty; but what of his abuse? a good cause in the end generally prospers.

Friday 24th. May

Richd. Marshall threshing wheat this day with a Machine: I think there is yet much corn to thrash; the sellers are sadly off on account of the low prices: I never yet could think that dear food was profitable for the Consumers.

Saturday 25th. May

Heard from Wm. this morning that he & little Mary are coming at Cave fair, we are very much rejoiced at the news. I hope they will both arrive comfortable and safely.

Sunday 26th May

A very windy dusty and cold day, the weather suddenly changed last night from hot to cold, in the morning it was so hot that clothes seemed a burden, but at night it was cold enough to wear a top Coat.

Monday 27th. May

I think I have nothing particular to notice today. A good many Pots for sale in the Market as usual before Cave fair; all ended quietly with the Potters.

---

[14] David Hume, *The History of England, from the Invasion of Julius Caesar to the Revolution in 1688*. London: Thomas Dolby, 1825. - 6 vols. The standard work on English history in the 18th and early 19th c.; first published in 2 parts, 1754-7, and then as a single 6-volume work by the London publisher, A. Millar, in 1762.

Tuesday 28th. May

Went to the Castle this Evening for Mr. Stourton's taxes but as he was not at home I went to see the Butler shoot Crows in the Rookery; the afternoon before he had shot Seventy two; but this night they were not good to find.

Wednesday 29th. May

I was at Brantingham this night after School time, for half a year's Rent for the Workhouse, which I received & then came home again; it was a very pleasant night, but the roads very dusty.

Thursday 30th. May

Here must be a Blank, for what with preparing for the Fair, and eating up the Cheer there has been no time for writing, so that I must pass on to Monday the 17th. day of June.

Monday 17th. June

Heard from Wm. that he and little Mary arrived safe at home on Saturday last about half past 12 O'clock, which was sooner than I expected they would, we are very glad that they met with no misfortune. I was at Beverley on Saturday. I rode Abm. Barff's Black meer (mare)—I arrived at home about Six O'clock. Mr. Stuparte's money was left for me at Beverley so that I got all comfortably settled.

Tuesday 18th. June

Our Red Roses are now for the most part in bloom and the tufts of London pride putting out their beautiful flowers, the weather keeps wet and rainy.

Wednesday 19th. June

A Boy who comes from Brantingham, to School was met about Ring Beck this morning by some tramp and robbed of his Shoes Hat and his Dinner— indeed they say most of his Clothes was taken, and the poor Boy sadly affrighted; he went home again.

Thursday 20th June

This day one of Mr. Robinson's Sons of Mount Airy, was married to Ths. Dyson's daughter, they were married at Hull, as the Curate here was not at home; at night there was running for Ribbons;[15] and Music in the Streets; all alive and much to the enjoyment of those who like a stir.

Friday 21st. June

This is the longest day how time slips along. Six months since was the Gloomy winter with little day light, but even in Winter there is enjoyment to sit at the fire side, and hear the blustering storm beating without—and if we look six months forward we shall see the dark hours once more; should we be spared.

Saturday 22d. June

I was at Ellerker this afternoon collecting the Church Sess, I cannot say that I was very successful. When I got home at night the Coachman brought a

---

[15] 'In the evening [of the day of the wedding], a race is run by men for a broad piece of ribbon, the ribbon being as carefully provided by the bride as the ring by the bridegroom, and the winner of the race has the privilege of kissing the bride, the ribbon being his passport' (Nicholson 3).

parcel from Wm. containing 1lb of Tobacco for which I thank little Mary, as I dare say she would have thoughts of her Grandfather and I am certain she would not forget her Grandmother, Ann is much delighted with the fine book, but her highest joy is to think that she will have a Pink Bonnet; a Pink Bonnet is her cry.

Sunday 23d. June

This afternoon about five O'clock we had a terrible storm of Thunder, Hail, and rain the Hail lay on the ground like snow; and put in the look of winter in the midst of Summer; it cleared up again about Six O'clock and became a fine night.

Monday 24th. June

It is all a Flam or Sham of the lad of Brantingham being robbed as he came to School, he had hid the Clothes himself, and went home and raised the report, they had a poor fellow before the Justices for the Crime, but he was proved innocent and liberated.

Tuesday 25th. June

I have been making a Bond for Mrs. Cook to the Club and have got it executed by her and her Brother who is bound with her for the safe custody of the Box &c.

Wednesday 26th. June

Abraham Barff who has been drinking and spreeing was at Fenwick's and found himself hungry, so he ordered some Beef steaks; but in the mean time poor Abe fell asleep, and Robinson of Mt. Airy happened to go in; and eat up the Beef steaks—which our friend had ordered.

Thursday 27th. June

I have been making out the Stamp Ac[count]ts. for the last Quarter; my Allowance this Quarter on £67–4–0 is £1–0–0½ together with 5s. additional for Receipts, it is mostly under one pound a Quarter.

Friday 28th. June

We were at Mr. Arton's at Provence last night at tea there were several others. It was ten O'clock or after when we got home; my wife thinks she shall never venture to go so far again for a Cup of tea, it is many years since she was there before ...

Sunday 30th. June

Very windy weather yet continues, yesterday clouds of dust were driven about; but last night it had been a little rain which settled the dust; which on that account is not so troublesome.

Monday 1st. July

Little Thomas went to Church yesterday afternoon with his Father, when he saw the Church and heard the Bells ringing, he says Hark! "Church is talking". He behaved very well.

Tuesday 2d. July

Recd. a returned Letter which I sent to Mr. Stuparte at Hornsea on the 27th. May last, it appears he has left Hornsea; but I know he was there on the 13th. June the letter had been sent to the Post office Leicester to be kept till called for, but it had not been called for; therefore it had been sent to London and I had 1s/7d to pay for it; with which I am not at all satisfied. I think single Postage would have been sufficient.

Wednesday 3d. July

Wm. Deloitte called this morning to see me he is going to Sydney. I was just reading the times, and told him I had frequently seen his name and the name of his Ship "Florentia" in the Paper; this is his third voyage he is going round the World, his Mother lives with him in London. I forgot to ask his address.

Thursday 4th July

This is again the Club night, the last monthly night in June Wm. & little Mary were here; but they are now far away: They came, they are gone, we met, but—when shall we meet once again?

Friday 5th. July

This is Beverley midsummer fair day a fine day it has been; I think there have many people gone, it is amongst other things a fair for Pigs, and several poor people who can raise as much money generally buy a Pig, to feed for the Winter.

Saturday 6th. July

My wife and Eliza were this afternoon amongst a few others at the Mill; it was very windy which made it very uncomfortable, the wind has been excessively Strong this Summer ...

Monday 8th. July

Two men who work for James Levitt fell from a Scaffold, or as I believe the fact was the Scaffold gave way, one of them had his leg broke in a dreadful manner; so that the bone on the front of his Leg came through his Stocking, it was said the other man had his thigh broke; but it appears he had no bones broken, but was dreadfully stunned.

Tuesday 9th. July

A letter from Skipton this morning saying that my Brother was so much better as sometimes to walk out in the Garden; — I hope it will not be long before he will bear to be removed here. He is not likely to preach again, his articulation being so defective.

Wednesday 10th. July

I wrote a begging Petition for the Poor man who fell from the Scaffold on Monday last and broke his leg, the bone came through his Trowsers (I said before his Stocking) I hope he will be successful Mr. Stourton at the Castle has proffered him any thing that his house affords, — The Poor fellow was very steady, and kept his aged mother, who had been left a Widow it is said with 12 Children.

Thursday 11th. July

This is the Club feast day, it was at B. Cook's; there were about 100 dined, a very good dinner, and agreeable, no squabling [*sic*] nor falling out; the Club has cleared since the last feast £15–13–0 so that it is yet prosperous.

Friday 12th. July

Recd. this night a Box from Wm. containing the Pink Bonnett for Ann with which she is highly delighted, she enquired if her Cousin had come, but when she found she had not, she said then my Cousin Mary will come again at sometime. — We set the slips which were sent but I am afraid they will not grow, but they shall have a fair chance.

Saturday 13th. July

One unlucky member of a Temperance Society at Preston was expelled for eating part of a Plum pudding in which was some Rum!!

Sunday 14th. July

Little Ann says she must have a <u>Pallisol</u> to be like her Cousin Mary, she has held up her head a great height today with her Pink Bonnet on ...

Tuesday 16th. July

The witnesses in the case of Rd. Franklin of Ellerker went to York yesterday, and were today examined before the Grand Jury, the result of which was that no Bill was found against the old man; so now the wise men who composed the Coroner's Jury will be at their wits' end or rather further; they certainly had taken leave of the little sense they ever had when they returned a Verdict of Manslaughter.

Wednesday 17th. July

This morning I see that the tyrant Miguel' Fleet is dished up in fine stile;[16] it is marvellous that a few frigates should thus conquer Ships of the Line. This Napier is a spirited and talented Man.

Thursday 18th. July

I have been pulling our Currant Berries today, we have not had many this year; but what we have are very fine. We shall have but little wine of them.

Friday 19th. July

Last night at the Workhouse with the Overseers taking an Inventory of all the Articles belonging to the Parish which was soon done. We then went to Jem Levitt's and had a Pitcher of Ale; it came on a fine Rain this night.

Saturday 20th. July

Measuring some grass mowing this afternoon for Mr. Elgie at Ellerker Ings about 15 Acres, it was a very pleasant afternoon, after having done I Stopped at Tea, there was the Old Popish Priest. Our talk a good deal was on Religious Subjects, the Old Man I dare say means well, but when hard pushed what he could say was that I was de Calvinist and talked de blasphemy. We

---

[16] This was the reactionary Marin Evarist Miguel (1802-1866), who had reigned as King of Portugal since 1828, after ousting his more liberal fellow claimants to the throne, Pedro I of Brazil and his daughter, Maria de Gloria. Dom Miguel's navy was destroyed by a small fleet, purchased on behalf of Dom Pedro and commanded by Captain (afterwards Sir Charles) Napier, off Cape St. Vincent on 5 July 1833. This was the first of a series of setbacks for Dom Miguel which culminated in his defeat at the hands of an allied army, formed by France, Spain, Great Britain and the Portuguese followers of Dom Pedro and his daughter, Maria, at Asseiceira in 1834 and his subsequent banishment from the Peninsula (*AR* 1833 Hist. 257).

parted very good friends, he had had an answer this morning to the letter he sent by Wm. to London.

Sunday 21st. July

This afternoon I did not feel very well so did not go to the Church altho' I went down for that purpose; I came home again and soon felt better. It is my old complaint in the Bowels; I am generally the worst on Sundays and Mondays ...

Tuesday 23d July

Mr. Stott brought up a letter to send to Wm. respecting some Books he had ordered and paid for beforehand, I promised to send the letter in the morning; I doubt the poor preacher will be taken in: I do not like these cheap Advertisers. I think they are not always upright. The Books were ordered at a Shop in Newgate Street. I forget the man's name.

Wednesday 24th. July

At Ellerker this afternoon at Mr. Arton's at tea, they appear to be just as usual. I think Eliza said there were about 40 great and small; all their own relations excepting us. I know there were 3 changes of Company at a large table. We got home about nine O'clock, little Ann was there and her Father and mother. My wife got wet through in going, as she was overtaken with a very heavy shower; I did not go until after; when it was fine.

Thursday 25th. July

The swelling in little Ann's neck is gone and she is now better; the Doctor gave her some Powders to take and she quitted a quantity of Worms.[17]

Friday 26th. July

The weather is extremely hot, it makes a fine hay time and is also favorable for the growing wheat: I hope it will be a plentiful harvest.

Saturday 27th July

The Doctors Carter & Hill were going this afternoon to Brantingham to open a young woman who had been buried some days, it is suspected she was poisoned, it is said a Man gave her poison when I get to know the result I will note it down.

Sunday 28th July

I think this has been the most sultry day we have had, it was so hot that one could not walk without sweating & being greatly relaxed.

Monday 29th July

The Coroner & Jury this day met at Brantingham on the young Woman who had been poisoned; the Jury gave in their Verdict that she died by taking Poison, but by whom administered, was to them unknown: — but it seems to be believed that the man that was suspected is guilty but there was not sufficient Proof to convict him, so he is left for the present to his own Conscience.

---

[17] It is likely that Ann was suffering from roundworms, which can occur in large numbers in the human body. The lump in her neck may have been caused by swollen glands resulting from a general lowering of her health. The treatment for roundworms, at that time, usually involved the administration of a potion including wormwood (*EB* xxviii. 832).

Tuesday 30th. July

Richd. Marshall had some wheat to sell yesterday at the Market for which he could not get so much by 5s. pr. Quarter as he could have had the week before; which he says has thrown him £20 away, he lays all the blame on Tommy Wride, who put him off with the Threshing machine. I think he is gone to Hull today to try to sell it.

Wednesday 31st. July

I have had an <u>official</u> account of the Repeal of Stamps for any Sum under five pounds, so that the lowest Rect. Stamp is now 3d. I have returned all the 2d. Rects. I had by me.

Thursday 1st. Aug.

Yesterday Mr. Stott's Books arrived, I sent them down to him, but have not yet seen him, they came by Cousens, altho' the direction was by Miles' Coach.

Friday 2d. Aug

Mr. Stott brought up a letter which had been sent by Wm. in his Parcel. I was not at home when he brought it, he had opened the letter, — it was the Club night.

Saturday 3d Augt.

Some thieves last night stole Wm. Loncaster's Bacon, it was in the Granary—4 Sides it is said and 5 Hams were taken away; I have not heard that suspicion has fallen on any person; but it has certainly been some who have been acquainted with the Premises.

Sunday 4th. Aug

Old Loncaster's Bacon was found this morning in a Barley Close of Teavil Leeson's in the new field, and all recovered except about half a Flitch.

Monday 5th. Aug

This is Pocklington fair day which has caused a very thin market here; it is a great fair for lambs, where they have sold pretty well, the weather still dry.

Tuesday 6th Aug

My wife was at Hull, this day, she has bought a <u>blue eyed Doll</u> for Mary, and material to dress her with, so that when she puts on her Clothes she is to go to London.

Wednesday 7th. Aug

I think harvest is begun in several places and the weather at present is very fine for it. It is said that the Wheat will be very good in quality; this is the report of some who would not make it, if not forced to Confess.

Thursday 8th. Aug.

What a deal of senseless jargon there has been about Beer Shops corrupting the morals of the Country. There certainly were opportunities sufficient before the establishment of Tom & Jerrys' for corruption Why cannot Beer be sold at Chandler Shops the same as other articles used by the poor? let me know that you men of much wisdom!!

Friday 9th. Aug

Ths. Marshall says he is "more plagued wi' feals than onny body"; he had sold some Oats to Mr. Spicer and sent his Waggon with his man to deliver them, when feal livered 'em to Mr. Brown, so now what is to be done he does not know; but however he went to Brough and found his Oats mixed among Mr. Brown's, so Spicer and Brown must agree between themselves who are to have them, but which of them will agree to pay poor Tom?

Saturday 10th. Aug

Wm. Cousens was leading Wheat today, he is the first in the town who is so forward; although there is a good deal of wheat cut; and the weather is very fine for it.

Sunday 11th. Augt

This day there were three or four Lads knocking down Apples from Mr. Barnard's trees at the fish pond end: I told Rd. Marshall; but before he could get at them, they made themselves scarce, and were not discovered so as to be known.

Monday 12th. Augt

This day F. Wood wanted the measurement of a Close which I measured a year ago; but as it is against the trade; to give up the contents where there is no profit—it is pretty generally relinquished, I advised him to have it measured over again; So that it will be a job for me or someone else.

Tuesday 13th. Aug

Mr. Stourton and his Gamekeeper went last week from home to shoot Moor Game: there was a letter this morning that the Keeper was very ill at Lord Stourton's at Allerton; and will not be ~~capable of being~~ able to be removed for a fortnight.

Wednesday 14th. Augt.

It has been a rather dull day particularly the afternoon, it came a little Rain about noon—which put a stop to leading wheat; at night it was fine and bright; I think some of the Farmers are not so thankful for fine weather as they ought ...

Friday 16th. Aug

I think the Beer Shops will, at least many of them be wrecked, by advancing the Licence to five Pounds—[18]

> "What little we have by industry made,
> "We must pay for a licence to set up a trade".

Saturday 17th. Aug

Measuring some Pease reaping this afternoon for Ned Coates, belonging Rd. Marshall, Ned promised to pay when he came back from Receiving his wages: but I saw no more of Ned, and I do not know when he will come back.

---

[18] The Beerhouses Act of 1830 was not amended until 1834 (4 and 5 Will. IV c. 85), when the duty for a licence to sell beer on the premises was raised from 2 guineas (£2 2s.0d.) to 3 guineas (£3 3s. 0d.), not 5 pounds.

Sunday 18th. Aug

This forenoon I went down to Church with my very oldest hat on without knowing any thing about it, until I got to the west end when Rd. Marshall asked me what sort of a Hat I had got on: and sure enough it was my old easy, greasy every day hat that I wear at home: I was in hope it would be rain at Noon when I could cover it with my Umbrella, but no: it came not; so I was obliged to walk home in public without any covering to my old Slouched head cover.

Monday 19th. Aug

Scarcely any Persons at Market today, all busy with the Harvest, nothing particular; light Crops as <u>usual</u>, but allowed to be of excellent quality.

Tuesday 20th. Aug

The old Coin which Wm. left when he was here, I sent to Mr. Baron of Drewton[19] to decipher, and here is his report—"On the Obverse is the head of Caligula with the words. C. Ceasar [*sic*] Aug. Germanicus Pont. M. T.R. Pot— On the reverse the emperor addressing soldiers—above the word adlocent."[20] He adds "in its present worn state he is sorry to say it is of no value". — This I expected viz. that it was worth nothing.

Wednesday 21st. Aug.

Brewster Sessions this day at Beverley, when the Landlords & Landladies, have to appear for Licences to sell Ale; those who obtain a licence for Ale; may then apply to the excise if they think proper for a licence to sell Liquors.

Thursday 22d. Aug

A fine harvest day much wheat having been got home, and I hope in good condition: but let the condition be what it may; I doubt not but it will be mixed with the sprouted of last year, so the bad will spoil the good.

Friday 23d. Aug.

We have some very fine Sun flowers in blossom now, and likewise Dahlias, the one that is set singly has the finest flowers, indeed it is a very fine dark coloured double one, viz the flower.

Saturday 24th. Aug

This day I was at the Castle collecting poor Sess, of the Honble occupier, I got a glass of Ale, which was nearly sour so I did not feel very much obliged for it, but as it was given I drank it.

Sunday 25th. Aug

Some body either in jest or earnest one night last week knocked against Abraham Barff's door about Eleven O'clock: Abe got up and fired his Gun at

---

[19] George Baron of Manor House, Drewton, had discovered Roman remains on his own estate which was in a Wolds valley about 1½ miles N.E. of South Cave (Allen 92–3; Hall 90–1).

[20] This coin, featuring Caligula addressing the guard, if genuine, would date from A.D. 37–38. The usual inscription on the obverse of this type of coin was 'C.CAESAR (not Ceasar) AUG GERMANICUS PON (not pont) M TR POT', and on the reverse 'ADLOCUT COH (not adlocent)'. If the mis-spellings in the diary entry are not simply transcription errors made by RS or Mr Baron of Drewton, they would seem to suggest that the coin was a forgery (Mattingly and Sydenham i. 112–17).

them, without however doing any mischief, but it is <u>too bad</u> to be thus disturbed.

Monday 26th. Aug

I had a man sent for me on Friday night last at Morley's, he is an Overseer from Abbey holme in Cumberland, he wanted a Man who was working at Thorpe Brantingham: he called this morning to say he had seen him and settled with him.

Tuesday 27th. Aug

I think most of the Wheat in this neighbourhood must be got in; there is a great outcry that Beans are devoured by insects, but this is so common a cry that it is little noticed: I have no doubt but there will be a sufficiency of Beans: the greatest scarcity appears to be money.

Wednesday 28th. Aug

There was a dismal letter from a Man who went from Leeds to Botany Bay as a free settler: he wishes he and his family were back again: for the Scoundrels there will not associate with him, telling him he was not wanted amongst them. I think it was in the last week's Packet ...

Friday 30th. Aug

I have seen Mr. Stott, who is sadly galled because he has had the Carriage of his Books to pay from London >1s/10d<; I paid for the Letter to London and he would not pay me again without a great deal of objections: Let Dowding have behaved as he would, I am convinced that he Stott has behaved as ill; he said he could have had the Books cheaper at Hull; I told him he was very silly then to order them from London—I have done with him; I do not think my wife will go to hear him any more.

Saturday 31st Aug

It began to rain gently last night about 5 O'clock but before ten it came on a perfect Storm; and continued all this day; it has blown down many trees; and abundance of Apples and Plums: indeed I never knew such a violent Storm.

Sunday 1st. Sepr.

The Storm still continues this day: but not so violent as yesterday; the wind is very strong, but not so much Rain; the poor Swallows seem to be starved and benumbed: they cannot bear cold especially when it is wet.

Monday 2d Sepr.

The Sportsmen have lost a day this year, yesterday having been the 1st Day of Partridge Shooting, so that this is the day when they sally forth, armed with death and destruction.

Tuesday 3 Sepr.

Tindale of Weedley who lives in an elevated Situation has not got a single Sheaf of his wheat home, neither has Tim. Turner of Riplingham grange: they are always later on the Hill than down below; there is sufficient time yet for fine weather, altho' at present it looks very gloomy, with every appearance of Autumn ...

Thursday 5th. Sepr.

I have told Frans. Ruston of Stott's behaviour, and in addition, he Stott went to the Post house, and asked Old Barnard whether I had post paid a letter to London; and as it happened the old Man remembered that I had: Frans. says he never knew such bad and ungrateful usage as I have met with from him: I think the same and nothing more will I have to say to him.

Friday 6th. Sepr.

I was at Mr. Turk's when he said he had a Newspaper sent him by Wm. Sharp, with which he was very much pleased they were Scotch Papers, which appeared to make them more valuable.

Saturday 7th. Sepr.

I was at the Common this afternoon at John Robinson's, where Laverack lately lived, they have been building a new Barn, Stables, and outhouses, all which appear very convenient.

Sunday 8th. Sepr.

The Parson this forenoon had a Sermon on the Rite of Confirmation; and it appears that he was much pleased with it; as he repeated it over in the afternoon: I can truly say that I should never wish to hear less Gospel in a Sermon; let alone the repetition.

Monday 9th. Sepr.

The Spirits of the Farmers were rather down this day on account of Wheat having been lower at Wakefield on Friday last 3s. pr. Quarter; for my part I am glad of it.

Tuesday 10th. Sepr.

When old Billy Gardam's wife died, Mrs. Barnard said to him "when do you bury your wife William" whya today he says, dear you are very soon with her funeral, she only having died the day before. Whya Billy says She stinks like an Otter!! O, for shame Wm. to say your wife stinks like an Otter, Whya she does however, and I'll have her buried for yan can't stay e house wiv her, she stinks sea. So Billy had her buried: he had invited her relations to come to her funeral the day after; but when they came Billy was left alone; and he told them they mud gang yam again.

Wednesday 11th. Sepr.

My wife was at Hull yesterday it was a very fine day, she went and came back by the Carrier, all safe and well ...

Saturday 14th. Sepr.

I was down at the Mill this afternoon, to see for some Money: but none did I see for the Poor man gave me none: I got tea with him and staid till about eight O'clock when according to Custom he set me back to the West end: much pleased I dare say that he quitted me so finely, as I was not in much want & did not expect he would pay so I was not disappointed ...

Monday 16th. Sepr

Ths. Marshall says if he have a piece of Beef before him at home he can't eat it with any enjoyment, for he begins to think what a devil of a Butcher's Bill he will have to pay!! now Bacon he can eat with satisfaction as he knows he will not be called on for payment for it: this paying is to him serving up his meat with sour sauce.

Tuesday 17th. Sepr.

Fine weather now very suitable for the latter harvest, there being much Barley and Oats yet out; together with Beans which are generally Condemned as a bad Crop; though opinion is veering about that they will not be so bad as were represented.

Wednesday 18th. Sep

When I am at a loss to make out any thing I am in search of; I examine what Books I have which are likely to give me information; and at times I find in some that are very unlikely what I am anxious to know. I found in the "Young Man's Companion"[21] an Account of the Olympic Games: it says they were established by Hercules in the year of the world 3228 or 776 years before Christ. — They were celebrated every four years near the Temple of Jupiter Olympus, in Elis, a Province of Peloponnesus.

Thursday 19th. Sep

Rd. Marshall has been today at Driffield fair. He brought some Sheep of a Man from Barmston. He had thoughts of me he told my wife when he bought them; I do not know whether he asked the man's name; If he had—I know him not ...

Saturday 21st. Sepr.

I was at the Mill again today; the Miller would willingly give me my tea if I would say no more about money that day: but I told him I would not be bribed, but I would make this bargain with him, I would favour him with my Company on condition that he would pay me after; but we could not agree on the terms; so like many other propositions this was abandoned, but he says it means nought what I have given nor how I am behaved to, for he says I am no better but just as bad as before, I teaze him to settle. Now he says he is quite different, for when he has wanted money, he has been invited in and a good <u>strang</u> glass or two given to him, when he has had no more thoughts of money than as though he had not gone for it: he felt so comfortable!!

Sunday 22d Sepr. [In red ink:]

This shall be a Red letter day with me, it is my birth day, I think I have completed my twelfth lustrum, or however within a year.

Monday 23 Sepr.

A traveller with Paper &c but not my old merchant, I bought nothing but a Paper of Slatepencils, small dutch 8d. pr. hundred ...

Wednesday 25th Sep

Weighton fair today for Cattle, Sheep, and Old Milk Cheese. Cheese sold for 3s/7d pr. Stone; it requires good teeth to encounter the Crust which is both hard and tough.

---

[21] William Mather, *The Young Man's Companion* ... 1681 and numerous subsequent editions throughout the 18th c., or possibly, J. A. Stewart, *The Young Man's Companion* – 2nd ed. 1814.

Thursday 26th. Sepr.

I am busy entering the Highway accounts, in order to balance the Book for the present year which is to be done tomorrow.

Friday 27th. Sepr.

A meeting this Evening at Morley's to Balance the Highway Accounts, there is more than £40 in hand which will be a good beginning for the next Surveyors.

Saturday 28th. Sepr.

The Jury list is today to be returned to Beverley one of the Overseers is gone with it; and one of the Surveyors with the Highway Book, to be examined and allowed by one Magistrate.

Sunday 29th. Sepr

Tom Leason of Ellerker was out shooting the other day, when by some accident his gun went off and shot his Dog—so that there was an end of his Sport for that time: it was a valuable Dog, his Father would not have taken 10 Sovs. for it.

Monday 30th. Sep

This day at the Market time the Surveyors of the Highways of Drewton wished I would balance their Highway Book for them, which I did in a very few minutes there not being more than 20 lines to Examine. I sat down with them and got for my trouble a Glass of wine & water.

Tuesday 1st. Oct 1833

The making up of the East India accounts puzzles me—for instance 104,25,000 Rupees, now what number is this? I frequently see Rupees cut off in this manner—this is about equal to a very intelligent man last week at a Sale at North Cave, who was fond of displaying his Silver Pencil case; the bidding was £610 which he put down carefully in his notes 600,10. This was weather cock Jack as Mrs. Tapp used to call him; to wit Jackey Stather, of Everthorpe.

Wednesday 2d Octr.

This day after schooltime I went to Mr. Bridgman's to balance the Churchwarden's accounts, preparatory to their being examined at a meeting to be held on Friday next; so that with different kinds of Parish Books I have had part employment.

Thursday 3d Octr.

Club meeting this Evening at old Bant's, there was one new member entered, got done in good time and at home shortly after nine; very fine weather.

Friday 4th. Oct

This Evening at [a] meeting at Fenwick's to Balance the Churchwarden's accounts, only six or seven people attended very little to do. I think I have been pretty well engaged this week.

Saturday 5th. Octr.

This afternoon I was at Ellerker Sands near the Humber measuring some land for Charles Rudd about 20 Acres of harvesting—wheat and Beans very pleasant it was but a pretty long walk—I staid tea at Ellerker and got home before it was dark.

Sunday 6th. Octr

Old John Lund commonly called Lundy was buried this afternoon he was in his 82d. year he had been about a month ill, having had a fit of some kind, he was born in the year that the Stile was altered viz. 1752. I had a letter this morning from London, which seemed to be a printed Catalogue of Novels & Romances; it was charged 11d: so I sent it back without paying for it, as 11d. is not so easily got as to be thus wasted; I think if the person who sent it wishes his Catalogue to be put in circulation he ought to have paid the postage.

Monday 7th. Octr.

Packed up the Box for London, containing Dolly and her Cradle, with a Goose & other eatables that she might not starve; carried it to Cousens to take with him to Hull tomorrow.

Tuesday 8th. Octr

A young man of the name of Lyon whose mother lives here, is dead this day in the Small Pox it is said; he lived Servant with Saml. Shaw.

Wednesday 9th. Octr.

Richmond Cousens this morning brought a Receipt for the Box going to London; so that now we expect it is on its way, a very fine day.

Thursday 10th. Octr.

Recd. a letter from Skipton this morning respecting my Brother saying that he had gone to Lodgings and was much better, but that he would not be able to come here before the Spring, he had not written the letter himself.

Friday 11th. Octr

I was at Brantingham last night at Mr. Ringrose's I wanted some money of him which he paid me after that I got a Glass of Rum & Water with him he appears to be much better than he was, but I think it is very probable that he will never be well again; his complaint is the Gravel; he says that it has been coming on for the last 40 years.

Saturday 12th. Octr.

At Weedley this day measuring some Rape land it came on rain pretty quick when we were knee deep in Rape, and by that means got much wet; we went into the Warren house or hut where there was a fire and staid till the rain abated, when I had done I went to Weedley about three O'clock and got my Dinner, and soon after came home; there was a little more than 20 Acres. it had been measured over twice before.

Sunday 13th. Octr

All the Strollers have not yet arrived from Hull fair, Jem Levitt went on the fair day and had not returned this day at noon; I am well assured that he is not at his own expence or else he would [have] been back before.

Monday 14th. Octr.

It is said that John Smith (commonly called Jack Smith) was robbed at Hull fair of ~~more than twenty pounds~~ ten pounds, which he had been receiving for Work done at the Common the last Summer. It is not surprising if he have lost his money, as he is not famed for keeping the best of Company; and then he is so cunning and shifty that he was very likely to be taken in: these shifty fellows are in general; (nay always) fools.

Tuesday 15th. Octr [Written in red ink:]

I have been making some Red Ink, which I now try, I expect it will prove very good, this is the date of it 15th. Octr. 1833. Good Red Ink.

Wednesday 16th. Octr.

Heard from Wm. this morning that the Box had arrived safe, and that they had the Goose to dinner on Sunday last; and it appears they were satisfied with it; as he says it was excellent. Glad to hear that little Mary is gratified with her Doll; I am not much of a judge of Dolls, but I think it looked very well, it will be a remembrance to her from her Grandmother.

Thursday 17th. Octr.

Our old Friend Mr. Atkinson, who has been at Malton fair with Mr. Bridgman, has arrived safe home again; his house as usual when he goes out has undergone a thorough cleaning which puts him to much inconvenience, as he cannot find many things, which have been put in fresh places; but on the whole it has undergone a great improvement.

Friday 18th. Oct

This is the Court day it was called in the Cross as usual; Joseph Kirby & Henry Arton, were sworn in Constables, and Saml. Langricke the Pinder or Pounder, further this deponent saith not.

Saturday 19th. Oct

I was at Ellerker this afternoon settling with Mr. Leeson for the Church Sess; I came away before tea, but just met with friend Watty—I went to tea with him, and got home about Six O'clock, after staying a short time at old Willy's.

Sunday 20th. Oct [20th–25th Oct. out of sequence]

[In margin in red ink:] I have turned over here to the wrong Page

Watson Arton generally knows about a week before hand what they are to have to dinner every day; on Saturday he told me they were going to have a Roast Goose as today; so that the Leg of Mutton is put off to another day.

Monday 21st. Octr.

A Certificate was wanted today, which had been given by Ellerker to So. Cave, above 17 years ago, and as I keep these kind of things, I was applied to for it, but I could not find it in fact I never had it, but I recollected that Rd. Kirby was at that time Overseer; It came into my Mind that he had it; so the Overseers went to Straker's at Riplingham, and it was soon found, and very glad I was to see it: I recollected that it had been given to Rd. Kirby, and he had neglected to deliver it to me; So much for a Memory of 17 years.

Tuesday 22d. Octr.

Robt. Marshall who is one of the Overseers, went to a Girl who is with Child, in order to remove her, when she swore she would lay the Child on him, and says that if he goes again she will split his head with a Poker; he ought to be supported by the Parish as he is only fulfilling his duty and I think he will, and not be outraged by an unprincipled & abandoned profligate.

Wednesday 23d Octr.

This morning received a letter from Wm., with a lb. of Tobacco; my wife says she will weigh it out for me One ounce a Week, and I desire no more, so that all will be right. Glad that Mary is so fond of her Doll & Wm. of his Stockings.

Thursday 24th. Oct

This is South Cave Cattle shew or the new fair, there was more company in the town than I expected, as yesterday was a very rainy day, there were a good many Cattle, which it was said only brought low prices, but I think most of them were sold.

Friday 25th. Octr

Robt. Marshall wanted me to go with him to Ellerker tomorrow to get a certificate signed but as I have to go out on a measuring expedition I cannot attend. [At foot of page in red ink: 'turn back one page'].

Saturday 26th. Octr

I was at Drewton this day measuring a following Crop on the Farm on which Frans. Wood entered last Lady day; it was a stiff day's work, and was dark when we got done; very tiresome rising the Hills; I had a lad with me who was so tired, that he said he should take to ploughing again on Monday, very gladly, for it is but playing he says to Surveying, he says he will not be a Surveyor, he always thought it was easy work — A66–R2–P3

Sunday 27th. Octr

Considering what a hard day I had yesterday, I did not feel at all tired, my feet did not hurt: neither did I feel at all fatigued a very fine day.

Monday 28th. Octr

A very wet rainy day, very few people at the Market, I do not know the Prices of Corn. Robt. Usher of Drewton has got notice to quit his Farm; it belongs to Captain Waller; there are many applicants for it; but it is said that Wm. Fisher who married one of Robinson's daughters of Mount Airy, is the first.

Tuesday 29th. Octr.

Drewton has been a place of more population than it is at present,[22] even now the Places where Cottages have been are to be seen; in one of the Closes that I measured on Saturday, there was a part not ploughed, on which I enquired the reason; and was told that it contained old Stone foundations which rendered it incapable of being worked. In another Close was an old fortification (I think Roman) perhaps I call it wrong, as it appears to have been a line of defence, which is here called "double diking", it consists of a trench with a

---

[22] Drewton was probably reduced at the Black Death as in 1354 its tax assessments were decreased by 50 per cent. In 1672, hearth tax records show that there were only 13 households and by the 19th c., the hamlet had further diminished to consist of only Drewton Manor and a single farmhouse (*VCHYER* iv. 22–3).

Bank on either side, (this kind of work is continued for Miles) the Banks have lately been levelled and thrown into the trench,[23] the Hills are all Chalk Rock.
Wednesday 30th. Octr.

All the talk about who is to be the tenant of Robt. Usher's farm at Drewton, but nothing yet made out: Charles Rudd of Ellerker has taken the land lately occupied by Rd. Kirby. I think if he had tried for any thing more inconvenient he could scarce have found it.
Oct. 31 Thursday

Charles Rudd was here wanting some alteration making in the Poor Rate of Ellerker, part of some land having been sold, which in that case was divided: and it is (the land) of different qualities something wants taking from the worst land and laying on the best, the whole is A20–R2–P25 the least & worst part contains 6 Acres which we fixed at 20s. pr. Acre, and the other part to be advanced proportianlly [*sic*]. the whole was valued at 37s pr Acre.
Friday 1st. Nov

There has been a brutal fight between two blackguards of Hull, somewhere in Holderness, it is said one of the fellows is killed, had they both shared the same fate, there would have been but little loss to the Community.
Saturday 2d Nov.

I was at Elloughton this forenoon measuring a bit of Land between 3 & 4 Acres, as awkward a piece as need to be seen, not a straight fence about it; I had rather have measured 20 Acres with straight boundaries. I got home about 2 O'clock.
Sunday 3d Novr

A Very windy day again, this is very uncomfortable weather being so windy, it blew dry, I see it had blown a tree top down in Mr. Bridgman's Cow pasture.
Monday 4th. Novr

A Rumour this morning that a Girl at the West end had had a Child and destroyed it, the Rumour continued to spread all the day, it is the Same Girl who abused Robt. Marshall her name is Sarah Dove.
Tuesday 5th. Novr

Last night Mr. Hill went down to the West end respecting the Child which was said to have been born, when he saw old Mary Dove who told him the Girl had had a miscarriage and she had buried it; he asked where and she said in the Garden, he then desired her to let him look at it, when she took a spade and a Lanthorn, it being dark and went about 7 or 8 yards into the Garden, and dug it up, on the Doctor seeing it he exclaimed this is no miscarriage the Child is

---

[23] Prehistoric linear earthworks, known as double dikes, are not uncommon in the Yorkshire Wolds. Possibly dating back to the late Bronze Age, many of them were extended during the Iron Age and Roman times or even later. Allen (1841) described a double dyke at Drewton, which ran in a NW to SE direction and could be traced across the Wolds from Newbald to Riplingham, a distance of approximately 4 miles (*ex inf.* Bryan Sitch, Assist. Keeper of Archaeology, Hull Museums, *in litt.*; Allen 64 and 95–6).

nearly full grown; he told her he should take it with him, to which she made no reply, so he wrapped it in his handkerchief & brought it away.

Wednesday 7th. [i.e. 6th] Nov

[In margin in red ink: 'I have again begun the wrong page']

The Coroner having been sent for yesterday came this day to Morley's[24] about 2 O'clock in the afternoon where a Jury was summoned to meet him, of which I was one; the first thing was to view the Child which was at Dr. Hill's it appeared to be very small, but its hair and nails were perfectly formed & the Doctors Hill & Carter had both examined it and pronounced it to be an eight month's Child, they both said they had seen as small Children as it live; they stated in their Evidence that it was their decided opinion the Child had been born alive. There was a Wound* on the back part of the Head about an Inch long with a Fracture, seemed they said to have been made with some sharp instrument, they talked a good deal of the turgidity of the vessels, the Parietal Bone, Membranes &c &c., but there was no extravasated Blood nor no Decomposition, I wished for the sake of the Jury they had delivered themselves more plainly—after their evidence the Jury about 6 O'clock went to the West end to Mary Dove's (Aunt of the Girl) when they that is the Aunt and Girl both said that they never hurt the Child; the Girl had no appearance of a murderer but seemed quite innocent and unconcerned; the Jury & Coroner then returned to Morley's, when the Coroner retired after having read the evidence and in a few minutes, the Jury being unanimous that there was no proof that violence had been used returned a verdict that the Child was found dead but from what cause was to them unknown,[25] the Coroner said he was quite of a different opinion but the Jury had nothing to do with his opinion and he doubted not it was a conscientious verdict. I ought to have mentioned that the Child was buried, without being wrapped in any covering, and being laid on its back, its head might have come in contact with a Stone & caused the wound. — It is altogether a melancholy affair, (or the spade in digging it up might have caught it up, by the Corner, of the spade).

* [In margin:] The Jurors did not see the wound nor heard of it until the Drs. gave their Evidence

Thursday 7th. Novr

After the business of the Club this Evening what should be the conversation of all things but Gulliver's travels, some of the learned disputers had read some parts of it, some of them saying they thought the Book could not be true, when I was asked if I had ever read it, I answered I had but it was a long time ago; I was then asked if I thought it was true, this was a home question, but I evaded it and asked if they thought any man would sit down to

---

[24] Coroners' inquests were usually held at public houses, there being no purpose-built coroners' courts until the late 19th c. (Rose 57).

[25] Jurors were notoriously reluctant to return verdicts of infanticide. The Offences Against the Person Act of 1803 enacted that infanticide should be proceeded against like any other form of murder, and unfortunately girls like Sarah Dove would in law merit the death penalty if convicted (Rose 59).

write a Book full of lies; especially a Clergyman and a Dean, the next in office to a Bishop—this hardly stopped them, for they said many a man would sit down and tell lies, and why not write them? they admitted that the Customs of various countries are different but there were some things they thought could not be true!!! — for my own part I have nearly forgot both all the truth and lies in it, so no more of Gulliver.

Friday 8th. Nov

Robt. Dunn or his Son Timothy who had been at Beverley fair on Tuesday last, and I dare say both of whom were drunk, the old Man especially who fell from his horse, when his Son Timmy took his purse from him, but did not examine it until the next morning, when there was nothing in it: — it should have contained £37 so how or where it was lost is all conjecture.

Saturday 9th. Novr

I was at the West end this afternoon; and as it was a fine moderate day, I came back by Peggy Medd's lane, and over Mr. Bridgman's Closes, and called at Mr. Atkinson's, where there was nothing particular transpired.

Sunday 10th. Nov

Last night I received an order to pay 20s each on the Conviction of Hawkers for selling unstamped Almanacks,[26] on the production of a certificate from the Magistrate so convicting, — from the Stamp office.

Monday 11th. Nov

Obed Martin was drunk in Brown's room at the Market, he is a sort of queer good natured fellow, he said he had more Sovereigns than any body— amongst other things he said that Mr. Rodmell the Curate, lived upon nothing but Dog Biscuits—I suppose the Parson has taken it in his head to live upon the vegetable diet only.

Tuesday 12th. Nov

This Evening Thos. Bird whose wife died last week, (she was one of Jos. Barrat's daughters) wanted to draw eight pounds out of the Club Box for her funeral; the Stewards and President, met at the Club room, and sent for me to take out the money, which was soon done, — David Dennis was in the House drunk, and he would sing Rule Britannia which he did as far as one verse went, I know very little of singing, but I know that I wished he would not make such a horrid noise.

Wednesday 13th. Nov

A meeting this Evening at Barnard Cook's respecting Composition for the Highways, there were eight or nine persons only, it was wished by some of them to raise the rate from 9d. to 1s. in the pound, but Robt. Marshall and I withstood it, and it was settled that it should be at the old rate of 9d. in the pound, which I know will be sufficient.

---

[26] The heavy stamp duty of 15 pence per copy on all almanacs, first imposed in 1710, was not repealed until 1834 by the passing of 3 and 4 Will. IV c. 57 (Dowell iv. 393).

Thursday 14th. Novr.

Sittings this day, and a Constable meeting at Morley's, there were 18 or 19 present, a very good dinner, which is all the Constables have to attend to, Mr. Smelt was not here, but sent his Clerk; I came away about four O'clock. Ths. Marshall came in about five O'clock to our house and staid until nine; as he was so comfortable at the fire side, that he had no thought it was so late.

Friday 15th. Nov

Val. Tindale had a hedge pulled up on the 5th. Novr. to make a Bonfire; he has been getting a Summons for the aggressors, they are to appear on Monday next at Riplingham, before the Magistrates.

Saturday 16th. Nov

I was at Welton this forenoon, swearing to the delivery of some Charges for taxes, before Mr. Thos. Raikes who is now one of the East Riding Magistrates, I got home about one O'clock; when I was going Timmy Dunn was coming home from airing one of his horses; I said I was going to Welton he offered me his horse to ride, which I accepted; I had to go round by Brantingham.

Sunday 17th. Novr.

A kind of wet slattery day, — it is said that Abm. Barff has got an order for Geo. Petfield and Jem. Levitt for breaking his door, some person had told him out of sport that it was they who had broken his door; but whether he has or not got the order is to me not certain.

Monday 18th. Nov

The Girl Sarah Dove who had the Child on whom a Coroners inquest was held a short time since, was this day committed to Beverley House of Correction for concealing the birth of the Child she will be tried at the Sessions;[27] she belongs to Ellerker.

Tuesday 19th. Nov

Val. Tindale yesterday before the Justices made nothing out against the hedge breakers he is to appear on Monday next with more Evidence, or otherwise be subject to the Expences.

Wednesday 20th. Nov

I have not been well this week, I have got cold which makes me very languid, being accompanied with my old complaint in the Bowels.

Thursday 21st. Nov

We have bought a pair of small hams at 6s. pr. Stone, it is said that Bacon Pigs are about 5s. pr. Stone. it suits us rather better to have hams than to buy a Pig, as the Bacon when fat cannot be eaten by us.

Friday 22d. Nov

I bought some Paper & Copy Books yesterday of my old travelling merchant, he complains much of the badness of trade: I should have bought a

---

[27] She was subsequently sentenced to 2 years with hard labour (see entry for 2/1/34), which was the maximum penalty for the crime of concealment of a birth (Rose 70).

little more of him, but his Paper was not such as I liked. Sittings yesterday again, very little Company.

Saturday 23d Nov

I had forgot to notice that James Levitt was buried on Thursday; he was 86 years of age; it is said he has left the farm to his daughter it is let for £100 a year. Wm. Cousens rents it. I was at Ellerker this afternoon, got home before dark.

Sunday 24th. Nov

It came on so rainy this afternoon that I did not go out, so I staid at home to tent Cat from the tongs!²⁸ I cannot say that I like to spend the day without going to a Place of Worship.

Monday 25th. Nov

Geo. Petfield & Jem. Levitt were at Riplingham this day to meet Abm. Barff respecting the breaking his door; but no sufficient evidence appearing, the Justices desired them to get some person to arbitrate for them to settle the matter, it was therefore put to Mr. Beaumont of Brantingham; when he thought that Abraham should pay the expences and treat them with a Glass a piece and be friends, which was done, Abm. & Jem both got drunk and the little Landlord fell down and came back as thick with mud as if he had been plastered.

Tuesday 26th. Nov

This evening I intended going to the Castle for Mr. Stourton's taxes, but just before I went out I heard he was gone from home and would not be back before Friday next, so I went to Mr. Atkinson's; and stopped till Seven O'clock then came home.

Wednesday 27th. Nov

At our old Friend's this evening, it was observed that Alexander was a very common name in Scotland; and it was added by our old friend that Mac. was very common in Scotland and Ireland of which he gave a few examples, as Mackenzie, Mackintosh, Maclartie &c and by way of crowning the whole Andrew Murdoch!! this Andrew was known to our old Friend, besides a great many more Macs.

Thursday 28th. Novr.

I think there is but little to do this Martinmas week; though there were two House warmings at the West end last night, at two Beer Shops, but what there was to do I know not. Charles Smith's (the fellow who fought with the little Nut man at Cave fair) is the landlord of one, the sign of the Carpenter's Arms. Robt Donkin is the other who displays the sign of the Gate, nay the Gate itself.

Friday 29th. Nov

Our old Friend had his half year's Rent to receive of Barnard Cook for his Close; so he would have Mr. Bridgman & me to go with him, which we did; I wrote him a receipt, & he treated us both.

---

²⁸ i.e. to sit idly by the fireside.

Saturday 30th. Nov

Henry Arton the Constable had to take a man by a Warrant which he did, it was for money in a Bastardy Case. The fellow got away this morning, & the Constable set off after him and overtook him in Bacchus Lane, where a scuffle ensued which ended in Poor Harry having had his face bitten, and the Prisoner got away, but was pursued and found at Broomfleet, where he was taken, and had to Beverley and committed to Prison for three months for not paying the money that was due ...

Monday 2d. Decr. 1833

I am now busy collecting the half year's taxes—I saw nothing done at the Market today in the Corn business, I understand there have been large Supplies and slack prices, which I am glad to hear ...

Wednesday 4th. Dec

Went out this Evening with an intention of going to the West end, but it came on so very dark, that I only went down the Lane a piece of the way, but I dare say I shall be soon enough another day for the West end Gentry, as they have a natural desire of keeping their money as long as possible.

Thursday 5th. Decr

Club night at Barnard Cook's, Jem Levitt painted 2 Club Staves[29] for which he charged and received 5s, now the great argument was how to make Jem. disgorge a part of the money as it is pretty well known that what he gets he keeps. I think it is safe in his hands.

Friday 6th. Decr

I have got a bad cold with one of my eyes very tender and a swelled face, my face is very subject to swell when I get cold, I am in hopes that I shall soon be better.

Saturday 7th. Decr

I was down at the Mill this afternoon and drew ten pounds from the Man of the Mill, when he saw my swelled face, he gave a recital of a Bad eye that he once had, it was ten times worse than mine he said, and unluckily he had it just at Cave fair time, but however it was so bad that he applied to the Doctor I think Day, he ordered him not to eat any flesh meat and not to drink any Spirits, so he was put upon a starving diet, but he said to the Doctor, now it is very hard to be debarred from eating and drinking this week which is the only week in the year that we live, but the Doctor was inflexible, — So the Miller said to himself or rather to his eye Thou is nea Ee for me if thou weant bide itting and drinking this weak, however I tell thee I'll it & drink as much as I can get; — So according to his promise or threat, he eat and drank heartily and lived well and got glorious, and over his eye he was victorious, for he and his Eee were quite comfortable together before the weeks end.

---

[29] The regalia of the club or village friendly society included banners, scarves, and staves, which were brought out for parades and feast days (Neave (1988) 29).

Sunday 8th. Decr

James Levitt at the west end is very ill this day, and has been a few days back his complaint is the Quinsies, a very troublesome and dangerous disorder, he has had them two or three times before.

Monday 9th. Decr

Complaints this day at the Market amongst the Farmers of the low price of Corn, which the Consumers look upon to be quite high enough. I think something will be done in the next Session of Parliament respecting the Corn laws, perhaps the best thing would be to have no Corn laws at all.

Tuesday 10th. Decr.

This Evening I was at the West end collecting; the taxes are to be paid in on Thursday at Beverley, but I think I shall not attend as Mr. Beaumont of Brantingham will take my money, and it will be a great deal shorter Journey there than to Beverley.

Wednesday 11th. Decr

I went to Brantingham this Evening to Mr. Beaumont's, he now lives on the Wold above the Spout Hill; he was not at home when I got there a little after four O'clock, but he soon after came, and I gave him £124–5–0 to pay in for the taxes at Beverley tomorrow.

Thursday 12th. Decr

I forgot to say that I stop'd at tea last night with Mr. Beaumont, and he sent two lads down the Hill with me (it being dark) as far as Brantingham Church, it being they say a little nearer than the Spout hill road the way that I went; I got home a little after Seven. A frosty night.

Friday 13th. Decr

Capn. Waller has let his farm at Drewton to a Man who is a tenant of his and lives at Stone ferry. Robt Usher has taken a Farm at Swanland, belonging Mr. John Todd of that place.

Saturday 14th. Decr

I was at the West end this afternoon. Js. Levitt has got better again. I went as far as Widow Dove's in the new field having no call to go any further so I came back by Peggy Medd's lane which is very bad travelling on it, it being very dirty.

Sunday 15th. Decr

I think there is nothing particular this day, it is tolerable fine weather, we have had no snow yet except a small shower one day last week: there was a sharp frost a night or two the last week.

Monday 16th. Decr

The Churchwardens have received a circular from Lord Althorpe, requiring a return of the Quantity of Land, Tithe &c,[30] — the quantity of Land

---

[30] Bills to commute the tithes were introduced in 1833, 1834, and 1835, but all failed. Lord Althorp, the Whig Chancellor of the Exchequer, introduced the 1833 bill, which involved commutation based upon a corn rent fixed upon the average of receipts over the previous 7 years. The circular referred to here requested the churchwardens in each parish to supply details of acreages of arable, meadow, pasture, and other types of land together with the rents per acre of

in this Township is 3931A–2R–31P and the Value £5376–3s–0d the average yearly value pr. Acre is 27s–4d. — the valuation of the great or Rectorial tithe is £463–3s–4d and the Vicarial tithe £44–11–1 — there are about 500 Acres of Grass land, and nearly that quantity on Wallingfen that is not subject to agistment tithe. The return is not yet made.

Tuesday 17th. Decr

The Churchwardens on Sunday last, came out of the Church in Service time, and visited the Public houses, but found all quiet; indeed they need not trouble themselves, for very few have any thing to spend other days, so that they need not to go to drink on Sundays. I suppose this is done to ape their betters in large towns.

Wednesday 18th. Decr

A Poor Woman from Hull this morning whose husband is ill & belongs this place, came for some relief, the man was formerly a Gardener with old Mr. Barnard his name is Peck; she has two Children ill one a Girl about 15 years old subject to fits, and a Boy of 8 years in the measles. I gave her a Sovereign without seeing the Overseer, as she had to walk back to Hull.

Thursday 19th. Decr

Capn. Waller has let his Drewton farm, to a tenant of his who lives in Holderness I think at Sutton: he appears to be a stranger here; the farm is either for himself or his Son. We have got a Goose and a Couple of Chickens to send to Wm., Hannah Martin is come to pull and prepare them so that we shall have plenty of intelligence this day of a domestic nature. I know not that I can add any more than that we are all pretty well, I myself am the worst, not having got entirely quit of my cold. Our best love to you all, I hope that little Mary is better in her Cough; her grand Mother has sent her some Bullace Cheese[31] which is all she had, for her to take a little when she goes to Bed at nights.

R: SHARP

Friday 20 Decr

Packed up a Hamper for London with Christmas Cheer, last night when carrying it to Cousens's I fell over a Box Standing in the House floor, and I and the Hamper both came down, I rather hurt my Ancle and Shoulder, but I feel no worse.

Saturday 21st Decr

Thos. Marshall was at Js. Levitt's this evening where there was a Rider from Hull, after Paint and Colouring. They disagreed and the Bagman called Tom an old Asshead and would fight him. I may give the particulars some other time.

Sunday 22d. Decr

A very wet day; there was a Daughter of William Langricke's about 18 buried this day, she died with the Small Pox, having been ill about a fortnight.

---

each category divided into highest, lowest, and average, and information on the value of the tithes (Evans 123).

[31] A cheese flavoured with bullaces or wild plums (*OED*).

Monday 23 Decr.

Very little to do at the Market today, Mr. Brown was not here; he was going to Wakefield the last week in a Gig, when his horse becoming restive he jumped out, and caught his finger in something or other which broke it (the finger) so that he could not attend the Market this Day.

Tuesday 24th. Decr

This being Christmas eve, most people according to Custom, have got a Yule Clog, and are preparing Furmety for Supper, which with a bit of Cheese and Apple Pye, for those who can get it, is a common set out.

Wednesday 25th. Decr

Christmas Day, Boys and Girls as usual, running shouting about for Christmas Boxes, which they wish to receive in exchange for their "wishes of a merry Christmas".

Thursday 26th. Decr

Now that we have Holidays, I am rather at a loss how to apply my time, indeed I do not feel so much in my element, when I have nothing to do, as when I am regularly engaged. I spent my spare time at Mr. Atkinson's.

Friday 27th. Decr

At west end this Evening, consulting with the Overseer, the Churchwardens wish to have a meeting before the Return of Land &c. be made to Government, so after the Return is made out a Meeting will be held on Tuesday next, this is wisdom!!!

Saturday 28th. Decr

My longest Journey this day was no further than Mr. Atkinson's, but as he is Churchwarden he makes it known that he has had a letter from Lord Althorpe, which raises him not a little in his own estimation;[32] he is afraid he says of making a wrong return, I told him to leave it to me and I would be answerable he should have no more trouble about it; but all would not do so a meeting we must have.

Sunday 29th. Decr

Newspaper missed coming again this morning; as it did on Friday; but on Saturday there were two packed together, so that one of them had not been stopped.

Monday 30th. Decr

I think I have very little to remark today—Farmers very low on account of the low price of Corn.

Tuesday 31st. Decr

A very stormy day, the wind excessively strong, several stacks were stripped, and buildings nearly uncovered, we sustained no damage; but a

---

[32] The circular began, 'Gentlemen, I shall be very much obliged to you', and concluded 'I have the honor to be, gentlemen, your obedient humble servant Althorp.' No doubt Old Willy was not alone in being flattered at being thus addressed. The circular is quoted in full in Cobbett's *Weekly Political Register*, vol. 82, no. 12, (21 Dec.) 1833, col. 707–8.

Chimney pot of Cousens's fell down, but luckily did not hit our kitchen window.

Wednesday 1st. Jan

A meeting last night respecting the return to be made to Government, of the Quantity and rental of Land; when it was carried that the highest Rental should be 50s. pr. Acre and the lowest 6s. and the average 20s. pr. Acre. I was not convinced that this was right, but as it did not affect me at all I was nearly silent, only I said if the land was mine I could let it for 30s. pr. Acre on the average: they all knew that they were giving this or more, (so much for public reports.)

Thursday 2d. Jan

This week which is a Holiday, has been most of it spent by me at Mr. Atkinson's—The Girl Sarah Dove, who was committed to Beverley for the concealment of the birth of her Child, pleaded guilty at the Sessions, and has been sentenced to two year's imprisonment and hard labour. A Pig Stealer of the name of Hotham from Welton has been sentenced to fourteen year's transportation.

Friday 3d Jan

George Metcalfe of Drewton died on Wednesday last; he had been ill a long time, with a Cancer in his back, he is about 38 years of Age.

Saturday 4th. Jany

A Set of Simpletons called Plough Boys went out this morning, (with Music and Fools;) they say to Market Weighton, not missing any of the Villages in the way—they get back about five O'clock; with nearly four Pounds in money, this shews that people are not in such a bad state as is sometimes represented!!!

Sunday 5th. Jany

A very fine mild day, those who are fond of frost and Snow, cry out that the weather is too fine; for my part I am always thankful for fine weather, be it at what time of the year it may: I have no great predilection for Frost and Snow.

Monday 6th. Jan

This morning again began School, but the Street being so crowded with Fools, music and Drums; it made being at School a very irksome concern: so we left pretty soon, and there was an end of this day's (no) work.

Tuesday 7th. Jan

The Plough Lads got in two days between eight & nine pounds!! they are to have a Supper this night at Fenwick's; where no doubt they will attend for the good of the house.

Wednesday 8th. Jan

Yesterday my wife and Eliza with little Ann were at the Mill, I was left Housekeeper, they got back about eight O'clock.

Thursday 9th. Jan

Mrs. Fenwick behaved uncommonly well to the Plough Boys, they had 10 Gallons of Ale and 10 Quarts of Gin mixed with it; after that they had a Gallon of Gin by itself: and all came away sober!! Now can any thing be said against this? Yes there can, for some of them wished to be drunk, but were kept sober against their minds.

Friday 10th. Jany

Very wet stormy weather, which makes the roads very dirty, down to Broomfleet and Faxfleet it [is] so deep and muddy that it is in some places, horse belly deep.

Saturday 11th. Jany

Measured part of a Close of Turnips this afternoon for Ths. Marshall, at the Sheep dike Close, it was very good measuring as the land is sandy and dry, about 8½ Acres of it: I did not go to the House, as it was nearly dark, so I came home quietly ...

Monday 13th. Jan

This day at the Market the Tradesmen collecting their Christmas Bills, which makes the farmers put on longer faces than usual, as the price of Corn yet is low: — and may it keep so.

Tuesday 14th. Jan

Ths. Marshall came last night for the measurement of his land, when he says what is this at the bottom, I told him it was the main line in measuring, viz. the charge: which was 2s. but he said I get too <u>awdfarrand</u> to ask for pay when wark was dean, no he could not pay then as he was in a hurry and wanted to see Ben Brown to sell him some Barley, he can put up with any thing but paying, except losing a Poke to Mill, this really vexes him.

Wednesday 15th Jan

We have expected a Parcel from Wm. for some time; I went to Cousens's again last night to see for one, but nothing had arrived so we must be patient, until the same come.

Thursday 16th. Jan

I had Rd. Marshall and Mr. Elgie this day to settle about the Sesst. for the following Crop; I believe they are both feared that one should get the advantage of the other, — I find that the Farm contains 243 Acres and the Rent is £320, which is about 26s–4d pr. Acre, some of the land is valued at 40s. — and some at 7s pr. Acre.

Friday 17th. Jan

A Fine Rainbow this forenoon, rainbows are not so frequent in the mornings as at afternoons, at least I have not observed them to be so

> "A Rainbow at night,
> Is the Shepherd's delight;
> A Rainbow in the morning,
> Is the Shepherd's warning."

Saturday 18th. Jan

At Ellerker this afternoon posting the Parish Books for Charles Rudd: Mrs. Rudd has a nephew (Emery) who was the Master of a Ship, when she was wrecked on the Coast of Valencia in Spain at a Place he calls Veneras[1] or

---

[1] i.e. Vinaroz.

something like it, but I cannot find the Place on a small Map that I have neither in the Gazetteer. He came to Ellerker when I was there, he had travelled home through France, with the loss of every thing belonging him. The Ship was insured, she had on board 100 Pipes of Wine all wasted, they were going to Rio Janeiro.

Sunday 19th. Jan

Ths. Marshall was at Hull on Friday when he bought some Bags (Pokes), he is afraid he says that he overbid himself for them. When he asked the Price the Man said 1s/10d each, which was the lowest selling price. Then I doubt says the Purchaser we shall not agree, as my price is 1s/9d—which was no sooner said than he was to take them. He should have liked better if the fellow had stood at 1s/10d and not have abated any thing, then he would have thought he had got them at the lowest price, but now he thinks he could have had them lower had he bid less.

Monday 20th. Jan

Abm. Barff has been at Justice today for assaulting Savage's wife, the assault was, he went to ask for pay for some Apples she had got of him, but she said he had broke 5s. worth of Pots—so poor Ab. had to appear and they say he got better, but I do not see much good that he got, as he had to pay the expences and was fined five Shillings for getting drunk. So that this Victory appears very much like a defeat!!

Tuesday 21st. Jan

Now if I was to give my Opinion on Church Establishment, I should most certainly be against any Establishment, especially, one supported by the State— Let the People Choose their own Ministers and if they have any feeling of Religion in them; they will Support their preacher without tithes—they will not think that he preaches any worse, if he does not appear in any of the cast off Robes of old Mother Rome—the father of us all.

Wednesday 22d. Jany

I wrote to Mr. Craggs yesterday respecting the Parcel sent by Wm. on the 30th. Decr. last; I recd an answer from him this morning saying that it had not been in his Parcel, so that it is probable it is yet at Whittaker's.

Thursday 23d Jany

Robt. Marshall has given a note for the Money that he has of ours, with which I am content. He has had it a long time without any security. It is the last time that I shall act with the like folly.

Friday 24th. Jan

John Murgatroyd's Son of North Cave, who now lives in London called the other day, saying he would take a letter to Wm. so I wrote one as I had to enquire about the parcel; but he has not called since, so I shall not put myself to any inconvenience in seeking for him, as I can write tomorrow.

Saturday 25th. Jan

This morning we received the Pocket Book from Wm. so where it had been delayed since the time that he sent it; we are ignorant—however it was received with pleasure when it did come, and was much valued.

Sunday 26th Jan

When I went down to the West end this morning, Richard Marshall was ill in bed with the Rheumatism, and a Cow had struck at him over his leg, so that he could not get out this day.

Monday 27th. Jan

What shall I say today? why very little, there is scarce any thing doing at the Market, perhaps the weather may occasion so few people being here, as it rains and storms a good deal; we have had abundance of Rain; but no frost this winter thus far.

Tuesday 28th. Jan

This evening I measured part of a Close of Turnips for Saml. Shaw, at the Trancledales, it was not so very wet as I expected. The piece contained 8A–1R–18P. As it was very good to do, I soon got it done.

Wednesday 29th. Jan

Some body has stolen Thomas Dyson's Ass last night out of his Baglett's Close, he thinks it has been taken by some Gipsey's. Mr. Bridgman said to Ob. Martin last night, cans't thou Rule Planets? because if thou can we may know who has got the Ass; but Ob. said he could not, only he said he was born in August under Venus, and Rd. Grasby tells him he will be lucky, for he Ob. says can Rule Planets, Ob. says he >Rd.< knows them all, he knows Juniper and Marvellous, and all rest of them!

Thursday 30th. Jan

Richd. Grasby is a great man at talking, and as is mentioned yesterday must know something as he can Rule Planets, now Rd. was holding forth as I am informed amazingly last Market day; when Ed. Usher who had not had either a Glass too little or too much, said to him there is one thing I cannot account for; — well what it is? Whya when Noah went into the Ark with his family he left his Grandfather behind him, — I don't remember says Richd. of reading about that, — whya but you may read about it, but I can't tell just now the Chapter and verse; but I think it was a shabby action of Noah, to leave his poor old Grandfather behind him. Poor Dickey could make very little answer or reply to the why or wherefore the old Man had been left.

Friday 31st. Jan

Last night there was a meeting to nominate Assessors for the ensuing year, when myself and Copartner Thomas Levitt were again appointed; I got home about nine O'clock; the meeting was called to be held at the Vestry: but got no further than the Bay horse; the Landlord was at Sancton Cockings[2] eating Willy Carr's neck Chine.

Saturday 1st. Feby

This day I had to make out the return of the Overseers of Broomfleet, of the Quantity & Value of Land, & tithes, in their Township, but as they are not famed for much intelligence in general, I had a good deal of trouble to get the

---

[2] Cocking, i.e. cock-fighting. Sancton was recorded as still having a cock-pit in 1890 (Nicholson 149).

information they gave me properly arranged, I made out the Quantity of Land to be 1088 Acres, when they said they had but 1100 Acres in the whole, so that they could not have 1,088 Acres! this is a Specimen of the knowledge of those who live, below the Mill Beck!!

Sunday 2d. Feb

There was a meeting yesterday at Beverley, respecting the Corn Laws, when I suppose the main consideration was to keep up the price of Land; consequently the Price of Corn; it will be long before a Glance of understanding enters the head of the Clodpoles, not to see that it is the Landlords who prompt them on.

Monday 3d. Feb

The market this day was kept up by the talk of Horses, their walking trotting & Galloping, some Wagers were made; Mr. Popple of Ellerker bet five Pounds with Mr. Brown that his mare should trot 15 miles within an Hour before this day month, likewise some other wagers. One of which was Brown bet Popple a Sovereign that he durst not start for the 15 miles race.

Tuesday 4th. Feb

A Canvasser this day getting instructions for Pigott's Northern Directory;[3] he is from Manchester, but they have an office in London No.1 Basing-lane Bread Street, Cheapside.

Wednesday 5th. Feb

This Evening there was an Exhibition of Legerdemain at Fewson's, and such feats to be performed and sights to be seen, as are not to be equalled by any other Professor of the Art; I think he had very little Company.

Thursday 6th. Feb

Club night at Barnard Cook's, this is one of the nights in which new Stewards are appointed, when the old ones, have to deliver up all money Books &c, to their Successors; the two new Stewards both live out of the town, one at No. Cave & the other at Ellerker.

Friday 7th. Feb

Ob. Martin has an Almanack that does not tell the Moon's age to a week, but he thinks it as good as one he has seen today, which says there will be a new Moon on the 32d. day of February 1834!!!

Saturday 8th. Feby

This morning being frosty & Clean, I had to measure a piece of Turnip Land for Lockwood, on his far Wold adjoining the Steep hill Road, it measured a little more than 6 Acres; I then went to the Tofts adjoining Bacchus Lane, and there measured a small piece a little more than 2 Acres. I then went to Thos. Marshall's close in Ruffham field, and measured 6A–2R–10P — and got home about half past one O'clock.

---

[3] *National and Commercial Directory ... of the Merchants, Bankers, Professional Gentlemen, Manufacturers and Traders ... in the Counties of Chester, Cumberland, Durham, Lancaster, Northumberland, Westmoreland and York ... London: Pigot and Co., 1834.*

Sunday 9th. Feb

Nothing particular this day—Only Jem. Levitt's Almanack, which is a Paddy,[4] says there will be a full moon on the 32d day of February, so that he can match Ob. Martin's Calendar!

Monday 10th. Feb.

It is pretty generally believed that Ministers will do nothing this year, towards repealing the Corn Laws; So that the Farmers have nothing to amuse themselves at the Market, but to drink their Glasses, and to Complain of bad times. — Now should the Corn law be altered and a fixed duty imposed on imported Corn, not the most raving could think of laying it, at what it is now brought to viz. above 30s. pr. Qr. — this is a complete prohibition: what could the growers or the growlers wish for more?

Tuesday 11th. Feb

Writing a notice to a Man of Newbald, to remove and take away some Ash trees, laying in the Swineskaif Road, within five days from the date, otherwise he will be liable to a penalty of ten Shillings.

Wednesday 12th. Feb

Ths. Marshall got to Abm. Barff's one night, and made strange Havock of Ab's Rum Bottle, and eat up his Roast Mutton which had been spared, at dinner; indeed he played his part so well that his Sister Beckey, went all the way home with him, as he was completely happy; he says he could ha dean varry weel wiv his self, but she wad gang with him for fear he should fall into the Sheep dike; but he says he always 'scap'd it yet, and he will warrant not to lig down there.

Thursday 13th. Feb

This Evening I was at the Castle, and the west end collecting Poor Sess: as there is a County Rate to be paid on Saturday next; which with the Fees &c will be about 22 Pounds.

Friday 14th. Feb

The Wager that was made between Mr. Brown & Mr. Popple, respecting the horse going 15 Miles within an hour, was a drawn bet, the parties agreeing to be each a bottle of Wine, and have their money again, they staid all the night at Morley's and some of them the next day and night until the morning after.

Saturday 15th. Feb

This afternoon Measuring a Close of Turnips for Jno. Stather of Everthorpe, it was part of it very dirty land one Corner of it so boggy, that one was in danger of sinking deep in the Mire, there was 8A–1R–0P of it, it is the first Close on the Everthorpe Road, from the Cross Roads.

Sunday 16th. Feb

This morning two Men came from Hull, with an Acct. that Mark Cousens who belongs this town, dropped down dead in Osborne Street at Hull, yesterday, they wanted some Money to bury him with, and they were given an Order to draw 30s. for that purpose at the Charity Hall, Hull.

---

[4] 'Paddy's watch' or 'Paddywhack almanac', i.e. an unlicensed almanac (*OED*).

Monday 17th. Feb

Papers handed out this day, inviting farmers to become members of an East Riding Agricultural Association;[5] to be composed of Owners and Occupiers of land; one of the Committee met with Rd. Marshall at Beverley and told him what benefit it would be to him, as well as others, so he was almost persuaded to sign his name, but he was given to understand that there would be five Shillings for him [to] pay, he immediately declined having either part or let in the matter, so his 5s. were spared.

Tuesday 18th. Feb

Wm. Fisher who lives at Brantingham, has taken the farm at Ellerker occupied by Ths. Allison (formerly Heselwoods) there is about 130 Acres of it; Allison gave £240 a year for it, but it is said Fisher has taken it at £200 a year.

Wednesday 19th. Feb

The House duty I see is to go—but I think of the two that the Window duty would have been more beneficial to the Country; but I think they might both have been spared.[6]

Thursday 20th. Feb

The Agriculturalists complain grievously of the Poor Rates but it appears, that with respect to this place, a very trifling reduction in the Rents, would save them from the burden, for in this town this year I do not think that the Poor rates will be more than 2s. pr. Acre; but certainly not more than 2s/6d pr. Acre; now it has never entered into their heads to demand this relief of their Landlords.

Friday 21st. Feb

I had a kind of breeder in my Arm, of which I did not take much notice, so that it never properly dispersed; and near it, five or Six Blisters have come out which are very sore, I am in hopes it will soon be better.

Saturday 22d. Feb

I went to Mr. Carter this morning to shew him my Arm, he has applied some Ointment and Linseed poultice to it, and given me Pills, and Mixtures to take, so that I am in the Doctor's hands—I went in the afternoon to measure a Close of Turnips besides the Ring Beck, belonging Ths. Robinson of Ellerker — 9A–3R–9P.

---

[5] The East Riding Agricultural Association was founded in 1834 and was active for the next 12 years. It organized ploughing matches and dinners for its members and held annual meetings at the Public Rooms in Beverley and exhibitions of stock and agricultural machinery. On the occasion of its 4th exhibition, the *Yorkshire Gazette*, in its issue of 29 July 1837, commented that 'the number of ... agriculturists present was immense, many ... from remotest parts of the county.' (Sheahan and Whellan ii. 285–6).

[6] Houses rated at £5–20 per annum paid 1s. 6d. in the pound with the tax rising proportionately on a sliding scale. The window tax which had been introduced in 1696 to replace the hearth tax was not abolished until 1851, although it was only applied to houses with 8 or more windows after 1825 (Dowell ii. 52, 279, and 303–4).

Sunday 23d. Feb

This day I did not go out of the House, and had but a sort of miserable day within, as my Arm was painful.

> "And 'tis a poor Relief we gain
>
> To Change the place but keep the pain".[7]

Monday 24th. Feb

This day I did not go out, again. It is a long time since I have missed the market, but this day I never attempted to go there; I was afraid that by some mischance I should have come too near some of my friends, and have suffered in my Arm by it.

Tuesday 25th. Feb

I really am very ill in my Arm, it is the left arm just above the thumb, on the side of the Shackle;[8] the Doctor says it is much better, but for myself I feel no betterness about it; this is like the report of a Victory, which the Soldiers all know to have been a defeat.

Wednesday 26th. Feb

I can scarcely lift a Pen in my left hand, it seems to weary it so much, had it been my right hand, I should have been disabled, and prevented from either making Pens or Ruling Books. But I am thankful it is not so bad. I believe I am very impatient when afflicted—it does me no good, but still it is so.

Thursday 27th. Feb

The Doctor has cut my hand today, in order that the corruption might be discharged, but I think there was no matter to discharge, nothing but blood proceeded from it. I have it now poulticed with a linseed meal Poultice.

Friday 28th. Feb

I can scarcely attend to any thing but my hand, and it is no better for my attention; I have some land to measure at Brantingham tomorrow, but shall be obliged to send word that at present I am not capable of doing it.

> "Pain is an evil"

Saturday 1st. March

Nothing to record but suffering, I went to the West end this afternoon, and took a walk with Rd. Marshall, on the Bean Lands end; he like me is an invalid, he had, had Coffee to his Dinner; and I have not eaten an Ounce of Meat this week.

Sunday 2d March

I did not go out today, I had some Fish to Dinner of which I eat very well. I do not know that we ever had Fish on a Sunday before—I likewise had an Orange or two today.

Monday 3d March

The Doctor says my Arm is much better, I think myself it is rather better; but no feeling much of better. I went into the Market this afternoon: and was pitied by one, and not noticed by another, but it was just the same to me, for pity

---

[7] See n.31 (1829).

[8] 'Shackle'—short for 'shackle-bone', that is the wrist or wrist-bone (*OED*).

did me no good and Contempt did me no harm. What an amazing deal of reputed ~~prescriptions~~ remedies I might have applied to my arm if I had followed the directions of all who prescribed. This arm appears to be the main object of attention to me, it is of very little consequence to me what is passing round me so long as I suffer from pain.

Tuesday 4th. Mar

I think my arm is something easier today; I hope it will continue to improve.

Wednesday 5th. Mar

My arm is certainly better than it was, as I can move it in different positions better than I could, it is yet far from well, but as it has got a turn for the better, I hope it will continue to mend.

Thursday 6th. Mar

This is Mr. Barnard's Rent day, he is as great a stranger here, as any Irish Absentee Landlord is on his own Estate in Ireland, not one Shilling of the Rents which arise from his Estate is spent by him here.

Friday 7 Mar

Abm. Barff came staggering in drunk this day to see me, I could have dispensed with his Company very well, for his presence is not the most agreeable when the little reason he had is drowned.

Saturday 8 Mar

This morning I went to Measure a piece of Land for Wm. Loncaster in the low Ruffham field Close, I was a good deal fatigued with it; and could not or would not go out in the afternoon to Brantingham where I had two or three Closes to measure.

Tuesday 11th. March

Sent by the Carrier this day 2 Hams for Wm. I hardly know whether they were a pair or not, as I was prevented helping to pack them on account of my Arm, which altho' it is better is far from well ...

Thursday 13th. March

The weather keeps very fine, we have been planting Dahlias, which I think is rather too soon as frost may yet visit us, however they must now take their chance; tho' I think it will be proper to cover them at nights for a while.

Friday 14th March

Our Pear tree shews but few Flower buds this Spring, and I think the Gooseberry trees will have but few Berries; but they may not yet be sprung out.

Saturday 15th. March

I was at Kettlethorpe Bar (Drewton)[9] this forenoon measuring the Garden taken from the Road side, as there is a dispute concerning the right of it; but this makes no difference to me, for if there had been no dispute perhaps I should not have had a job. Towards night I was called to measure some turnip Land above Beverley Plump. It came on dark before I had done and I was put to

---

[9] Located on the Brough–Newbald turnpike *c.* 2 miles north of South Cave, and shown on the 1855 O.S. 6-in. map of the area.

it to complete the measurement. This had been measured before, but I know that sooner or later they will come to <u>my</u> Shop!!

Sunday 16 March

One day when my Arm was very painful, I was complaining, when little Ann said you must not cry: I said to her dost not thou cry when thou art ill? She said no, I get some Sago to make me better; and you must have some and some Chamomile tea to mend you.

Monday 17th. March

Ralph Martin was buried the last week; he had been ill a long time he was 78 years of Age: many a funeral he has attended and sung before the Corpse to the Church: then he was never slack at taking his lowance after the funeral, as it is customary to give the Singers something to spend; but now Ralph has sung his last Burial Psalm.

Tuesday 18th. Mar

We have had frosty nights for some time, but the days have been very pleasant; I am afraid that the frosts will injure the fruit trees in flower, as there are several Plum trees in full Bloom.

Wednesday 19th. Mar

I was at the west end this Evening, I saw Ben. Tapp he was at the Bay horse soliciting Orders for his inflammable goods; He says his Brother John lives at Saint Alban's, he is in business for himself.

Thursday 20th. Mar

Measured a piece of Turnip Land for Wm. Cousens this Evening, in Mr. Levitt's Close at the Garth end, it was very pleasant and the ground dry & clean. There was about Six Acres of it.

Friday 21st. Mar

My hand or Arm is a great deal better, but I have it yet bandaged up; My eye is again very tender, and the Cold weather is not much in favour of it, however I hope it will soon be better.

"Hope springs eternal in the human breast" ...

Sunday 23d March

A very cold blustering day, but I was twice at the Church; as it refreshed me a little to go out; I had a Chicken to dinner, as I can eat no butcher's meat; I dare say I have not eaten half a pound for the last month.

Monday 24th March

Not much doing at the Market today, Mr. Brown would not give 45s. pr. Quarter for wheat today. Mr. Beaumont of Brantingham has got his Arm broken, by his horse falling with him: I have been prevented some time by my Arm from measuring some land for him; and now I doubt he is worse than I am.

Tuesday 25th. March

A very hard frost last night and cold all this day[.] I was at the west end this Evening, my Arm is much better, but not yet well by a good deal, However I have little pain in it, and can move it about pretty well, but cannot yet use a fork at meat, but this does not mean much, as I eat very little meat.

Wednesday 26th. March

I was at Beverley this day with my Partner Ths. Levitt getting sworn in as Assessors, we had a Gig the honest miller lent me his horse as I wanted a trifle of him for measuring but he complained so poor that he said he had no money, but he <u>wad</u> lend me his horse, for if he had money he said he did not like to pay it. We got home about three O'clock we did not stay to Dine; as it would have been very little profit to me to pay for my Dinner when I was not disposed to eating.

Thursday 27 March

I think I have not noticed that we received a parcel from Wm. on Monday night last, all safe & sound. The Biscuits are very good but rather too hard for me, those that he brought were of a thinner kind; — I am sorry that he is going again to remove, as the distance will be greater from the Shop, and in any situation there will be some inconvenience.

Friday 28th. March

This is what is called Good Friday—there is Service at the Church, but as I am not in very good condition I stay at home—Conder is going to <u>flit</u> to where Charles Jenkinson lived; the house round the old Glazier's Corner, it is Mr. Barnard's house; they have not been well used where they are, and I dare say would have staid if they could have been comfortable, but this with the neighbour they have was not very probable; however there is one satisfaction I know that Fewson's (the Bear) cannot stay long where they are to be a plague to any one long: they have contrived so well that they have nearly lost the little custom that was at the House.

Saturday 29th March

I was at the West end this forenoon, and at Ellerker in the afternoon, balancing the Poor Book for the Overseers—I think I have said nothing about my Arm for some time, the fact is, it has been pretty free from pain, but it is yet an ugly looking place.

Sunday 30th. March

This is Easter Sunday, which is, or rather <u>was</u>, noted for Children having on new Clothes, whose parents could afford to purchase them; but I think this fashion is not so much followed as formerly; It is the approach of Spring, and the little human flowrets, used to look gay.

Monday 31st. March

This is a day here for Horses being shown, there were not many, but there was as usual a considerable bustle, Fewson's appeared to be not much esteemed by the Horsemen for they had not so much as a single horse.

Tuesday 1st. April

This is the day for Penny Rolls being given away at the Church to any who will hold out a hand for one, there appeared to be plenty of bread as there were a few Rolls to spare. There were 30 Dozen or 360 Penny loaves. The Easter Dinner was at Barnard Cook's. There were only nine or ten dined, I have not attended the dinner for some years past.

Wednesday 2d. April

This Evening I intended going to the West end, and set off for that purpose; but meeting Jack Smith, he had so many lies to tell and so much "what I was observing" that Robt. Marshall, came up and I turned back with him, so bidding friend Smith Good night, I quitted him.

Thursday 3d. April

There was a Man at Mr. Atkinson's this evening, who was going about with a Basket and Brush which he said contained Japan Varnish,[10] which he would undertake to varnish furniture with, and render it he said incapable of receiving any Stain, besides making it look so shining that it would save the trouble of rubbing: he was a Foreigner and said he came from Paris.

Friday 4th. April

Last night was the Club night, it was held at Morley's. I had a Bond to prepare for him, for Security of the Box and its contents. The Bonds formerly have been kept in the Box, which is a sort of queer place for them; because if the Box should happen to be lost, the Bond would be with it, then where would the Security be? but this will be amended.

Saturday 5th. April

A letter from my Brother informed us that he was much better, he had written the letter with his left hand, he says he is not yet in a fit state to come to Cave; I shall write to him in a Day or two, he wishes to know about Mary's affairs but I can import to him little intelligence on that head, only to say that the £500 at Liverpool is not likely to be had without having recourse to the Law.

Sunday 6th. April

Richard Marshall, and the Gamekeeper had gone this morning to Skidby to hear a preacher there, who attends occasionally. A very fine day, but I kept on my Great Coat, as I am rather fearful of getting cold.

Monday 7th. Apl.

A great hurry again today to see Horses shewn, If none were more pleased to see them than I am, there would I know be very few Spectators. I had some Fish to dinner today, as I cannot yet fancy Beef or Mutton. I have got the Handkerchief from my Arm today for the first time, and a Broad Ribbon bound round it ...

Thursday 10th. Apl.

I went down to the West end this Evening, intending to see the Overseer, but when I got there he had not got from the Common (or as the phrase is, "from the Farm") so I came back without waiting, and spent a little time at our old friend's.

---

[10] A varnish of exceptional hardness, which originally came from Japan; also used to describe similar hard varnishes, especially black varnish (*OED*).

Friday 11th. Apl.

I was sent for this evening to Fewson's by a man who wished to treat me with a Glass of Liquor, but I declined it as I have not tasted or taken a Drop of Spirits or Ale for many weeks past.

Saturday 12th. Apl.

It is announced (it is said) in the York papers today that Mr. Barnard has got married to an Irish Lady[11] this is all that is known at present about it.

Sunday 13th. Apl.

Mr. Creyke has resigned the Vicarage of So. Cave but who is appointed in his room to the living is not yet known. Rd. Marshall is very glad that he shall quit Jack, (as he calls him) the Curate.

Monday 14th Apl

This day at Noon I went to measure the Breadth of the Road at Kettlethorpe bar, and in 5 other places between there and Drewton Beck; it was a pleasant day.

Tuesday 15th. Apl.

After School time this afternoon I measured a piece of Turnip Land of Mr. King's on the North Cave road, it was a very fine evening, there was about five Acres of it.

Wednesday 16th. Apl.

A Circular has been received from the House of Commons headed Medical Returns; it requires to know if a Medical man was engaged by the Parish for the year ending Lady day 1834. together with the amount of the Salary given to such Medical man for one year. But as we have not had a Doctor engaged for the Parish we shall have but little to answer. There are a variety of questions which seem to be

"Propounded by a fool,

which a wise man cannot answer for his Soul!

Thursday 17th. Apl

Eliza's are very throng flitting they got to sleep at their new house a few nights ago, a Tailor has taken their old house, but I think his prospect of a living is very small; as I am certain there is no occasion for another tailor in the town.

Friday 18th. Apl.

It is said that Bessy Pinder is going to give up the Shop-keeping business; a man at Hull has taken it, and will enter on it in a short time; perhaps before the fair.

Saturday 19th. Apl.

I went to Brantingham this forenoon to measure some ornamental Plantations; I dined with Mr. Beaumont after measuring a small triangular plantation taken off for the purpose of feeding Pheasants in, after dinner went to

---

[11] Henry Gee Barnard was married at Paddington Church, London, on 8 Apr., 1834 to Elizabeth Mary, daughter of Henry Elliot of Clonmel, Ireland. There were no children from the marriage (Hall 29).

measure 3 more plantations almost as far as Brough: there were two closes to measure but as I was obliged to go again to the Wold I left them undone; and got done with the Laurel and Sweet Briar Plantations, about 7 O'clock when I returned home, pretty well tired; when I got some Coffee and refreshed myself, I felt no more of the fatigue.

Sunday 20th. Apl.

I had forgot to state that the Man who trailed the Chain for me yesterday, in getting over a hedge discovered a Snake or Serpent, which he immediately struck at with a hedge Stake, but it eluded the stroke and came out on the Side of the fence where I was standing. I had one of my Poles in my hand Shod with Iron, with which I struck it, and pierced it through, the Man then struck it over the head and dispatched it; I think the reptile was nearly a yard long.

Monday 21st. Apl

Benjn. Brown has got married again, about a fortnight since; he was treating his friends with a Glass a piece today; I got a Glass of Wine and Water, as Spirits are out of my way at present, and I think it will be some time before I take any more.

Tuesday 22d. Apl.

My wife has gone to Hull today, so that I am left alone I had a little Beef pie to my Dinner, and an Orange after it, I having eaten an Orange a day for some time, as it is considered beneficial to my Arm, it is not yet well, but has no pain in it; it has yet a wound on it.

Wednesday 23d. Apl.

My wife arrived safe at home with the Carrier last night, between nine and ten O'clock; she bought some Sugar and tea, and a new Bonnet for herself, and an Orange for little Ann with which she was much pleased.

Thursday 24th. Apl

I think this day has passed without anything remarkable my Arm continues much as it has been some time back viz. without pain but not healed, and my eye still continues tender, in fact I have to be nursed and fed with Sago &c. ...

Saturday 26th. Apl.

This day I spent chiefly at home, little Ann was very sick and ill today, we thought she was going to have the Small Pox; but after getting a sleep she was something better towards night.

Sunday 27th. Apl

Mr. Barnard has appointed a new Vicar for So. Cave,[12] he is a Son of Admiral Sir William Hotham (whom I do not know) I suppose he is a relation at least by marriage to Mr. Barnard. The Revd. has not yet come but is expected shortly.

---

[12] Edwin Hotham was the vicar of South Cave from 1834 until 1844 when he was appointed rector of South Dalton, the family seat of the Hothams. He was the cousin of the wife of the late Henry Boldero Barnard, the church's former patron and Lord of the Manor. (See Appendix 2) (Foster iii. section on Hotham family).

Monday 28th. Apl.

I had a Gentleman from London today a Stamp Inspector he came without my having any notice, but this did not put me about for I had nothing but what was right, he was very well satisfied with the manner in which the Accounts were kept, and said he wished he had no more trouble than he had here.

Tuesday 29th. Apl.

A Stormy rainy night last night, it has continued to rain moderately the greatest part of today, Rain it is said has been much wanted, though I think myself warm weather would be more beneficial.

Wednesday 30th. Apl.

What a deal of trouble several people seem to give themselves, on the immorality of Beer Shops: was the Beer all <u>drugged</u> there could hardly be a greater outcry made. I do not believe one word of the <u>general</u> bad effects which are said to arise from the Beer houses: they like others of their elder brethren the Publicans, are desirous of disposing of as much of their Liquor as they can.

Thursday 1st. May

This is the day sung by poets, but I think in a more genial Clime than ours, however it is very fine weather, we have had a fine rain, and every thing seems favorable for a display of spring flowers.

Friday 2d. May

The Churchwardens & Ministers have been begging for the building & repairing of Churches[13] they never came to me, as I gave the Churchwardens notice not to trouble themselves to call as not one Penny would I give for the Purpose—There have been let loose upon the Population of England and Wales this week more than 30,000 beggars to support old Mother Church and to try to support her with rotten props. I wish that Constables in every Parish had had the resolution to have taken up 10,000 of these sturdy beggars in black.

Saturday 3d. May

I was measuring some land this afternoon at Brantingham: it was low land and Tufits cried hard with the same cry, as in Southfield bottom and the same sprightly appearance when running, as I well recollect fifty years since.

Sunday 4th. May

Nothing particular this day, Rd. Marshall says the new Vicar will be here shortly, he intends doing duty himself for the present.

Monday 5th. May

A very fine day, but little doing at the Market. There was a meeting of the Trustees of the Turnpike when it was agreed not to suffer any encroachments, on the road, I shall I expect have another job at the road.

---

[13] The newly reformed parliament was unwilling to vote more money for the building of new churches (see n.48 (1831)). Accordingly the 'King's Letter for the Incorporated Society for the Enlarging, Building and Repairing of Churches and Chapels' was circulated to all parishes to encourage voluntary subscriptions (Soloway 311).

Tuesday 6th. May

This Evening after School time I went to Brantingham with an intention to measure a plantation, but I could do without as I had the notes from the last time I was there—Geo Holborn is the Gamekeeper to Mr. Shaw.

Wednesday 7th. May

This Evening there was to have been a meeting at the Church respecting the Court of Sewers but there was nobody attended, I was at the West end and saw no company, that were inclined to attend.

Thursday 8th. May

The new Shopkeeper I think has come to Mrs. Pinder's Shop; the Windows are whitened as they are taking the Stock; the man's name is Harland.

Friday 9th. May

At Kettlethorpe Bar again last night setting out a Garden of 20 Perches, which is allowed to be taken off from the road Side adjoining the house, I think I go oftener than I get any thing; I had one of the Trustees with me last night ...

Monday 12th. May

There was not at the Market today a single Corn buyer, as the markets do not get up in price the Factors are not willing to purchase, as they cannot send it where they can get more than they give for it. I am glad that Corn is cheap.

Tuesday 13th. May

At Beverley fair the last week there was a man of the name of Baitson who lived at Hotham, a butcher, he dropped down dead in the Street at Beverley when looking at some Sheep.

Wednesday 14th. May

This is Weighton fair day and very fine it is, it was a fine rain yesterday which will (they say) benefit the Country; I believe there are many people gone from here to the fair.

Thursday 15th. May

This is the day for the holding the Spring Court the meeting is at the Bay horse at the West end, little Jemmy is throng today providing for the Steward, Bailiff, Jury &c, &c.

Friday 16th. May

Went to the West end with some tax Papers for my Partner Ths. Levitt to take to Beverley tomorrow, but at night he sent them back, as he could not go; so that I must even go myself.

Saturday 17th. May

This morning I set off to walk to Beverley and got there very well and soon had my business done, I got a glass of Wine and Water and then set off for home, where I arrived safe about half past three in the afternoon.

Sunday 18th. May

I felt not in the least tired this morning with my walk yesterday; I did not hurry but walked slow and regular, which I find to be the easiest; and perhaps the soonest—according to Mr. Barnard's Motto, Festina Lente, — which means a slow haste.

Monday 19th. May

There was abundance of Pots at the Market today, preparatory for the fair; good Wheat this day sold at 44s. pr. Quarter.

Tuesday 20th. May

The Farmers are sadly sore at the low price of Wheat, and are wishing they had fat Oxen to sell instead of Corn; as they can sell them readily at 7s. pr. Stone.

Wednesday 21st. May

We have beautiful fine weather, every body cleaning and colouring for the fair, both inside and outside of their houses; so that we look like a Dutch town now for cleanliness.

Thursday 22d. May

This day or at least in the Evening we leave off for Cave Fair; that we may have time to get all put in order for the approaching throng.

Friday 23d May

Hannah Martin has come today to clean the School so that we are in no lack of noise; however little we may have of reason or argument. She is a famous dabbler amongst whitening and colouring.

Saturday 24th. May

This day according to custom on the Saturday before the fair is the market day; but there is a very thin attendance in the Street; We have had all the Arton's of Ellerker and Provence at tea as usual on this day.

Sunday 25th. May

This is Cave fair Sunday, when there was no want of Hull gentry, coming to stuff themselves with Cheesecakes, and who are particular not to forget their Cave friends at this time, we have had none of them.

Monday 26th. May

Very dry and dusty, a great Shew of Beasts, a good deal more than was sold, as the weather is so dry the pastures are not good, which made the Sale Slack, — we have had Js. Ramsdale and his two Sons; we have had no other Company, but comers and goers.

Tuesday 27th. May

John Ramsdale and his Sister Mary were here today, they dined and drank tea at Eliza's, and went home in pretty good time perhaps between eight and nine O'clock.

Wednesday 28th. May

It was expected there would have been some Races today, but neither horses nor Asses came forward so that there was no sport (as it is called) of that kind.

Thursday 29th. May

There are two rival Beer Shops at the west end, one of them Charley Smith's (who was the opponent of the little Nut man at the last fair) got some Ribbons to Run for; which when his adversary discovered, he immediately got some Tobacco to Smoke for, which drew away Charley's Company, but he no ways daunted brought out a bowl of Treacle, and some Rolls; for the lads to eat, they who eat the most in the least time to bear away the prize; this turned the scale again in his favour.

Friday 30th. May

Went down to the west end this forenoon, to see if there was any thing for me, that is what I wanted was money, and I came on full as well or better than I expected; and had Cheesecakes and liquor brought out, but the latter I never tasted at all this fair, nor have done for some months past.

Saturday 31st. May

This forenoon I think I spent chiefly in reading the newspapers—by the way the Paper did not arrive on Monday last nor has it at all come to hand—In the afternoon I went to measure a small Close on the little Wold for Ths. Wride about 6 Acres, thus ends the week.

Sunday 1st. June

This day we were invited to tea at the Bay horse but as we do not make a practice of going out on Sundays, we declined attending. Eliza and little Ann were there.

Monday 2d. June

The Market here today very thinly attended, and very little business done, a farmer shewed a sample of Wheat which had been thrashed about two months; he asked 43s. pr. Qr. for it; but Mr. Brown to whom he offered it did not bid him any thing for it, as he said he had too much of the same sort.

Tuesday 3d. June

Our old friend Mr. Atkinson was taken suddenly ill yesterday; he has been bled, he looks very poorly but he says he is better; he would not have any person to stay with him last night, as he said he was not afraid of dying by himself.

Wednesday 4th. June

I went this morning to see Mr. Atkinson, he looks better than he did yesterday, and says he feels much better.

Thursday 5th. June

Mr. Atkinson is much better but his complaint seems to have fallen into one of his eyes which is very tender and much inflamed, but he can now eat well.

Friday 6th. June

Last night was the Club night, when two new members were admitted; after that a sort of stormy discussion arose respecting a Man who had been on the Box and had picked up a Stick or two when receiving pay, but as the Club hours were over nothing was done the fine is One Guinea for any person doing any thing when receiving the benefit. To me it seems to have been a malicious information.

Saturday 7th. June

I was at the Mill this afternoon, the Miller was very poorly with a sore mouth and throat, and so pestered that it was not possible for him to pay any money, as when he is well it frequently makes him ill when paying, but when he is ill it endangers his life to pay in that state, and certainly his friends can never be so thoughtless as to teaze him to pay, when he runs the hazard of his life.

Sunday 8th. June

A Methodist Preacher and his hearers rushed into the Cross this Evening like Soldiers entering a besieged fortress, as I happened to be at home I went out to the Man of words and told him I should not permit him to preach there, he said he had a Licence, I asked him if his Licence gave him authority to preach on my premises; to this he made very little answer, and said that he would preach in the Street. I told him I should not interfere where I had no authority, so he preached in the Street opposite to Cousens's; the Chapel would have contained a great deal more than were there assembled to hear him. I fancy I shall be pretty well called for opposing the whole tribe; but it was as little I think as they could have done to have asked leave; and had they done so I dare say I should not have refused them; but they shall not have that as right which ought to be granted as a favour.

Monday 9th. June

A very thin attendance at the Market today, it seems that wheat is better to sell than it has lately been; and Oats are scarce and expected to fetch high prices.

Tuesday 10th. June

We have had a fine Shower, which will make vegetation again bloom; it is said that the Crops never looked better, the wheat Crop is very forward, it is now shooting into the ear, which is at least three weeks sooner than common.

Wednesday 11th. June

I was at Beverley this day paying in the taxes, I walked there and back again; I arrived at home about four O'clock in the afternoon. I did not hurry nor fatigue myself, I was caught in a Shower near Tim Turner's. I got into a plantation till it was over.

Thursday 12th. June

There was a Parish meeting this Evening at Cousens's[.] Ths. Marshall was there, but he said there was a strange want of sense; the result was like the ending of long Passages (I think; nay I do not know the name of the Poet) that lead to nothing.

Friday 13th. June

Recd. instructions from the Secretary of State's office relative to the making out the annual list of Voters for the Knights of the Shire for the East Riding of Yorkshire[14] ...

Sunday 15 June

Conder went to West Ella today, as Eliza and the Bairns are gone to Swinefleet. Last night we had a dreadful thunder storm: it rained uncommonly

---

[14] Section 12 of the Reform Act of 1832 (2 Will. IV c. 45) provided for 6 'Knights of the shire' for Yorkshire (instead of the previous 4) with 2 for each riding. The overseers of the poor in each parish and township were responsible for drawing up and publicizing the lists of voters in accordance with a strict timetable and method of procedure dictated by the Act. (See also n.16 (1835).

fast and swam down the Street like a torrent. The Storm began between seven &
Eight and continued till about nine; it lightened I dare say most of the night
after, but without thunder.

Monday 16th. June

It is three years this day since Norrison Marshall was killed by lightning.
A Rainy afternoon very few people at the Market, the farmers throng sowing
Turnips.

Tuesday 17th June

The Visitation this day, it is at Morley's (viz the Dinner). I think there will
be a very thin attendance, our old friend Mr. Atkinson, as one of the
Churchwardens has got himself ready for the feast; I do not attend, it is many
years since I gave up.

Wednesday 18th. June

So we have two more runaway would be Kings coming amongst us.[15]
England appears to be a refuge, for the Offscum ~~Off~~ or Scum of all nations.

Thursday 19th. June

I had my Paper merchant, he has a Son a Wood engraver; I shewed ~~some~~
~~of~~ the Specimens of Northcotes fables: with which he was much taken, indeed
they are very fine.

Friday 20th. June

This day I put up a notice on the Church Door for those who have not put a
claim in for Voting, for members of Parliament, may give in their Claim
together with a Shilling, that they may be registered as Voters.

Saturday 21st. June

This afternoon I was at Ellerker collecting the Church Sess for Ellerker, I
got most of what I wanted, and then came home again, it was a very warm day.

Sunday 22d. June

This day very hot, altho' it had been part rain the last night. I think there
is nothing particular today.

Monday 23d June

Wheat seemed very bad to sell today at the Market indeed I do not know
that any was sold; I saw one Man offer Samples to two factors but neither of
them bought it.

Tuesday 24th. June

I have been making up the Quarterly stamp Acct. which is generally a
tedious concern, as every particular stamp is to be looked over, and an account
taken of them. I have now on hand in Stock to the amount of £204–19–0.

---

[15] Following their defeat by a Spanish army led by General Rodil, both Don Carlos, pretender to
the Spanish throne, and Dom Miguel, claimant to the throne of Portugal, had embarked on British
men of war. Don Carlos was taken to England aboard the 'Donegal', which arrived at Spithead
on 13 June 1834. He remained in this country only until 1 July, when he left for Spain to resume
the struggle. Dom Miguel was taken from Sines on another vessel on 2 June and landed at Genoa
(*AR* 1834, Hist. 394–5 and 434).

Wednesday 25th. June

Eliza and her Mother and little Ann were at the Mill yesterday at tea, it was rather rainy as they went, but it became very fine afterwards they got home between eight and nine O'clock.

Thursday 26th. June

Little Ann and her Grandmother went this afternoon to Mount Airy, to see Mrs Robinson, she has been and indeed is yet very ill; she thinks she overset herself at Cave fair, having had a good deal of Company.

Friday 27th. June

The Chinese beat all the Geologists hollow including the Rev. Somebody of Cambridge[16] who has preached a sort of Geological Sermon to disprove the History of the Mosaic Creation. Send him to China, where he will find that the Emperor She-nou — reigned there 20,000 years before the Creation of the Moon!! Now who can come up to this?

Saturday 28th. June

Heard from Wm. that he had again removed, I think he is like Tommy Gray who no sooner gets into a house; but he is contriving how soon he can get out again. — But it is a serious distance is three Miles to walk twice every day.

Sunday 29th. June

Francis Ruston has been very ill for about a week past, he is something better today, it is an inward complaint with which he has been frequently troubled.

Monday 30th. June

At the Market today no wheat sold as the factors are not free to buy, because they say if the weather continues fine, the prices will be lower, it is said if the weather continues favorable, the harvest will be begun in a month from this time, the Crops of Wheat look uncommonly fine ...

Wednesday 2d. July

It seems the Poor Law, (miscalled amendment Bill) has passed the house of Commons,[17] if this Bill be a boon to the Poor, it is the queerest piece of good that I ever heard of; it will increase the Poor Rates, instead of diminishing them.

---

[16] The Revd Adam Sedgwick (1785–1873), professor of geology at Cambridge University, was famous both for his sermons and lectures. He made important discoveries in the study of stratigraphy and became president of the Geological Society in 1831 and of the British Association in 1833 (*DNB*).

[17] The Poor Law Amendment Act (4 & 5 Will. IV c. 76), which followed the Bill on 14 Aug. 1834, embodied the recommendations of the Commission on the Poor Laws appointed by the Government in 1832. Its main recommendations were: the establishment of a central board to administer the Poor Law on a national basis; outdoor relief for able-bodied paupers to be abolished (except for medical aid), and replaced by indoor relief to be provided in workhouses. As well as incorporating in full these recommendations, the Act also provided for groups of 20 or 30 parishes to join together to form unions with one workhouse to each union, whilst administration within a union would be carried out by a board of guardians who would include all the local Justices of the Peace plus members elected from local ratepayers and property owners within the area.

Thursday 3d. July

This night was the Club meeting before the feast, there was a large attendance of members: it is required for all to be paid up and cleared off at this night, which was accordingly done.

Friday 4th. July

The weather still keeps very dry, and the Wind very generally strong: the Wheat crop looks uncommonly well, as dry weather is in its favour; I hope that Providence will favour us with a fine harvest.

Saturday 5th. July

This day I have been a kind of prisoner at home, as last night I had a toe that rather hurt me, so I cut it; but going too deep I made it bleed, and this morning, I could not bear my Shoe on, so I slittered about with an old Slipper on.

Sunday 6th. July

It is said that the new Vicar will not be here in less than a fortnight's time, — Rodmell is going to do duty at Brantingham and Ellerker as the Vicar is ill and incapable of preaching.

Monday 7th. July

I did not see a single sample of Wheat at the Market today; indeed there was no factor that I saw to buy any; this fine weather has extinguished Speculation.

Tuesday 8th. July

Turnip hoeing and Haymaking, are now the order of the days, very fine weather for carrying on the different (operations) works: some complain that the Grass mowed (or mown) does not hay very fast that is it does not die fast enough.

Wednesday 9th July

Miss Leeson of Ellerker was married today to John Scholefield of Faxfleet; after the ceremony they went to Burlington it is said; but I saw nothing of them.

Thursday 10th. July

This is the Club feast day, I did not go to the Church, as it began to rain, but did not come much wet; I was there at the Dinner there were nearly 100 members present. The Club has cleared since the last feast £23–14–11 — At the feast all very quiet. Jn. Cousens and Mrs. Akam's daughter were married this day.

Friday 11th. July

I was not very well this day, being troubled with an inward pain; but before night I was better; very fine weather yet continues; the Farmers are throng with their Hay & Clover; and also Turnips.

Saturday 12th. July

This morning for the first time I saw in the Hull Packet that Lord Althorpe & Lord Grey had resigned their Places;[18] it appears that O'Connell has been

---

[18] Lord Althorp resigned from his ministerial post after failing to persuade the government to remove the clause prohibiting public meetings in the Irish Coercion Act, which was due to be

the Instrument: of the Ministers giving up. I think the Irish Secretary did wrong in having any communication with the Irish Agitator.

Sunday 13th. July

Mr. Wilson, master of the Hull Grammar School[19] preached at the Church this morning, and in the afternoon Mr. Rodmell read over his farewell address, which I dare say he called a Sermon, and intended it to be pathetic; but he fell short in moving the Passions.

Monday 14th. July

The Wheat trade seems to be at a stand, as the Prices at present are regulated by the weather, the Factors will not purchase on Speculation, indeed they seem to have too much in hand already ...

Wednesday 16th. July

I have been pulling Currant berries today, a tolerable Crop from two trees, one of them is a great height that against the House side, beside the Pear tree; I contrived when on the Ladder to reach the top branches, and cleared them of the fruit ...

Friday 18th. July

This morning and all the forenoon the wind very strong, and at noon came on a heavy rain and continued all the remaining part of the day, it was such a storm as is seldom experienced at this time of the year; it must have laid the Corn very much.

Saturday 19th. July

This morning still rainy, it stormed most part, or all of the last night, a great deal of rain has fallen; it cleared up about noon; and in the afternoon I went to measure a Grass Close at Broomfleet about 10 acres.

Sunday 20th. July

The new Vicar the Revd. Edwin Hotham this day did the <u>duty</u> at the Church; he read the 39 Articles and gave his assent and consent to all and every thing in the Book of Com. Prayer; of course to that part amongst others which denominates Charles the 1st the blessed Martyr!! I was called on in the afternoon to witness with my hand; his adhesion to the Rites & Ceremonies of the Church.

Monday 21st. July

This day a very thin attendance at the Market; On Saturday last I went to put the Paper into the Post office a little after Eleven O'clock, I was informed that the time was altered, and the Post had gone out at Eleven, so that I was too late for that day's Post.

Tuesday 22d. July

The Poor law Bill seems as though as it was a thorough Racer; it will run through the Lords and beat in a Canter; I think after all the warning that

renewed at the end of the session. Since Althorp was leader in the House of Commons, Grey was unable to continue, and resigned his ministry, which was succeeded by that of Lord Melbourne (July–Dec. 1834).

[19] Revd William Wilson, headmaster of Hull Grammar School, 1822–1836 (Lawson 194–8).

Parliament has had, they ought to have paused and not have gone on in such a hurry.

Wednesday 23d. July

Very fine hay weather, a great deal of the Hay is now safe at home in very good condition, it is said not [to] be a very large crop.

Thursday 24th. July

Saml. Bridgman came to day from Malton to see his Brother; he looks very well, and appears just as usual; his Brother went to meet him at Beverley.

Friday 25th. July

I was at the West end this Evening: where I met with nothing in particular; I wrote 7 Notices to different Persons to remove their Manure heaps out of the Street, they are under a Penalty of ten Shillings if they do not comply with the notices.

Saturday 26th. July

I was at Ellerker this afternoon settling with Mr. Leason for the Church Sess, I got home about five O'clock, when the Revd. Vicar called to say he wished I would sign another paper for him tomorrow; as the last had been read over in the Church at the wrong time—he stopped about two hours, and we had a good deal of conversation on various subjects—he asked me if I was a Whig or a Tory; I told him I certainly was in favour of Whig sentiments. I asked him whether he was an Oxford or Cambridge man; he said Oxford to which I replied that it was scarcely necessary to ask him whether he was a Tory or not: he did not give an Answer; but smiled.[20]

Sunday 27th. July

This afternoon I again signed the Vicar's Assent and Consent to all and everything contained in the Book of Common prayer, much good may it do him.

Monday 28th. July

Strong talk of the beginning of Harvest, I think there is none yet begun in this neighbourhood, the weather continues fine for the Crops.

Tuesday 29th. July

Mr. Bridgman has been this day at Skelton where he has some land, it is somewhere towards Howden; he says several People have Commenced Harvest; the Crops very good on the strong Wallingfen land.

Wednesday 30th. July

After School time this Evening I measured a Close of Turnips for Ths. Robinson of Ellerker, adjoining the Road to Brantingham, the Land before the Inclosure was called Holgates and is still known by that name; there is about 8 Acres of it; It was very hot; I saw the first beginning of harvest this year in a Close of Wheat near the Ring beck; it is Mr. Popple's Close.

---

[20] Of the 2 universities, Cambridge was inclined to evangelicalism, latitudinarianism and whiggery, whilst Oxford was the seat of the High Church party and traditional toryism.

Thursday 31st. July

Saml. Bridgman intends going away again tomorrow there is a conveyance from Hull to Malton twice a week, so he is going to meet it at Beverley tomorrow morning: He keeps house at Malton now and is not at lodgings; as general he has given me an invitation to get to see him; which I think is very unlikely that I shall go.

Friday 1st. Augt.

This afternoon I was at Ellerker Wold measuring some Turnip Land for Wm. Fisher, it was very hot, and came on a heavy Shower of Rain; but we got under a hedge and kept dry; it did not continue long; — There was about 12 Acres or rather more ...

[*3rd–8th August*—no entries]

Saturday 9th. Augt.

This day I again resume my scribbling; — Wm. went away this afternoon very shortly after I went to Beverley, (now I think this is not quite plain, I went first viz. before he set off) It was a fine day I hope he would have a pleasant Journey, It was past Six O'clock when I got home.

Sunday 10th. Aug

A very fine day, I dare say many Farmers grieved that it happens to be Sunday; for their thoughts are all on the harvest; There was new Wheat yesterday at Beverley Market; one man had 47s. pr. Quarter bid; but did not take it.

Monday 11th. Augt

A Farmer of the Name of Kirk who lives at River Bridge sold at Howden Market on Saturday last 30 Quarters of New Wheat at 47s. pr. Quarter; there was nothing done at this Market today.

Tuesday 12th. Aug

This day I stirred out very little, only went according to Custom to Mr. Atkinson's in the Evening, a very fine day for the Harvest, several Stacks of Wheat have been got up.

Wednesday 13th. Aug

This morning received a letter from Wm. giving an Account that he arrived safe at home on Sunday. I think he has done right in leaving his Money in the Custom house bank: for the differences in the Interest of £500 between being there and in the Stocks will only be 33s/4d reckoning the 3 pr. Cents at £90. and should the Stock come down to 60 or even 70 then there would be a large Slice of the principal gone.

Thursday 14th. Aug

The weather still remains fine, and all busy employed in Harvesting, a great deal of the Wheat has been secured in excellent Condition; Mr. Bridgman this day leading Pease.

Friday 15th. Aug

This day wrote to my Brother at Skipton and amongst other things I pressed him to apply to the Club for relief as he is unfortunately justly entitled thereto. I wrote him a Certificate to get signed for that purpose so that I hope either he or his friends will attend to it.

Saturday 16th. Augt.

I measured the Road from So. Cave to River Bridge this afternoon, but I was not satisfied with the Result so that I will not try to satisfy others, but will again measure it over; I only set down every Mile, but in my next expedition I will put down the distance at every 10 Chain's lengths so then I shall be certain ...

Monday 18th. Aug

There was new Wheat sold in the Market today from Broomfleet, both white and Red,[21] I think the Red was sold at 44s. pr. Quarter, the White was superior and was sold for more.

Tuesday 19th. Aug

My wife intended going to Hull today, but as the morning was stormy, it prevented her, and as she is not very particular to the time another day will do just as well.

Wednesday 20th. Aug

This afternoon I measured some Turnip Land for Rd. Marshall about 9 Acres, in the great Wold, it was a very pleasant day.

Thursday 21st. Aug

I have at present very little to do, as all the Scholars are either gleaning, or otherwise engaged in the Harvest.

Friday 22d. Aug

This morning there was a letter from my Brother in answer to one which I wrote some days since. It is rather more intelligible than the last; he says he is better in health, but continues lame; he has given up the Club three years ago; he wishes me to tell Wm. to take care of his money.

Saturday 23d. Aug

This forenoon I set out 2½ Acres of Potatoes in the Hall Garth opposite Mr. Turk's. Charles Rudd has sold them to Rd. Thomas & Jerh. Kirby. In the afternoon I measured accurately the Road from the Cross to the River Bridge, the distance is 5 Miles and 44 Yards.

Sunday 24th. Aug

I had forgot to notice that my wife was at Hull on Friday last, she went with and returned by the Carrier, got back about nine O'clock very well, she bought me a pair of new Shoes which I have had on today.

Monday 25th. Aug

Our old Friend complained when at his tea this afternoon that it was disagreeable, but could not tell the reason until he saw the paper in which had

---

[21] Strickland, writing in 1812, noted that the variety of wheat usually grown in the Wolds was Red Kent, so called because much of the seed-wheat was annually imported from that county. He also wrote that 'the red wheats are generally more productive than the white ones, but they command less price in the market'. The downy (white) wheats were found in the north to be more prone to mildew and quicker to sprout or grow in the ear in wet harvests (Strickland 122).

been an Ounce of tea, when he found out that he had put the whole ounce into the Teapot at once; so then he knew it was so strong that made it disagreeable.
Tuesday 26th. Aug

I am nearly as weary with doing nothing as some people are with working: however I do not put myself forward to fall in for a job at harvesting, as I know I should get nothing for it; but perhaps blistered hands.
Wednesday 27th Aug

I went to the West end this afternoon, and there I found David Dennis asleep at the Bay horse he had been employing himself in swallowing Ale to keep it from turning sour this warm weather!!
Thursday 28th. Aug

Sent to the Stamp Office at Hull this Evening £28–10–0 likewise sent a pair of Hams to Wm. to go by the Carrier in the morning, together with the old Gazetteer.
Friday 29th. Aug

A Shower of Rain came on this afternoon which put off those who had not got their harvest home, the Rain will be very acceptable to those who have strong land to plough, as some of it had got too hard for working.
Saturday 30th. Aug

Measuring some land at Drewton (harvesting) this afternoon about 22 Acres for Mr. Cook on the farm late Usher's, in coming home it came on a heavy Shower which wet me through, (I mean my Clothes) I got home about four O'clock ...
Monday 1st. Sepr.

There was but little done at the Market today, Now wheat is bad to sell, it is said that it is worth no more pr. Stone than Oats are.
Tuesday 2d Sepr.

I was settling the Church accounts with Mr. Atkinson, the Churchwarden, this evening, the Rate has been one penny in the pound.
Wednesday 3d Sepr.

Ths. Marshall was one day leading Wheat, and about four O'clock in the afternoon, lowance time a Pie and some Ale were sent into the Close and just put down within the Gate, when a lahtle nasty beast of a lad of Jes. Leighton's was tenting Pigs for Halliday ("but I will yark that Devil",) let his Pigs get in, when they found out the Basket, and eat up all the Pie: whea the Devil can stand sike as that and nut be mad.
Thursday 4th. Sep.

This morning recd. the Morning Chronicle, so I suppose the Times is gone overboard for abusing its own late Pet Lamb, the Lord Chancellor.[22]

---

[22] i.e. Lord Brougham. Until about Easter 1834, he had been strongly supported by *The Times*, but Barnes, its editor, had been sent the pasted fragments of a letter written to Brougham by Lord Althorp asking whether they should 'come to terms ... or make war' on *The Times* over its vehement opposition to the New Poor Law bill. Barnes concluded that Brougham had advocated war and thereafter attacked him in a series of hostile articles (Campbell viii. 413, 440–4).

Friday 5th. Sep

Last night was the Club night, and as is usual this month there were a very few members attended, two fresh members were proposed, who are to be ballotted for it the next monthly meeting.

Saturday 6th. Sep.

This forenoon I spent at home, and in the afternoon went to the West end; Mr. Turk has had about four quarters of Wheat stolen from him out of the Barn, but at what time or by whom he does not know.

Sunday 7th. Sepr.

Tailor Waudby has opened a Beer Shop, in the house where James Milner used to live; his sign is the Half Moon, which shines day and night.

Monday 8th. Sepr

I wonder we have not yet heard whether Wm. has received the Hams we sent on the 28th. of last month perhaps the Paper has not been marked; I thought it might have been in the Paper which came on Saturday: but I examined it and there was nothing to be found. I begin to be uneasy and fear they have not arrived.

Tuesday 9th. Sepr.

Hannah Martin's daughter Mary was married on Saturday last, she had another daughter married a few Weeks ago; so she is in hopes of quitting them now to make room for others.

Wednesday 10th. Sepr.

A very Rainy day but moderate, there was a Man at Mr. Atkinson's who had to go to Broomfleet that had been waiting for fair weather from three O'clock in the afternoon, but as it did not come, he set off in the rain about Six O'clock so that he would have the pleasure both of wet and darkness before he got home.

Thursday 11th. Sepr.

This Evening a Parish meeting at Barnard Cook's to balance the Church accounts for the last year, there were about twelve people, I came away about nine O'clock.

Friday 12th. Sep

Last night we had Church reform talked over, and it was nearly resolved that the Ringers should not be paid for their Services in making "the merry Bells ring round". It was in like manner moved by our friend of the Mill, that the Easter and Visitation Dinners should be discontinued, at the Parish expence; but the Churchwardens who like the rest of their brethren in office in other Parishes, did not appear to sympathise with the Man of the Mill.

Saturday 13th. Sepr.

Heard this morning from Wm. that he had got the hams which we are glad to hear. He says he wrote on the 3rd. Sepr. but there being no mark, I never examined further.

Sunday 14th. Sepr

Yesterday afternoon I was at Ellerker, balancing nay only posting up the Highway Book, I came home without my tea, as I did not wish to stay.

Monday 15th. Sepr

A very fine day, but few people at the Market, most of the talk was of Doncaster Races which begin today, some of the amateurs are going tomorrow to see the Saint's Race (St. Leger.)

Tuesday 16th. Sepr.

I wonder we have not yet recd. a Copy of the new Poor Act, with the list of interrogatories, there are plenty of Abridgements for Sale, but I will keep clear of them until I see the <u>matchless</u> act itself.

Wednesday 17th Sep

The Poor act has arrived together with questions to be answered, I suppose it is much like other Acts, nearly past all human comprehension, however I have not yet read it.

Thursday 18th. Sepr

This afternoon after School time measured a Close of Turnips for Ths. Wride on the little Wold, between 6 & 7 Acres, very bad travelling among them, as in many places they were higher than my knees ...

Saturday 20th. Sepr.

Here is great talk of the Musical Festival which is to take place next week at Hull;[23] I think there will be some of our wise ones will go to have their ears tickled; some of them who know about as much as I do of the Harmony of Pipes and Whistles, will no doubt be enraptured.

Sunday 21st. Sep

I have had a toe very painful, and have cut it two or three times until it bled, but it was no better, so I thought I would examine it again and behold it was not in the Part where I had cut it that the pain was, but quite on the other side of the toe; I think it is rather better than it was.

Monday 22d. Sep

The Market still remains dull and thinly attended—Corn is but at a low rate; in fact it can scarcely be turned into money.

Tuesday 23d Sep

Dr. (Joseph) Galland had a Patient that was ill and did not recover so readily as the Dr. could wish, so he (the Dr.) says to his Patient—Curse lit o thee get yam wi thee for thou'll dee onder me hands, thou nasty <u>Davel</u> get away with thee or thou'll dee afore thou gets yam, get away with thee. I'll ha na mare o thee.

Wednesday 24th Sepr

I do not know that any of our musical friends are gone to Hull today. Some of our neighbours as well as others did not like the tune at Hull Market yesterday, for they had all been keeping their good things against the throng

---

[23] The 'Grand Musical Festival' took place in Holy Trinity Church on 24, 25 and 26 Sept. 1834. It was held in aid of the fund for completing the restoration of the church's great east window. Unfortunately, however, although 'the performances went off with the greatest ECLAT ... the receipts did not amount to much more than the expenses', so the fund received little benefit from the occasion. Greenwood's *Picture of Hull* (1835) has a fine engraving of the interior of Holy Trinity, depicting the players and audience at this festival (Greenwood 132).

time, gaping for great prices, when it was found the market was so stocked with Geese Chickens, butter, fruit, &c that it was impossible to sell the greatest part of it.

Thursday 25th. Sep

This is Market Weighton "back end fair" day and a fine day it is, yesterday was a new fair there for Cattle which were low, but Sheep today were much wanted and dear.

Friday 26th. Sep

Horses for Howden are going through today, the Shew begins today and holds for a week, I suppose it is nearly as great a fair for Horses as any in England,[24] several dealers from London attend.

Saturday 27th. Sep

I was this afternoon measuring some Land for the Man of the Mill about 11 Acres in the new field before you come to the Mill, the Close is Turnips; now says he what sort of land do you call this? whya says he here is whicks, and a deal of feals calls me for nut getting 'em out, but curse 'em if they had it some of 'em; the devil a Turnip wad they get.

Sunday 28th. Sep

The new Vicar is very busy with a Sunday School at the Church, but is rather short of teachers; let them work on the Sabbath who please, I have enough of it not to covet Sunday employment.

Monday 29th. Sep

There was a Farmer from Newbald with a Sample of new Barley for sale, but he did not sell it, the Price talked of was 30s. pr. Quarter.

Tuesday 30th. Sep

I have been two or three mornings at the Castle teaching two of Mr. Stourton's Son's to write; I am to attend 3 mornings a Week from 8 to 9 O'clock, I cannot say that I am very fond of the Job, nevertheless I shall attend; as one cannot always have what they like.

Wednesday 1st. Oct

Wrote 2 notices for Mr. Bridgman to two of his tenants to quit, his Cottage tenants in general pay their Rents so badly that he is obliged to quit them if he can; and then perhaps meets with no better. Cottages are a bad speculation. Wrote another for Wm. Kirby to quit a house at the west end. Only the day before I wrote a notice from the Landlord to the same Wm. Kirby to quit.

---

[24] In the *Sporting Magazine* for 1807, it is described as 'indisputably the largest fair for horses in the kingdom ... It commences annually on September 25th, being attended by all the principal dealers from London, Edinboro', and from several of the great towns ... in England. During every night there are not less than 2,000 horses in the inn stables and sent out to grass. The stables of the public-houses in the adjoining villages to the extent of 10 miles round Howden are also completely full, so that it may be estimated that 4,000 horses are every day exposed for sale, 16,000 being disposed of at the last fair, worth altogether not less than £200,000.' (Fairfax-Blakeborough 16–17).

Thursday 2d. Octr.

I have got a bad toe, I cut it two or three times but it got no better, so when I examined it Closely the sore place was not where I thought it was but on the other side of the toe, now this may appear singular, but it is true, and even now it hurts more in the place where it is not bad than in the other where it is.

Friday 3rd Oct

Last night was the Club night when two more members were admitted, it was a throng night being the third from the feast.

Saturday 4th. Oct

I was at Beverley this day, carrying in Notices of Exemption from [i.e. for] the Farmers only, from Shepherd's Dogs, Ride horses, and Windows.[25] I rode a horse of Ths. Marshall's, which he let me have instead of paying for his Turnip Land measuring, as he had rather do any thing than part with his money. I believe he has given notice to quit his farm ...

Monday 6th. Oct

We have got Hannah Martin this morning to dress the Goose and Chickens to send to London she had the Goose to fetch from Provence this morning, the Chickens we got at Mr. Bridgman's very fine ones they are.

Tuesday 7th. Sep [i.e. October]

Last night I took a little bit of small candle with me to bed; I having just before lighted a thick one and as old Alison Wilson said it was a moulded one, well I was admonished not to take up the thick candle for fear of it dropping on the Stairs, so I took the wee bit, but unfortunately left the whole thick one burning, it being in a flat Stick, in the morning behold the bottom of the Candlestick full of tallow but no Candle left; well I was chided for >having< being so careless and thus ended the Candle.

Wednesday 8th Sep [i.e. October]

Last night we received the Box from London by Cousens, with the new tippet, I do not know how such an odious name as Boa[26] has been so prevalent for things of this Sort, for my part when I see one I am reminded of the dreadful Boa Constrictor But fashion sanctions many odd things. The Basket with the Goose & Chickens would leave Hull today for Wm. which we hope will arrive safe.

Thursday 9th Sepr [i.e. October]

We had our friend the Miller today telling us of his having given notice to quit his farm my wife told him that he had plenty and if he said he had not he was denying God's mercies; but he said God had not been merciful to him, for suffering him to stay so long where he had been, <u>weashiped</u> every day; besides

---

[25] These tax concessions, granted to farmers, were included in the provisions of the Act to Grant Relief from the Duties of Assessed Taxes in Certain Cases (4 & 5 Will. IV c. 73) passed on 14 Aug. 1834.

[26] The earliest reference to the noun 'boa' ('a snake-like coil of fur worn by ladies as a wrapper for the throat') is in Charles Dickens, *Sketches by Boz* (1836): 'Ladies' boas, from one shilling and a penny half-penny'. However, 'boa'd', meaning 'provided with or wearing a boa', appeared in 1831, in the *Blackwoods Magazine* xxx, 967 (*OED*).

it would have shewn more mercy if he had left some years since then he could have left with some hundreds more than he will now have, he does not wish to have any more mercies of that kind!!

Friday 10th Octr

Ths. Marshall's wife had a legacy left by some man of Nafferton, and they were sent for to Driffield to receive it; but neither he nor his wife went, but as one of the Executors lived at Hull, the Miller and his wife called on him for the legacy, he telling the Executor he had never called on Miss Horsley the Executrix, when the Man told him that Miss Horsley was dead—dead says he why she can't be dead; for I expected she would leave me five or six hundred pounds, and I have never heard of her death; well but she is dead without a Will; Why damn the awd Bitch what did she dee without making a will for? Damn her she cam to our house at Cave fair and eat and drank what she liked of what we had; now I'se all that out of Pocket for the Devil of a farthing did I ever get for it; but I expected th'awd Bitch wad leave me plenty for it and now damn her she's dead without a Will, O, Lord O Lord, what a Creature she was. — but he got his legacy and was treated with a good dinner, and so when all was over he says now as you've been so kind as [to] give us a good dinner we will send you some <u>Sausinges,</u> so they were all satisfied as far as this went. — I have only give an abridgment of the above transaction as it was a long tale.

Saturday 11th. Octr

This is Hull fair day and very fine weather, whether there be many people gone or not I cannot say. I think this day has been with me a day of leisure; I have not had a job.

Sunday 12th. Oct

A little Boy of David Dennis's who brings Milk every morning: he had a lamentable tale of the death of Waudby's white Calf—the poor thing was playing and broke its leg and died the same day, Billy Langricke bought it skin and all for half a Crown, and then sold half of it for as much money as he gave; so Waudby was the loser.

Monday 13th. Octr

Holliday who lives at the West end—down the lane where Mr. Turk used to have his farm yard, has got notice to quit he has been little more than a year.

Tuesday 14th. Oct

Beverley Sessions this day. Rd. Marshall and Robt. and Teavil Leeson are on the Jury: Rd. had got back soon; I was at the West end, he and Teavil had been on the grand Jury; which is the place attended with the least trouble.

Wednesday 15 Octr.

Our old friend being out makes me keep close quarters at nights, I expect he will be at home tonight; then the house will be opened with new decorations.

Thursday 16th. Octr

This and tomorrow are the Court days at the Bay horse at the west end, when the Steward of the Lord of the Manor receives the Court fees, and admits new tenants to Copy hold property.

Friday 17th. Octr

John Elgie and Obed Martin have been Sworn in Constables of So. Cave this day, for the ensuing year: there have been two Pinders also sworn in viz. Saml. Langricke and John Wilson.

Saturday 18th. Octr.

I was at Ellerker this afternoon looking for some money I got five Pounds, out of £15 and odd, however it was made less, but I should like to have the remainder.

Sunday 19th. Oct

Mr. Rodmell preached at the Church today the Vicar being at Scarbro, where his Father is at present.

Monday 20th. Octr

This morning received the Paper with an account of the Conflagration of the two houses of Parliament.[27] Matty Moody says they have blown up Parliament; but he says nought better can be expected, however it happens that the fire has been purely accidental; I am glad to find that no lives have been lost

...

Wednesday 22d. Octr

Great conversation about what is to be done now, that the Parliament house is destroyed. Some say that there will not be another house built to meet in, and others say that it will most likely cost a thousand pounds before another as good can be built!!

Thursday 23d. Octr

What am I to write today? I don't know yet it is even as my pen pleases; Tomorrow is to be the new fair here, it appears there is very little preparation for it.

Friday 24th. Oct

There are a good many Cattle in the Street this morning, a very cold frosty day with a high wind that blows the dust like showers of snow: Js. Ramsdale and his Son John are here.

Saturday 25th. Oct

It came on a very heavy rain last night; I dare say it was ten O'clock or after before Jack set off home; he and a young man of the name of Wood (I think) were at Eliza's[.] Jn. is very anxious to have a letter from Wm. he is not so very anxious what it contains as to have a letter from London; I think I would oblige him.

Sunday 26th. Oct

This forenoon I was very bad in my Bowels I was obliged to come out of the Church, but I was better in the afternoon.

---

[27] Westminster Palace, including St. Stephen's chapel used for the meetings of the House of Commons, and the apartment used for the meetings of the Lords, was burnt down and, apart from Westminster Hall, almost totally destroyed by the fire of 16 Oct. 1834 (Walpole iv. 7–9).

Monday 27th. Octr

There was a sale today of some Household goods; and Jno. Wilson the Bellman was reading and <u>spelling</u> over the Notice for sale; when Ob. Martin was coming by him; Jack says to him, I lay thou wouldst give a good deal if thou could read as well as I can; whya says Ob. I ought to be very thankful that I can neither read nor spell as thou canst!!

Tuesday 28th. Octr

Here is a man walking here from Howden, some round about way, to near the Ring Beck, to make 15 Miles; he walks from Howden and back again twice a day which makes Sixty miles a day, this is his second day; he is going to walk for 3 days: I know not (neither do I care) whether it be for a wager or not; but I am fully satisfied it is connected with gambling.

Wednesday 29th. Oct

Mr. Abbs the tailor who lived in the house which Conder's left; has this day gone away and taken his goods with him; after paying half a year's Rent; It is said the little fellow has got into part debt; more the fools they who trusted him.

Thursday 30th. Octr

Little Ann has had the yellow Jaundice and has been ill with it a few days, but is now better we think; She has taken some medicine for it; but she is no ways a lover of Physic.

Friday 31st. Octr

A little Boy who comes to School, has been at Balkham[28] seeing some Relations; I asked him if he had spelled when he had been out; he said no there was no spelling at Balkham! he said they had some books but he did not know what they did with them; for he saw nobody look at them; — on the whole he did not dislike Balkham, for he was free of Books.

Saturday 1st. Nov

I was at Ellerker Sands this forenoon measuring some Wheat Stubble land on which a following Crop had grown, I likewise measured the foreshore of the same land; it had been a very high tide the night before; I got wet over my feet which was of no service to me, as I had a Cold before; got to Ellerker and dined there at Wm. Fisher's, and went to the Wold in the Afternoon, and measured another small piece of Wheat Stubble and then came home, about four O'clock.

Sunday 2d Nov

A very fine day it still keeps so dry that there is much land that cannot be sown with wheat, on account of its being so dry; the Clay land on the Sands has large cracks in it; which will take part Rain to fill them up.

Monday 3d Nov

Mr. Brown was not at Morley's this day, it is said that he is going to be at Fenwick's one Monday and at Morley's the other; Fenwick being a Customer of his for Ale.

[28] Balkholme is a small hamlet 2 miles east of Howden and *c.* 8 miles west of South Cave.

Tuesday 4th. Nov

There was a fire at Brough last night, a Farmer of the name of Jefferson had his Stacks burnt; the Servant Girl is suspected of setting them on Fire; but it is said there is no evidence to implicate her.

Wednesday 5th. Nov

A kind of stormy blustering day—a Bonfire at night as usual on this day; together with Hare feasts at the public houses; which would all be better dispensed with.

Thursday 6th. Nov

The Club night, it is the most agreeable night to me of any in the year, as on the first Thursday in November I receive my Salary which is 30s. yearly, and a pint of Ale each meeting night.

Friday 7th. Novr.

A very stormy night last night with a great deal of rain, which I think will effectually soften the land which has been so long dry, it continued raining all this forenoon, but in the afternoon the Sun Shone very pleasant.

Saturday 8th. Novr

I think I have been this day without a Job from home; I went to the West end in the afternoon but staid, stayed or stopped a very little while and then came back, and spent an hour or two with Mr. Atkinson ...

Monday 10th. Nov

I think there is nothing particular to day, I did not see a single sample of Corn shewn, the farmers think that prices will be higher and those that can keep, will not bring their Corn to market yet ...

Wednesday 12th. Nov

There was a meeting this evening for the purpose of fixing the Rate of Compensation and Statute duty for the Highways for the present year, but it was nearly a failure, as only five or six attended so nothing was finally determined upon.

Thursday 13th Nov

This is the Sittings day, there was a Constable meeting at Morley's[.] Mr. Smelt the Chief was not there his Clerk attended in his stead, there were twenty one Constables dined their whole business this day being eating and drinking. I attended as usual.

Friday 14th Nov

I bought a pair of Silver Spectacles of our old friend Mr. Atkinson, which he bought a short time since second handed, he could not see in them very well so I gave him the money they cost him which was five Shillings; Mr. Bridgman bought a pair at the same time for the same money.

Saturday 15th. Nov

I thought I should have had to gone [*sic*] to Beverley today but one of the Overseers went, so that I had no occasion to go, which pleased me better than having to go there ...

Monday 17th. Nov

I did not see a single sample of Corn shewn today, although there was Barley sold in the Market for 33s. pr. quarter. Wheat is yet low in price: but not too low for those who have it to purchase.

Tuesday 18th. Nov

It is said that Scarlet fever is prevalent in the Neighbourhood particularly at Hotham, Stather's have lost one Child in it; and some more are very ill.

Wednesday 19th. Nov

Saml. Ringrose of Brantingham died this morning, he has been severely afflicted a long time and suffered very much, his complaint was the Gravel.

Thursday 20th. Nov

I was at Welton this morning swearing to the delivery of some Surcharges, before Mr. Ths. Raikes. I got home about 10 O'clock, it being the last Sittings, we had a holiday.

Friday 21st. Nov

Some of the farmers are pleased at the Duke being at the head of affairs,[29] for they say he will keep up prices, and send out One pound notes as in the prosperity times!!!

Saturday 22d. Nov

This day I was collecting the taxes for the half year due at Michs. last; in the forenoon it came on a Shower and I got rather wet which was not very agreeable ...

Monday 24th. Nov

This is what is called Martinmas Monday there were plenty of Stalls, all wanting the same thing viz. money, I have seen a good deal more company as this day: all went off tolerable quiet; a little liquor made some of the rabble shout a little.

Tuesday 25th. Nov

A good many Servants today have gone to Hull market, where there is expected to be much stir, as it falls at a favorable time from Martinmas; the Hullers will be as glad to receive money, as the Company to spend it: whether the satisfaction will be mutual or not I cannot say.

Wednesday 26th. Nov

There was shooting at the Beer Shops this afternoon for a Cheese and Tea kettles and other articles, I saw nothing of it, but heard there was a good deal of stir, it being Martinmas week.

Thursday 27th. Nov

The Duke of Wellington seems to be somewhat like Dr. Sonley's Servant when his master entered him in every Capacity.

---

[29] Following the succession of Althorp to the House of Lords and the King's dismissal of his ministry, the Duke of Wellington was summoned to form a government on 15 Nov. 1834 (Walpole iii. 479–80 and iv. 1–2).

Friday 28th. Nov

I think upon the whole there has been as little stir this Martinmas week as I ever knew.

Saturday 29th. Nov

I was at the west end today, collecting money for the taxes, which I received pretty well. I got home about dark, and then spent an hour or two at Mr. Atkinson's.

Sunday 30th. Nov

The Churchwardens on Sundays in Service time visit the public houses, which is not very pleasant to the Landladies, Mrs. Cousens told them she wished they were as well employed as she and her husband were; who were reading the Bible when the Churchwardens were looking for Company.

Monday 1st. Decr

The Market very thinly attended today on Account of Martinmas; the Factors seemed in no spirit for purchasing.

Tuesday 2d Decr

Eliza Turk was married this morning to a Gentleman (of course) from Bradford who is in some way of trade; he keeps a Carriage, I suppose it was a very gay wedding.

Wednesday 3d Decr

I was at Brantingham last night taking my Money for taxes to Mr. Beaumont to pay for me at Beverley which will save me a Journey there; Conder went with me, we got home about Seven O'clock.

Thursday 4th. Dec

John Clark of Anlaby (Son of the late Mr. Clark of Riplingham) had Seven horses suffocated in the Stable last night, it is supposed that a spark had dropped in the litter or bedding when a Boy was in the Stable; in going about two hours afterwards they were all dead; the fire had done no more harm. He was insured.

Friday 5th. Decr

Mr. Beaumont came this morning and brought the receipt from the Receiver of taxes: so that as the Coachmen say all's right ...

Sunday 7th. Decr

I think Richard Marshall has turned Churchman, as he was at the Church twice today, — perhaps it may be that the Vicar occupies his Lodgings.

Monday 8th. Dec

As Mr. Brown this day was forward to shew his Wakefield letters, I knew as soon as he pulled them out that the Market had been lower; because had it been higher he would not have divulged the information.

Tuesday 9th. Decr

My Paper Merchant was here today; it is rather before his time; but he was forced out for want of Money. I bought what Copy Bks he had viz 2 Dozen; paper I did not want.

Wednesday 10th. Decr

The Vicar's horse has run away with his Gig and broke it; when it was done he said to his Servant an old fashioned lad, "Wm I think we shall get over it for twenty pounds;" Twenty pounds the lad says we shall get over it for five Sir!

Thursday 11th. Decr

Thos. Grasby came from the West end this morning with a piece of Bride Cake for Wm. from the late Miss Eliza Turk, now Mrs. Rand: it seems we are not so much in favour as we have had none; indeed I don't think they have sent to any of the Town-<u>Folk</u>.

12 Decr Friday

Some lads, & even Men who ought to have known better have been calling Loncaster "Cuckoo", they get him cried as strayed or conveyed; it is said he has got an order for them.

Saturday 13th. Decr

This forenoon about ten O'clock I went to Drewton to measure the land on which Robt. Usher had his following Crop; very hilly land, about 30 Acres; got home about three O'clock pretty well tired: ready for my dinner when I arrived

...

Monday 15th. Decr

Very little doing at the Market today. I think the Market people decline attending; Eliza's have been killing a Pig today, about 17 Stone weight.

Tuesday 16th. Decr

Loncaster and his adversaries were yesterday at Riplingham, but they got nothing decided Mr. Burland the Attorney was retained on Loncaster's part: the Justices wished them to agree, but they did not as Loncaster wanted five pounds to make it up, they have to attend again next Monday: if they do not agree.

Wednesday 17th. Decr

Recd. a Precept from the Inspector of Weights and Measures that he will be at Morley's on Tuesday next to inspect and mark the different weights and measures—I think the wise men in Parliament have found something out that will not be easily practised viz. no upheaped measures to be used after the 1st of Jany. next,[30] it will require some skill to strike Coals, Potatoes Apples, &c &c.

Thursday 18th. Decr

This day we packed up a Basket for Wm. containing a Goose &c, we had Hannah Martin to dress it. Carried the Basket to Cousens's at night and wished it a prosperous Journey or Voyage to London.

---

[30] In section 4 of the Weights and Measures Act of 13 Aug. 1834 (4 & 5 Will. IV c. 49) heaped measures and the use of lead and pewter weights were abolished from 1 Jan. 1835. This Act was repealed on 9 Sept. 1835 (5 & 6 Will. IV c. 63) but the ban on heaped measures and soft metal weights was re-affirmed with provision being made for a fine to be imposed on shopkeepers illegally using heaped measures while goods which could not conveniently be sold by weight were allowed to be sold by the bushel.

Friday 19th. Decr

Sir Robt. Peel has been sent for from Italy,[31] a wise Man said nay he was gone to Rome, I asked was not Rome in Italy? Whya it was some ways about the Outskirts!!!

Saturday 20th. Decr

Measured the Hall Garth at the West end today for Charles Rudd; about 4 Acres, went to Charley Smith's at the West end and got a Pint of Ale between us ...

Monday 22d. Decr

Notwithstanding all the talk of Patriotism, there are always numbers of the Electors, who are as ready to take Bribes, as any Candidate can be to offer them; the poor for want, and the corrupt for <u>want</u> of principle (good) viz <u>good principle</u>.

Tuesday 23d. Decr

Charley Smith undertook one night to break his Chairs &c, when Ths. Clegg was called in to him, but Charley who is a bruiser shewed fight: so Clegg caught up a kettle, and let fly at Charley and dropt him; and at the same time broke a looking glass: but Charley not daunted, strip'd and would have a go at Clegg, but they were both prevented; but their Choler did not subside.

Wednesday 24th. Decr

This Evening we had as customary with ourselves and neighbours a <u>Yule Clog</u>—and Furmenty to Supper, it is very fine weather, no frost as yet of any consequence this winter.

Thursday 25th. Decr

Christmas Day. The Waits or Singers went about last night; and this day were begging for their Musical exertions.

Friday 26th. Decr

Last night there was much fighting and uproar in the Street, but we never heard it. It is said that the Constable has gone for a Summons for four or five of those who were engaged in the fight.

Saturday 27th. Decr

Went down to the Mill this afternoon, but the Miller was not at home; I think he will not take his farm again, — a Man of the name of Cade at Welton has been looking at it; and it is said is likely to take it.

Sunday 28th. Decr

We had a discourse last night on the word Hustings at Mr. Atkinson's. One said they were going to erect <u>Huskins</u> on the Cornhill at Beverley when another more knowing said it was <u>Hoskins</u> (but pronounced like <u>Horse-Skins</u>,) but our old friend who has long been used to Elections said that Hastings was

---

[31] Having been asked by the King to form a ministry, Wellington sent for Peel to head the government in the House of Commons. At the time, Peel was in Italy and it was impossible for a messenger to reach Rome in less than 8 days. Peel was contacted there on 25 Nov. and reached London on 9 Dec. 1834, taking the offices of Prime Minister and Chancellor of the Exchequer. He issued his famous policy statement, the Tamworth Manifesto, on 17 Dec. 1834 (Walpole iv. 2–6).

the word; as the work was executed hastily; there was no withstanding this which was like a Mathematical demonstration to which I said that when a pudding was made quickly it was called <u>Hasty pudding</u>, so the weighty war of words was settled!!

Monday 29th. Decr

The Rioters or fighters this day went to Riplingham but as there was but one Justice[32] the case was put off to the 12th. Jany next.

Tuesday 30th. Decr

We have now Holidays so that I have little to do; Conder's has sold a fat pig to Jem Levitt 19st. 5lb a very fine one at 5s. pr. Stone.

Wednesday 31st. Decr

We are now come to the last day in the present year: we have been long spared, but what good use have we made of our time? may we so live that at the last we may not look on our time as having been ill spent.

---

[32] A minimum of 2 magistrates was required to constitute a court of petty sessions at which minor crimes could be judged without reference to a jury (See also n.41 (1826) and n.42 (1826)).

Thursday 1st. Jany

Mr. Barnard's tithe Rent which is the first Thursday in January happens this year on the very first day of the month: I did not go to the West end today so that I cannot tell what sort of a Company there was, but I understand the Money was seldom paid better ...

Saturday 3d. Jany

I was at the Mill yesterday afternoon on the old Errand for Money I staid about five Hours and got tea with the honest Man; he thought I got well paid as I received a pound an hour for stopping, he said for his part he would not find fault if he could get as well paid!!

Sunday 4th. Jany

I am dull of hearing in one of my Ears having I think got cold in this Ear; I have always a Bit of Wool in it as I know I am liable to be troubled with it if I get cold.

Monday 5th. Jany

This day we began School again so that my time will now go on as usual; I shall not now be at a loss where to spend my time, indeed regular employment seems to be the best both for me and others.

Tuesday 6th. Jan

I think I have not noticed that Mrs. Akam died and was buried a short time since, she was buried at Brantingham: there is little to be said for her and not much against her. So no more; as it will avail nothing what is said or left unsaid.

Wednesday 7th. Jany

Beverley Election was on Monday last when Hogg & Burton were returned;[1] Joseph Sykes was too late in the field, but it is said he stood out the contest till the last man was polled.

Thursday 8th. Jany

I have not heard who are the successful Candidates at Hull; but it is said that Carruthers was the first on Tuesday; there had been Windows broken where Carruther's Colours or Flags were exhibited.

Friday 9th Jany

Carruthers and Hutt have been elected at Hull, Hill who appears to be a very independent man has been rejected.[2] Ths. Levitt, Cousens & V. Tindale have

---

[1] Both the successful candidates were Tories: James Weir Hogg, who topped the poll, was a wealthy East India Company director; Henry Burton of Hotham Hall was a local landowner. Hogg was subsequently re-elected in 1837 and 1841. Joseph Sykes of Kirk Ella, a Whig, was the nephew of the former Hull and Beverley MP, Daniel Sykes (*VCHERY* vi. 130–1; Markham (1982) 46–7).

[2] David Carruthers, a Tory candidate and London shipowner and insurance broker, who had been narrowly defeated in the 1832 election, this time defeated the unsuccessful sitting candidate, Matthew Davenport Hill (brother of Rowland Hill), also by a narrow margin. William Hutt, elected in 1832, was again returned. Both Hill and Hutt were Whigs. Carruther's triumph was

been canvassing for Mr. Langdale[3] for the East Riding—but it appears that Mr. Langdale has resigned.

Saturday 10th. Jany

A meeting has been held at Hull to nominate Henry Broadley of Melton Hill[4] as a Candidate for the East Riding; but it is said only in case Mr. Langdale came forward; the day of nomination is fixed for Tuesday next at Beverley.

Sunday 11th. Jany

The Chronicle is generally correct as to facts but as to speculation and Prophesying, it is as often wide of the mark as Cobbett used to be in that line.

Monday 12th. Jany

This day at Riplingham before the Justices—three of the fighters on Christmas day at night were fined 50s. each, and one of them 10s. the other one was cleared. They have a fortnight given to pay the fine, or otherwise at that time to be committed to the tread Mill for 2 months each.

Tuesday 13th. Jany

All Eliza's Children are very poorly; little Ann has not been here today, we think she is going to have the Scarlet fever; — however she has a great deal of fever on her.

Wednesday 14th. Jany

Little Ann is very poorly today and cannot bear to hold up her head; the other two are better and we hope she will be better soon, I think her illness proceeds from a Violent cold.

Thursday 15th. Jany

Joseph Galland says he hates these Papishes, — I yance says he had a Papish Patient, but I was resolved I wadent cure him, for I saw him make his Papish signs about my table; Sea I gav him a few Pills to Physic him pretty weal, and told him to be off, for I couldent cure him: — Nea, Nea, I'll cure nean of these Papish devils, Curse 'em, I hate 'em.

Friday 16th. Jany

Mr. Bethell and Mr. Beilby Thompson were nominated at Beverley as Knights of the Shire for the East Riding,[5] but as there was not a third Candidate, they were declared duly elected.

---

short-lived as he died almost immediately after the election (of a broken heart caused by the election expense, it was said) and a by-election had to be held later in the year on 19–20 June (Markham (1982) 49; *VCHERY* i. 206, 242–3).

[3] Charles Langdale of Houghton Hall, Sancton, was a local landowner and a Roman Catholic. He had stood for election in Beverley in 1832—a rather surprising candidate in such a staunchly Protestant borough—but after spending over £3,000 in election expenses, he was duly elected. Daunted by the prospect of a comparable election bill in 1835, he withdrew from the contest (*VCHERY* vi. 126, 130–1).

[4] Henry Broadley, chairman of the Hull and Selby Railway Company, did not stand for this election but was later returned as MP for the East Riding in 1837, 1841, and 1847 (Markham (1982) 9 and 44).

[5] Both candidates were members of local landowning families. Richard Bethell of Rise Park was a Tory, and Paul Bielby Thompson of Escrick Park was a Whig. They had first been elected to

Saturday 17th. Jany

A very cold day. I was at the West end in the afternoon but did not stop long; I then went to Mr. Atkinson's, he keeps a good fire and his house is very warm.

Sunday 18th. Jany

Mr. Rodmell preached at the Church today. Mr. Hotham has gone to London; which at this time cannot be very pleasant.

Monday 19th. Jany

Mr. Brown says that Mr. Hume is elected for Middlesex by a Majority over the Tory candidate of four hundred ...

Wednesday 21st. Jany

Cousens had a Supper this night when the tradesmen who want Bills attend to settle; The Supper is given them, and what drink the[y] have they pay for themselves. Val. Tindale was it is said most conspicuous as a Trencher man, having nearly demolished a whole Chine.

Thursday 22d. Jany

I think there is nothing particular that I have seen or heard this day—The Muff & tippet came on Tuesday night, and made at least one happy; they are both very neat, but we do not know the price, glad that Wm. & all are well.

Friday 23d. Jany

Mrs. Burland died this morning, she has left five small Children, she got her bed about ten weeks ago, and has not been well since ...

Sunday 25th. Jan

Mr. Hotham has not yet got back, so that Mr. Rodmell was at the Church again today.

Monday 26th. Jany

Spilman the Ellerker Miller at the Market today said that he could eat a Quartern of Apples every day; he has lately been ill; and was limited in his Apple eating to six Apples a time, four times a day!! but he said he always liked them to be as large as he could get.

Tuesday 27th. Jan

There were two of the Christmas fighters committed to the House of Correction yesterday in default of paying the Penalty, a warrant granted for another of them, and the fourth had a fortnight longer given him, either to pay or suffer.

Wednesday 28th. Jany

I have sometimes wondered why Milton, makes Satan appear as a Cormorant on the tree of life; it is well known to those who know the Bird that it is a Water fowl, and I believe never settles on Trees.[6] — I have seen many of them on the Shore at Barmston, and we used to remark that when there was a

---

represent the East Riding in the election of 1832. Both the 1832 and the 1835 elections were uncontested (Markham (1982) 9 and 44).

[6] This is incorrect. At the present day, cormorants have been observed to roost in trees bordering Hornsea Mere on the Yorkshire coast, approximately 7½ miles south of Barmston.

funeral a Cormorant was generally seen; but of them I think they would have appeared the same had there been a wedding.

Thursday 29th. Jany

Mrs. Coates was buried today, she had been ill a long time before she died. Ann and her Grandmother went to the Church to see her buried.

Friday 30th. Jany

Thos. Marshall's farm is let to Cade of Welton; it will go very near him if he have his Stock to sell; he will be far from right in leaving.

Saturday 31st. Jany

Measured some Turnip Land for Mr. Lockwood this forenoon, in two lots, one of them at the bottom of the Wold just below the round plump (or Clump) the other at the Garth end; it was very dirty; — about 8 Acres of them both.

Sunday 1st. Feb

Mr. Hotham has got back again and preached at the Church today: a fine Winter day, very moderate.

Monday 2nd. Feby

It is said that Cade has given up the Mill farm and that Ths. Marshall has taken it again; he says he will give more for it than it is worth on purpose to keep such a Hobkite out of the town ...

Wednesday 4th. Feb

There has been great talk this week that the Money left by Mrs. Banks (Mr. Barnard's Aunt) to the Poor was to be given away this week but I have not yet heard of its distribution.

Thursday 5th. Feb

It is reported that Frans. Wood of Drewton has married Mrs. Hodgson (late Mr. Barnard's Housekeeper) at York and brought her home either yesterday or this day. <u>This is true</u>.

Friday 6th. Feb

A meeting this Evening to nominate Assessors for the taxes for the following year, when I, myself I, and my partner Ths. Levitt were again chosen ...

Sunday 8th. Feb

The money to the Poor was most of it given away yesterday, but to say that all were pleased is more than could be expected; but some that have received & others who have not, are equally dissatisfied.

Feb. 9 Monday

The Market this day pretty well attended, but very little business done; one of the Factors who was at Wakefield market on Friday last, said that he would not give more than 38s. pr. quarter this day, for the best red wheat that he could lay his hands on.

Tuesday 10th. Feb

It is reported that David Morley has taken a Public house at Beverley, whether it be so or not I don't know, but most likely soon shall.

Wednesday 11th. Feb

I had Mr. Pratt the Bookseller of Howden here today I owed him 10s. which I paid him but did not give him another order as I am better served with my old Paper merchant.

Thursday 12th. Feb

Went this day at Noon with the Steward to the Club room to pay a young man the Sum of twelve pounds for the funeral of his Father who was a member; his name was Dayson Brigham he lived I think at Whitgift.

Friday 13th. Feb

It is thirty one years this day since I came to Cave; many changes there have been since that time, — It was a great deal of frost and Snow after this time in 1804.

Saturday 14th. Feb

I was at Ellerker this afternoon measuring some Turnip Land, between 9 and 10 Acres; it was a fine moderate day; I was not long about it as it was very good to measure.

Sunday 15th. Feb

We had a letter from Hull yesterday giving an account that Jn. Read my wife's Brother was dangerously ill with a dropsical Complaint, she will go to see him very shortly, I am fearful he and his family are in a distressed state.

Monday 16th. Feb

Very little business done at the Market today, the complaint is that there is too much Wheat, these murmurers at the bounty of Providence if they had their deserts, ought never to be permitted with the indulgence of again tasting wheaten bread.

Tuesday 17th. Feb

My wife is gone to Hull this day with the Carrier, to see her Brother who is very ill I am by myself with a cold Pork pie to my dinner.

Wednesday 18th. Feb.

John Read my wife's Brother died yesterday morning before she got to Hull, of a dropsy in the Chest; he has left a wife and six or seven Children very ill provided for; One of the Boys is a Cripple, and a Girl is so very ill that she is not expected to live long: — this is the fruit of an Old man marrying a young wife; he has played the fool exceedingly.

[No entry for Thursday, 19 Feb.]

Friday Feb. 20th

This day we sent off a Package to Wm. containing a Ham, a Leg of mutton, and a pair of Stockings and the Journal up to this time.

Saturday 21st Feb

I was at Elloughton this afternoon measuring some land, it came on a very stormy afternoon a great shower of Snow; I got under a hedge till it rather abated, and then proceeded to work, the land was like plaster, it was very dirty, however I soon got it done, there was about eight acres.

Sunday 22nd. Feb.

Eliza got her bed this morning of another Boy, so that they have now three Boys they talk of calling it John.

Monday 23d. Feb

An uncommon high wind today, and part of the last night; it has ruffled a good many Stacks; and the Street has an accumulation of leaves and Straw; these high winds are very disagreeable ...

Wednesday 25th. Feb

The weather continues very boisterous. As to Politics we appear to take very little interest in them: the Election of a Speaker, cannot awake us from our Apathy: however I am myself pleased at the choice of Mr. Abercrombie.

Thursday 26th. Feb

Before this time the address, and its amendment has been decided—it is wonderful that so many of the Parliament's proceedings, want so much mending. I think the Ministers themselves want mending: they are little better than Patch-work ...

Saturday 28th. Feb

This afternoon and part of the forenoon I was collecting the Poor rate; I did not stay long in one place: and got home before five O'clock, and then went to Mr. Atkinson's ...

Monday 2d March

Wm. Hudson of Everthorpe has taken Morley's house, he is a farmer but going to give up this Lady day, he is a young man, with a wife but no family.

Tuesday 3d March

The votes of the House of Commons bid fair as a notice to Sir Robert to quit the Place he holds;[7] which the Chronicle thinks will be in a short time.

Wednesday 4th. March

Mr. Hume is a right-un, he is a mixture of the English Bull Dog and terrier, he bites some of the Curs sharply, they run away and grumble, but this annoys him very little; for when they turn back he will bite of them again.

Thursday 5th. March

This is Mr. Barnard's Rent day, the tenants to have a Dinner at James Levitt's—The Club Box this Evening has been removed to Fenwick's so that the next meeting will be held there.

Friday 6th. March

It is said that David Morley has let his Blacksmith's Shop to a stranger on lease for 13 years; the same time as he has taken the Public house at Beverley.[8]

---

[7] At the opening of Parliament on 24 Feb. 1835, the Whig opposition's amendment to the King's Speech, deploring the unnecessary dissolution of Parliament, was carried by a majority of 7 votes. This followed the Tories' failure to secure the election of their own candidate, Manners Sutton, as Speaker of the House of Commons. The Whig leaders' choice, James Abercromby, was elected by 316 to 306 votes (Walpole iv. 9–12).

[8] David Morley became licensee of the King's Head in Saturday Market Place, Beverley. In 1852, whilst retaining the King's Head, he purchased on behalf of his son, also David, the

Saturday 7th. March

This day I was at Beverley paying the County Rate; the Overseer sent me his horse to ride on; it was very bad going as it had been a good deal of Snow the last night and no horse had been on before me: I got home again about three O'clock in the afternoon.

Sunday 8th. March

This was a very fine Sunny day but cold, it having been a frost the last night. The Crows this day (for the first time that I have heard them) are very clamorous, on building Speculations: by this I hope we shall have some settled weather.

Monday 9th. March

A very windy stormy day again so that the Crows must be deceived—very little doing at the Market.

Tuesday 10th. March

A good deal of Snow last night, I am afraid the Winter is coming at the wrong end of the Season, now when the days have got a good length; it makes cold weather very disagreeable.

Wednesday 11th. March

This morning we recd. the small parcel from Wm. and am glad to hear that they are all tolerably well; the London Cries have set little Ann up a great height; she says she must have it covered; Sweep, Soot, O, seems to take her attention most, as it is a well known subject to her.

Thursday 12th. March

Wm. Hudson's Sale at Everthorpe is this day previous to his coming to the Fox. I think it is not a good Speculation; but he must a bide by it.

Friday 13th. March

I had my old paper merchant again last night. I laid out with him 9s/3d— this day he was going to North Cave and Hotham and from thence to Hull; he went to Mr. Atkinson's and eat his Supper, having provided some bread & Cheese and two Eggs, which the Old Gentleman boiled for him ...

Monday 16th. March

There appears to be no alteration in the price of Corn; One of the Factors today said he wished he might not see a Sample of Corn again for a month to come.

Tuesday 17th. March

This has been a rainy day (moderate) from morning to night; it came on very dark in the Evening. There was another Sale at Everthorpe yesterday, where Stock and other articles sold well.

Wednesday 18th. March

Eliza's had what is called the Child's Christening today, his name is John that is about all I know of the matter—I served a charge of a Game certificate on Tom Langricke for snaring.

Beverley Arms hotel in North Bar Within, Beverley, which remained in the family's hands until 1920 (Pigot and Co. 17; Markham (1986) 8).

Thursday 19th. March

There was a Sale at North Cave today of farming Stock &c. belonging to George Carbut who is declining business: he has plenty to keep him, & seems not much calculated for a farmer.

Friday 20th. March

It appears that the Church reform is to be begun by making two new Bishopricks, I think the Bishops are a useless Set, and should have thought better of the reform if the present number had been lessened or totally abolished: for I cannot conceive of what use they are: Except to eat our Beef and Pudding.

Saturday 21 March

Went to Welton this morning to swear to the delivery of the Game Certificate Charge to Langricke—In the afternoon measured 3 acres of Turnips in the Ruffham field for Holliday. After that measured the Park Close for Charles Rudd, at the Sheep Dike about 6 Acres.

Sunday 22d March

A very fine day, the Crows very busy, we have now twelve hours Sun (when it shines) our Pear tree this year has a fine Shew of Flower Buds, if the weather come favorable it is likely for a fine Crop.

Monday 23d March

This is a cold day: the farmers enquiring for Seed Corn; but they are not very anxious to sell one to another as some of them take longer Credit, than they are willing to give to the Factors.

Tuesday 24th March

At the west end this Evening arranging with Tommy Levitt for our Journey to Beverley tomorrow; we intend going in a Gig.

Wednesday 25th. March

This day me and my partner were at Beverley getting sworn in Assessors, we soon got done; We dined at the Cross Keys, and got home about four O'clock in the afternoon all safe it was a very fine day; but I was troubled as usual with a Bowel Complaint, which is not very agreeable at any time, but is particularly disagreeable when from home ...

Friday 27th. March

A man >a sort of Captain< the day I was at Beverley who had he said passed Cape Horn, was telling the Company he had been in the Latitude 71° South before making the passage, I said I thought, that was an odd way of finding a passage to go nearly a thousand miles further South than there was any occasion, indeed I disputed that he had ever been so far South; he took it very mildly.

Saturday 28th. March

This day I had nothing to do from home, I was engaged a good part of the day with taking my Stock of Stamps and making out the quarterly Account; so thus went this day.

Sunday 29th March

This was a fine day the trees are putting out their buds, preparatory to their appearing in their green Spring clothing. (cloathing)

Monday 30th. March

There were a few Horses shewn today for the first time this year; which caused a little more stir than common.

Tuesday 31st. March

I hope the Irish Church will be reformed and the immense income it possesses will be applied to more useful purposes than it is at present.

Wednesday 1st. April

Measured some Turnip land this Evening for Miss Cooper in what is now called the Ellerker Close (7a–2R–16P) but before the inclosure at Ellerker it was called Dunsdale.

Thursday 2d. April

I want various articles at times and they perhaps would make any person smile to hear them mingled together—A map of the World on Mercator's projection, the Canons of the Church, the 39 Articles a chronological table &c. &c. &c. and a pencil Case.

Friday 3d. Apl.

A very stormy day, however I ventured to Ellerker after School time in the Evening, but I should have been more comfortable at home, as I got nothing for going.

Saturday 4th. Apl.

Measured 2 Closes for Jn. Stather of Everthorpe this afternoon (one near the Low Closes—formerly occupied by Jn. Crathorne) about nine Acres, the other Close near Mr. Barnard's Beanlands 7 Acres.

Sunday 5th. Apl.

A fine day but I still keep to my great Coat on Sundays, as we have not much preaching to keep one warm.

Monday 6th. Apl.

At the Market this day a young man who was propping about with, Tom Leason, Scholefield and Ben. Brown, talking as much or rather more than they knew about Politics; one of them said to me, this Gentleman is the Editor of the Hull Packet;[9] I then said I thought he could not do less than treat me with a Glass; as I read over his Paper every Saturday morning and sometimes it was so tedious and dull it exercised my patience to get through with it. — This raised the laugh against Mr. Editor; + I own I was rather forward with him but I measured him in my mind before I spoke, and found there was nothing to fear: thus ends the introduction of the Editor of the Hull Packet to me.

+ [In margin in red ink:] I understand this fellow is not the Editor.

---

[9] At this time, the *Hull Packet* was owned by William Goddard and Robert Brown. (See n.107 (1827)).

Tuesday 7th. Apl.

A meeting this Evening at Fenwick's to balance the Poor Book, all comfortably settled, I got home a little after nine. John Elgey and Thomas Fisher are the two first on the list for Overseers for the ensuing year.

Wednesday 8th. Apl.

When the meeting was over last night and after I came away David Dennis was drunk, and called the whole of the Company, they threatened to turn him out and I wonder they did not; for I dare say he deserved it.

Thursday 9th Apl.

Wm. Wilkinson it is reported stole four Sheep from a Close on the little Wold, and drove them to Hull where they were found; and the Owner claimed them; I suppose he does not intend to follow up the Charge; but several of the Town's people think he ought to be prosecuted.

Friday 10th Apl.

Last night there was a meeting to let the Lanes when they were all taken by different persons for the Sum of £7–4–0 which Sum was then paid.

Saturday 11th. Apl.

This afternoon measured a small piece of Land for Ths. Fisher, at the Bottom of the Cliffs rather more than three Acres; part of the Land that Henry Arton had; Ths. Fisher having taken the farm that he (Arton) had belonging to Mr. Collinson. Hen. Arton has gone to live at Sandham; he has taken a small farm of about 40 Acres.

Sunday 12th. Apl.

So the Tories are out again,[10] and long may they keep so, they are not calculated nor qualified for the good of the Country; I hope there will be a thorough reformation of the Church; I mean the overgrown bloated Bishops &c. &c.

Monday 13th. Apl.

The new Landlord[11] is now at the Fox, but I think there was not much custom today there not being a single Corn factor there this day; indeed there was very little doing at the Market today.

Tuesday 14th. Apl.

It is said that Wm. Wilkinson the Sheep stealer has set off and left the town; and that he is going to America, but I think he has not money sufficient to pay for his passage; except he can persuade some of his friends to assist him; however let this be as it will he cannot shew his face here again, except he has an uncommon share of assurance ...

---

[10] Peel's brief ministry lasted only 4 months. He had been defeated on the election of the Speakership, on the amendment to the opening Address, on the proposal for a charter of incorporation for London University, and finally on the question of the distribution of the wealth of the Irish Church in the Irish Tithes Bill. His cabinet was succeeded by that of Viscount Melbourne (Walpole iv. 21–5).

[11] William Hudson.

Thursday 16th. Apl.

Went to measure a Close this Evening after School time, as I was going it snowed fast and was very cold, but before I got to the Close it cleared up, it was between Ellerker and Elloughton I got done before dark there was about 10 Acres of it.

Friday 17th. Apl

This day being a Holiday I went with an intention of going to the Mill but met with the honest man in a Close in the new field leading Turnips, and as it frequently happens no money with him nor had he any at home—I got back about four O'clock when a Man of Drewton was waiting for me to measure some land for him he said about an hour's work so I went with him by the way of the little Wold as the Land adjoins the Swineskaife road, we wrought at it till about Seven O'clock and did not get it half done, as there was a dismal hill side; indeed I could not see in some places more than a Chain length before me, so that we had all the lines to run before we could begin which is a tedious and tiresome concern.

Saturday 18th. Apl

Went again this morning after breakfast to finish my last night's job and completed it about noon, when I returned home to dinner having got very well tired there was a little more than 31 Acres of it.

Sunday 19th. Apl

This is Easter Sunday, not very warm weather however I have been without my great Coat today though there has been finer Sundays when I have had it on.

Monday 20th. Apl

No great Market today as Easter is so late that there were very few Horses shewn, however there was no want of Rabble the whole Pepper Gangrils noising about the Street.

Tuesday 21st. Apl.

This is the day when the Churchwardens are chosen, when the two old ones were again appointed viz Mr. Atkinson & Lockwood the Easter Dinner was at Barnard Cook's I was not there. I have not attended some years.

Wednesday 22d. Apl

This is or used to be the night for the Tansy but this day I have not seen or heard of any preparations for it: so that it appears it is about worn out or obsolete.

Thursday 23d Apl

I was at Ellerker this Evening but did not stay long I got home about Seven O'clock; it was a very fine still night; the Pear, Plumb, and Cherry trees appear to be very full of Blossom.

Friday 24th. Apl.

Our Tories some of the knowing ones have prophesied that the present Ministry will not continue for five weeks; I do not know how they have got the odd week, as a month would just have sounded as well.

Saturday 25th. Apl.

This day I think I have not had a job so I can hardly say how I have spent the day, so I even took a walk to the Mill but the Miller was so throng he could not get time to pay, but threatened that he would break the Sabbath and come and pay tomorrow, but I told him I knew him better, than that he would break the Sabbath and part with his money both together; and I dare say in this respect he will keep the Sabbath holy.

Sunday 26th. Apl

A very cold day, so that I wrapped myself up in my great Coat again, and I was none overwarm with it, the wind from the north west being very piercing, or in our language pearching ...

Tuesday 28th. Apl.

Some lads who had been making a hurry at the west end on Sunday last: were complained of to the Magistrates yesterday, when four or five of them were summoned to attend on Monday next; Charley Smith's beer Shop as usual is blamed for the misdemeanor [*sic*].

Wednesday 29th. Apl.

It still continues very cold and stormy though not much rain falls. I have been no further this week than Mr. Atkinson's, where we generally have a good fire and are comfortable.

Thursday 30th. Apl.

The Spring Court is held this day at Js. Levitt's there is a full attendance which will please the little Landlord; I went down in the Evening but did not go into the inner apartment, I wanted to see Mr. Hudson, and sent for him out; I wanted some land tax of him, and he came out and paid me ...

Saturday 2d. May

This forenoon I have been entering a poor-rate in the Book, and in the afternoon getting it signed by the Churchwardens and Overseers previous to its being allowed by the Magistrates, so thus ended the day.

Sunday 3d. May

A rather more moderate day than we have had, as most of the last week was very cold and stormy; but I am in hopes that the Spring will again revisit us, dressed in living green.

Monday 4th. May

This Evening they have the House warming at the Fox, I never came near them, but I hear there was no lack of Company.

Tuesday 5th. May

A new Coach from Hull commenced running yesterday through to No. Cave,[12] I think there will not be sufficient encouragement to keep two Coaches on the road.

---

[12] The *Hull Advertiser* (8 May 1835) carried an advertisement (dated 4 May) by the Hull coach operator, R. J. Chaffer, for a 'New Four-Inside Post-Coach' which was to start from the White Hart, North Cave at 7. 15 a.m. every morning except Sunday and return there at 4. 15 p.m., calling at South Cave en route. He claimed that no coach had hitherto run between North Cave and Hull.

Wednesday 6th. May

The Lads who were making a hurry on Sunday night week, were taken to the Justices on Monday last; three of them were fined Five pounds each; one of them Tailor Waudby's Son paid the Money, another (Barratt) had a week given him to pay the money, another Son of Jno Holborn's was committed to the house of Correction for two months in default of paying, but this day they have paid his fine and he is liberated: two more one of Holborn's and Duffin had only three Shillings each to pay, so thus ends this prank ...

Monday 11th. May

I did not see much of the Market today and indeed there was not much to be seen; I saw our old friend the Miller, who paid me five pounds, but he could not clear all off at present.

Tuesday 12th. May

This day or part of it I was making out the Assess'd tax Bill for the present year; it is to be returned on Saturday next, so that I shall be ready; as when I have any thing to do I do not like to put it off until the last moment.

Wednesday 13th May

This Evening I did not get to Mr. Atkinson's, being at the west end, and did not get back until Eight O'clock, when I thought it was too late so I came home, and took a Voyage to New Albion on the west Coast of America, and went to bed—at Nootka Sound!!

Thursday 14th. May

Heard this Evening that Lord Morpeth[13] had lost his Election for the West riding; when within less than a quarter of an hour another account was that his Lordship was elected by a Majority of 3008; so which of the Accounts is true, must be left a little longer to decide.

Friday 15th May

Lord Morpeth now it is certain has been returned by a Majority of 2800 and odd, so say the liberals, but the absolutes protest the Majority is not so large; but this is certain he is a long way ahead.

Saturday 16th. May

I was at Beverley today. I walked in the morning with Wm. Hudson who has come to Morley's house, he went to Hull and I came back alone, and got home very well about five O'clock.

Sunday 17th. May

Yesterday was a very fine Spring day, but this day is again cold. I do not feel at all tired with my journey to Beverley yesterday.

---

[13] George William Frederick Howard, 7th Earl of Carlisle (1802–64), a prominent Whig politician, was at that time known by the courtesy title of Lord Morpeth. First elected to represent the West Riding in 1832, he was again elected in Jan. 1835, but following his appointment as chief secretary in Ireland, he was called on to defend his seat under a new writ in May that same year. He successfully beat the Tory politician standing against him, the Hon. John Stuart Wortley, by polling 9,066 votes to his rival's 6,259 (*DNB*; Dod 360).

Monday 18th. May

On Saturday at Beverley I had to take up a Bill[14] or rather to pay the value of it; Our old friend like an old fool suffered himself to have a Bill drawn on him at two months, which has cost him 3s/9d it is the first Bill transaction in which he has been engaged and it will be the last.

Tuesday 19th. May

This Evening I was at the west end it was very cold; I went with my partner Ths. Levitt to demand some Money for a Game Certificate, but we did not get it; so I suppose it will be settled by a committal to York Castle, <u>until it be paid</u>.

Wednesday 20th May

Wm. Wilkinson the Sheep man is now at home and they say very little abashed, I have not seen him since his freak, but it appears he again shews himself in the Street.

Thursday 21st. May

This Evening I was collecting the half yrs. taxes and was as successful as I expected or rather more so; I came home about eight O'clock, and went out no more this night; so I sat until ten O'clock and then went to bed ...

Saturday 23d. May

At the west end this afternoon, spent a little time with Mr. Turk, he is cheerful and lively as usual; I went down no lower this day but came home and got my tea, then spent the Evening at Mr. Atkinson's ...

Monday 25 May

There is nothing any way new at the Market this day; perhaps there was some little Corn sold but I dare say no variation in the Prices.

Tuesday 26 May

This Evening I was at the west end collecting[.] Wm. Loncaster has been very ill, but is now recovering he has had some kind of a fever which has brought him very low.

Wednesday 27 May

This day my Partner Ths. Levitt went to Beverley instead of me to swear to the Ass'd tax Bill, he was at home pretty early but I did not see him after he came back, this night.

Thursday 28th. May

Francis Ruston is very ill with a complaint with which he is often troubled being the passing a Gall stone; to this is added a Liver complaint he has likewise Hiccup very violently and almost incessantly: I think he is dangerous.

---

[14] Bills of exchange were commonly used in financial transactions, in a similar manner to the modern system of bank cheques, as a money substitute. The bill was considered 'an obligation, whereby the drawer directs the acceptor to pay a certain sum at the day and place therein mentioned, to a third party, or his order' (Baines ii. 639–41).

Friday 29th May

The Commissioners of taxes have granted a Warrant to take Ths. Langricke on account of his not having paid the charge of the Game Certificate made on him; so that there is no alternative but either paying or York Castle.

Saturday 30th. May

This day we had a Crow pie to Dinner, about once in a Season is sufficient for me, I believe the time is about over for them.

Sunday 31st. May

This day it was very cold, and not like the last day in May; we still keep a fire in the Room on Sundays; which with it, is not too warm.

Monday 1st. June

There was but very little market today excepting Pots for Cave fair, — I gave Mr. Beaumont my taxes to pay in on Thursday next, to save me a Journey to Beverley.

Tuesday 2d. June

The Farmers very busy sowing Swedish Turnips it is a fine time for them they require being sown earlier than white Turnips.

Wednesday 3d. June

This day there was a flower Shew at Beverley,[15] but as yet I have not heard any particulars, the Races at Beverley likewise begin today.

Thursday 4th. June

This is the day for paying in the Taxes at Beverley; I sent mine with Mr. Beaumont of Brantingham, who is very trust worthy and thus saved myself a Journey, when if I had gone there would have been no allowance which is the case when money is paid in.

Friday 5th. June

John Elgie the Constable took Langricke to York Castle, but he (Langricke) paid his money before he went in. It is said that the Constable did not take his Warrant of Commitment with him; so to make the best of it he took Langricke's word to pay when he got home; which he has since done.

Saturday 6th. June

There was a meeting last night at the Vestry respecting a claim made by the Surveyor of the Turnpike road; for money and Statute work for the Swinescaife road; Tindale of Weedley is gone to Beverley today to appeal against the claim: and if he does any good I shall be surprised. I am convinced that they can claim more than they have done ...

Monday 8th. June

The fair is coming is almost every one's cry, for my own part I am no lover of it; but to be neighbour-like we must prepare for it like others.

---

[15] The show was held under the auspices of the East Riding Floral and Agricultural Society. See n.20 (1836).

Tuesday 9th. June

Mr. Leeson of Ellerker has had some kind of a fit, a night or two ago: it appears he had fallen out of the Bed, and was found about six O'clock in the morning it is said unable to speak: but he is now something better.

Wednesday 10th. June

James Pearson of Everthorpe died last Thursday, he had been very ill a long time; his was a dropsical case; he was a member of the Club; and the Money for his funeral was paid last night.

Thursday 11th. June

We left off this afternoon for the fair, we want the School cleaning, we expect a Bricklayer to white wash the top tonight.

Friday 12th June

We did not get the School cleaned until this morning, we had Hannah Martin at it as usual; she drives away, — It has been very hot weather all this week, but it is rather cooler today.

Saturday 13th. June

This is the Market day this week, here is not much stir, we had Mrs. Arton & Co. to tea as is customary on the Saturday before the fair.

Sunday 14th. June

A very warm day people begin to throng in for the fair; a good many Cattle have got here to be in readiness for tomorrow.

Monday 15th. June

Cave fair day the Street thronged with Cattle. I never went out amongst them. We had John Swift, James Ramsdale and John and Robert at Dinner, they none of them staid tea, so that after dinner we had no throng, with which we were as well satisfied.

Tuesday 16th. June

This was a very fine day, but dusty, there was a great many people in the town—we had but two at tea, but the School Windows were filled with gazers and lookers out. All ended very peaceably.

Wednesday 17th. June

This day there were Ass Races and Foot races; and other amusements for those who delight in them, so that they may sing.

> What care I for Epsom Green,
> Or what is Ascot heath to me;
> For all their frolics I have seen,
> In Cave fair yearly Revelry.

Thursday 18th. June

Some attempts were made to have a stir this night at more racing; but I believe the West end Beer Shops got all the Company; various diversions were going on but the particulars I have not learned if there should have been any thing extraordinary, that I shall hear, I will note it down.

Friday 19th. June

This day we were invited to tea at Provence but did not go, as it is so far off, so we even staid at home and got tea by ourselves.

Saturday 20th. June

This day the 20th. June I put a notice in the Church door, for any persons who had not made a claim for Voting; to put in their Claims before the 20th. July next, that is if they think proper.

Sunday 21st. June

A sort of gloomy day which is in accordance with the feelings of many, who contrast this day with the last Sunday, when all were busy with preparing.

Monday 22d. June

It is hard to say whether there was any market or not today, all is dulness at present; some enquiries for Wool, but no sellers at present prices.

Tuesday 23d. June

The weather this day has changed from very hot to remarkably cold for the Season; fires are very necessary Articles now; when the last week I could scarce find a fire to light my pipe.

Wednesday 24th. June

Yesterday was the Visitation; the Dinner was at the Fox; there was but a small company consisting of the Parson, Clerk & Proctor and the Churchwardens, of So. Cave, Broomfleet and Faxfleet, and Wm. Green the tenant of the Bread Land: in all ten persons.

Thursday 25th. June

A very rainy day yesterday, and all the last night, and it yet rains this morning accompanied with a high wind: it is a long time since we have had so much rain; It will be likely to lay the wheat.

Friday 26th. June

I mentioned some time since that Tindale of Weedley went on the part of the Town to appeal against a charge made by the Trustees of the Turnpike Road; but all the comfort and relief he got was that a very moderate Charge had been made; they told him the Surveyor had been very moderate and might have charged as much more, which they (the Magistrates) would have allowed.

Saturday 27th. June

This day I have been engaged making up the Quarterly account of Stamps: that is about all this day I have attended to.

Sunday 28th. June

Wm. Turk M.D. was at Cave today, I met him he seemed to be very glad to see me, he enquired kindly after Wm. and desired me to make his kindest respects to him, which I here do, not knowing when I shall have a better opportunity.

Monday 29th. June

Wm. Turk has been seeing Francis Ruston yesterday and it [is] said has given his opinion that he will recover: he is I understand yet very ill.

Tuesday 30th. June

I am Housekeeper this day, my Wife has gone to Hull, it is a fine day, but I care not how soon it is over.

Wednesday 1st July

This day there is a meeting at Beverley for some purpose or other to petition for the support of the Protestant Religion; I do not think it is any danger; excepting that it be overburdened with wealth & leisure, like the English Church establishment.

Thursday 2d. July

I understand that three or four leaders of the Beverley meeting yesterday, were at Cave today for what purpose I cannot say, but most likely to procure Signatures to their precious petition.

Friday 3d. July

Last night was the Club meeting before the feast, when all is required to be paid up, there was not one defaulter; I came away about ten O'clock; but some of the Company I heard was much later, even until this morning.

Saturday 4th. July

I was at Ellerker this afternoon, and got tea with Watson Arton; then came home I arrived at Mr. Atkinson's about Six O'clock and staid there till nearly eight, then went home in peace.

Sunday 5th. July

A very rainy morning, on account of the wet I did not go out this forenoon, it cleared up about noon, and I went to the Church in the afternoon. — Francis Ruston is (it is said) much better.

Monday 6th. July

This being Beverley Midsummer Fair day we had but a thin attendance at the Market; Mr. Leason of Ellerker was here, but he seems far from being yet well.

Tuesday 7th. July

The Tories seem to be exerting themselves to get all who they think will vote for them, to claim being registered in the List of Voters;[16] will not the Reformers likewise exert themselves?

Wednesday 8th. July

This afternoon I and my wife went to Tea at Robt. Arton's at Provence; it is a long way I went after School time, and we got home between nine and ten O'clock very well.

Thursday 9th. July

This was the Club feast day, there were present 95 Members. — On the Sick list seven; fined for non attendance five, and fifteen who live at a greater distance than five Miles from Cave; which makes up the number of Members at

---

[16] In the counties, persons who possessed the requisite qualifications to vote were required to send to the overseers of the poor a formal claim to registration, and an annual list of voters and claimants (which could be disputed) was displayed at the church door. Since not all of those qualified to vote sent in their claims, and not all of the actual claimants were qualified, there was considerable inducement for political agents both to make sure that all of their own supporters were duly registered, and to scrutinize closely the qualifications of their opponents. This aspect of the Reform Act of 1832 gave great impetus to the development of local party organization (Markham (1982) 16–17).

present 122: there are also 5 free or honorary members; the Dinner was at Fenwick's, all very quiet, I came away about five O'clock in the afternoon.

Friday 10th. July

The Reformers are wishful to have the claims of their friends as voters, put in the List, Mr. Popple of Welton, seems active in the business. I think he might be more seriously engaged.

Saturday 11th. July

I was at Ellerker this afternoon, and got tea at Mr. Levitt's, which was about all I fell in for. There was a Coroner's inquest at Ellerker this afternoon at Ellerker [*sic*], on a Servant Girl who lived [at] Mr. Popple's, she had taken poison the last Saturday, and continued living until this morning; The Cry was raised by those who either knew or ought to have known better, that she was very ill with the Cholera. The Verdict was; Insanity ...

Monday 13th. July

The market full as badly attended as last week, and no more done: although it is said that Wakefield Market was from 2 to 3s. higher for wheat the last Friday than the week before.

Tuesday 14th. July

Most of the Farmers have begun to mow their Clover, and some of them their Grass, it is a tolerable fine time, being part wind and sunshine.

Wednesday 15th. July

We went to tea this afternoon at Ellerker to Mr. Watson Arton's; and if we had not anything very intellectual, we had much that was substantial; and old told tales varied in no new ways. — It rained as we were going but cleared up before we came back; where we arrived about nine. P.M. that is 9 Hours past noon; which means in plain Yorkshire, East Riding language, nine at night!

Thursday 16th. July

I was at West end this Evening, I went by the Park to see if I could find some Crow Quills, but I was very unsuccessful, but very few of them were to be found; so I gave up the search.

Friday 17th. July

Mr. Hotham has a Brother[17] come to see him, Rd. Marshall says he is an officer in the Navy, — which is very likely for any thing I know to the Contrary to be the case.

Saturday 18th. July

I was pulling Currant berries today, I cannot say that it was a very pleasant job, however I got done, but not before it came on rain, which obliged me to leave off until it became fair weather, when I went again to work and finished.

Sunday 19th. July

We had today at Church an old Gentleman who preached. It is said he is Vicar of Chelsea, he has taken a house at Ferriby; his name is Fisher:[18] he appears to be about 70 years of age he wears Glasses, and seems infirm.

---

[17] Edwin's younger brother, John William Hotham (b. 30 Mar. 1809), attained the rank of Captain in the Royal Navy (Foster iii. section on Hotham family).

[18] Revd Thomas Fisher (White (1840) 197).

Monday 20th. July

This is the last day for delivering in the claims for Voters; I have received the Papers for Ellerker to make out a List for that place, there are Eighteen voters.

Tuesday 21st. July

I have been making out our List of Voters today there are this year 26 fresh claims; the last year's list contained 33 names, so that this year there are 59 names on the List.

Wednesday 22d. July

I was at Brantingham this Evening, and came home by way of Ellerker; I was not above an hour and half from going out to getting home.

Thursday 23d. July

All the talk now is chiefly of a Murder having been committed on the Person of Mr. Beilby Thompson's Gamekeeper of Escricke;[19] the last week: it is said that three Farmers' Sons were the Murders; they had cut the poor Man's throat. I think this murder may vie with any Irish murder.

Friday 24th. July

I have not heard one word from the Assizes at York which are held this week: I suppose there is nothing going on very extraordinary ...

Monday 27th. July

Scarcely any Market today, indeed I did not see a Corn factor here: it is said that the Farmers have not much Wheat in hand; but I know some have a good deal.

Tuesday 28th. July

Charles Barff who went a Missionary into the South Sea Islands, has two Sons in England,[20] who are expected on Thursday next, by their Grandfather at Newbald; they are going to a School near Wakefield.

Wednesday 29th July

It has been a very fine time for Hay and Clover most of which are now got in, this sort of Weather must hasten the Harvest, it being very hot in general, in the day time, but it turns cooler in the Evening especially when the wind gets Easterly, which is frequently the Case.

Thursday 30th. July

Went to the West End this Evening to get the Overseers to sign the List of Voters, but did not meet with any one of them at home, so that I did not succeed

---

[19] Thomas Robinson was killed whilst investigating shots in the night thought to have been made by poachers. A young man, named Morley, was later arrested and charged with murder (*HA* 24 July 1835).

[20] Charles Barff (see also n.23 (1831)) and his wife had a total of 9 children of whom 5 (Charles, John, Richard, Rowland Hill, and George) were boys. At least one of the sons, John, followed in his father's footsteps and became a missionary (Richardson (1895) [Article on Charles Barff], *Hull and District Congregational Magazine*, July and Aug. 1898).

in getting their Signatures so it must be put off, perhaps to the last period of time limited for their signing.[21]

Friday 31st. July

Wm. Loncaster has had 18 or 20 Fleeces of Wool and a Quarter of Wheat stolen; but he cannot tell to a week when it was lost: it appears he does not live in a very good neighbourhood.

Saturday 1st Augt.

Search was made yesterday for Loncaster's stolen goods, but nothing of them was found—a Bag was found belonging to Mr. Elgey, which had contained part of a Sack of Barley that he had lost some time since.

Sunday 2d. Augt.

The Lists of Voters were put up on the Doors of the various places of Worship this day. A Camp meeting of the Ranters was held this day at Newbald; I do not know whether any persons went from here or not.

Monday 3d. Augt.

This day I shall say nothing of the Market. — We had a meeting this Evening to consult about building a new Pinfold, out of Porter hole end, which was agreed to. It was likewise wished for by some that the Market place beck should be arched over from one side of the Street to the other, this was opposed by Mr. Bridgman on account of being a hindrance to the People getting water; when it was found this could not be carried at the Parish Expence; it was proposed that the Job should be done by voluntary Subscription; but this was worse relished by Mr. Bridgman than having it done by the Parish; and he would not consent to having it done in any manner, which was generally approved, so that the Water is yet to run through the Street for the refreshment of the Inhabitants and their Cattle. I think the thanks of the inhabitants, at least some in the Market place are due to him. Mr. Bridgman does not oft put himself forward, but this time he was in his right place.

Tuesday 4th. Aug

This Evening being at Mr. Atkinson's Rd. Marshall called in, who said he was going to see a Close of Oats in the Tofts, so I went with him, we went round by Mr. Bridgman's pasture, we parted when we got into the road each homeward.

Wednesday 5th. Aug

It is said that Captain Shaw of Brantingham has bought the Farm where Tim. Turner lived which belonged to the late Mr. Wilberforce; there is about 500 Acres of it; the Price I do not know, I suppose it is let for 20 Shillings an Acre.

---

[21] Schedule H of the Reform Act of 1832 (2 Will IV c. 45) prescribed the wording and format of the notices which the overseers had to publish annually, listing those claiming the right to vote and those already listed as voters. These model notices specified a requirement for the signatures of the overseers. Section 38 of the Act stipulated that the list of those claiming eligibility to vote had to be made out by the overseers on or before 31 July.

Thursday 6th. Aug

A Letter from Wm. yesterday, glad they have all got home again, he wants his Mother to go to London but I am afraid she will not be able to get.

Friday 7 Aug

Yesterday was Mr. Barnard's Rent day, I dare say the Rents were well paid; and this day the Money will be carried to Hull; where it will be drawn by Mr. Barnard in London.

Saturday 8th. Augt

I was at the West end this morning, being nearly out of Money; I recd. five Pounds of Mr. Leeson part of what he had to pay. In the afternoon I measured some land for Ths. Robinson of Ellerker, about 12 Acres, it was very hot; It was good to do; I staid on my way coming back at Mr. Atkinson's, and arrived at home; rather tired and languid.

Sunday 9th. Aug

I had the List of Voters on the Doors of the Places of Worship again today for the last time. Richd. Marshall is poorly this day.

Monday 10th. Augt

Scarcely any Market today, the Harvest has begun, pretty generally outcries as usual of the badness of the Wheat Crop, the heads not being well filled; so the discontented Creatures amuse themselves and endeavour to gull others; but it won't do.

Tuesday 11th. Aug

This Evening I measured the Road from the Ellerker lane end nearly opposite to the Sand holes to Ring Beck, which is 1400 yards or 3 Quarters of a mile & 80 yards. — And from Ring beck through Ellerker to the place I began at namely Ellerker lane end which is 2647 yards or one Mile and a half & 7 yards; so that the difference is 1247 yards or three Quarters of a Mile wanting 73 yards. I was employed by the owners of the new Coach,[22] as they have, or had some thoughts of going by Ellerker to Hull.

Wednesday 12th. Aug

Robinson of Mount Airy is very ill, not likely it is said to get better, but [that] is generally the cry when a person falls ill here; it is said the complaint is an inflammation, and to be fashionable it is a Liver complaint; It may be a drinking complaint.

Thursday 13th. Aug

All very busy at Harvest work, the weather is very favourable for it, although the Farmers are crying out for Rain, because their turnips do not grow so rapidly as they wish, in dry weather ...

Saturday 15th. Aug

This afternoon I went to measure a little Shearing[23] for Rd. Marshall; little Ann went with me she said she could trail the Chain, for she had found it one

---

[22] See n.12 (1835). The detour to Ellerker, between South Cave and Brantingham, would have added less than one mile to the total journey.

[23] i.e. an area of land that had been 'sheared' or cut with a sickle.

day tied up, and trailed it in the passage. We staid tea, and then returned home, with a few wheat ears which she gleaned.

Sunday 16th. Aug

A very hot day, I went as usual twice to the Church where there is not a single Window that opens to admit the least breath of Air, so there we were like Bees in a hive.

Monday 17th. Aug

I have just come in from the Market, and Wm. Cousens has been asking if I had any thing to send so I have even packed up my Journal, nay I have not packed up yet but am preparing at Eight O'clock on Monday night 17th. Augt. 1835.

Tuesday 18th. Aug.

This day Wm. Cousens and his Brother John has set off for London; I entrusted him (Wm.) with my Journal made up to yesterday to deliver to Wm. ... I had written a few lines to accompany it, but after I had sent the Parcel, I found I had not enclosed the letter, which certainly was an oversight.

Wednesday 19 Aug.

The Farmers very busy getting in their Wheat, which must be in good condition, as there has been very little Rain lately; indeed some of the knowing ones say that a rainy day would be of great service to the Wheat, in making it more kindly: but should this be the case, the cry would immediately be that the Wheat was sprouted!!

Thursday 20th. Aug

Fine weather the Farmers still throng leading wheat which is a fine time for it, I hope it will be got well in.

Friday 21st. Aug

Mr. Turk says he never knew in his life finer Crops of all sorts of Corn, God help that poor old fellow Ths. Marshall says; for he has lived till he is superannuated, what does he talk of eight or nine quarters of Oats on an Acre and Seven Quarters of Barley, and wheat four Quarters, when a deal of land will not have more than twelve Bushels!! ...

Monday 24th. Aug

Thos. Marshall says his Father had two remedies for all Complaints, one was Rum and new Milk for a Medicine which he said would cure ought but broken bones, for Dr. Sonley told him so. Aye but says Tom if the Dr. had told him to take any thing he did not like he would have Pish'd and thaw'd about it: but he liked it and he stuck to it, he never got it over often, Morning Noon and night it was always in season with him. The other remedy was a Bunch of Thorns for all kinds of Gaps, Broken Gates or fallen down walls, there he was with his bunch of Thorns to stop up all mischances; a Bunch of Thorns was his sovereign Remedy for all out of doors work[.] When he got his skin full of Rum and milk and his Bunch of Thorns in his hand he was master of all.

Tuesday 25th. Aug

The Overseers have got a Notice of objection against a person on the list of Voters of the name of Cade who lives at Welton; so that there will be lists to make out and fix on the Doors of Places of Worship on the first two Sundays in September.

Wednesday 26th. Aug

John Cousens and Francis Ruston arrived at home this Evening from London their stay has been very short; Cousens says he saw Wm. once but he was so far off five miles that he did not see him any more, indeed their time was very short, for in going staying and returning they were only nine days.

Thursday 27th. Aug

There was a special Court one day this week to admit two Copyholders; one in the room of the late John Broadley Wilson Esqr. of Clapham Common; and the other on the death of Mrs. Smith of Willerby, of whose farm Loncaster is tenant.

Friday 28th Aug

I was at James Levitt's this afternoon when the honest Miller came in after having tied his Horse to a staple near the Window, but whether the Horse did not like waiting or not I don't know but he turned himself round and thrust his back into the Window and broke two Squares of Glass, the Miller went out to see what was the matter; and his first salute to his old Horse was "Now d—n thee I wesh onny body had shot thee before I com;["] then says he to me this is all with your drawing me in: so he mounted his old horse swearing all the way I could see or hear him.

Saturday 29th Aug

It is said that Fewson is going to leave the House where he now lives, the sign of the Bear and it is said Val. Tindale is about taking it.

Sunday 30th. Aug

I was obliged to come out of the Church this forenoon being ill in my Bowels, I did not go in the afternoon. Mr. Hotham is now in London, the old Gentleman from Ferriby preached this day.

Monday 31st. Aug

All throng with the Harvest, I never saw fewer persons at the Market than this day, nothing done at all in the Corn line.

Tuesday 1st. Sepr

The first Partridge Shooting day, but I have never heard so much as a single Shot, so what sport the Murderers have had I cannot tell.

Wednesday 2d Sepr

I have now very little to do all the Scholars being gleaning, harvesting or tending Pigs.

Thursday 3d. Sepr

This afternoon measured two Closes on the Common, down Jarratt-Hill's lane, about twelve acres, occupied by Charles Rudd, and at present belonging to Jn. Butler Esqr. Cheltenham: this and other property formerly belonged to the

Family of Lloyd's, who had a Hall at the West end, called West Hall;[24] one of the Manors in South Cave is still called the Manor of West Hall.

Friday 4th. Sep

I was going to the West end this afternoon when Lockwood was going down in his Waggon in which he invited me to Ride; so up I mounted and off he went in a trot; It was like being electrified, I got out at Church Hill, and they will be cunning to catch me again jolting in a Waggon at such a pace.

Saturday 5th. Sepr

A very warm day, I wanted to measure some land this afternoon but as the Stooks were not taken away it was put off.

Sunday 6th. Sepr.

Notice of an objection against a claim for voting on the Church Door today, nothing particular.

Monday 7th. Sep

No attendance at the Market again today, a little new Wheat from Broomfleet was sold at two pounds a Quarter.

Tuesday 8th. Sep

The York Musical Festival begins today,[25] there were several Carriages came through yesterday, with Company, to have their Ears tickled with sweet sounds and some perhaps not sweet.

Wednesday 9th. Sep

The Parliamentary Session appears to be drawing to an end, the Commons have taken what they could get of the Corporation Bill:[26] a mighty hubbub there has been made about it, and what is it all for—I say nothing at all—mind I say nothing, that is I do not speak about it.

Thursday 10th. Sep

A Person at Ellerker got his leg broken today when out shooting, in getting over a hedge, he comes from Hull, and is Father in law to Mr. Ellerker.

---

[24] The manor of South Cave West Hall was held by the Lloyd family from 1717, when Richard Lloyd (d. 1724) was named sole lord of the manor, until 1764, when it was sold by his son, also Richard, to a certain John Dunn, one of whose sisters, Mary, eventually sold it to Henry Boldero Barnard in 1784 (*VCHERY* iv. 44–5).

[25] This was the 4th, and last, of the York musical festivals to be held in the series from 1823 to 1835. It was on the same elaborate scale as its 3 predecessors (in 1823, 1825 and 1828), and took place from 8 to 11 Sept. It was attended by the young Princess Victoria (soon to be Queen) with her mother, the Duchess of Kent. Vocalists and instrumentalists numbered over 600. A surplus of £4,000 was raised and on this occasion the Minster Restoration Fund (because of the fire in 1829) benefited equally in its distribution with the 4 hospitals (York, Hull, Leeds and Sheffield). (See also n.66 (Letters)) (Knight 626–7).

[26] The Corporation Bill, which was concerned with the reform of the administration of municipal corporations, had been steered through the Commons by Lord John Russell, and was broadly supported by Peel on the Tory opposition benches. It was, however, drastically amended by Lyndhurst in its passage through the Lords. When the Bill returned to the Commons at the end of Aug., Russell rejected most of the Lords' amendments, and as he was supported in his stand by Peel, the Lords were forced to capitulate and the Bill became law on 4 Sept. 1835 (Walpole iv. 31–46).

Friday 11th. Sep

This afternoon measured part of a Close on the Wold about nine acres being a following Crop belonging Mr. Hudson; Thos. Dyson has taken the Farm.

Saturday 12th. Sep

At the Sands this afternoon measuring some more land for Mr. Hudson, Wheat & Oats, nearly nine acres, very warm weather.

Sunday 13th. Sep

This day fixed up as well as last Sunday the List of Persons qualified to serve on Juries in this Township of South Cave.

Monday 14th Sep

Danl. Foster at Market today was observing and asse[r]ting that it would be no rain as the Glass was rising, and he had noticed then when it rose in foggy weather it would be no rain; so said the wise man—Obed Martin went out but was soon back in a hurry—and said Daniel Ise cum to tell you to break your Glass, for I'll swear it rains fast and your Glass is a Liar.

Tuesday 15th Sep

It was expected yesterday that the new Coach from Hull to Selby would commence yesterday but it has not come, and is put off for another week.

Wednesday 16th. Sep

Here is and has been much rattling about to and from Doncaster Races, I do not know that any Person from this town has been there.

Thursday 17th. Sep

I had my old Paper merchant again today I laid out with him 10s/6d which lightened him of much of his load, I do not know how he makes a living with such a small Stock.

Friday 18th. Sepr

My wife was at Hull today and I was left to be Housekeeper, an office of which I am no great admirer, she went and came back with the Carrier, got home well about nine at night ...

Monday 21st Sep

I think we have nothing to [be] called Market now. Mr. Leeson of Ellerker was not here to day he is ill in the Gout.

Tuesday 22d. Sep

There was a meeting called at the Vestry this day at Eleven O'clock in the Forenoon to nominate Surveyors of the Highways, but as there was a very slight attendance the meeting was adjourned to a future time, I was not there.

Wednesday 23d Sep

The new Coach from Hull to Selby has commenced running,[27] it came from Hull the first time on Monday morning last about half past seven O'clock

---

[27] The 'True Briton' provided a daily service from Hull to Liverpool, via Selby, Leeds, Huddersfield, and Manchester. It was still in operation in 1840, but in that year passengers to Selby had the choice of travelling by rail, following the opening of the Hull to Selby railway (White (1838) ii. 713; White (1840) 183).

and returned again about Eight at night instead of Six as was proposed. This night and the last it returned between Seven and Eight.

Thursday 24th Sep

Obed Martin one night had got rather more liquor than was conducive to Wisdom, his wife told him she would stay no longer with him it was just as the Coach came past; so Obed called the Coachman to stop as here was a passenger a Woman to go with him, she may get up and I will bring all her Boxes and parcels in two minutes—But the wife when it came to it would not go; she has been very quiet since and never once talks of quitting ...

Saturday 26th. Sep

I went to the West end this afternoon and fell in with the old Miller, he complained of being ill, So he got some Rum and Water he had four Glasses, he got gloriously drunk, and was then rather better!!

Sunday 27th. Sep

At Church this forenoon, a Sermon on Catechising, in which it was proved (nay) that the Catechism, of our Church is a glorious Composition, and happy are they who can repeat it, and more learned are they who can understand it.

Monday 28th. Sep

Mr. Brown at the Market today said he would give no more than 11d. pr. Stone for good Wheat; I dare say he bought none.

Tuesday 29th. Sep

Howden Shew for Horses is this week, there have [been] a good many come through here; Good Horses are good to sell, but the Ordinary ones are not good to turn into money. I think I have written good oft enough today.

Wednesday 30th. Sep

Mr. Bridgman fell from his Horse today the Saddle turned when he was getting down but he fell soft among some straw, he has hurt his thigh, but I think he is no worse.

Thursday 1st. Octr

Now we are packing up for London, a pair of Hams and some Pears of our own growing for the Bairns I think they will be very good for they are not over ripe.

Exit 4 Oclock

[*2nd October to 17th December*: This section of the Diary is missing and was presumably destroyed in the fire aboard the steam packet conveying it to London; see the entries for 18th, 23rd and 24th December below]

Decr. 18th Friday

Sent off a Basket this day for Hull to go by the Steam Packet tomorrow, containing a Goose dressed a Standing Pork Pie some few fine apples—a little Spice loaf and a Sovereign and a half together with my Journal up to this time and a letter for a few popular Books such as Cock Robin, little Red Riding Hood &c. &c.

Saturday 19th Decr.

This day very cold weather I went no further from home than to Mr. Atkinson's; where we always have a good fire; and a Pipe of Tobacco if we choose to find it ourselves.

Sunday 20th. Decr.

I was not very well this morning so did not go out; in the afternoon I went to the Church; having on my great Coat, and being armed with an Umbrella.

Monday 21st. Decr

I saw very little of the Market this day having been no further than Cousens's where there was not much Company, I came home about Six O'clock.

Tuesday 22d. Decr

One of the Greenland Ships that was left in the Ice has escaped from her confinement and arrived at Hull;[28] I am glad at her arrival.

Wednesday 23d. Decr.

This Evening heard that the Steam Packet the London, had taken fire and been run ashore at or near Grimsby; which is heavy news to us as the Basket we sent is on board her; little Ann was the first to tell us that the letter for the Books was either burnt or lost; but I yet hope for the best.

Thursday 24th. Decr

All last night I was balancing probabilities I said if the Packet was lost on Saturday morning we should have heard before today as bad news always flies fast; I nearly convinced myself that the event had not happened but Wm. sent word this morning of the same disaster and blew up my hopes.

Friday 25 Decr

This is Christmas day plenty of Christmas Boxers running about, little Tom has got 11½d I am not fond of the Practice. My Mother never would suffer us to run about begging at Christmas nor the new year.

Saturday 26th. Dec

A very cold day as was yesterday I was at Ellerker in the afternoon and from thence went to the Mill but the careful Miller had no Money to spare, so I came back without.

Sunday 27th. Decr

I was at the Church twice today, and that is about all I have to observe, as nothing particular has taken place.

Monday 28th. Decr

It is now Holidays this week with us I attended the Market as usual, but there was but little Company, came home about Six O'clock and went out no more this night.

---

[28] This was the Hull whaler, the 'Alfred', which had arrived from the Davis Straits in the previous month. Her captain, R. W. Humphreys, reported 11 ships still beset in the Greenland ice, including 6 vessels from Hull. On 12 Dec. 1835, a public meeting was held, in Hull's Guildhall, to organize a petition to urge the government to mount a rescue expedition and to raise a subscription for the relief of the families of the detained seamen (*HP* 20 Nov. and 18 Dec. 1835).

Tuesday 29th. Decr

Mr. Hotham has been given [*sic*] Coals away to the Poor it is said to the amount of £20. without distinction, to all the Poor whether they belong the Town or not.

Wednesday 30th. Decr.

I have been making out this day my Quarterly Account of Stamps and have on hand Parchment and Paper Stamps amounting to £239–11s–9d.

Thursday 31st. Decr

Recd. the Hull Observer[29] this morning, it is the first time I have seen anything of it; It appears to be a violent Radical; they call one another (viz. the Papers) this is not very intelligible writing in using the Pronoun before the Substantive, but one frequently sees it done.

---

[29] The *Hull, East Riding, and North Lincolnshire Observer* was published weekly by the proprietors of the *Hull Advertiser* from May 1834 until 1841, when it was incorporated into that newspaper (*VCHYER* i. 429).

Friday 1st. Jany

This is the beginning of another year, plenty of Boys and Girls too running about for New year's Gifts, some who have got more than others look very lofty and look more with disdain than pity on the less fortunate. This day sent a small Hamper containing a Goose to Wm.

Saturday 2nd. Jany

There was a beggar going to Rd. Marshall's door, just as Tom Levitt was coming up; when the Servant Girl was coming with a halfpenny to the beggar, when Tom said to him we go shares you know: The fellow said he would go shares with nobody; then says Tom you have run off your or our bargain for we agreed last night at North Cave to go shares. Thou's a liar for I never saw thee in my travels before just now. Nay, Nay says Tom what deny all: you know we both lodged at one house last night and were as thick as thieves tho' we are only beggars: Now says the beggar to the Girl with the halfpenny this Rascal here is the biggest liar I ever heard in my life—and with that he got his stick to strike at Tom, when he told the Girl to throw up the Halfpenny which she did, and Tom in his old Ragged Coat picked it up and ran away, and left the poor fellow distracted, saying thou said we were to share and now thou hast turned thief and stolen all, thou thief I'll report thee and give a description of thee at every lodging house I come to ...

Monday 4th. Jany

Beverley Sessions begins this day the Overseer is gone this day to have an Order of Maintenance made on a Man in a Bastardy Case;[1] I am sure there is more trouble and expence too in these Cases than under the old law; as an Attorney has gone with the Overseer.

Tuesday 5th. Jan

The Plough Lads were about yesterday, and this night, they have a Supper at Fenwick's, they have five pounds to Spend so no doubt they will enjoy themselves: as Money will command both attendance and luxuries.

Wednesday 6th. Jan

Conders killed their Pig on Saturday last it weighed nearly 23 Stones (of 14lb to the Stone) that is our way of reckoning Stones and not the London weight of Eight pounds to the Stone.

Thursday 7th. Jany

This morning heard that Wm. had received the Basket safe on Saturday last; it has been more fortunate than the Steam Boat Basket—Ann is overjoyed to hear that her Books will soon be sent.

---

[1] The Poor Law Amendment Act of 14 Aug. 1834 (4 & 5 Will. c. 76) provided detailed instructions for the conduct of overseers or guardians in cases of bastardy where paternity was disputed (sections 69 to 76).

Friday 8th. Jan

Last night was the Monthly meeting of the Club a pretty large Company, I got done and got home about nine O'clock as there was nothing material going on.

Saturday 9th. Jany

I was at the Mill this afternoon, where I got a little money, and bought a small parcel of Quills, of two or three years' produce; I did not stay tea but got home about four O'clock, and the remainder of the Evening I partly spent at our Old Friend's Mr. Atkinson.

Sunday 10th. Jany

Mr. Hotham has been giving away a Quantity of Coals this winter to the Poor, which is a kind action, but perhaps will not please all who have received of the Bounty, and assuredly some will be displeased who have received none.

Monday 11th. Jan

This morning the Ground is covered with Snow, at which I do not wonder, as it was very cold yesterday, and looked black as a Winter's Storm, — Mr. Brown gave 20s/6d pr. Quarter for Oats this day at the Market.

Tuesday 12th. Jan

I read in the Paper a while since of a search having been made for smuggled Goods, where the Officers found an empty Brandy Cask with some Bladders in it.

Wednesday 13th. Jan

We received the small parcel from Wm. this morning with the Books, which was highly pleasing; the Mercators Map is just what I wanted: the last two parcels have been charged 6d. each to Hull.

Thursday 14th. Jan

Henry Arton's wife was buried today, she has been ill a very long time; she was entirely worn away. Ann & her Grandmother went to the funeral ...

Saturday 16th. Jan

I was no further from home this day, than to Mr. Atkinson's, where one is sure of a good fire side, and very often no lack of Company.

Sunday 17th. Jan

I was at Church twice today in the afternoon an old Gentleman from Ferriby preached. On a Sunday I never stir out after leaving Church in the afternoon.

Monday 18th. Jan

At the Market as usual, where Tradesmen were presenting their Christmas Bills to their Customers, and endeavouring to get them discharged I did not stay long, but got home about Six O'clock.

Tuesday 19th. Jan

Obed Martin said one day to the old Popish Priest that he thought he would turn Catholic; the next day the old Priest gave him a good glass of Gin, and Obed was in a fair way of conversion and thinks if he had had a whole Bottle set before him, it would have gone hardly with him—But all is quite changed again and Obed is a true Protestant for Mr. Hotham has given him some Coals!!!

Wednesday 20th Jan

Very dirty at the breaking up for the present of the Frost. I went down to the West end this Evening, but came back very soon as it was so disagreeable walking, I did not like to be out after dark.

Thursday 21st. Jan

There was no Paper yesterday, so that I had two Blank days together as Tuesday is always one—but they both came this morning so that I have as much news as could be reasonably wished.

Friday 22nd. Jan

We have sent off a Ham today for Wm. which Mr. Turk presented him with hope it will arrive safe, we have sent it to go by the Barton Coach.

Saturday 23d. Jan

An uncommon windy day but dry, it blew Straw and light substances about very much; I went out no further this day than Mr. Atkinson's, so that I did not travel far ...

Monday 25th Jany

A kind of dark dull day and very little doing in the Market; Mr. Barnard has sent Richd. Marshall a Gold watch as it is said; I have not heard him say any thing of it himself; some of the tenants think it would have been better to have had something deducted from their Rents.

Tuesday 26th. Jan

This day I did not stir out at all any further than to get tea at Eliza's, as I was left to be Housekeeper, my wife having gone to Hull. She went and came back with the Carrier she got home just at nine O'clock at night.

Wednesday 27th. Jan

We had a very small meeting this Evening at Mr. Atkinson's two of our members Mr. Bridgman and Obed Martin had been at Beverley fortnight Cattle market, and Timy. Dunn has got married.

Thursday 28th. Jan

This Evening the Box arrived with the Muff which is much liked and highly prized it was not at all crushed, but in as good condition as though it had not been carried ten yards it appears to have left London only yesterday upon the whole it has been very expeditious.

Friday 29th. Jan

A Letter from my Brother this day, who says he is in good health and free from pain, but continues lame; I am glad to find that he is so well as [to] have the use of his faculties so much better than he had, it appears he writes with his left hand.

Saturday 30th. Jan

A very cold day which makes fire side a comfortable place; I stirred out very little today; I went in the forenoon as far as Ths. Fisher's with the Poor book; he is Overseer.

Sunday 31st. Jan

There is generally a larger Congregation at the Church in the afternoon of the last Sunday in the Month, which is called the Bread Sunday,[2] this causes a greater attendance.

Monday 1st. Feb

Wheat which was reported to be higher in price than it was, did not meet with purchasers today at any advance, indeed it could scarce support its former price.

Tuesday 2d Feb

This is what is called new Candlemas day[3] the weather is very cold and boisterous: the days may now be perceived to be a good deal longer.

Wednesday 3rd. Feb

This day and last night it has rained & stormed without ceasing, it is a very long time since we have had so much Rain, the Beck was full to overflowing ...

Saturday 6th. Feb.

I was at Everthorpe this afternoon measuring a little Close about seven Acres and setting out 6 Acres in another Close, as soon as I had done I came home, being as near Cave as Everthorpe.

Sunday 7th Feb

The old Gentleman of the name of Fisher preached at the Church this afternoon: they say the old Man goes a Foxhunting in his Gig, or at least to see the Sport as it is called. I had more thoughts of Foxhunting than the Sermon when he was preaching.

Feby 8th Monday

The farmers today elevated with the thoughts of Corn soon being higher— I hope they will be deceived—Barley seems to be at a remunerating price 30s. pr. Qr.

9th Feb. Tuesday

I have an Ancle at present rather troublesome, I think I knocked the Skin off it sometime ago, by hitting my other foot against it; it is rather swelled but has not much pain in it.

10th. Feb Wednesday

I am glad to find that the Unitarian Trustees in Lady Hewley's Charity are to be removed;[4] this is as it ought to be. I dare say that Lady Hewley abhorred Socinian doctrines.

---

[2] Bread was distributed free at church on the last Sunday of each month by the 2 churchwardens. It is probable that the money for this charitable practice came from the surplus funds of Jobson's Charity, which was established specifically for the free distribution of penny bread rolls to the poor annually on Easter Tuesday. (See n.51 (1827)).

[3] i.e. the Roman Catholic feast of the Purification of Our Lady.

[4] Lady Sarah Hewley (1627–1710) had left a substantial estate in trust, particularly for the support of 'poor and godly preachers'. By the end of the 18th c., all the trustees and a majority of the Presbyterian recipients were Unitarians. The direction of the Hewley Fund was the subject of protracted litigation, which began in 1830, and was not finally settled until 1842, when according

Thursday 11th. Feb

In my Mercator's Map I cannot find Nootka Sound, I know it is known also by the name of King George's Sound. There is a place marked King George Archipelago, not far from the place, perhaps it may be the same. — In my Geography I cannot find Behrings Straits which I rather wonder at. I have been lately on a Voyage to the North West of America, and find that the distance between Asia and America is only about forty miles in the narrowest part.

Friday 12th. Feb.

My Ancle is a good deal swelled but not much pain, I have had it poulticed, but the swelling does not settle.

Saturday 13th. Feb

I had some land to measure today but was prevented from going on Account of my Ancle; as the land was on the Wold, I durst not venture.

Sunday 14th. Feb

Mr. Rodmell preached at the Church this morning, he never was very good to understand but he has marvellously improved shall I say in pronunciation as for instance Gloory for Glory, Amang for among Fauther for father &c. &c. I cannot endure such minced meat.

Monday 15th. Feb

I think I saw very little of the Market today, I soon came home my Ancle rather troubles me, but I do not want for prescriptions, for every one I talk to has a remedy of their own.

Tuesday 16th. Feb

Eliza's youngest Child is very ill he has lost his flesh very much and can take very little support; I do not know whether the Doctor understands his complaint or not.

Wednesday 17th. Feb

A very stormy day which makes it very cold, with Showers of Snow, indeed it is a real Winter-day This windy weather is at all times disagreeable to me.

Thursday 18th. Feb

This is what is called Beverley Candlemas fair it is not so stormy as it was yesterday, but so cold that it feels like skinning one's face; several People are gone to the Fair.

Friday 19th. Feb

Mr. Bridgman bought some Sheep at Beverley fair yesterday and ordered them to be taken to Walkington to come home this morning; he sent a man for them but the man not coming back at the time expected Mr. Bridgman went to meet him; when they got to Walkington the Sheep were not there at the place appointed, but somewhere else in the Town where he met a man who claimed one lot of them, but they got the Sheep and arrived at home soon after dark.

to a judgement in the House of Lords, the monopoly of the Unitarians was broken and 3 orthodox Presbyterians, 3 Congregationalists and one Baptist were appointed as trustees (*DNB*).

Saturday 20th. Feb

I was twice at the West end this forenoon and at Ellerker in the afternoon, I am afraid I have taken too much exercise for my Ancle, though I feel no inconvenience to arise from my Walk.

Sunday 21st. Feb

I think I have nothing to remark particularly today; I have got a little Bottle of some kind of Oils at Rd. Marshall's which he says will cure my Ancle, but I think I shall not yet apply it as it is suitable for fresh wounds and mine is not of that description, I rather begin to think it is some kind of a Blain or Botch[5] with which I am sometimes troubled.

Monday 22d. Feb

A Son of John Wride's who was Shepherd to Mr. Turk when we came to Cave has been stealing 30 Sheep: and sold them to a Butcher of Beverley he has been apprehended, he lived near Driffield.

Tuesday 23d Feby

Some women for breaking down Trees were taken to Riplingham yesterday, and reprimanded and fined some trifle: and threatened to be more severely punished if they transgress any more.

Wednesday 24th. Feb.

The Rail Roads drag heavily along at present it appears that they are a Speculation to take money from those who are willing to be Share holders, for my part if I had money to spare I would not embark it in any such scheme.

Thursday 25th. Feb

Obed Martin has taken a House that was Jno. Gardam's with the Garden, it formerly belonged to Joshua ˙Cade, he >Cade< lately lived at Hull, but died about a week ago, he was it is said 79 years old.

Friday 26th. Feb

We have very cold weather but not what may be called severe winter weather; it frequently is frost at night, after rain in the day time.

Saturday 27th. Feb

This afternoon I measured some land called little Cardales, nearly opposite to the Mill some parts of the Land were very wet, the others sandy and dry, it belongs to Mr. Levitt of Ellerker. Teavil Leeson's Sheep had eaten the Turnips that grew on it. — I went to the Mill after I had done and staid tea.

Sunday 28th. Feb

This was a very cold day and stormy, Teavil Leeson has gone to York as a Juryman, but not on the Grand Jury, as he has given out.

Monday 29th. Feb

As my Ancle is not yet well, I never taste either Liquor or Ale, and it is very seldom that I can come at Wine so that Water is my chief Beverage which I believe is the best Liquid I can take.

---

[5] 'blain', an inflammatory swelling or sore; 'blotch', an inflamed eruption or discoloured patch on the skin, a pustule, boil, or botch (*OED*).

Tuesday 1st. Mar

Yesterday was the 29th. Feb. consequently this is Leap year, and this is the Rule to find when it is Leap year, divide the year by 4 if nothing remain it is Leap year, if any thing remain it is the 1st—2d—3d after leap year.

Wednesday 2d March

Some people have begun to work their Gardens and to set and sow, but they are too forward so long as this weather continues, for if the Seeds be saved from perishing that will be all, they will not be so well as in Bags or Boxes, and sown when fine weather comes.

Thursday 3d March

Club night this first Thursday in the month it has been held at Fenwick's but removed to Barnard Cook's for the next year ...

Saturday 5th. March

This forenoon I measured a Close of Turnips for Lockwood, the left hand top Close going up to Mount Airy it was 10A–1R–8P. I had a Shoe on that let in the wet in going over the Cow pasture.

Sunday 6th. March

At Church this forenoon a Sermon was preached nay read and not very well neither from the words of Balaam "Let me die the death of the righteous and let my latter end be like his". But not one word about living the life of the righteous; Balaam was a crafty time serving Sycophant and would willingly have received the wages of unrighteousness, but was compelled against his mind to speak truth.

Monday 7th March

I was at the Market as usual but saw no business done. It is said that the Wheat looks very ill this year; but much notice need not be taken of this.

Tuesday 8th. March

Thos. Marshall's Daughter was married this morning to John Elgey, they set off after the Ceremony to York: we had a slice of Bride-Cake with Mr. & Mrs. Elgey's Compliments.

Wednesday 9th. March

When the Newspaper arrives in a morning Ann who has a taste for news, enquires if there be any Wants; which most takes her attention, I let her have an old Paper sometimes, but she notices nothing but "Wanted places &c." this is about the last article I care anything about, but she is vastly delighted to read this part of the Paper.

Thursday 10th. March

Very unkindly spring weather cold blustering winds and rain, with frost almost every night, so that nothing makes any progress in growing.

Friday 11th. Mar

There was a Sale of Farming Stock at Newbald yesterday when Sheep sold at higher prices than they would have fetched in a fair, such is the folly of one person bidding against another.

Saturday 12th. Mar

This forenoon I measured Thomas Fisher's little Wold farm from the Beverley road at Bottom to the Plantation at the top about 10 Acres. It was tolerably fine weather but the land was ploughed which made it heavy walking.

Sunday 13th. March

A tolerable fine morning, I generally take my Umbrella with me on Sundays; but today I went without it, and had no occasion for it. It was dry all the day, but it came on Rain at night.

Monday 14th. March

There was a meeting of the Turnpike Trustees this day to let the Brough Toll bar,[6] it was put up at the last year's rent but there was no bidder.

Tuesday 15th. March

My Ancle is much better indeed I hope it is nearly well, I still keep a rag on it to keep my Stocking from it, it seems to be healed.

Wednesday 16th. March

Mr. Beaumont of Brantingham is gone to London respecting some Selby Rail way in the West Riding[7] I suppose he is an advocate for it.

Thursday 17th. March

I am not one that wish for the total repeal of the Stamps on Newspapers: it would not benefit us who live in the Country, as we should have to pay more for the Postage than for the Stamp, therefore I hope the duty will be reduced, & the Paper sent free as usual ...

Saturday 19th. March

I went down to the West end this afternoon but did not stay long, I came home before tea, as I was collecting and the Present Overseers have not much time to turn their hands in ...

Monday 21st. March

The Days now are of a sufficient length for a person who begin work at Sunrise and continues to work all the day till Sunset to tire himself provided he works with exertion.

Tuesday 22d March

Ann and her Mother were at Hull today for the first time in her (Ann's) life they went and came back by the Coach, it was in general a Wet day but they were in the inside. Ann had seen King William[8] she said he had not a hat on.

---

[6] The practice of leasing tolls was sanctioned by the General Turnpike Act of 1773, which laid down that advance notice of forthcoming tolls auctions had to be announced in the press by the turnpike trustees, and intending bidders were required to put down a deposit in testimony of their good faith. The Brough toll bar was leased by the Brough Ferry–Newbald Holmes Turnpike Trust (1771–1872) (Macmahon 52–3 and 70).

[7] The Hull and Selby Railway Company had been formed in 1834, and succeeded in obtaining an Act on 21 June 1836, but despite the relatively short distance between the 2 towns (just over 30 miles) and the relatively flat terrain (the difference in height over sea level between Hull and Selby is only 12 feet), it took 4 years to lay the line. The railway was formally opened on 1 July 1840. Thanks to this new rail link, it became possible for the first time for travellers to journey from Hull to London in less than a day (Macturk 36–79; *VCHYER* i. 392–3).

[8] This was the equestrian statue of King William III (still standing 1996) in Hull's Market Place, south east of Holy Trinity church. It was erected by public subscription in 1734, being designed

Wednesday 23d. March

The Surveyors of the Highways of Ellerker brought me their Book to balance previous to closing their Accounts, which is not a very long Job.

Thursday 24th. March

I had my Paper merchant this day in a state of mental elevation, for he expects to succeed to a fortune of 10 or perhaps 30 thousand pounds; I told him I thought he had not very good grounds to go on, being derived from an Advertisement in the Papers about 30 years ago, for a Person of the name of Graham, and he supposes he is the man. I wish for his sake it may be so.

Friday 25 March

Very Stormy weather again—I think there is very little of importance going on in the Political World, those who are in power wishing to keep it and those who are out, striving with all their might to get in; the wise ones seem bewildered and the fools are always so.

Saturday 26th. March

I have been about with the Overseers this day to collect all the Arrears of Poor's Rates we could, but I am never anxious of succeeding when I have any of the Parish Officers with me, and this day I certainly got as little as could be expected.

Sunday 27th. Mar

A very cold day a great contrast between this and the last Sunday; the Rooks are very busy in building and Repairing their old habitations; the young ones of last year are obliged to edge off to the outside trees.

Monday 28th. March

Hull and Selby Railway is a good deal talked about now[.] Some are positive the Bill will pass, and others who are adverse to it are as sure it will be thrown out, for my part I think it will pass.

Tuesday 29th. March

We had a meeting last night to balance the Poor Books and Highway Books and to nominate Overseers of the Poor, the two first names on the list are Robert Marshall and Thomas Leaper. The meeting under the new Highway act appointed Thomas Wride and John Elgey as Surveyors.[9]

Wednesday 30th. March

The Overseers and Surveyors were at Beverley this day to get their Books signed by the Magistrates and the two first on the Overseers list were appointed to the Office, they have only been one year out ...

---

and produced by the Flemish sculptor, Peter Scheemakers, who was paid £893 10s. 0d. for it. The statue was first ordered to be gilded in 1768. The rider is mounted without stirrups, and local tradition has it that when the sculptor realized his omission, he was so distraught that he committed suicide! (Pevsner (1995) 540).

[9] The Highways Act of 31 Aug. 1835 (5 & 6 Will. IV c. 50) empowered parishes to appoint salaried highway surveyors (section 9) as an alternative to the traditional annual election of surveyors at the parish vestry meetings, which was still permitted by the Act (section 6). Parishes were also allowed to merge into a single district for the purposes of highway maintenance with a district surveyor being appointed by the Justices of the Peace (sections 13–15).

Friday 1st. April

I was at the West end this forenoon seeing for my Partner Thomas Levitt to go to Beverley tomorrow to be sworn in Assessors. I did not go to the Church, very few attended there.

Saturday 2d. April

I walked to Beverley this morning a sort of disagreeable day, sometimes Rain, sometimes Snow, sometimes Sleet, at others sunshine; I got home about five O'clock, the roads were very bad but I was not much tired.

Sunday 3d. April

This is Easter Sunday, but so cold and stormy that the weather is more like Christmas than Easter, I was at the Church twice.

Monday 4th. Apl.

This is the day of the greatest Horse Show, I suppose there were several to be seen but I saw none of them for I am not at all fond of being near such Animals.

Tuesday 5th. Apl.

This day there was a Coroner's inquest on a new born Child found in the Beck at the west end on Sunday afternoon; the mother was discovered being a Servant Girl living with Thos. Dyson—the Jury met at half past ten in the forenoon and it was between five and six in the afternoon before a Verdict was returned, which was that the Child was still born but the Mother was guilty of concealing the Birth;[10] she will be taken to Beverley to be tried at the Sessions next week. For the first time there was Reporter here (from the Yorkshire Gazette)[11] so you see how we were honoured.

Wednesday 6th. Apl.

The Tansy this Evening was at Barnard Cook's but what Company there was I wot not. I heard a noise but saw nothing: I suppose it was kept up most of the night.

Thursday 7th. Apl.

The Black Bear opposite to us has acquired another new tenant; a person of the name of Turner a Blacksmith has taken it, he has been in the Town a few years, he succeeded Matthew Pickering.

Friday 8th. Apl.

Our Old friend has been amused by a Man who has been shaved with the new Shaving Stone; whether he will purchase one or not I cannot tell ...

Sunday 10th. Apl.

I was not at Church on Easter Tuesday when the Church Wardens were chosen; The old ones stand again for another year viz Mr. Atkinson and Jn. Lockwood.

Monday 11th. Apl

My Ancle is now quite settled and has been healed some time, but there still remains a large Scar on it; in the place where the Breeder was.

---

[10] See n.25 (1833).

[11] Weekly newspaper, 1819–1954 (See Appendix 3).

Tuesday 12th. Apl.

The Girl that was taken to Beverley last week for concealing the Birth of her Child, was this day tried at the Sessions, and sentenced to two years confinement.

Wednesday 13th. April

This Evening I measured some Turnip Land for Wm. Cousens; part of the Beck Tofts formerly old Mr. Js. Levitt's, and part of Frans. Ruston's Close, the whole between 11 and 12 Acres ...

Friday 15th. Apl.

I had Mr. Pratt the Bookseller of Howden to solicit an Order but I did not give him one of any kind he says he will be here in about three weeks time again, but he once sent me some very ordinary Copy Books, and I have no mind to have any more of him.

Saturday 16th. Apl.

I went to the Castle this afternoon as I wanted to see the Honble Mr. Stourton but he was from home so I came back again without going any further. He is going to leave in the beginning of May ...

Monday 18th. Apl

A very thin attendance at the Market today, it being the new Howden fair day, which took away many of the Farmers from us.

Tuesday 19th. Apl

It is said that Mr. Barnard is coming to Cave in a little time but it is not expected that he will reside here the Castle is not yet let, Mr. Stourton is going to remove into Northumberland, the Place I do not know, but it is said to be a large Heath or Moor of some thousands of Acres.

Wednesday 20th. Apl

The old Catholic Priest is going to leave Mr. Stourton and is going into France, there is a Catholic Priest at the House Mr. Stourton is going to, it belongs to a Catholic who is a minor.

Thursday 21st. Apl.

The Carlow Election Committee, I think will quit Mr. O'Connel, although it has been a shabby affair in which he and his quondam Friend Raphael has been engaged[12] ...

---

[12] After the result of the 1834 election at county Carlow had been declared void, in May 1835, O'Connell invited Alexander Raphael, a London sheriff, to stand as a candidate. After paying £1,000 to O'Connell for election expenses, Raphael was duly elected, but the result was contested by his opponents, and he was required to pay a further £1,000 in order to defend the return. The defence was unsuccessful, and the disgruntled Raphael wrote a letter to the *Times* (31 Oct. 1835), in which he complained that part of the money that he had paid over to O'Connell was unaccounted for. The letter caused great scandal, and in 1836 O'Connell's conduct was referred to a parliamentary committee, which subsequently exonerated him completely (MacDonagh (1989) 139–42).

Sunday 24th. Apl.

I am greatly troubled with tooth Ache and a pain in my Gums which makes it very distressing when I eat any thing; I think it is cold that has flown into my mouth.

Monday 25th. Apl.

This Evening the new Tenants at the Black Bear have their House warming but I see no stir of any of the thoughtless attending. I am inclined to think there will be very little Company.

Tuesday 26th. Apl.

My wife was at Hull today so I was the Housekeeper with Ann as my Assistant. I was charged to lock the Room doors when I was at School, but it unfortunately happened I could not find the Key, indeed it was not likely I should as my wife had it in her Pocket.

Wednesday 27th. Apl

I have had Watson Arton with all his Tax papers, as he is the Assessor; I have made out his accounts many years; and he gets credit for the Correctness with which he presents them and I am content with the Profit which is not much.

Thursday 28th. Apl.

I received this morning for Mr. Levitt a Sydney "Commercial Journal and Advertiser"[13] there appears to be as much puffing in it as in any old World Newspaper. Several Advertisements where rewards are offered for Stolen Horses and other Articles.

Friday 29th. Apl

I have now two bad Ancles, I believe I have knocked the Skin off by striking one foot against the other Ancle: it has not been done in any kind of Spite, but so it is I have to bear it.

Saturday 30th. Apl.

I was at Brantingham Sands this afternoon measuring, when there it was a smart Shower of Hail, there was no shelter so we had to bear the pelting of it. It was soon over, there was rather more than 11 Acres and a half of Dibbled Beans.

Sunday 1st. May

This is the time of the year when one may expect fine weather, but as yet we have very cold North East Winds, and still makes Fire Side a comfortable place.

Monday 2d. May

We generally have had done with a Fire in the School at this time, but at present we cannot dispense with it, so that it is still continued.

---

[13] Apart from the fact that it was still being published in 1839, very little bibliographical information on this newspaper has been found. (See Appendix 3).

Tuesday 3d. May

I have seen very few Cowslips this year, the weather I think has been too cold for them, therefore they do not shew their beautiful flowers, these nearly first wild flowers of the Spring.

Wednesday 4th. May

Obed Martin has been at the Cattle market at Beverley with a Cow that he bought of Lockwood, to sell. Mr. Bridgman told him he would get nothing by her but Obed thought otherwise; however if he got what he gave for [her] that was all, being his time and expences out of Pocket.

Thursday 5th. May

I was at Frog Hall this Evening, it is taken by a Lady of Sutton (of course I must not say a Woman) I went to enquire about the number of Windows, which is 20 mind number is the Nom. case.

Friday 6th. May

Very cold weather yet; at Mr. Atkinson's as usual when I have nothing particular to attend to, I generally leave between seven and eight O'clock then return home, and read something till ten O'clock.

7th. May Saturday

I was at Weedley Warren this forenoon where I was measuring some Paring, about 14 Acres, there is some more yet not Pared; I should have liked it better had it all been done, as most likely I shall have another Journey to it: it is a Wild looking place ...

Monday 9th. May

The Corn sellers this day wanted higher Prices for their wheat than they could get, they would not take less than 50s. for good Wheat, but the buyers would give no more than 48s.—so there it remained.

Tuesday 10th. May

Recd. an annual Letter from the Schoolmasters' Association of which I am a member giving an Account of the number of members which is 30. The amount of Stock £926–19–8. Annuities have been paid the last year to Members and Widows amounting to £36–10–0. On the whole the concern is prosperous.

Wednesday 11th. May

This Evening I have been in the Market place (only) collecting taxes &c I was satisfied with my work, so went to Mr. Atkinson's and smoked a pipe, mind we all provide our own Tobacco as we are not very generous one to another.

Thursday 12th. May

This appears to have been a Crow shooting Day after School time I heard several Guns fired it was no war but murder that was going on who the Assassins were I know not, neither did I enquire.

Friday 13th May

I have a deal of trouble with my Ancle but not much pain, it is a good deal swelled, I have had it poulticed and plastered, I hope it will soon be better; I cannot bear a Shoe on so I am obliged to have a light Slipper ...

Sunday 15th. May

At Church this morning, there was no service in the afternoon, so the congregation might view the Eclipse[14] or not just as they liked: I got a piece of smoked glass to view the Sun. Some people said they saw stars at the time, but I did not.

Monday 16th. May

A large assortment of Pots at the Market today as is usual before the fair, but all was pretty quiet, there is no such uproar as there used to be with the Blackguards who attended: I think the Potters are rather more respectable than formerly.

Tuesday 17th. May

Very fine warm weather now, quite favorable for the growing wheat, some people are wishing for rain, I am not one of them, all I wish is for fine warm weather, which we are at present favoured with.

Wednesday 18th. May

Some of the Butchers have been at Beverley fortnight market today to buy Cave fair Beef or rather oxen which produce the Beef. One of them it is said has bought an old Cow.

Thursday 19 May

I was to have gone to Weedley again this afternoon to have measured some more paring, but my Ancle was not in a fit state to suffer me[;] the swelling has rather abated.

Friday 20th. May

Dry cold weather again with blustering North and east winds which makes fire Side yet desirable, as it becomes very cold at nights ...

Monday 23d May

Market for Pots as usual in anticipation of the Fair all appears now to be animated with the thoughts of Pleasure in the forthcoming week.

Tuesday 24th May

Mr. Beaumont of Brantingham and a Butcher of Welton named Bartram are now in London as witnesses for the Hull and Selby railway; Mr. Raikes opposes it.[15]

Wednesday 25th. May

Butchers running about with Beef for Cave Fair, we have many of them now, we have engaged some of Obed Martin as it is capital he says, it wants nothing of his recommendation.

[14] It was while observing this same annular eclipse that the astronomer, Francis Baily (1774–1844), first discovered the phenomenon known as 'Baily's beads', an apparent string of separate portions of light, which may be seen just before the final disappearance of the solar crescent, and which are caused by the inequalities of the lunar surface (*EB* iii. 221).

[15] See n.17 (1836).

Thursday 26th. May

The weather yet is very dry, we have a fine display of Tulips at least I think so; I suppose they are not what are called Prize Flowers but they are very gay and gaudy; We have a great deal of Lilac and Laburnum.

Friday 27th. May

This day we have Hannah Martin cleaning the School and Passages she seems to be in her glory when one can hardly stir for dust and colouring.

Saturday 28th. May

This is the Market day, this week we have two Market days and the next there will not be one, we have had as customary the Artons to tea.

Sunday 29th. May

Coaches, Gigs and Horses in full requisition this day to bring the Hull Gentlemen Barbers and Bottle washers to get drunk here and make fools of themselves and then go home if indeed they are able.

Monday 30th. May

An uncommon dusty day there are many Beasts in the fair but it is not a good selling day on account of the dry weather and scarceness of grass. We had James Ramsdale and his two Sons and Hugh Carr the younger, together with John Swift at dinner.

Tuesday 31st. May

This day we have had very little company, indeed we had not any either to dinner or tea, which we did not at all regret, as it made it much easier, than otherwise would have been.

Wednesday 1st. June

This day there were Ass Races, and Foot races but no Horses could be found to run, there was not much Company in the town as the Riverbridge People call this their Fair day which draws a good deal of Company there—I believe this is wrong it was yesterday for Bridge Fair.

Thursday 2d. June

There were Races this afternoon or Evening at the West end, but they were not calculated for my presence. It was the Club night which being the last before the Feast, was a throng night.

Friday 3d. June

We have had a fine Rain which has laid the Dust in the Street, and will be very acceptable to the Farmers; they are a discontented set, and the weather is seldom right for them.

Saturday 4th. June

I was at the West end this forenoon collecting, as the taxes are paid in the next week, I came on full as well as I expected or rather better, so came home Satisfied in this point.

Sunday 5th. June

I had forgot to notice that Mr. Barnard and his Lady came last Monday, this day they were at the Church. I suppose there were many there to see them more than for Religion's sake; I suppose the Lord of the Manor is not going to make any long stay, but this I know very little about.

Monday 6th. June

At the Market as usual there was very little done or even to do. I was no where but at Cousen's I got a Glass of Brandy and water as it was long since I had tasted Liquor of any kind.

Tuesday 7th. June

The indulgence of a Glass of Liquor last night prevented me from sleeping, and caused me to suffer much pain in my Ancle; this is from experience, or I could not have believed that taking so small a quantity of Liquor would have had such an effect.

Wednesday 8th. June

Yesterday we had a Poor Law Commissioner or otherwise a Lacquey belonging to them he is going to establish a Union of Parishes and have a Workhouse at So. Cave,[16] he proposed sending Letters to the different Parishes to meet to consult or rather to hear instructions, for I do not suppose that if they were opposed to the project they would be attended to. Talk of Irish Oppression indeed when every Parish in England is prevented from conducting their own affairs!!

Thursday 9th. June

Eliza and her Mother were yesterday at Provence I was prevented from attending by my Ancle, so that I escaped the Effects of a Thunder shower which wet them through, and diminished the pleasure of the Party.

Friday 10th. June

Yesterday was the Receiving day for the Taxes at Beverley, I was not there I sent my Money with Mr. Beaumont of Brantingham. I have not seen him since.

Saturday 11th. June

I was at the West end this morning, and at Ellerker in the afternoon, but home about four O'clock in time for tea, then spent the remainder of the Evening at the Old place viz. Mr. Atkinson's.

Sunday 12th. June

There was an Advertisement yesterday in the Packet for letting Cave Castle, so that it seems Mr. Barnard is not for staying here. He has taken a House in London in Queen Anne's Street Cavendish Square.

Monday 13th. June

It is said that Mr. Raikes has withdrawn his Opposition to the Hull and Selby Rail way having compromised with the Railway Company who give him ten thousand pounds to withdraw his opposing them and 3000 pounds for Expences he has incurred in opposing them.[17]

---

[16] See n.17 (1834) on the provisions of the Poor Law Amendment Act. The workhouse was eventually established at Beverley, not South Cave.

[17] The Act for Making a Railway from Kingston-upon-Hull to Selby was passed on 21 June 1836. Robert Raikes (d. 1837), a Hull banker, succeeded in having clauses inserted into it which were designed to minimize disturbance to his family estate at Welton, and in particular to ensure that no railway station would be built there. The figure of £10,000, as the price paid to secure his consent to the

Exit

Tuesday 14th. June

My wife this morning went by the Coach to Hull, on her way to London by the way of Barton: it is a warm day and there is but little difficulty in keeping ones selves warm.

Wednesday 15th. June

This morning I got up at Five O'clock not knowing what time it was; I made a Fire and had my Breakfast at Seven O'clock: I should not have risen so soon if I had known what the time was, however I felt no worse for it: I was at Mr. Atkinson's about an hour, then came home, and went no more out this night.

Thursday 16th. June

It is really very hot weather but I have felt no inconvenience from it. Conder's mother is dead and they are gone to her funeral.

Friday 17th. June

I water the Garden and likewise the Flowers in Pots every day, they are not at all neglected, they look very fine most or all of them, the Geraniums are very fine: heard my wife arrived safe at London on Wednesday about 2 O'clock, very glad she is well.

Saturday 18th June

It began to Rain last night about eight O'clock and I think rained most of the night, indeed the land has got very well watered; it will spare me some water fetching.

Sunday 19th June

It rained uncommon fast this forenoon, and I was not in a situation to go out with my old Slipper without being wet at the first step, I even stopped at home, and did not go out at all except to Eliza's to Dinner at Noon, when the Rain had abated a good deal, but it still kept wet so I staid in the house all the afternoon.

Monday 20th. June

The assistant Poor Law Commissioner has sent notices to twenty Townships or Parishes or more for the Overseers to meet him on Monday next the 27th. June at the School Room, to consult with him, on the Union of Parishes. I think Dis-union would be as proper a name.

Tuesday 21st. June

This has been the Visitation here, our old Friend was there as one of the Churchwardens, I went to his house at night after he had got home, I thought he had got too much Wine, as he was gasping & gaping very much.

Wednesday 22d. June

I did not go out at all today but staid a home like an excellent Housekeeper, I had Ann & Thos. at tea with me yesterday having found some Spice bread so I told them both to stay and help me to eat, it was very good.

Act. is also cited in the standard published work on Hull railways (Macturk), although no mention is made in it of an additional sum for expenses (Macturk 36–48).

Thursday 23d. June

Got a new Rope for the Bell and had it fixed up this evening, I secured all the old Rope which is a Prize but little worth ...

Saturday 25th. June

I kept house very close today, after the Rain last night it is quite dry today, and again dusty, Mr. Hood has opened the Shop where Collinson lately lived with an Assortment of various Articles, Ann finds out that he has Confectionary Goods.

Sunday 26th. June

I was at the Church twice to day as usual, I dined at Eliza's, but I cannot but say I like to be at home full as well; she is very attentive to any thing she thinks I may want.

Monday 27th. June

A meeting in the School this Evening of several Overseers to meet the Assistant Poor Law Commr. when it was settled that a Union of several Parishes is to take place and most probably a Workhouse will be provided here for the Union, there did not appear to be the least Opposition; for all were complying and quiescent.

Tuesday 28th. June

I am engaged today taking my Quarterly Stock of Stamps, which I have nearly finished in a satisfactory manner to <u>myself</u> and hope it will meet the approbation of the Stamp distributor.

Wednesday 29th. June

Wrote a letter to the Overseers of South Hiendly a Parish or Township near Barnsley respecting a Man who lives here and is at present very ill and who says his Settlement is at the above place.

Thursday 30th. June

Heard that my wife intends to leave London on Tuesday next by Steam for Hull, I shall be very glad when she arrives. I neither like to go out of the house, nor yet to come in when she is not here.

Friday 1st. July

The weather now is very hot and sultry, I do not stir out much so that I feel as little of it as I can, my longest Journey today has been no further than Mr. Atkinsons in the Evening.

Saturday 2d. July

Went this afternoon to measure some Clover land for Joseph Kirby in the Close below his house, Heard when I came back that a Son of Capn. Waller's, had got drowned when out fishing somewhere not far from River Bridge, the Cpn. is from home in London.

Sunday 3d. July

Tailor Waudby made a pair of Breeches for me which are nearly long enough for Trowsers, I sent them back to be made shorter, but when I sent for them which was not till this morning he sent word that they were only half done, so that I could not put them on very well with a long Step and a short one, so I was obliged to do without them this day.

Monday 4th. July

At the Market today a good deal of drunken fellows, I got tea when I came back, and went no more out this night, but adjourned quietly to bed.

Tuesday 5th. July

This is Beverley Midsummer Fair day, a good many persons have gone, Mr. Bridgman went with Val. Tindale in a light Cart; when going down a Hill the Horse fell down and they both fell from the Cart. Mr. B's hand appears to be rather strained; I saw him after he came back.

Wednesday 6th. July

Barnard Cook this day has Workmen fitting up a tent or Booth in the yard for the Club feast tomorrow.

Thursday 7th. July

Eliza (& Ann) went to meet her Mother this morning by the Coach. I did not go to the Church with the members of the Club*, but attended to call over the names. I went to dine, and came home about Four O'clock, between Six and Seven the Coach arrived with the delighted London visitor, very weary, having been Sick all the way from London to Hull without tasting food of any kind.
*This was the Club feast Day.

Friday 8th. July

My wife has been employed this day in thinning the Garden of Superfluities, it had grown up like a Wilderness in the time she had been away. The Flower plants she brought with her are all in good condition.

Saturday 9th. July

I have a London plaster on my Ancle which I hope will perfectly cure it. It sticks on very closely and I intend letting it stay on as long as it will ...

Monday 11th. July

The Assistant Poor Law Commissioner was this day at the Fox, respecting the Union of Parishes, the Workhouse it is settled is not to be here at So. Cave, but it is thought it will be at No. Cave as more centrical. I am glad it will not be here; though many of our Neighbours, would wish it to be here.

Tuesday 12th. July

Mr. Hotham the Vicar is gone out it is said to London, and is going to stay a month or five weeks away. I had my old Merchant with Paper and Copy Books I laid out with him 9s/8d.

Wednesday 13th. July

There was an old Parson who formerly lived at Brantingham, within living memory, who had an old Lady to his wife, with an old Carriage and two old Horses who never travelled above five Miles an Hour, driven by an old Coachman called Tommy Andrew, (who died at Matthew Kirby's since we came to Cave,) he was footman, Butler &c &c, and used to carry a Pie when hot into the Room by taking hold of it with his Coat Laps. The old Lady had company one day, when she said to her waiter "Thomas there are some Cheese-cakes you may bring them in" To which Thomas answered "I have brought them in Madam" well she says I dont see them. Tommy replied I have them in my Pocket Madam!!!

Thursday 14th. July

All the Plants which my wife brought with her from London, seem to be in a growing State. The Convolvulus has put out two or three flowers: I think the Dahlias will be late; we have been taking up the Tulip Roots which have done flowering ...

Saturday 16th. July

This forenoon I did not go out at all, but in the afternoon I went as far as Miss Cooper's but as usual she was without money, but she has still plenty of Dogs, Birds &c. which takes her money which is wanted for other purposes.

Sunday 17th. July

A very high wind this day, which blows about the dust that makes it very uncomfortable; I had both my Shoes on today for the first time I think for nearly three months, I hope my Ancle is about well, I have the London Plaster on it, which sticks very close and I intend to let it stay on till it will hold on no longer.

Monday 18th. July

At the Market this day as usual; I was no further than Cousens's, I got a Bottle of Ginger Beer as I dare not taste any Liquor, knowing that it would be detrimental to my Ancle.

Tuesday 19th. July

I took to my Slipper again as my Shoe kept my Ancle too tight, it is much easier without my Shoe than with it; I hope and think it is nearly well.

Wednesday 20th. July

Very wet weather which causes Haymaking to proceed very slowly, some has been got pretty well home, but there is yet the greatest part of it out.

Thursday 21st. July

I hear no more of the Poor Law Union nor where the Poor house is to be, but at present it is reported that it is to be at Market Weighton, but neither I nor any Person in the Town know for any certainty where the Union is to be formed. We had rather hear no more about it: as we can with satisfaction to our selves manage our own Parish affairs.

Friday 22d. July

It is said Mr. Barnard is either going to build a Wall or raise a high Paling on the Plantation by the Road side[18] ~~and on the new Road to the Fish Pond end~~ for the Purpose of keeping out of the Park, the Idlers who cut the Trees, with which he is much vexed.

Saturday 23d. July

I was very little out this day. Eliza and her Children are gone to Swinefleet, they went the day before yesterday in a Cart, Conder's Brother came

---

[18] At enclosure, 1785–7, the Barnards' park was enlarged and the 'Fish Pond', an ornamental lake, was created at the same time. The village street was re-aligned so that it ran in a hollow on the far side of the lake. The plantation began at the eastern edge of the lake and encircled much of the park on its northern and eastern sides. Mr. Barnard, an absentee for much of the time, was apparently taking a renewed interest in his property at this period. See also the entries for 26/7/36 and 7/8/36 (Neave and Turnbull (1992) 26–7).

for them. It was a very heavy shower after they went; we do not know whether they got wet or not.

Sunday 24th. July

It was a very rainy forenoon this day, so I did not go out; it was fair weather in the afternoon but very dull without any Sunshine, I went in the afternoon to Church then came home and kept myself quiet at home till bedtime.

Monday 25th. July

I did not see one Sample of Corn shewn today, the Farmers are holding back in expectation of higher prices, and praying (if they ever pray) for bad weather, that their old Stock may be more valuable; they can hardly trust the new Crop to the care of Providence.

Tuesday 26th. July

It is said that Mr. Barnard wants to let, or has let the Manor for Shooting, but not the Castle, as it seems he is not for leaving it yet, he is making some improvements (or alterations) about the Grounds in forming flower Beds, Gravel Walks &c &c.

Wednesday 27th. July

This is the Agricultural meeting day at Beverley[19] when premiums will be given, for different animals to be shewn; much good may the Prizes do those who get them, but as for good to the Country but little can be expected. I think the Country was just as prosperous when Farmers never exhibited their Stock, but When they took their Cattle or Sheep to a Fair for Sale.

Thursday 28th. July

We have had some very heavy Showers lately, which will have laid the Corn, some of which will not get up until it be helped up; fine weather would bring the Harvest on very fast.

Friday 29th. July

Mr. Levitt it is said has sold most of his Land, indeed all but a Close at the Sands, to the Trustees of George Shonswars Son; the Land sold is Hilldales 13 Acres and a half, & Cardales & Pigdam 34 Acres.

Saturday 30th. July

This afternoon I was at Ellerker, but did not stay long, it was a great Shower of Rain while I was there, but being under cover I did not feel any of it; I got home to tea.

Sunday 31st. July

I was out this forenoon at the Church, but in the afternoon I was locked up at home, so that I could not get out into the Street: My wife went out and locked the Door not knowing that I was at home, so that like a Child I was forced to wait till my <u>Mam com yam</u>.

---

[19] The East Riding Agricultural Association held its annual show at Beverley. See n.5 (1834) (*HA* 29 July 1836).

Monday 1st Augt.

I have my Shoe on regularly every Day, so that I think my Ancle is very nearly well only the Shin is tender, and I still keep on the London Plaster.

Tuesday 2d. Aug

This morning I wrote a Letter to my Brother, as it is long since we heard from him, and we wish to know what state he is in, we hope he is tolerably well.

Wednesday 3rd. Augt.

I was invited this afternoon to tea at Wm. Cousens's but I did not go—my wife was there, where there was part Company, visiting is out of my way and drinking rather more so at present.

Thursday 4th. Aug

This is Mr. Barnard's rent day, he did not appear to receive the rents himself—the tenants as usual had a Dinner at the Bay Horse. I do not know at what time they broke up. — Club night nothing particular. I got home soon after nine O'clock, thus ended this day.

Friday 5th. Augt

I sent a list of Voters to John Martin to put upon the Chapel Door on Sunday next; I saw him afterwards when he asked me what the voting respecting Popery meant[.] I told him it had nothing to do with either Pope or Popery, he said he thought it was to vote in respect of Popery, but I told him it was in respect of Property within this Parish, so we made it out between us.

Saturday 6th. Augt.

I was at the West end this afternoon, it is very fine weather. I called at James Levitt's, he has got one of his feet crushed with a piece of Wood, and is so lame that he cannot set his foot down nor bear his Shoe on.

Sunday 7th. Augt

I think I mentioned before that Mr. Barnard was going to build a Wall, (on the new Road) but I understand this is not correct, as it is only to extend from where James Milner lived, to the end of the Plantation, opposite Frog Hall.

Monday 8th. Aug

Very few persons at the Market today, the Weather being fine those who have Hay are throng securing it, this weather is very favourable for bringing on the Harvest, it is expected that the Harvest will be very good.

Tuesday 9th. Aug

I had the Stamp Inspector this forenoon, looking over my Stamps, the Gentleman comes from York he is the Receiver General of taxes, and has had this place put to his other, I suppose that the Receivers General in the several Counties, are thus appointed.

Wednesday 10th. Augt

We had a Couple of Summer Rabbits from Weedley for an Oil Cask, which he (Tindale) got more than three years since, so that we are now even; or at least we shall get no more.

Thursday 11th. Augt

Very fine weather; A man who came from Brantingham this evening, said he had seen Stooks of Wheat both there and at Ellerker; so that the harvest appears to have commenced.

Friday 12th. Aug

My wife and Ann were at Ellerker this Evening and I was left at home to be the Housekeeper; I was very attentive to the charge for I locked the Door and went out, but I got home before they arrived.

Saturday 13th. Aug

I did not stir out this forenoon, but in the Afternoon I went to Ellerker to settle with Mr. Leason I did not stay to tea; but got home before Six O'clock, having settled our business very soon.

Sunday 14th. Augt.

I was at the Church as usual twice today, it was very warm; I have seen no Stooks yet, but Thos. Dyson's were at Harvest work on Saturday, in the Park Close near the Sheep Dike: it is said that Wheat was from 3 to 4 Shillings pr. Quarter lower at Wakefield Friday last.

Monday 15th. Aug

This day we are going to send off a Ham to Wm. so for the present I must close my Diary, and send it with the Ham. —

Tuesday 16th. Aug

This day we packed up a Hamper for London, containing a Ham, a Spice Cake and a few Summer Apples, and an order for two Penknives, for which I sent 2 Shillings, as I was informed that it was very <u>unlucky</u> to receive such things as a present: so to insure <u>good luck</u>, I sent pay for them.

Wednesday 17th. Aug

When Mr. Atkinson was a young man in London, he had a Brother a Joiner who went to the great City to work, and was astonished at the various Cries he heard in the Streets, in coming home from his work one night a Woman was going about selling or crying Pease Soup, she was bawling out Hat, Hat, Hat, (for Hot) the Countryman not knowing well what she said or meant, thought he would be a customer then he should know what she was calling out; accordingly he asked for a Pennyworth, when the woman asked him what he had to put them in; he said he would take them in his hand; so the woman soused a tinful of Hot Soup into his hand, the thin matter ran out between his fingers, but what with blowing and hitching about he retained some of the Pease, and went to his Brother with his fingers scalded to shew him his purchase; for which he was laughed at!!

Thursday 18th. Aug

Very fine harvest weather, many people have begun their Harvest work, and I hope Providence will favour us with fine weather for the ingathering of the Fruits of the earth.

Friday 19th. Aug

I went this night to see Mr. Robinson's Garden, or Mr. Marshall's rather, he has certainly a fine display of Flowers, he will be a candidate for the Prizes at the Shew in Beverley on the 7th 8th Sepr. next, the flower shew.[20]

Saturday 20th. Aug

We had a Letter this morning from my Brother he is free from pain, this is about all I can understand in it; I think he has a very deficient memory, as the letter is written just in the same unconnected manner as he has written before.

Sunday 21st. Aug

At the Church this morning Mr. Rodmell read the Prayers if reading it could be called; had I boy that read so ill I certainly should flog him; it was to me very disgusting to hear and see so much affectation and Pride, in the place where there ought to be humility and plainness. Heard from Wm. on Friday that they were well.

Monday 22d. Aug

The Harvest has generally commenced, as usual it is said that the Wheat ails something, it is this year said there is a great deal of Smut in it / here called Fuss-balls; there has been an unusual quantity of poppies amongst the Corn, here popularly called Headwarks.

Tuesday 23d. Aug

I have very little to do at present for most of the Scholars are out in the Fields either at one thing or another, or some of them perhaps doing nothing. — Mr. Bridgman is gone to York this day with Mr. Robinson, but on what business I am not informed.

Wednesday 24th. Augt

Hudson at the Fox has got his Sign Post taken down and the Sign put out against the House side, which is I think rather disadvantageous to the House, as any Person coming into the town, cannot discover that [it] is a Public house.

Thursday 25th. Aug

The first load of Wheat this year that I have seen was today; Ths. Wride, and Giles Bridgman, have both been leading, and have got up two or three Stacks, it has been a fine working day, not hot but dry weather and a brisk wind.

Friday 26th. Aug

Several Persons at Beverley are canvassing for the Office of Clerk to the Poor Law Union there, amongst the rest is a Clerk of Mr. Smelt's at the Tax office.

Saturday 27th. Aug

Rd. Marshall has got three or four Irishmen to shear this Harvest;[21] I met with them today they not being at work as it is a wet day; I asked them from

---

[20] The flower show was held under the auspices of the Beverley and East Riding Floral and Horticultural Society in the old Assembly Room and an adjoining marquee on 7 Sept. It was a major event in Beverley's calendar of social events, and included impressive floral displays, speeches, a range of classes for competing gardeners, and prizes for the winners in all classes (*HP* 9 Sept. 1836, 2).

[21] See n.33 (1831).

what part they came they said from the North of Ireland, what do you know Newry? (I asked) No master we come from the County of Mayo; I replied that is from the west, aye sure and so you are right for we come not far from Westport, — I then turned and left them after saying Success to you—One of them said God bless you master for that then, — and long life to you.

Sunday 28th. Aug

Mr. Hotham has not yet got home, and the Old Gentleman from Ferriby; preached as usual, a tolerable fine day: twice at the Church.

Monday 29th. Aug

Brewster Sessions this day at Beverley, the Constable and all the Landlords there to procure Licences a very thin Market; not a brisk harvest day.

Tuesday 30th. Aug

I dare say the Landlords who were at the Brewster Sessions yesterday, had applied their time so well, that some of them at least were top heavy, Obed the Constable and Hudson of the Fox, were so far taken with drought after having had Wine and Liquor at Beverley, pulled up at Walkington and partook of two Bowls of Punch, to steady them on their way home!!

Wednesday 31st. Aug.

Capt. Waller sent for me last night when I was nearly fit for Bed; I do not like messages of this sort either from Capts. or their superiors; he wanted a Game certificate which he could just as well have had in the morning, and I was to send him a Receipt Stamp after I got home but I told him I had no one to send it with, so he said he would send his Groom for it; which he did not that night; this morning I carried it.

Thursday 1st. Sepr.

Only three Persons in So. Cave have taken out Game certificates viz. Mr. Barnard's Gamekeeper Capn. Walker and Geo. Scholfield, I think no more will be wanted here this year.

Friday 2d. Sep

Mr. Bridgman has been at York for the purpose of getting some new teeth put in his mouth, I have not yet spoken [to] him since the operation; but he is almost the last person I should have thought of being supplied with artificial teeth.[22]

Saturday 3d Sepr.

Last night we recd. a parcel from Wm., the Carriage only charged 2d.—as to the Registration and Registrars the Medical Gentlemen have the first offer,

---

[22] Various types of artificial teeth were available at this time. Probably the most popular were those fashioned of ivory and held in place by coiled springs. More durable but less natural in appearance were the so-called 'mineral' or porcelain teeth, originally pioneered in the late 18th c. by French dentists, but still being 'plentifully manufactured' in England. Also in demand because of their natural-looking appearance and durability were the so-called 'Waterloo teeth', made from re-used human teeth set in an ivory base. Dentists generally had a low reputation in the 19th c., as many of them were without skills or specialized training, which may perhaps account for RS's seemingly critical attitude to the 'operation' (Woodforde 46–68).

and most likely they will accept of it, for my part I think it would not at present suit me.

Sunday 4th. Sepr

Mr. Hotham has got back, and this day read prayers at the Church, but Mr. Fisher from Ferriby preached or rather read over something meant for a Sermon.

Sep 5th. Monday

At the Market today I got a glass of Cyder, the first I ever had, it was very pleasant, I have when I get any thing to drink lately, had Ginger Beer, but it appears the Season is nearly over for that beverage.

Tuesday 6th. Sepr

My Wife is at Hull today, she went with the Carrier it is rather an unfavourable day, being at times rainy. I am not very partial to being left as the Housekeeper.

Wednesday 7th. Sepr

Dull weather again for the Harvest which prevents the Farmers leading home their Corn, but they still continue mowing, and are in hopes of finer weather.

Thursday 8th. Sepr

Yesterday was the Flower Shew at Beverley. Mr. Marshall got the first Prize for a Dahlia, and ten other Prizes for various Articles. Mr. Champney of Ellerker got the second prize for a Basket of cut Flowers: Mr. Marshall having got the first.

Friday 9th. Sepr.

I have read over most of the Edinburgh Review, the Article I most approve is Capn. Back's Northern Discovery,[23] it seems that there is not much likelihood of any thing satisfactory being made out as the Eternal Bars of Ice stop all progress.

Saturday 10th Sepr.

I was out this afternoon at the west end, when it came on a heavy Shower of Hail and Rain, accompanied with some claps of Thunder; I took Shelter in the House near the Pinfold as I had been in the New Field Lane.

Sunday 11th. Sepr

A Stormy Forenoon, but I ventured out as I had some Papers to put up on the Church Door, or else I think I should have staid at home; however I did not get wet.

Monday 12th. Sepr.

Several Petty Creatures who would wish to put off themselves as Gamblers have had a Lottery something about the Horses that are to run for the <u>Saints</u> stakes at Doncaster have put in half a Crown each; and been drawing the names

---

[23] Captain George Back (1796–1878), later promoted to Admiral and knighted, was a notable Arctic explorer, who had served with Franklin on his expeditions to Spitzbergen and the Mackenzie River. Between the years 1833 and 1837, he led a series of expeditions to map and explore the rivers and coastline of the Canadian Arctic (*DNB*).

of the Horses; there were about 75 Tickets. 73 of which were blanks. I know no more about it; but this I think is no credit to our neighbourhood to find so many fools as about 35 for some of them were so infatuated that they had three or four tickets!!

Tuesday 13th. Sepr.

Jos. Coltman (the Revd)[24] has sent out Papers containing an Account that the Babel of the Conservatives has fallen and it is said has killed one Workman[25]—but the Revd. assures the Con. Gulls that all will be secure against tomorrow his Reverence likewise gives notice of a Ball on Thursday.*

[In margin:] * will his vicarship dance?

Wednesday 14th. Sepr.

This is the day for the Conservatives' Dinner at Beverley, many are gone to be enlightened in the Tory mysteries of Church and State; but who from here I hardly know, except Teavil Leeson: who says he is both a Conservative and Reformer!! he would gladly have Tithe abolished as he is a tithe payer.

Thursday 15th. Sepr.

Mr. Levitt of Ellerker was yesterday one of the individuals wearing Tory colours; and hearing speeches that perhaps would have been as well not spoken. I asked him who made the best Speech, but out of so many good ones he could not say who made the best harangue, but he told me there was an honest Captain of a Ship, who sat besides him that pointed out the decidedly best speech that was made. A man with a Trumpet stood behind the Chairman to announce the Toasts: after blowing a blast, he shouted out Gen-tale-men — Chaarge your Glasses: the Sailor said well done my Lad that is the best Speech I have heard today: I would sit here and attend to what thou sayst until to morn at this time if thou makest Speeches as good as this!!

Friday 16th. Sepr.

I was this afternoon measuring Mr. Levitt's Crop at Cardales which he has sold, consisting of Oats, Beans and Line,[26] about 11 Acres, only a dull day but not much Rain.

Saturday 17th. Sep

I was measuring off some harvest work this afternoon at Drewton, it came on a heavy shower, and I and the man that was with me got under a Stook for

[24] The Revd Joseph Coltman held the living of Beverley Minster from 1813 to 1837, and despite his immense corpulence (he weighed 37 stones), managed to lead an active and productive life. His bulk was so great, that he was unable to climb the steps leading to his pulpit, and thus, every Sunday in order to deliver his weekly sermon, he had to be vigorously propelled up a ramp, while sitting astride a dandy horse, by 3 of his vergers. He met an untimely end, when he accidentally rolled over in bed and, being unable to rise of his own accord, suffocated before his menservants were able to roll him back again (Markham (1992) 35–7).

[25] The accident occurred on 9 Sept. 1836, when the roof of the old Assembly Room in Beverley, in which the Conservatives were to hold their dinner on 14 Sept., collapsed. The young workman, who was killed in the fall, was named Burton Monckman. Several other people were injured, and had to be extricated from the debris (*HA* 16 Sept. 1836).

[26] i.e. flax (*OED*).

Shelter and kept pretty dry, then proceeded to work up hill and down there was about 9 Acres of Barley and 4 of Wheat, but not all in one Close.

Sunday 18th. Sepr.

A fresh Clerk at the Church today, Jn. Reynolds fell down from a load of Straw on Thursday and has broken his Collar bone, so Frankish Cross officiated for him today.

Monday 19th. Sep

A Cold day; it being Driffield fair day took some of our ordinary Market attendants from us, but some of them contrived to get home before Six O'clock; Watson Arton had bought some Sheep &c.

Tuesday 20th. Sepr.

Mrs. Cousens & her Daughter in Law in Company with John Hall have this morning set off on a Journey to London; I have given her Wm's address.

Wednesday 21st. Sep

Mr. Bridgman has this day been at Beverley fortnight market, I sent some Papers with him. He has bought 36 Sheep.

Thursday 22d Sepr

This Evening a Vestry meeting was held (or rather called) by the Churchwardens to lay before the Landowners the Notices they had received respecting the Commutation of tithe,[27] but as there was no attendants nothing was done.

Friday 23d Sepr.

I was getting tea at Eliza's this afternoon, as it was Thomas' Birth day he is four year's old, he is a strong lad and a tolerable dunce.

Saturday 24th. Sepr

I was at Beverley today swearing to the Jury list, it was the Overseers' duty, but as they could not attend I went instead of them, I had a Horse, I did not stay to dine, but came home as soon as I had done. The Parish officers there had to wait two hours before the <u>unpaid</u> were ready.

Sunday 25th. Sep

I do not feel at all put out with my Journey yesterday—there was very little talk at Beverley where I was, of any thing but the Doncaster Races and this was kept up I dare say in an animating way by the Speakers, but very disgusting to me.

Monday 26th. Sepr

Weighton Fair this day which causes a very thin attendance at the Market; Mr. Leason and myself constituted the whole of the Company for a good while at Cousens's, but towards night some few more came in.

Tuesday 27th. Sepr

I never saw such innumerable Companies of small Flies as now fly about, they are very annoying, flying into people's Eyes, at biting them.

---

[27] The Act for the Commutation of Tithes in England and Wales (6 & 7 Will. IV, c. 71) had been passed in the previous month, on 13 Aug.

Wednesday 28th. Sepr

Strings of Horses are daily coming through here to Howden Shews, which are this week; it is a very large meeting for the Sale and buying of Horses.

Thursday 29th. Sep

Conder's Sponge [?] arrived this Evening by Miles' Coach, it is very fine and much liked; I think myself it is a very dear Article.

Friday 30th. Sep

We had intended to have sent a Goose to Wm. shortly but he wrote that he thought it would be better not to send it till the weather was colder, it is postponed at present.

Saturday 1 Octr.

A very rainy day, I have been engaged in making out the Quarterly Stamp account, so that the weather did not incommode me much; at night the weather was rather brighter.

Sunday 2nd Octr

Still rainy and very windy; I had my Umbrella up as I went to the Church and likewise when I came back again, I did not suffer by the wet.

Monday 3d. Octr

This is Howden Fair day; these Monday fairs cause our Market to be nearly forsaken; — Mrs. Cousens has arrived from London, she had seen our Wm. she says she never saw him look better, we are glad to hear of his being well.

Tuesday 3d Octr.

Mostly Frost at night with white Rime, but the days are pretty fine, and the Autumnal Flowers have not yet parted with all their beauty; China Asters look yet very fine. Sun Flowers are getting full ripe in their Seeds.

Wednesday 5th. Octr.

This Evening I went to measure a small Close for Thomas Fisher, a little further than the Sand holes; it being very fine Ann went with me as it was a Grass Close and very clean, and she had not before been with me when measuring.

Thursday 6th. Oct

This morning I went to Ellerker, to meet a Surveyor who had promised to be there this morning at nine O'clock to measure the Land which Mr. Levitt has sold, but as he had not arrived by half past ten, I came home again, till a future opportunity offers ...

Saturday 8th. Octr.

I had two Jobs measuring today one at the Common and Sands, and the other at Drewton, but as it was so very rainy I was prevented from attending at either Place; we cannot contend against the weather, so the best way is to submit patiently; at least I think so ...

Monday 10th. Octr

Went to Ellerker this morning and from thence to the Cardales and Pigdam in company with Mr. Wilkinson (who is now a professed Land

Surveyor,[28] he was formerly a Schoolmaster at Hull) from thence we went to the Hilldales Close and it was very dark when we got done, then we went to Mr. Levitt's where a Beef Stake was prepared for us. I then came home about eight O'clock, it was very dark and stormy.

Tuesday 11th. Octr

This is the Hull fair day and a wet morning it is, yet it does not prevent much Company from going. Miles has two Coaches both well loaded with passengers, who I think would have a very uncomfortable Journey.

Wednesday 12th. Oct

A fine morning the Hull fair mania is still raging the Coach was again crowded with Company, for the little Fair day, it is certainly a great deal pleasanter than it was yesterday.

Thursday 13th. Octr

A tremendous stormy night it blew dreadfully, it has almost finished the late sprung flowers having blown them about so much as nearly to destroy them.

Friday 14th. Octr.

A Parish meeting this Evening at Wm. Cousens's to balance the Poor accounts from Lady day last to this time, which was very shortly accomplished: after some more talking the Company separated.

Saturday 15th. Oct

Yesterday at Noon I went to measure some harvesting at Drewton it was very fine and sunshining, I soon got it done and got home before three O'clock, there was about 11 Acres of it ...

Monday 17th. Oct

Not being satisfied with the measuring last Monday I went again today and measured part of it over again so that I shall rely and stand to my own work, I went in the afternoon and got home about seven O'clock.

Tuesday 18th. Oct

Mr. Levitt has gone to Hull with my measurement this day, what Mr. Wilkinson's is I do not know, but think it will not agree with mine: if so, an Umpire must decide the matter.

Wednesday 19th. Oct.

This day the Overseer is gone to Beverley to meet the Revising Barristers, who have to examine the List of Voters: Robt. Marshall is gone to answer what questions may be put to him—if he can ...

Friday 21st. Oct

The weather now is very fine indeed it is like Summer and has been for a few days past; it is very favourable for Wheat sowing, and the Land I dare say is in good condition for the work.

---

[28] The first professional association of surveyors, the Land Surveyors' Club, was formed in London in 1834. Its members aimed to 'advance the dignity and status of their profession' (Thompson 94–5). It does seem, however, unlikely that the Club had reached East Yorkshire by 1836, and RS probably meant only that Mr Wilkinson had served an apprenticeship with an experienced surveyor.

Saturday 22d. Oct

This day I went to Ellerker in the afternoon but did not make any stay; I was not very well pleased with my Reception so I even turned Round and came back, there is so much self interest in the world that some people will suffer no wrong and neither will they do right.

Sunday 23 Oct.

Robt. Marshall was much gratified when taking in the List of Voters before Barrister; when it was opened out and laid before him he said this is the best List and made out in the most correct manner of any one I have this day seen; were they all like it my trouble would be reduced to a very little.

Monday 24th. Oct

This is what is called the Back-end fair day, here, there was a good shew of Cattle; we had Js. Ramsdale and his two Sons at Dinner: John staid tea at Eliza's, what time he went away I don't know, — but Robt. and his Father went away about three O'clock—in the afternoon.

Tuesday 25th. Oct

Several persons say that there were more Cattle at the Fair yesterday, than what were shewn as the same day last year, I think there was not much difference, as far as I saw for myself; but the Opinions of many often put individual knowledge.

Wednesday 26th. Oct

I think I have very little to notice this day in passing events and as to begin to prophesy, I will not so far disgrace myself; notwithstanding the multitude that pretend to foretell the weather: when to their discomfiture the very reverse happens to what they prophesied; yet they are so given up to the Spirit of lying, that they still keep prating on; and happy are they if they sometimes hit on, Then it is "you know I said it would rain" &c.

Thursday 27th. Octr.

This is the Court day held at the usual place viz. at the Sign of the Bay horse at the Church Hill. I have seen no stirrings about it; there is a Dinner at which the Jury attends; as eating generally is resorted to, when any meeting of a public nature is in hand.

Friday 28th. Octr

This is also the Court day, the Steward came in to the Cross about one O'clock to call over the names of those who owe Suit and Service; and those who do not attend are threatened with Amercement except some friend will pay a Penny for their non appearance.

Saturday 29th. Oct

A Stormy night last night, a great deal of Snow has fallen last night or this morning, and looks very wintry like. I never knew so much Snow at this time of the year, it is a hard frost.

Sunday 30th. Octr

There was a begging Sermon (it is said) preached at the Church this forenoon; I was there but did not hear it as it was delivered in a sort of whisper;

NOVEMBER 1836

the Poor Parson had no voice or no exertion; he was a Stranger, and comes from Cottingwith where John Turk lives ...

Tuesday 1st. Novr

I have been reading the life of Colonel Hutchinson,[29] it is a Book of which I am partial; he was one of the Judges of King Charles the first—His life is written by his Widow Lucy.

Wednesday 2nd. Novr.

A Packet this day from the Poor Law Commissioners, commanding the Rate payers of this Parish to elect a Guardian, to the Beverley Union, which consists of 36 Parishes or Townships, the day of Election is fixed by them (the Comms.) for the 15th. Novr.

Thursday 3d Nov.

Another packet of Explanations and Instructions from the Poor Law Commrs. which only makes confusion worse confused; however dark it is we shall grope our way out in some manner.

Friday 4th. Novr

Last night was the Club night when one new member was admitted: and a new Treasurer chosen; as John Murgatroyd has given up, & Geo. Petfield is chosen in his place.

Saturday 5th. Novr

I was at the West end this afternoon placing a Notice on the Church door, according to the orders of the Lords in the ascendant viz. the Poor Law Comms. — Preparations making for a Bonfire according to Custom.

Sunday 6th. Novr.

I think none of the Publicans had a Supper last night or as it is called a Hare feast, except Barnard Cook, who had the Ringers; all was very quiet, and I did not know any thing of it till this day when I heard one of the Ringers lost the use of his Legs and was carried home and thrust up Stairs in the best manner he could be bundled up. It was Frankish Cross.

Monday 7th. Novr

A very cold day it having been a frost last night, although it has been a fine Sunshine at times. Mr. Hotham did not preach yesterday, he having got cold. Mr. Fisher supplied for him.

Tuesday 8th. Novr.

Thos. Leaper has been nominated to be Guardian for this Parish which is to join the Beverley Union, so that we shall soon have the Machinery in progress.

Wednesday 9th. Novr

Thos. Marshall says he is going to leave his Farm at Lady day next. Jn. Elgey who married his Daughter has taken it as is reported; so that it is a family affair.

---

[29] Lucy Hutchinson, *Memoirs of the Life of Colonel Hutchinson, Governor of Nottingham Castle and Town* ... 4th ed. London: Longman etc., 1822. – 2 vols. First ed. published 1806.

Thursday 10th. Novr.

I had my old Paper merchant last night, I laid out with him 9s/6d for such articles as I wanted. I wonder how he makes a living, I think he could not have had with him more than two pounds worth of Goods; but so it is he continues the trade.

Friday 11th. Nov

Yesterday was the Sittings and it is said there was a good deal of Servants hired. I was at the Constables' meeting as usual, there was a larger Company than formerly as Seven Villages in Hullshire are now joined to the East Riding in our Division of Hunsley Beacon ...

Sunday 13th. Nov.

A wet rainy morning but it rather cleared up and I went to the Church, the text was, "Feed my Lambs["] and the Diet that the preacher prescribed was the Church Catechism or the Catechism of "Our Church" the poor Lambs were so stuffed that they stared and "thought, and knew not what to think".

Monday 14th. Nov

All the Farmers in high Glees at the rise of Price in Corn. I hope they will be deceived in the Price still advancing indeed they seemed more wishful to sell than the Factors to purchase.

Tuesday 15th. Nov

Our old Friend has got some Leather packed in three old London newspapers with which he is much lifted up he has them spread about as though he kept a news Room.

Wednesday 16th. Nov

The first meeting of the Guardians elected for the Beverley Union is this day held at Beverley, when they meet to obey the commands of their Superiors the high & mighty the Commissioners of the Poor Law: I like none of the set.

Thursday 17th. Nov

This is the last Sittings day here, a very dull wet morning, and very little Company in the Town, for which I am not sorry; it turned out very fine in the afternoon, and at night there was dancing & rattling at the Bear ...

Saturday 19 Novr

Obed Martin surprised us one night in saying that "Mr Lord John Russell" was going to have a Roaring Police in every Parish; I suppose he meant Rural; and Obed being Constable he says Mr Lord John might as well be quiet; for he himself has not half the employment he might have, if all was not so quiet!!

Sunday 20th. Nov

A tolerable fine day. I went out without my Umbrella, and did not want it; I bought an Almanack one day for a Penny; and am informed that it tells about the weather as well as Francis Moore, Physician; I am inclined to think it does so quite as well.

Monday 21st. Nov

This day the Factors and Farmers are on a very flat Key this day on account of the bad market at Wakefield on Friday last, I saw nothing done in the Corn line; it requires something to keep Corn from the Market, which some Farmers have not, viz. money.

Tuesday 22d. Nov

I think the War in Spain for the Queen[30] is like the improvement which the Captain of an Irish Regiment discovered amongst his men: for he said they improved in growing worse.

Wednesday 23d. Nov

This is Martinmas day when the Servants here are their own masters and Mistresses for at least one week, which is quite long enough for some of them to quit all the[y] have been working for the whole year.

Thursday 24th. Nov

We had some information from our old Friend this night respecting <u>Algerine</u> Percy,[31] who was in the American War, and got home again, which is more than many could do.

Friday 25th. Nov

The Spanish Warriors seem to be afraid of hurting each other, they seem to do little more than play at Leap Frog; jumping over each others Back, and away as fast as they can ...

Sunday 27th. Nov

This forenoon at the Church there was a begging Sermon, for the Building, repairing &c of Churches, there was a Collection after the preachment, I think there was very little given, however I gave nothing so the Beggars were no better for me. Let the Church maintain the Church.

Monday 28th. Nov

This is what is called Martinmas Monday, there are a great many Stalls with various Articles for sale, but the day is not very favourable either for Shew or Business. Upon the whole the attendance was very small.

Tuesday 29th. Nov

A very wet morning, still there are a good many going to Hull with the Coach, to the Market at Hull, as the poor Silly Lads and Lasses cannot settle so long as the[y] have any money left.

Wednesday 30th. Nov

This is the last day of this gloomy month, it has indeed been a very stormy time, abundance of wind and rain the land has not been so wet for some years; in some places it is so Soft that the wheat cannot yet be sown.

---

[30] The Carlist war in Spain was a long-running series of guerrilla-style operations between the anti-government Carlists (and their clerical allies) and the Liberal supporters of Queen Isabella II and her mother, the regent, Maria Christina, who were known as Cristinos. Great Britain and France gave some help to the young queen, but hostilities continued until Aug. 1839, when the Carlists made a reluctant peace at the convention of Vergara (Carr 184–92).

[31] Probably Lord Algernon Percy (1750–1830), the second son of Hugh Percy, First Duke of Northumberland. Unlike his elder brother, who was a Whig, Lord Algernon was a Tory and supported Pitt. He was created Earl of Beverley in 1800 (Brenan ii. 463).

Thursday 1st. Decr.

Mr. Barnard's Sale is to take place next Thursday, several Pictures and Articles of Furniture are for sale, the Catalogue contains nearly 300 Lots, and the sale to continue two days I expect I shall be there as writer.

Friday 2d. Decr

Last night was the Club night there was nothing very particular stirring, I got home a little after nine O'clock, all well Sat a while then took my departure up stairs to bed.

Saturday 3d. Decr

This forenoon measured a Turnip Close at Ellerker, it was very dirty, I fell amongst the dirt but was no worse I got home before noon, and like the last Saturday, went to the west end and got wet.

Sunday 4th. Dec

A Sermon at the Church more to the purpose than I have lately heard, the Parson begged his hearers to pay their taxes without grumbling at the time they are due.

Monday 5th. Decr

This day I was collecting the half year's Assd. taxes and Land tax due Michaelmas last; I was tolerable fortunate having got settled with a good many of my Customers.

Tuesday 6th. Decr

[This entry and the rest of the sheet and next sheet are blank. There is a gap until 10th December, 1836].

Saturday 10th. Decr

I think I am in arrears with my Journal a day or two, having been engaged at Mr. Barnard's Sale the last two days; I was not very fond of my employment, for sometimes I could scarcely get the names of the Purchasers, and at others hardly the prices however I got through. The amount of the two days Sale was £586–15–7d. ...

Monday 12th. Decr

I did not see any business done in the Corn line today—at night the Ranters had a Missionary meeting at the west end Chapel (which they borrowed)[32] there was I understand a large Congregation and a tolerable Collection. We neither of us were there.

Tuesday 13th. Decr

I think I got cold last week at the Sale, as my head is rather affected, and my nose is sore, I have not much Cough but I am not very right, This night I attended as usual at Mr. Atkinson's, having been absent two or three nights, indeed I never attend on Sundays and Mondays.

---

[32] This was the Independent (Congregational) Chapel which had been built in *c.*1718 and remained in use until it was replaced in 1873. The Primitive Methodists were to have their own chapel in South Cave just one year later, in 1837, when one was built behind 2 cottages in Church Street. It too was replaced, later in the century, in 1877 (Trout 4, 16; Neave (1984) 50).

Wednesday 14th. Decr

Beverley fortnight Market today Obed (who generally attends with us at our old friend's) was there (at the Market) with eight Sheep for Sale, which he sold: but he would not say what he got for them, he sold them in three lots.

Thursday 15th. Decr

This Evening at West end, I gave Rd. Marshall (the Steward) an Account of the Sale, and I likewise wanted an account of 2 Horses charged by the Surveyor of taxes on Mr. Barnard, they are Horses which Mr. Barnard borrowed in London for a year, which makes him liable to the Duty ...

Saturday 17th. Decr

This morning I went to measure some Land at Riplingham Grange on the Farm, which Capn. Shaw has bought; about 30 Acres which he is going to plant, it adjoins Weedley Warren, and in the valley, Hunsley, it is the same Valley in which are Weedley Springs, which expand into the Drewton Beck. — I got home between three and four O'clock in the afternoon. I had Adam with me to trail the Chain.

Sunday 18th. Decr.

We had two Sermons at the Church this day, exhorting the hearers to be very zealous for the Prayer Book, which it was contended contained the Doctrine once delivered to the Saints; the Scripture seem only to be secondary to the Old Mass Book.

Monday 19th. Decr

I think there is very little doing in the Market now, the Farmers are not willing to sell, nor the Factors free to purchase at present, I hope the Prices will not get higher; I shall be more pleased if they lower.

Tuesday 20th. Dec

Ann and her Grandmother went this afternoon to Ellerker to Mrs. Rudd's it was a very sweet day, they got home about eight O'clock, it being very Moon light ...

Thursday 22d Decr

Rd. Marshall was at Hull on Tuesday, he had my account of the first day's sale at the Castle, which the Auctioneer's Clerk examined, and for which I got much credit for the exact manner in which it was made out; he said it agreed with his account exactly, but if it did it was more correct than when it was here as I know there was 5s. diffrence [*sic*]. On the whole sale he says there is £1–11–6 difference, but I know the difference is but 12s/9d.

Friday 23rd. Decr

A cold blustery day looking much like a Storm, we have this day left off for Christmas: In former years I used to go the Hull at this Season; but that time is past.

Saturday 24th. Decr

Last night was stormy with a great fall of Snow, and very cold and piercing; I was no further out than Mr. Atkinson's went home at night and had Furmenty and Apple pie and Cheese to supper, we had a Youle Clog on the Fire according to Annual Custom here.

Sunday 25th. Decr

This is Christmas day and a very Stormy day it is; In coming from the Church it was almost past getting on; for the Wind was high and the Snow deep and snowing fast; however I went again in the afternoon.

Monday 26th. Decr

Still Stormy and Snowing and blowing boisterously, more people at the Market than I expected to see; indeed the weather must be very bad if the Broomfleeters stay at home; no Coaches nor post today so that we are entirely without any knowledge of what is passing in the Country.

Tuesday 27th Decr

The weather a little more moderate today but the Roads are quite impassable. Labourers are employed in cutting Snow on the Highways, all men in the Town are at Work: I have orders to pay them at night for their work.

Wednesday 28th Decr

The Post came in today but brought no London Papers nor Letters as the Mail had not arrived at York: the Mail cannot travel between Hull and York on Account of the Snow.

Thursday 29th Decr

The Snow cutters still at Work and not likely yet to have done as the drifts are both deep and high, and what roads were at first cut have been again filled up by the Wind drifting the Snow into them, it is indeed a còld white time.

Friday 30th. Dec

We have had the Papers this week very irregular, only two Papers since Sunday, but I hope the weather seems rather more settled, and the wind not so high, it appears to be settling into a regular Frost.

Saturday 31st. Decr

A very cold day, no Hull papers this day so that it appears there is yet some impediment in the way; indeed I hardly know how the world is wagging for the Papers this week have come very irregularly.

1837

Sunday 1st Jan

Last night I had to go round the Town to invite the Members of the Club to attend, at the Club room on Monday at One O'clock to accompany the Body of James Drury to the Church; he died yesterday morning. I got about 4s/6d for my trouble; at 1d each member.

Monday 2d. Jan

The Members attended according to invitation, except ten who were fined Sixpence each, I called over the names, but did not go to the funeral.

Tuesday 3d. Jany

Two men who think they have good Horses made a Match to ride to Hull, to set off this morning from the Beck Bridge when the Bell rung, I never looked out to see them, but I understand only one of them was ready at the time, but the other set off when the other had at least got a mile before him.

Wednesday 4th. Jan

The Relieving Officer from the Beverley Union was here paying the Poor yesterday morning,[1] some were satisfied who got the same pay as before, and others were not at all pleased who got nothing.

Thursday 5th. Jan.

A rather softer day than it has been, but one can scarcely tell whether it be a frost or a thaw, some say it is not a hard frost; but I never knew a soft one! — This is Mr. Barnard's tithe rent day.

Friday 6th. Jan

Robt. Marshall has paid the Money he had Of us, for which we are not at all sorry; Although we have had a Note for it, yet Promissory Notes are poor Security where there is no property.

Saturday 7th. Jan

Eliza's have been killing their Pig today, it weighed 20st.–9lb and a piece of good furniture it will be when they get it hung up in the house far more useful than Ornaments.

> "In some Irish houses, where things are so so,
> "One Gammon of Bacon hangs up for a show
> "But, for eating of what they take pride in,
> "They'd as soon think of eating the pan it is fried in".[2]

[1] According to the provisions of the Poor Law Amendment Act of 14 August 1834 (4 & 5 Will. IV c. 76), the Poor Law Commissioners were empowered to appoint their own officers (section 9), and had sole responsibility for the administration of relief through their boards of guardians and executive officers, although it was permissible for parish overseers to administer temporary relief in cases of emergency (section 54).

[2] This is a quotation from Oliver Goldsmith's poem, 'The Haunch of Venison: a Poetical Epistle to Lord Clare'. The 1st line should begin, 'As in some Irish houses' and the 3rd line should read 'But, for eating *a rasher* of what they take pride in' (*EP*).

Sunday 8th. Jan

A very hard frost the last night, and indeed continues the same all this day, it is uncommonly slippery walking but I managed to get twice to the Church and kept the right end uppermost viz. I did not get a fall ...

Tuesday 10th. Jany

I have been busy with making out a Poor's Rate in the new Book which is furnished by the Beverley Union. I do not know whether I understand it or not, indeed I think the inventors of the Form would be at a loss to explain it. I asked no advice but set to work on it in my own way.

Wednesday 11th. Jany

The Relieving Officer for the Beverley Union, comes here to pay the Paupers on Tuesday mornings, I think he does not much like his office, indeed the first who had the Office, resigned after his first Journey: He has to be from home five days in the Week, and on Saturday to attend the Board of Guardians I expect he will give up.

Thursday 12th. Jany

I think it mostly a waste of time to read over the long and often dull repetitions of many public Speeches, there is very seldom any thing new in them; but the Conservatives alias Tories roaring out "Church and State" this is the burden of their blarney. The Liberals shouting out against the "Tricks of Tories["] it is all "Preaving and fending".

Friday 13th. Jan

Obed the Constable has been at a Justice meeting with Ann Savage to Market Weighton for breaking Fenwick's Windows she was drunk and said she paid Mrs. Fenwick a Sovereign instead of a Shilling, which Mrs. Fenwick denied; so she Mrs. Savage broke the Window and pelted in Snow Balls through the breach. She was committed to the House of Correction for a month ...

Monday 16th. Jany

I think there was very little doing at the Market today Corn has been kept back from the Markets on account of the late bad weather, and it is expected when the Rivers are free from ice there will be large supplies which make the Factors keep from purchasing.

Tuesday 17th Jany

Mr. Barnard has sent £20 to be laid out in Coals to be distributed amongst the Poor, which will be found very serviceable to those who are in want of firing but I do not know that every one will be satisfied.

Wednesday 18th. Jany

Mr. Bridgman is not very well, and he thinks himself worse than he is, he is naturally timorous when he is ill; his appetite is not good; I have told him that for being ill he looks no worse than common; then he grasped his waistcoat and said he must have it taken in, but I told him as the Buttons were so tight he would have to have it let out!!

Thursday 19th. Jany

Many people are troubled with colds and coughs, but I think not more than common in such variable weather; for my Part I have suffered nothing in my health this winter, bless God ...

Saturday 21st Jany

Sam. Langricke was buried today, so after all his tricks there is an end of Poor Sam. He was once I understand put in the Spiritual Court for putting a little Stone at the head of a Child's grave the Stone contained only two letters, but he did not ask leave to put it down, and what aggravated the case did not pay for it; how it was settled I cannot tell, but he died a good member of the <u>Church</u>.

Sunday 22nd. Jany

A rainy day however I put on my great Coat and took my Umbrella and went to the Church, and heard what was meant for a Sermon, where the only piece of Scripture it contained was the text!!

Monday 23d. Jany

At the market as usual but soon came away, and went to see Mr. Bridgman, he is no worse, but he has got the Doctor to visit him, and if he escape being ill I shall be rather surprised, for I think he has no more Occasion for the Doctor than I have.

Tuesday 24th. Jany

Our old friend Mr. Atkinson is very poorly, indeed the old Gentleman looks ill, he has a bad Cough and can not rest at nights, this to a good Sleeper as he has been is very trying. He has not yet employed the Doctor.

Wednesday 25th. Jany

My spare time is much taken up at present with visiting my sick friends, Mr. Bridgman thinks himself much worse than I think he is; the weather is so bad that he cannot get out; and being confined at home; is as much suffering to him as imprisonment would be to some Vagabonds.

Thursday 26th. Jany

Mr. Atkinson is yet no better he cannot eat much and his Cough annoys him, he appears to be very weak, and is drowsy; but I think does not sleep much.

Friday 27th Jany.

The weather very unpleasant mostly Rain, Snow and Sleet, which makes it very uncomfortable   stirring about, it has been a very long severe winter already, and appears to be not yet over.

Saturday 28th. Jan

Mr. Atkinson has got the Doctor to him, but what success he will have I cannot anticipate, he is troubled with a little fever, and most likely will be bled; He has had some persons to sit in the house at nights lately.

Sunday 29th. Jany

A very stormy day, I was at Church in the forenoon but did not go in the afternoon, I spent the afternoon at Mr. Bridgman's, as he appears to be very glad of my Company when I came away he says pray you come in at night, so I went after the Methodist Chapel was over, and left him comfortable.

Monday 31st. [i.e. 30th] Jan

Mr. Atkinson has got a bed in the house[3] which I think will be a great deal more convenient than going up stairs every night; but he seems to rebel against it. I have plenty of employment in visiting our sick friends.

Tuesday 1st Feb [i.e. 31st Jan]

February has come in very full of tears and with a good deal of blustering, indeed the weather is very disagreeable.

Wednesday 1st. Feb

I perceive I have missed the 30th. January, but not out of any superstitious regard to the "blessed Martyr". however let that pass.

Thursday 2nd. Feb

This is the Club night and the Month when new Stewards are appointed for the next Months; all went off in very good order.

Friday 3d. Feb

This Evening a meeting to nominate Assessors for the ensuing year when I and my old Partner Thos. Levitt were again chosen to the honourable Office.

Saturday 4th. Feb

This was a very fine day, it seemed to be the approach of Spring; I was measuring some Land today at Weedley Warren nearly fifty Acres, I went in the morning, and got home between 3 and 4 O'clock in the afternoon.

Sunday 5th. Feb

I was at the Church twice today, not very fine weather today, however I managed pretty well, not getting much wet, I spent the evening with Mr. Bridgman, who may (as I dare say he does) think himself obliged to me, as I scarcely ever stir out on a Sunday.

Monday 6th. Feb

I saw no business at all done this day at the Market the Corn buyers seem to be very easy at bidding, and this wet weather makes the Corn in bad condition.

Tuesday 7th. Feb

This is Pancake Tuesday, and we had some to dinner, how it happens that Pancakes are more general on this day than any other, I cannot tell.

Wednesday 8th. Feb

Some people (certainly not sensible people) appear to have a great satisfaction in being killed: for Duellists appear to have a great delight in firing Pistols one at another; I envy them not their satisfaction.

Thursday 9th. Feb

Our two Friends Mr. Atkinson and Mr. Bridgman keep very poorly; indeed Mr. Atkinson is very ill so much so that I think he will scarcely recover, he slumbers and sleeps the whole days and does not talk much; he appears pleased when I go to see him.

---

[3] i.e. in the living room.

Friday 10th. Feb

Mr. Hood who lives in Grayson's Shop has had it shut up some time, whether he will open it any more or not, is more than I can say ...

Sunday 12th. Feb

A very pleasant sunshiny morning, with a cold drying wind it dried so much that the Roads before night became quite clean, I was twice at the Church; and spent the Evening with Mr. Bridgman, I think he has not been so well today as he has been.

Monday 13th. Feb

This Evening I got upon a Chair with a little Stool upon it, to cut down a piece of Bacon; when the Stool slipped and I came down, backwards over the top of the Chair, and fell with my head against the Wall, which hurt me a good deal; but I hope I am not much worse.

Tuesday 14th. Feb

A wet morning, but it cleared up before noon. I have a slight pain in my breast, which I think proceeds from the fall I had last night, but I think it will go off.

Wednesday 15th. Feb

This morning we received the Parcel from Wm. the Letter was very gloomy, we are truly sorry that Mary is so ill, but hope she will get better as fine weather comes. Her mother has had a sorrowful time for 10 Weeks: but we are in great hopes of her speedy recovery. May Providence soon restore her.

[*Thursday 16th Feb.* omitted]

Friday 17th. Feb

This day we sent off a Box to Wm. with a Piece or Pieces of fine thin Bacon, which we hope he will receive safe.

Saturday 18th. Feb

The Overseer is gone today to Beverley to pay the County Rate he called on me for the Money when I gave him twenty one pounds for that purpose.

Sunday 19th. Feb

A very stormy day with abundance of rain, however I went twice to the Church, I got my Umbrella very wet. Our two sick Friends are not yet well; Mr. Atkinson is I think very weak, but Mr. Bridgman is much better.

Monday 20th. Feb

Butter this day at the Market scarce and dear, it is 16d. pr. lb. I saw nothing done in the Corn line. I paid Mr. Leaper £22–4s–0d which he had paid to the Beverley Union[.] Confusion attend them!!

Tuesday 21st. Feb

I think Lord John Russel has not nerve enough for his Situation, he has made a Speech with which Sir Robt. Peel seemed to be gratified; I do not think this will add much to his popularity.[4]

---

[4] The Whig government of Lord Melbourne, led by Lord John Russell in the House of Commons, held power by only a slim majority, and was dependent on the support of the Radicals. The House's attention at this time was focused on legislation to introduce a poor law for

Wednesday 22d. Feb

I do not think that Mr. Atkinson is much better, although he rests pretty well at nights, and eats his meat much better than he did; yet he still keeps very weak, and drowsy.

Thursday 23d. Feb

It keeps very wet weather the ground is soaked with wet it is a long time since we have had such a wet time, but we live in hope that we shall soon have fine weather.

Friday 24th. Feb

I have been viewing the <u>Picture</u> and the Plan of the new Houses of Parliament[5] but I know very little about it, and there is a very meagre explanation attending it.

Saturday 25th. Feb.

Mrs. Tapp was buried this forenoon in the Chapel: my wife was there, having received a Pair of Gloves, as a testimony of old Friendship, but that Cord is for ever severed.

Sunday 26th. Feb

A very fine dry day but cold; I went out today without my Umbrella, and did not need it. Mr. Atkinson I think is not much better, although he was this morning reading in his Bible.

Monday 27th Feb

I saw very little of the Market today, indeed I do not think there was much doing altho' there were three Cornfactors in the town, but I dare say they bought but little.

Tuesday 28th. Feb

This afternoon I measured some turnip Land, adjoining the Beverley Road, on the other side of the steep hill; there was Eight Acres, which I had to set out.

Wednesday 1st. March

Mr. Marshall (the Dandy) is begging about the Town for money to buy a Covering I suppose of Velvet for the Cushion in the Church. I am sure I am not inclined to give any thing for such a purpose.

Thursday 2d. March

This is Mr. Barnard's Rent day, the tenants are going with their money. I think he has as good a set of tenants as any Gentleman could wish for.

Ireland and the reform of Irish municipal government. Lord John Russell had made an important speech on Irish affairs on 14 Feb. 1837, which was severely criticized in a letter to the *Times* written by 'Britannicus' (*TM* 18 Feb. 1837, 2 c). It was probably this letter that occasioned RS's comment.

[5] In 1835, the year after the conflagration of the Palace of Westminster, a competition was held to select a design for a replacement building for both Houses of Parliament. The winner was Charles Barry, who, with the assistance of A. W. N. Pugin, produced a much-praised series of drawings. The foundations of the new building were begun in 1837, and the first stone of the superstructure was laid in 1840. The House of Lords opened in 1847, but the entire building was only finally completed in 1867, at a total cost of almost 3 million pounds (Pevsner (1973) 521–5).

Friday 3d March

Last night was the Club night, when the Box was removed from Barnard Cook's to Jn. Fenwicks for the next Six months, there was nothing particular.

Saturday 4th. March

This afternoon I went to measure some Turnip Land for Thomas Dyson, in the Close just above Beverley Plump, it was not a very pleasant day; There were about Eight Acres and a half.

Sunday 5th. March

A very fine moderate day, it had been a slight frost last night, but it was very clean walking. I saw Billy Bullock; who said they have begun in good <u>Yannest</u> this morning, I asked who, when he said Craiks had begun building, he said they had been contriving a good while but now they were at work.

Monday 6th. March

I saw Mr. Jno. Scholefield of Faxfleet at the Market today, he was telling me he had been at London with Mr. Bowser, and had seen Wm.—he said he was well: this is some time since he was there.

Tuesday 7th. March

The weather still keeps very cold and gloomy with Frost mostly at nights, some people are beginning to Garden but I think they are premature, as the weather is not favorable for any thing growing in the open Ground.

Wednesday 8th. March

Measured some Turnip Land last night for Ths. Fisher the Turnips were eaten by Mr. Bridgman's Sheep the Close is at Ryland hills adjoining the Brough road the part measured was about Six Acres.

Thursday 9th. March

Mr. Atkinson I think continues to get better, but he does not gather much Strength. Mr. Bridgman is about recovered again he rides out daily.

Friday 10th. March

I had my Old Paper Merchant this day, he has been very ill this Winter, and now looks very ill, I laid out Eleven Shillings with him, and away he went with the Money in his Pocket ...

Monday 13th. March

A very cold day which makes one almost shiver with cold, but hope speaks fair for finer weather; I have promised Charles Rudd to measure some Land for him on Saturday next <u>if nothing better hand out</u>; but I expect I shall have another job.

Tuesday 14th. March

I should wish very much that the Petitioners for the continuance of the Church Rates could be so far gratified as to have to pay as usual, in their own particular cases; and as they wish for the impost to continue it will be very hard if they cannot be obliged.

Wednesday 15th. March

Ann her Mother and Grandmother were at Ellerker yesterday afternoon, the[y] drank tea at Mrs. Arton's they got home at Nine O'clock. I set off to meet them, but I got no further than the Town end before I met them.

Thursday 16th. March

Mr. Atkinson is much better today, he almost seems to be well again, he thinks he will be able if he continues improving to get to the Church on Easter Tuesday to give away the Penny Rolls.

Friday 17th. March

We recd. the Parcel from Wm. on Wednesday morning last, we are sorry to hear that the Bacon is not good, I thought when we got it that it was excellent, indeed I got a piece or two broiled and thought it capital, but it seems I was deceived; — The Flower Seeds are very acceptable.

Saturday 18th. March

This morning I went to measure some Land at Brantingham for Mr. Beaumont; it was not a very agreeable day, but full as good as I expected; I dined there after measuring one Close, and measured another after dinner; there were about 33 Acres; I got home about five O'clock.

Sunday 19th. Mar

A very clean dry day but remarkable cold; I went out without my Umbrella, and did not want it. Rd. Marshall was at Hull on Friday last, sending some of Mr. Barnard's best Looking Glasses to London, this does not look like his coming here at present.

Monday 20th. March

A good deal of Snow last night, and this is a stormy snowy day, which caused very few people to be at the Market, I think there was nothing particular going on.

Tuesday 21st. March

Ths. Marshall was at Cousens' one night when a Miller of Newbald said to him how do you go on with grinding now to which the long Miller replied, whya I could eat all the Moulter I get and not have enough, and I think I could eat all that both thee and I get: and thee and I together would eat all the Corn we both get, and we should both be hungered.

Wednesday 22d March

A Snowy morning I had to go to Beverley this day, and rode a Horse of Saml. Shaw's, it was a very cold day, I got home again about five O'clock safe and sound.

Thursday 23d March

I am rather stiff today with my Journey yesterday. The weather keeps very severe. Frost and Snow with Sunshine at intervals to enliven us.

Friday 24th March

Mr. Bridgman is quite recovered and Rides out every day amongst his Flocks & Cattle; Mr. Atkinson is a great deal better indeed he seems to be as well as before, only he is weak.

Saturday 25th. March

This day I was measuring some land at Ellerker, it was mixed with Snow, which was not very pleasant, it was on the whole a dirty job there was about 12 Acres of it[;] it belonged Charles Rudd.

Sunday 26th. March

Easter Sunday very wintry weather, the Church is decked out today with a Velvet (Scarlet) Cushion and Cover &c. to please some who think that Religion consists in a fine Appearance. I am not one of those who so think.

Monday 27th. March

A very cold day and very little Company at the Market it being too stormy for shewing Horses indeed there were very few in the town, so that the day passed quietly.

Tuesday 28th. March

This is the day for choosing Churchwardens, when Richard Marshall was appointed by the Vicar and Jno. Lockwood for the Parish. Easter dinner as usual at Barnard Cook's there were only eight persons there, I was not one.

Wednesday 29th March

This is the day or night on which the Tansy is kept, but it is much fallen into disuse, altho' there were fiddling and dancing and all very lively when I went to bed about ten O'clock, and I suppose long after that time.

Thursday 30th March

A meeting last night to Balance the Highway Accts. and to nominate Overseers of the Poor for the ensuing year; Teavil Leeson & Thomas Levitt were the two first names on the list.

Friday 31st. March

Mr. Atkinson has got that he can nearly do by himself as before his illness, he was at the Easter dinner on Tuesday last; but declined being Churchwarden again.

Saturday 1st. April

I was measuring Wm. Cousens' Turnip Land this forenoon; the first Close adjoining the Swineskaife Road, it was ploughed and very dirty which made it very disagreeable there was about 10 Acres—after that measured a part of Tofts near Bacchus Lane nearly 3 Acres: got done about noon or soon after ...

Monday 3d April

Several Horses shewn today but I never went out to see them, as they are Animals to which I am not partial, there was part Company today.

Tuesday 4th. Apl.

This night after I came in I had a sudden pain came into my back, which pestered me a good deal but I hope it will go off suddenly as it came.

Wednesday 5th Apl

The Pain in my back continued at intervals most of the night which made me uneasy: however I think it is rather better, I have got a Plaster put on it.

Thursday 6th. Apl

The Constable is gone to Beverley with the nomination of Overseers: I have sent with him to Weedley the appointment of Guardian to Robt. Tindale of Weedley.

Friday 7th. Apl

I think there is very little <u>Flitting</u> this Lady day, though I have seen some loads of Furniture pass by, but whose they were or where they came from or where going, this deponent sayeth not.

Saturday 8th. Apl.

This day which was very winterly, I measured the Stone Pit Close opposite Beverley Plump Seven–acres, and after that another small Close on the little Wold containing Six Acres they had both had turnips, belonging Richd. Marshall—who trailed the Chain.

Sunday 9th. Apl.

Mr. Jarratt of North Cave preached at the Church this forenoon he is they say very popular, but it has been long fixed in my mind that a low Speaker cannot be a good preacher. Mr. Jarratt's Journeyman alias his Curate preached in the afternoon, with rather a more elevated voice than his master.

Monday 10th. Apl.

The Overseer has been at Beverley with the Poor Book to the Auditor, who has not passed the Accounts, so that I shall have to go to Beverley on Saturday to <u>explain</u> what is at present <u>plain</u> enough.

Tuesday 11th. Apl

Music meetings Concerts &c And horse Racing & Sporting in the Newspapers are generally passed over by me, those accounts may amuse some people but they have no attraction for me ...

Thursday 13th. Apl.

The Vicar has been round with a Petition to sign for the Continuation of Church Rates or as he termed it to keep things as they are but I refused signing it: Mr. Burland then came but I told him I would sign it no more than I had signed it: but as he is a good Stamp Customer I gave him my name under a protest, that it was with a delusive intent that the Petition was to be presented, so much for (my) Consistency.

Friday 14th. Apl.

Still very bad cold weather with Frost, Snow & Sleet which keeps back all vegetation there is not so much as a blade of Grass yet sprung out.

Saturday 15th. Apl.

I was at Beverley this day to explain (and help) the Auditor to balance the Poor Accounts which we soon settled, I cannot say much in praise of his knowledge of Book-keeping as he had written down "By" on the Dr. Side of the Account, which I told him was not right, as "To" should be on the Dr. Side and "By" on the Cr. I likewise told him whatever was received belonged to the Dr. Side, and whatever was delivered to the Cr. Side, and also that the left hand folio was Dr. and the Right Cr.

Sunday 16th. Apl.

I rode Robt. Marshall's Horse to Beverley yesterday I came home without dining and arrived safe about Five O'clock. I am never disposed for eating when I am out stirring about.

Monday 17th. Apl.

Mr. Leaper one of the Overseers was at Beverley today swearing to the Accounts before the Magistrates, he said I had been greatly praised by the Auditor, so it seems he was grateful for what I had told him on Saturday.

Tuesday 18th. Apl.

Mr. Atkinson has nearly got into his old way of living only he has still his Bed in the House, but he talks of removing it up stairs very shortly, provided the weather becomes a little warmer, it (the bed) lumbers his house very much.

Wednesday 19th. Apl

My wife was at Hull yesterday she went and returned with Cousens the Carrier; it was near ten O'clock at night when she arrived at home laden like a honey Bee.

Thursday 20th. Apl

The Eclipse of the Moon took place tonight but it was thick and Cloudy I did not see it, tho' some people who can see a long way before them avouched that they fairly saw it, which I am certain was not the case.

Friday 21st. Apl

There is a man come into the Town with a travelling Bazaar, which he is setting up for the good of the Public and likewise he hopes for his own private Advantage, I think little of his See-Saws and Tee-taws.

Saturday 22d. Apl.

This afternoon I was measuring a Close at Brantingham it was a finer afternoon than we have had of late, but very dirty: there was nearly 12 Acres Mr. Green is the tenant, it was Turnips the last year.

Sunday 23d Apl

I was not out this Forenoon, it was so very stormy and wet with Snow and Rain. I went to the Church in the afternoon, it was uncommonly dirty on the Road.

Monday 24th. Apl

A very little Company today at the Market, I saw nothing doing in the Corn line: the Farmers are generally busy in getting their Seed Corn into the Ground.

Tuesday 25th. Apl.

Searching the Club Box this evening for an Admission Copy of Copyhold land belonging a Person who has £200 belonging the Society on Mortgage he has now sold the land and wants to give a title to the purchaser, but is prevented at present by not knowing where the Court Roll Copy is.

Wednesday 26th. Apl.

Mr. Bridgman was at Mr. Atkinson's this Evening for the first time since he has been ill, so that we looked something like what we had been. Mr. B's Old Dog was also there stretched on the Hearth.

Thursday 27th. Apl.

The Admission Copy of the Copyhold land for which the Club has a Mortgage has been found, having been in the hands of the Bailiff of the Newbald Court: and not been delivered to the proper party ...

Saturday 29th. Apl.

I went to Brantingham this forenoon to measure some land it was not a very pleasant morning, and before noon it began to rain, we left off for about two hours, and went again about three O'clock, it looked very black, and about Four O'clock the Rain came on very heavy, when we were obliged to give in; I got completely wet through, and when I got home, I had all my Clothes to change ...

Monday 1st. May

The Swallows these welcome Summer Visitors have made their appearance, though not yet in great numbers, there were very few people at the Market today.

Tuesday 2nd. May

I have been making out the Land tax Bills for So Cave, Ellerker, and Broomfleet, and have finished them so that they are nearly ready to be put on the Church Door on Sunday next.

Wednesday 3d May

Obed Martin has bought Fifty Sheep of Richd. Marshall and is going to take them to Pocklington Fair on Saturday next, with the hope of making a profit of them.

Thursday 4th. May

The Club night this Evening a good deal of Company there were two fires in the Room, but it did not feel too warm, so it may be inferred that the Weather is not yet very mild.

Friday 5th. May

Mr. Atkinson has now got his Bed removed up Stairs so that his house is now something like what it was before he was ill, it seems that he has not yet got his Articles yet into order; but I think he will in a little time, what is meant by order is having his things lumbered up as much as possible; and more than can be convenient, but every one has his hobby.

Saturday 6th. May

I was at Brantingham this day measuring Land, I began at ten in the forenoon, and continued until Six or after in the Evening. I did not get a single morsel to eat all the time—nor until I got home a short time after Seven at night. I got a glass of Ale at Noon, while the man I had with me went to his dinner. There was about 72 Acres measured.

Sunday 7th May

I do not feel tired this day with my yesterday's work, tho' it was very difficult and tiresome. It was a favorable day for the purpose which made it more agreeable.

Monday 8th. May

A Cold day. Fires kept in the Public houses, to warm their Customers; part Pots at the Market today, so that those who have money need not want for Brittle ware.

Tuesday 9th. May

People throng Colouring and painting against the Fair, which this year will be very soon in the Season; indeed we have but very little Spring weather yet.

Wednesday 10th May

I was at the West end this Evening but soon returned, it was very cold. I think it has been a frost almost every night for a long time past; still the Grass land, looks green, but not very luxuriant.

Thursday 11th. May

One of my Penknives which Wm. sent, and which I had just begun to use and I think was a very good knife but the blade broke off close to the handle, so that there was an end of it, almost before it had been used; I am sorry that it has so happened, but I must put up with the inconvenience.

Friday 12th. May

Mr. Leeson of Ellerker is very ill, he is confined to his bed he has had a Physician to see him Dr. Chalmers of Hull, it is said he is a little better. I have been to enquire after him as I am very busy this week with the Assessed taxes duplicate.

Saturday 13th. May

I was at Beverley this day with the Land tax and Assd. taxes Bills, I walked, it was a very fine morning, but in coming home about three O'clock in the afternoon it was a smart Shower: I had got to within about three Miles of home, when a Man overtook me with a Gig, and asked me to ride so I got in and Rode home.

Sunday 14th. May

We had a fresh Preacher (or reader) at the Church today. The Vicar is gone out it is said into Scotland. I can say very little for the Stranger's performance to day, he is a very sleepy reader.

Monday 15th May

This being both Weighton fair and Driffield fair, made a very thin market here today, indeed the Market falls off a good deal.

Tuesday 16th. May

I went this Evening to Ellerker to enquire how Mr. Leeson was. I did not see him as he was in Bed, but it was thought he was rather better, what his complaint is I do not know.

Wednesday 17th May

When public meetings are called, I think it has become fashionable for those Gentlemen who have given in their names to attend to send a Letter to the Chairman excusing themselves; that their letters may be read to the public, and to shew what Clever Letter writers they are, — But as Jos. Leighton says this is, "Humbugging".

Thursday 18th. May

We are nearly finished preparations for the Fair—Hannah Martin is to come tomorrow to clean and colour the School, that we may appear to have nothing out of order.

Friday 19th May

This day I went to Brantingham to measure some Land, it came on wet in the morning which prevented my beginning so soon as I wished; however the after part of the day was tolerable fine. I left off about One O'Clock when I got a glass of Ale as the man I had with me went to his dinner: we got done just about Seven at night and I got home shortly after eight, when I got dinner, tea, and Supper, altogether, as I did not eat a single morsel all the day, after breakfast—There was rather more than 72 Acres.

Saturday 20th May

The market day today, very few attended; we had the Artons at tea as usual, but not the old Lady. I think it is the first time I have known her miss.

Sunday 21st May

Coaches and Gigs rattling about this morning as if "South Cave was mad". Two of John Read's Sons came from Hull they were here as soon as I got up.

Monday 22d May

Cave Fair day, and very cold it was, a great Wind and mostly the Men had on great Coats it was excessive dusty; We had James Ramsdale and his Son Robert, and Mr. Swift to dinner, but none of them staid to tea.

Tuesday 23d May

A Change of the weather since yesterday, this indeed is a fine mild day with a brilliant Sun; a good deal of Company in the town in the afternoon, all appeared delighted with the Fair & perhaps the Weather.

Wednesday 24th May

This Afternoon or Evening there were some foot Races in a small way, but neither Horses nor Asses Run indeed there would not any start. There is a booth or something boxed up, where there are some strollers they say acting something or another I don't know what and perhaps they know little more of it themselves.

Thursday 25th. May

I think the Fair appears to be nearly over, and we are settling into our own old habits, for which I am not at all sorry; as I do not like to be put out of my old track.

Friday 26th May

Eliza, her Mother and Ann were at Provence today, dining and drinking tea, it is a long way to walk there and back; they arrived at home about nine at night all safe and sound and pretty well tired.

Saturday 27th. May

This day I did not stir far from home, as I had not much to do, so I kept myself still; all seems very dull; and people are making long Faces, because the days of pleasure are past for this year.

Sunday 28th. May

Two fresh Parsons at the Church today one in the morning and another in the afternoon; the weather continues fine, but very dry; some people are continually wishing for rain; but I think fine warm weather would be as great a blessing.

Monday 29th May

This day I gave Rd. Marshall a letter for Wm., he sets off tomorrow for London and expects to be there on Wednesday afternoon, he intends going by the Express Coach from Boston.

Tuesday 30th May

There was an old Miser who lately died; some Relation to Ths. Marshall's wife, and left some trifle to her; but the bulk of his fortune to others: one of the Executors has nearly killed himself with drinking, and his Son follows his Father's Example and Tom thinks neither of them will be long in this world. He says the old man who left them the Money, were he now alive ought to be hanged for Murder: "for he mud be certain when the fellow got the money that he wad never give up drinking as long as his money lasted. A Cursed awd Feal to leave his money to be so wasted. D—n him if he had left me it says long Tom, I wad ha taen care ont [of it] but to leave it to this drunken Feal vexes me past biding".

Wednesday 31st. May

They are about to Value over the Township of Broomfleet, and they I think want me to be their Clerk, provided they can get me to do a good deal of work for a very little money; but this will not do as I know by near what work it will take: I will not undertake it without having a bargain with them: I mean the Broomfleeters; This is a very bad sentence ~~paragraph~~, for there is no Substantive to which the Pronoun refers, so I have added it at the last viz. Broomfleeters.

Thursday 1st. June

There was a strong meeting at the Club this evening, but nothing particular occurred, a diversity of Opinion whether there would be another meeting night before the feast, which is the first Thursday after Old midsummer day: the next Club night will be on that day, so consequently the Thursday after will be the Feast day, nothing can be plainer.

Friday 2d. June

This day appeared my travelling merchant with Paper &c. I laid out ten Shillings with him, he was forced from home sooner rather than his usual time, as he wanted to raise a Sum; he went away rather lighter than he came.

Saturday 3d June

This day I think I have not been very busy, I went to the West end in the afternoon, but got home before tea time; and went no more out except to our old Friend's for a short time.

Sunday 4th. June

No newspaper this morning, so I went out in good time, there was a letter from Rd. Marshall this morning, giving an account of his arriving in London, but no particulars.

Monday 5th. June

This day, I saw a nephew of Mr. Beaumont's at the Market who comes from London, he is with Twinings at Temple Bar in the Banking line, he will

take a parcel to Wm. with pleasure so I will send this with him; and not begin
another Sheet.

APPENDIX I

Glossary of East Yorkshire Dialect Words

Many of the words and expressions listed below are still in daily use by modern dialect speakers. The meanings of words which have fallen out of current usage have been taken mostly from F. Ross, R. Stead and T. Holderness (eds.). *A Glossary of Words Used in Holderness in the East Riding of Yorkshire* (London: Trübner and Co. for the English Dialect Society, 1877) and J. Wright (ed.) *The English Dialect Dictionary*. 6 vols. (London: Frowde, 1898–1905).

Afore, *adv.*, before

Aneuf, *adj., adv.*, enough

Awd, *adj.*, old

Awdfarrand, *adj.*, old-fashioned, forward (often applied to precocious children)

Ax, Ax'd, *v.*, ask, asked

Back end, *n., adj.* autumn, autumnal

Badly, *adj.*, unwell, sick, poorly

Baulk, *n.*, an omission, something left undone; slipshod work

Bayn, *n.*, baby, child (*cf.* Scots. bairn)

Beal, Bealing, *v.*, cry out or shout aloud, crying out, shouting

Beath, *adv., pron.,* both

Belly Wark, *n.*, belly ache, stomach ache

Bink, *n.*, bench

Blashkite, *n.*, a noisy, nonsensical talker

Brantling, *adj.*, strutting, conceited

Breeder, *n.*, a boil

Call, Calls, v., call names, criticize adversely

Cam, *v., p.p.,* came

Casion, *n.*, occasion

Chimler, *n.*, chimney

Clease, *n., pl.*, clothes

Click, *v.*, to snatch at, seize hold of

Craiks, *n., pl.*, crows, rooks

Creak, *See:* **Reckon Creak**

Creakum-Croakum, *n.*, crow, rook

Davel, *n.*, devil

Dea, Dean't, *v.*, do, don't

Dean, *v., p.p.*, done

Dee, *v.*, die

Fand, *v., p.p.*, found

Feal, *n.*, fool

Fending, *See:* **Preaving and Fending**

Flam, *n.*, cheat, subterfuge

Flit, *v.*, to move from one house to another

Fog, *n.*, autumn-grown grass, after the hay-harvest

Fond, *adj.*, daft, foolish, stupid

Fonnitery, *n.*, furniture

Furmity, frummaty, *n.*, a preparation of wheat which was 'cree'd' or parboiled in the oven, then boiled in milk and spiced. (It was traditionally eaten on Christmas Eve)

Fuss-Balls, *n., pl.*, wheat smut

Gain , *adj.*, handy, convenient

Gang, Gan, *v.*, to go

Gang, Gang-Rail, Gangeril, n., vagabond, vagrant or wandering beggar

Gavelock, Gavlac, *n.*, an iron crowbar or lever

Glorin, Glooarin, *v., pres.p.*, staring or gazing intently or rudely

Hae, He, *v.*, have

Hand Ganging, *v., pres.p.,* going around as a rumour

Headwarks, *n., pl.,* headaches; corn poppies

Hobkite, *n.*, rascal, greedy fool

Hotch, Hutch, *v.*, shake up or lift with a sudden jerk, jog, jolt

Hoving, *adj.*, stupid

Innow, *adv.*, presently, shortly, after a while

Intiv, *prep.*, into

Itting, *v., pres.p.*, eating

Jolterhead, *n.*, a dullard or blockhead

Jowl-Head, *n.*, blockhead (probably from 'jowl' meaning to knock together, usually with reference to heads)

Kennel, *n.*, open drain at side of street, gutter

Knoppy, Noppy, Nappy, *adj.*, slightly intoxicated

Lahtle, *adj.*, little

Lead, Leading, *v.*, to carry corn etc. from the harvest-field to the stack-yard; when used to refer to the transportation of other than harvest produce, the name of the article being carried is always specified

Lewance, Looance, *n.*, lit. 'allowance', refers to the allowance of free meat and drink provided by the farmer for his workers, especially at harvest time, between meals at the morning and afternoon breaks

Lig, *v.*, to lie (as in bed), to place or lay down

Liverin, *v., pres.p., n.*, delivering, delivery

Mak, *v.*, make

Mam, *n.*, mother

Mare, *adj., adv.*, more

Mawker, Mawkin, *n.*, a scarecrow

Mense, *n,* tidiness, decency, state of being presentable

Mesan, Mesen, Mysen, *pron.*, me, myself

Met, Mett, *n.*, a measure of two bushels

Mowdart, Mowdiewarp, *n.*, a mole

Moulter, Moother, *n.*, the toll of flour taken by millers in payment for grinding

Mucked, *v., p.p.*, dirtied

Mud, *v.*, must

Mun, *v.*, must

Musling, *v., pres.p.*, musing

Nae, Nea, *adv., adj.*, no, not any, none

Neabody, *n.*, nobody, no-one

Nean, *n.*, not one, none

Neet, *n.*, night

Nobbut, *adv.*, only

Notish, *n.*, notice

Nut, *adv.*, not

On, *prep.*, of

Onny, Ony, *adj., pron.*, any

Ower, *adv.*, over, too

Pearching, Peeachin, *adj.*, keen, piercing: used generally in reference to wind

Pepper gang, *n.*, (strictly) a gang who sell inferior horses for sound ones (from 'pepper' a thief, a cheat, especially a cheating horse-dealer), used as a general term of contempt

Pick, *n. and v.*, a sudden push; to push

Poke, *n.*, bag or sack

Preaving and Fending, *v., pres.p.*, lit. proving and defending (as in a quarrelsome dispute), arguing, verbally sparring

Raffled, adj., upset, disturbed, confused

Raffling, adj., loose, disorderly

Rag, See: **Shale Rag**

Raggal, Raggil, n., rascal, a mean, saucy or mischievous person

Ratten, n., a rat

Reckon Creak, n., a pot-hook of adjustable length

Runagate, n., deserter, fugitive, run-away, vagabond; also general term of abuse

Sadly, adv., very, extremely, seriously, urgently

Sall, v. aux., shall

Same, Seeam, n., lard

Sawney, n., a simpleton

Sconce, n., a screen or thin partition

Scrubby, adj., mean, shabby, shallow or ungenerous

Sea, adv., so

Seave, Seeave, n., a rush (plant of genus *Juncus*)

Seer, adj., sure

Shabby, adj., mean, ungenerous

Shale Rag, adj. + n., a shambling worthless crew (from 'shale' shuffle, stagger, shamble, and 'rag' a low worthless person)

Sham, n., a shame

Sike, adj., adv., such

Sippyty, adj., weak, as in, e.g., 'sippety-soss' weak, insipid food

Skeal, n., school

Slattery, adj., wet and splashy

Slitter, Slither, v., to slide

Snaffling, adj., whining, snivelling, canting

Spre, Spree, Spreeing, v. + n., frolicking, making merry, joining in drunken mirth

Steck, v., to fasten; to shut or close

Steg, Awd-Steg, n., a gander

Stoving, adj., big and awkward, ungainly, loutish

Strang, adj. strong

Sud, v., should

Swab, n., a drunkard, a low ill-mannered person

Taen, v., p.p., taken

Tak, v., take

Team, Teem, v., (1) to pour copiously (e.g. with rain), (2) to unload

Tent, v., tend, care for, guard or protect

Theesen, pron., thyself, you

Throng, adj., busy, occupied with

Till, prep., to

Tiv, prep., to, towards

Tomorn, n., tomorrow

Tudder, adj., the other

Tufit, n., the lapwing or peewit

Varry, adj., adv., very

Wad, v., would

Ware, Waring, v., expend, lay out money

Wark, n., work

Weal, Weel, adj., adv., well

Weant, v., will not, won't

Weashipped, v., p.p., worshipped

Wesh, v., wash; (also) wish

Whea, pron., who

Whicks, n., couch grass

While, adv., until

Whya, interj., why (a common prefatory interjection)

Wi, prep., with

Yam, n., home

Yam, Yam'd, v., guess(ed), believe(d), opine(d)

Yan, adj., n., one

Yance, Yanse adv., once

Yannest, n., earnest

Yark, v., jerk; strike with stick or whip

Yet, adv. still, up to this time

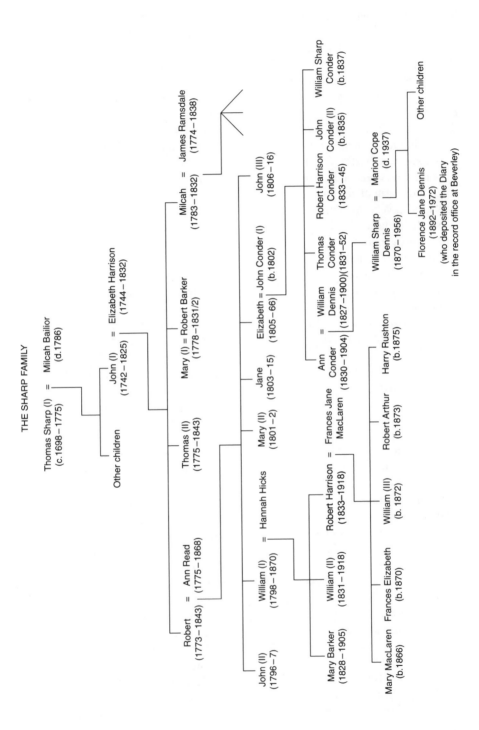

THE SHARP FAMILY

APPENDIX II

Brief Biographies of Local People in the Diary

Individuals included in this biographical list were mentioned in the diary on several occasions or were important people locally. Where it could be ascertained, for each entry the information has been given in the following form:

> SURNAME, first name, maiden name if appropriate (familiar name if any), (the year of birth/baptism and death/burial if known); occupation or status; address in South Cave or elsewhere; family relationships; religious allegiance if not Anglican.
>
> Further biographical information such as the individual's role in local affairs, personality and activities, principally as derived from Robert Sharp's (= RS) remarks in the diary.

Apart from the diary itself, the sources used include parish registers and other parish records, nonconformist registers, directories, land tax returns, census, monumental inscriptions, wills, and the tithe award of 1839.

Persons with identical names are distinguished by capitalized Roman numerals after the name. Within the entries, italicized names indicate that an individual appears as a separate entry in the list.

AKAM, Ann I, (old Mrs Akam), (*c.* 1743–1829); Market Place, South Cave; widow of John I (*c.* 1730–1818), farmer of Brantingham, sons *William* and *John II*.

'Both her sons have done as ill for themselves as possible' (25/10/29).

AKAM, John II, farmer; Everthorpe; son of *Ann I* and John I; probably the John Akam named as the reputed father of John Akam Garton (bapt. 1811) and Mary Garton (bapt. 1813), illegitimate children of Mary Garton; by 1815 married to Ann II, several children; Independent.

Ann Akam II was described as 'very extravagant' (25/10/29). In 1830 the Akams decided to emigrate to America (25/1/30) holding an unsuccessful auction sale at the Duke of York, Everthorpe (16/2/30), and leaving for America with some debts unpaid (8/4/31). Akam returned from America, reporting that he had bought and cleared 170 acres near Philadelphia (23/9/31).

AKAM, William, (1776–1820); son of *Ann I* and John I, married to Elizabeth (1772–1835); Independent.

'poor simple Willy he cut his throat—and there was an end to him' (25/10/29). William's children inherited his mother's house, and his widow, Elizabeth, and her sister Rachel (dubbed by RS 'the Holland toys') lived there (25/10/29, 26/3/30). A daughter, Mary Paulina (bapt. 1809), married *John Cousens* in 1834.

ARTON, Ann, *née* Arton (Mrs Arton), (*c*. 1790–), Castle Farm then Provence
Farm, South Cave; married *Robert II* in 1812, mother of at least 12
children of whom most died in infancy.

The Sharps and the Artons were on very friendly terms. Mrs Arton often
sent greetings and presents, for example, ducks, to *William Sharp I*
(3/12/29).

ARTON, Elizabeth, *née* Watson (Mudda or Old Mrs Arton), Ellerker; married
John in 1776, mother of *Henry* and *Watson*, with whom she lived on the
family farm at Ellerker.

Frequently visited by the Sharps, and especially at fair time the Artons
came to South Cave.

ARTON, Henry (*c*. 1780–); farmer; Market Place, South Cave until 1835, when
he moved to Sandholme near Gilberdyke; son of *John* and *Elizabeth*,
cousin of *Robert II*; married Sarah Levens (*c*. 1781–1836) in 1801.

South Cave constable 1833/4. His children attended RS's school, fees
usually being paid much in arrears and often in kind, 'he owes for
Schooling between two and three pounds for a long time past, he promised
last week to let us have some Wheat for it' (11/10/29). Relationship with
brother *Watson* apparently acrimonious (11/10/29).

ARTON, John (1747–1825); farmer; Ellerker; son of Robert Arton of Hayton,
brother of *Robert I* of Provence Farm, married *Elizabeth* Watson in 1776,
father of *Henry* and *Watson*; Independent.

Left most of his property to his widow and his son *Watson* (letters
25/12/25).

ARTON, Robert I (1742–1814); farmer; Provence Farm, South Cave; brother of
John, married Elizabeth Brown (1747–1835) in 1777, father of *Robert II*.

ARTON, Robert II (Dab), (1779–); farmer; Castle Farm until 1831, when
moved to Provence Farm, South Cave; son of *Robert I*, cousin of *Henry*
and *Watson*, married *Ann Arton*, (his cousin?), in 1812. Independent.

Overseer of the poor for South Cave, 1828/9. His 16-year old daughter,
Mary, eloped with young *John Robinson IV* of Mount Airy (3/3/32,
7/3/32). RS and *Ann Sharp* regularly visited the Artons and were visited
by them in their turn.

ARTON, Watson (Watty), (1781–1842); farmer; Ellerker; son of *John* and
Elizabeth, cousin of *Robert II*, unmarried and lived with his widowed
mother.

Surveyor of the highways for Ellerker 1826/7. Constable of Ellerker
1827/8. Assessor of Ellerker 1836. On his father's death in 1825, Watty
inherited most of his property. Acrimonious relationship with brother
Henry in 1829–30 (11/10/29, 27/9/30). Watty and his mother (Mudda)
were great friends of the Sharp family. RS often measured his land and
visited them at Ellerker. *Ann Sharp* also visited them, whilst the Artons
always visited the Sharps at fair time.

ATKINSON, William (Old Willy), (*c.* 1751/2–1838); boot and shoe maker;
Market Place, South Cave; married Mary (*c.* 1751–1813) at St. Martin's,
London. Freeman of Bristol and of Beverley.

Churchwarden 1827/30 and 1833/37. Popular host, who provided in his
house a good fire and company for those such as RS and *Giles Bridgman*,
who liked to gather there in the evenings to smoke their pipes and discuss
local and national events.

AYRE, Samuel, (the Old Sinner, the Old Blashkite), (1747–1826); farmer;
West End, South Cave; married Elizabeth Wilkinson (*c.* 1745–1827),
father of *Wilkinson*.

Churchwarden in 1817, when the school became a National School. On
hearing of his death, RS recorded that he was 'satisfied that he was gone',
he had 'lifted his Arm against me as much as he could' (28–29/11/26) —
probably a reference to the period when the church school was run under
the National Society system (see Introduction).

AYRE, Wilkinson, (1784–); farmer; South Cave and Ellerker; son of Elizabeth
and *Samuel*, married Ann Tindle in 1807, several children.

He was extravagant (e.g. 18/2/27, 11/4/33). Sold his property and was said
to have moved to Hull (13/4/33).

BARFF, Abraham (Abe), (1771–1846); farmer; Church Street, South Cave;
illegitimate son of Ann Barff (old Nanny) (1750–1828). His housekeeper,
from at least 1834, was *Rebecca Marshall*.

Highways surveyor 1828/9, and possibly churchwarden 1830. Frequently
recorded as drunk by RS. Regular supplier of pigs to Sharp family, usually
at Christmas (e.g. 25/12/25, 15/12/26).

BARKER, Mary *née* Sharp, (1778–1831/2); daughter of *John I* and *Elizabeth I*,
born 18 October 1778, baptized at Barmston 22 October 1778, married
Robert in 1804. *William I* lodged with her when he worked in Hull, as did
John Ramsdale. She died between October 1831 (after *William I's* visit)
and 3 April 1832 (when *William I* is reported to have received her legacy).
She left silver plate and money as a legacy to the Sharps and the
Ramsdales.

BARNARD, Revd Edward William, (Revd Mr Barnard), (1792–1828); curate
of Brantingham 1814–17; domestic chaplain to Philip Henry, Earl
Stanhope from 1817; vicar of South Cave 1817–28, but left the parish
owing to ill health in 1827, dying of fever in Chester in 1828; JP 1820–8;
lived at Brantinghamthorpe Hall from 1818–27; son of *Henry Boldero*,
brother of *Henry Gee*, married Philadelphia Wrangham, daughter of the
Archdeacon of York, their eldest son, Charles Edward Gee Barnard
(1822–94), inherited the estate on his uncle *Henry Gee's* death in 1858.

A minor poet, he wrote *Trifles, Imitative of the Style of Meleager,* and
translated the *Poems of Flaminio.* His only prose work was *The Protestant
Beadsman.* Barnard was apparently responsible, when he took over the
living in 1817, for associating the school with the National Society,
though at some point thereafter RS succeeded in detaching the school from

that system. RS's comments on Barnard are few, and cease altogether after 1827, when Barnard left South Cave.

BARNARD, Elizabeth Mary, *née* Elliot, (1808–71); married *Henry Gee Barnard* in 1834.

BARNARD, Henry Boldero (old Mr Barnard), (1755–1815); owner of Cave Castle, which he rebuilt in the late 18th century; married Sarah Gee (who died at Worthing in 1832), father of *Henry Gee*, Charles Leuyns (1790–1815) and *Edward William*.

RS's references to him suggest a higher regard for old Mr Barnard than for either of his sons, probably because the former spent most of his time in residence at Cave Castle.

BARNARD, Henry Gee (Mr Barnard), (1789–1858); largest landowner in South Cave; Cave Castle; eldest son and heir of *Henry Boldero*, married *Elizabeth* Elliott, an 'Irish lady' in 1834, no children.

Barnard spent much of his time away from South Cave. In 1829 he closed the Castle, and left to live in York, later moving to London, only returning home occasionally. He let the Castle for several years to the Hon. Christopher Stourton (11/3/32). RS was very critical of his absences—'he stays in London and seems hardly to know ... anything of his Estate' (21/4/33), 'he is as great a stranger here, as any Irish Absentee Landlord ... not one Shilling of the Rents which arise from his Estate is spent by him here' (6/3/34). In 1836 Barnard had a sale of many household items, including furniture and pictures (1/12/36; 10/12/36; 13/12/36). RS's comments in the diary suggest little enthusiasm for Barnard, but record that he treated his tenants fairly well and gave money to the poor occasionally.

BARRATT, Joseph, butcher; Market Place, South Cave; married Joanna, daughter of *Richard Newlove*, the landlord of the Bear.

BEAUMONT, Joseph (Mr Beaumont), (*c.* 1783–1859); substantial farmer; Thorpe Wold, Brantingham.

Promoter and advocate of railways. RS measured his land regularly, and often dined with him afterwards. Mr Beaumont usually took the tax money to Beverley for RS in the 1830s. His nephew took the last instalment of the journal to *William Sharp I* (5/6/37).

BENTLEY, Henry (Harry), (*c.* 1746–1819); parish clerk for 36 years.

BRIDGMAN, Giles (usually Mr Bridgman), (*c.* 1767–1843); substantial gentleman-farmer; Market Place, South Cave; brother of Samuel, married Elizabeth Hood in 1796, no surviving children. After Elizabeth died in 1801, he was looked after by a housekeeper, who also cleaned *William Atkinson*'s house occasionally.

Foreman of the water jury 1827. Juryman at Beverley sessions 1827. Overseer of the poor 1829/30. Surveyor of highways 1831/2. Churchwarden 1823/7 and 1830/3. Very close friend of both RS and *William Atkinson*, at whose house he was a regular visitor. Every October he took *William Atkinson* to Malton Fair, where they visited Bridgman's relations.

BROWN, Benjamin (d. 1879); corn factor, brewer, maltster; Brough.

Regular attender at South Cave market. Visited Wakefield market on Fridays, South Cave market on Mondays, and Hull market on Tuesdays. Read several of the newspapers that RS read, and discussed current affairs with him.

BURLAND, Joseph Blanchard (Mr Burland), (1803–68); attorney, partner in firm of Walmsley and Burland from *c.* 1827; lived at Everthorpe until 1827, then Market Place, South Cave; later Drewton Manor; married first, in 1825, Mary King (who died 1835 aged 28 after childbirth, leaving five small children including *Thomas Blanchard Burland*), and secondly another Mary who died 1839, aged 38.

He took over as steward of the manorial court from Robert Spofforth in 1832, and was a regular stamp customer of RS (13/4/37).

BURLAND, Thomas Blanchard, (1827–91); solicitor, Market Place, South Cave; son of *Joseph Blanchard Burland*; married Margaret Ann MacTurk in 1856.

Not mentioned in diary, but in 1859, when *Ann Sharp* made her will, she devised 'all estates vested in me as mortgagee or trustee to my friend Thomas Blanchard Burland of South Cave aforesaid gentleman', and appointed him her sole trustee.

CADE, Joshuah, (1756–1836); boot and shoe maker; Market Place, South Cave; father of *William*.

RS recorded that he had got through all his property and was 'a sort of butcher's Cad' to his son, *William* (23/4/27).

CADE, William, butcher; Market Place, South Cave, but left for Hull 1829; son of *Joshuah*.

CARTER, Dr Samuel, surgeon; Market Place, South Cave.

Treated RS for a boil (22/2/34, 25/2/34, 27/2/34, 3/3/34).

CLEGG, Michael, (*c.* 1787–1843); inn-keeper/publican *c.* 1810–13; farmer; West End, South Cave; married Mary Pinder 1808, who died 1827, after birth of 12th child; Independent.

Acted as 'bum bailiff' to *Teavil Leason I* (12/10/29) and appointed pinder (28/10/29). One of his children was refused burial in South Cave graveyard because it was baptized at the Chapel (2/12/26).

COATES, Edward II (Ned), (1798–); surgeon and farrier; Market Place, South Cave; son of Edward Coates I, surgeon and apothecary (d. 1807), married Mary Swindell, several children. Possibly died in Beverley workhouse in 1880.

Noted for his drunkenness and bad debts (e.g. 24/7/29, 6/5/31, 17/8/33).

CONDER, Ann (little Ann), (1830–1904); daughter of *Elizabeth* (Eliza) and *John Conder I*, granddaughter of *Robert* and *Ann Sharp*, married *William Dennis* in 1863, son *William Sharp Dennis,* born 1870. Probably baptized as an Independent.

Little Ann figured frequently in the diary. She lived near to her grandparents, and saw them often. Her childhood ailments—measles (26/4/32), threat of chicken pox (9/6/32), worms (25/7/33), threat of small pox (26/4/34), yellow jaundice (30/10/34), threat of scarlet fever (13/1/35, 14/1/35)—were all recorded by RS. She sometimes accompanied her grandmother on visits to neighbours. In 1835, she helped RS with measuring (15/8/35), and in 1835 and 1836 went with *Ann Sharp* to funerals (29/1/35, 14/1/36). After RS died, Ann lived with her grandmother in Church Street, South Cave, probably until she married in 1863. It was through Ann's son, *William Sharp Dennis*, that the diary descended.

CONDER, Elizabeth, *née* Sharp (Eliza), (1805–66); born 11 April 1805, baptized 2 May 1805 at the Independent Chapel, South Cave; third daughter of *Robert* and *Ann Sharp*, but the only one to survive to adulthood, married *John Conder I* in 1829, mother of *Ann* (b. 1830), *Thomas* (b. 1831), *Robert Harrison* (b. 1833), *John II* (b. 1835) and *William Sharp* (b. 1837). Died at Drypool, Hull, but buried at South Cave, 11 December 1866.

Eliza assisted her father in the school, probably by looking after the younger children. RS's comment in 1821, when she was 16, that 'Eliza could read your letter nearly as well as myself' (letters 25/12/21), suggest that his educational expectations of her were not high. Eliza was often recorded as helping her mother in the kitchen, visiting neighbours and family with both of her parents, and attending the Independent Chapel, usually with her mother; she also went to some Methodist meetings. Eliza's marriage to *John Conder I*, a saddler, does not appear to have met with her father's approval since neither the impending marriage nor its actual occurrence was recorded in the diary. A certain coolness can be detected in RS's references to her husband, always referred to by his surname. This coolness also applied to their sons, but not to little *Ann*, who was a clear favourite of her grandfather. For her part, Eliza was very attentive to her father: he noted her concern for his welfare when he took a meal at Eliza's during his wife's absence in London (19/6/36).

CONDER, John I, (1802–); saddler; Market Place, South Cave from *c.* 1826, and in 1846 and 1848 was also recorded as landlord of the Windmill, Market Place, South Cave (directories); son of Thomas Conder, miller at Whitgift, near Goole, married *Elizabeth Sharp* by special licence, 4 April 1829, witnesses being *James Levitt,* landlord of the Bay Horse and *John Reynolds,* the parish clerk. Father of *Ann* (b. 1830), *Thomas* (b. 1831), *Robert Harrison* (b. 1833), *John II* (b. 1835) and *William Sharp* (b. 1837).

The Conders lived opposite the Sharps in the Market Place, next door to the Bear, until 1834, when they moved into Porter Hole, just round the corner from the school. In 1830, Conder took a shop at Market Weighton, intending to open it every week on market day, but the experiment was short-lived (10/5/30, 15/5/30). With Eliza and the children, he visited his relatives at Swinefleet annually. RS's attitude to his son-in-law was rather distant, and often critical (for example 9/8/29).

CONDER, John II, (1835–); third son of *John I* and *Elizabeth Conder*, grandson of *Robert* and *Ann Sharp*.

RS referred to him twice, once when he was born—'they talk of calling it John' (22/2/35), once when he was christened (18/3/35).

CONDER, Robert Harrison, (1833–45); second son of *John I* and *Elizabeth Conder*, grandson of *Robert* and *Ann Sharp*.

His birth recorded briefly (13/2/33). Named, as was *William Sharp I's* second son, after his grandfather's favourite uncle and mentor, *Robert Harrison II*. He died, aged only 12 years old, in 1846. The verse on his grave is now unfortunately illegible.

CONDER, Thomas, (1831–52); eldest son of *John I* and *Elizabeth Conder*, grandson of *Robert* and *Ann Sharp*.

Died, aged 21, in South Cave. RS recorded 'I was getting tea at Eliza's this afternoon, as it was Thomas' Birth day he is four year's old, he is a strong lad and a tolerable dunce' (23/9/36). It was in fact his fifth birthday.

CONDER, William Sharp, (1837–); youngest son of *John I* and *Elizabeth Conder*, grandson of *Robert* and *Ann Sharp*.

Born late 1837 after the diary finished.

COOK, Barnard I (old Barnard or old Bant), (1760–1840); inn-keeper, post-master and farmer; landlord of the Fox and Coney, Market Place, South Cave until 1829 (when he assigned it to his daughter-in-law, *Sarah Cook*), and of the Blacksmith's Arms from 1831 to 1833 (when his daughter-in-law took it over); married first Jane Gardam in 1784, son *Barnard II* and other children. When Jane died, aged 35, in 1798, he married Ann Skaife. She died, aged 52, in 1817, and he may have married a third time to another Ann, who died, aged 74, in 1847.

Churchwarden 1820/9. During the years of the letters and the early years of the diary Barnard Cook was landlord of the Fox and Coney, managed the post office, was a substantial tenant-farmer, and was consequently an important person in South Cave. However, in 1829, he was arrested for debt (14/5/29). In 1830 at the age of 70 he was in the Fleet prison for 'a debt of liquor', put there by *Ben Tapp* and his partner McBride. He was tried at York (21/6/30) but returned to South Cave in July 1830. In 1831 he took over the Blacksmith's Arms, though from 1833 the licence was in the name of his daughter-in-law, *Sarah Cook*.

COOK, Barnard II (young Barnard), (1788–1828); farmer; South Cave; twin son of *Barnard* and Jane, married *Sarah* Sissons of Wallingfen in 1819.

A habitual drunkard, he was described as having 'a strange sottish look and quite shrunk away' (15/6/26). In August 1826, he had a fit allegedly caused by drink (3/8/26). His wife, *Sarah*, was a much greater support to old *Barnard*, his father, than he was himself.

COOK, Sarah, *née* Sissons (Mrs Cook), (*c.* 1793–1880); licensee of Fox and Coney May–Aug. 1829, of the Blacksmith's Arms 1833–1840s; married *Barnard Cook II*, who died in 1828, daughter-in-law of *Barnard Cook I*.

In May 1829, she was assigned the licence of the Fox and Coney by her father-in-law, when he fell into debt. She took over the Blacksmith's Arms from him in 1833, though it continued to be described by RS as *Barnard Cook's*. In 1826, RS described Mrs Cook as giving *Robert Dunn I* a black eye (8/11/26), and in 1829, Mrs Cook, turning *Ned Coates* out of the house, was 'as drunk as he' (24/7/29).

CORNER, Christopher (Kit or Old Kit), (*c.* 1750–1827); shopkeeper and agent, Market Place, South Cave; married Mary, father of *Mary*.

Steward to Mr Barnard. Disliked by RS, who recorded of his funeral — 'Kit Corner's funeral this forenoon, he was taken in a Waggon, Miss went in the Chaise, Farmer's on horseback, Beggars on Foot. Hangers-on, waiting about the door for a drink of ale: but as I did not belong to any of these Classes, I staid at home and did not attend at all ... I ... left the mourning department to those who were paid for it' (21/5/27).

CORNER, Mary (Miss Kitty), (1786–1844); Market Place, South Cave; daughter of *Christopher Corner*. Independent.

'a Lady ... who aspired to more gentility than her neighbours', and made advances to *Robert Marshall* (20/5/26). A little later, in 1826, she was apparently setting her cap at *John Hall* (22/8/26, 8/9/26), and in 1832, *Richard Marshall* was 'rumoured to be marrying' her (10/10/32). In 1841 she was still unmarried, and died at Bridlington Quay in 1844, aged 59.

COUSENS/COUSINS, John, (1807–58); grocer and draper; Market Place, South Cave; son of *William I*, married Mary Paulina Akam in 1834. Both Independents.

Took over William Hewson's shop in 1831, when RS feared that 'he will do us down' (7/4/31). In 1835 he and his brother *William I* visited *William Sharp I* in London, taking with them an instalment of the diary (17–18/8/35, 26/8/35).

COUSENS/COUSINS, Richmond, (1811–74); carrier in business with his father, *William I*; Market Place, South Cave.

COUSENS/COUSINS, William I, (1780–1852); landlord of the Windmill, carrier and farmer; Market Place, South Cave; married Ann (d. 1856), father of *John*, William II (1813–90), George (1815–67), and *Richmond*. Independent.

Overseer of the poor 1830/1. RS's next door neighbour. Figured frequently in the diary, both as a carrier taking letters and parcels to Hull and London, and as the landlord of the Windmill. Noted as 'very subject to liquor when he goes to Hull, but never at home' (11/8/29).

CRAGGS, John I, bookseller, binder, stationer and music-seller in Silver Street, Hull, paper-maker in North Cave; married first Margaret (d. 1826) and a second wife (d. 1831), father of John II.

William worked for him as apprentice from *c.* 1813 until he left to go to work for the publishers, Longman's, in London in 1821. RS sold prepared quills to him (e.g. 11/8/27). In 1826, Craggs offered *William Sharp I* a business partnership, which he declined, because 'he knows the Man—and his wife—and their manners. I remember the agreement that was made with him before and the manner in which it was fulfilled, he Wm. was to have an increasing Salary for 3 years, but that cringing fellow Wells wormed himself in, the Salary instead of an increase, fell off more than the last quarter's revenue, even to nothing. These things cannot easily escape my memory' (19/10/26). His son John II apparently went to work in London with *William Sharp I*, but the association was short-lived (10/4/33).

CREYKE, Revd Stephen, vicar of South Cave, 1828–34; married Sarah Hotham, the Barnards' cousin.

Creyke lived at Ripon and left the work in South Cave to his curate, *John Rodmell*, though he himself pursued with vigour those who did not pay their church rates and dues. On his resignation in 1834, the living passed to his wife's cousin, *Edwin Hotham*. RS had a low opinion of Creyke, 'a poor Creature he appears as a preacher, he was they say reading himself in, I suppose he read over the 39 Articles, but I am certain I did not hear ten Words' (9/1/31). This estimation rose a little when the vicar disagreed with his curate on the burial of dissenters in the churchyard (18/3/32).

CROSS, Frankish or Francis, (1784–1862); agricultural labourer; West End, South Cave; married Ellen.

Stood in for *John Reynolds* as parish clerk (18/9/36). Sold a pig to the Sharps. One of the ringers on fifth of November 1836 (6/11/36).

DAY, Francis, (1790–); surgeon; Market Place, South Cave.

Qualified as a surgeon in London, 1811. Practised in South Cave from 1813 to 1823, when he sold the practice to *Edward Tinsdill*. Qualified as physician in Glasgow in 1824, and afterwards travelled to France, Germany and Jersey.[1] Re-visited South Cave in 1831 (6/2/31).

DENNIS, Ann, see: *Conder, Ann*.

DENNIS, David (*c.* 1800–53); wheelwright and joiner; Market Place, South Cave, married Jane Todd in 1824, father of *William Dennis*, who married *Ann Conder*, RS's granddaughter.

Most references in the diary relate to his drunkenness (e.g. 12/8/26, 31/7/32, 27/8/34).

DENNIS, Florence Jane, (1892–1972); daughter of *William Sharp Dennis*, granddaughter of *Ann Conder*, great-granddaughter of *Elizabeth Conder* (*née* Sharp), great-great-granddaughter of *Robert Sharp*. She deposited the diary in the Record Office at Beverley (ERYARS).

DENNIS, William, (1827–1900); gardener; Church Street, South Cave; married *Ann Conder* in 1863, father of *William Sharp Dennis*.

---

[1] *Ex inf.* W. E. Browne.

DENNIS, William Sharp, (1870–1956); son of *William* and *Ann Conder*, married Marion Cope, father of *Florence Jane Dennis*.

DOVE, Sarah; Ellerker, but living with her aunt Mary at West End, South Cave, when accused of infanticide (18/11/33).

Acquitted of child murder but sentenced to two years' imprisonment for concealment of birth (2/1/34).

DUNN, George, (*c.* 1787–1863); horse-dealer; Market Place, South Cave.

In debt in 1829/30 (e.g. 19/12/29, 6/1/30), served 6 months' imprisonment with *Timothy Dunn II* in 1830 for obstructing sheriff's officer (14–15/1/30, 11/7/30).

DUNN, Robert I, (1770–1842); weaver and small farmer; Market Place, South Cave; married Mary, father of *Timothy II* and *Robert II*.

References in diary are mainly to his drunkenness (e.g. 23/12/30, 8/11/33).

DUNN, Robert II, (1795–); son of *Robert I* and Mary.

Emigrated to Quebec (5/9/29).

DUNN, Timothy I (old Timothy), (1772–); farmer; South Cave; married Mary Ruddock.

RS witnessed his and his wife's signatures to property deal (13/7/26). Referred to several times in friendly manner.

DUNN, Timothy II, (1805–); horse-dealer; Market Place, South Cave; son of *Robert I*.

Imprisoned in 1830 with *George* for obstructing a sheriff's officer (14–15/1/30, 11/7/30). A regular at Old Willy Atkinson's by 1836.

DYSON, Thomas, (d. 1844); farmer; West End, South Cave; his daughter Sarah Bathia married *Thomas Robinson II*, son of *Thomas Robinson I* (of Mount Airy) at Hull in 1833. Independent.

Figures several times in diary. His servant girl was accused of concealing a birth (5/4/36).

ELGIE/ELGEY, John, (*c.* 1809–73); farmer; West End, South Cave and Ellerker; married first, the sister of *Thomas Marshall*'s wife, and second, Elizabeth Marshall, (1813–83) *Thomas Marshall*'s daughter, (his first wife's niece), in 1836.

Constable for South Cave 1834/5. Overseer of the poor 1835/6. Highways surveyor 1836/7.

FENWICK, John, carrier in partnership with *William Cousens*, landlord of the Three Tuns from 1831; Market Place, South Cave.

FEWSON, Edward, horse-breaker and landlord of the Bear 1832–5; Market Place, South Cave.

FISHER, Thomas, (1774–1846); farmer; Church Street, South Cave; married Elizabeth Broader in 1811.

Constable 1825/6. Juryman at Beverley sessions in 1827. Overseer of the poor 1835/6. RS measured for him.

FISHER, William, (*c.* 1797–); farmer; Brantingham (1827), Drewton (1833), Ellerker (from 1834); married Hannah, daughter of *Thomas Robinson I* of Mount Airy, in 1826.

RS measured for him.

GALLAND, Joseph ('Doctor' Joseph Galland), (1762–); shopkeeper, tea-dealer, tailor, and self-professed doctor; Market Place, South Cave.

Accounts of Galland's doctoring, quoting him in dialect, paint a telling picture of village medical practice for the poor, for example, in giving medicine to a young girl—'I will give you some medicine for her, it will be very nasty, and very like she will not take it (she was about 12 or 13) but never mind her mak her tak it, Gang you tiv her, and throw her down, get a stride on her, nip her nose and team it intiv her, Od rot her never mind her noise, nip her nose well and team it in, tak no notice of her roaring and screaming' (6–7/11/30).

GARDAM, John, (1787–); wheelwright and joiner; Church Street, South Cave; father of John who went to America in 1830; Independent.

GARNONS, Revd Daniel, (d. 1817); vicar of South Cave, 1783–1817.

HALL, John, (1803–); Faxfleet.

Friend of the Sharps, the Corners, and the Cousens. Appears in the diary several times, mainly as looking for work in various parts of the country (e.g. 17/9/26, 1/10/26).

HARPER, Thomas (Tommy), (1802–); traveller in tea in 1827.

Went to London for work in 1825. Came back, having married, in 1827, to sell his South Cave property. RS recorded that he was drinking heavily (11/11/27).

HARRISON, Elizabeth, mother of RS, see: *Sharp, Elizabeth.*

HARRISON, Robert II, (1736–1812); schoolmaster; Barmston; son of Robert I and Mary Harrison of Beeford, brother of *Elizabeth Sharp*, beloved uncle and mentor of RS.

'let me not forget him. No never so long as Memory holds her seat. He spent his time at Barmston from the time that I, and my Brother were fit to go to School; until the time we both left, when he went to either Skipsea or Ulram. He never went into Company: I never knew him go to a Market Town. Whatever I know, the foundation of all was laid by him' (22/12/31). In 1812, RS walked from South Cave to Barmston (a journey of about 30 miles) to attend his funeral, but arrived only as the grave was already half filled (22/12/31). Both *William Sharp I* and his sister, *Elizabeth,* named a son after Robert Harrison II.

HILL, John, MRCS, (c. 1802–65), surgeon; Market Place, South Cave; son of a Cottingham builder, married first, Elizabeth, who died 1846, then in 1848, Louisa (c. 1815–93), daughter of *Teavil Leeson I.*

He had a bailiff into his house collecting debts in 1829 (5/11/29).

HOLBORN, Catherine *née* Stephenson (old Kate, Mrs Holborn), (c. 1765–); Market Place, South Cave; married *John*, in 1783; Quaker.

HOLBORN, George, (1789–); gunsmith and gamekeeper; Market Place, South Cave; son of Charles and *Grace Holborn.*

Gamekeeper to Lord Muncaster in 1827 and to *Captain Richard Shaw* of Brantingham in 1834.

HOLBORN, Grace *née* Stodart, (1766–1843); married Charles Holborn (1751–1811), South Cave watchmaker, in 1785.

HOLBORN, John (the Old Cardinal, the Old Monk, Old Broad Brim), (*c.* 1758–1838); plumber and glazier; Market Place, South Cave; married *Catherine* Stephenson; Quaker.

He was the landlord of the Sharps when they had the shop, living next door on the corner of Market Place and Porter Hole. Many stories of him in the diary. In the early years RS was quite friendly with him, but in 1832, the references to him had become quite antagonistic (e.g. 12/8/32, 11/9/32, 19/12/32).

HOTHAM, Revd Edwin, (1807–); vicar of South Cave, 1834–44, of South Dalton, 1844–54, then rector of Crowcombe, Somerset; son of Sir William Hotham (1772–1848) and related both to the Barnards and to his predecessor, the *Revd Creyke*.

RS was quite complimentary about Hotham, in marked contrast to his usual attitude to clerics (e.g. 26/7/34). Hotham established a Sunday school, and gave coals away to the poor at Christmas—'a kind action' (29/12/35) .

HUDSON, John (Mr Hudson), draper; Market Place, Hull; farmer, South Cave, from 1831.

HUDSON, William, (*c.* 1809–); farmer at Everthorpe until 1835, then landlord of the Fox and Coney, 1835–1840s.

JACKSON, Frank, shopkeeper and schoolteacher; Market Place, South Cave; married Mary Wilson in 1804 by whom he had several children, and was the reputed father in 1814 'of Ann Foster's daughter 'got in adultery'.

Left South Cave in debt in 1826.

KELSO, Revd Seth, (*c.* 1748–1831); minister of Independent Chapel, South Cave, 1824–8.

When he arrived at South Cave from the South Seas missions, he was already in his late 70s. In 1827, soon after his resignation as minister at South Cave, he was robbed, and a chest containing money (said to be about £500) was taken. At that time Kelso stated that the registers of the chapel had also been stolen, but the volume dating from 1791 was found with his possessions on his death in 1831.

KEMP, Robert (the lantern-maker), (*c.* 1798–1873); tinner and brazier; Market Place, South Cave; married Elizabeth, daughter of *Thomas Robinson I* of Mount Airy in 1829.

In 1827 RS lent £100 on a mortgage of Kemp's newly built house 'a very important transaction in my life' (3/3/27, 28/3/27)

KING, Revd John; farmer and landowner; Frog Hall, Church Street, South Cave.

In 1816 bought South Cave property from Timothy Newmarch's son. Described as 'formerly of Kentish Town, now of Leeds' in deeds. In 1823 directory described as minister of St. James's Church, Leeds. King stood in for Barnard as minister at times 1821–2. One of the surveyors of the highways 1826/7. RS measured for him.

KIRBY, Joseph, (1802–); farmer; West End, South Cave; son of *Richard* and Mary.

Constable 1833/4.

KIRBY, Richard, (1769–1831); substantial farmer; Common Farm, South Cave, until 1829, West End 1829–31; married Mary Hesp in 1792 (d. 1828), father of Robert, Hannah, John, *Joseph* and Mary.

Overseer of the poor in 1816. RS made his will (3/4/30) and an inventory of his goods, and he 'expected that he died worth in money (exclusive of his real property) £1100, there will be I think £200 each to his children' (2/2/31). Quarrelsome (e.g. 15/7/26, 28/10/26).

LANCASTER, William, see: LONCASTER, William.

LANGRICKE, Frances I, *née* Sanderson (c. 1773–); married to *Samuel.*

LANGRICKE, Frances II (Fanny), (c. 1780–1837); married to *William.*

Stole currants at Beverley (30/4/32) and imprisoned for three months (7/7/32).

LANGRICKE, Samuel, (c. 1772–1837); labourer; West End, South Cave; married *Frances I* in 1792.

Children were Hannah (1792), Sarah (1795), Samuel (1797), John (1800), William (1802), *Thomas I* (1804–77), Robert (1810), Elizabeth (1813), and Mary (1818).

Pinder from 1833.

LANGRICKE, Thomas I, (1804–77); labourer; West End, South Cave; son of *Samuel* and *Frances I*, married Mary Tindale in 1835, two days before their son, Thomas II, was born.

Charged with poaching (18/3/35, 21/3/35, 19/5/35).

LANGRICKE, William, (c. 1773–1846); land-dealer, horse-dealer, and labourer; West End, South Cave; married to *Frances II.*

LAVERACK, William; substantial farmer; Cave Common and Everthorpe; married Mary, father of Joseph (1813), John (1814), Thomas (1819), and others.

LEAPER, Thomas, (c. 1798–); farmer; Cave Sands and Ellerker; married Mary Blashill in 1821.

Juryman at Beverley sessions in 1827. Surveyor of highways 1831/2. Overseer of poor 1833/4. Overseer and guardian 1836/7.

LEASON/LEESON, Robert I, (1784–); attorney in partnership with Mr Walmsley, Market Place, 1818–23, South Cave; illegitimate son of Teavil Appleton and Ann Leason (see below).

LEASON/LEESON, Robert II, (1818–); son of *Teavil I.*

LEASON/LEESON, Teavil I, (1779–1865); army captain, gentleman-farmer; the Hermitage, West End; illegitimate son of Ann Leason and Teavil Appleton, a Beverley banker and landowner, who, on his death in 1800, provided amply for his housekeeper, Mrs Leason, and his seven surviving illegitimate children by her.[2] Teavil Leason married Elizabeth Green (*c.* 1782–1847), father of *Teavil II*, Isabella, Maria, *Robert II*, and Louisa (who married *John Hill*).

In 1813 he was in St. Helena, and a tradition exists in South Cave that he was the officer in charge there during Napoleon's captivity. There is no evidence to support this, although he may have been on the island when Napoleon arrived in 1815. He was certainly back in South Cave in 1816. In 1827, RS described him as 'the West End self-styled esquire' (7/12/27). Surveyor of the highways 1829/30. Juryman at York assizes in 1831 and at Beverley sessions in 1834. Overseer of the poor 1837/8. RS measured land for him.

LEASON/LEESON, Teavil II, (1806–); West End, South Cave; son of *Teavil I* and Elizabeth.

In 1826 he had returned from London 'long before his time is out' (24/9/26). From other references it seems likely that he was studying law (e.g. 27/10/26) in London, and when he returned to South Cave, he was employed for a time in debt-collecting. In 1830, he went to America (28/7/30).

LEASON/LEESON, Thomas I (Mr Thomas Leason of Ellerker), (*c.* 1774–1837); gentleman-farmer; Ellerker; illegitimate son of Teavil Appleton and Ann Leason (see above), married Elizabeth Levitt (d. 1824) in 1805, father of *Thomas II*.

LEASON/LEESON, Thomas II, (1809–42); Ellerker; son of *Thomas I* and Elizabeth.

In 1835 he was 'propping about Cave market with young men' (6/4/35).

LEVITT/LEVETT, Ann, (Nancy) *née* Marshall, (1800–76); daughter of *Richard* and *Hannah Marshall*, married *Thomas Levitt* in 1818, mother of *Norrison Marshall Levitt I*.

LEVITT/LEVETT, Christopher (Kester), (*c.* 1760–1803); blacksmith and landlord of the Bay Horse, West End, South Cave; married *Rachel* Grasby in 1786, father of *James III* and *Hannah*.

LEVITT/LEVETT, Hannah, (1797–1867); Bay Horse, South Cave; daughter of *Christopher* and *Rachel*, mother of illegitimate twins, *Norrison Marshall Levitt I* and Marshall Norrison Levitt, by *Norrison Marshall*, who was struck by lightning, and died before they were born (24/9/31, 8/1/32, 15/1/32). *Norrison's* father, *Richard Marshall II* was 'much taken with' the twins and when one died lavished affection on the one remaining (26/1/32).

LEVITT/LEVETT, James I, (Old Mr Levitt, Old Jemmy Levitt); (*c.* 1747–1833); gentleman-farmer; Market Place, South Cave.

His death recorded by RS (23/11/33).

---

[2] There is a possibility that Mrs Leason's children were fathered by Teavil Appleton's brother, Robert (*c.* 1722–87), and that Teavil took over responsibility for them after his brother's death, *ex. inf.* K. Q. Appleton.

LEVITT/LEVETT, James II; farmer; West End, South Cave.

His illness and recovery recorded by RS (8/12/33, 14/12/33).

LEVITT/LEVETT, James III, (little snaffling devil, Jem) (1791–1848); joiner and landlord of the Bay Horse; West End, South Cave; son of *Christopher* and *Rachel*.

His mother had sent him to London for improvement in 1827, but he returned apparently unimproved (11/7/25). In 1826, he set up in business in Hull, in partnership with a Mr Kidd, but the partnership was dissolved the following year (3/8/26, 25/2/27). On his mother's death, he took over the Bay Horse (21/7/27). He was a rival to RS for Post Office vacancy in 1829 (24/5/29), but by 1830 RS was visiting him every Sunday after church (12/12/30).

LEVITT/LEVETT, John (Mr Levitt of Ellerker), (1793–); farmer; Ellerker. Independent.

RS often measured his land. Throughout the diary period, John Levitt was not in a prosperous condition. In 1826 his land was heavily mortgaged, and he sold portions of it to *Richard Marshall II* (26/10/26, 8/6/27), to *Teavil Leason I* (11/4/27), and to *Samuel Ringrose* (1/11/27, 20/3/34, 27/2/36). In 1827, he sold his mother's house to *John Hill* (14/12/27). He owed RS tax money (8/11/29), and was described as 'slow to pay his debts' (12/1/33). By 1836 most of his land had been sold (29/7/36).

LEVITT/LEVETT, Norrison Marshall I, (1820–98); West End, then Castle Farm, South Cave; son of *Thomas* and *Ann*, grandson of *Richard Marshall II*.

LEVITT/LEVETT, Norrison Marshall II, (1832–1905); Castle Farm, South Cave; illegitimate son of *Hannah Levitt* and *Norrison Marshall*, who was struck by lightning before he and his twin brother were born; grandson of *Richard Marshall II*, with whom he lived as a child.

LEVITT/LEVETT, Rachel *née* Grasby (Old Rachel), (1757–1827); landlady of the Bay Horse; married *Christopher* (d. 1803) in 1786, mother of Mary (1789), *Thomas* (1790), *James III* (1791), Elizabeth (1795), Joanna (*Hannah*) (1797).

LEVITT/LEVETT, Thomas, (1790–1870); blacksmith, shopkeeper and farmer; West End, South Cave; son of *Rachel* and *Christopher*, married *Ann (Nancy) Marshall* in 1818, father of *Norrison Marshall Levitt I*. From 1833 they lived with *Richard Marshall II* at Castle Farm.

Constable 1828/9, 1829/30 and 1832/3. Overseer of the poor 1837/8. Assessor (with RS) 1832–8.

LOCKWOOD, John (Mr Lockwood), (*c*. 1800–); gentleman-farmer; Market Place, South Cave.

Arrived at South Cave in 1831 having taken Scatcherd's farm. Overseer of the poor 1832/3. Churchwarden 1834/8.

LONCASTER/LANCASTER, William (Old Lonc, Cuckoo), (1772–1854); farmer; West End, South Cave.

Constable 1826/7 'to his satisfaction' (30/10/26) but was regarded as unsuitable. He was served a summons for assault in April 1827, the 'second time since he came to office' (7/4/27), and after a troublesome year, he was thrown out in November 1827 (2/11/27, 9/11/27, 25/11/27, 6/12/27). He was churchwarden 1829/32. RS's references to him are generally affectionate. The impression given, however, is that he was the village fool.

MACTURK (i.e. TURK in diary).

MACTURK, Ann *née* Grasby, (*c.* 1762–1822); married *George* in 1788, mother of Benjamin (1789), *Thomas* (1792), William (1794), *William* (1795), Ann (1797–1858), who married Henry Bowser of Market Weighton in 1826 and 'presented her husband with a young Bowser, but the Old Women say it should not have been a Christmas Box—but come it is that's truth' (27/12/26), John (1799), Helen (1800), *John* (1802), and Eliza (1809), who married John Rand of Bradford in 1834.

MACTURK, George (George Turk, Georgy), (*c.* 1750–1845); farmer; West End, South Cave; married *Ann* Grasby in 1788, father of large family (see under *Ann*). Independent.

George and his brother James came from Scotland to work on the digging of the Market Weighton canal. James opened the first pub in Newport (Turk's Head), and George became a large tenant farmer in South Cave, first at Mount Airy, then at the West End. By the time of the diary, the MacTurks were a well established and prosperous family in South Cave— 'they have had 5 Servants this year not all at a time mind you, but fairly one after another, the old cry is still kept up, Servants are but little worth, and how should they be any otherways in the manner they are brought up!!' (29/9/25). RS's references to George MacTurk in the diary were generally very friendly—'cheerful and lively as usual' (23/5/35). The MacTurk children were contemporaries of the Sharp children, and like them were baptized as Independents.

MACTURK, John (1802–); traveller for a sugar house in 1827, farmer from 1833 (22/4/33); son of *George* and *Ann*. Independent.

A school friend of *William Sharp I*. though apparently not his equal scholastically (24/4/22).

MACTURK, Thomas (Tom Turk), (1792–1857); woollen merchant and draper with business in Market Place, Hull and connexions with Bradford; from 1827 he lived at West End, South Cave; son of *George* and *Ann*, married Jane Gladstone in 1823, father of George Gladstone (1831–1911) and Margaret Ann (1833–), who married *Thomas Blanchard Burland* in 1856. RS said that he 'has taken Saml Ayre's house for a country house, so that he must have done pretty well since he commenced measuring yards of cloth' (20/6/27).

MACTURK, William (the physician), (1795–); doctor in Bradford; son of *George* and *Ann*, his first wife, Catherine, died in 1829, and was buried in

South Cave (30/7/29, 3/8/29); he married for a second time, another Catherine, and had several children in Bradford.

MARSHALL FAMILY. Major South Cave farming family. RS recorded that 'the Marshall's spread and occupy farms here like a hungry Colony in a new Country' (10/11/30), and in 1832, he wrote 'Richd. Marshall has three farms ... Robt. Marshall has two Farms ... then the Farm at the west end where Jn. Crathorne lived is divided amongst Ths. Marshall, Rd. & Robt. so that Rd. has 3 Farms and one third of another, Robt. has 2 and one third and Ths. has one & one third of another in all 7 amongst them' (11/1/32). All three brothers were great friends of the Sharps. *Richard II* and *Robert* were the more sober and respectable characters, and both had wives with social pretensions, somewhat despised by RS. Thomas, the 'Long Miller', was altogether a more rumbustious personality, and RS affectionately recorded many of his drunken exploits and stories in dialect.

MARSHALL, Ann, daughter of *Richard II* and Hannah, see: *Levitt, Ann.*

MARSHALL, Elizabeth (first husband's name Leak), (*c.* 1773–1862); married *Thomas* in 1812.

MARSHALL, Hannah *née* Jubb (*c.* 1778–1831); married *Richard II* in 1800, mother of *Ann* and *Norrison*. Independent.

RS commented when she was ill that 'pride has brought much of it on, for they have got a Parlour fitted up with a good Carpet, the Walls painted, fine Window Curtains, polished Irons, grand Glass ... the Lady about Christmas thought she was not very well so she adjourned to the Parlour and sat in state, where her neighbours had an opportunity of seeing her and her furniture together; but, lo & behold! she really grew ill from the dampness of the Room, and the Doctor was obliged to be had, and her display brought down by bleeding and blistering' (19/1/29). She died only a week after her son, Norrison, was killed by lightning (24/6/31, 26/6/31).

MARSHALL, James, (1783–1825); son of *Richard I* and Susannah.

RS mentioned that his death caused dissension in the family—'Since James's death the different branches of the family can hardly agree; Mrs. Bellard the Sister from Hessle has been here a month without ever speaking to the Miller' (11/11/26). The dispute centred on the division of his legacy—'I do not think James Marshall will be found to be worth so much as he valued himself at, which was £800 in ready money, exclusive of a small Estate at Newbald' (20/5/27).

MARSHALL, Jeremiah, (1781–1854); would-be farmer in 1827, working at livery stables from March 1827; son of *Richard I* and Susannah, brother of *Thomas, Richard II*, Elizabeth (Mrs Bellard), *Robert, James, Rebecca,* and *William.*

MARSHALL, Norrison, (1806–31); son of *Richard II* and *Hannah,* fathered twins by *Hannah Levitt* before his death. One, *Norrison Marshall Levitt II,* survived. Independent.

Killed by lightning at age 25—'Norrison Marshall was at Hull yesterday on business. I think buying bones for Manure, he set off for home between five and six O'clock in the Evening, when it came on a thunder Storm, he took shelter under a tree just at the end of the town of Hull when a flash of lightning struck both him and his horse dead' (17/6/31). RS described him most affectionately and was deeply distressed at his death. *John (III) Sharp* and he were 'like Brothers and of the same age within a month'.

MARSHALL, Rebecca (Aud Beck, Sister Becky), (1786–1866); daughter of *Richard I* and Susannah. Unmarried, and in the 1820s she was housekeeping for her brother *Robert* (25/12/25, 16/9/26) probably until he married in 1828, but by the 1830s she was housekeeper for *Abraham Barff* (12/2/34, 1841 census).

MARSHALL, Richard I, (1734–1819); farmer; West End, South Cave; married Susannah Grasby (1740–1815), in 1764, father of *Thomas, William, Richard II*, Elizabeth (married Bellard), *Robert, Jeremiah, James*, and *Rebecca*.

RS reported his son Thomas's comment that 'his Father had two remedies for all Complaints, one was Rum and new Milk for a Medicine which he said would cure ought but broken bones, for Dr. Sonley told him so ... the other remedy was a Bunch of Thorns for all kinds of Gaps, Broken Gates or fallen down walls, there he was with his bunch of Thorns to stop up all mischances; a Bunch of Thorns was his sovereign Remedy for all out of doors work[.] When he got his skin full of Rum and milk and his Bunch of Thorns in his hand he was master of all (24/8/35).

MARSHALL, Richard II, (1776–1864); corn-miller at South Cave water-mill (Low Mill) in 1801/2, substantial farmer at West End during diary years; from 1833 lived at Castle Farm, West End, South Cave; son of *Richard I* and Susannah, married *Hannah* Jubb in 1800, father of *Ann* and *Norrison*, grandfather of *Norrison Marshall Levitt I* and *Norrison Marshall Levitt II*. Independent until *c.* 1834 when RS recorded that he had the vicar lodging with him and 'he was at church twice today' (7/12/34). In 1837/8, he was the vicar's churchwarden (28/3/37).

A great friend of RS, as were his brothers, *Robert* and *Thomas*. The three brothers quarrelled over brother *James's* will in 1827 (e.g. 23/5/27, 8/6/27). RS often measured his land. Succeeded *Christopher Corner* as steward to Mr Barnard in 1827. Overseer of the poor 1829/30. Surveyor of highways 1829/30. Juryman at Beverley sessions in 1834. Churchwarden 1837/40. Very badly affected by his son *Norrison's* death by lightning in 1831 and his wife's death the following week (e.g. 16/7/31), but comforted by his late son's illegitimate son (24/2/32).

MARSHALL, Robert, (1778–1842); farmer; West End, South Cave; son of *Richard I* and Susannah, married *Susannah* Foster in 1828 (d. 1856). Constable 1820. Tax assessor 1825/31 with RS. Surveyor of highways 1826/7. Overseer of the poor 1833/4 and 1836/7. Juryman at Beverley sessions in 1834. One of RS's closest friends. They worked as parish assessors together, visited each other frequently, smoked a pipe and dined at each other's houses. Robert Marshall was unmarried during the early

years of the diary, and RS recorded that *Mary Corner* was setting her cap
at him (11/7/25). From 1829, when Robert's wife made her first
appearance in the diary, RS spent rather less time with him.

MARSHALL, Susannah *née* Foster, (1782–1856); married *Robert* in 1828.

Robert and Susannah were married in the year for which no diary
survives. RS apparently had a low opinion of his friend's new wife—'Mrs.
Robt. Marshall got an Apple to eat but she says she is not much of an
apple eater: but I found there was something more, for it was attended
with a little display, she pulled a small case out of her Pocket in which was
a silver fruit knife, this was enough!' (12/9/29).

MARSHALL, Thomas (the Long Miller, the Man of Dust), (1768–1851);
farmer and miller; Low Mill, South Cave; son of *Richard I* and *Susannah*,
married as first wife possibly Mary Foster (at Hull in 1802) by whom he
had a son, Thomas, and daughter, Elizabeth (d. 1847), who married *John
Elgie*. In 1812 married as second wife, *Elizabeth* Leak (*c.* 1771–1862).
Independent.

Overseer of the poor 1830/1. A close friend of RS, and frequently
mentioned in the diary. Most of his appearances feature his drunken
exploits, his use of dialect, his extreme parsimony, and his rustic humour.
RS was clearly very fond of him, but seems to have regarded him with
rather less respect than he accorded to his brothers, *Richard II* and *Robert*.

MARSHALL, William (1775–1828); son of *Richard I* and *Susannah*.

MARTIN, Hannah *née* Downs, (*c.* 1791–1880); West End, South Cave;
married *John* in 1816, mother of Adam, Mary, and several other children.
Independent.

Hannah worked for the Sharps, cleaning the school and performing other
domestic duties (e.g. 3/12/29, 20/4/31, 23/5/34).

MARTIN, John (*c.* 1789–); agricultural labourer; West End, South Cave;
married *Hannah* Downs in 1816, father of *Adam* and other children.
Independent.

Compared to his wife Hannah, he seems to have been a somewhat
unenterprizing character—'he has nea Spirit for ought to dea ony good'
(11/10/31).

MARTIN, Obediah (Obed), (1787–1873); butcher; Market Place, South Cave;
son of *Ralph*, married Margaret (d. 1863).

Constable 1834/7. A regular at Old *Willy Atkinson's*. Described by RS as a
'queer good-natured fellow' (11/11/33), but often the worse for drink (e.g.
29–30/8/36).

MARTIN, Ralph, (1754–1834); tailor; South Cave; married Catherine Oliver
(1760–1846) in 1784 .

RS described his new wig, in which 'he looked as wild ... as though he had
escaped from some Lunatic Asylum' (12/2/32). Was one of the regular
singers at funerals (17/3/34).

MILNER, James, (1773–); bricklayer; Church Street, South Cave; son of *Richard*, married Jane Story in 1796, father of *Thomas* and others; Independent.

Emigrated to Canada in 1830 after applying for and receiving money from 'the Club' (4/2/30). At first reported to be doing well, 'he is clearing 4 or 5 acres a week in Canada' (14/1/31), but his wife, who did not want to go, died there, and he was later said not to be in his right mind (26/8/31).

MILNER, Richard, (1745–1829); born at Flamborough, formerly of Barmston; Church Street, South Cave; father of *James*. Methodist.

RS wrote that 'Richd. has been a member of the Methodist Society considerably more than half a Century. He remembers his Mother taking their part from the very first, but his Father was very much against them. Richd. is a very worthy old Man' (5/9/27). RS also recorded that he used to work for the Barnards but 'having more Zeal than humility he offended Mr. Barnard and lost his situation' (17/8/29).

MILNER, Thomas, (1806–); Church Street, South Cave; son of *James* and Jane. Formerly Independent but became a Methodist.

Emigrated to Canada in 1830 with his father.

MILNER, William (Willy Milner, the little Waller), bricklayer; Church Street, South Cave; possibly son of *James* and Jane, married Mary Pickering in 1826.

RS recorded a dispute with *Thomas Marshall* about his bill (17/4/29) and a drunken scene with a saddler and two dogs (20/1/32).

MOODY, Matthew I (Matty Moody), (1763–1845); tailor and merchant; Market Place, South Cave; married first Elizabeth, and after she died, Ann Martin in 1801, father of *Matthew II* (Mails).

Considered emigration in 1831 (21/2/31, 28/2/31), but was unable to sell his house, and apparently gave up the idea (7/3/31).

MOODY, Matthew II (Mails), (1809–); son of *Matthew I* and Ann.

Former pupil of RS. Emigrated in 1830 (12/5/30).

MORLEY, David, blacksmith and later (from 1829) landlord of the Fox and Coney; Market Place, South Cave; married Sarah Moody in 1820, their son David (b. 1828) later became landlord of the Beverley Arms, Beverley. In 1835 he left South Cave and took over the King's Head, Market Place, Beverley.

NEWLOVE, Richard, landlord of the Bear until 1832 and tenant of churchwardens' land until 1831; Market Place, South Cave; his wife, Ann, died 1831 and was buried at Rowley. Their daughter, Joanna, married *Joseph Barratt*.

RS did not like Newlove, whom he described as an idle fellow (e.g. 15/5/29, 4/2/30). In 1829, business at the Bear was poor. RS recorded that they only used one cask of ale (4/11/29). At the end of the year, presumably to improve business, Newlove was holding 'balls' (19/11/29, 22/12/29). In 1831, he had taken out a mortgage with the brewery of £200 after changing his mind about selling the house (17/2/30, 16/12/31). In 1832 he left, and the Bear was taken by *Edward Fewson*.

NICHOLSON, Robert I, (1773–); South Cave; married Rachel Smith in 1796, father of *Robert II*.

Emigrated to America in 1831, his son and family having gone there the previous year (26/11/29, 1/3/31, 4/3/31, 15/3/31).

NICHOLSON, Robert II, (1798–); South Cave; son of *Robert I* and Rachel, married Anne Pickering, one of *Matthew Pickering*'s daughters, in 1823.

Emigrated to America in 1830 despite his wife's apparent reluctance (26/11/29, 22/3/30, 11/4/30). Followed in 1831 by his father and his father-in-law, *Matthew Pickering*, and family.

NICHOLSON, William (Mr Nicholson); Frog Hall, Church Street, South Cave. Leased Frog Hall from *Revd John King*. Said to be from Hull (13/7/31). Churchwarden 1832/3, but left in March 1833 for Lund, because he could not agree with his landlord (9/3/33).

OXTOBY, Robert, grocer, tea-dealer, and seedsman; Market Place, Beverley. The Sharps bought groceries from him, when they had the shop (e.g. 6/9/30, 2/6/31, 14/12/31).

PETFIELD, George, (1792–1859); wheelwright and joiner; Church Street, South Cave.

Constable 1828/33. Treasurer of the South Cave Friendly Society in 1836. Petfield made coffins as part of his business. In 1832, he said of Samuel Leighton that 'he was as much like himself as ever he saw a Corpse' (30/6/32). His account book[3] includes an entry which shows the cost of RS's coffin as £3 10s.

PICKERING, Elizabeth *née* Robinson (old Betty), landlady of the Blacksmith's Arms, village midwife; Market Place, South Cave; married *Matthew* in 1802, mother of '5 or 6 daughters'. One of her daughters, Anne, married *Robert Nicholson II* and emigrated to America in 1830. She and her husband followed in 1831.

RS wrote in 1830 of her horror, when one of her daughters had an illegitimate child (20/3/30, 23/3/30). She delivered *Elizabeth Conder's* first baby—'there was old Betty Pickering there in a twinkling after she was called, and as soon as it was over, she set on and got breakfast ready in a jiffy' (17/7/30).

PICKERING, Matthew, blacksmith, small-holder, landlord of a new public house, the Blacksmith's Arms, from 1825 until 1831 when *Barnard Cook I* took it over; Market Place, South Cave; married *Elizabeth* Robinson in 1802, father of large family (see under *Elizabeth* above). The Pickerings emigrated to America in 1831, presumably encouraged by their daughter Anne Nicholson's success there.

---

[3] Partly transcribed in the notes of Archibald Trout kept in the Hull Local Studies Library.

PINDER, Elizabeth *née* Dyson (Bessy), (*c.* 1800–); grocer and draper until 1834; Market Place, South Cave; married *Thomas Pinder* in 1821, daughter Hannah. When *Thomas* died in 1827 she continued to run the shop, and in 1830 married *John Pinder II*, her husband's brother. In 1832, he too died.

PINDER, John II, (1795–1832); tailor, then from 1830, grocer and draper; Market Place, South Cave; son of John I and Ann, brother of *Thomas*, whose widow he married in 1830. RS described him as a Quaker (29/9/25, 30/10/30), but in 1832 he attended the Independent chapel (15/9/32).

RS disliked him, describing him as 'a little quack' (29/9/25). RS's friendship with his late brother, *Thomas*, may explain RS's hostility.

PINDER, Thomas (Tommy), (1793–1827); grocer and draper; Market Place, South Cave; son of John I and Ann, brother of *John II*, married *Elizabeth* Dyson in 1821. Independent.

A friend of RS. When he died, at the age of 33, RS reported that 'I really feel sorry for the loss of him. It is said he has been subject to drink much Liquor unmixed to the amount as report says of ten Glasses a day at times. However I can say I never saw him drunk, though several people have' (13–15/1/27). Over 200 people attended his funeral at Brantingham (17/1/27).

POPPLE, Revd Edmund, (1797–1829); curate of All Saints' Church, South Cave 1821–5; son of *Miles* and Josepha l'Oste.

RS had a very favourable opinion of him, in contrast to his usually critical attitude towards parsons. When he died suddenly, RS commented that 'he was a very excellent Character, feeling and humane' *(*13/9/29).

POPPLE, George Wetwang (Mr Popple of Ellerker), (1797–); substantial farmer; Ellerker.

RS often measured his land.

POPPLE, Revd Miles (old Mr Popple), Welton; married Josepha l'Oste, father of *Edmund*.

Preached at South Cave in 1827 (3/6/27).

PURDON, William, (1775–1856); farmer; Broomfleet; married Elizabeth (*c.* 1770–1865).

RS measured his land and occasionally dined with him.

RAMSDALE, James, (1774–1838); probably butler for the Sykes of West Ella, later a keeper of chaise and post horses, and from 1829 a farmer; West Ella; son of Robert I of Holme-on-Spalding-Moor, married *Milcah Sharp*, RS's sister, in 1808; father of *John*, *Mary*, and Robert III (b. 1819).

Visited the Sharps, especially at South Cave fair time.

RAMSDALE, John, (1809–); West Ella; son of *Milcah* and *James*, nephew of RS.

Like William, he lodged with his aunt, *Mary Sharp*, in Hull for a time (28/12/26).

RAMSDALE, Mary, (1814–); West Ella; daughter of *Milcah* and *James Ramsdale*, niece of RS.

RAMSDALE, Milcah *née* Sharp, (1783–1832); West Ella; daughter of *John I* and *Elizabeth Sharp*, born 22 February 1783, sister of *Robert, Thomas* and *Mary*, married *James* in 1808, mother of *John, Mary*, and Robert III (b. 1819).

Her mother and father lived close by her until their death. When RS visited West Ella, he went to see his sister and her family, and then his mother. He reported that she 'has 3 Cats a Dog and a Nanny Goat ... [and] some Ferrets' (15/11/30). In 1831, she had a mastectomy, from which she apparently recovered for a time, but in 1832, at the age of 49, she died (21/10/31, 26/10/32).

RAMSDALE, Robert II, (1772–); horse-dealer and innkeeper of the Old King's Arms; Market Weighton; son of Robert I.

A colourful personality in the horse-breeding trade in Market Weighton.

READ, Ann, see: *Sharp, Ann.*

READ, John, (1774–1835); Hull; son of *Richard* and Mary of Bempton, brother of *Ann Sharp,* married a young wife, and when he died, 'left a wife and six or seven Children very ill provided for' (18/2/35).

RS disapproved of his marriage, and when he left his family destitute wrote 'this is the fruit of an Old man marrying a young wife; he has played the fool exceedingly' (18/2/35).

READ, Richard; farmer; Bempton; married Mary Gibson of Carnaby in 1771, father of *Ann Sharp* and *John.*

REYNOLDS, John, (*c.* 1787–1877); blacksmith and grocer; West End, South Cave; married Mary Levitt (1789–) in 1810.

Parish clerk during the period of the diary. His tombstone records that he was parish clerk for 58 years.

RINGROSE, Samuel, (1762–1834); farmer; Brantingham; married Sarah/Sally Kirk in 1801.

ROBINSON. Several Robinsons feature in the diary, but RS was always careful to identify each one: *John Robinson III,* the attorney, was always 'Mr. Robinson'; *Thomas Robinson I* of Mount Airy was 'Robinson' or 'Mr. Robinson of Mount Airy'; *Thomas Robinson III* of Ellerker was usually 'Tom Robinson', or 'Robinson of Ellerker'.

ROBINSON, Ann (Mrs Robinson), (*c.* 1785–1857); Mount Airy, South Cave; married to *Thomas I.*

ROBINSON, Fenlay (1795–); farmer; South Cave; married to Hannah. Independent.

ROBINSON, John I, (d. 1798); superannuated officer in the Customs; father of *John II.*

ROBINSON, John II, (*c.* 1757–1814); attorney; South Cave; son of *John I,* married Elizabeth, father of *John III.*

ROBINSON, John III (Mr Robinson), (1784–1838); attorney; Market Place. South Cave; son of *John II* and Elizabeth.

RS copied deeds for him, witnessed his will twice, used his services when he lent £100 on mortgage, and gave him a parcel for *William Sharp I*, when he went down to London.

ROBINSON, John IV, (*c.* 1810–); Mount Airy and then Common Farm, South Cave; son of *Thomas I*, eloped with Mary Arton in 1832 (3/3/32, 7/3/32).

ROBINSON, Thomas I (Mr Robinson of Mount Airy), (*c.* 1782–1842); farmer; Mount Airy; married *Ann*, father of *John IV* (who eloped with Mary Arton), Joseph, Daniel, Hannah (who married *William Fisher*), Elizabeth (who married *Robert Kemp*), Thomas II (who married Sarah Bathia, *Thomas Dyson's* daughter in 1833).

Juryman at Beverley sessions in 1827. Assessor with RS 1831/2. Overseer of the poor 1831/2. RS measured for him. On one memorable occasion, the diarist travelled as a passenger in Robinson's gig on a visit to Beverley. On the return journey, Robinson was drunk, and drove the gig so erratically that RS was forced to jump out of it, causing him to injure his foot, and swear never again to travel in a gig driven by his fellow assessor (30/3/31).

ROBINSON, Thomas III (Robinson of Ellerker), farmer; Ellerker.

RS often measured for him.

RODMELL, Revd John, (1793–); curate of All Saints' church, South Cave, 1826–34); son of Thomas Rodmell, Hull postmaster.

RS at first described him as 'a good natured young man' (9/7/26), but his opinion of the curate deteriorated as Rodmell's rigid doctrinal views, especially on baptism, became apparent (17/9/26, 29/10/26, 2/12/26). In 1829, RS noted his 'affected pronunciation' (16/8/29). In 1832, the question of the burial of people baptized as dissenters again surfaced in relation to *Hannah Levitt's* son by *Norrison Marshall* (24/2/32, 18/3/32). The vicar, *Revd Creyke*, did not agree with his curate's obdurate attitude, and RS commended him for it. In 1833 Rodmell was reported to live 'upon nothing but Dog Biscuits', which RS interpreted as his apparent predilection for a vegetarian diet (11/11/33). Preached farewell sermon in 1834, but twice recorded as preaching at South Cave in 1836.

RUDD, Charles, (*c.* 1780–); farmer; Ellerker; married Ann Elizabeth Forbes in 1805.

Overseer of the poor and surveyor of the highways for Ellerker in 1832 (when RS assisted him with the accounts) and in 1834. RS measured for him regularly, and *Ann Sharp* and *Ann Conder* visited his wife in 1836.

RUSTON, Francis, (*c.* 1769–1838); joiner; West End, South Cave; Independent, but reported to have given up going to the chapel because the preacher (*Revd Seth Kelso*) was dirty (25/2/27).

SHACKLETON, James, (*c.* 1786–1835); gentleman; West End, South Cave; brother of *William*.

RS found him to be of a higher intellectual level than most of his neighbours (23/10/30).

SHACKLETON, William, gentleman-farmer; Provence Farm, South Cave, until 1831 when *Robert Arton II* took it.

SHARP, Ann *née* Read, (1775–1868); baptized 30 December 1775 at Bempton, daughter of *Richard* and Mary Read, married *Robert Sharp* at Priory Church, Bridlington, 5 May 1795. They had six children: *John II* (1796–7), *William I* (1798–1870), *Mary* (1801–2), *Jane* (1803–15), *Elizabeth* (1805–66), and *John III* (1806–16). After RS's death in 1843, Ann probably moved to Church Street, South Cave, where she was living in 1851 with her granddaughter *Ann Conder*. Ann Sharp was buried 3 December 1868 at South Cave.

SHARP, Elizabeth I, *née* Harrison, (1744–1832); born April and baptized 6 May 1744 (RS recorded incorrectly that she was born on the '7th day of old May 1745', i.e. 25 April 1745), daughter of Robert I and Mary Harrison of Beeford, sister of *Robert Harrison II*, married *John Sharp I* on 20 December 1770 at Barmston (in the register, she wrote her name, but John Sharp signed with a cross). Mother of *Robert, Thomas II, Milcah,* and *Mary*. Elizabeth and *John I* moved to West Ella some time after their daughter, *Milcah*, had settled there with her husband, *James Ramsdale*. *Robert* and *Elizabeth II* visited her regularly during the period of the diary, by which time her husband, *John I*, had died. She still read without spectacles in her eighties. RS's report of the conversation, which took place, when the minister of Swanland and his wife visited her, in order to distribute religious tracts, shows her to have been an intelligent and forthright person, well capable of holding her own, despite her age (9/7/29). When writing of the tufits (lapwings) of Barmston, RS recorded that when, as a boy, he caught them, and carried them home 'My Mother has frequently carried them back to their breeding place for fear they should be destroyed, (was not this trait worth recording? Yes there was pure feeling here).' (13/12/31). She was buried at Kirk Ella on 7 August 1832 (7/8/32).

SHARP, Elizabeth II (Eliza), (1805–66); daughter of *Robert* and *Ann*, see: *Conder, Elizabeth.*

SHARP, Jane, (1803–15); daughter of *Robert* and *Ann*, born 28 April, baptized 19 August 1803, at the Zion Independent Chapel, Bridlington, buried 3 March 1815 at South Cave. Jane Sharp's sampler has been preserved in the family.

SHARP, John I, (1742–1825); son of *Thomas I* and Milcah Bailior, baptized 28 June 1742 at Reighton, married *Elizabeth* Harrison on 20 December 1770 at Barmston. Worked as a shepherd at Barmston, and also held some closes there. Father of *Robert, Thomas II, Milcah,* and *Mary*. Died at West Ella on 23 June, and buried at Kirk Ella on 25 June 1825. RS described him as a 'remarkably quiet and peaceable man ... his Father was a Shepherd and lived at Reighton' (11/7/25). 'I recollect my Father talking of having Tansy pudding to dinner on the Sunday called Tansy Sunday, he was brought up a Shepherd and continued so as long as he was able, he aspired to nothing but honest rural manners' (18/4/27). 'My Father was the last Cottager I believe who had a small Close about 3 Acres, which grew Wheat, Potatoes, Grass &cs' (7/11/31). 'I said nothing of South Field where my Father for more than forty years, spent the greatest part of his time with his Flock; he was no Arcadian Shepherd; but up late and early attending to the wants of his charges; there are no such Shepherds in this Country as we find painted or described in the Poets; their Pastorals are what poor Shepherds never experience' (7/12/31) 'My Father was the best Clipper of Sheep in the Country; he could Clip a Sheep better and sooner than any Man he ever wrought with' (15/12/31).

SHARP, John II, (1796–7); eldest son of *Robert* and *Ann*, born 27 May 1796, baptized 15 June 1796 at Zion Independent Chapel, Bridlington, buried 9 February 1797 at Priory Church, Bridlington.

SHARP, John III, (1806–16); third son of *Robert* and *Ann*, born 28 March 1806, baptized at Independent Chapel, South Cave, buried 29 February 1816.

RS recalled him, in the diary, when *Norrison Marshall* was killed. He wrote that 'he and our poor dear John were like Brothers and of the same age within a month' (17/6/31).

SHARP, Mary, (1778–1831/2); daughter of *John I* and *Elizabeth I*; see: *Barker, Mary*.

SHARP, Mary, (1801–2); first daughter and third child of *Robert* and *Ann*, born 8 May 1801, baptized 24 July 1801 at Zion Independent Chapel, Bridlington, died of measles and buried 10 June 1802.

SHARP, Mary Barker (little Mary), (1828–1905); daughter of *William I* and Hannah Hicks, sister of *William II*, and *Robert Harrison*, unmarried. At her death she was living in Penge, Kent, with her brother *William II*.

In her childhood she seems to have suffered many ailments. In 1832, she was sent to Wales for her health (30/7/32). She visited her grandparents at South Cave in 1829, 1833, and possibly 1834. *Ann Sharp* went down to London to see her and her family in 1835.

SHARP, Milcah, (1783–1832); daughter of *John I* and *Elizabeth I*; see: *Ramsdale, Milcah*.

SHARP, Robert, (1773–1843); son of *John I* and *Elizabeth*, born 22 September 1773, baptized 1 October 1773 at Barmston, brother of *Thomas II*, *Mary* and *Milcah*, married *Ann* Read at Priory Church, Bridlington 5 May 1795. Six children: *John II* (1796–7), *William I* (1798–1870), *Mary* (1801–2), *Jane* (1803–15), *Elizabeth II* (1805–66), and *John III* (1806–16). He was educated at Barmston school by his uncle, *Robert Harrison II*, the village schoolmaster. He left Barmston in 1786, when he was 13, and went to Bridlington. He worked as a shoemaker there, before taking the post of schoolmaster at South Cave on 13 February 1804. He died on 5 May, and was buried on 7 May 1843.

SHARP, Robert Harrison, (1833–1918), son of *William I* and Hannah Hicks, grandson of *Robert* and *Ann*, married Mary MacLaren, five children.

SHARP, Thomas I (*c.* 1698–1775); shepherd at Reighton; probably born Burton Fleming, married Milcah Bailior (d. 1786), in 1732 at Bridlington, father of *John I*, grandfather of *Robert*, buried at Reighton 13 September 1775.

SHARP, Thomas II, (1775–1843); Independent minister at Skipton; son of *John I* and *Elizabeth I*, baptized 2 June 1775, brother of *Robert*, *Mary* and *Milcah*, died 24 April 1843 in Skipton.

Thomas was in Bridlington with RS during his late boyhood, apparently remaining there until 1805, when he decided that he wished to train for the Independent ministry. In 1806, he went to Idle College, where he remained as a student for five years. In 1809 and 1810 he preached at Skipton chapel, and in 1811 was chosen as its minister. He remained minister until 1833, when as a result of a dispute, an attempt was made to replace him.[4] He refused to resign, but later, in the same year, he suffered a paralytic stroke, and became incapable of carrying out his duties. He received an annuity from his sister, *Mary Barker*, and remained in Skipton until his death on 24 April 1843, just 11 days before his brother *Robert* died.

SHARP, William I, (1798–1870); son of *Robert* and *Ann*, born 17 June 1798 at Bridlington, baptized 29 June 1798, married Hannah Hicks 12 April 1828 at St. Luke's, Old Street, London, daughter *Mary Barker* (1828–1905), son *William II* (1831–1918), son *Robert Harrison* (1833–1918), died 6 September 1870. William began work, *c.* 1812, in Silver Street in Hull, where he was employed by *John Craggs*, of North Cave, who operated in Hull as a bookseller, binder, stationer, and paper manufacturer. William was staying with his aunt *Mary Barker*, RS's sister, when he received the first letter in the collection in 1812. From November 1821 he was living in London, and working for the publishing firm of Longman's, where he held the post of 'Head of Counter', until his death, when his address was given as Paternoster Row, London.

SHARP, William II, (1831–1918); son of *William I* and Hannah, grandson of *Robert* and *Ann*. Like his father, he worked at Longman's as 'Head of Counter'. He entered as a boy on 5 April 1847, and retired 'by request' on 30 June 1896. He lived with his sister, *Mary Barker Sharp*, from at least 1881 until his death in 1918, in Penge, Kent.

SHAW, Samuel; farmer; Brantingham, Drewton from 1832. Independent.

SHAWE/SHAW, Nathaniel II (Mr Shaw), (*c.* 1794–); farmer and yeoman; Swanland; son of Nathaniel I and Margaret, brother of *Richard*.

SHAWE/SHAW, Capt. Richard Fleetwood (Captain or Mr Shaw), (1804–72); gentleman and army officer; Brantinghamthorpe Hall and Brantingham Hall from 1832; son of Nathaniel I and Margaret, brother of *Nathaniel II*, married Anna (1809–97).

Shawe bought Brantinghamthorpe Hall from *Revd Edward Barnard's* devisees in 1832, and then, later in the same year, Brantingham Hall from

---

[4] Dawson 55, 73–84.

Revd James Simpson, who had been declared bankrupt. He also bought more land and property in the area (e.g. 5/8/35, 17/12/36). RS stated that 'there is a Gentleman come to Brantingham-Thorpe who has bought the House & Land of the late Revd. Mr. Barnard's he has also bought all the Estate of the Revd. Mr. Simpson he is making great alterations and has a number of Labourers employed, which is a great relief to the Poor men both at Brantingham & the neighbouring Parishes' (10/4/32).

SIMPSON, Henry, (1777–1842); gentleman-farmer; Brantingham Grange; married Elizabeth Nichols in 1805.

SIMPSON, Revd James; curate of All Saints, Brantingham, and farmer; Brantingham Hall from 1816 until 1832, when he sold it to *Captain Shawe*; married Mary, by whom he had several children.

He officiated at South Cave at various times until 1832, when he got into financial difficulties. RS recorded that *Samuel Ringrose* stood surety for him, but Simpson absconded, and was subsequently apprehended in Lincolnshire (8/12/31).

SMELT, Robert; high constable of Hunsley Beacon Division; Wednesday Market, Beverley; married Ann Sentoff in 1830.

RS was quite friendly with him. He dined with him at Beverley (24/5/26), and Miss Smelt and a niece dined at the Sharp's house (9/11/26). Smelt was a supporter of the abolition of slavery (19/11/30). When the Sharps were found to have low weights in their shop, RS wrote to Smelt, and was not fined (21/11/31).

SMITH, Charles (Charley Smith), (1803–74); carpenter and joiner, then from 1833, landlord of a beerhouse—the Carpenter's Arms; West End, South Cave; married Hannah.

RS described the rivalry between the two beerhouses at the West End (29/5/34). Smith's beer shop was blamed for an occurrence of riotous behaviour in 1835 (28/4/35).

SMITH, Matthew, (d. 1829); cooper, but by the time of the diary, probably too old for work.

Most references in the diary concern his drunkenness (e.g. 2/2/27,12/7/27). In 1829, RS recorded that 'he hanged himself on Friday morning in *Grace Holborn*'s Garret where he lodged. A Coroner's inquest was held on him yesterday, when the Jury of which I was one brought in the verdict temporary insanity, he has been ill and in a low way for nearly a year past' (15/3/29).

SONLEY, Elizabeth, *née* Huntington, (Mrs Sonley), (*c.* 1752–1827); gentlewoman, widow of physician; Market Place, South Cave; married as second wife, Dr William Sonley, who practised in South Cave for 50 years until his death in 1813, step-mother of Sarah, who married Aldcroft Waller. Their son, also *Aldcroft Waller*, inherited her property.

In 1826, at the age of 74, she had her breast removed to treat cancer, but died the following year (31/8/26, 23/8/27).

STATHER, John (Jackey or Weather cock Jack), farmer; Everthorpe.

STOTT, Revd William, (*c.* 1788–1839); minister of the Independent Chapel, South Cave 1828–39.

Described as 'a very big man, with stout legs encased in knee breeches, silk stockings, and shoes with large buckles'.[5] In 1833, RS had a dispute with Stott about some books ordered from London (e.g. 23/7/33, 1–2/8/33).

STUPARTE, Dr James, surgeon; Market Place, South Cave; married Elizabeth. He succeeded *Dr Edward Tinsdill* in 1829. Treated RS for various complaints (30–31/1/30). Left in 1832 to live in Elloughton, and was succeeded by *Dr Samuel Carter.*

SYKES FAMILY. Those members of the family mentioned in the diary were distant cousins of the Sykes of Sledmere, both branches being descended from Richard Sykes, Hull merchant (1678–1726). Members of the Sledmere branch were Tories, whilst those of the West Ella branch were Whigs.

SYKES, Daniel, (1766–1832); attorney, recorder of Hull, MP for Hull 1820–30, MP for Beverley 1830–2; Raywell House; fifth son of *Joseph I* (1723–1805) and Dorothy *née* Twigge of West Ella, married Isabella Wright (1766–1844) in 1795.

He was a much respected radical MP, involved with the promotion of parliamentary reform, Catholic emancipation, the abolition of slavery, and free trade. RS thought highly of him (e.g. 11/6/26) and recorded on hearing of his death 'Mr. Danl. Sykes died on Tuesday morning last, I am sorry for his death, he was a kind Man and very useful Magistrate, & will be greatly lamented' (27/1/32).

SYKES, Joseph I, (1723–1805); gentleman; West Ella; married Dorothy *née* Twigge, father of *Revd Richard, Nicholas, Daniel* and others.

SYKES, Joseph II, (1796–1857); gentleman; Swanland Hall, then, after his uncle *Daniel's* death, Raywell House; son of *Nicholas*, married Elizabeth Egginton, daughter of Gardiner Egginton of Aston Hall, North Ferriby, by whom he had 12 children. After her death, in 1851, he married Anne Broadley of South Ella.

RS recorded his failure to be elected as MP for Beverley in 1835 (7/1/35).

SYKES, Nicholas, (1764–1827); gentleman, lieutenant in 1st Dragoons, alderman and mayor of Hull; Swanland Hall; son of *Joseph I* and Dorothy, father of *Joseph II*, married Mary Cam (*c.* 1769–1844), by whom he had 13 children, many of them dying in infancy.

SYKES, Revd Richard, (1756–1832); rector of Foxholes; eldest son and heir of *Joseph I* and Dorothy, married Mary (*c.* 1752–1831).

SYKES, Major Richard, (1783–1870); gentleman; West Ella; son of *Revd Richard*, never married; inherited West Ella Hall on the death of *Joseph I* in 1805.

[5] Trout 13.

The *Ramsdales*, in-laws of the Sharps, probably worked for him. In 1814 *Robert Ramsdale's* occupation was recorded as 'butler'. Major Sykes passed on information of *William Sharp I*, whom he had seen in London in 1826 (5/8/26).

TAPP, Benjamin, (1801–); travelling salesman; son of *Revd William* and *Sarah*, brother of John. Independent.

    RS received news from him of his brother, *Thomas*, in Skipton (4/2/27). He sued *Barnard Cook I* for debt in 1830 (21/6/30).

TAPP, Sarah *née* Ansley, (d. 1837); married *Revd William* in 1785.

    Mrs Tapp and her daughters visited the Sharps (19/7/32). When she died *Ann Sharp* attended her funeral 'as a testimony of old friendship' (25/2/37).

TAPP, Revd William, (1756–1819); minister of Independent chapel, South Cave (1791 to 1819); married *Sarah* Ansley in 1785, father of John (1798–) and *Benjamin*.

THORNHAM, William I, (*c.* 1777–); boot and shoe maker; Church Street, South Cave; married Ann Petfield in 1799, father of *William II*.

    RS recorded him as having broken his arm whilst drunk (17/3/30).

THORNHAM, William II, (1799–); boot and shoe maker, Church Street, South Cave; son of *William I*.

    RS recorded his drunkenness (30/3/32).

THORNTON, Ann *née* Leaman (old Nanny Thornton), (d. 1829); cow-keeper; Church Street, South Cave; married *Richard* in 1803, mother of *Robert* (Bobby) and 'fond' Jacky.

    RS recorded her quarrel with *Abraham Barff*, when he called her 'thou old yellow faced rubbish' (9/8/26). RS made out her will shortly before she died.

THORNTON, Richard (*c.* 1760–); boot and shoe maker; Church Street, South Cave; married *Ann* in 1803, father of *Robert* and Jacky

THORNTON, Robert (Bobby); boot and shoe maker; Church Street, South Cave; son of *Ann* and *Richard*.

    His dandified appearance in church described graphically by RS (12–13/4/29).

TINDALE/TINDLE/TINDALL, John (Cooper Tindale), (*c.* 1783/6–); cooper and landlord of the Three Tuns until 1831; Market Place, South Cave; possibly brother of *Valentine*, married Elizabeth, father of Thomas (b. 1817).

    Emigrated to America in 1831.

TINDALE/TINDLE/TINDALL, Robert, farmer; Weedley Farm.

    Constable 1827/8. In 1829, RS commented, 'I do not like this same Tindale for there has been nothing but disturbance in the Parish since he came into it' (21/4/29), but his attitude improved, when he knew him better. Tindale was overseer of the poor and surveyor of the highways 1832/3. In 1837, he was appointed guardian of the poor.

TINDALE/TINDLE/TINDALL, Valentine (Val Tindale), (1789–); butcher; Market Place, South Cave; possibly brother of *John*, married Ann Elizabeth Chapman in 1817.

An argumentative character according to RS's accounts.

TINSDILL, Edward Windle, (1798–); surgeon; Market Place, South Cave; married Elizabeth.

He bought the practice of *Dr Francis Day* in 1823. A friend of the Sharps and intellectual companion of RS, who wrote 'he still reads Cobbett, and is a great admirer of him. I like him pretty well at times, but he is continually bawling against Bank Bills' (29/9/25). He treated the Sharps for various ailments. The Tinsdills left South Cave in 1829.

TODD, Robert (Bobby), labourer; Church Street, South Cave; married Ann Grasby in 1803, his daughter Jane, his 'lahtle lass', married *David Dennis*.

TURK, see: MACTURK.

TURNER, John, blacksmith and farrier (succeeded *Matthew Pickering*), then landlord of the Bear from 1836; Market Place, South Cave; married Elizabeth.

USHER, Edward, (1776–); farmer; Drewton; probably brother of *Robert*, married Mary Tindale in 1818.

RS measured his land on several occasions.

USHER, Robert, farmer; Drewton; probably brother of *Edward*, married Rachel Walker in 1823.

WALLER, Captain Aldcroft, (1781–); army half-pay pensioner, gentleman-farmer; his mother, Sarah Sonley, daughter of Dr William Sonley, married Aldcroft Waller in 1779. When Dr Sonley's second wife, *Mrs Elizabeth Sonley*, died in 1827, Captain Waller inherited her house in South Cave Market Place, Frog Hall, and a farm at Drewton.

WAUDBY, John (Tailor Waudby), (*c.* 1789–1879); tailor and beerhouse keeper of the Half Moon, Church Street, South Cave; from 1834; but before then resident in Market Place, South Cave; married Jane Brown in 1814.

WILKINSON, William, butcher; Market Place, South Cave.

Accused of stealing sheep (9/4/35).

WOOD, Francis, farmer; Drewton; married Sarah Shaw in 1802, then, in 1835, married Ann Hodgson, Mr Barnard's former housekeeper, at York (5/2/35).

WRIDE, Thomas, (*c.* 1778–1856); farmer; Church Street, South Cave; married Elizabeth Forge in 1802.

Churchwarden 1833/4. Overseer of the poor 1831/2. Surveyor of the highways 1836/7. RS measured for him regularly.

APPENDIX III

List of Authors and Works Cited by Robert Sharp in the Letters and Diary

Books (including poems and plays)

Listed here are all the books (and their authors unless the works are anonymous) referred to by Robert Sharp together with the date in the letters or diary on which the first reference is made to a work. In some cases a work is referred to specifically by its title, whilst in other cases the reference is implicit in the form of a quotation. In order to avoid unnecessary complexity, no attempt has been made to identify the different categories of reference, especially since the diarist frequently quoted from works which he also explicitly cited. A dagger sign (†) after the date indicates that the passage or diary entry containing the reference has been deleted from the text in accordance with the principles listed in the section on editorial method.

It has not always been possible from the diarist's reference to determine the precise edition or even the exact identity of a particular work. When there are several editions, as far as possible, the most likely edition (usually the one published most recently before the date of the reference in the diary) of the work to which the diarist referred, is the one cited in the list. The date of the first edition is also given with some indication of the dates of intervening editions, where this is appropriate. A question mark in parentheses after a title indicates that some element of doubt remains on whether the listed title corresponds to the diary reference. Such cases have occurred either when more than one work has been located with the same title, or when some variation appeared in the wording of the listed title and the diary citation.

Where Sharp has made a reference to or quoted from a poem (often unidentified in the text), it is listed in the same way as any other work if published separately. When, however, a poem has not been published separately, it has been listed simply under its title; where possible, bibliographic details have been supplied of at least one work in which the poem has been published, but not necessarily the same work in which it was encountered by the diarist. Dates of birth and death are added to the names of less well known poets.

No attempt has been made to supply bibliographical details to the titles of the various Shakespearean plays referred to, or quoted, by the diarist.

Allestree, Richard. *The Whole Duty of Man, laid down in a Plain and Familiar Way* ... New ed. London: J. G. and F. Rivington, 1832. Pp. xiv, 374. (8°). First published in 1659, this popular devotional work, attributed to Richard Allestree, was re-issued in numerous editions during the remaining decades of the 17th century and throughout the 18th and 19th centuries. (31/7/32).

Anon. 'The Pilgrim' [poem] (10/3/29).

The Arabian Nights' Entertainments, consisting of One Thousand and One Stories [from the French translation of Antoine Galland]. London: F.C. and J. Rivington, 1821. – 3 vols. – Numerous editions of the 'Arabian Nights' appeared in the early 19th century, many of them translated from the French, as in this example. (29/9/25).

Arnold, Richard (d. 1521?). *The Customs of London, otherwise called Arnold's Chronicle, Containing among Divers other Matters the Original of the Celebrated Poem of the Nut-brown Maid.* Reprinted from the first edition with the additions included in the second. London: Longman, Hurst, Rees, Orme and Brown, 1811. Pp. lii, 300. (4°). Originally published under the title, *In this Booke is Conteyned the Names of ye Baylifs, Custos, Mairs and Sherefs of the Cite of London* ... London: Richard Arnold, 1502. Other editions published Antwerp: A. van Berghen, [1503?] and Southwark: P. Treveris, [1525?]. (23/5/31). †

Bailey, Nathan, *comp. An Universal Etymological English Dictionary.* London, 1726. – Variously entitled *The New Universal Etymological English Dictionary* etc., more than 30 editions of this popular dictionary were published throughout the 18th and early 19th centuries. (24/5/30). †

Beverley, Robert Mackenzie. *A Letter to His Grace the Archbishop of York, on the Present Corrupt State of the Church of England. Beverley:* W. B. Johnson, 1831. (8°). (30/6/31).

Beverley, Robert Mackenzie. *The Tombs of the Prophets: a Lay Sermon on the Corruptions of the Church of Christ.* Beverley: W.B. Johnson, 1831. Pp. 59. Also 2nd ed, 1831. Pp. 51. (22/7/31).

Boswell, James. *The Life of Samuel Johnson LL.D.* ... 2nd ed., revised and augmented. Copious notes and biographical illustrations by [Edmond] Malone. London: J. Richardson and Co., 1821. – 5 vols. – Several editions of this work were published and current in the early 19th century of which this one is representative. (13/9/26).

Britton, John *and* Brayley, Edward Wedlake. *The Beauties of England and Wales; or; Delineations, Topographical, Historical and Descriptive of each County* ... 18 vols. London: Vernor, Hood and Sharpe, 1801–15. – Volume 9 (1807) by John Britton covered Lancashire, Leicestershire, and Lincolnshire. From a parallel 18-volume edition of the same work published in London by George Cowie and Co., the section on Lancashire, pages 5–312 from volume 9, was re-issued as a separate volume, entitled *A Topographical and Historical Description of the County of Lancaster* [*c*.1815]. Sharp might have been referring to either of these volumes in his letter. (10/2/20).

Burns, Robert. 'Aloway Kirk; or, Tam O'Shanter: a Tale' [poem]. (16/3/27).

Carr, John. *A Northern Summer; or, Travels Round the Baltic, through Denmark, Sweden, Russia, Prussia and Parts of Germany in* ... *1804.* London, 1805. – Also another edition in 1810. – John Carr was an indefatigable traveller and published other books of his travels in Spain, France, Holland and Ireland; it is impossible to know to which book Sharp was referring and the work cited here is intended to be only a representative example. (30/6/29).(?).

Cervantes Saavedra, Miguel de. [*El Ingenioso Hidalgo Don Quixote de la Mancha*]. Originally published in two parts, the first in 1605 and the second in 1615, this work was translated into English by several translators including Thomas Shelton, J. Philips, Peter Motteux, Charles Jarvis, and Tobias Smollett and innumerable editions were published from the 17th century until the period of this diary. A representative contemporary edition of the version by Peter Motteux is: *The History of the Ingenious Gentleman, Don Quixote of La Mancha ...* A new edition, with copious notes ... [by J. G. Lockhart]. London: Hunt, Robinson and Co., 1822. – 5 vols. (8⁰). (19/8/27).

Church of England. *Book of Common Prayer.* Oxford: University Press, 1831. Pp. 263. One of several editions available at this period. (18/12/36).

Church of England. *Constitutions and Canons Ecclesiastical.* 1828. (8⁰). Various editions available. (2/4/35).

Clare, John. 'The Workhouse Orphan: a Tale' 1821 [poem]. (14/4/33). (?).

Cobbett, William. *The Beauties of Cobbett.* London: H. Stemman, [1820?]. – 3 pts. (25/12/21).

Cobbett, William. *Cottage Economy: Containing Information Relating to the Brewing of Beer, Making of Bread, Keeping of Cows, Pigs, Bees, Ewes, Goats, Poultry and Rabbits, and Relative to other Matters Deemed Useful in the Conducting of the Affairs of a Labourer's Family.* London, 1822. – This work was originally issued in seven monthly parts (1821–2). (25/12/21).

Cobbett, William. *The Emigrant's Guide; in Ten Letters, Addressed to the Tax-payers of England; Containing Information of Every Kind, Necessary to Persons Who are About to Emigrate ...* London: published by the author, 1829. Pp. 153. – Also a new edition, 1830 with 168 pages. (5/9/29).

Cobbett, William. *A History of the Protestant "Reformation" in England and Ireland; Showing how that Event has Impoverished the Main Body of the People in those Countries and Containing a List of the Abbies, Priories, Nunneries ... Confiscated ... by the Protestant "Reformation" Sovereigns and Parliaments ... In a series of letters ...* London: the author, 1829. – 2 vols. – Originally published in parts by Charles Clement, 1824–6. (12⁰). – Also part 2, containing a list of the abbeys, etc., was separately published by Cobbett in 1827. (16/6/30).

Cobbett, William. *The Poor Man's Friend; or, Companion for the Working Classes, Giving Them Useful Information and Advice: being the System of Moral and Political Philosophy Laid Down and Exemplified by William Cobbett.* London: H. Stemman, 1826. (17/8/26).

Cobbett, William. 'Rural Rides'. – Originally published in serial form in *Cobbett's Political Register*, a selection of the original articles was later reprinted as: *Rural Rides in the Counties of Surrey, Kent, Sussex ... with Economic and Political Observations Relative to ... the State of those*

Counties Respectively. London: William Cobbett, 1830. Var. pag. (12⁰).(9/10/26).

Cole, John. *The Antiquarian Trio, consisting of Views and Descriptions of 1. Duke of Buckingham's House. 2. Rudston Church and Obelisk. 3. Effigy in the Old Town-hall,* with observations on the latter by the Reverend J. L. Sisson. To which is added a finale called *The Poet's Favourite Tree* by the Reverend Archdeacon Wrangham with a brief description of Hunmanby ... Scarborough: John Cole, 1826. Pp. ii, 28. (13/8/26).

Collins, William (1721–59). 'Eclogue the Second, Hassan; or, The Camel Driver' [poem]. (25/12/21)

Crabbe, George. *The Borough: a Poem in Twenty-four Letters.* London: J. Hatchard, 1810. Pp. xli, 344. (8⁰). – Further editions (2nd to 6th) published by the same publisher between 1810 and 1816. (23/3/32).

Crabbe, George. 'The Tale of Jesse and Colin' [poem]. (25/1/33).

Defoe, Daniel. *The True-Born Englishman: a Satyr.* London, 1700 [i.e. 1701]. Pp. 71. (4⁰). – More than 25 separate editions of this work were published throughout the 18th century. (25/9/35). †

Dryden, John. 'Prologue – Sophonisba'; in his: *Prologues and Epilogues.* (13/1/29).

Edgeworth, Maria. *Vivian.* – First published, with *The Absentee* and *Mm. de Fleury,* in the author's *Tales of Fashionable Life,* 2nd series, in 1812 but not published, except in translation, as a separate work until 1856. (21/8/32). †

Evans, John. *An Excursion to Windsor in July 1810, through Battersea ... and Hampton Court ... Also a Sail down the River Medway, July 1811, from Maidstone ... to the River Nore, upon the Opening of the Oyster Beds.* To which is annexed, *A Journal of a Trip to Paris, by Way of Ostend ... and Waterloo,* embellished with woodcuts by John Evans (jun.). London: Sherwood, Neely and Jones, 1817. Pp. x, 558. – Also a 2nd ed. in 1827. (31/1/25).

Fielding, Henry. *The History of the Adventures of Joseph Andrews, and of his Friend Mr. Abraham Adams ...* London: Andrew Millar, 1742. – 2 vols. (12⁰). More than 20 separate editions of this work had been published by the end of the 18th century, and it continued to be popular throughout the period of the diary. (21/2/30).†

Fielding, Henry. *Journey of a Voyage to Lisbon.* London: A. Millar, 1755. Pp. iv, 245 (12⁰). – This edition was published in December but was preceded by a shortened version published in February 1755. Another ed. 1785 and reprinted in Mavor, William. *A Collection of Voyages and Travels ...* vol. 11 (1810), pp. 201–52. (27/2/35). †

Franklin, Benjamin. *Poor Richard's Maxims of Industry and Frugality* – Aphorisms originally published in *Poor Richard's Almanack,* 1758, and subsequently collected and published under a variety of titles such as *Father Abraham's Speech, The Way to Wealth, Poor Richard's Maxims* etc. (25/12/21).

Goldsmith, Oliver. *The Citizen of the World; or, Letters from a Chinese Philosopher, Residing in London, to his Friends in the East.* London: printed for the author, 1762. – 2 vols. (12⁰). – Originally published serially under the title, 'Chinese Letters' in John Newbery's *Public Ledger* Jan. 1760—Aug. 1761, it was later republished in numerous editions in the later 18th and 19th centuries. (4/7/27).

Goldsmith, Oliver. *The Deserted Village: a Poem.* London: W. Griffin, 1770. Pp. vii, 23. (4⁰). – Published in several later separate editions, until at least 1793, as well as in the poet's collected works. (2/7/27).

Goldsmith, Oliver. *Edwin and Angelina: a Ballad.* By Mr. Goldsmith printed for the amusement of the Countess of Northumberland. London, [1764 or 1765]. Pp. 8. – Followed by several later editions and printed in numerous collective works that would have been available to Sharp. (12/8/27).

Goldsmith, Oliver. *The Haunch of Venison: a Poetical Epistle to Lord Clare ...* London: G. Kearsly; J. Ridley, 1776. Pp. 11, plate. (4⁰). (24/4/29).

Goldsmith, Oliver. *The Vicar of Wakefield* [with engravings from designs by Richard Westall]. London: John Sharpe, 1828. Pp. 226. – First published in two volumes, 1766. (29/11/30).

Heber, Amelia. *The Life of Reginald Heber ...* By his Widow. With Selections from his Correspondence, Unpublished Poems and Private Papers ... London: John Murray, 1830. – 2 vols. (4⁰). (See also: (1) Heber, Reginald. 'Critique on Scott's "Force of Truth" ...' and (2) Scott, Thomas. *The Force of Truth: an Authentic Narrative.* 2nd ed. London: Religious Tract Society, 1831). (8/12/32).

Heber, Reginald, *Bishop of Calcutta.* 'Critique on Scott's "Force of Truth" [originally written as a letter addressed to Miss Charlotte Dod, 1819]' *in*: Heber, Amelia. *The Life of Reginald Heber ...* By his Widow ..., London: John Murray, 1830, vol. 1, pp. 533–53. (See also: Scott, Thomas. *The Force of Truth: an Authentic Narrative.* 2nd ed. London: Religious Tract Society, 1831). (8/12/32).

Holy Bible (quoted, e.g. 23/7/29).

Hone, William. *The Every-Day Book; or, Everlasting Calendar of Popular Amusement.* London: published for William Hone by Hunt and Clarke, 1826. (19/9/26).

Hone, William. *The Man in the Moon,* with fifteen woodcuts [by George Cruikshank]. London: William Hone, 1820. – Satirical verses on George IV and others. There were at least 27 editions or impressions of this work up to 1825. (10/2/20).

Hone, William. *The Political House that Jack Built ...* London: William Hone, 1819. Some 49 separate editions or impressions of this satirical work were published by the author between 1819 and 1820; they were illustrated by 13 woodcuts executed by George Cruikshank. (10/2/20).

Hume, David. *The History of England, from the Invasion of Julius Caesar to the Revolution in 1688.* London: Thomas Dolby, 1825. – 6 vols. – The standard work on English history in the 18th and early 19th centuries; first published in two parts, 1754–7, and then as a single six-volume work by the London publisher, A. Millar, in 1762. (16/8/26).

Hunt, James Henry Leigh, *see*: Sprat, John, *pseud.*

Hutchinson, Lucy. *Memoirs of the Life of Colonel Hutchinson, Governor of Nottingham Castle and Town* ... 4th ed. London, Longman etc., 1822. – 2 vols. – First edition published 1806. (1/11/36).

Johnson, John. *Typographia; or, The Printer's Instructor* ... London: Longman and Co., 1824. – 2 vols. (31/1/25).

Johnson, Samuel. *A Journey to the Western Islands of Scotland*, with remarks by the Rev. Donald McNicol ... Glasgow: R. Chapman, 1817. Pp. vi, 504. – First published London: J. Pope, 1775. Pp. 268. Also 'New ed.' Edinburgh, 1819. (16/1/29).

Johnson, Samuel. *The Lives of the Most Eminent English Poets* ... A new edition, corrected [etc.]. London: J. Nichols and Son, 1810. – 3 vols. (8⁰). – Originally published as *The Lives of the English Poets* ... Dublin: Whitestone, 1779 – 3 vols. (20/9/32). †

Junius, *pseud. The Letters of Junius.* 1772. – Collection of anonymous abusive letters attacking the ministry of the Duke of Grafton, as well as King George III himself (letter of 19 Dec. 1769). The letters were originally published in the newspaper, the *Public Advertiser*, from 21 Jan. 1769 to 21 Jan. 1772 and subsequently in numerous official and unauthorized editions after 1772. There has been much speculation on the identity of the author who is now generally believed to be Sir Philip Francis (1740–1818). (9/4/32).

Knapp, Andrew *and* Baldwin, William. *The Newgate Calendar, Comprising Interesting Memoirs of the Most Notorious Characters who have been Convicted of Outrages on the Laws of England* ... with Anecdotes and Last Exclamations of Sufferers. London, 1824–6. – 4 vols. (8⁰). – There were several editions and versions of the 'Newgate Calendar' by Knapp and Baldwin as well as by other compilers. An earlier edition entitled: *The New and Complete Newgate Calendar; or, Villany Displayed* ... compiled by William Jackson was published in six volumes in 1795. (21/3/27).

L'Estrange, (Sir) Roger. *Tyranny and Popery Lording over the Consciences, Lives, Liberties and Estates Both of King and People.* London: printed for Henry Brome, 1678. Pp. 94 (4⁰). – Also published under the title: *An Account of the Growth of Knavery, under the Pretended Fears of Arbitrary Government and Popery* ... (22/8/35).†

Leybourn, William. *The Compleat Surveyor, Containing the Whole Art of Surveying of Land by the Plain Table, Circumferentor, Theodolite, Peractor and other Instruments* ... 3rd ed. ... London: by E. Flesher for George Sawbridge, 1674. – Sharp mistakenly gave the author of this work as Thomas Manley, although all his other bibliographical details are correct. (13/11/32).

London Melodies; or, Cries of the Seasons. Part 1. London: William Darton, Jun., [1825]. 12⁰. This title is representative of the many different editions of collections of London cries then available. (11/3/35).

Mackenzie, Henry, *et al. The Mirror: a periodical paper published at Edinburgh in the years 1779–80* ... London, 1809. – 3 vols. – Reprint in book form of an original literary periodical. Re-issued in various editions between 1781 and 1827. (See also under *The Mirror* in section below listing newspapers and other periodicals). (6/9/31). †

Manley, Thomas, *See:* Leybourn, William. *The Complete Surveyor* ... – 3rd ed. (1674). (13/11/32).

Mather, William. *The Young Man's Companion* ... 1681. – Numerous subsequent editions throughout the 18th century. (20/2/27). (? *See also:* Stewart, J.A. *The Young Man's Companion*).

Mills, Charles. *The History of Chivalry; or, Knighthood and its Times.* London, 1825. – 2 vols. Also another ed. 1826. (30/1/27).

Milton, John. *[De Doctrina Christiana]. A Treatise of Christian Doctrine.* Compiled from the Holy Scriptures alone ... Translated from the original by C. R. Sumner. Cambridge University Press, 1825. Pp. xlii, 711. (4⁰). (23/10/30).

Milton, John. 'L'Allegro' [poem] (4/11/27).

Milton, John. *Paradise Lost* ... with a biographical account of the author and his writings [by Elijah Fenton]. London: A. Millar, 1780. Pp. xviii, 313. – This is one of several editions which would have been available in 1786, when Sharp was aged 13. (23/10/30).

Moore, John. *A View of Society and Manners in France, Switzerland and Germany* ... 6th [i.e. 9th] ed. London: W. Strahan and T. Cadell, 1800. – 2 vols. (19/8/27)

Moore, Francis. *Moore's Almanac Improv'd* ... by ... J. Trusler etc. [1789?] – And numerous later editions. – The original almanac by Francis Moore was entitled: *Kalendarium Ecclesiasticum ... a Kalendar ... for 1699* ... by Francis Moore. (1/1/32).

Moore, Thomas. *The Memoirs of the Life of the Right Honourable R. B. Sheridan.* London: Longman, 1825. (4⁰). Two subsequent two-volume 8⁰ editions appeared in 1825 and a 4th edition, also in two volumes in 1826. (17/10/26).·

Moxon, Edward (1801–58). *The Prospect and other Poems.* London, 1826 (12⁰). (5/7/26).

Mudford, William. *The Life of Richard Cumberland, Esq.* ... London: Sherwood, Neely and Jones, 1812. Pp. xxiii, 621. (7/9/30).

Mudie, Robert. *The Picture of Australia, Exhibiting New Holland, Van Diemen's Land and All the Settlements, from the First at Sydney to the Last at the Swan River.* London: Whittaker, Treacher and Co., 1829. Pp. x, 370. (12⁰).(20/11/29).

Nicholls, Thomas. *The Steam Boat Companion; or, Margate, Isle of Thanet, Isle of Sheppey, Southend, Gravesend and River Thames Guide ... with*

Descriptions of Every ... Place ... on Each Side of our River, from the Custom House to Margate ... London, 1823. (31/1/25). (?).

Northcote, James. *One Hundred Fables, Original and Selected* ... embellished with two hundred and eighty engravings on wood [from drawings by William Harvey]. London: Geo. Lawford, 1828. Pp. iii, 272. (8⁰). Also 2nd ed. 1829. Pp. viii, 272. Another edition sub-titled 'Second Series' published London: J. Murray, 1833. Pp. liv, 248. (8⁰). (19/6/34).

Otter, William, Bishop of Chichester. *The Life and Remains of Edward Daniel Clarke, Professor of Mineralogy in the University of Cambridge.* London: Cowie and Co., 1825. – 2 vols. (8⁰). – Originally published in 1824 as a single-volume 4⁰ edition. (18/11/26).

Pigot and Co. *National and Commercial Directory ... of the Merchants, Bankers, Professional Gentlemen, Manufacturers and Traders ... in the Counties of Chester, Cumberland, Durham, Lancaster, Northumberland, Westmoreland and York* ... London: Pigot and Co., 1834 (8⁰). (4/2/34).

Plutarch. [*Vitae Parallelae*]. *Plutarch's Lives.* Translated ... with notes ... and a life of Plutarch by John and William Langholme. A new edition, carefully revised and corrected. London, 1831–2. – 7 vols. (16⁰). (29/8/33). †

Pope, Alexander. *The Dunciad: an Heroic Poem,* in three books. Dublin printed; London reprinted for A. Dodd, 1728. – Numerous subsequent separate editions; also reprinted in various collective works, e.g. in *British Satirist,* 1826. (9/7/32). †

Pope, Alexander. *An Essay on Criticism.* London: printed for W. Lewis, 1711. Pp. 43 (4⁰). With numerous subsequent editions printed throughout the 18th century. (20/7/32). †

Pope, Alexander. *An Essay on Man* [in 5 parts]. Dublin: Powell for G. Risk, 1733. (8⁰). Frequently republished both in separate editions and as a part of the author's collective works. (11/5/27).

Pope, Alexander. *The Rape of the Lock: an Heroi-comical Poem.* In Five Cantos. London: Bernard Lintott, 1714. Pp. 48 (8⁰). – With numerous later editions and inclusions in collective works. (16/7/32).†

Reynard the Fox. *This is the Table of the Historye of Reynart the Foxe* (tr. W. Caxton). fol. Westminster: W. Caxton, 1481. (11/2/27).

[Scott, Thomas. *The Force of Truth: an Authentic Narrative.* 2nd ed. London: Religious Tract Society, 1831. First published in 1779, it had been republished in some ten or more editions since that date]. (See: Heber, Reginald, *Bishop of Calcutta.* 'Critique on Scott's "Force of Truth" '). (8/12/32).

Scott, Sir Walter. *Chronicles of the Canongate.* [First Series. *The Highland Widow. – The Two Drovers. – The Surgeon's Daughter.*] By the Author of Waverley ... Edinburgh: Cadell and Co., 1827. – 2 vols. (6/11/27).

Scott, Sir Walter. *The Fortunes of Nigel.* By the Author of "Waverley" ... Edinburgh: A. Constable and Co., 1822. – 3 vols. (8⁰). – 2nd ed., Edinburgh and London, 1822. – 3 vols (12⁰). Also published in his:

Novels and Romances ... Edinburgh: A. Constable and Co., 1824. – 7 vols. (23/8/26).

Scott, Sir Walter. *The History of Scotland.* London: Lardner, 1830. – 2 vols. (Dionysius Lardner's Cabinet Cyclopaedia). (22/6/30). †

Scott, Sir Walter. *The Life of Napoleon Buonoparte, Emperor of the French, with a Preliminary View of the French Revolution.* By the Author of "Waverley". 1827. – The Diary reference is to an advance notice for this work. (8/11/26). †

Scott, Sir Walter. *St. Ronan's Well.* By the Author of "Waverley" etc. Edinburgh: Constable and Co., 1824. – 3 vols. (11/7/25). †

Scott, Sir Walter. [Waverley Novels]. *Novels and Tales of the Author of Waverley.* Edinburgh: A. Constable and Co.; London: Longman, Hurst, Rees, Orme and Browne, 1819. – 12 vols. – And various subsequent editions. (19/7/26). †

Scott, Sir Walter. *Woodstock; or, The Cavalier: a Tale of the Year Sixteen Hundred and Fifty-one.* By the Author of "Waverley". Edinburgh, 1826. – 3 vols. (18/7/26). †

Secker, Thomas, Archbishop of Canterbury. *Lectures on the Catechism of the Church of England.* 14th ed. London: Rivington, 1821. – The standard Anglican catechism, first published 1769. (3/9/26).

Sewel, Willem: *The History of the Rise, Increase and Progress of the Christian People Called Quakers.* 5th ed. London, 1811. – 2 vols. One of several editions in an English translation from the Dutch original first published in Amsterdam in 1717. (15/11/29).

Shakespeare, William. *Hamlet, Prince of Denmark* (20/7/26).

Shakespeare, William. *Julius Caesar.* (2/6/32).

Shakespeare, William. *King Henry IV,* Part Two (27/7/26).

Shakespeare, William. *King Henry V.* (24/2/35).†

Shakespeare, William. *King Henry VIII.* (15/5/27).†

Shakespeare, William. *Macbeth.* (25/8/27).†

Shakespeare, William. *The Tempest* (4/6/31).

Shakespeare, William. *The Works of Shakespear.* Collated and corrected by the former editions, by Mr. Pope. London: Jacob Tonson, 1723–5. – 6 vols. (4⁰). (2/8/26). †

Shrubsole, William. *Christian Memoirs; or, A Review of the Present State of Religion in England, in the Form of a New Pilgrimage to the Heavenly Kingdom of Jerusalem* ... Rochester: the author, 1776. – 3rd ed., with the life of the author [by his son, William Shrubsole, the younger]. London, 1807. (2/10/31).

Smith, Adam. *An Inquiry into the Nature and Causes of the Wealth of Nations.* New ed. Edinburgh, 1828. – 4 vols. – First published in two volumes, London, 1776. (16/5/32).

Smollett, Tobias George. *The Adventures of Sir Launcelot Greaves;* published as vol. 9 of *The Miscellaneous Works of Tobias Smollett, M.D.*, with a life of the author. London: Otridge and Rackham, 1824. – 12 vols. – First published in *The Select Works of Tobias Smollett, M.D.*, 1776. (6/6/27).

Speculum Humanae Salvationis. Augsburg: Gunther Zainer, [1471?]. 269 leaves. – Numerous commentaries on and translations of this Latin devotional work were subsequently published. (11/2/27).

Sprat, John, *pseud.* [i.e. James Henry Leigh Hunt]. *The Rebellion of the Beasts; or, The Ass is Dead; Long Live the Ass!!!* By a late Fellow of St. John's College, Cambridge. With dedicatory epistle by John Pimlico. London: J. H.L. Hunt, 1825. Pp. 165. – Also a 2nd ed., 1825. Pp. 165. James Leigh Hunt was the editor of the Radical anti-government newspaper, *The Examiner*. (11/7/25).

Stanhope, Louisa Sidney. *The Crusaders: an Historical Romance of the Twelfth Century*. London, 1820. – 5 vols. (29/9/25).

Sterne, Laurence. *A Sentimental Journey through France and Italy*. By Mr. Yorick [pseud. of Laurence Sterne]. London: T. Becket and P.A. De Hondt, 1768. – 2 vols. (8⁰). Numerous later editions. (31/1/25).

Stewart, J. A. *The Young Man's Companion; or, Youth's Instructor* ... To which are added *The Elements of Natural Philosophy*. 2nd ed. Oxford: Bartlett and Newman, 1814. Pp. 861. (20/2/27). (? *See also*: Mather, William. *The Young Man's Companion*).

Swift, Jonathan. *Travels into Several Remote Nations of the World*. London: for Benjamin Motte, 1726. – 2 vols. in 4 parts. (8⁰). – Original edition of 'Gulliver's Travels', followed by at least 30 separate editions prior to the reference in RS's diary entry. (7/11/33).

Walker, George (1772–1847). *The Battle of Waterloo: a Poem*. London, 1815. (16/11/15). †

Ward, Edward (1667–1731). 'The ambitious mercenary; or, The climbing lawyer' [poem] published in his: *The modern world disrob'd; or, Both sexes stript of their pretended virtue* ... London: printed for G. S. and sold by B. Bragge [etc.]. 1708. (30/8/31).

Ward, Thomas (1652–1708). *England's Reformation from the Time of King Henry VIIIth to the End of Oate's Plot*. 4 Cantos. London, 1804. – First published in Hamburg in 1710 with numerous subsequent editions as follows: London, 1715 (2 vols.), 1716, 1747; Dublin, 1814 (2 vols.) and Manchester, 1815. (31/1/25).

Watts, Isaac (1674–1748). 'The Beauty of the Church; or, Gospel, Worship and Order' [poem]. (3/3/27).

Watts, Isaac (1674–1748). 'Frail Life and Succeeding Eternity' [poem]. (1/1/29).

Watts, Isaac (1674–1748). *Hymns and Spiritual Songs*. In three books ... London: John Lawrence, 1707. Pp. xxiv, 276. – There were 15 numbered editions of this popular work in the author's own lifetime. (1/4/29).

Wentworth, Thomas. *The Office and Duty of Executors; or, A Treatise of Wills and Executors* ... To which is added an appendix by Thomas Manley. London, 1676. – The earliest edition of this work had been published in

1641 and numerous other updated editions continued to be published well into the 19th century. Although Sharp does not specifically cite this work, it is likely that it is his 'treatise on Wills ... the only law Book [he] ever had'. He also cites Thomas Manley as the author of William Leybourn's *The Compleat Surveyor* ... (1674) so that it is possible that he was confusing the authorship of two almost equally old works in his possession. (14/1/29). (?)

Wesley, John. *The History of Henry, Earl of Moreland*. [Abridged, with a preface, by John Wesley from *The Fool of Quality* by Henry Brooke] London: J. Paramore, 1781. – 2 vols. (12⁰). (29/6/33). †

White (William) and Co. *The Directory, Guide and Annals of Kingston-upon-Hull ... together with the Neighbouring Towns and Villages* ... Leeds: William White and Co, printed by Edward Baines, 1826. (27/6/26).

Wickes, John Wight. *Accipe si vis. A Letter Addressed to the ... Lord Bishop of Peterborough, in Answer to the Opinion of Sir William Scott ... as to the Legality or Illegality of Refusing Church Burial to Dissenters*. Stamford: printed and sold by J. Drakard, [1809]. Pp. 44. (8⁰). (4/1/27).

Young, Edward (1683–1765). 'To His Grace the Duke of Dorset' [poem] (28/11/27).

Young, Edward (1683–1765). 'To the Right Honourable Sir Spencer Compton' [poem] (28/3/29)†.

Newspapers and other Periodical Publications
The main sources used for the information in this section are: (1) Wolff, Michael, *et al.*, comps. *The Waterloo Directory of Victorian Periodicals, 1824–1900*. Phase 1. Waterloo (Ont.): Wilfred Laurier U.P. for the University of Waterloo, 1976; (2) British Library Network On-Line Public Access Catalogue (BLOPAC). Prototype Version 1995–. (3) British Library. *Catalogue of the Newspaper Library, Colindale* (London: BL, 1975). – 8 vols.; (4) Watson, George, ed. *The New Cambridge Bibliography of English Literature*. Vol. 3: *1800–1900* (Cambridge: at the UP, 1969), Section 15: *Newspapers and Magazines*, columns 1755–1884; and, for Hull newspapers, (5) *Victoria History of the Counties of England (VCH). A History of the County of York, East Riding;* edited by K. J. Allison. Vol. 1: *The City of Kingston upon Hull* (London: OUP, 1969), pp. 428–32 [section on newspapers].

When the first and last dates of publication of a periodical title are unknown, the earliest and latest dates held by any major British library as published in the *British Union Catalogue of Periodicals* (BUCOP) or in the British Library's *Catalogue of the Newspaper Library, Colindale* (Colindale) or in any other specified source, have been supplied instead.

Aberdeen Observer: a commercial and political journal
Mar. 1829–Mar. 1836. (1/6/31).

Bell's Life in London and Sporting Chronicle

3 Mar. 1822 – 29 May 1886. Sunday newspaper founded by Robert Bell and later acquired by William Clement. In 1827 absorbed rival newspaper, Pierce Egan's *Life in London* taking on its editor, William Clement. Eventually incorporated into *Sporting Life*. (25/1/27).

Bell's Messenger = *Bell's Weekly Messenger* (?)

1 May 1796 – 28 Mar. 1896. Continued as: *Country Sports and Messenger of Agriculture*. 4 Apr. 1896 – 31 Dec. 1904. (16/12/30).

The Chronicle, See: *Morning Chronicle*

Cobbett's Political Register

Vol. 1–89, 1802–1835. Widely read Radical journal, published weekly and written by William Cobbett as a vehicle for his ideas and a commentary on the political scene. It was variously entitled: *Cobbett's Annual Register, Cobbett's Weekly Political Register, Cobbett's Weekly Political Pamphlet, Cobbett's Weekly Register*. (11/7/25).

Commercial Journal and Advertiser (Sydney)

New ser., no.414–416, 420, 428, 12–19 Oct., 2 Nov., 4 Dec. 1839 (Colindale) (28/4/36).

The Courier

Sept. 1792 – 6 July 1842. One of the foremost London evening daily newspapers. Founded by James Perry who remained its proprietor until 1799. He was succeeded by Daniel Stuart, who owned the paper from 1799 to 1822 and edited it from 1803 to 1811; Peter Street was editor from 1811 to 1822; he was succeeded by William Mudford. It was finally incorporated into *The Globe*. (30/11/26).

Doncaster, Nottingham and Lincoln Gazette

[179–?]–Dec. 1881. Continued as: *Doncaster Gazette*. Jan. 1882 – in progress. (25/12/25).

Edinburgh Review; or, Critical Journal

Oct. 1802–Oct. 1929. Important literary quarterly attracting many famous writers, including (briefly) Sir Walter Scott, Lord Brougham, Carlyle, Hazlitt and Macaulay. It was first edited by Sydney Smith, who remained as one of its regular contributors, but was quickly succeeded as editor by Francis Jeffrey, under whose management (1803–1829) it acquired its pronounced Whiggish character. (29/9/25).

Englishman's Magazine

Vol. 1–2, no.2, Apr.–Oct. 1831. Published in London and edited by Edward Moxon. (6/10/31).

The Examiner

3 January 1808 – 26 February 1881. Strongly anti-government, radical weekly newspaper originally owned and edited by John Hunt and his brother James Henry Leigh Hunt (1808–1825). They were succeeded by Robert Fellowes (1828–1830?) and Albany Fonblanque (1830?–1865). (24/4/22).

Foreign Literary Gazette

No. 1–13, 6 Jan.–31 Mar. 1830. Published in London. (21/1/30).

Freeman's Journal

10 Sept. 1763 – 20 Dec. 1924. Irish daily newspaper published in Dublin and originally entitled: *Public Register; or, Freeman's Journal.* Successively owned and edited by Francis Higgins (1783–1802), Philip Whitfield Harvey (1802–1826), Henry Grattan (1826–1830), and Patrick Lavelle (1830–1837). (16/5/31).

The Globe

1 Jan. 1803 – 28 Dec. 1822. Continued as: *Globe and Traveller* 30 Dec. 1822 – 5 Feb. 1921. Absorbed: *The Traveller* (1822), *The True Briton* (1823?), *The Statesman* (1824), *The Evening Chronicle* (1824), *The Nation* (1824), and *The Argus* (1828). *The Globe* was London's oldest evening newspaper and was owned during the period of the Diary by Robert Torrens. It was eventually incorporated into the *Pall Mall Gazette* and shortly afterwards merged into the *Evening Standard*. (19/6/26).

Hull Advertiser and Exchange Gazette

July 1794–1867. Originally intended by its first printer and publisher, William Rawson, as a medium for agricultural and commercial information, it became more political in tone under Isaac Wilson who gained sole control of the paper in 1821. He gave strong support to the Tories throughout the Reform Bill crisis, but when William Kennedy became proprietor and editor in 1833, the *Hull Advertiser* was transformed into a Radical organ and remained so until at least 1858. The newspaper appeared weekly on Saturdays until 1820 when it began to be published on Fridays instead. It was finally incorporated in the *Eastern Morning News*. (18/6/26).

Hull, East Riding and North Lincolnshire Literary and Scientific Panorama

No. 1, 1812 (Hull) This is the only number held by the British Library (BLOPAC). The publication is cited by Sharp as simply the *Literary Panorama*, but he refers to an issue of January 1812 (8/9/30). †

Hull, East Riding, and North Lincolnshire Observer

May 1834–1841. A Radical Hull weekly newspaper appearing weekly on Tuesdays. It was printed and published by the proprietors of the *Hull Advertiser* and was eventually incorporated into that newspaper. (31/12/35).

Hull Packet and Humber Gazette

May 1787–1886. Weekly Hull newspaper which lasted, with various slight changes of title, for almost one hundred years before it was eventually incorporated in the Hull *Daily Mail*. In addition to commercial and political news, it contained correspondence and became a medium for agitation against slavery. At first the paper appeared on a Tuesday but from 1832 onwards it was issued on a Friday. (24/10/27).

*The Imperial Magazine; or, Compendium of Religious, Moral and
Philosophical Knowledge*
> 1819–1830 (in 12 volumes); 2nd series, 1831–1834 (in 4 vols.). The
> second series was edited by Samuel Drew. Published in Liverpool until
> 1832, then London. (11/7/25).

Leeds Mercury
> May 1718 – 25 Nov. 1939. Variously entitled *Leeds Mercury; or, General
> Advertiser* and *Leeds and Yorkshire Mercury*, it was finally incorporated
> into the *Yorkshire Post*. Originally a weekly newspaper, and for a time
> thrice weekly, it became established as one of the foremost provincial daily
> newspapers, especially under the proprietorship of Edward Baines (senior)
> who built up its circulation considerably after taking it over in 1801. He
> continued to run it single-handed until 1827, and in conjunction with his
> son, Edward Baines (junior), from 1827 onwards, throughout the period of
> the Diary. (20/10/27).

Literary Gazette
> 25 Jan. 1817 – 26 Apr. 1862. Famous weekly literary review founded by
> Henry Colburn, its principal editor for more than thirty years (1817–1850)
> was William Jerdan, who attracted many famous contributors, including
> the poet, George Crabbe. (31/1/25).

London Magazine
> 1820–1829. Originally known as Baldwin's *London Magazine* to
> distinguish it from its short-lived rival, Gold's *London Magazine*. Its first
> and most successful editor was John Scott, who died as a result of a duel
> occasioned by a quarrel with Lockhart of the rival *Blackwood's Magazine*.
> Among the *London Magazine*'s many illustrious contributors were Charles
> Lamb, William Hazlitt, John Clare, De Quincey and Carlyle. (10/2/20).

London Mercury
> 12 Aug. 1826 – 23 Dec. 1826. Finally incorporated into the *Weekly Times*.
> At least five other short-lived journals with this title were published later
> in the 19th century. (14/8/26).

The Mirror [By Henry Mackenzie and others]
> No. 1–110, 1779–1780. Edinburgh. Re-issued in book form in various
> editions from 1781 to 1827. (See also under Mackenzie, Henry in section
> for books above). (6/9/31).

Monthly Magazine
> 1796–1843. Particularly successful under the proprietorship of its founder,
> Sir Richard Phillips, the *Monthly Review* had an enthusiastic following
> among nonconformists, radicals and freethinkers and attracted many
> famous contributors, including Malthus, Godwin, Hazlitt and Southey.
> After it was sold in 1824, the periodical changed its political stance and
> adopted a more sober style, and never thereafter enjoyed great success.
> (11/7/25).

Morning Chronicle

28 June 1769 – 20 Dec. 1862. London daily morning newspaper. Proprietors: James Perry (1789–1821); William I. Clement (1822–1834); John Easthope (1834–). It was edited from 1819 to 1843 by John Black. (10/10/31).

Morning Herald

1 Nov. 1780 – 31 Dec. 1869. One of the principal London daily morning papers. Founded by Sir Henry Bate Dudley, then editor of the *Morning Post* and retained by him until his death in 1824. (29/9/25).

Old Whig

No. 1–2, 1719. A periodical publication commenting on the state of the peerage by Joseph Addison. London. (20/9/32).

Penny Magazine

Vol. 1–14, 1832–1845. Continued as: *Knight's Penny Magazine*. Vol. 1–2, 1846. This was one of the most popular (circulation 200,000) and successful of the 'useful knowledge' miscellanies of the period. It was published weekly and edited by Charles Knight. (3/4/33).

The Plebeian

No. 1–3, 1719. A political periodical published in quarto format, it was later reissued in the same year in four numbers in octavo. It was written pseudonymously by Sir Richard Steele and is notable for involving its author in a dispute with his former ally, Joseph Addison. (20/9/32).

Political Protestant's Register

Untraced. It may have been a publication of the General Committee of Political Protestants who published in Newcastle in this same year (1819) their pamphlet, *The Loyal and Constitutional Declaration of the Political Protestants of Newcastle* ... (17/5/19).†

Port Hope Telegraph

Canadian newspaper. Bibliographical details untraced. (30/9/31).

Rockingham and Hull Weekly Advertiser

2 Jan. 1808–1828. Continued as: *Hull Rockingham and Yorkshire and Lincolnshire Gazette*, 6 Apr. 1828–1844. Said to have been founded by members of the Sykes family and John Cowham Parker, this weekly Hull Saturday newspaper was a Whig organ. (6/6/27).

Society for Promoting Christian Knowledge. *The Annual Report*. 1814– Continuation of: *An Account of the Origin and Designs of the Society* ... 1733–[1813?]. (29/3/29).

The Spectator

1 Mar. 1711 – 6 Dec. 1712; 18 June 1714 – 29 Sept. 1714. Edited by Joseph Addison and Sir Richard Steele and others as a successor to *The Tatler*, this famous literary journal had been republished in a new edition in 1827, which was probably the version read by Sharp. (31/8/27).

The Standard

  21 May 1827 – 29 June 1857. Continued as: *The Evening Standard*.
  London evening newspaper Proprietor: Edward Baldwin, 1827–1857;
  editor: S. L. Giffard, 1827–1845. (18/11/30).

The Sun

  1 Oct. 1792 – 15 Apr. 1876. Daily London evening newspaper, entitled
  The Sun and Central Press from 1871 to 1873. (24/4/31). Proprietors:
  Patrick Grant, Apr. 1826–1831; Murdo Young, 1832–1850. (24/4/31).

The Tatler

  No. 1–271, 12 Apr. 1709–Jan. 1711. Originally published thrice weekly as
  a newspaper and society journal with general essays on manners and
  morality, it was later reprinted as a collective work: *The Tatler; or,
  Lucubrations of Isaac Bickerstaff, Esq.* [By Sir Richard Steele and others].
  London: Jacob and Richard Tonson, 1759. – 4 vols. (8⁰). There were
  several subsequent editions, e.g. Dublin, 1777; London, 1786, in 6 vols.;
  and London, 1789, in 4 vols. (15/2/29).

The Times

  1 Jan. 1785– onwards. First published under the title *Daily Universal
  Register* (until 31 Dec. 1787). *The Times* was the principal London
  morning newspaper and generally a staunch supporter of the government
  of the day. It was taken regularly by Sharp. (5/7/26).

Weekly Miscellany

  16 Dec. 1732 – 27 June 1741. Originally published as *The Miscellany:
  giving an Account of the Religion, Morality and Learning of the Present
  Times* ... By Richard Hooker of the Temple [pseudonym of William
  Webster, D.D. (1689–1758)], it was later entitled *The Weekly Miscellany*,
  but was more popularly known as 'Old Mother Hooker's Journal' on
  account of the large number of religious essays that it contained. (9/7/32).

York Herald

  2 Jan. 1790–Dec. 1889. Continued as: *Yorkshire Herald*. Jan. 1890–1954.
  Published weekly. Its editor from 1813 to 1846 was William Hargrove. In
  1954 it was incorporated with the *Yorkshire Gazette* to form the *Yorkshire
  Gazette and Herald*. (10/6/29).

Yorkshire Gazette

  24 Apr. 1819–1954. Weekly newspaper established by a group of members
  of the York Book Society. John Wolstenholme was the newspaper's first
  manager and publisher; he was succeeded in July 1828 by Henry Bellerby
  who continued to publish it until 1851. In 1954 it was incorporated with
  the *Yorkshire Herald* to form the *Yorkshire Gazette and Herald*. (4/7/27).

INDEX

This index combines persons, places, and subjects in one sequence. Names of persons who are listed in Appendix II appear in bold in the index. The author of the diary, Robert Sharp, is referred to as RS throughout, but is not indexed separately. The entries for William Sharp and South Cave are selective.

A

Abbeyholme (Cumberland), 425

Abbott, Mr: wine merchant, 109

Abbs, Mr: a tailor, 454, 475

Abercromby, James: elected Speaker of the House of Commons, 487

Aberdeen Observer, 313

Achilles, statue of, 17

Acland, James, 384, 385n

actors, 94, 181, 214, 561

acupuncture, 266

Adrianople, treaty of, 230

Ady, Joseph, 370, 373

agricultural unrest. *See*: unrest, agricultural

air gun, 36

Akam, Ann, 164, 229, 253

Akam, Elizabeth, 229, 371, 482

Akam, John, 230; buys land near Philadelphia, 330; emigrates to America, 306; land owned by him, 355; preparations for emigration, 244, 247, 304; returns from America, 329; sale of his property at Everthorpe, 333

Akam, Mary Paulina, 463

Akam, William, 206, 229–30

Alderson, Dr John: called to treat Mrs Turner, 98

ale: price of, 281; RS receives one pint per month as friendly society's secretary, 281. *See also*: Food and drinks: ale and beer

Aleksandr I, Tsar of Russia: death of, 31

Alfred (Hull whaler): returns from Greenland, 509

All Saints' Church (Barmston), 344, 352

All Saints' Church (North Cave), 274

All Saints' Church (South Cave), xliv–xlv, 274

Allison, John: criticizes the Marshall brothers, 287

Allison, Thomas, 62, 276, 323, 407, 448; fights with W. Green, 335; his bullock shot, 329

almanacs, 324, 347, 446–7, 543; convictions for sale of unlicensed, 434

Almorah (ship), 301n

Althorp, Lord. *See*: Spencer, John Charles, Viscount Althorp

Ambrose, Mr, 31, 89

America, 199, 235, 241, 244, 246–7, 251–2, 269, 295, 299–301, 303–4, 306, 312, 314, 318–19, 326, 329; dismal account of by returned emigrants, 325; its roads worse than those of Broomfleet, 324

American War of Independence, 544

Amsterdam, 268

anatomy, 197

Ancient and Honourable Lumber Troop, 333

Anderson, Evelyn: MP for Beverley, 401

Andrew, Thomas: servant of vicar of Brantingham, 529

Anson, William, 411

Anthony, John (of Barmston), 351

Antiquarian Trio (by J. Cole), 56

Antwerp, siege of, 390, 394, 397, 406

apples, 484; price of, 97, 324; theft of, 423; varieties of, 322, 403

Arctic exploration, 536

Arminians, 395

arsenic, 164

Arton, Ann, 236, 285

Arton, Elizabeth, 31, 38, 59, 230; visited by the Sharps, 49, 160, 323, 554; visits the Sharps, 497, 525

G

S

54, 58, 68, 72, 94, 148, 157, 160,
179, 204, 240, 268, 285, 365

Sharp, Hannah (née Hicks, daughter-in-law of RS), xxvi, 211, 213, 215, 296; birth of her first son, 304: takes her sick daughter to Wales, 379–80

Sharp, Jane (daughter of RS), 23, 216, 379; letters to her brother, William, 1–3

Sharp, John (father of RS): death of, 23; RS's recollections of, 59, 126, 336, 341, 351, 404

Sharp, Mary (daughter of RS), 369

Sharp, Mary (sister of RS). *See*: Barker, Mary (née Sharp, sister of RS)

Sharp, Mary Barker (granddaughter of RS), 228, 270, 279, 302, 304, 307, 313, 345, 354, 370, 387, 394, 418, 430–1, 439; ill health of, 295–6, 380, 386, 552; taken to Wales to recuperate, 379–80; visits South Cave with her father, 416–17

Sharp, Milcah (sister of RS). *See*: Ramsdale, Milcah (née Sharp, sister of RS)

Sharp, Samuel (of Barmston), 336

Sharp, Revd Thomas (brother of RS), xxv, 42, 78, 104, 113, 268, 344, 366, 402, 466–7, 532, 534; Ann Sharp visits, 396, 413–14; concerned with sister's legacy, 376, 378, 453; ill health of, 392, 399, 405, 413–15, 419, 429, 513; preaches at South Cave chapel, 50; visits RS, 59, 151, 212, 266, 319, 321; writes to RS, 96, 382

Sharp, William (of Barmston), 351

Sharp, William (son of RS), xxvi; character of, 31; his job at Longman's, 9; his tour of Wales, 149, 153; inherits from his aunt Mary, 366, 378, 388–90, 466; involved in coach accident, 213, 215; reports birth of son, 304; travels to Liverpool, Dublin, etc., 331; visited in London: (by his aunt Mary), 313, (by his mother), 503; visits his aunt, Mary, in Liverpool, 327; visits to South Cave, 211–12, 416–17, 466

Sharp, William (the younger, grandson of RS), 304, 307, 309, 313, 326–7, 370

shaving stones, 520

Shaw, Jenny, 227

Shaw, Nathaniel, 26, 94, 236

Shaw, Capt. Richard Fleetwood, 457, 502, 546; buys Brantingham and Brantinghamthorpe Halls, 367

Shaw, Samuel, 75, 114, 145, 153, 329, 386, 392, 445, 555

Shaw, Thomas, 227; his niece removed to Ellerker, 248; receives news of legacy, 262

sheep and lambs, 116; at Caistor sheep fair, 124, 134; price of, 53, 67–8, 89, 124, 131, 134, 137, 155, 162, 168, 191, 224, 232, 311, 380, 471, 517

Sheep Dike, 489, 533

Sheep Dike Close, 357, 443

sheep shearing, 210, 343

Shen Nung, legendary 2nd emperor of China, 462

Sheridan, Richard Brinsley, 77

Sherwin, Dr Henry Charles, 22

ships (named): Alfred, 509; Almorah, 301n; Aurora, 301; Blonde, 66n; Brothers, 107, 109; Donegal, 461n; Ebenezer, 126; Enterprise, 415n; Florentia, 419; Freak, 327; Graham, 82n; Jubilee, 113; London, 509; Triton, 301; United Kingdom, 82n; Westmoreland, 300; Wilberforce, 252

ships' figureheads, 338

Shipton, Old Mother: her prophecies, 283

shoemakers and cobblers: at Walkington, 202, 284; evidence for RS's early career as one, xxv–xxvi; murder of one at Newbald, 406–7. *See also*: Atkinson, William

shooting: accidentally of bullock, 329; accidents, 506; dangers of, 93; hares, 86; partridges, 61, 158, 274, 382, 505; pheasants, 93; rights over H. G. Barnard's land, 327, 531, 531; rooks, 36, 132, 257, 417, 523; runaway bull, 256; sparrows, 398; start of season, 220, 274

RECORDS OF SOCIAL AND ECONOMIC HISTORY
(New Series)

24. *The Register of Thetford Priory, Part 1: 1482–1517*. D. Dymond. 1995
25. *The Register of Thetford Priory, Part 2: 1518–1540*. D. Dymond. 1996